365

DOWN-TO-EARTH

GARDENING

HINTS AND TIPS

SUSAN MCCLURE, M.S.

C. COLSTON BURRELL, M.S., CONSULTANT

PUBLICATIONS INTERNATIONAL, LTD.

CONTRIBUTORS:

Susan McClure has an M.S. in botany and is the author of more than a dozen gardening books including the *Herb Gardener* and *Culinary Gardens from Design to Palate.* She also writes for magazines and newspapers, teaches at the Chicago Botanic Garden and Morton Arboretum, and is a regional director of the Garden Writers of America.

C. Colston Burrell is a Master of Landscape Architecture and has an M.S. in horticulture. He is a garden designer, writer, consultant, and photographer, and is president of Native Landscape Design and Restoration, Ltd. He coauthored the *Illustrated Encyclopedia of Perennials,* contributed to the *New Encyclopedia of Organic Gardening* and *Landscaping with Nature,* and has served as consultant to many gardening books, including *Treasury of Gardening.*

PICTURE CREDITS:

Front cover: **Heather Angel Photography**

Back cover: **Marlene Hill Donnelly**; **Derek Fell** (bottom)

Heather Angel Photography: Contents, 25, 38 (bottom), 126, 144, 145 (bottom), 155, 199 (top), 201; **Derek Fell:** 11, 14, 17, 34, 36, 40 (bottom), 42, 47, 50, 52, 57, 70, 76, 80 (bottom), 84 (top), 85, 112, 114, 116 (top), 118 (top), 130, 131, 134 (top), 137, 140, 146 (top), 157 (top), 168 (bottom), 183, 193; **Pamela Harper:** 106, 108 (top), 116 (bottom), 200 (top); **JRM Chemical:** 206; **Jerry Pavia:** Contents, 24, 54, 56, 59 (top), 60, 91 (bottom), 92 (bottom), 94, 96 (bottom), 99, 120, 139, 148, 153, 160 (bottom), 165, 166, 167, 175, 185, 191; **Photo/Nats, Inc.:** Gay Bumgarner: 21, 66 (top); George & Judy Manna: 84 (bottom); Ben Phillips: 66 (bottom); Ann Reilly: 178; **Richard Shiell:** 128, 162, 170, 173, 197 (top), 200 (bottom); **Carol Simowitz:** 96 (top), 110, 149 (bottom), 208; **SuperStock:** 82, 186, 199 (bottom)

Illustrations: **Marlene Hill Donnelly**

Louis Weber, CEO
Publications International, Ltd.
7373 North Cicero Avenue
Lincolnwood, Illinois 60712

Permission is never granted for commercial purposes.

Manufactured in China.

8 7 6 5 4 3 2 1

ISBN-13: 978-0-7853-2436-2
ISBN-10: 0-7853-2436-4

Library of Congress Catalog Card Number: 97-69450

CONTENTS

INTRODUCTION

If you enjoy working in the yard and are thinking about starting a new garden or improving an existing landscape, you'll find a wide array of fun and easy projects in this book. *365 Down-to-Earth Gardening Hints and Tips* provides special tips on how to employ useful gardening tools and techniques for every element in your landscape. We'll give you information about new types of flowers and plants, many of which have been specifically bred to be more resistant to pests and diseases, and we'll also tell you about new methods of improving your garden.

Many of the hints in this book only require everyday household items or a simple change in the way you're already gardening! Our goal is to make gardening easier and more fun while you're doing it so that it will be even more pleasurable once you're done.

Inside this book, you'll find a number of ways to make garden upkeep easier, like letting snow serve as a winter mulch, allowing toads to tackle insect pests, or using a perforated pipe to aerate your compost pile. In *365 Down-to-Earth Gardening Hints and Tips,* you'll learn surprisingly simple tricks of the trade, such as using a clear plastic bag to make a miniature greenhouse, shaping the lawn so it's easily mowed, and positioning warm-colored flowers for increased impact in distant gardens.

This book is divided into two sections. The first section, "Gardening Basics," is all about those elements of gardening that seem so elementary, we may want to take them for granted! But by focusing just a little extra attention on fundamental things like soil, water, and light, you can make a major difference in your garden.

Perhaps you need to do a soil test to determine if you should adjust the nutrients in the dirt, or maybe you need to switch the time of day that you're watering your plants. Any extra time and effort you spend in the garden early on will ensure an even greater reward at bloom or harvest time. We'll also discuss how to prevent pests and diseases from ruining your handiwork, how you can propagate your plants to increase your own supply or share with a friend, and how organic and low-maintenance gardening can add to the ease and enjoyment of this popular hobby.

The second section of the book, "Types of Gardens," focuses on the various elements included in the landscape, such as shade trees and evergreens, annual and perennial flowers, herbs and vegetables, and, of course, the lawn. Each part of the landscape is important, and we'll help you decide how to make the very most of your garden. We'll also give you hints about bulbs, roses, ground covers, and vines. Just because these elements may seem fancy doesn't mean you can't grow them beautifully—and easily! With a little planning and our helpful hints you can create a landscape filled with an abundance of flowers, trees, and greenery. Dig in!

GARDENING BASICS

There are libraries full of how-to books that explain the things you *need* to know for an outstanding yard and garden. But this book goes beyond that, featuring hints and tips you'll *want* to know—those little extras that can make a big difference. You'll discover ways to do things better, easier, or faster with new products, new techniques, and new plants. The practical advice offered here will help you enhance the growth of your flowers, vegetables, herbs, and other plants—often with less work than you were doing before!

But even the best tips can't change the fundamentals of gardening. Most plants need good soil with suitable drainage, texture, and fertility. They need moisture, light, nutrients, and occasional pruning to keep them healthy and thriving. These basics provide an important foundation for any yard or garden, and with our helpful hints, you'll be sure to get started off right. The tips included here will help you enhance your landscape—and maybe even your enjoyment of gardening.

THE DIRT ON SOIL

Children who are scolded for running into the house in dirty shoes may come to believe dirt is a bad thing. But just the opposite is true as long as dirt remains outdoors where it belongs. In the garden, dirt is transformed into soil, a complex and beautiful (at least to experienced gardeners) blend of animal, vegetable, and mineral material. Good soil is the first step to a great garden.

The loose, dark earth of fabulous gardens seen on television and in magazines doesn't usually just happen. It is created by gardeners improving their native soils. Soils can be amended with sand to make them looser and drier or with clay to make them moister and firmer. They can be given plentiful doses of organic material—old leaves, ground-up twigs, rotted livestock manure, and old lawn clippings. Organic matter improves and nourishes any kind of soil which, in turn, encourages better plant growth.

1

USE PLANTS ADAPTED TO THE CONDITIONS RIGHT OUTSIDE YOUR DOOR. When plants prefer your native soil and climate, no matter how difficult these conditions may be, they are likely to grow beautifully with little effort. Native plants—shade trees, shrubs, or flowers that arise in the nearby countryside—are good options. Or, try less common plants from faraway places with conditions similar to your own.

To identify suitable plants, begin by identifying your garden conditions. Have your soil tested or do your own tests (see Hint 5) to determine if you have a light and sandy soil, a moderate and productive soil, or a heavy clay soil. Watch the site to see how sunny it is, and select plants that need full sun, partial sun, or shade, accordingly (see Hint 31).

Finally, find your location on the United States Department of Agriculture hardiness zone map (see pages 210–211), which measures winter coldness. Make a note of the light levels, soil conditions, and climatic zone information you've found. Check through nursery catalogues and gardening books to find plants that thrive in every one of the elements particular to your yard. Use these plants as a shopping list for all of your future gardening projects. A little extra legwork in the beginning makes garden-ing much easier over the coming years.

2 **GET A SOIL TEST** before you start adding fertilizers and amend-ments to your garden soil. This follows the old advice, "If it ain't broke,

Make sure your soil has been thoroughly prepared before you start to plant.

don't fix it." Sometimes unnecessary tampering with nutrients or soil acidity can actually create more problems than benefits.

Soil tests tell you the nutrient levels in your soil, a plant version of the nutrient guides on packaged foods. They also note pH and organic content, two factors important to overall smooth sailing from the ground up.

To have your soil tested, call your local Cooperative Extension Service, often listed under federal or county government in the phone book. Ask them how to get a soil testing kit, which contains a soil collecting bag and instructions. Follow the directions precisely for accurate results.

The results may come as a chart full of numbers, which

SOME SOURCES OF SPECIFIC NUTRIENTS

Many of these fertilizers are available processed and packaged. You don't have to harvest your own.

NITROGEN: livestock manure (composted), bat guano, chicken manure, fish emulsion, blood meal, kelp meal, cottonseed meal

PHOSPHORUS: bonemeal, rock phosphate, super phosphate

POTASSIUM: granite meal, sulfate of potash, greensand, wood ashes, seabird guano, shrimp shell meal

CALCIUM: bonemeal, limestone, eggshells, wood ashes, oyster shells, chelated calcium

BORON: manure, borax, chelated boron

COPPER: chelated copper

MAGNESIUM: Epsom salts, dolomitic limestone, chelated magnesium

SULFUR: sulfur, solubor, iron sulfate, zinc sulfate

ZINC: zinc sulfate, chelated zinc

IRON: chelated iron, iron sulfate

can be a little intimidating at first. But if you look carefully for the following, you can begin to interpret these numbers:

- If the percentage of organic matter is under 5 percent, the garden needs some extra compost.
- Nutrients will be listed separately, possibly in parts per million. Sometimes they are also rated as available in high, medium, or low levels. If an element or two comes in on the low side, you'll want to add a fertilizer that replaces what's lacking.
- Soil pH refers to the acidity of the soil. Ratings below 7 are acidic soils. From 6 to 7 are slightly acidic, the most fertile pH range. Above 7 is alkaline or basic soil, which can become infertile above pH 8. Excessively acidic and alkaline soils can be treated to make them more moderate and productive (see Hints 7 and 8).

3   **ADD ONLY THE NUTRIENTS YOUR SOIL TEST SAYS ARE NECESSARY.** More is not always better when it comes to plant nutrients. Don't feel compelled to add a little bit more of a fertilizer that promises great results. Too much of any one nutrient can actually produce toxic results, akin to diseases or worse. Buy only what's required and save the rest of your money for a better use, like more plants.

4   **LOOK FOR THE TALES WEEDS HAVE TO TELL** as they grow in your garden. Weeds are opportunists, taking advantage of any vacant soil to make their home. (Just think of how well this strategy has benefitted the dandelion, a native of Eurasia that has swept through America.)

Although they seem to grow everywhere, dandelions prefer fertile, often heavy soil. Likewise, other weeds favor certain kinds of soil. For instance, acidic soil can encourage the growth of crabgrass, plantains, sheep sorrel, and horsetails. Alkaline soil (also called sweet or basic soil) is favored by chamomile and goosefoot. Fertile near-neutral soils can provide a nurturing environment for redroot pigweed, chickweed, dandelions, and wild mustard.

These unwanted plantains are a sign that the soil may be acidic.

Even if you can't tell one weed from the other, you can find out important information by looking at them closely. If a vacant garden area has few weeds taking advantage of the opening, the soil is likely to need plenty of work. If they are growing, but only sparsely, and have short, stunted stems and discolored leaves, the area may have a nutrient deficiency, and a soil test is in order. If, in newly tilled soil, weeds sprout up quickly in certain areas and more slowly in others, the weedy areas are likely to be moister and better for seed germination.

5   **CHECK THE TEXTURE OF YOUR SOIL** in a jar filled with water. This test is simple to do at home and provides important information about your soil.

Gather up some soil from the garden, choosing a sampling of soil from near the surface and down to a depth of 8 inches. Let it dry, pulverize it into fine granules, and mix well. Put a 1-inch layer (a little over a cup) in a quart glass jar with ¼ teaspoon of powdered dishwasher detergent. (Dishwasher detergent won't foam up.) Add enough water to fill the jar two-thirds full. Shake the jar for a minute, turning it upside down as needed to get all the soil off the bottom, then put the jar on a counter where it can sit undisturbed.

One minute later, mark the level of settled particles on the jar with a crayon or wax pencil. This is sand. Set an alarm for 4 hours, and when it goes off, mark the next level, which is the amount of silt that has settled out. Over the next day or two, the clay will slowly settle out and allow you to take the final measurement. These measurements show the relative percentages of sand, silt, and clay, or the texture of your soil.

- Soil that has a high percentage of sand (70 percent or more) tends to be well aerated, ready to plant earlier in spring. But it also tends to need more frequent watering and fertilization than heavier soils.
- Soil that has 35 percent or more clay retains more moisture, so it takes longer to dry in spring and may need less watering in summer. It can be richer and more likely to produce lush growth with just the addition of compost and, occasionally, a little fertilizer. The compost is important. It helps break up clay so the soil won't be too thick and poorly aerated.
- Soil that has more equal percentages of sand, silt, and clay can have intermediate characteristics and is generally well suited for good gardening.

6 **TEST YOUR SOIL'S DRAINAGE** by digging a hole, filling it with water, and watching how quickly the water disappears. All the soil tests in the world won't do a better job than this simple project. It tells you how quickly moisture moves through the soil and whether the soil is likely to be excessively dry or very soggy—neither of which is ideal.

When it hasn't rained for a week or more and the soil is dry, dig several holes that are 1 foot deep and 2 feet wide. Fill them to the top with water and keep track of how long it takes for the holes to empty. Compare your findings to the following scale:

- 1 to 12 minutes: The soil is sharply drained and likely to be dry.
- 12 to 30 minutes: The soil has ideal drainage.
- 30 minutes to 4 hours: Drainage is slow but adequate for plants that thrive in moist soil.
- Over 4 hours: Drainage is poor and needs help (see Hints 13 and 14).

7 USE GROUND LIMESTONE TO RAISE THE pH OF ACIDIC SOILS.

Limestone is nature's soil sweetener, capable of neutralizing overly acidic soils. It's best to add limestone in the fall to allow time for it to begin to dissolve and do its job. The amount of limestone you use will vary depending on the specific soil conditions. Simple home test kits, or a professional test, can be used to determine the soil's pH. If you dump limestone on soil randomly, you run the risk of overdosing the soil with lime. Follow guidelines on the limestone package or on a soil test.

Maintaining the new and improved pH is an ongoing project. Recheck the soil's pH every year and continue to add limestone as needed.

Apply only as much limestone as your soil requires.

8 **TO LOWER THE ALKALINITY** and increase the fertility of limestone and other soils with very high pH, add cottonseed meal, sulfur, pine bark, compost, or pine needles. Garden sulfur is a reliable cure when added as recommended in a soil test. It acidifies the soil slowly as microbes convert the sulfur to sulfuric acid and other compounds. Soil amendments such as compost, decaying pine bark, and ground-up pine needles gradually acidify the soil while improving its texture.

9 **ADD A THICK LAYER OF MULCH** and let it rot to improve the soil of existing gardens. Minerals, released as the mulch is degraded into nutrient soup, soak down into the soil and fertilize existing plants. Humic acid, another product of decay, clumps together small particles of clay to make a lighter, fluffier soil. For best success, remember these points:

- Woody mulch such as shredded bark uses nitrogen as it decays. Apply extra nitrogen to prevent the decay process from consuming soil nitrogen that plants need for growth.
- Don't apply fine-textured mulches, like grass clippings, in thick layers that can mat down and smother the soil.

   🍃 Use mulch, which helps keep the soil moist, in well-drained areas that won't become soggy or turn into breeding grounds for plant-eating slugs and snails.

10   GET LOCAL COMPOST from your city or town hall service department. Made from leaves and grass clippings collected as a public service, the compost may be free or at least reasonably priced for local residents. To find other large-scale composters, check with the nearest Cooperative Extension Service; they are up-to-date on these matters. Or try landscapers and nurseries, who may compost fall leaves or stable leftovers for their customers, and bulk soil dealers, who may sell straight compost or premium topsoil blended with compost. Don't give up. Yard scraps are discouraged or banned in many American landfills, so someone near you is composting them.

11   PLAN AHEAD FOR BULKY ORGANIC SOIL AMENDMENTS—compost, manures, and leaves—that may be added by the wheelbarrow-load to

---

SOURCES OF ORGANIC MATTER

Compost
Livestock manure
Straw
Grass clippings
Salt hay
Shredded bark
Bark chunks
Shredded leaves
Seedless weeds
Peat moss
Kitchen vegetable scraps
Mushroom compost
Agricultural remains such as
peanut hulls or ground corn cobs

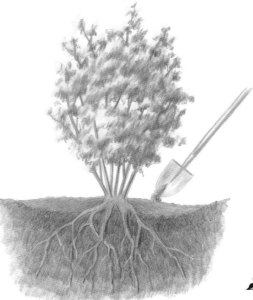

improve the soil. This will raise the soil level, at least temporarily. As the organic matter decays, the soil level will lower.

🍂 If soils rich in organic matter drop to expose the top of a newly planted shrub or tree roots, add more soil or organic matter to keep the roots under cover.

🍂 If your garden is beside a house or fence, keep the soil level low enough so it won't come in contact with wooden siding or fencing that isn't rot resistant.

🍂 When planting around existing trees, shrubs, and perennial flowers, avoid covering the crown—where stems emerge from the ground—with organic material. This helps prevent disease problems.

I2 | **DON'T WALK ON WET SOILS,** especially clay soils. The footprints you leave are evidence of compression—packing the soil particles tightly and squeezing out vital oxygen. This is not a desirable quality in a garden. Put walkways or stepping stones in the garden for easy access and to keep your shoes clean and dry. When planting, cover the soil with a board to kneel or stand on.

13 **TEST YOUR SOIL BY FEEL** before and after the soil is amended to judge the extent of the change. Take a small handful of lightly moist

This stone pathway is both attractive and useful.

soil from several inches below the soil surface. Squeeze it into a ball in your hand and watch the results when you open your fingers. Sandy soils, which can have a scratchy feel, will fall apart. To enrich a sandy soil, apply a several-inch layer of compost and even an inch or two of clay, then try again. When the soil is improved, the ball will cling together better.

Clay soils, which have a slick feel, will form a tight ball that's not easily broken up. To lighten clay soil, add extra compost and coarse sand. When the soil is light enough, the ball will break up with a tap of a finger.

14 **TILL OR SPADE A THICK LAYER OF COMPOST** into lightly moist (never wet) soil to bring it to life before planting a new garden. The going may be rough at first if you are starting with hard, compacted soil. Use a rototiller and tough it out. Go over the area, removing weed roots and other underground vegetation as you go. Then go over it again cross-wise, until you break up the soil into reasonably small pieces.

Your well-tilled soil, like screened topsoil, may look great at first, but silt or clay soils are likely to get stiff, crusty, and hard after a few heavy downpours. The best way to keep soil loose and light is to add organic matter.

Add a 4- to 6-inch-deep layer of compost to the soil and work it down until it's 10 to 12 inches deep. The soil will become darker, moister, and spongier—a dramatic conversion right before your eyes. As long as the organic matter remains in the soil, the soil is likely to stay loose. But since it slowly decays, you will have to continue to add organic matter—compost, mulch, or shredded leaves—in order to maintain the desired texture.

15 **TRY SPADING OR NO-TILL SYSTEMS TO PRESERVE THE TEXTURE AND ORGANIC CONTENT** of thriving garden soils. Once the soil is loose, light, and rich, minimal disturbance will help preserve the levels of organic matter. Avoid repeated tilling, which breaks healthy soil clumps and speeds up decay.

Instead of tilling, loosen rich soil before planting by turning the surface shallowly with a shovel and breaking it apart with a smack from the shovel backside. Very loose soil can be made ready to plant by combing it with a hoe or cultivator.

16 **DOUBLE-DIG GARDEN BEDS** to make high-performance gardens for deep-rooted plants like roses, a tradition in many beautiful English gardens. The average rototiller works the soil only 8 or 10 inches deep and won't break up compacted soil below. But double-digging will.

Double-digging requires of a bit of what the British call a stiff upper lip, because it takes a lot of manual labor. Do a little at a time so you don't overdo it, or hire a professional landscaper if you have health restrictions.

Start with vacant soil that is stripped of grass or other vegetation. Beginning at one end of the garden, remove a strip of soil a spade's length deep and a spade's width wide. Put it in a wheelbarrow. Use your shovel to turn the soil below it (likely to be one of the heaviest parts of the job) and break it up. Another (sometimes easier) option is to jab a garden fork (like a big pitchfork) into the hard lower soil and rock it around until the soil breaks up. If organic matter is needed, you should add it to the lower level at this point.

Do the same thing to the second strip of soil next to the first row. But turn the surface topsoil into the first trench, adding organic matter as desired. Then loosen and amend the exposed subsurface soil. Continue filling each trench from the adjacent row and loosening the soil below. Fill the final strip with the soil from the wheelbarrow.

17 **BUILD RAISED BEDS** where the soil is too hard, rocky, poor, or wet for plants to grow well. Instead of struggling to change these bad conditions, construct a great garden bed over them. In vegetable gardens, simply mound up planting rows 6 to 8 inches high and 2 to 3 feet wide. (You can walk in the paths beside the planting rows without compressing the raised soil.) Permanent and decorative gardens can be set in handsome raised bed frames built of timbers, logs, rocks,

In urban areas, or where the soil isn't usable, a raised bed garden is a good alternative.

or bricks and varying from 4 inches to 4 feet high. Don't hesitate to ask for professional help for big building projects, which need strong structures in order to last.

CHAPTER 2

THE WAYS OF WATER

At least 90 percent of every plant is composed of water, which should give you some idea of how important this substance is. No plant can live without some moisture, and certain plants use it in amazing ways. Orchids and bromeliads that live on tropical trees absorb rainwater through their foliage. Succulent plants and cacti store reservoirs of water in their swollen stem tissues so they can go for a month or more without rain. Prairie flowers such as butterfly weed store water in their fleshy taproots. And daffodils store water in their bulbs.

Without water, plants wilt and die. But too much water can be as bad for plants as not enough. If land plants are submerged in water for too long—even if just their roots are submerged—they may rot or drown from lack of oxygen.

Balancing plants' water needs is like having a healthful diet. Everything should be consumed in moderation. Provide your plants with enough water for good health, but don't flood them with it.

How and when you water your plants can make a big difference.

18 **APPLY WATER IN THE COOL OF THE MORNING OR EVENING** when the wind is calm, the sun is less hot, and water loss through evaporation is minimal.

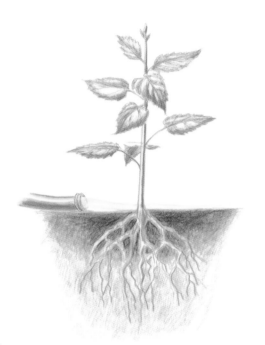

PLANTS TO WATER IN THE MORNING, NOT AT NIGHT

Roses	Tomatoes
Apples	Cucumbers
Pears	Melons
Peaches	Beans
Plums	Begonias
Cherries	Geraniums
Grapes	Peonies
Strawberries	Dahlias
Raspberries	Chrysanthemums
Blackberries	

19   **AVOID WATERING DISEASE-SUSCEPTIBLE PLANTS AT NIGHT.** If water sits on plant foliage for hours, it can encourage fungal diseases to attack leaves, buds, flowers, and fruit. Plants susceptible to leaf spots, fruit rots, and flower blights are best watered in the morning, when the warming sun will quickly dry off the leaves and discourage fungus development.

20   **PROVIDE AN INCH OF WATER A WEEK** for many plants and lawn grasses. The idea is to keep the soil lightly moist and to prevent it from drying out completely, which would be damaging to most plants. But because plants don't always follow the rules, there are exceptions to this general guideline:

- Hot weather, dry sandy soil, or crowded intensive plantings or containers may make more than an inch of water a week necessary.
- When the weather is cool, the plants are widely spaced, or the soil is heavy and moisture-retentive, less water may be required.
- Young or new plantings require more moisture at the soil surface to help their budding roots get started. You should water lightly and more frequently to accommodate their needs.
- Mature plantings with large root systems can be watered heavily and less often than younger plants. The moisture soaks deep into the soil and encourages the roots to thrive.

21 **SET A RAIN GAUGE IN AN OPEN AREA OF THE GARDEN** to learn how much water the garden receives each week. You can purchase one at a garden center or use a topless coffee can. After each rainfall, check the depth of the rain inside. A commercial rain gauge is calibrated and easy to read. To read rain levels in a coffee can, insert a ruler and note how high the water has come. Judge the need for supplemental irrigation accordingly (see Hint 20).

Rain gauges are also helpful when trying to determine when you have watered enough with an overhead sprinkler. Since some sprinklers apply water unevenly (more up close and less farther out), you could set several rain gauges around the garden and compare the amount of moisture each one collects. If the readings vary widely, move the sprinkler more frequently or invest in a more efficient model.

22 **USE GRAY WATER** on potted plants or small gardens to reduce water use. Gray water is the leftover tap water from activities such as rinsing vegetables at the kitchen sink. However, avoid water contaminated with water-softener salts, harsh detergents, fats, oils, or other extras that would harm plants. Gray water has been used successfully in arid parts of the United States and is well worth taking advantage of anywhere. It helps prevent stress on wells during drought and lowers utility bills for people with municipal water lines.

Capture gray water in a basin stored close to the sink, where it will be handy to pull out and use. Transfer the gray water to a watering can before watering potted plants or new plantings. A little moisture in a time of need will make a big difference.

23 **CATCH WATER FROM A DOWNSPOUT** into a container. This unfluoridated, unchlorinated water is ideal for watering plants. It comes at an ambient temperature, not shockingly cold from the tap—which is hard on warmth-loving plants. And perhaps best of all—at least from the gardener's perspective—it's free!

The easiest way to collect downspout runoff is to put a container at the bottom of the downspout. A topless bucket or barrel with a sturdy spigot at the bottom can be set in place permanently. Simply drain the water from the spigot into your watering can. To handle larger quantities of water, look for a 30- to 50-gallon barrel or drum. It's helpful to keep a large cup or other dipper on hand for transferring the water into a watering can.

You can tap every downspout around your house for maximum water yield or, if you prefer, just use the downspouts in the private parts of the landscape, the back and side yards.

24 **STRETCH SOAKER HOSES THROUGH THE GARDEN** to provide water directly on plant roots. Soaker hoses are made of water-permeable fabrics, perforated recycled rubber, or other porous materials. When attached to a hose with the water turned on low or medium, moisture droplets weep out along the length of the hose. Very little evaporates and none sprays on plant foliage, helping discourage diseases (see Hint 19). But it may take an hour or more to moisten nearby areas of the garden thoroughly.

Soaker hoses require a little special attention in order to work properly. Here are some hints:

- Run soaker hoses straight through the garden. If set to turn or curve too sharply, they will kink and won't fill with water.

- Expect more water to be released from the end closest to the hose and less to be released from the far end.

- If the hose is moistening only one side of a plant root system, move the hose to water the dry side before you consider the job done.

- To determine if the soil has been watered enough, dig into the soil beside the hose. If the water has seeped 12 inches down, it's about time to turn the hose off. Remember how long this took for the next time around.

- For faster results, look for flat hoses that are peppered with small holes. Of course there's a trade-off: These hoses do provide water more quickly, but they are not as gentle on the soil.

- If you like soaker hose results, you can upgrade to permanent or semi-permanent drip irrigation systems. Although more expensive, these systems are custom designed for vary-

MOISTURE-LOVING PLANTS

Louisiana and Japanese irises	Impatiens
	Hostas
Foamflowers	Ferns
Marsh marigolds	Joe-pye weed
Solomon's seal	Astilbes
Sweet flag	Umbrella plant
Horsetails	Ligularia
Swamp hibiscus	Mint
Chameleon plant	Cordgrass
Cardinal flower	Willows

ing soil types and individual plant water needs. They also don't require shuffling around the garden.

25 **WHEEL HOSE CARTS AROUND THE YARD** instead of dragging armloads of hoses and causing wear and tear on your back. Hose carts consist of a reel with a crank that you can use to neatly coil the hose, eliminating tangles, knots, and kinks. This reel is set on a two- or four-wheeled base with a handle for easy pulling. Look for large-wheeled types if you're rolling the cart over the lawn or rough ground. Smaller wheels are fine on a paved path or patio.

26 **PLACE HOSE GUIDES AT THE EDGES OF GARDEN BEDS** to keep the hose from crushing nearby plants when you pull the hose taut. Hose guides, such as a wooden stake pounded into the ground at an outward angle, prevent the hose from sliding into the garden. More decorative hose guides (stakes carved like decorative animals, elves, or flowers) can be found at some garden centers, mail-order garden suppliers, or craft shows. You could also improvise by using things like plastic pink flamingos, garden statues, or birdbaths.

27 **SAVE WATERING TIME BY USING SELF-WATERING PATIO PLANTERS.** These pots aren't smart enough to turn on the faucet and water themselves, but they do have a lower-level moisture reservoir that's available to plants at any time. A wick, which may resemble fabric or rope, pulls the water up into the rooting area when the soil begins to get dry. Many different styles are available—and more kinds are becoming available every year. Another option is to buy a converter kit that turns regular planters into self-watering pots.

28 **USE A WATER BREAKER ON THE END OF YOUR HOSE** to change heavy water flow into a gentle sprinkle. This helps prevent soil compaction and spreads the water more evenly across planting areas. Put an adjustable spray nozzle on the end of the hose, watering only with the setting that produces fine droplets in a gentle spray and wide arc. Save the strong blasts for washing the car.

Or, look for spray heads developed specifically for garden use. Some are set on angled bases, making it easy to reach in between plants. Others are on long poles for watering hanging baskets.

Water breakers should be put on watering cans, too, especially when watering young plants such as seedlings, which can be broken or uprooted with a strong drenching.

29 **REDIRECT RUNOFF FROM DOWNSPOUTS INTO FLOWER BEDS OR LAWN AREAS** to give plants extra water every time it rains. Flexible tubing could be connected to the end of the downspout and directed into nearby plantings around the foundation of the house or to flower or vegetable gardens. For maximum benefits, shape beds like a shallow bowl to collect the water and give it time to soak in. Or, as an alternative, the garden could be made fairly level with lower, moisture-gathering saucers made around newly planted trees or shrubs or plants with high moisture needs.

In dry climates, the tubing could be covered with soil or mulch and kept connected all the time. In climates with periods of overly wet weather, the tubing should be disconnected during soggy seasons to prevent oversaturation of the soil, which causes plants to rot.

30 **DROP THE SOIL LEVEL IN THE BOULEVARD STRIP,** the row of grass between the sidewalk and the street, so it will collect runoff rainwater that otherwise would be lost to street sewers or roadside ditches. A small 1- to 2-inch drop in soil level will be enough to do the job. If planting sod, make the soil level even lower to account for the extra height of sod roots. In cold climates, you may have to remove sand or grit that can accumulate after winter snowplowing to maintain an appropriate height.

SHEDDING SOME LIGHT ON LIGHT

While sunshine may not literally make the world go 'round, it does power the process of photosynthesis, which makes many things possible. Photosynthesis allows plants to make their own food, using only air and water. As they grow, plants provide food for grazing animals who in turn provide sustenance for higher levels of the food chain. Since sun provides the start for the whole food pyramid, it's vital to give it the respect it deserves in the garden.

Many plants, especially lawn grass, flowers, roses, vegetables, fruit trees, and conifers (needle-leaved evergreens) thrive in bright sun, which provides abundant energy for growth, flowering, and fruiting. But some plants, particularly those native to forests and glens, need shadier conditions. Learn the sun requirements of any plant you intend to grow so you can put it in the right place.

31 **WATCH HOW SHADOWS AND SUNLIGHT HIT THE GROUND** to determine how much shade exists during the growing season under deciduous trees (which drop their leaves in fall). This test will determine which shade-loving plants will thrive there.

The shade in your yard will help you determine which plants can grow there.

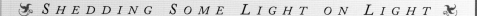

Some suggested plants for varying degrees of shade are found in the list at right.

- Full shade is found under thickly branched trees or evergreens. A garden that's located here will receive little or no direct sun and remain gloomily lit. Only a limited number of plants are suitable for this situation. You should choose flowers and ferns with evergreen leaves.

- Partial shade can be found under trees that allow sunlight to penetrate through the canopy and dapple the ground throughout the day. A garden grown under a lightly branched honey locust tree would fall into this category. A larger selection of plants are capable of growing under these conditions than in full shade.

- Light shade is found in places where plants are in direct sun for a portion of the day. This could be found in a garden under mature trees with long barren

> ## SOME PLANTS FOR SHADY CONDITIONS
>
> **PLANTS FOR FULL SHADE:**
> - Ferns, ivy, pachysandra, periwinkle
>
> **PLANTS FOR PARTIAL SHADE:**
> - Spring wildflowers: trout lilies, bloodroot, bellworts, Solomon's seal
> - Shrubs: rhododendrons, azaleas
> - Shade-loving perennials: bleeding heart, hostas, mint, bergenia, sweet woodruff, astilbes
> - Annuals: impatiens, browallia
>
> **PLANTS FOR LIGHT SHADE:**
> - Annuals: begonias, coleus, ageratum, sweet alyssum
> - Herbs: basil, parsley, bee balm
> - Vegetables: lettuce, spinach, arugula
> - Perennials: daylilies, hostas, anemones, hardy geraniums, coral bells, lobelia

trunks. The sun can shine in under the high leaf canopies. Light-shade conditions also exist on the east or west side of a wall or building. Here you can grow many shade-loving plants as well as shade-tolerant plants, which are sun-lovers capable of growing moderately well in light shade.

32 **GROW SUN-LOVING SPRING BULBS AND WILDFLOWERS** beneath deciduous shade trees to make the most of the sun before the tree leaves emerge. This is a great strategy for people who have a shady yard and therefore have trouble getting flowers to grow during summer and fall. Crocuses, squills, Spanish bluebells, daffodils, windflowers, glory-of-the-snow, and wildflowers such as bloodroot, squirrel corn, and other local natives thrive in spring sun. When tree

These spring flowers will thrive until the leaves in the tree above them begin to bloom.

leaves emerge and the setting grows dark, many of these spring growers fall dormant and lie quietly below the ground until spring sun arrives again.

33 **PAINT A DARK WALL WHITE** to reflect more light onto plants. Just like the silver solar reflectors used by sunbathers to intensify their tans, a light-colored wall will reflect additional light onto nearby plants. Similarly, using a mulch of white pebbles, sand, or gravel will reflect light up through the bottom of plants, a technique often used in gardens of Mediterranean herbs or silver-leaved plants that thrive on plenty of sun.

34 **LIMB-UP TREES** or remove smaller, scraggly, or unwanted saplings and brush to brighten a densely shaded spot. Tall, mature shade trees can have their lower limbs removed (a heavy job requiring a professional arborist) to produce light shade (see Hint 31). For even more light, arborists can thin out overcrowded branches in the canopy, leaving some openings in the foliage for sun penetration.

Removing unwanted tangles of young trees, wild shrubs, and other woody growth is a project you can do yourself. Look for self-sown seedlings around trees such as maples, oaks, ashes, and elms. Crabapples will send up vertical sprouts called suckers, turning the tree into a bush. Get a pair of long-handled pruning lopers to trim out the smaller growth and a pruning saw to remove larger trunks. When finished, you can admire the newly revealed shape of the tree trunk and the ferns, hostas, and other shade plants that can grow beneath it. Be sure not to overthin; you should leave enough saplings to replace older trees as they die.

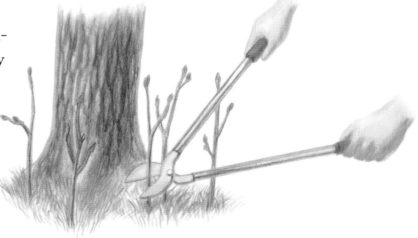

35

PRUNE LOW-HANGING BRANCHES ON A SUNNY DAY so you can see how the light changes. This way you can watch the shade lighten. You also can keep an eye on the shadows, which will dance from one side of the tree to the other, changing with the time of day and position of the sun. Their silhouettes can be a beautiful part of the garden, especially in winter when the dark shadows stand out on the white snow.

36 **DO NOT PRUNE OAKS IN SUMMER.** Even though this may be when you are anxious to lighten shade the most, it will make your trees susceptible to oak wilt disease. Prune, instead, in late winter.

37 **CONSIDER DIFFERENCES IN SUN INTENSITY WHEN PLANTING ON THE EAST AND WEST SIDE** of shade-casting trees or buildings. Even if east- and west-facing sites receive the same number of hours of sun, they will not produce identical results.

   ❧ Gardens with an eastern exposure are illuminated with cool morning

You need to consider sun exposure when planting directly against the house.

sun, then shaded in the afternoon. They are ideal locations for minimizing heat stress in southern climates or for plants such as rhododendrons that can burn in hot sun.

🌢 Gardens with western exposure are shaded in the morning and drenched in hot sun in the afternoon. Sunburn, bleaching, and sometimes death of delicate leaves can result, especially in warm climates and when growing sensitive young or shade-loving plants. Afternoon sun can also cause brightly colored flowers to fade. However, the west side of a building is the ideal place for sun-loving plants.

38 **TRY EXPOSING FLOWERING SHADE PLANTS TO A HALF DAY OF MORNING SUN** to encourage better blooming. Extra light can also keep the plants more compact, tidy, and self-supporting.

SOME PLANTS FOR SUNNY CONDITIONS

EVERGREENS: boxwood, junipers, false cypress, yews, arborvitae

CONIFERS: pines, spruces, firs

TREES: maples, oaks, elms, magnolias, crabapples, hawthorns, apples, pears, peaches, plums

SHRUBS: roses, barberries, potentilla, spirea, lilacs

PERENNIALS: yarrow, sea thrift, Shasta daisies, chrysanthemums, coreopsis, pinks, coneflowers, blanketflowers

ANNUALS: portulaca, gazania, gerbera, marigolds, zinnias, dahlias

HERBS: lavender, astilbes, thyme, sage, rosemary

39 **PROVIDING 6 TO 8 HOURS OF DIRECT SUN A DAY** is sufficient for most plants that need full sun. The term "full sun" doesn't actually mean plants must be in bright light every moment of the day, only most of the day. The 6 to 8 hour minimum must be met, however, even during the shorter days of spring and fall for perennials, trees, and shrubs.

40 **WHEN GROWING POTTED PLANTS INDOORS,** supplement natural light with fluorescent or grow lights. Sometimes in winter the weather may be cloudy for days, even weeks. This creates problems for tropical plants, potted flowers, and even foliage plants which need light to remain healthy.

    The solution is to hang a fluorescent shop light directly over your indoor plants. Special grow lights or full spectrum bulbs (formulated to produce light wavelengths that plants need most) can be used in place of fluorescent bulbs for spectacular results with flowering plants. For extra-easy maintenance, plug the lights into an automatic timer, then set them to turn on for 14 to 16 hours a day and off again at night.

Indoor potted plants may require a supplemental light source.

CHAPTER 4

MAINTENANCE AND PRUNING

Like playing a lively game of tennis, keeping your garden looking great depends on having the right equipment, developing a good technique, and being organized enough to do the right things at the right time. This may sound like a lot to juggle, but once you understand the basics, it's easy.

For a start, you need good hoes, spades, rakes, pruners, and a sturdy wheelbarrow. Then you need to learn how to control weeds with cultivation and mulch (Hints 48 and 49). A few basic pruning cuts will help you rejuvenate and control the size of your shrubs and trees (Hints 50 to 55). Other helpful suggestions in this section will help you polish up the rest of the landscape.

Watch the calendar and note the dates things need to be done in advance. This lets you encourage desirable plant growth and deter difficulties before they happen, thereby keeping your maintenance chores to a minimum.

41 **PILE DUG-OUT EARTH ON A TARP** instead of on the grass when digging a hole for planting or excavating a garden pool. You can easily drag away any excess soil, and you won't have to rake up little clods trapped in the turf. Don't waste that soil. You can use it to build a waterfall beside the pool or to fill a raised bed for herbs or vegetables.

42 **BUY THE BEST TOOLS** you can afford. There is no substitute for good tools. Tools that cost half the price but last only two years (instead of 22 years) are not cost-effective in the long run. They may also fail you in the middle of a big project, just when you need them most.

One way to ensure good quality is to buy tools from a reputable dealer willing to guarantee their performance. For another quality test, look at the way tools are made. Tools with steel blades are strong enough to last for years without bending. Stainless steel is even better, because it won't rust. Spades, shovels, and forks with hard ash handles are unlikely to splinter or break in the middle of a heavy opera-tion. People with smaller builds can find specially designed tools with smaller blades and shorter handles, which are easier to control than oversized tools.

43 **KEEP HAND TOOLS IN A BASKET** on the garage or pantry shelf so they are always easy to find. Nothing is more frustrating than seeing a

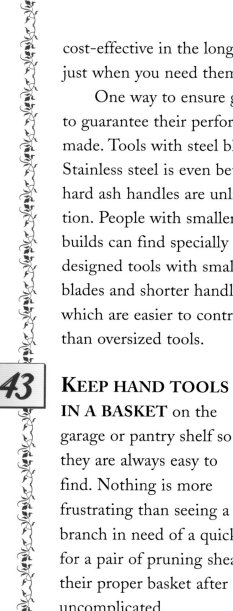

A basket keeps hand tools neat, accessible, and easy to carry.

branch in need of a quick trim but having to search all over the house and garage for a pair of pruning shears. If all your tools are kept together—and returned to their proper basket after each use—simple garden projects will stay quick and uncomplicated.

44   USE WIRE GRID SUPPORTS instead of individual stakes to easily hold up bushy but floppy perennials such as peonies. You can buy commercial grid supports, which are handsome round or square grids neatly set on legs; green grids are more camouflaged amid the foliage than metallic grids. Or you can make your own grid supports out of a sheet of wire mesh, cut a little wider than the plant it will support. The extra length can be bent into legs.

The supporting process takes one simple step. Set the grid over a newly emerging perennial in spring. The stems will grow up though it, retaining their natural shape while staying firmly upright.

The alternative (which occurs when you let the plant sprawl before staking it) is more difficult and less attractive. Corsetting the drooping limbs with twine and

PERENNIALS THAT OFTEN NEED SUPPORT

Shasta daisies
Asters
Bellflowers (taller types)
Garden phlox
Pyrethrum daisies
Yarrows
Balloon flowers
Sedums (taller types)
Hollyhock
Foxglove

hoisting them up with a stake of wood can result in broken stems and a miserable-looking specimen.

45 **ALWAYS SET HOES, SOIL RAKES, AND OTHER TOOLS WITH HORIZONTAL TEETH OR BLADES FACE DOWN** on the ground when not being used. If stepped on, the teeth or blades sink harmlessly into the soil. But if left upright, an unwary walker might step on the teeth, making the tool tip and the handle spring up into his or her face. This hurts!

For an even more organized approach, attach a topless and bottomless coffee can or similarly shaped plastic container to a fence post, securing it with wire. You can slip in the handles of rakes, shovels, and hoes, keeping them together, upright, and out from underfoot.

46 **KEEP A BUCKET OF CLEAN SAND AND MACHINE OIL** in the garage to cure tools after each use. This is particularly helpful for rust-prone digging instruments such as shovels, garden forks, and hoes. After use, rinse with water and dry the blades. Then insert them in the oil/sand mixture. The sand will scour off debris, and the oil will coat the metal, retarding rust.

Keep the tools together in one place, preferably close to your basket of hand tools (see Hint 43) so they will be easy to find when needed.

47 **USE A SHARP HOE TO CUT OFF WEEDS,** especially annuals, instead of stooping and pulling them. Using a hoe is quicker and easier than hand-weeding, plus it does a superb job. If you catch weeds when they are young seedlings, a single swipe will be all it takes to eliminate them. If they are older, cut them down before they go to seed to prevent future generations of weeds.

Perennial weeds such as dandelions may have large underground roots that will resprout after hoeing. You can keep hoeing in hopes of wearing them down. Or, as a faster alternative, when the soil is moist, use a corner of the hoe blade to dig down and help you loosen the root, then pull it up by hand.

When the hoe blade begins to get dull and takes more effort to use, sharpen it like a knife with a sharpening stone.

48 **COVER GARDEN BEDS WITH A LAYER OF MULCH** to keep weeds down and reduce the need for water. Annual weed seeds are less likely to sprout when the soil is covered with enough mulch to keep the soil surface in the dark.

When it comes to water, even a thin layer of mulch—nature's moisturizer— will reduce evaporation from the soil surface. Thicker mulches can reduce water use by as much as 50 percent.

Mulches vary in their appearance, makeup, and texture, which will influence how you use them. Here are some examples:

- Varying appearances: For a soothing, natural-looking garden, use dark-colored organic mulches made of bark or compost. For a brilliant-looking garden,

consider a mulch of bright gravel. In
utilitarian gardens like a vegetable
garden, plastic or straw makes an
excellent mulch.

❧ Soil improvement: This calls for
the use of organic mulches
that break down to add
organic matter to the soil
(see Hint 9).

❧ Texture: For maximum
effectiveness with only a thin
mulch layer, look for fine-
textured mulches such as twice-
shredded bark, compost, or cocoa hulls. For an airy mulch, try thicker layers
of coarse-textured mulches such as straw or bark chunks.

49 **KILL OFF SOD OR DENSE WEEDS** by layering newspaper, compost, and
mulch directly on the garden site. This treatment cuts off the sunlight to unwanted
vegetation, which will eventually decay and add organic matter to the garden. The
newspaper decomposes, too. (What a bargain!)

If you build the compost layer at least 4 inches high, you can plant shallow-
rooted annuals or vegetable seedlings into it. In a year or so, loosen the soil deeply
or build it up into a raised bed if you want to grow deeper-rooted perennials,
shrubs, and trees.

50

PRUNE WITH TOP-QUALITY PRUNING SHEARS, LOPPERS, AND A SAW.

Sharp blades and sturdy handles make pruning a breeze. Dull blades—rusty and sticking—make projects harder than they need to be. They can also cause wood to be crushed or torn, which is damaging to the plant. Look for hard, durable blades capable of being resharpened and a sturdy,

Use loppers on branches up to 1¹/₂ inches thick.

smoothly operating nut holding the blades together. Hand shears should also have a safety latch to keep the blades closed when not in use.

Hand pruning shears are used for small stems under about a half-inch in

Hand pruning shears work well on smaller stems.

diameter. Look for scissor-type blades, which make sharper, cleaner cuts than the anvil type with a sharp blade pressing on a flat blade. Also check out new ergonomically designed pruning shears that minimize repetitive motion stress.

Loppers are long-handled pruning shears with larger blades for cutting branches up to about 1¹/₂ inches in diameter. Pruning is easier if you buy a model with ratcheting action for more power with less effort.

Pruning saws should have narrow blades, be easy to maneuver into tight spaces, and be toothed on one side only.

51 **CANDLE-PRUNE PINES TO CONTROL THEIR SIZE** or make them branch more thickly. Candle-pruning (also called candling) refers to manipulating the candle-shaped new shoots that arise in spring. Before the needles enlarge, use your pruning shears to cut off a little, half, or most of the soft candle, depending on how much you want to limit size. The cut should slant at an angle instead of slicing straight across the candle. Come the following spring, clusters of new side branches will appear. Continue candling each year for more dramatic results.

Candling is especially handy for keeping mugo pines small enough for use near the house or in a mixed border. It also can help lanky, open-branched pines fill in to form a more solid and substantial cone.

52 **RENEWAL-PRUNE FLOWERING SHRUBS** by removing one-third of the stems once each year. This modest effort acts like a fountain of youth, keeping these shrubs young. It's much better than shearing, which reduces flowering, has to be repeated frequently, and can even accelerate aging.

Use pruning loppers or a pruning saw to cut the oldest stems off at the ground, ideally in early spring before the shrubs break dormancy. This timing encourages quick renewal, but a few spring flowers will be sacrificed on early bloomers. If you can't bear that thought, wait to prune until after flowering. As spring and summer progress, new branches will take the place of the old branches. If pruned every year, the shrub will be continually rejuvenated, remaining healthy and beautiful.

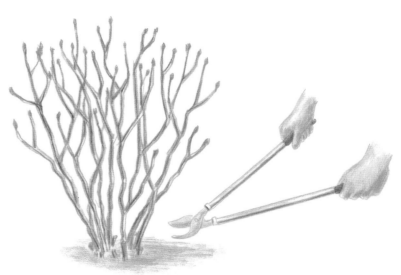

53 **REJUVENATE TIRED, OVER-GROWN, OR WEAK SHRUBS** by cutting them to the ground. Although this may sound like giving up, just the opposite is true. It can be the start of a whole new shrub. This technique works well

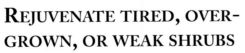

SPRING-BLOOMING SHRUBS

Azaleas
Flowering quince
Cotoneasters
Forsythia
Fothergilla
Japanese kerria
Rhododendrons
Pussy willows
Lilacs
Viburnums

with easy-growing shrubs such as lilacs, viburnums, butterfly bushes, and boxwoods but is generally not effective with evergreen shrubs (except boxwoods).

The idea is similar to renewal-pruning, only more radical. It should be done in early spring before leaves or flowers emerge. Shrubs with strong root systems will resprout with a fountain of new stems. So that they don't crowd each other out, you should thin out excessively thick clumps to allow the strongest to continue growing and form the foundation for the new shrub.

Cut worn-out or overgrown shrubs to the ground to rejuvenate them or thin them out.

Shrubs with weak root systems or disease problems may not resprout. If there are no signs of life a month or two after cutting the shrub back, start looking for a replacement plant.

54 **PRUNE TO THE OUTSIDE OF A TREE'S BRANCH COLLAR** for fast healing and good tree health. The branch collar is the swelling located at the base of the branch, where it arises from another limb or the trunk. The branch collar is like a hospital isolation ward; it houses protective chemicals that help keep diseases from invading the parent limb. When removing a branch for any reason, leaving that branch collar in place shuts out any passing pathogens.

55 **SLANT PRUNING CUTS AWAY FROM THE BUD** to encourage water to run off. This helps keep the bud healthy so it can grow and prosper.

56 **USE A LAWN MOWER EQUIPPED WITH A BAGGER** when you mow the grass and any fallen leaves in autumn. The mower will begin to shred up the leaves and mix them with the grass. This does twice the good of ordinary mowing: It saves you from raking, and the blended leaves and grass clippings are a dynamite combination for making compost. Empty the mower bag in an out-of-the-way place to make a compost pile. Use a garden fork to fluff the pile occasionally during winter, and you could have great compost by spring or summer.

57 **GROW A PLANT FOR AT LEAST TWO OR THREE YEARS** before you decide to remove it. It can take that long for a perennial plant to get comfortable in a new home and begin to really show what it can do. Allowing a trial period of several years also lets the plant get beyond setbacks from difficult weather—slow growth after an exceptionally cold winter or poor flowering during a long drought, for instance.

58 **DON'T ASSUME YOU CAN'T GROW A PLANT** if it dies once. If you like that plant and are willing to buy another one, put it in a different place—one better suited for its light and soil needs.

59 **MULCH NEW PLANTS WITH STRAW OR CHOPPED LEAVES AFTER PLANTING IN THE FALL** to prevent root damage during winter. A little mulch used immediately after planting can help to keep the soil moist and encourage continued root growth.

Mulch fall plants to protect them from damaging winter cold.

But the main reason to mulch lies ahead, in winter. Alternately freezing and thawing, expanding and contracting soil can break new roots or even push new plantings out of the ground, a process called soil heaving. By mulching generously with an airy material like straw when the soil first freezes, you can help keep the soil frozen until winter ends, at which point the mulch can be removed.

60 **IN WINTER, MULCH EVERGREEN PERENNIALS AND GROUND COVERS WITH EVERGREEN BOUGHS** to protect them from winter burn (the cold-weather opposite of sunburn). When the soil is frozen, the wind is strong, and the sun is bright, moisture is pulled out of the vulnerable leaves and cannot be replaced by the frozen roots. A protective layer of evergreen boughs, possibly obtained by recycling the branches of a Christmas tree, forms a protective shield over vulnerable greenery. Straw will also do the job, especially in colder areas where there is less chance of rot in winter.

61 **CELEBRATE IF YOU LIVE IN A SNOWY AREA.** Snow is the best mulch of all, and it may allow you to grow plants that won't survive winter in snowless areas farther south.

CHAPTER 5

LOW-MAINTENANCE GARDENING

If you are used to cutting your lawn every week and shearing your shrubs once a month, you may be relieved to know that there are easier ways to keep your yard looking nice. Low-maintenance gardening begins with choosing plants ideally suited for your yard's conditions so they won't need coaxing to stay alive.

Beyond that, some plants are naturally easier to keep, requiring little but suitable soil and sun exposure to grow and prosper. You can plant them and let them be without worrying about pests and diseases or extensive pruning, watering, fertilizing, or staking. Spending a little time finding these easy-care plants will prevent hours of maintenance in coming years.

Selecting the right style of planting for any given area can also reduce maintenance. Instead of lawn grass that needs regular fertilizing, watering, and mowing, a self-sustaining meadow area can be appealing and leave you with plenty of time for your other interests. Or grow dwarf shrubs that don't need pruning for a trouble-free planting next to the house. These and other tips will help your landscape look great with less effort.

Dwarf shrubs require less pruning than their full-size counterparts.

62 CHOOSE DWARF AND SLOW-GROWING PLANTS to eliminate the need for pruning and pinching. Tall shrubs just keep growing, and growing, and growing…sometimes getting too big for their place in the landscape. Lilacs, for example, commonly grow to 12 feet high. If planted by the house, they could cut off the view from the window. The only solution is regular trimming or replacement. A better option is to grow dwarf shrubs or special compact varieties that will only grow 2 to 4 feet high. They may never need pruning and won't have to be sheared into artificial globes.

Tall flowers and vegetables may not be able to support the weight of their flowers and fruit. They might need staking, caging, or support with a wire grid (see Hint 44) to keep them from falling flat on their faces. Flowers such as

---

COMPACT SHRUBS FOR FOUNDATION PLANTINGS

Dwarf balsam fir	Hydrangea, French and oakleaf	Mugo and other small pines
Compact azaleas	Hypericum	Potentilla
Compact barberries	Compact hollies	Pyracantha
Compact boxwood	Compact junipers	Roses
Heather	Leucothoe	Spirea
Compact false cypress	Mahonia	Stephanandra
Cotoneasters	Dwarf Korean lilac	Compact viburnums
Daphne	Dwarf spruce	
Deutzia	Japanese andromeda	
Fothergilla		

delphiniums, asters, and Shasta daisies are now available in compact sizes that are self-supporting. And shorter types of daylilies are less likely to become floppy in light shade than taller types. Compact peas and tomatoes, while not entirely self-supporting, can be allowed to grow loosely on their own, or they may need only small cages or supports to be held securely upright.

63 **PLANT WEEDY SPOTS WITH THICK-GROWING GROUND COVER** to avoid becoming a drudge to weeding. Ground cover works well on banks, in sun or shade, under fencing where it's hard to keep weeds down, beside outbuildings, and even under trees where it's too shady for grass to grow.

It's important to start the ground-cover bed in weed-free soil, however, so the ground cover can take over without competition. One easy way to get started is discussed in Hint 49. Another option is to clean up the soil. Turn it over with a rototiller or spade, let the weeds sprout, and then turn it again. Repeat the process until the weeds are almost gone.

Ground cover looks neat and keeps weeds to a minimum.

Choose a ground cover that will thrive in the site. It needs to spread vigorously and grow thickly enough to crowd out any weeds that may try to work their way in. In shady areas, try ivy, pachysandra, barrenwort, wild ginger, or periwinkle. In sun, try creeping junipers, daylilies, ground cover roses, or other plants that are specifically suited for your climate.

For good results fast, buy plenty of plants and space them relatively close together. If this is too expensive, spread plants farther apart, and mulch the open areas to discourage weeds. Plan to keep a close eye on the new garden for the first year and pull up or hoe down any weeds that appear. Water and fertilize as needed to get the ground cover plants growing and spreading quickly. Once they've covered the soil solidly, there won't be any space for weeds.

64 AVOID FAST-SPREADING AND AGGRESSIVE PERENNI-

ALS such as yarrow, plume poppy, 'Silver King' artemisia, and bee balm. Although these plants are lovely, they have creeping stems that can spread through the garden, conquering more and more space and arising in the middle of neighboring plants. Keeping them contained in their own place requires dividing—

Yarrow can be problematic if it's not controlled.

digging up the plants and splitting them into smaller pieces for replanting. This may need to be done as often as once a year. It's better to just avoid them.

65 **AVOID DELICATE PLANTS** such as delphiniums, garden phlox, and hollyhocks, which need extra care and staking. Although spectacular in bloom, these prima donnas require constant protection from pests and diseases, plus pampered, rich, moist soil and, often, staking to keep them from falling over. If you simply have to try one, look for compact and/or disease-resistant cultivars, which are easier to care for.

66 **IN AREAS DISTANT FROM THE HOUSE, PLANT NATIVE MEADOW GRASSES AND FLOWERS** that only need to be mowed once a year. Then have fun watching meadow garden flowers come and go throughout the season.

You can find seed mixes or prestarted turflike carpets of meadow plants specially blended for different regions of the country. To feature your location's unique meadow plants, just let the area grow wild, and meadow plants will come on their own. (Be sure to explain what you are doing to your neighbors so they won't think your lawnmower is broken!)

While they are getting started, newly planted meadows will need weeding and watering. Once in the late fall, after the flowers and

---

SOME MEADOW PLANTS

Black-eyed Susan	Snow-in-Summer
Dame's rocket	Butterfly flower
Evening primrose	Maiden pinks
Coreopsis	Penstemon
Blanketflower	Rock cress
Asters	Wild lupine
Coneflowers	Gayfeather
Shasta daisies	

Wildflowers add a unique touch to a lawn.

grasses have all set seed, mow them down and let the seeds scatter to come up next year. Purchased wildflower carpets and mixes may contain colorful flowers that disappear after several years. You can sprinkle new seeds or plug in new clumps of a wildflower carpet to reintroduce them for color if you want.

67 **MOW DOWN OLD FLOWER STALKS IN LATE FALL** to clean up a flower garden. Before mowing anything but grass with your mower, make sure it has a safety feature that will prevent debris from being thrown out at you. Using suitable lawn mowers can save you plenty of time compared with cutting back the flower stalks by hand. If you allow the old stems to scatter around the garden, instead of bagging them, you may find an abundance of self-sown seedlings arising in springtime.

68 **BUILD GARDEN PATHS** anywhere that gets enough foot traffic to wear out the grass. Paths make pleasant straight or curving lines through the yard and make it easier to get where you need to go in wet weather.

They also save you the trouble of having to constantly reseed barren, footworn areas.

Paths are useful elsewhere too. A path in the middle of a wide garden gives you access without having to walk through the soil. A narrow path can run along the front of a garden, serving as an edging, making the garden look neat, and keeping the grass out.

At its simplest, a path can be made with a surfacing of mulch or gravel. More elaborate paths can be made from stone, brick, or pavers.

69 **TURN A LOW, MOIST SPOT INTO A BOG GARDEN** for plants that need extra moisture. You can even excavate down a little to create a natural pond. Plant the moist banks with variegated cattails, sagittaria, bog primroses, marsh marigolds, and other moisture-loving plants. See the list on page 30 for additional plants.

Take advantage of wet soil by planting a bog garden.

70 **SPEED UP THE COMPOST-MAKING PROCESS** by chopping up leaves and twigs before putting them on the compost pile. The smaller the pieces are, the faster they will decay. Chopping can be easily done with a chipper-shredder or a mulching mower.

ORGANIC GARDENING TECHNIQUES

Organic gardening is popular today, and for good reason: It works wonderfully! Organic gardeners shun the use of synthetic chemicals to keep their yards free from potential hazards. But the real success of organic gardens lies in the methods used to keep plants growing vigorously, without a heavy reliance on sprays. Organic gardening cuts right to the heart of the matter: soil.

Soil is the life force of the garden. When enriched with organic matter, the soil becomes moist, fertile, and airy—ideal for healthy plants. It also nourishes a rich population of beneficial organisms such as earthworms and nutrient-releasing bacteria. And it harbors root-extending fungi that help make growing conditions optimal.

Organic gardeners also stress problem prevention in the garden. Putting plants in the right amount of sun, along with suitable soil, proper spacing, and ideal planting and watering, allows most plants to thrive with minimal upsets.

71 **MAKE COMPOST THE LAZY WAY** by layering leaves, lawn clippings, and kitchen waste. Then simply leave it until it's ready. Nature's recyclers will take organic matter no matter how it is presented and turn it into rich, dark compost. This process just takes longer in an untended pile.

To begin your compost heap, dump yard scraps in a far corner of the yard. An ideal blend would be equal amounts of soft or green material (manure and fresh leaves) and brown or hard material (dead leaves and chopped twigs); see the list on page 64. Or, if you prefer, keep the compost materials neatly contained in a wooden slat or wire mesh bin. If you put an access door on the bottom of the bin, you can scoop out the finished compost at the bottom while the rest is still decaying.

72 ADD COMPOST STARTER or good garden soil to a new compost pile to help jump-start the decay of organic materials.

Compost starter, available in garden centers or from mail-order garden catalogues, contains decay-causing microorganisms. Some brands also contain nutrients, enzymes, hormones, and other stimulants that help decomposers work as fast as possible. Special formulations can be particularly helpful for hard-to-compost, woody material like wood chips and sawdust or for quick decay of brown leaves.

> ### OPTIONAL COMPOST-MAKING EQUIPMENT
>
> Wire composting bin
> Stackable composting bin
> Wooden composting bin
> Vented plastic bins
> Worm boxes
> Compost tumbler
> Compost inoculant
> Garden fork
> Compost thermometer
> Sifting screen

Good garden or woodland soil, although not as high-tech nor as expensive as compost starter, contains native decomposers well able to tackle a compost pile. Sprinkle it among the yard scraps as you are building the pile.

73 **USE PERFORATED PVC PIPES** to aerate compost piles. An ideal compost pile will reach three to four feet high, big enough to get warm from the heat of decay. Why is heat important? High temperatures—when a pile is warm enough to

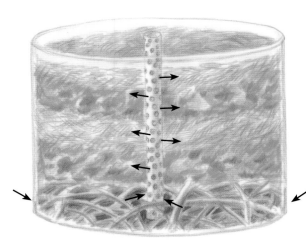

steam on a cool morning—semi-sterilize the developing compost, killing disease spores, hibernating pests, and weed seeds.

But the problem is that in order for decomposers to work efficiently enough to create heat, they need plenty of air—and not just at the surface of the pile. Aeration is traditionally provided by fluffing or turning the pile with a pitchfork, which can be hard work. But with a little advance planning and a perforated pipe, this can be avoided.

Start a compost pile on a bed of branched sticks that will allow air to rise from below. Add a perforated pipe in the center, building layers of old leaves, grass clippings, and other garden leftovers around it. The air will flow through the pipe into the pile.

74 USE ON-SITE COMPOSTING for easy soil improvement. Gather up old leaves, livestock manure, and/or green vegetable scraps and let them lie in or beside the garden until they rot, then work them into the soil. Or just heap them on the garden in the fall and till them into the soil. They will be decayed by spring. You can also dig a hole, dump in the yard waste, cover it with a little soil, and let it rot in privacy.

75 EXPECT TO USE MORE ORGANIC FERTILIZER, by volume, than synthetic chemical fertilizers. That's because organic fertilizers contain fewer nutrients by weight, averaging from 1 to about 6 or 7 percent. Contrast this with an inorganic lawn fertilizer that may contain up to 30 percent nitrogen, more than four times as much as organic fertilizer.

More is not always better when it comes to fertilizers. Lower-dose organic fertilizers are

---

COMPOST BLENDS

Organic material decays most quickly if blended with approximately equal parts of the following:

NITROGEN-RICH SOFT AND GREEN MATERIAL
Manure from chickens, cows, horses, rabbits, pigs, guinea pigs, and other herbivores
Fruit and vegetable peels
Grass clippings
Green leaves
Strips of turf
Alfalfa

CARBON-RICH BROWN AND HARD MATERIAL
Wood chips
Ground-up twigs
Sawdust
Pruning scraps
Autumn leaves
Straw

unlikely to burn plant roots or cause nutrient overdoses. Many forms release their components slowly, providing a long-term nutrient supply instead of one intense nutrient blast. Organic fertilizers may also provide a spectrum of lesser nutrients, even enzymes and hormones that can benefit growth.

For details on how to use fertilizers properly, read the package labels. The volume of fertilizer required may vary depending on the kind of plant being fertilized and the time of year.

76 **USE FISH EMULSION FERTILIZER** to encourage a burst of growth from new plantings, potted flowers and vegetables, or anything that is growing a little too sluggishly for your taste. High-nitrogen fish emulsion dissolves in water and is easily absorbed and put to immediate use by the plant. For best results, follow the package directions.

77 **ADD TOAD HOUSES** to the garden to attract toads for natural pest control. Just as fairy-tale toads can be turned into handsome princes with just a kiss, ordinary toads become plant protectors just by hopping into the garden. They may not be pretty, but toads eat plenty of bugs, so you'll be glad to see them.
To encourage toads to come to live in your garden, try the following:

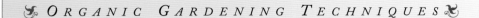
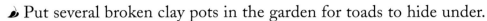

❧ Put several broken clay pots in the garden for toads to hide under.

❧ Water when the ground gets dry to keep the environment pleasant for amphibians.

❧ Avoid spraying toxic chemicals on the garden.

❧ Watch out for toads when tilling, hoeing, or shoveling.

This deer looks cute, but it's a nuisance in the garden.

78 **USE ORGANIC REPELLENTS** to chase away rodents and deer. Sprays made out of hot peppers, coyote or bobcat urine, rotten eggs, bonemeal, or bloodmeal—even castor oil—can make your garden plants unappetizing to herbivores. Reapply the repellents frequently, and always after rain, to maintain high protection levels.

79

French marigolds

GROW FRENCH OR AMERICAN MARIGOLDS to kill any nematodes in the garden soil. Nematodes—microscopic wormlike pests that can damage tomatoes, potatoes, and other crops—are killed by chemicals that are released by marigold roots and decaying foliage. You can plant marigolds in and around other nematode-susceptible plants. Or just till marigolds into the soil and let them decay before planting potatoes or tomatoes.

CHAPTER 7

PROPAGATION

S tarting your own plants from seeds, cuttings, divisions, and layering saves money and expands options. But be prepared to give propagation a certain amount of attention. Young plants, like young children or young puppies, need tender loving care to get them off to a good start.

Many plants grow well from seeds, especially annual flowers, herbs, and vegetables. You can find dozens of new, rare, or old-fashioned varieties in seed catalogues that aren't available in the local nurseries. Seed sowing allows you to grow a few, dozens, or even hundreds of seedlings from a seed packet costing a dollar or two. That's economy!

Certain special plants don't grow from seeds. They need to be cloned (vegetatively propagated). This is done by rooting sections of stems or sprouting chunks of roots. Clump-forming plants can be divided into several pieces, and some stems can be rooted while still attached to the mother plant. The tips included in this chapter will help make the transition from old plant to new as smooth as possible.

80 **KEEP A NOTEBOOK, CALENDAR, OR ADVANCE PLANNER** to remind you when to plant seeds or take cuttings. For example, seeds such as tomatoes and peppers need to be planted six to eight weeks before the last spring frost, but squash and cucumbers need to be planted only three weeks before the last spring frost. It can be hard to remember everything (and squeeze it into your schedule) unless it's written down.

81  **KEEP GOOD PROPAGATION RECORDS** to track how successful each operation has been and how the young plants are proceeding through the seasons. These records will guide you about when to plant, divide, start seeds, or collect seeds for future years. Jot down your observations weekly in a notebook. Or keep an index card on each plant you propagate so it's easy to find the next time. Some gardeners may want to computerize their records. Here are some things to note:

- How long seedlings grew indoors before being transplanted outdoors, and whether that timing allowed enough, too little, or too much time for a great performance outdoors.
- When you planted seedlings outdoors and how well they responded to the weather conditions at that time.
- When the first shoots of perennial flowers and herbs emerged in spring and were ready to divide.
- When you took stem cuttings from roses, lilacs, geraniums, impatiens, chrysanthemums, dahlias, and other plants. Rooting success often depends on the season in which the cuttings were taken.
- When seed pods matured and were ready to harvest for next year's crop (see Hint 82).

82 **WATCH THE COLOR OF RIPENING SEED PODS,** which is the clue to when seed is ripe. When dry pods turn from bright green to dull green or brown and succulent fruits turn bright colors, the seeds are mature and ready to harvest.

83 **TO KEEP RIPENING SEEDS FROM ESCAPING** when a pod dries and splits open, slip a net made from an old nylon stocking over the seed head. Secure it to the stem with a twist tie.

84 **KEEP DRY SEEDS DRIER** by refrigerating them. This works with both seeds you've collected from dry pods in the garden and leftover packaged seeds. Keeping these seeds in low humidity will encourage a long lifetime. Put collected seeds in dry envelopes. Keep packaged seeds in their original packets as long as they are dry. Enclose them in a sealed plastic bag or glass jar and put them in the refrigerator, where the air is extra arid. Avoid putting them in the humidified produce keepers.

85 **WHEN PLANTING, LABEL ALL SEEDS** with plant and cultivar name and date sown. Because many seedlings look alike, facing an unlabeled flat would be a nightmare. Labels help you remember such things as which little green sprouts are the zinnias and which are the marigolds.

The cultivar name lets you tell hot peppers from sweet peppers (very important!) and red pansies from blue pansies. Since cultivar names like Hungarian Wax pepper may be too long for short plant labels, come up with code abbreviations (such as "HW pep") and note them in your propagation records for future reference. Write on wooden or plastic tags with permanent ink.

86 **MAKE YOUR OWN LABELS** out of milk cartons or plastic jugs instead of buying them. Simply wash them out, cut them into strips about 1 inch wide and 4 to 6 inches long, and write right on them with permanent ink or wax pencil.

87 **LABEL LIKE THE PROS.** When planting in a flat (see Hint 85), organize plant tags neatly so you can remember which plants they are referring to. If planting the flat with the long side closest to you, run rows of seeds from the front to the back, starting at the left side and ending at the right side. Insert a new label in the planting row each time you start using a different seed. This technique also works for flats of cuttings.

Keep your seed flats well organized and clearly labeled.

88 SOW PERENNIAL AND WILDFLOWER SEEDS OUTDOORS in raised beds or spacious nursery pots (the kind you get big flowers in at the nursery) and let nature get them ready to sprout. Hardy perennials and wildflowers often have a special defense called dormancy that keeps them from sprouting prematurely during a temporary midwinter thaw (which would be damaging when the frost returned). They require a certain amount of cold—or alternating freezing and thawing—to indicate when winter is truly over and spring has begun. The easiest way to accommodate the cold requirement is by putting them outdoors. (For other ways to provide cold treatments, see Hints 90 and 91.)

89 INSTEAD OF BUYING POTS OR CELL PACKS, recycle household containers for starting seedlings. Try some of the following:

- Egg crates or milk cartons cut lengthwise
- Clear plastic bakery containers with lids that provide a green-houselike atmosphere
- Yogurt cups
- Cottage cheese containers
- Plastic foam coffee cups

Wash the containers out thoroughly with soapy water, then sterilize them with a solution of 1 part bleach to 10 parts water. Poke holes in the bottom to allow excess water to drain out.

GIVE CERTAIN SUMMER BLOOMING PERENNIALS A BRIEF COLD CHILL to synchronize their germination. Provide four weeks of cold, moist conditions (a process called stratification, detailed in Hint 91) to perennials such as asters, goldenrod, sneezeweed, and blazing stars before encouraging them to grow.

TO STRATIFY PERENNIAL SEEDS that require a cold treatment to germinate, sow them in a community flat of moist seed-starting mix. Label as explained in Hint 87. Wrap the entire flat in a plastic bag and close with a twist tie. Set the flat in the refrigerator for the time indicated on the seed packet or in a seed-sowing handbook. When the recommended stratification time is up, move the flat into warmth and bright light so the seeds can sprout and grow.

SOME PERENNIALS THAT DON'T NEED STRATIFICATION

Lavender
Fennel
Chives
Lemon balm
Oregano
Sage
Catmint
Germander
Valerian
Butterfly weed
Purple coneflower
Orange coneflower
Rock cress
Mountain bluet
Tickseed 'Early Sunrise'
Shasta daisy 'Snow Lady'

IF STARTING SEEDS IN A WINDOW, take extra care to maximize light. Use a south-facing window that will receive sun all day. It should not be blocked by a

protruding roof overhang or an evergreen tree or shrub. (Without a south-facing window, it's worth considering building a light garden; see Hint 93.)

Hang foil reflectors behind the flat to keep seedlings from leaning toward the sun. If the seedlings are sitting on a windowsill, make a tent of foil behind them, with the shiny side facing the seedlings. This will reflect sunlight and illuminate the dark side of the seedlings. They will grow much sturdier and straighter as a result.

93 **START SEEDS INDOORS UNDER LIGHTS** rather than in a window for even, compact growth. Seedlings must have bright light from the moment they peer up out of the soil. In climates with cloudy weather or homes without south-facing windows, sun may not be reliable enough. A light garden is an ideal solution.

Set seedlings snugly under a fluorescent shop light. You could place seedlings on a table or counter and suspend the shop light from the ceiling over them. Or you could set up three or four tiered light stands. You can adapt ordinary shelves by attaching lights to the bottoms of the shelves and growing trays below each light. Put the lights on a timer set to turn them on for 14 hours a day and off again (one less job for you). You can't beat the results!

94 **MAKE A MINI-GREENHOUSE UNDER LIGHTS** with a clear plastic garment bag. This traps humidity near seedlings, helping to protect them from wilting. To cover nursery flats full of seedlings, bend two wire coat hangers into arches and prop them in the corners of the flat, one at each end. Work the plastic over the top of the hangers, and tuck the loose ends in below the flat.

It's even easier to make a green-house cover for individual pots. Slide two sticks (short bamboo stakes work well) into opposite sides of the pot. Then top with the plastic and fold under the pot.

95 **START SEEDS OR CUTTINGS IN AN OLD AQUARIUM OR CLEAR SWEATER BOX** to keep humidity high. Aquariums or sweater boxes are more permanent alternatives to the makeshift options above. They are particularly good for cuttings that may need more overhead and rooting room than seedlings. To reuse these containers, wash them with soapy water, rinse, and sterilize with a solution of 1 part bleach to 10 parts water.

96 **DON'T TRANSPLANT SEEDLINGS** into a larger pot until they have one or two sets of true leaves. This allows seedlings to develop enough roots to be self-supporting even if a few roots are lost in the process. It's also a time when seedling roots are fairly straight and compact, making them easy to separate from nearby plants.

How can you tell when the time is right? It's not as simple as counting the number of leaves on the stem, because the seedling usually has an extra set of leaves called cotyledons or seed leaves. They emerge first and store food that nourishes the sprouting seedlings. When you look closely, you can see that cotyledons are shaped differently from true leaves. Squash seedlings, for instance, have oval squash-seed-shaped cotyledons that are easy to spot. But the true leaves are broad and lobed.

97 **TO AVOID BURNING SEEDLING STEMS** with the salts on your hands or breaking an irreplaceable stem, handle young seedlings by the cotyledon or seed leaf (see Hint 96).

98 **TAKE SOFTWOOD STEM CUTTINGS IN LATE SPRING OR EARLY SUMMER** for fast rooting. New spring shoots are vigorous but soft and succulent. They may wilt before they root. But if the shoots are allowed to mature for a month or two, they firm up slightly and are ideal for rooting.

PROPAGATION

99 TAKE STEM CUTTINGS IN THE MORNING when they are fresh and full of water. Once the stem is severed from its root, it will not be able to soak up moisture for several weeks or until new roots develop. If cuttings are started without enough stored moisture, they will simply wilt and die.

Stems should be strong and moist before they are cut.

100 USE ROOTING HORMONE ON OLDER OR HARD-TO-ROOT CUTTINGS. Rooting hormones, available in powdered and liquid forms, contain chemicals (called auxins) that allow cut stems to begin to produce roots. They must be applied as soon as the cutting is taken and before the cutting is put into sterile planting mix. Not all stems need rooting hormone (mints and willows, for instance), but it can make slow starters much more reliable.

SOME PLANTS SUITABLE FOR SOFTWOOD STEM CUTTINGS

Willows	Chrysanthemums
Maples	Dahlias
Serviceberry	Mints
Clematis	Bee balm
Bugleweed	Catmint
Asters	Lavender
Bellflowers	Bedding geraniums
Blanketflowers	Fuchsias
Hardy geraniums	Tomatoes
Russian sage	Blueberries
Plumbago	

IOI **AVOID FEEDING SOFTWOOD SHRUB CUTTINGS ANY ADDITIONAL NITROGEN** after rooting. A little nitrogen, which is available in nutrient-enriched planting mixes, can help the rooting process proceed. But excess nitrogen can encourage fast, tender new growth that is vulnerable to winter damage. Once the cuttings have survived the winter, transplant them into the garden or a larger pot and fertilize them normally.

IO2 **SET A CLEAR GLASS JAR** over cuttings of roses, willows, dogwoods, or other easily rooted stems put directly in the garden. The jar will maintain high humidity around the cutting and help prevent wilting. But be sure to protect the jar from the hot sun so the cuttings don't get cooked.

IO3 **TEST IF A CUTTING HAS ROOTED** by gently tugging on the stem. If it shows resistance, roots have formed. After first rooting, allow the roots to develop for several more weeks, if possible, before transplanting.

IO4  **TAKE ROOT CUTTINGS** when stem cuttings are not possible. Some perennials, like Oriental poppies and horseradish, have clusters of foliage close to the ground without any stems at all. You can dig up a root and cut it into pieces that may sprout into new plants. With horseradish, you can cut off a side root in the fall and replant it for a new start in the spring. But root cuttings of most other perennials need more help than horseradish. Here's how to do it:

- Dig the root in early spring before shoots begin to emerge.
- Cut the roots into pieces an inch or two long.
- Lay them horizontally in a flat of well-drained propagating mix such as perlite or coarse sand. Cover lightly.
- Keep slightly moist but not wet (to prevent root rot) and watch for new sprouts to emerge.
- When the new plants are growing strongly, transplant them into individual containers or put them out in the garden.

105 **"HARDEN OFF" SEEDLINGS AND CUTTINGS** before they go out into the garden. When growing in the protection of a windowsill, light garden, or greenhouse, young plants are tender and can be easily damaged by strong winds or sun. Toughen them up (a process called hardening off) to make the transition from indoors to outdoors successful.

- Days 1 and 2: Put well-watered young plants outdoors in a shady location for several hours. Bring them back indoors when the time is up.

- Days 3 and 4: Increase the length of time seedlings stay outdoors in the shade.
- Days 5 to 7: When well adjusted to shade, gradually move sun-loving plants into brighter light, starting with an hour of sun the first day.
- Days 8 and beyond: When seedlings can stay out all day without burning or wilting, they are ready for transplanting.

106 **EASILY DIVIDE DAYLILIES, HOSTAS, ASTILBES,** or other clump-forming perennials with a sharp shovel. Just slice off an edge of the clump in spring or late summer. Uproot it and replant elsewhere. Keep the new division watered for at least several weeks or until it has regenerated lost roots.

107 **DIVIDE A LARGE PERENNIAL CLUMP** into small divisions to get many little plants fast. This is a quick and easy way to make enough plants for the big drifts, clumps, or ground covers that are so popular in landscaping today.

A mature bee balm clump might contain 50 rooted sprouts, each of which can be separated off and grown into a new plant. Other easily divided perennials include asters, daylilies, yarrow, phlox, lady's mantle, salvia, coreopsis, hardy geraniums, irises, mint, thyme, oregano, and winter savory. Here's how to make smaller divisions:

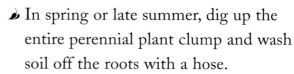

❧ In spring or late summer, dig up the entire perennial plant clump and wash soil off the roots with a hose.

❧ If dividing in late summer, cut back the foliage by half or more.

❧ Use your hands to break rooted sprouts into individual pieces. If roots are too hard to work apart by hand, slice them free with a knife or pruning shears. Each section should contain at least one leafy sprout and one healthy root.

❧ Replant very small divisions into pots of peat-based planting mix and tend them carefully until they get a little bigger. Larger divisions can go right back into the garden if kept moist until they become reestablished.

108 ROOT THE PLANTLETS ON SPIDER

PLANTS and strawberry begonias, which grow from the parent plant on arching stems. These pretty plantlets have leaves but no roots, a condition that's easy to correct. Put a pot of peat-based potting mix beside the parent plant and set the plantlet in it. Firm the mix around the lower part of the plantlet and keep it moist. Once the plantlet roots, snip the stem and enjoy.

You can grow new spider plants by using the attached plantlets.

109 **USE LAYERING TO PROPAGATE HARD-TO-ROOT SHRUBS** like azaleas. Layering also works well with shrubs that have low-growing or creeping branches, like creeping rosemary. Layered stems develop roots while still connected to the mother plant, which helps nourish the rooting process.

- In spring, select a low, flexible branch that will bend down to the ground easily.
- Prepare well-drained but moisture-retentive soil where the stem will touch the ground.
- Nick the bark off the side of the stem that will touch the ground and remove the leaves near the nick. Dust the cut with rooting hormone (see Hint 100).
- Cover the barren and nicked stem with soil. Top it with a rock or pin it in place with a stake or metal pin.
- The branch tip will become the new plant. If it is an upright grower, stake the tip upright to give it a good shape.
- Keep the rooting area moist for several months, until roots develop and become large enough to the support the new plant.
- Cut the new plant free from the parent branch and transplant it to a pot or new site in the garden.

PESTS AND DISEASES

Growing healthy plants is the first step toward a great garden. In order to achieve this, it's important to prevent diseases and pests through careful plant selection, planting, and care. It also helps to use some of the environmentally safe new products and techniques described in this chapter.

Among the most important considerations when preventing diseases is soil drainage (see Hint 6); soggy roots lead to rot in almost every instance (though there are some plants that need the extra water). Sunlight is also essential. It must keep the plant well nourished (by photosynthesizing) so it can stay robust enough to resist diseases that attack weak plants.

Plants with enough space to reach maturity without overcrowding are likely to be healthy. They suffer less competition with their neighbors for sun, water, and nutrients, and they enjoy plenty of fresh air. In an overcrowded garden, airflow stagnates, just as it does in an overcrowded room. Without free air circulation, foliage dampened by dew, rain, or sprinkling will stay wet longer and be more susceptible to fungus and other diseases.

110 **CHOOSE DISEASE-RESISTANT CULTIVARS** whenever possible. They are bred to resist infection—an ideal way to avoid diseases. Growing disease-

Many tomatoes are specifically bred to resist disease.

resistant vegetables prevents chemical tainting of your food. Disease-resistant varieties of popular flowers such as roses save you time, trouble, and expense.

There are varying levels of protection available:

- Some cultivars have multiple disease resistances for maximum protection. The 'Big Beef' tomato, for instance, resists various types of wilts: tobacco mosaic virus, nematodes, and gray leaf spot. Little is left that can harm it.
- Some cultivars resist only one disease. But if that disease is a problem in your area, then these plants will be worth their weight in gold.

SOME DISEASE-RESISTANT CULTIVARS

ROSES: 'The Fairy,' 'Red Fairy,' rugosa roses, 'Carefree Delight,' David Austin English Roses, Town and Country Roses, Meidiland roses

ZINNIAS: 'Star Gold,' 'Star Orange,' 'Star White,' 'Crystal White,' 'Cherry Pinwheel,' 'Salmon Pinwheel,' 'Rose Pinwheel,' 'Orange Pinwheel'

CUCUMBERS: 'Park's All-Season Burpless Hybrid,' 'Fancipack,' 'Homemade Pickles,' 'Tasty King,' 'Sweet Success,' 'Salad Bush'

PEAS: 'Super Sugar Snap,' 'Sugar Pop,' 'Maestro,' 'Green Arrow'

BEANS: 'Florence,' 'Buttercrisp,' 'Jade'

TOMATOES: 'Celebrity,' 'Better Boy,' 'LaRossa,' 'Enchantment,' 'Sunmaster,' 'Mountain Delight,' 'Big Beef,' 'Beefmaster,' 'Sweet Million,' 'Viva Italia,' 'Roma'

APPLES: 'Liberty,' 'Jonafree,' 'MacFree,' 'Freedom'

STRAWBERRIES: 'Surecrop,' 'Cavendish,' 'Redchief,' 'Allstar,' 'Guardian,' 'Scott,' 'Lateglow,' 'Delite'

❧ Other plants are disease tolerant, meaning they may still get the disease but should grow well despite it.

To find out more about disease-resistant cultivars for your area, ask your local Cooperative Extension Service or a knowledgeable professional grower. Or get your name on the mailing list for nursery and seed catalogues that describe disease-resistant cultivars.

Interplanting adds color and texture to the garden—and also helps deter pests.

III INTERPLANT HERBS AND FLOWERS WITH VEGETABLES to help reduce pest problems. This gives the vegetable garden a colorful patchwork look and helps confuse problem pests. The varied aromas of interplantings make it hard for pests to find their favorite food by scent. This works particularly well if you interplant with powerfully fragrant herbs and flowers such as mints, basils, lemon geraniums, garlic, or onions.

Ladybugs are beneficial insects.

II2 ATTRACT BENEFICIAL INSECTS. Sprinkling flowering plants amid the garden helps draw ladybugs, spiders, lacewings, and tiny parasitic wasps who prey on plant-eating pests. The flowers provide shelter plus nectar and pollen, an alternative food source.

Once beneficial insects are at home in your garden, keep them there. Remember, they can be killed as quickly as plant pests by broad-spectrum pesticides, which kill indiscriminately. It's best to avoid pesticides or use targeted pesticides such as Bt (a bacterial disease of caterpillars that won't harm other insects) to protect beneficial insects.

113 **USE FLOATING ROW COVERS** to keep pests off vegetables. This simple idea works so well it's a wonder nobody thought of it years ago. Floating row covers are lightweight fabrics that you can drape over plants. They allow sun, rain, and fresh air to penetrate, but if secured to the ground with rocks, bricks, or long metal staples, they will keep flying insects out. Here are some great ways to use floating row covers:

Floating row covers let sun, rain, and air get through while keeping plants safe from pests.

- ❧ Eliminate maggots (fly larvae) that will tunnel into the roots of radishes, turnips, carrots, onions, and other vegetables. Row covers keep egg-laying female flies away from the vegetables. If there are no eggs, there are no maggots.
- ❧ Keep potato beetles from eating the foliage off potato leaves and vines. Pin the row cover edges down tightly so the beetles can't crawl under.

🌿 Protect cucumbers, squash, and pumpkins from cucumber beetles, which carry a wilt disease capable of killing entire vines. Since flowers of these vines need insect pollination for fruit set, the covers must be lifted for several hours at least every other day for honeybees to do their work.

114 USE BARRIERS OF COPPER STRIPS OR DIATOMACEOUS EARTH to

keep slugs away from plants. Slugs are voracious plant eaters. They eat almost anything, ganging up on tender succulent plants and eating them down to the ground. They thrive where soils are damp, spending sunny days under rocks, logs, or mulch and coming out to eat when it's rainy or cool and dark. Any slug control measures you use will work better if you clear out excess mulch and any dark, dank hiding places where slugs might breed.

🌿 Diatomaceous earth is a gritty substance that pierces the skin of soft-bodied slugs. Sprinkle it on the soil, encircling plants plagued by slugs. Use horticultural-grade diatomaceous earth, not the kind sold in swimming pool stores.

🌿 Copper strips, set around the edge of the garden, prevent slug trespass by creating an unpleasant reaction when touched with the mucus on the crawling slugs. Set copper strips an inch deep and several inches high, so that slugs can't get over or under.

115 **KILL EXISTING SLUGS** by trapping them in deep saucers of beer. Slugs love beer, and that can be their downfall. Bury an empty plastic margarine tub in the garden soil. The top rim should be level with the soil surface. Fill the tub with beer (any kind will do) and leave it overnight. The slugs will crawl in and drown. Empty the tub every day or two and refill with beer until the tub comes through the night empty.

116 **SPRAY APHIDS OFF PLANTS** with a strong stream of water. Aphids, small sap-sucking insects with soft, pear-shaped bodies, cling to succulent young stems and buds. They reproduce quickly, sometimes covering stems that curl and distort in protest. Because aphids can multiply into swarms almost overnight, it's important to eliminate any that you find.

Before hauling out any pesticides, try a strong blast of water from the hose. Aphids are easily dislodged from plants. This method works best on mature or woody plants that won't be damaged by the force of the water blast. Repeat every couple of days or any time you see new aphids arriving.

117 SPRAY PLANTS SUSCEPTIBLE TO FOLIAGE FUNGUS with wilt-proofing solution before disease strikes. This product is a pine oil modified to spread into a film coating that protects evergreen foliage from drying out during winter. An unexpected side effect of the film is that it keeps fungus spores from penetrating into susceptible leaves. Mix according to label directions and try it on phlox, bee balm, cucumbers, watermelons, tomatoes, and apples. Do not, however, spray plants with hairy leaves.

118 EXPERIMENT WITH BAKING SODA SPRAYS to prevent fungus diseases. Mix two teaspoons baking soda in 2 quarts of water with $\frac{1}{2}$ teaspoon corn oil. Shake well, put in a sprayer, and go to work. Spray susceptible plants often and always after rain to help keep diseases such as powdery mildew from getting started.

119 THIN STEMS ON DISEASE-PRONE PLANTS to improve air circulation. Mildew-susceptible phlox and bee balm, for instance, can grow into clumps so thick that

> ### SOME PLANTS PREFERRED BY DEER
>
> (Based on Cornell Cooperative Extension Service research)
>
> | | |
> |---|---|
> | Fraser and balsam firs | Evergreen azaleas |
> | Norway maple | Hybrid tea rose |
> | Redbud | European mountain ash |
> | Clematis | Yews |
> | Winged euonymus | Arborvitaes |
> | Wintercreeper | Asters |
> | English ivy | Hostas |
> | Apples | Phlox |
> | Cherries | Lilies |
> | Plums | Tulips |
> | Rhododendrons | |

they block air flow. This encourages fungus attack, but it is easily corrected. When new growth is coming up in the spring, cut out every third stem, targeting those that are weak or in areas of the thickest growth.

120 **USE BAGS OF SOAP OR HUMAN HAIR** to repel deer. Sometimes called jack rabbits on hooves, deer can be a nuisance. They seem to enjoy dining on cultivated plants and are worst in the winter, gobbling evergreens when their native food supply dwindles. But they are also a problem in spring and summer, when they like to munch tender flowers and new growth. In fall, males rub their antlers on wood and can damage small trees and shrubs. However, they don't enjoy strong-smelling soaps and human hair.

Powerfully scented soap can be stuffed in a mesh bag and dangled from branches about 3 feet high. You also can set soap bars directly on the ground. Replenish the soap supply frequently so it won't dissolve away or lose its smell.

You can also fill mesh bags with human hair. Hang them outside (like a furry scarecrow) so deer wonder if you are hiding in the garden. Refill bags as soon as you pull another handful from your hairbrush.

GARDEN DESIGN

Growing plants beautifully is a wonderful thing, but arranging them in a handsome landscape is even better! A good landscape design plays many roles. It blends the house into the yard, making the entire property look good and increasing property values. Through the design of the landscape, you can create outdoor privacy with hedges, fences, vine-covered trellises, or informal clusters of plants that act like walls of an outdoor room. You can seclude certain areas of the yard or buffer the entire property perimeter.

Landscape designs might include work areas, places for composting or vegetable gardening, even areas for storing trash cans and other less-than-decorative necessities. You can designate places for entertaining—decks, patios, barbecue pits, or perhaps a white garden for guests to enjoy on a moonlit night. You can even have areas groomed especially for the dog or the children's play equipment.

Once you make a list of what you want in your yard, you can begin to find the room for it all and start getting all the elements in place.

121 **DRAW A MAP OF YOUR PROPERTY** and choose where the new beds and plantings will go before you start buying and planting. The map needs to be to scale, an exact replica of your property in miniature. Many designers use a scale in which 1/4 inch on the plan equals one foot in your yard. This scale usually provides enough room to show considerable detail but is likely to require the use of oversized paper to fit everything on one sheet.

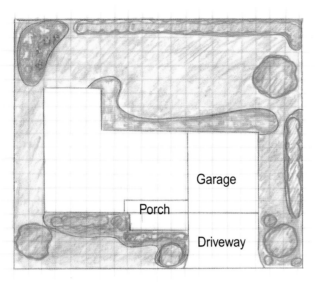

Measure the yard using a measuring tape (50-foot lengths work well) and sketch the perimeter on graph paper. Draw in existing trees, shrubs, fences, and other features you intend to keep. Make some copies so you can experiment with designs. Then pencil in possible bed outlines and imagine how they will look. Once you've decided on the location of the beds, pencil in the plants you want to add (at the proper spacing) and get an accurate count of how many plants you'll need before you start shelling out any money.

122 **PLAN THE SHAPE OF THE LAWN,** which is usually the biggest feature in a yard. The lawn's shape is more important than the shape of the beds. If it's designed with straight or gradually curving lines, the lawn can make a pretty picture and remain easy to mow. Avoid sharp turns, wiggly edges, and jagged corners that are irritating to the eye and extra work to mow.

A rounded lawn is pleasing to the eye.

123 **TAKE PHOTOS AND PHOTO-COPY THEM.** You can shoot the entire front yard or backyard, the plantings around the house's foundation, or individual gardens. Enlarge them on a color copier, if one is available. Then you can sketch in prospective new plants and get an idea of how they will look. A great time to do this is in winter. Although the yard may be dormant, you won't forget how it looks.

124 **BORROW IDEAS FROM NEIGHBORS' GARDENS.** There is no better way to learn what grows well in your area. You also can get great design ideas from other people. Remember, mimicry is the greatest form of flattery.

125

Public gardens can provide inspiration for the garden in your own backyard.

VISIT PUBLIC GARDENS and nurseries with display beds for inspiration. These professionally designed gardens may have the newest plants and creative ideas for combining them. Look for gardens about the same size as your yard so you can apply what you learn directly.

126 **MATCH THE FLOWERING PLANT TO THE SITE.** Most flowers are high-performance plants, especially sensitive to inadequacies in light, moisture, soil, or other elements. Give them exactly what they need to thrive (see Hint 1).

127 **SELECT FLOWERING PLANTS WITH A RANGE OF BLOOM TIMES** to keep the garden interesting through the seasons. Many perennials, shrubs, and trees will flower for a maximum of three weeks per year. (Some exceptions are in the list on this page.) On paper, list those that bloom in early and late spring, early and late summer, early and late fall. Then when you plant your garden, you can develop a sequence so one kind of flower will fade as another begins to open.

> ### *PERENNIALS WITH EXCEPTIONALLY LONG BLOOM*
>
> | | |
> |---|---|
> | Orange coneflowers | Blanket flower |
> | Purple coneflowers | 'Stella de Oro' daylily |
> | Coreopsis | Russian sage |
> | Rose mallow hibiscus | Stoke's aster |
> | Lenten rose | Pincushion flower |
> | Violet sage | 'Sunny Border Blue' |
> | Sedum x 'Autumn Joy' | veronica |
> | Asters | Spiderwort |
> | 'Luxuriant' bleeding heart | |

Annual flowers are great for filling the gaps. Pansies, sweet alyssum, and calendula thrive in cool spring and fall weather. Petunias, marigolds, zinnias, geraniums, and other annuals will fill the frost-free summer months with color. And tender bulbs such as dahlias and cannas can also provide bright color through much of the warm summer season.

128

Variations in foliage can provide as much visual interest as the flowers themselves.

CHOOSE FLOWERING PLANTS with good foliage as well as flowers. The foliage will still be on display long after the flowers are gone. For starters, find plants with foliage that stays healthy, lush, and green and won't become off-colored, ragged, or diseased after flowering. Then you can expand to add plants with golden, silver, bronze, blue, or multicolored leaves that fit the garden color scheme.

129 **PLANT TREES AND SHRUBS FIRST,** then add flower gardens. Woody plants are the bones of the garden, the bold foundation that will be there summer and winter to enclose your yard or blend your house into the property. They are also the most expensive and permanent features and, as such, need to be given special priority. Plan well, find top-quality trees and shrubs, and plant them properly where they can thrive.

130 **MAKE ISLAND BEDS HALF AS WIDE** as the distance from where you view them. Island beds, often oval or kidney-shaped, are situated in areas of lawn where they can be viewed from all sides. They may be near a corner of your yard or by your driveway or entrance walk.

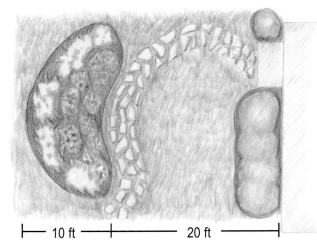

⊢— 10 ft —⊣⊢——— 20 ft ———⊣

No matter where you put it, an island bed needs to be wide enough to look substantial from your house, patio, or kitchen window—wherever you usually are when you see it. A tiny garden located far from the house is more comical than beautiful. So, for example, if an island bed is 20 feet away, make it 10 feet across. In very large yards, keep island beds closer to the house if you don't have time to tend a large island bed.

131 **MAKE BORDERS UP TO HALF AS WIDE** as the total space in a small- or medium-sized yard. For example, a 40-foot-wide yard could have one border 20 feet wide or two borders 10 feet wide. Borders—traditional gardens usually set at the edge of a yard, fence, or hedge—also need enough size to be in scale and make an impact in the yard. Wider borders can accommodate taller plants, including trees, shrubs, and large clumps of perennials and ornamental grasses, taking on a rich diversity.

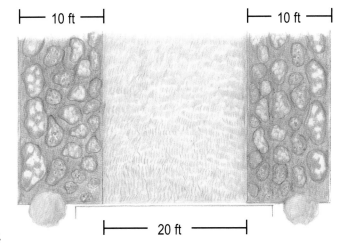

⊢— 10 ft —⊣   ⊢— 10 ft —⊣

⊢——— 20 ft ———⊣

132 **USE WARM COLORS AND COOL COLORS** to give the garden just the right amount of emphasis. Warm colors such as yellow, orange, and red are bold and appear visually to be closer to you than they are. This makes them ideal for a garden located farther away from your house. Cool colors such as blue and purple recede from the eye and look farther away than they really are. They make pleasant, quiet gardens close to the house, but they may be lost farther away.

You can blend cool and warm colors to give a feeling of movement and depth in the garden. Color blends also provide vivid contrast, which some people find exhilarating.

Experiment with a mixture of warm and cool tones in your flower garden.

133 **CONSIDER VARYING LEAF SIZES** for more design interest. Large leaves like those on hostas or oak leaf hydrangeas advance and stand out (similar to warm-colored flowers). They are striking in prominent locations, but if overused they will lose their impact.

Small or finely textured leaves, as on thread leaf coreopsis or carrot tops, recede from the eye and look farther away. They can best be appreciated up close. Or if you are trying to make a garden look deeper, these varieties might be used toward the rear as a floral optical illusion. But when used exclusively, fine textured leaves may look busy and weedy.

Use plants with various leaf sizes for visual impact.

134 **ADD IN THE IMPACT OF FLOWER SIZE** to get another variable for an interesting design. Large flowers are bold and prominent. Smaller flowers and fine flower clusters recede. Blending airy small flower sprays with large, bold flowers combines the best of both textures. Planting larger flowers toward the front of a garden and smaller flowers toward the rear increases visual depth.

135 **USE A COLLECTION OF POTS** to end cut-throughs and shortcuts. Gaps in the shrubbery or fencing around your yard are an invitation for neighborhood kids to slip through. Even adults will be tempted to shortcut across the lawn instead of following a longer path up the walk. Reroute traffic by blocking openings and detours with large pots of plants, flowers, herbs, or even your indoor floor plants brought outside in the summer. Cluster them together in a barrier that's not easily skirted. As a bonus, you'll have a dynamic plant grouping with maximum impact in the landscape.

136 **USE OLD CONCRETE** from a poured sidewalk as stepping stones in a bed or border. This faux stone is either given away or sold inexpensively by communities conducting sidewalk renovation. Other people may have the same idea, so call well before you need the concrete and get your name on a waiting list if necessary.

137 **CREATE A SHADE GARDEN WITHOUT TREES** by planting under a vine-covered arbor. Shade gardens can feature serene blends of ferns, hostas, and woodland wildflowers, plus a few dazzling bloomers such as azaleas and rhododendrons. Although these plants usually grow amid trees and shrubs, they can thrive in shadows cast by other structures—walls, fences, houses, or a vine-covered arbor.

The advantage of an arbor shade garden is that fewer roots are competing for moisture and nutrients. And unlike a planting close to a wall or building, the arbor shade garden has plenty of fresh air circulation. In addition, an arbor looks great when clad in flowers and handsome foliage.

VINES FOR AN ARBOR

Clematis	Kolomikta vine
Trumpet creeper	Silver-lace vine
Honeysuckle	Wisteria
Climbing roses	Jasmine (warm
Kiwi vines	climate only)

---

138 **COVER ROCKS AND BRICKS WITH MOSS** using a buttermilk-moss milkshake. A soft green moss veneer adds an air of antiquity, permanence, and beauty to walls, walks, or woodland rock gardens. You can wait a few years for moss to naturally creep into moist and shady places, or you can encourage a quicker appearance. Gather local cushion-forming mosses, the kinds that thrive in your climate, and find a garden location similar to where they naturally grow. Mix the moss with butter-milk in a blender and pour the concoction onto the appropriate rocks or bricks in your garden. Let it dry thoroughly. Keep the area moist, but not so wet that the milkshake washes off the bricks or stones. New moss will soon make an appearance.

139 **REDUCE THE VOLUME OF STRONG WINDS** by planting a layered assort-ment of plants as a windbreak. Wind can knock down and dry out plants, gener-ally making it harder to get the garden to grow well. Layered plants—taller trees with shade-tolerant shrubs planted under them—create an irregular barrier that gently stops wind. Solid fences, in contrast, allow wind to slip up and over and swirl back in on the other side.

140 **PLANT BAMBOO FOR A QUICK SCREEN.** Bamboo has handsome foliage and grows in upright thickets that can provide quick and easy privacy. But most types of bamboo are vigorous spreaders. To keep them from overwhelming a gar-den, plant them in large, submerged tubs or pots that keep the roots contained.

These mid-sized bamboo plants provide fast, attractive privacy in the yard.

141 **DON'T FORGET TO PLACE A BENCH** in the garden. You can sit and admire your handiwork, which always looks best up close. Your bench, even a rugged one, can double as garden sculpture.

TYPES OF
GARDENS

A landscape is the sum of its many parts: lawn; flower and vegetable gardens; vines and ground covers; shrub borders and hedges; and shade or ornamental trees. Each is an important element in its own right, and each contributes to the collective beauty and usefulness of the landscape.

A lush, green lawn enhances the beauty of all else around it, and though it may be overlooked for other, more "showy" forms of vegetation, the lawn is the basic element in your landscape, bringing everything else together.

Vegetable, fruit, and herb gardens yield flavorful harvests. They can be simple working gardens or handsomely constructed decorative elements. Flower gardens provide color, beauty, bouquets for the house, and food for birds and butterflies. Shrubs can be backdrops for flower or vegetable gardens, or they can serve as ornaments in their own right.

Knowing the potential of each landscape element allows you to utilize them for the best effect, making the most out of your home and garden.

CHAPTER 10

LAWNS

The emerald green lawn that spreads across most peoples' yards serves many purposes: It gives us places to play, filters air pollution, cools the air, and softens harsh light. But healthy, beautiful lawns don't just happen; they require work—more than just about any other part of the yard.

We have become accustomed to fertilizing, spraying, and mowing, mowing, mowing. This kind of pampering can result in a lush and pristine lawn, but it may also be more time-consuming than is necessary.

If you're planting a new lawn and want it to be low-maintenance, choose the right kind of grass for the site, plant at the ideal time, and use organic and slow-releasing fertilizers. Or, if you're dealing with an existing lawn, follow our easy hints to learn how to minimize maintenance.

142 **USE A MIXTURE OF TURF GRASSES** for a disease-resistant lawn. Diseases that attack one type of grass may not affect the others, so you are reducing risks.

Grass blends also increase versatility. Fine fescues mixed with bluegrass, for instance, are less likely to turn brown in summer heat. Read the labels on lawn grass seed packages closely to identify which grass mixtures are used and how they might affect performance.

143 **PLANT CREEPING RED FESCUE** in a lightly shaded lawn where bluegrass is likely to fail. For best results, provide well-drained, slightly acidic soil.

144 **CONSIDER THE MERITS OF SOD, SEED, AND PLUGS** before choosing which to use to start a new lawn:

- Sod: Sheets of prestarted turf can be purchased ready to be laid out on pre-pared soil, where they will take root and grow. Sod is expensive, but it pro-vides an "instant lawn," and many people like that. It's great on a slope where grass seed can be washed away with the first heavy rain. But sod has a few potential problems in addition to its high cost. It may fail to thrive on diffi-cult soils, and your selection can be limited to a few varieties and blends.

- Seed: Grass seed is inexpensive and available in a wide variety of custom mixes; there's something for every kind of lawn. It is best planted in warm,

---

GRASSES FOR DIFFERENT PURPOSES

COOL CLIMATES: SUN
Kentucky bluegrass

COOL CLIMATES: SUN OR LIGHT SHADE
Chewings fescue
Creeping red fescue

MODERATE CLIMATES: SUN OR LIGHT SHADE
Hard fescue
Tall fescue

WARM CLIMATES: SUN
Bermuda grass
Zoysia grass

WARM CLIMATES: SUN OR LIGHT SHADE
St. Augustine grass

BALL FIELDS
Perennial ryegrass

GOLF COURSES
Creeping bent grass

mild weather and must be kept constantly moist to germinate. The grass needs to become well established before summer heat or winter cold push it to the limits.

🌢 Plugs: These are small clumps of sod that can be planted like a ground cover in prepared soil. If kept moist and fertilized, the plugs will spread to form a solid sheet of turf. Plugs are an important way of starting warm-climate lawns and a way to economize in cooler climates.

 145 **USE SEED RATHER THAN SOD** to establish grass on poor soils. Sod roots may never grow into stiff clay soils, which puts a damper on their future if drought strikes. Spend a little extra time and money to improve poor soil with compost and peat moss. Then plant seed of suitable grasses and tend the lawn well (feeding, watering, raking, and weeding, as necessary) until it is growing strongly.

146 **USE EDGINGS** to keep grass out of garden beds. A physical barrier can prevent sprigs of grass from spreading to unwanted areas where they can make bed edges look ragged or spring up amid other plants.

Edgings made of 5- to 6-inch-wide strips of fiberglass, metal, or plastic—even stones or brick—can line the perimeter of a garden bed. Let the upper edge emerge a little above the soil (but well below the level of the mower) and the lower edge sink securely into the ground. More expensive edgings should last longer than cheap plastics, which can shift out of place during winter.

147 **TOP-DRESS THE LAWN** with compost or rotted manure to keep it healthy. Unlike super-concentrated fertilizers that stimulate rapid growth, these natural fertilizers provide light doses of nutrients and improve soil conditions. Make sure the compost or manure is finely screened so it will settle down to the soil without packing on top of the turf.

148 **FERTILIZE LAWNS WITH SLOW-RELEASE NITROGEN FERTILIZER.** Slow-release products gradually emit moderate amounts of nitrogen over a period of weeks or months, so you won't need to fertilize as often. The nitrogen levels in slow-release products are high enough to keep your yard green and healthy, but not so high that the lawn is stimulated to grow rampantly and require continual mowing. Read fertilizer bag labels carefully to determine which brands contain slow-release nitrogen.

149 **FILL IN LOW SPOTS** in uneven lawns by spreading sand evenly over the lawn area with a metal rake.

You can sprinkle grass seed on the sand or wait for the surrounding grasses to send out new tillers and colonize the fill.

150 **LEAVE GRASS BLADES LONGER** for more drought resistance and better root growth. Longer blades shade the soil and roots, keeping them cooler and moister, and the grass roots may grow deeper. In contrast, close-cropped lawns can dry out quickly in summer heat. The stubby leaves expose grass-free openings where crabgrass and other weeds can grow.

Longer grass is healthy for the yard—and it means less mowing for you!

151 **KEEP YOUR LAWN MOWER BLADES SHARP.** Like a sharp razor on a day-old beard, your mower will slice through grass blades, giving a clean, level cut. Dull blades tear grasses, which can increase their susceptibility to diseases.

152

Thatch, the dead grass trapped at the soil's surface, needs to be removed periodically.

DETHATCH YOUR LAWN once a year or as needed to keep it healthy. Thatch is a layer of dead grass stalks that can build up at the soil surface, cutting off air, water, and fertilizer when it becomes thick and matted. Thatch can also harbor pests.

A vigorous raking can help break up small amounts of thatch. For big problems, you can rent dethatching machines. Use them in mild weather and plan to reseed if necessary to refill gaps left behind. Once thatch is gone, the clippings can rot to enrich the soil.

153 **DON'T MOW THE LAWN DURING DROUGHT.** Without rainfall, the grass is unlikely to grow much, if any.

154 **WATER SPARINGLY DURING DROUGHT.** Providing about a half inch of water every two weeks can keep grass alive without encouraging growth.

155 **AERATE COMPACTED LAWNS** to keep them healthy. With a lot of foot or wheel traffic, soil can become hard-packed, creating a poor environment for grass roots. To help air reach the roots (and also to cut out old thatch), run over the lawn with a core cultivator. This is a machine that pulls up small cylinders of soil, creating breathing spaces. Do-it-yourselfers can buy or rent a core cultivator (see the illustration at right). As an alternative, have a landscaper or lawn-care company core your yard.

156 **TRY A FRAGRANT HERBAL LAWN** for a change of pace. Herbal lawns release delightful fragrances when you walk on them or

HERBS FOR A
FRAGRANT LAWN

Creeping thyme   Clover
Roman chamomile   Yarrow
Mint   Pennyroyal

Try planting herbs such as thyme—rather than grass—to create a plush, fragrant lawn.

mow them. But few herbs will tolerate as much traffic as grass, so it's best to keep them out of the mainstream. You can blend low-growing creeping herbs into grass or plant a smaller area entirely in herbs.

157 **TURN A RAGGED LAWN INTO A MEADOW** by killing the grass and planting perennial wildflowers and grasses (see Hint 66). This works best in the privacy of your backyard or in country settings.

158 **CONSIDER MOWING WITH A HAND-POWERED REEL MOWER.** On a well-tended lawn, reel mowers provide an especially polished cut. They are also quiet and energy efficient.

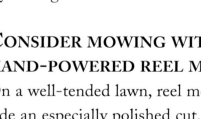

CHAPTER 11

VEGETABLES

Whether you like to cook or just to eat, a vegetable garden can be the perfect addition to your yard. Situate it in a sunny place, raise the beds so you can start growing food early in spring, then keep planting all summer long so something fresh is always ready to harvest.

Spring is a wonderful time for succulent, tender lettuces, spinach, and asparagus. In summer, you can pick juicy tomatoes and fruity ripe peppers. And in fall, salad gardening time returns with great radishes, carrots, and more lettuce.

But fresh and flavorful produce is just the beginning. Growing your own vegetables organically ensures healthful produce and saves you the high prices of organically grown produce at the grocery store.

Add walks and arbors and interplant with beautiful flowers and herbs to make the vegetable garden both pretty and productive.

VEGETABLES: FLAVORFUL AND ATTRACTIVE

Experiment with vegetables that are extra pretty or extra flavorful, such as the following:

- Ruby- and pink-leaved lettuces
- Green, yellow, and purple snap beans; the purple ones turn green when cooked
- Crimson, white, gold, and red-striped beets
- Violet, neon pink, soft pink, and white egg plants
- Peppers ranging from sweet to mild spicy to super hot—something for everyone
- Red, orange, yellow, pink, or cream tomatoes; for exceptional flavor, try 'Brandywine' and 'Sweet 100' cherry tomatoes

159 **KEEP THE GARDEN NEAR YOUR KITCHEN.** It will be easy to run out and pick a few things you need, and you can spy on the garden from your window. Picking tomatoes after you see them blush crimson is a perfect way to get them at their best.

Plant your garden near the house so you'll have easy access to the vegetables.

160 **SOAK SEEDS** to get a jump on the season. Before germinating, seeds need to drink up moisture, just as if drenched by spring rains. Once they become plump and swollen, the little embryo inside will begin to grow.

Seeds such as broccoli, cabbage, and arugula use moisture efficiently and germinate promptly without presoaking. But slower-starting parsley and parsnip seeds benefit from presoaking. Dunk them in room-temperature water for several hours or even overnight, but don't forget them and leave them in too long. Drain and plant the seeds immediately.

161 **PRODUCE LATE FALL, WINTER, AND EARLY SPRING LETTUCE** by growing extra-hardy varieties such as 'Artic King' or 'North Pole,' and creating sheltered planting places for them:

- Raised beds covered with heavy-duty floating row covers can provide protection from frosts and light freezes in early to mid-spring and mid- to late fall, or even winter in mild climates.

❧ Cold frames, heated by the sun, make it possible to grow lettuce early in spring and later in fall or winter. Cold frames are translucent rectangular boxes, about 2 feet wide, 4 feet long, and 18 inches high. The top is hinged to open so you can tend plants inside or cool the cold frame on mild, sunny days. Plant seeds or seedlings of lettuce in the frame and shut the lid to hold in the heat.

❧ A hot bed, which is a souped-up cold frame, is a great place for winter lettuce. Lay a heating cable under the cold frame. Cover with wire mesh to prevent damage to the cable, and top with a layer of sand mixed with compost.

162

USE WATER-FILLED TEPEES around tender vegetables for protection from the cold. You can buy inexpensive plastic sheets of connected tubes that, when filled with water, form self-supporting walls around seedlings. The clear walls allow sun to penetrate to the plant inside while the solar-heated water stays warm into the night.

163 **START WITH LARGE SEEDLINGS** for quick results in cold climates. This strategy works well for tender vegetables like beefsteak tomatoes and chili peppers that take a long time to ripen but must squeeze in their performance before the last frost does them in for the season.

For some vegetables, it's better to plant seedlings.

Look for seedlings grown in large pots (indicating a strong root system) with healthy green leaves and a sturdy constitution. Avoid neglected, overgrown seedlings.

Note that not every seedling transplants well when older. Cucumbers, squash, zucchini, pumpkins, and gourds are best started from young seedlings planted carefully to minimize root disturbance.

164 **MULCH ASPARAGUS EVERY SPRING** with several inches of compost or decayed livestock manure. Asparagus, a greedy feeder, will use all the nutrients it can get its roots on and grow that much better for it. By mulching in the spring, you can fertilize, help keep the soil moist, and reduce weed seed germination all in one effort. The shoots that arise through the mulch will grow especially plump and succulent.

Nutrient-rich mulch helps asparagus thrive.

165 **MAKE FANCY WHITE ASPARAGUS SPEARS** with a simple blanching basket. This European connoisseur item is easy to do at home. When the spears first emerge in spring, cover them with a bucket, basket, or mound of soil that will exclude all light. Harvest when the spears reach 8 to 10 inches tall and before the ferny leaves begin to emerge.

166 **TEAR THE TOPS AND BOTTOMS OFF PEAT POTS** when setting out vegetables. Peat pots, which are supposed to decay when submerged in the soil, don't always break down the first year they are planted. This leaves plant roots captive inside. To complicate matters further, if the peat rim emerges above the soil surface, it can dry out and steal moisture from the surrounding soil and nearby roots. Peat pot problems are easily solved by tearing off the top and bottom of the pot before planting. This helps eliminate the danger of drying out and gives roots a way to escape if the peat pot persists.

167 **PLANT LEGGY VEGETABLE SEEDLINGS DEEPER** to provide a stronger start outdoors. Seedlings started indoors or in crowded greenhouses, places without enough light, may develop lanky, barren stems that topple over in the garden. As long as they grow from a single stem (rather than a rosette of leaves) and go into well-drained soil, leggy seedlings can be submerged slightly deep for extra support.

For flexible-stemmed seedlings like tomatoes, a horizontal planting trench is better than a vertical one. It is warmer and better aerated than deeper soil, encouraging good root growth and fast development.

168 **KEEP CUTWORMS AWAY FROM SEEDLINGS** with the cardboard centers of toilet paper rolls—recycling at its best! Cutworms, which are moth caterpillars, creep near the soil surface, eating tender stem bases of young seedlings and cutting sprouts off the roots.

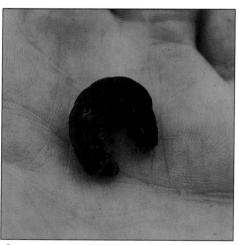

Cutworms are common garden pests.

It doesn't take barbed wire or an electric-shock fence to get cutworms to detour away from your seedlings. After planting, just set a 3-inch-long cardboard tube around the seedling. Push the tube down so half is submerged, thus preventing underground attacks. Then once the seedling has grown into a plant, you can remove the cardboard collar.

169 **FOR AN EXTENDED LETTUCE HARVEST,** pick the largest leaves from the outside of the plant and allow the younger inner leaves to continue growing. But when springtime weather begins to get warm, you need to take the opposite strategy. Cut off the entire plant before it begins to send up a flower stem (a condition called bolting) and turns bitter.

170 **PRUNE TOMATO PLANTS** to direct maximum energy into tomato production. Choose your pruning plan based on what you want from your tomatoes. For larger and earlier (but fewer) tomatoes, remove any shoots that emerge on or beside the main stem, and tie the stem to a stake. For more tomatoes later, let plants bush out and support them in tomato cages. Pinch off any flowers that open before July 4.

171 **CHOOSE BETWEEN DETERMINATE AND INDETERMINATE TOMATOES** according to the way you prefer to harvest.

Determinate tomatoes (such as 'Celebrity') tend to stay compact and produce most of their

EARLY, MIDSEASON, AND LATE TOMATOES

EARLY
'Early Girl'
'Early Pick'
'First Lady'
'Glacier'
'Oregon Spring'

MIDSEASON
'Better Boy'
'Big Beef'
'Big Boy'
'Big Girl'

'Celebrity'
'Delicious'
'Floramerica'
'Heatwave'

LATE
'Homestead'
'Oxheart'
'Wonderboy'
'Supersteak'
'Beefmaster'
'Brandywine'

'Better Boy' tomatoes

tomatoes at about the same time. This is convenient for freezing, canning, and sauce making.

Indeterminate tomatoes (such as 'Big Beef') keep growing and developing new tomatoes as they go. They produce a greater yield but spread it over a longer harvest period.

Dozens of different cultivars are in each class—plenty to pick from. You might have to check seed catalogues to find out whether a particular tomato is determinate or not.

172 **STAKE YOUR TOMATO CAGES** so a bumper crop won't pull them over. Work a tall stake through the wire mesh near the perimeter of the cage and stab it 4 to 6 inches deep in the ground. This will anchor the cage (and the plant inside) firmly despite the pull of strong winds and branchfuls of ripening tomatoes.

173 **PLANT VERTICALLY TO SAVE SPACE.** Instead of letting beans, cucumbers, melons, and squash sprawl across the ground, you can let them climb up a trellis or arbor.

This attractive trellis is a real space saver.

I74  **ADD HEIGHT TO A VEGETABLE GARDEN** with a tepee covered with bean and pea vines. This space saver works similarly to a trellis but has a different look. Make the tepee of six or eight 6-foot-high poles tied together at the top. Plant pole beans, lima beans, or peas around each pole, and they will twine up to the top.

I75 **PLANT MORNING GLORY SEEDS AROUND THE STEMS OF SUN-FLOWERS.** Lanky  sunflowers can look quite barren once the flowers are done blooming. But when clad in morning glories, their beauty lasts for the rest of the growing season.

I76 **SIDE-DRESS LONG-GROWING CROPS,** such as indeterminate tomatoes, eggplants, and peppers, with a balanced vegetable-garden fertilizer in order to keep them producing. After the first harvest, sprinkle some granular fertilizer around the perimeter of the plants, then work it lightly into the soil, and water well. The extra nutrients can encourage blossoming of new flowers and development of fruits afterward.

177 **PLANT POTATOES IN RAISED BEDS,** covering them with a little compost-enriched soil. As the potato vines arise, surround them with straw until the layer reaches about 12 inches in thickness. New tubers will develop in the straw, which can be brushed away for a super-simple harvest.

Grow potatoes in a raised bed for easier harvesting.

178

USE NEWSPAPER covered with straw between garden rows to eliminate weeds and retain moisture. This dynamic duo works more efficiently together than either one alone. At the end of the growing season, rototill the paper and straw into the soil to decay.

179 **PLANT MELONS AND CUCUMBERS** in the compost pile. (They might grow there anyway if you toss old fruits on the pile in the fall). Warm, moist, nutrient-rich compost seems to bring out the best in melon and cucumber vines.

180 **GET TWICE THE HARVEST** by planting a lettuce and tomato garden in an 18- or 24-inch-wide pot. You can pick the lettuce as it swells and leave extra growing room for the tomatoes. Here's how to proceed:

- Fill the pot with a premoistened blend of $\frac{1}{3}$ compost and $\frac{2}{3}$ peat-based potting mix.
- Plant several leaf lettuce seeds or small seedlings around the edge of the pot and a tomato seedling in the middle.
- Place the pot in a sunny, frost-free location.
- Water as needed to keep the soil moist, and fertilize once a month or as needed to encourage good growth.

181 **EXTEND THE FALL HARVEST SEASON** for crops such as cabbage, Brussels sprouts, and broccoli with a warm coat of straw. Although it may never be fashionably chic, straw does trap heat effectively.

Put bales or piles of straw around the plants, leaving the south side open to the warm sun. Thus treated, these naturally frost-tolerant plants may stay in good condition deep into fall, or even into winter in warmer climates.

CHAPTER 12

HERBS

H erbs are useful for cooking, crafting, and decorating—coming boldly out of the garden into your home. A separate herb garden is wonderful, but herbs can also be blended with flowers and vegetables in a kitchen or a cottage garden. You can also slip herbs in flower or shrub beds, or even into the plantings around your foundation.

Culinary herbs are a mainstay of most herb gardens. The garden-fresh flavors of thyme, basil, savory, oregano, and marjoram are incomparable. You can also grow gourmet varieties of these classics—lemon thyme, cinnamon basil, and Sicilian oregano, for example—to add to your cooking pleasure.

Once your kitchen is well stocked, try lavender and scented geraniums for their sweet perfumes. Add some herbal teas, such as stomach-soothing peppermint and calming chamomile. One of the best and easiest ways to enrich your life is to grow more herbs!

182 **PLAN AN HERB GARDEN** before you plant. Some of the most charming herb gardens have formal beds or geometric patterns that show off the beauty of herbal foliage. Here are some examples:

An herbal knot garden

- Knot gardens interweave herbs with contrasting leaf color and textures into simple or intricate patterns, many of which are taken from embroidery schemes. Simple knot gardens can be made with two overlapping circles or squares set on a background of mulch or gravel. An easy way to make a knot is with annual herbs such as bush basil, summer savory, or sweet marjoram, or even annual flowers such as French marigolds or ageratum.

- Formal herb gardens generally have symmetrical planting plans, with matched herbs on either side of the garden like reflections in a mirror.
- Formal and patterned herb gardens often include neat, clipped edgings of boxwood, teucrium, santolina, thyme, winter savory, or other neat herbs suitable for shearing.

183 **PROVIDE SANDY SOIL** for herbs that need well-drained soil of moderate fertility. If kept in soil that's lean and light and drenched in hot sun, these herbs develop excellent flavor and stay free from disease.

If your soil is naturally sandy and well drained, you're in luck. If, instead, it's damp clay, raise the herb garden and add a 3-inch layer of coarse sand and 2 inches of compost to improve drainage. Avoid excessive use of fertilizers, especially those high in nitrogen.

184 **GROW HERBS THAT NEED LIGHT SOIL IN POTS.** When planted in well-drained, peat-based potting mix, herbs such as thyme, lavender, and rosemary thrive—and they look great!

185 **PLANT PERENNIALS THAT DOUBLE AS HERBS IN FLOWER BEDS AND BORDERS.** Some herbs masquerade as perennials (and vice versa) because they can be used for decorating, fragrance, or cuisine. Some examples include the following:

- Sweetly fragrant bee balm has flowers and foliage wonderful for tea or drying for potpourri.
- Yarrow bears everlasting flowers for dried arrangements. Air drying is fine for golden-flowered forms. To preserve the color of pink, red, and white-flowered yarrows, dry them in silica gel.
- Lady's mantle is a historical herb with lovely scalloped leaves and small sprays of yellow-green flowers for cutting.
- Pinks have fragrant flowers that can be used fresh for cut flower arrangements or dried for potpourri.

SOME HERBS FOR LIGHT SOIL

Lavender	Lamb's ears
Sage	Teucrium
Santolina	German
Thyme	chamomile
Oregano	Coriander
Sweet fennel	Hyssop
Marjoram	Tarragon
Winter savory	Rosemary
Yarrow	Artemisias

SOME HERBS FOR MOISTER SOIL

Mints	Lady's mantle
Angelica	Lemon balm
Basil	Parsley
Bee balm	Sorrel
Chives	Sweet woodruff
Horseradish	

186 **USE HERBS WITH ATTRACTIVE FOLIAGE** for season-long color in perennial gardens. Amid the comings and goings of perennial flowers, neatly or colorfully clad herbs maintain enduring style and beauty.

Some of the best herbs to grow for decorative foliage include globe basil (small mounds of emerald green), bronze leaf basil or perilla, ornamental sages (with purple leaves, variegated gold leaves, or tricolor green, white, and pink leaves), and silver-leaved herbs such as gray santolina and lavender.

For a great overall color scheme, complement the color of the foliage with nearby flowers.

187 **PLANT A COLLECTION OF COMMONLY USED CULINARY HERBS** in a clay planter by a sunny kitchen window. They will be right at hand when you need them.

188 **RESTRAIN RAMPANT HERBS** like mint and bee balm so they can't take over the garden. These plants need firm limits to keep them in their proper place.

Plant rampant herbs in large plastic pots with the bottom removed and the top rim emerging an inch or two above the soil surface. The container will slow down spreading growth enough so you can see trouble before it spills over the edge. Cut back any errant sprouts and use them for tea or to garnish a fruit salad. Divide to renew the chastised plant every year or two.

189  **PINCH BACK ANNUAL HERBS,** such as basil, to keep them from blooming. If allowed to channel energy into seed production, the foliage will grow skimpy and so will your harvest. Pinching off the shoot tips from time to time provides sprigs for herbal vinegars and pestos and inspires the plant to grow back bushier than ever.

190 **REMOVE A FEW BRICKS** in a garden path to make places for low-growing thyme or oregano. Either herb will thrive in this warm, well-drained location and will give a charming natural look and wonderful fragrance to the walkway.

191 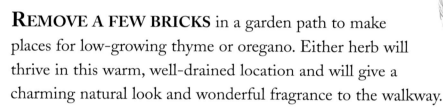 **PLANT MORE PARSLEY, DILL, AND FENNEL** than you think you will use to attract swallowtail butterflies. The beauty of the butterflies and fun of watching the caterpillars develop can be worth the foliage that they eat.

192 **HARVEST PERENNIAL HERBS** as they develop flower buds. This is the time when the fragrant and flavorful oils in the plants are at their peak of intensity, providing a gourmet experience. Because fresh herbs taste so good, even at other times of the growing season, it's perfectly acceptable to continue harvesting whenever you feel the urge. In cold climates, however, hardy perennial herbs need a break from heavy harvesting beginning 45 days before the first frost in order to prepare for winter.

CHAPTER 13

FRUITS

So many different kinds of fruit are available—how do you begin to decide which to grow? Start with quality. When soft berries are homegrown, they can be harvested when fully ripe, plump, and sweet, without concern for shipping and perishability. The flavor is outstanding!

The amount of yard space available will be another deciding factor. Choose between growing small fruits—berries that grow on small plants, vines, or bushes— or larger tree fruits. Start with easily raised, space-efficient small fruits such as strawberries, blackberries, and raspberries. But if you have a place in your landscape for a fruit tree or two, don't pass up the opportunity. Look for easy-care fruit trees, or even nontraditional trees such as mulberries or crabapples.

Traditional orchard trees such as apples, peaches, and pears require some knowledge and attention to pollination, pruning, spraying, fertilizing, and other kinds of care. To minimize or eliminate spraying for disease, look for new disease-resistant cultivars of apple trees.

> ### DISEASE-RESISTANT APPLE CULTIVARS
>
> 'Liberty'   'GoldRush'
> 'Macfree'   'Enterprise'
> 'Freedom'   'Jonafree'
> 'Pristine'

193 **MULCH STRAWBERRIES** with straw to keep the fruits clean. Straw keeps soil and disease spores, which cause berries to rot and mold, from splashing up onto the berries. As a result, they look nicer and keep longer. Straw also keeps the soil

Straw helps berries stay healthy and attractive.

194

moist, so the berries can plump up, and it helps reduce weeds.

GROW DAY-NEUTRAL STRAW-BERRIES for a summer-long harvest. While June-bearing strawberries bear fruit heavily in early summer, and ever-bearing strawberries bear in June and again in fall, day-neutrals can keep flowering and fruiting throughout much of the summer.

Plant day-neutral strawberries as early in spring as possible and pinch off all the flower buds for six weeks afterward. This lets the plants grow strong before they begin to fruit. Once the plants are flowering, fertilize them monthly to keep the plants vigorous and productive.

Heavy producers such as these may not keep up the pace year after year. When you notice berry production diminishing, consider starting a new strawberry patch with fresh plants.

SOME JUNE-BEARING AND DAY-NEUTRAL STRAWBERRY CULTIVARS

JUNE-BEARING	DAY-NEUTRAL
'Honeoye'	'Tribute'
'Earliglow'	'Tristar'
'Annapolis'	'Fern'
'Redchief'	'Selva'
'Cardinal'	
'Surecrop'	
'Guardian'	
'Lateglow'	

195 **PLANT STRAWBERRIES IN A STRAWBERRY JAR** for an edible feast on a patio. Strawberry jars stand about two feet high and have openings along the side, perfect for planting with strawberry plants. They look especially charming when little plantlets sprout on runners and dangle down the sides.

Plant in peat-based potting mixed with extra compost. To make watering easier, run a perforated plastic tube down the center of the pot before planting. You can pour water down the tube to moisten the entire container from the inside out.

196 **CUT THE CANES** on blackberries and raspberries when first setting out new plants. The canes are the elongated flowering stems. Leave just a few of the leafy buds at the base of the stems. This eliminates any cane diseases that may have hitchhiked to your garden on the plant. It also discourages spring flowering, letting the plant become well established before moving on to berry production.

197 **THIN OUT ONE-THIRD OF ALL BLACK-BERRY AND RASPBERRY CANES** each year to keep them productive. If you've ever tried to walk through an abandoned farm field bristling with blackberry thickets, you know what a thorny tangle these plants can grow into.

Not only does crowded growth make blackberries and raspberries hard to work around, but it forces canes to compete for sun, nutrients, moisture, and fresh air. The result can be smaller berries and more diseases.

As soon as canes are done bearing fruit, you can cut them off at the base to provide more space for new canes. Remove any sick, weak, or scrawny canes. Then selectively remove additional canes from areas that are crowded or creeping into other parts of the garden.

Pruning is easier if you wear thick, thornproof gloves and use long-handled pruning loppers. A pair of sunglasses to protect your eyes won't hurt either.

198 **PLANT DWARF FRUIT TREES,** which stay small enough for you to pick the fruit from the ground. This is a safe, easy way to harvest. You won't have to lug around ladders or balance on them while working. Another advantage of dwarf fruit trees is they begin to bear fruit much younger than full-sized trees do. And if

Dwarf fruit trees are a practical choice for small lawns.

your lawn is small, a dwarf tree, which takes up less space than its full-size counterpart, is a good alternative.

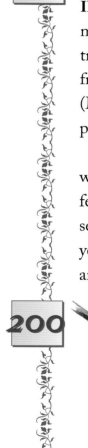

199 **TRY GROWING A SUPER-DWARF PEACH TREE IN A POT.** Super-dwarfs are extra-miniature trees that may reach only about 5 feet tall. Although other fruit trees come as super-dwarfs, peaches produce flavorful fruit with only one tree and are great for beginners. (Many other fruit trees require a second cultivar for pollination.)

Plant your super-dwarf peach in a 24-inch-wide tub with drainage holes in the bottom. Keep it moist, well fertilized, and in a sunny location during the growing season. If your tree doesn't bear fruit the first year, give it time. It may need another year or two to start its career. During winter in cold climates, store the tree, tub and all, in a cool but protected location.

200  **USE STICKY RED BALLS** for control of apple maggots on apple and plum trees or blueberry bushes. Apple maggots are fly larvae that tunnel into developing fruit, making it disgusting and inedible.

Apple maggot flies are easily tricked, however. If you put out sticky red balls (homemade or purchased through a garden supply catalog), the egg-laying females will be attracted to the ball and get stuck. (This will end their egg-laying career!) Hang at least one sticky red ball in a dwarf tree and six or more in larger trees.

201 **USE TREE BANDS TO CATCH CRAWLING PESTS** climbing up fruit tree trunks. Sticky plastic bands will catch and hold ants carrying aphids and creeping caterpillars such as gypsy moths and codling moths.

202 **COVER RIPEN-ING BERRIES** with fine netting to keep birds away from strawberries, blueberries, raspberries, blackberries, cherries, and grapes. Birds love the juicy, sweet flavor of berries and begin to be attracted to them as

Cover your berries with netting to protect them from hungry birds.

soon as the berries start to color. If the netting is in place, they won't be able to get close enough to do much damage.

ANNUALS AND BIENNIALS

Annuals are flowers that bloom the first year they are planted, often flowering just a couple of months after sowing. Most annuals are started indoors or in greenhouses in late winter or early spring. But when spring frosts are over, plants such as zinnias, nasturtiums, and cosmos can be sown directly in the garden for a summer full of flowers.

In colder climates, tender perennials such as alstroemeria, wax begonia, and some species of impatiens will behave like annuals and must be cultivated as such. These same plants, however, will grow as perennials in their native hot climates.

Biennials like cup and saucer, some foxgloves, and some hollyhocks produce greenery the first year only. During the second year of growth, they flower and set seed destined to become the next generation. If you allow plants to self-sow for at least two years, you will have a steady supply of blooming plants.

203 **RE-CREATE A FAVORITE PATTERN** from a family crest, piece of fabric, or needlepoint with annuals in your flower garden. You've seen similar patterns at amusement parks and public parks. Why not do the same with a pattern that is meaningful to you?

Gardens don't have to be rectangular—use your imagination to come up with a creative pattern.

204 **USE PALE SAND TO OUTLINE THE PLANT GROUPINGS** before planting when laying out annual beds. This is like making a pencil sketch of a painting before stroking on the oil paints.

Whether you're planning to put blue ageratums in edging rows, make a teardrop of red zinnias, or create a sweeping mass of pink impatiens, you can adjust and fine-tune the overall shapes before filling them in with colorful flowers. After

making the sand outlines, stand back and look at the results objectively. If you don't like the first attempt, cover the sand with soil and try again.

205 **PLANT STAGGERED ROWS OF ANNUALS** to create a fuller look. A single marching line of annuals such as French marigolds set side by side can look weak in a bigger garden. You can beef up their impact by planting a second

> ### *FRAGRANT ANNUALS*
>
> Why not plant some perfumed flowers under an open window or beside the patio? Here are some good choices:
> Pinks
> Heliotropes
> Petunias
> Moonflowers
> Lemon and Orange Gem marigolds
> Fragrant White flowering tobacco
> Stocks
> Sweet peas

row behind the first, with the rear plants centered on the openings between the front-row plants.

Staggered rows are also nice for showcasing taller annuals, such as blue salvia or snapdragons, set in the rear of a garden. A double row of spider flowers can become so full and bushy it resembles a flowering hedge.

206 **CHOOSE HEALTHY PLANTS** when shopping at the garden center or nursery in spring. Here is a checklist to use before buying any new plant:

- Leaf color: The foliage of naturally green-leafed plants should be bright green, not faded yellow or scorched bronze or brown.
- Plant shape: The sturdiest seedlings will be compact, with short stretches of stem between sets of leaves. Slenderness may be an admirable quality on high-fashion models, but a lanky, skinny seedling is weaker and less desirable than a short, stocky one.
- Pests: If you shake the plant, no insects should come fluttering off. Inspect the stem tips and flower buds for aphids, small pear-shaped sap suckers. Look for hidden pests by turning the plant upside down and looking under the leaves and along the stem.
- Roots: An annual with ideal roots will have filled out its potting soil without growing cramped. When roots are overcrowded, the plant is root-bound—the roots have consumed all soil space and grown tangled and ineffective. The best way to judge root quality is to pop a plant out of its container (or ask a sales clerk to do this) and check to see how matted the roots have become. (Light tangles can be corrected; see Hint 209.)

207  **CHOOSE SHADE-TOLERANT OR SHADE-LOVING ANNUALS** for a lightly shaded garden. Among the annuals that prefer shade are impatiens, browallia, and torenia. Other annuals, the most versatile of the bunch, will grow in sun or light shade. They include wax begonias, sweet alyssum, ageratum, coleus, forget-me-nots, and pansies.

Bright-colored impatiens are good flowers to have in a shade garden.

208 **CREATE THE MOST EXCITEMENT** with your shade garden by choosing flowers with white, pastel, or brightly colored blossoms. Dark burgundy leaves and cool blue or purple flowers won't shine the way brighter blooms do from shady garden depths.

209 **GENTLY BREAK UP THE ROOT BALL** of annuals grown in cell packs or pots before planting them. Often, the roots have overgrown the potting area and become matted. You'll have to pull off the tangles so the roots will be able to grow free into the soil.

If roots are wound around the bottom of the root ball, use your finger to gently work the roots free of each other. If they are matted over the entire root ball, you'll need to tear or cut the mats off, leaving the roots below intact.

210 **SNIP BACK LEGGY ANNUALS** when you plant to encourage bushy new growth. Don't hesitate—it's really for the best! Removing the growing tip of a stem stimulates side shoots to sprout, which makes annuals fuller. Since each side shoot can be full of flowers, the whole plant will look better.

211 **USE A SPACING AID** to plant annual displays and cutting gardens in even rows. Even the most beautifully grown annuals can be distracting if they are spaced erratically. Fortunately, spacing is one element you can easily control. Here are some options:

- Make a planting grid by stapling a large piece of wire mesh over a wooden frame. If the mesh openings are 2 inches square and you want to plant ageratums 6 inches apart, you can put one seedling in every third hole.
- Make a spacing rope. Tie knots in the rope to mark specific measurements, for instance, noting every 4 or 6 inches. You can stretch the rope between two stakes to make even measurements along a straight line.
- Take a yardstick with you when you go to plant. Measure the distance between each plant in a row and between rows rather than simply eyeballing it.

212 **FERTILIZE ANNUALS PERIODICALLY** during the growing season to keep them producing. This is particularly helpful after the first flush of blooming flowers begins to fade (which often marks the beginning of a quiet garden during hot summer months).

For best results, deadhead (see Hint 213), then fertilize with a balanced water-soluble or granular fertilizer. A balanced fertilizer contains similar percentages of nitrogen, phosphorus, and potassium. Check the fertilizer package label for application instructions.

213 **REMOVE SPENT BLOSSOMS** from geraniums and other annuals to keep them blooming and tidy. The bigger the flower, the worse it can look when faded, brown, and mushy. Large, globular geranium flowers are particularly prominent when they begin to discolor. Snip off the entire flower cluster. Take off the stem, too, if no other flower buds are waiting to bloom.

This process, called deadheading, is more than mere housekeeping. By removing the old flowers, you prevent seed production, which consumes a huge amount of energy from the plant. Energy saved can be channeled instead into producing new blooms.

214 **PINCH ANNUALS** like coleus, browallia, and petunias to keep them full. These plants can get tall and gangly as the growing season progresses. A little pinch, removing the top inch or two of stem, will soon correct this problem.

More is at work here than merely shortening the stem. Removing the terminal bud (at the stem tip) allows side branches to grow and make the plant fuller.

215 **PLANT NATURALLY SELF-BRANCHING ANNUALS.** Your mother may have pinched all her flowers throughout the summer. But many modern types of impatiens, begonias, multiflora petunias, and other annuals have been bred to be self-branching. They stay fuller naturally and may not need any pinching, or at least very little.

Some petunias are self-branching.

216 **TAKE STEM CUTTINGS OF TENDER FLOWERS** in late summer before temperatures drop below 50 degrees Fahrenheit. You can root them indoors and enjoy their greenery and perhaps a few flowers during winter. Then you can take more cuttings of these plants to set out next spring. Cuttings are more compact and versatile than old garden plants dug up and squeezed into a pot. They can thrive with less effort and space.

Fresh-cut annual stems may root if you put them in a vase of clean water. But stems can root more reliably in a sterile, peat-based mix.

ANNUALS SUITABLE FOR LATE SUMMER CUTTINGS	
Geraniums, ivy-leaf and standard	Coleus
	Asters
Impatiens	Petunias
Fibrous rooted begonias	Portulaca
	Verbena

217

HAVE FLOWERS BLOOMING IN SUNNY WINDOWS during fall and winter by starting new seedlings outdoors in pots in mid- to late summer. Bring them indoors several weeks before the first autumn frost. They will begin to bloom as frost arrives, perfect for brightening the autumn transition period. This works well with French marigolds, pansies, petunias, nasturtiums, violas, impatiens, compact cockscomb, and annual asters. Simply discard the plants later when they get ratty-looking.

218

GROW SOME ANNUALS WITH EVERLASTING FLOWERS to dry for winter arrangements. There are many wonderful annuals to choose from. Those listed at right are easily dried if spread out in a warm, dark, airy place. Grow a few for yourself and some extras to give away as gifts.

If seedlings of everlasting annuals are not available at your local garden center, consider starting your own seedlings indoors (see Hint 93).

SOME EVERLASTING ANNUALS

COCKSCOMB: plume or comb-shaped flowers in bright red, orange, or yellow

ANNUAL BABY'S BREATH: cloudlike drifts of small white flowers

BELLS OF IRELAND: spikes of green trumpet-shaped flowers

GLOBE AMARANTH: ball-shaped flowers of white, pink, purple, and orange

LOVE-IN-A-MIST: maroon-striped seed pods

STATICE: bright sprays of pink, purple, yellow, white, and blue flowers

STRAWFLOWERS: double daisylike flowers with straw-textured petals in red, pink, white, gold, and bronze

219 **RELIVE A LITTLE SLICE OF HISTORY** by growing a few heirloom flowers. These are flowers your ancestors may have enjoyed. Many of these plants are

returning to popularity, thanks to their interesting appearances. Some heirlooms are only slightly different from modern flowers—taller, larger- or smaller-flowered, or more fragrant. But other heirlooms are quite distinct and unusual. Here are some examples:

- Love-lies-bleeding: Long, dangling, crimson red seed heads form colorful streamers.
- Kiss-me-over-the-garden-gate: These six-foot-tall plants have pendulous pink flowers.
- Balsam: This impatiens relative sprinkles flowers amid the foliage along the stems.

Staking sweet peas to the house adds a lovely, old-fashioned touch to the garden.

- Sweet peas: Vining pea-shaped plants that bear colorful pink, white, purple, and red flowers with delightful fragrances.

220 **IN INFORMAL GARDENS, PLANT NONHYBRID ANNUALS** that may return from self-sown seeds allowed to mature and fall to the ground. Suitable annuals include the heirlooms love-lies-bleeding and kiss-me-over-the-garden-gate; wildflowers such as cornflowers, California poppies, and verbenas; and open-pollinated annuals such as snapdragons, portulaca, cockscomb, and spider flowers.

CHAPTER 15

PERENNIALS

Perennials are distinct from annuals in that they return year after year, eliminating the need to buy new flowers every spring. Unlike annuals, perennials generally bloom only one or, at the most, two seasons per year. There are spring bloomers, summer bloomers, or fall bloomers. When they're not in flower, perennials are enjoyed for their foliage, which is at least as important a consideration as the blooms.

Perennial shapes and sizes also add to the mix. There are tall perennials like plume poppy that tower over your head and creeping perennials like moss phlox that carpet the ground.

Perennials may grow and expand each year, eventually filling more space than you might expect. To keep perennials under control and growing well, many need division (digging up the root clump, dividing it into sections, and replanting the best sections in freshened soil). This can provide a harvest of new plants for use elsewhere in the garden.

Plant according to height, so that all the flowers will be clearly visible.

221 **ARRANGE THE PERENNIAL GARDEN** so that you can see and enjoy every plant—regardless of how small it is. Place the tallest plants in the rear of a border that is viewed exclusively from the front. In an island bed viewed from all sides, place tall plants in the middle.

Work medium-height plants into the middle of a border or island bed, filling out the garden in front of the taller plants. Set small plants up front, where they won't be hidden by taller leaves or flowers.

The neat progression of short to tall gives a garden a sense of order and tidiness many people appreciate. Don't be too rigid, however. You can work some medium-size varieties into the plants up front to add interest (see Hint 222).

222 **BRING A FEW TALL PLANTS FORWARD** to break up any tendency to make height organization rigid. A garden can look more natural and interesting if it's allowed a few height variations. Here are some ideas to try (also see Hint 223):

- Plant some medium-height early bloomers such as columbines toward the front of the garden. They will flower before the other perennials are stirring and can be cut back after flowering so that only compact leaves remain.
- Swing an arc of medium-height plants up toward the front of the border, making a gentle curve that softens height restrictions but doesn't extend so far into the front of the border that it becomes restrictive.
- Loop a small drift of shorter edging plants back into the medium-height flower section to ease the dividing line between the two.

223 **USE PLANTS WITH AIRY SPRAYS OF SMALL FLOWERS** at the front of the garden. Perennials like baby's breath and coral bells have see-through veils of blossoms that don't obscure what's behind them. This can make the garden sparkle.

224 **COMBINE SEVERAL DIFFERENT PERENNIAL FORMS** to keep the garden from being monotonous. Diversity provides spice to perennial gardening.

Many perennials fall into the following shape categories. But you should expect variations as the seasons progress. Perennials usually stretch up to flower and then fade back to their foliage after the bloom is through.

    🍂 Mats: Perennials such as lamium, bugleweed, and plumbago form low carpets suitable for ground covers or the front of the border.

    🍂 Mounds: Nicely rounded perennials such as coreopsis and hostas provide a soft look.

    🍂 Flower sprays with low foliage: Perennials such as yarrow, sea thrift, and coral bells bear taller flowers over neat low foliage. Height is dramatically reduced when the old flower stems are removed.

    🍂 Vase shapes: When in bloom, plants such as garden phlox and Shasta daisies grow in an inverted triangular shape.

    🍂 Spikes: Plants such as salvias, lupines, gayfeathers, and delphiniums have slim, vertical flowering stems that contrast well with more horizontal forms.

225 **CHOOSE HEALTHY PLANTS.** For the inexperienced buyer, this may be easier said than done in the spring. Potted perennials may be showing only a little foliage, not providing much information about the health of the plant. Here are a few things you can do to get a better picture:

- Look at the plant crown, the place where the shoots emerge from the soil. The emerging stems and leaves should be nicely green and showing no sign of wilting or rotting.
- Study the foliage and soil surface for signs of pests, which might be feeding on the crown, beneath the leaves, or fluttering up when you move the pot. If you find extensive evidence of pests, buy your plants elsewhere.
- Ask a sales clerk if you can look at the plant roots. Turn the pot over and slip the root ball out. The roots should fill the pot, but not be crammed into it, and they should be healthy and firm.

226 KEEP YOUR EXPECTATIONS FOR PLANT LIFE REALISTIC. Although perennials like daylilies and hostas can live for decades, some perennials live only a few years. Perennials with short-but-sweet lives include columbine, blanketflower, and some chrysanthemums. Propagate new plants using division, cuttings, or seed to

PERENNIALS WITH WIDE-RANGING FLOWER COLORS

DAYLILIES: pink, yellow, red, purple, cream
IRIS: purple, red, yellow, white, blue
LUPINES: yellow, red, pink, orange, blue
LILIES: pink, red, white, yellow
POPPIES: pink, red, white, cream, orange
PHLOX: pink, orange, purple, white, blue
POTENTILLA: pink, white, red, yellow
PEONIES: white, pink, red, yellow

have replacements ready when needed. (See Chapter 7, "Propagation," for more detailed instructions.)

227 **AVOID WILDFLOWERS COLLECTED IN THE WILD.** Some people snatch wildflowers from native areas instead of propagating them in a nursery. This

Don't remove wildflowers from their natural environment—buy them from a reputable nursery instead.

depletes the natural environment and can result in inferior plants not prepared for garden life. Buy from a reputable garden center or nursery. Ask where they got the wildflowers and whether they were nursery propagated.

Be suspicious if you see pots with several small plants packed irregularly, which may have been taken from the wild. Flowers that are poorly rooted may have been recently dug and stuck in a pot.

If you see wildflowers sold for less than a comparable perennial, it's a sign that they may have been harvested in the wild.

228 **CHOOSE SINGLE-FLOWERED PEONIES** over the double-flowered types. A single-flowered plant has a solitary row of petals (or several rows, in the case of peonies) around the perimeter of each blossom. Double-flowered plants have many rows of petals, which form a full, fluffy-looking flower.

The big advantage of single-flowered peonies is weight. With fewer petals, the flowers stay lighter and are less likely to fall over when in full bloom. This means they don't need staking. The flowers are also less likely to trap moisture and, consequently, tend to suffer from fewer diseases.

229 **PLAN AHEAD TO COVER THE GAPS** left by perennials that go dormant in summer. Two of the most common now-you-see-them-now-you-don't perennials are sun-loving Oriental poppies and shade-loving old-fashioned bleeding hearts.

Old-fashioned bleeding hearts

When done blooming, both plants slough off their old foliage and hibernate underground. This creates vacant places in the garden. But with a little planning, you can easily work around them.

➤ Plant Oriental poppies or bleeding hearts individually instead of in large clumps or drifts, which leave larger holes.

➤ Organize gardens so that neighboring plants can fill in and cover for the missing greenery. In shade, the ample foliage of hostas and ferns can move into voids left when old-fashioned bleeding hearts go dormant. In sun, hardy geraniums, frothy baby's breath flowers, and spreaders like dragon's blood sedum can fill in for Oriental poppies.

🍂 Set a potted plant, such as a house-plant spending the summer outdoors, temporarily in the opening.

Plant a disease-resistant cultivar of phlox.

230 **CHOOSE DISEASE-RESISTANT CULTIVARS** of garden phlox and bee balm. Both perennials can be troubled with mildew diseases, which cover the plants with ugly white fuzz. Fortunately, developing disease-resistant cultivars has become a priority in the nursery industry. Check perennial catalogues to identify the best new cultivars for your climate.

231 **SOAK BARE-ROOT PERENNIALS** in a bucket of water for an hour before planting. Bare roots have been out of their element (moist soil) while handled and shipped. Letting them soak up a little extra moisture can refresh moisture levels so the roots can grow vigorously in the weeks ahead.

232 **MOLD THE PLANTING HOLE** to provide the proper support for a bare-root perennial. When planting potted perennials, the shape of the pot is a good match

for the hole you dig. But bare-root perennials tend to have octopuslike roots that
need different treatment.

- Dig a wide, shallow
  hole in well-prepared
  soil.
- Form a cone of soil in
  the center of the hole.
  Make the cone high
  enough to hold the crown
  (where the shoots emerge from the roots) at the soil surface.
- Spread the roots around the perimeter of the cone so that each has its own
  space. The hole should be deep enough to accommodate the entire root
  length without a lot of cramming, twisting, and turning.
- Fill in around the roots with soil, and keep it moist.

233 **SHAKE THE POTTING MIX** off the roots of potted perennials and plant them
like bare-root perennials. Larger perennials sold in 1- or 2-quart-size containers
are perfect candidates for this. The reason for doing this is that peat potting mixes
can complicate plant establishment in the soil. The roots of perennials grown in
peat-based mixes can have difficulty growing out of the peat and into the native
soil. In addition, peat can quickly become parched in drying soils, causing root
damage. Getting the peat out eliminates both of these problems and can help new
perennials get established faster than you ever thought possible.

234 **START A SHADE GARDEN UNDER TREES** by adding 4 inches of compost over the tree roots before planting. Rich, moist compost provides a fast start for newly planted perennials. This is important—the flowers need to be growing strongly before tree roots move in and capitalize on their growing space. Compost also helps keep the garden moist in summer, when the trees and perennials may compete for water. Just be careful when planting not to damage the tree roots.

Purple coneflowers tolerate drought.

235 **USE PLANTS ADAPTED TO DRY CONDITIONS IN DROUGHT-PRONE CLIMATES.** Perennials such as butterfly weed have deep or moisture-storing roots that allow them to weather dry conditions. Other drought-survival specialists have leaves that are modified to reduce moisture loss. Silver leaves reflect hot sunlight, and needle-shaped leaves have less surface area for moisture loss. Moisture is stored inside succulent leaves, and moisture loss for furry leaves is slowed by their furry coating.

DROUGHT-TOLERANT PERENNIALS

Yarrow	Purple coneflower
Artemisia	Gayfeather
Butterfly flower	Lavender
Sea pink	Russian sage
Orange coneflower	Sedum

236 SPACE LARGE, SLOW-GROWING PERENNIALS PROPERLY at the start. Big hostas, goat's beard, gas plants, and roses, for example, can be hard to move once they are established. Ask at the nursery or check in a garden encyclopedia for information on how big the plant will get. Then be sure to allow enough space for the plant to reach its mature limits without overcrowding.

237 AVOID DENSE TREE ROOTS by planting a shade garden around the outside of the tree canopy rather than directly underneath. Many tree roots cluster under the branch canopy, and active feeding goes on near the drip line, the place where rainwater drips off the leafy branch tips. Gardening beyond the shadow of the limbs reduces root competition, and the plants will get more light.

238 CONVERT YOUR FRONT YARD TO A COTTAGE GARDEN. Tending flowers is much more fun than mowing grass!

239 PLANT SHADE-LOVING PERENNIALS ON THE SHADY NORTH SIDE OF SHRUBS if you don't have trees. Perennials such as anemones, astilbes, hostas, Lenten roses, and violets can look

A well-tended cottage garden can serve as an attractive front yard.

lovely against a backdrop of evergreen shrubs. Flowering deciduous shrubs such as viburnums or hydrangeas can be even more beautiful.

240 **MAKE AN ARTIFICIAL BOG** for plants that need constantly wet soil. Then you will be able to grow swamp irises, variegated cattails, ligularias, and other water-loving plants.

Begin by deciding where you want the bog garden to be located. They are natural companions for fountains, water gardens, bridges, or streams. Dig out a deep trench or swale for the bog garden, then line the hole with plastic. Set a perforated hose in the bottom, with an end emerging from one side to connect with your household hose. Fill the hole with rich soil and plant bog natives. You can irrigate through the submerged hose as needed to keep the garden constantly moist.

241 **INTERPLANT PERENNIALS WITH RESEEDING ANNUALS** for a lush look that changes every year. For more on these annuals, see Hint 220.

242 **PLANT PERENNIALS INSTEAD OF GRASS** in the boulevard strip. The boulevard strip is the very public space located between the sidewalk and the road. It can be hot, dry, and heavily trod upon, which makes it difficult to keep grass looking healthy and nice.

Instead of fighting a constant battle with turf, use a different tactic. Plant the boulevard strip with low but bushy perennials that people won't walk on. Choose heat- and drought-tolerant perennials such as coreopsis, 'Silver Mound' artemisia, and sea thrift. Now the problem area can become a pretty garden.

243 **USE SALT-TOLERANT PERENNIALS** in cold-climate roadside plantings. Roads heavily salted during winter snowstorms often leave salt residue in the soil. Perennials such as sea thrifts, bearberry, and rugosa roses thrive in soils that are salty enough to kill other plants.

244 **LESSEN THE IMPACT OF WIND** by planting tall perennials and ornamental grasses to shelter a garden full of more delicate plants. Sturdy-stemmed perennials, which are not likely to topple over with the first big gust, grow large enough to curb the wind faster than most shrubs and trees. Some perennials to try are maiden grasses, pampas grass, boltonia, goat's beard, and large hostas.

This tip also works on a smaller scale. You can plant smaller, delicate flowers beside sturdy medium-sized plants like purple coneflowers and irises for wind protection.

245 **SUPPORT FULL, FLOPPY PERENNIALS WITH PRUNED TWIGS.** This is an old British trick called pea staking. It helps perennials stay upright and look natural without glaring metallic stakes or forced shapes that result from corseting with twine. Even better, pea staking costs nothing but a little time.

When the perennials begin to arise in spring, set the ends of sturdy branched twigs around the plant. The twigs should be about as long as the height of the perennial. As the stems grow, they will fill out to hide the twigs. You can cut off any errant woody stems that remain in sight after the perennial reaches full height.

246 **PLANT TALL PERENNIALS TOGETHER** so they can support each other and need no staking. Combinations such as boltonia and asters, yarrows and butterfly weed, or daisies and irises can result in pretty blends of flowers and foliage.

247 **AVOID OVERFERTILIZING** sun-loving prairie plants like coneflowers, yarrows, and coreopsis. Excess fertilizer stimulates taller growth, making these plants more likely to weaken and flop over.

248 **PINCH ASTERS AND MUMS.** Pinching is one of the handiest things you can do in the garden (see Hint 214). Removing the stem tip, with a pinch of your fingernails or with pruning shears, makes plants more compact and bushy.

Pinching is particularly helpful for mums and asters. Flowering plants purchased in a pot have been specially treated to make the plants bushy and full. If left untouched the following year, they will grow fewer, taller, scraggly stems that are more likely to need staking for support.

When pinching, scheduling is important. You want to start early enough to make an impact. And you need to stop by July 1 so flower buds can develop before heavy cold strikes. Start with this pinching schedule but feel free to modify it as you gain experience:

- Pinch shoot tips when the stems are 4 to 6 inches high.
- Pinch again three weeks later.
- Pinch a final time in late June.

249 **SHEAR REBLOOMING PERENNIALS** such as catmint and 'moonglow' coreopsis to promote a second flush of flowers. Getting rid of the old flowers and seed pods encourages new growth, new buds, and new flowers. This is a great reward for a small amount of effort.

Cut the old flowers off reblooming perennials to encourage new growth.

250 **RENEW A DECLINING CLUMP OF PERENNIALS** by division. As many perennials grow, new shoots emerge at the perimeter of the clump, which keeps spreading outwards. The center becomes increasingly older—sometimes woody, sometimes completely barren.

The solution is division. In spring, late summer, or fall, dig up the entire clump. Cut out the old heart, refresh the soil with organic matter, and replant healthy young pieces. (Also see Hints 106 and 107.) You may have enough good divisions left to share with friends.

251 **USE A STRING TRIMMER** to cut back ornamental grasses in spring. The golden leaves and seed plumes are a great winter attraction. But in spring, the old growth must be removed before the new shoots begin to sprout. The string trimmer quickly cuts through grass stems. Rake them up and toss them on the compost pile—job finished!

252 **MAKE PLANTERS OUT OF OLD TREE STUMPS** that are next to your house, in a mixed border, amid a grove of shade trees, or in a woodland edge. In nature, old stumps slowly begin to decay and provide fertile places for ferns and other interesting small plants to grow. You could plant flora native to your area or fill the opening with brightly colored annual flowers and vines.

Follow nature's lead and you will get several benefits: You won't have to pay to have the stump ground out; you can grow plants that need good drainage or special soil mixes right in the trunk; and you create an interesting, sculpturelike structure.

Chip some wood out of the top of the stump to create rooting space. Fill with a soil mix that's appropriate for the plants you intend to grow. After planting, water as necessary to keep the soil moist.

CHAPTER 16

BULBS

When winter finally melts away, crocuses, daffodils, and tulips are quick to appear. The earliest spring bloomers come from bulbs and other allied structures such as tubers, rhizomes, and corms, which lie underground ready to grow as soon as the weather breaks.

When planted in a compatible site, daffodils, snowdrops, and crocuses can spread into large clusters that paint the landscape with their early color. Long-stemmed tulips and daffodils are wonderful flowers to cut and bring indoors. Hyacinths, dwarf irises, and some daffodils have sweet fragrances, making them pleasurable indoors or out.

Summer is made more cheerful with brightly colored summer-flowering bulbs such as caladiums, dahlias, cannas, and gladioli. These bulbs are native to warmer climates and won't survive winter in cold areas. But they can be dug up, stored in the basement, and replanted when warm weather returns.

When heat has other plants resting, summer-flowering bulbs can continue to thrive. Their bountiful blooms make splendid bouquets.

253 **PLANT SPRING-FLOWERING BULBS** to give early seasonal color to lifeless perennial beds. While the perennials are just beginning to stir and

As these tulips fade, the irises are ready to bloom in their place.

arise, the bulbs are decked with color. As the bulbs are fading, the perennials are beginning to come on strong. It is an ideal partnership.

254 **PLAN AHEAD TO FIND THE BEST PLACE** for interplanting bulbs with perennials. Although they bloom in the spring, early flowering bulbs must be planted in the fall. They look best set in clumps around or between perennials such as hardy geraniums, daylilies, and Siberian irises that don't need frequent division (which would disrupt the bulbs).

Don't wait until the bulbs arrive in October. Mark ideal planting places with a tag or stake in spring or summer, when your existing bulbs are blooming and clumps of perennials are still small. Later in the autumn, when the perennials are dormant, you'll already have the best planting places marked.

255 **CHOOSE HEALTHY BULBS.** Use the same criteria you would use if shopping for good-quality onions in the grocery store.

- Look for plump bulbs without soft spots or dark, diseased blotches.
- Check the basal plate, where the roots will emerge. It should be firm and undamaged.
- Daffodil bulbs with two noses will provide twice the bloom, but tulip bulbs should have only one nose. With two, they won't flower.

COMBINE BULB ORDERS WITH YOUR FRIENDS to buy wholesale and save money. One bulb catalog sells 100 tulip bulbs for just a few dollars more than 50 tulip bulbs. You should order early to get the best selection and prompt delivery.

A bulk order of bulbs saves you money.

SOAK FALL-PLANTED BULBS for 12 hours in warm water before planting. This

moisturizing method works with tunicate-type bulbs (neatly enclosed round or teardrop-shaped bulbs) and is not suitable for lily or other bulbs with loose, fleshy scales. Soaking allows suitable bulbs to absorb enough water to begin growth immediately, saving two or three weeks of time. This is particularly helpful in northern climates, where early-arriving winter weather limits leisurely rooting.

ADD LIQUID RODENT REPELLENT to bulb-soaking water (at the lowest recommended concentration) to make the treated bulbs unappetizing to rodents.

Bitter-tasting rodent repellent is absorbed by the bulbs, which then become unattractive to mice, chipmunks, rabbits, raccoons, skunks, and most other animals. It's particularly helpful for crocuses and other edible, shallowly planted bulbs that are easily unearthed and eaten by passing critters.

259 **PLANT A DOUBLE LAYER** of 'Paper White' narcissus bulbs for twice the flower display. 'Paper White' narcissus, with sweetly scented clusters of small, white daffodil flowers, are warm-climate bulbs that naturally bloom during winter. Pot them in late fall or early winter, and then watch them come to life in a sunny window, even as the snow falls outside.

Most people plant five or six bulbs in an 8-inch bulb pot or forcing dish, which makes a nice enough display. But if you can find a deeper nursery pot, you can plant a bottom and top layer of bulbs to produce awe-inspiring results.

- Put several inches of moist, peat-based potting mix in the bottom of a deep pot.
- Set bulbs in the mix, with the flat rooting plate down and the pointed nose up. Put the bulbs side by side around the perimeter of the pot and fill the center with one or several bulbs (the number will vary depending on the size of the pot).
- Cover the lower-level bulbs with an inch or two of moist potting mix.
- Set the upper layer of bulbs in this mix, positioning them between (not over) the sprouting noses of the lower-level bulbs.
- Cover the upper level with potting mix, allowing any lanky green sprouts to emerge uncovered.
- Set the potted bulbs in a cool location to root for several weeks. Keep the pot moist but not wet. Then bring the pot into a warm, sunny window and let the growth begin!

260 **PLANT A TRIPLE LAYER OF BULBS** in the garden. The technique is similar to that in Hint 259 but the characters differ.

The idea here is to have a shallowly planted layer of early bloomers like crocuses, snowdrops, or squills for early spring color. Just below them, planted about 5 or 6 inches deep, put daffodils that bloom in mid-spring. Underneath the daffodils, plant late-blooming tulips, which benefit from deep planting and finish up the flower display. You can also plant up a large pot in the same fashion for a burst of early color.

261 **MAKE INTENSIVE BULB PLANTINGS WORK SMOOTHLY** (see Hint 260) by discouraging competition or disease spread. Use only well-drained soil for bulbs (see Hint 6). In wet soils, bulbs will rot. Plan to fertilize in the fall with a product formulated for bulbs so they won't have to compete for nutrients. Water during spring while bulbs are actively growing, but allow the soil to dry out in summer, when they are dormant.

262 **DISCOURAGE RODENTS FROM EATING CROCUSES** and other bulbs by planting them in fine-mesh wire

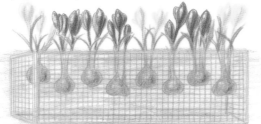

BULBS NOT PRONE TO RODENT ATTACKS

Squills
Flowering onions
Colchicums (autumn bloomers)
Crown imperial
Daffodils (narcissus); also called jonquils

baskets. If animals can't dig the bulbs out, they can't eat them. Wire cages also help prevent accidental human damage with shovels and hoes.

263

8-10"

PLANT TULIPS 8 TO 10 INCHES DEEP to prolong their life and protect them from rodents. When set deep, tulip bulbs are slower to split and stop flowering. They also take some serious digging to be reached by rodents. It's a win-win situation.

264 **PLANT THE SAME CULTIVAR OF DAFFODIL TOGETHER** in groups of 10, 20, or more. Then all the flowers will bloom together—at the same time, in the same color—making a maximum impact. Just a few daffodils look lonely, and a clump of mixed colors and cultivars looks chaotic.

265 **DIVIDE OR FERTILIZE CROWDED DAF-FODILS** to increase their bloom. Daffodils that have multiplied to form a large clump may have

A beautiful bloom of daffodils.

depleted the soil nutrients and riddled all the rooting space in the process. The result may be plenty of green leaves but few or no flowers. The solution is as easy as fertilizer or as down-to-earth as division.

Start by applying fertilizer. Slow-release bulb fertilizers can be used in fall for good root growth and continued effectiveness in early spring. Or you can use an

all-purpose, balanced fertilizer when growth begins in the spring.

To divide daffodils, dig up the bulbs as the foliage fades. Separate old and new bulbs, refresh the soil with organic matter, and replant with generous spacing.

266 **REMOVE THE BULBILS** from the stems of lilies and plant them to make new plants. These bulbils, or secondary bulbs, look like small, dark berries but contain no seeds at all. They are similar to miniature bulbs and have the ability to sprout into new plants. Give them a chance, and watch them grow.

267 **CUT LILY STEMS TO THE GROUND** in fall to avoid stem rot. It's better to be safe than sorry!

268 **MARK THE LOCATION OF BULBS** with a stake, stick, rock, or tag so you know where they are while they're dormant. Without an above-ground reminder, it's easy to dig into the bulbs by mistake when planting other flowers or vigorously hoeing out weeds.

269 **COVER LARGE PATCHES OF BULBS** with a ground cover that will fill the void when the bulbs go dormant. Bulbs brighten the ground cover in spring, and the ground cover helps keep the bulbs cool and dry in summer. You may need to

Bicolored tulips and snow-in-summer

270

fertilize more often since twice the amount of plants will be growing in the same space.

CUSTOMIZE BULBS AND GROUND COVERS by considering their height, sturdiness, and foliage thickness.

Bulbs with weak stems cannot emerge through heavy-leafed ground covers such as pachysandra. Small-leafed ground covers with more open growth, such as periwinkle, can be more suitable.

Bulbs must be tall enough to grow up and over any ground cover surrounding them. Short, early spring bloomers like crocuses may be better placed with deciduous ground covers like epimedium (which die back to the ground in winter) than with evergreen ground covers like ivy.

271 **LEAVE BULB FOLIAGE LOOSE** to ripen properly. Cutting off the foliage before it yellows severs bulbs' food supply and weakens them. Putting

---

SOME TULIPS WITH HANDSOME, COLORED FOLIAGE

GREIGII TULIPS
'Donna Bella'
'Red Riding Hood'
'Grand Prestige'
'Margaret Herbst'
'Oratorio'

SPECIES TULIPS
Tulipa linifolia
Tulipa maximowiczii

FOSTERIANA TULIPS
'Easter Moon'
'Juan'

KAUFMANNIANA TULIPS
'Showwinner'
'Johann Strauss'

daffodils in bondage by tying up their leaves also reduces food production and makes them more prone to disease attack. Taking care of bulb foliage, even though the bloom is gone, helps ensure more flowers in the years to come.

272 **CUT THE TALL, SPENT STEMS OF TULIP FLOWERS** down to the first leaf. This removes the old flower, an important task called deadheading (see Hint 213). It also leaves the attractive broad foliage to ripen in the garden as nature intended.

273 **BRIGHTEN UP DULL SPOTS IN THE GARDEN** with pots of tender bulbs such as agapanthus, tuberous begonias, caladiums, pineapple lilies, or tuberoses. The versatility of pots combined with the bright blooms of summer-flowering bulbs keeps gardens looking exceptional all summer and fall.

274 **STORE TENDER BULBS IN VERMICULITE OR PEAT** to keep them from drying out. These materials are a packing cushion and more. They help keep the bulbs from drying out and rotting. Peat moss, which is naturally disease-resistant, is particularly good for this job.

> ❧ Dig the bulbs when the soil is relatively dry so they won't emerge caked with mud. Follow the timing recommended in Hints 277 and 278.
> ❧ Gently brush off any extra soil, and remove any old vegetation. Throw out any damaged bulbs.

❧ Prepare a place for winter storage. Place a layer of vermiculite or peat in the bottom of a plastic storage box. Use one kind of bulb per box or one kind per layer, making sure to label each layer so you know which is which next spring.

❧ Set the bulbs in the peat or vermiculite, keeping bulbs an inch or two away from each other.

❧ Cover with a thick layer of peat or vermiculite and add another group of bulbs, repeating this process until all are packed.

❧ Store in a cool, but not cold, place during winter.

❧ Check the bulbs at least once a month (preferably more often). Remove any that may have rotted. If all the bulbs begin to shrivel, dampen the packing medium slightly to prevent further moisture loss.

275 **DIVIDE DAHLIAS** to make more plants every year. Dahlias contain underground food-storing rhizomes—a modified form of stem that looks a little like a potato. The rhizomes connect to a central stalklike crown, which contains all the growth buds. Look closely to find the small scaly bumps or sprouts that indicate where a new shoot will arise. Both rhizomes and shoots are necessary for a new division to succeed.

In the spring, take dahlia rhizomes out of storage. Cut the crown longitudinally into several pieces, each with at least one rhizome and growth bud. Now each division can act as an independent plant.

276 **PRESTART DAHLIAS INDOORS** six weeks before the last spring frost arrives so you can have extra-early flowers.

- ❧ Plant the tubers in large nursery pots filled with compost-enriched peat-based potting mix.
- ❧ Put the pots in a warm, bright location. The plants will begin rooting and sprouting.
- ❧ Dahlias can stay in large pots all summer, as long as you keep the soil moist and add extra fertilizer. Or you can transplant them outdoors into the garden when the danger of spring frosts pass.

For beautiful dahlias early, start them inside.

277 **DIG COLD-SENSITIVE TROPICAL BULBS** such as cannas and caladiums before the first fall frost to prevent damage to the bulbs. Damaged bulbs are likely to rot in winter storage.

278 **DIG COLD-TOLERANT TENDER BULBS** such as dahlias and gladiolus after a light frost has killed the foliage.

279 **POINT THE SHOVEL BLADE**—not the handle—straight down into the soil when digging bulbs. This prevents the shovel from angling into nearby bulbs and slicing them in half.

CHAPTER 17

GROUND COVERS AND VINES

Ground covers spread across barren patches of soil, coating them with greenery. Some ground covers offer a tapestry of both colorful flowers and foliage. The varying colors, heights, and textures contrast with the nearby lawn, highlighting the shape of the ground-cover bed.

Some ground covers also grow where no grass can thrive. In shady areas under trees, dead nettle and periwinkles are at home. On steep banks, where lawn mowing is difficult, great-looking daylilies or junipers can grow thickly enough to stop erosion. Some also double as vines, growing vertically as easily as horizontally. They can even blend tree trunks, walls, and fences into the scenery with a patina of greenery.

Other vines may have flowers, colorful foliage, or fruit that make them spectacular vertical accents to train on a fence, trellis, or lamppost. Some climb freely by twining or with tendrils. Others, like climbing roses, need your assistance to assure their secure ascendance.

Use your imagination to create a dramatic garden centerpiece.

280 **ADD HEIGHT TO A PERENNIAL BORDER**
with annual or perennial vines on wire cages, tepees, or scrims. When you want a dynamic high point for a flower garden, an upward-trained vine will be

effective throughout the growing season and sometimes beyond. In contrast, many of the tallest perennials reach their maximum height only when in flower, which may last for just a few weeks. Here are some support options to consider:

- ❧ Wire cages: These work like tomato cages but can be made from wire mesh in any height or shape. A narrow, upright pillar shape is elegant in a formal garden.
- ❧ Tepees: Make a support of angled posts tied together at the top. Plant one or several vines at the base and let them twine up and fill out to cover the post (see Hint 174).
- ❧ Scrims: These are open-structured, see-through supports that vines can climb and still provide a veiled view of the scene beyond. With imagination, scrims can be made of braided wire or other creative materials.

281 **CREATE SUMMER SHADE** on a porch with a string trellis covered with vines. String trellises, available from garden centers or mail-order garden catalogues, can be hung from a roof or held upright with posts. Set the trellis to the south or west side of the porch to block the most sun.

Hide an unattractive utility pipe with a trellis of dazzling vines.

282 **USE A WIRE TRELLIS AND VINES** to cover a blank, dull wall or a utility pipe. A trellis-covered wall comes to life with greenery. Just make sure the trellis is far enough away from the wall; a trellis snug against a wall is not good for either the build-

283

ing or the vines. If you are screening a utility pipe, be sure to leave access openings for maintenance.

PIN PERENNIAL VINES LIKE CLIMBING HYDRANGEA TO THE WALL to help them get started. Check a complete garden supply catalog or garden center for various hooks and loops that can be set into your wall to start vines out.

In the beginning, climbing hydrangea might set off in any direction, so guiding it in the right direction is worthwhile. Once it has started, climbing hydrangea ascends by clinging and is well able to scale solid walls or tree trunks.

284 **USE VINES TO COVER** a chain-link fence or other backyard eyesores. They can screen off your garage from view (or your neighbor's garage), make a hidden alcove for your garbage cans, or cover a barren-trunked tree or a fenced dog run. Remember to plant vines that twine or have tendrils on open supports like chain-link fencing and vines that climb on solid supports like walls.

An ugly chain-link fence becomes a lush green wall when it's covered with vines.

285 USE VINES TO MAKE A DEAD TREE DISAPPEAR into a mass of blooms. Just as grapevines in the woods can cover trees and turn them into a dripping mass of green vines, an old stump can become a garden pillar.

In mild climates, evergreen vines can provide reliable cover year-round. In cold climates, some evergreen vines can be more prone to dieback when temperatures really drop. Look for extra-hardy vines for this job.

HOW DIFFERENT VINES CLIMB

TWINING: NEED SOMETHING TO TWIST AROUND
Kiwi
Bougainvillea
Bittersweet
Morning glory
Honeysuckle
Wisteria
Black-eyed Susan vine

TENDRILS: NEED SUPPORT TO GRASP
Clematis
Passion flowers
Grapes

CLINGING: CAN STICK TO SOLID OBJECTS
Ivy
Climbing hydrangea
Trumpet creeper
Wintercreeper
Virginia creeper

286 **PLANT VINES ON AN OPEN PERGOLA FRAME** to create a cool, shaded retreat. A pergola is an arborlike structure with an overhead trellis that forms a garden roof. It can make a shady place to sit outside in summer and give the garden elegant architecture at the same time.

This open pergola frame is covered with Chinese wisteria.

To fill out the roof with foliage and flowers, try planting vines that have abundant growth, so they will be well able to go the distance needed. Some possibilities are wisteria, silver fleece vine, kiwi vine, hops, and grapes.

287 **TRY AN EXTRA-EASY WAY TO SUPPORT ANNUAL VINES** with a trellis made from biodegradable twine. Set two 4-foot-high posts about 4 feet apart, pounding their bases about 10 inches deep into the ground. Run the twine between the posts, knotting it around the posts occasionally to keep the twine from slipping down. You may want to make vertical webbing by working the twine up and down

between horizontal strands, which helps some vines climb more efficiently.

Plant annual vines such as sweet peas, cardinal climbers, or black-eyed Susan vines beneath the new trellis, and allow them to grow and cover it. When frost arrives or the vines begin to look shabby, simply cut off the twine trellis and throw it, vines and all, in the compost pile.

GROUND COVER FOR SHADY PLACES

Boston ivy	Golden star
Virginia creeper	Epimedium
Periwinkle	Sweet woodruff
Wintercreeper	Pachysandra
Lily-of-the-valley	Woodland phlox
Dead nettle	Hardy geraniums
Sedges	(some species)
Wild ginger	

---

288 PLANT GROUND COVER IN POCKETS OF SOIL BETWEEN TREE ROOTS. Soil pockets are easiest to find near the trunk of the tree, where roots

have become stout and no longer riddle the earth. Just add some organic matter, as necessary, to get ground cover off to a good start, and then water as needed during dry weather.

Pocket plantings are great places to try less common and especially beautiful ground covers like European or American gingers, epimedium, and golden star.

289 USE LANDSCAPE FABRIC instead of plastic to reduce weeds in large plantings. Landscape fabric has pores that allow free air and water movement, a big advantage over impenetrable plastic. Lay it down before planting and then cut holes in the fabric. Plant your ground cover in the holes. When covered with mulch, landscape fabric, like plastic, prevents light from reaching the soil, which will stop the sprouting of most weed seeds.

290 HOLD BARREN SOIL IN PLACE WITH BURLAP when planting ground cover on a slope. This will prevent erosion while the ground cover is getting established. You should pin the burlap securely into the soil so that it won't slip off when rain makes the soil heavy and wet. Cut modest openings in the burlap and plant ground cover in each.

Once the ground cover establishes a strong root system and is able to secure nearby soil from erosion, you can gradually enlarge the openings and allow it to spread until it fills out the slope.

291 SET GROUND COVER PLUGS IN PLACE USING A WIRE GRID stretched over the bed for fast, easy planting. The regularly spaced openings will help you to coordinate spacing without need for a measuring tape (see Hint 211 for more information about spacing aids).

292 HELP GROUND COVERS SPREAD by layering stems as they grow. Layering, a propagation method detailed in Hint 109, encourages stems to root while still connected to the parent plant.

Ground covers such as pachysandra and periwinkle are easily rooted simply by covering barren portions of the stem with soil and keeping them moist. For harder-to-root ground covers like wintercreeper, you can remove a small piece of bark from the bottom of the stem and treat the opening with rooting hormone before covering the stem with soil.

293 SPREAD NETTING OR OLD SHEETS OVER GROUND COVERS during autumn leaf drop. It can be difficult to rake leaves out of thick ground covers, and allowing the leaves to sit and mat on the ground-cover bed creates unhealthy conditions. But planning ahead to catch leaves as they fall allows you to gather up all the leaves in one easy move and keeps the ground cover uncluttered.

With proper care and cultivation, ground cover such as periwinkle will make a lovely addition to your landscape.

294 REJUVENATE WINTER-BURNED GROUND-COVER PLANTINGS BY MOWING. If a cold winter causes evergreens like ivy to grow brown and unsightly, don't give up hope. There is a good chance that the roots are still alive and will send up fresh green growth come springtime. Mowing off the old leaves gives the new leaves plenty of space and keeps the bed tidy.

CHAPTER 18

ROSES

The rose, one of the most glamorous garden flowers, continues to evolve into a more versatile part of the landscape. The earliest roses usually bloomed only once a year, but they gave off wonderful aromas. Old-fashioned roses can grow into large, thorny bushes, more vigorous than a modern hybrid tea rose.

In the early 1800s, reblooming roses from China were discovered and interbred with old-fashioned European roses to extend their bloom period. These hybrids had fewer thorns and petals but rebloomed through the summer. Breeding efforts focused on improving flower form and expanding color selection. The results were grandifloras, hybrid teas, and other long-blooming plants that required high maintenance.

Recently, to create hardier roses that need less spraying, have more fragrance, and bloom all summer, breeders began to infuse blood lines of the old-

---

CLASSIC OLD-FASHIONED ROSES

ALBA ROSES
'Semi Plena'
'Konigin von Danemark'

BOURBON ROSES
'Louise Odier'
'Variegata de Bologna'
'Madame Isaac Pereire'
'Honorine de Brabant'

CENTRIFOLIA ROSES
'De Meaux'

DAMASK ROSES
'Madame Hardy'
'Comte de Chambord'
'Celsiana'

GALLICA ROSES
Rosa gallica officinalis
'Cardinal de Richelieu'

MOSS ROSES
'Mundi'
'Empress Josephine'

fashioned roses back into modern hybrids. This has created land-scape roses, large or small bushes that bloom all season and have increased disease resistance. Many, but not all, are fragrant. They are a wonderful way to enjoy the long-bloom beauty of the rose.

295 **CHOOSE SHRUB ROSES** over hybrid tea roses for low mainte-nance and disease resistance. Look for the following brands of high-quality shrub roses: David Austin English roses (from England), Town and Country Roses (from Denmark), Meidiland Romantica roses (from France), rugosa roses (developed from Oriental *Rosa rugosa*), and Explorer roses (extra-hardy hybrids from Ottawa Experiment Station in Canada).

David Austin English shrub roses

296 **PROTECT A ROSE GRAFT,** the swollen knob near the base of the plant, from winter damage. Not all roses have grafts, but most hybrid teas, grandifloras, stan-dard (tree form), and some miniatures are grafted. When planting, check for the graft and make arrangements to keep it from harm, if necessary. There are several options:

- In well-drained soil, you could plant the rose slightly deep, covering the graft with insulating soil. In cold climates, the graft union should be planted 2 to 3 inches below the soil line.
- Mound soil up over the graft in late fall and pull it back in spring.
- Surround the graft with shredded leaves, and hold the leaves in place with wire mesh.
- Buy plastic foam rose cones to cover the entire plant for extra insulation.

297 **TAKE GOOD CARE OF YOUR ROSES** so they will stay pest- and disease-resistant. Roses can be susceptible to a wide variety of problems, especially if they are growing weakly. Make sure they have well-drained, fertile soil. Water roses during dry weather and mulch them to conserve moisture. Prune to ensure each cane receives sun and good air circulation. With this kind of treatment, problems will be few and far between.

298 **PRUNE HYBRID TEAS, FLORIBUNDAS, AND OTHER ROSES** requiring heavy shaping back to 12 inches tall while they are dormant in spring. These roses flower on new growth, and nothing encourages new growth more than heavy spring pruning. While you are cutting stems back, take some time to remove any dead, diseased, or overcrowded canes. For shrub roses, pruning can be as simple as cutting out old and dead canes with long-handled pruning loppers.

299 **REMOVE ROOT SUCKERS** from grafted roses to keep them true. Many hybrid tea and flori-bunda roses are grafted on the extra-vigor-ous and disease-resistant roots of other species such as multiflora or rugosa roses. These root stocks may send up sprouts of their own, called suckers, which are easily identified by the different-looking foliage and flowers. Upon close inspection, you can see root suckers emerge from below the swollen graft. Clip suckers back as soon as you see them to keep the inferior sprouts from competing with your rose cultivar.

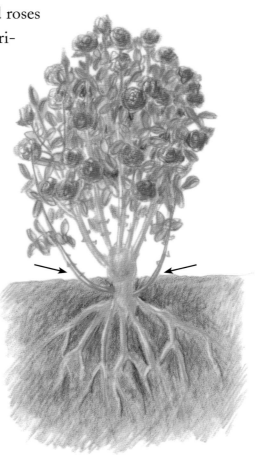

If the only sprouts that arise from the plant are off the roots, the graft has been damaged—which can occur during winter—and the original rose top is dead. If the root is a rugosa rose, you might try to grow it—it's a pretty plant. But if the root is a multiflora rose, it is a weed that is best taken out early.

300 **CONTROL BLACK SPOT** by planning ahead. Black spot, which marks leaves with black spots and then kills them, can spread up the plant and cause complete defoliation. Its damage is not pretty! But it can be avoided. Buy disease-resistant roses, including many of the landscape roses, polyantha roses such as 'The Fairy,' and even disease-resistant hybrid tea roses like 'Olympiad.' Sprays with baking soda can prevent black spot infection.

Preventive measures will keep black spot away from your roses.

Even disease-resistant shrub roses can benefit from this in extra-humid or wet weather. See Hint 118 for directions.

Rake up and destroy any leaves infested with black spot. This helps eliminate spores that would otherwise reinfect healthy leaves.

301 **PLANT AROUND ROSE BUSHES** with low or medium-height fragrant herbs such as mints, sweet marjoram, oregano, thyme, bush basil, and German chamomile. These herbs provide an attractive cover for the barren bases of many roses and release an odor that can screen the plant from rose-eating pests. They will also provide a nice harvest for the kitchen. Forget about eating the herbs, however, if you spray the rose with chemicals unsuited for edible plants.

IMPROVED CULTIVARS OF DISEASE-RESISTANT RUGOSA ROSES	
'Blanc Double de Coubert'	'Linda Campbell'
	'Topaz Jewel'
'Fru Dagmar Hastrup'	'Alba'
EASY-CARE POLYANTHAS	
'The Fairy'	'Red Fairy'

302 **LAYER RAMBLERS** and other roses to make new plants. Ramblers have long, limber canes that can be tied to a fence or trellis like a climbing rose. These flexible canes make them perfect for layering. Notch the bark beneath the stem, remove nearby leaves, pin the stem to the ground, and mound over it with soil (see Hint 109).

Once rooted and cut free from the mother plant, you'll have a new plant growing on its own roots. It will have no need for graft protection!

303 **USE THE MINNESOTA TIP METHOD** in cold climates for winter protection of hybrid tea roses. In well-drained soil, dig a trench on one side of the rose. With your foot, gently push the rose canes into the trench, where they will be insulated underground. Mound soil over the canes and graft and mark the burial site with a stake so you can free the canes in early spring.

CHAPTER 19

SHRUBS

While you may think of shrubs as "just bushes," they are actually much more. Shrubs come in a variety of shapes and sizes, with many different types of foliage. Some shrubs produce berries, and others even provide fragrance! No matter what effect you are trying to achieve, there is undoubtedly a shrub that will fit the bill.

Creeping shrubs, like junipers, can serve as evergreen ground covers. Low, bushy shrubs like Japanese spirea and potentilla blend nicely into flower gardens or the front of a planting around the house. Larger, rounded shrubs can be grouped into clusters to define space or create privacy. More compact cultivars that mature when around 4 feet high, like 'Newport' viburnum, can be used around a house without any pruning. Taller shrubs, like Allegheny viburnum, are best kept at some distance from the house, where they won't block the views. They make good screens for the property perimeter. Vertical shrubs that are shaped like an upright cone or pillar, such as 'Skyrocket' juniper, create formality or emphasis in the yard. They can be striking when placed on either side of a doorway or garden gate.

Using a medley of shrub shapes offers design interest that goes much deeper than the leaves and flowers. And when you also take into account the other qualities shrubs have to offer, you'll see that they are an asset to any kind of garden.

304 **PLANT FRAGRANT FLOWERED SHRUBS** near doors or windows so you can enjoy their perfume both indoors and out.

305 **CUT FLOWERING STEMS** from your shrubs and bring them indoors to use in big bouquets. If you have large vases that dwarf ordinary annual or perennial stems, fill them with long branches of forsythia, lilacs, or viburnums. What a wonderful way to celebrate spring!

> ### SOME SHRUBS WITH FRAGRANT FLOWERS
>
> Butterfly bush
> Blue spiraea
> Summersweet
> Fothergilla
> Honeysuckle
> Fantasy lilac
> Dwarf Korean lilac
>
> Miss Kim lilac
> French lilac
> Witch hazel
> Burkwood viburnum
> Fragrant snowball
>   viburnum
> Korean spice viburnum

306 **SLICE OFF CIRCLING OR TANGLED ROOTS** before planting shrubs grown in containers. Potted shrubs fill the pot with roots, which then twine around and around. New roots may continue this destructive pattern even when planted if the old circling roots are not removed. Eventually, the crown may be strangled by its own roots.

Use a pair of sharp pruning shears to slice off circling roots and loosen up matted roots. Releasing the healthy roots inside the root ball, planting the shrub in good soil, and keeping the area moist will encourage vigorous new root growth.

307 · SOAK THE ROOTS OF BARE-ROOT SHRUBS BEFORE PLANTING.

Bare-root shrubs are dug in fall or spring, washed clean of soil, and shipped directly to mail-order catalog customers. Shrubs commonly sold bare-root include Chinese abelia, bloodtwig dogwood, buttonbushes, viburnums, some forsythias, winterberry holly, and beauty bush, as well as hedge shrubs such as privet.

To ensure good results after planting, don't let the roots go into the soil dehydrated. An hour in a bucket of room-temperature water is all it takes. Plant immediately after soaking and keep moist through the entire first growing season.

308 · SCORE THE SIDES OF THE PLANTING HOLE

to encourage root penetration. In clay soils, slick-sided holes can dry to a glaze that is difficult for young roots to penetrate. Slicing into the hole perimeter with your shovel breaks up the glazing and creates openings where roots can burrow out.

309 · THIN OUT A THIRD TO HALF OF THE BRANCHES of bare-root shrubs

before planting. Your pruning shears will become one of your best planting tools, helping you put the shrub into a healthy balance before planting.

When shrubs are dug from the nursery field and processed for shipping, they lose most of their feeding roots, the delicate young roots responsible for absorbing moisture. Until the shrub is replanted and reestablishes new feeding roots, it can't support all the growth it once did. Pruning trims back shoots to balance root loss.

When pruning, begin by removing old, weak, damaged, or crowded branches at their base. But don't indiscriminately shear off the top of the plant. The terminal buds on the branch tips release hormones that encourage root growth and maintain a slow, orderly pattern of growth. These are both desirable qualities worth preserving in your shrubs.

310 **D**EADHEAD HYBRID RHODODENDRONS AND MOUNTAIN LAURELS to increase next year's bloom. Once the flowers begin to fade, use your thumb and forefinger (or pruning shears) to cut off the soft, immature flowering cluster. Just be careful not to damage nearby buds or shoots, which will soon be sprouting into new branches.

311 **C**ONSIDER CHANGING AN OVERGROWN SHRUB into a multi-stemmed tree. This works nicely with flowering plums, black haw viburnums, winged euonymus, and lilacs, all of which can grow to be 12 to 15 feet tall.

Begin by removing small, crowded upright stems to reveal a handful of shapely mature branches that can serve

A winged euonymus shrub can become a tree.

as trunks. Cut side shoots off the trunks up to about 5 feet off the ground, creating a tree form. Continue pruning as needed to keep the trunks clear of growth.

312 **WRAP BOXWOOD** and other evergreen shrubs with burlap to prevent winter burn. When the soil is frozen, the sun is bright, and wind is strong, evergreens lose moisture from their exposed leaves and cannot replace it through frozen roots. The foliage scorches to brown and the stems may die back—or even worse, the whole shrub may die. Burlap, although far from elegant, makes a neat coat for the shrub and ensures that you will have a nice-looking plant waiting for you when spring arrives. This also works for coniferous evergreens like arborvitae. Be sure to water these shrubs well in the fall so they'll have plenty of moisture stored.

313 **BUILD A TEMPORARY WIRE FRAME** around tender shrubs—the species most likely to suffer winter damage in your area—and fill it with straw or leaves for winter protection. Like padding a carton of valuables, this provides insulation from winter's worst cold.

> ### SOME SHRUBS FOR SEASONAL BLOOMS
>
> **SPRING**
> Azaleas
> Rhododendrons
> Ornamental quince
> Cotoneaster
> Forsythia
> Fothergilla
> Lilac
> Viburnum
>
> **SUMMER**
> Butterfly bush
> Scotch heather
> Blue spirea
> Summersweet
> Hydrangea
> Rose-of-Sharon
> St. John's wort
> Potentilla
> Spirea
>
> **FALL**
> Butterfly bush
> Rose-of-Sharon
> Witch hazel

314 **DO NOT PLANT BOXWOOD** and other brittle-stemmed shrubs near the foundation of your house. Heavy, wet, melting snow or chunks of ice can slip off the roof and flatten shrubs residing below.

315 **PLANT SHRUBS THAT WILL FLOWER IN SUCCESSION** through the growing season. Get some spring, summer, and fall bloomers—then play them up, using other plants as supporting characters. Match the flower color of a viburnum with a cluster of daffodils. Echo the color of a rhododendron with a pot of pink pansies.

316 **PLANT A CONIFEROUS SHRUB GARDEN** for winter fun. Use evergreens with a variety of different shapes and leaf colors—gold, blue, gray, and green. In northern climates where winter is long, this kind of garden brightens the yard.

Suitable shrubs include dwarf firs, pines, hemlocks, spruces, heathers, junipers, arborvitaes, and false cypress. Specialty nurseries and catalogs abound with other, less common conifers as well. Interplant cone-shaped and vertical evergreens with low and mounded forms. Add in some spectacular weeping conifers for

This shrub garden looks dazzling in any season.

excitement, and contrast blue and gray foliage against green and gold. In summer, add some interplanted annuals, perennials, and ornamental grasses for variety.

CHAPTER 20

FLOWERING TREES

Flowering trees can be one of the most memorable elements of the landscape. Fragrant flowering crabapples, frothy, aromatic fringe tree flowers, and weeping cherries dripping with pink blossoms can linger in the mind well after the flowers are gone.

For a lofty layer of flowers and greenery, flowering trees are magnificent when mixed with flowering shrubs, annuals, and perennials. But they are even more important in a yard with few flowers. Tree bark—silver, black, red, or green, either smooth or textured—can also be beautiful. Consider, for example, stewartia's peeling bark of gray, brown, orange, or red, as well as its creamy summer flowers and great fall color. The paper bark maple, with only small, early spring flowers, has glowing exfoliating, rust-colored bark and leaves that light up orange and red in fall. And colorful fall fruits provide a feast for the eyes as well as for the birds.

This strong tree has wide crotch angles.

317 CHOOSE TREES THAT HAVE WIDE CROTCH ANGLES to avoid weak branches and ice damage. The crotch (or branch) angle measures the distance between the trunk and the base of the branch. An

186

upright branch has a narrow crotch angle of less than 45 degrees. A sturdy, wide-angled branch has a 45- to 60-degree crotch angle.

The problem with branches that have narrow crotch angles, a common occurrence on trees like Bradford pears and plums, is that they are not well supported on the trunk. If coated with ice in a winter storm, they may split off. The narrow branching angle can also catch moisture and encourage diseases.

Another problem arises when upright-growing branches with narrow crotch angles near the top of a young tree begin to grow as fast as the main trunk. Prune the branches back to keep the trunk taller and dominant. If allowed to continue in this way, the tree develops a split leader, two trunks growing side by side. In severe weather, the trunks can crack apart, and the tree may be finished for good.

318 **USE SPREADERS ON YOUNG FRUIT TREES** to correct narrow branch angles. Fruit trees are particularly prone to developing upright branches. Not only do these branches have all the problems mentioned in Hint 317, but they also grow tall and wild instead of slowing down to flower and fruit. Shifting them into a more productive mode begins with creating a wider branch angle.

When the tree is young and flexible, you can prop short struts in the gap between a shoot and the trunk to force the branch down into a better 45-degree angle.

Slightly older branches can be tied to a stake or weight to pull them down into position. Once the branches mature enough to become firm and woody, you can remove the spreaders, and the branches will stay in place.

SOME SMALLER FLOWERING TREES

Crabapples	Redbud
Hawthorns	Dogwoods
Yellowwood	Mountain ash
Palo verde	Tree lilacs
Flowering cherries	Star magnolias and
Flowering plums	other magnolias

---

319 CHOOSE A FLOWERING TREE OVER A SHADE TREE for a small garden. Not only is the size right—you'll also get beautiful flowers as a bonus.

◦ Trees that stay under 15 feet tall include 'Spring Glory' amelanchier, 'Crusader' hawthorn, and 'Camelot' crabapple.

◦ Trees that stay between 15 and 30 feet include 'Autumn Brilliance' amelanchier, redbuds, and kousa dogwoods.

320 CHOOSE TREES THAT CAST LIGHT SHADE if you want to plant a flower garden below them. Some trees allow sunlight to filter down between light branches or small leaves. Small, weeping, or long-trunked trees allow light to reach the flowers from the side during the morning and afternoon. Some good choices for mixed flower beds include crabapples, flowering plums, flowering cherries, franklin tree, golden chain tree, and Japanese tree lilac. Among the shade trees, consider honey locusts, ironwood, and birches.

321 **AVOID PLANTING LARGE-FRUITED TREES OVER PATIOS AND DECKS.** Large crabapples, apples, pears, and other fruits and berries can mar the patio and furniture, drop on people, and make steps slippery. Sweet, ripe fruit can attract yellow jackets and other critters. Let large fruits look pretty from afar, where they can drop unheeded in mulch, lawn, or ground cover. For outdoor living areas, choose tree cultivars with small or persistent fruit that won't drop and cause a mess.

322 **BUY FLOWERING TREES IN THE SPRING.** Trees purchased in the fall have probaby been sitting in the nursery lot all summer.

323 **PULL OR CUT OFF THE BUR-LAP BEFORE COVERING THE ROOTS WITH SOIL** when planting balled and burlapped stock. This simple bit of house-keeping can mean the difference between success and failure for the tree. Some trees are wrapped with synthetic burlap, which will not

---

SOME CRABAPPLES WITH SMALL FRUIT

'American Masterpiece'
'American Salute'
'Christmas Holly'
'Donald Wyman'
*'Louisa'
M. sargentii
'Weeping Candied Apple'

*'Camelot'
'Cankerberry'
*'Cinderella'
*'Excaliber'
*'Guinevere'
*'Lancelot'
*'Snowdrift'

*Excellent choices for disease resistance

decay and allow the roots to grow free. Even natural-fiber burlap left around the roots can be slow to decay. It can wick moisture away from the young roots, a sure way to cause damage.

324 **CAREFULLY CONSIDER PLANTING DEPTH** before digging the planting hole for a new tree. You should make the hole twice as wide but no deeper than the root ball. Setting the ball on solid ground that has not been fluffed by tilling or shoveling will provide a firm foundation. If the soil underneath settles or shifts, the tree can sit too deep.

If planting in heavy clay soil, you can plant high so that the top third to half of the root ball is above the soil surface. This allows some roots to get up and out of soggy, poorly aerated soil. Fill in around the exposed roots with good soil, and top with mulch.

325 **CHECK THE ACCURACY OF YOUR PLANTING HOLE DEPTH** using a shovel handle. When you think the hole may be deep enough, set the root ball inside. Lay the shovel handle across the top of the hole. It should be even with or slightly lower than the top of the root ball.

326 **PLANT GROUPS OF FLOWERING TREES IN BEDS.** When growing in clusters or groves, flowering trees look spectacular in the landscape, much more so than isolated individual trees. There are other advantages to groupings:

- In poor soils, roots can grow freely through the entire amended bed.
- You can water and fertilize the entire group at the same time.
- The problem of mowing or trimming around the trunks is eliminated, saving time and damage to the bark.
- You can plant a shade garden in the grove.

327 **PLANT BENEATH YOUR TREES WITH GROUND COVERS** if you don't want a sea of mulch under them. Ground covers become a carpet of greenery and prevent mowing compli-

Planting ground cover under your trees, rather than adding mulch, has a number of benefits.

cations and root competition that can plague trees planted in turf.

C H A P T E R   2 1

SHADE TREES AND EVERGREENS

Shade trees and evergreens are the largest elements in the landscape, well able to complement even the biggest house. Use them to frame your home, but plan ahead to ensure that the trees will not become overwhelming; if you have a smaller house, you should plant smaller trees than if you have a very large home. With each passing year, big trees grow more valuable, increasing the worth of your house and property.

In winter, large trees have additional benefits. The lofty greenery of a big pine, spruce, or fir, or the dark, widespread limbs of a handsome oak stand out amid a landscape of brown, white, and gray. Their very stature demands respect, and in winter you will have the luxury of enjoying them without rivalry.

But large trees do more than look elegant. Did you know that large trees can help lower your energy bills? Shade-casting trees to the south or west of your house can keep the house 10 degrees cooler in the summer. By starting some shade trees now, you are making an investment in the future.

328 **CHOOSE PEST- OR DISEASE-RESISTANT SPECIES OR VARIETIES** instead of problem-plagued trees. When you take the time to select a tree ideally suited for your site, your chances of long-term success are great. But they're even better when you check the track record of the tree you have in mind. If it's prone to insect or disease attack, continue your studies to find alternative, untroubled species or varieties. Because large shade trees can live for decades, even centuries, spending an extra hour or two determining the best tree to plant will pay off for a long, long time.

Instead of European white birch, try disease-resistant river, 'Monarch,' or 'Avalanche' birches. A substitute for a silver maple tree is 'Celebration' maple. Try substituting 'Crusader' hawthorn for rust-susceptible hawthorns, and 'Metroshade' plane trees for disease-susceptible London plane trees.

329 **CHOOSE YOUNGER AND SMALLER TREES** to plant over larger ones. The motto "bigger is better" is not true in this case. Although you can have nearly full-sized trees planted in your yard (at a whopping price), smaller trees transplant more easily and grow more quickly than

This European white birch could be replaced by a disease-resistant cultivar of birch.

larger trees. They also cost less and are easier to handle without hiring landscapers.

It's best to start with a tree that has a 1- to 1½-inch trunk diameter (officially called its caliper). Very small seedlings—the kind given away by forestry departments on Arbor Day—are a little too diminutive. They take a long time to grow large enough to be noticed in the yard, especially if hidden amid grass.

330 **WHEN PLANTING FAST-GROWING TREES,** start with economical and quick-developing bare-root saplings. Fast-growing trees will increase in height by several feet a year. Under ideal conditions, a young tree that stands 3 feet tall upon planting will be up to 5, 6, or 7 feet tall the next year. The following year, it may be 10 feet tall or larger.

All trees require time to reach their prime, but fast growers stay on the move and hardly test your patience at all.

331 **LOOK TO SLOWER-GROW-ING TREES** for long, trouble-free lives and enough strength to withstand wind and ice storms.

332 **INSPECT TREES FOR ANY GIRDLING ROOTS.** Just as a tight girdle can be oppressive to wear, girdling roots can squeeze a tree trunk and cut off its food supply.

Girdling roots are common on container-grown plants. It all begins when circling roots (see

---

FAST-GROWING TREES

These can fill the yard fast, but they may not be as sturdy and long-lived as slower growers.

Ash	Hackberry
Poplars	Red mulberry
Willows	Tulip tree
Arizona cypress	Cork tree
Eucalyptus	Japanese pagoda
Catalpa	tree
Honey locust	

SLOWER-GROWING TREES

Red maple	Pin oak
Sugar maple	English oak
Ginkgo	Pines
Sycamore	Spruces
White oak	Sourwood
Bur oak	Lindens

Hint 306) reach upward and loop around the bottom of the trunk. As the trunk grows wider, the roots cut into it and can strangle it. In less severe cases, girdling roots may only cut into one side of the tree, causing death of limbs serviced by the damaged wood.

If you inadvertently buy a tree with girdling roots, use your pruning shears to cut them off where they emerge from the crown before planting.

333 **CHECK TREES FOR DEEP ROOT COLLARS.** The root collar is the junction of roots and trunk, an important place that should be kept level with or above the soil surface when planting (see Hint 324).

Sometimes when nurseries cultivate between rows of field-grown trees and shrubs, extra soil may be thrown up above the roots and around the base of the trunk. When the root ball is dug up and wrapped in burlap, the bottom of the trunk (and the top of the roots) may actually be deep in the ball, with only barren soil above. This leaves the tree short-changed on roots and the root collar unnaturally deep.

To test the depth of the root collar, rotate the trunk and see if it shifts deep in the ball, a sure sign of a deep root collar. Or, if the nursery will allow, pull back the burlap and brush back the soil to look for the junction of root and trunk.

334 **PLANT FAST-GROWING TREES** with slower-growing species to get shade fast. As the slower-growing trees get large enough to make an impact on the yard, cut out the weaker fast growers. You end up with the best of both worlds—quick greenery and lasting strength. See page 194 for a list of possible trees to plant.

335 **PLANT TREES IN A WIDE, SHALLOW HOLE,** at least twice the width of the root ball (see Hint 324). In the past, gardeners have been advised to plant trees in holes of many different shapes and sizes. But contemporary recommendations reflect new findings in how tree roots grow. Many trees concentrate their feeding roots in the top foot of soil. A wide hole loosens up an open, surface-hugging expanse for the early growth of these roots and will help young trees get established more quickly. There is no need to amend the soil—trees thrive best when they are established in native soil.

336 **SKIP STAKING** unless you are planting young trees in areas prone to strong winds. Staking can actually do more harm than good for young trees. If staked improperly, with rubbing or tight wires, the bark and trunk can become damaged, sometimes irreparably.

Staking also interferes with the natural movement of a tree swaying in the wind. Recent research has shown that swaying helps trees develop stronger, tapered trunks that will serve them well and keep them sturdy for decades.

Where staking is unavoidable, use flexible stakes and ties that have a couple inches of slack so the tree can continue to move. Pad the trunk or slip a section of rubber hose over the supporting wire so it won't damage the tree. Remove the stakes as soon as the tree has rooted enough to become self-supporting.

337 **WRAP THE TRUNK OF THIN-BARKED TREES,** most notably fruit trees, in winter to help keep the bark from splitting. Tree wraps and firmer

If you need to stake a tree, do it gently so the tree can still move.

plastic tree guards can also discourage rabbits and rodents from chewing on the bark and can prevent accidental damage from mowers.

Remove the tree wrap in the spring so it won't get too tight on the swelling trunk or provide a hiding place for pests.

338 **ADJUST HOW YOU WATER A YOUNG TREE** as it gets established. When it is first planted and for the following growing season, provide water directly on the planting site. You can allow a hose to trickle gently over the root ball, making a shallow saucer of soil below the leafy canopy to keep the water from running off (see Hint 29).

Once the tree has established enough new roots to grow vigorously, use soaker hoses to water just outside the perimeter of the tree canopy. This will encourage the roots to spread outward, providing a stronger foundation for the tree.

339 **MULCH THE TREE PROPERLY.** Spread a layer of bark mulch, wood chips, or compost from the drip line (below the perimeter of the branch canopy) to 4 inches from the trunk (not too close or problems can arise). Mulching will help eliminate weeds and keep the planting site moist. It also looks good and gives the landscape a polished feel.

Avoid excessively thick layers of mulch, which can limit soil aeration in heavy ground and cause roots to smother. Another problem occurs when thick heaps of mulch break down into rich organic matter. Shallow-rooted trees like maples can grow thick root mats in the mulch (which is not good), and some of those roots may start to girdle (which is even worse!—see Hint 332). Shallow roots are also subject to excessive drying in summer.

340 **PLANT EVERGREENS IN SPRING OR SUMMER** up to about mid-August, but no later. To support their foliage through winter, they need to have a well-established root system and plenty of internal moisture before the ground freezes.

341

Deer prefer certain trees—like yews—so you should plant trees they'll avoid.

AVOID PLANTING TREES THAT DEER ESPECIALLY ENJOY EATING where deer are abundant. Some of their favorites include yews, arborvitaes, and some pines. Concentrate instead on some of their least favorite trees, including maples, beech, ashes, ginkgo, honey locust, tulip tree, sour gum, spruce, sycamore, oaks, willows, and bald cypress.

342 **HELP PREPARE EVERGREEN TREES FOR DRY WINTER WEATHER** by watering them more in the fall, especially when rainfall has been limited. It's also helpful to spray leaves with an antitranspirant coating, which limits evaporation from the foliage.

Prepare your trees for winter weather so they will stay moist and healthy.

343 **DON'T PLANT SALT-SUSCEPTIBLE EVERGREENS NEAR THE STREET** in cold climates. Salt used for snow and ice control will splash up on the needles and drip into the soil. It won't be long before a thriving tree begins to brown out and then fail. Look for trees that can withstand salt spray. An example of a salt-susceptible evergreen is white pine. Some other possibilities include sycamore maple, shadblow, Austrian black pine, Japanese black pine, Red mulberry, and sour gum.

344 ENJOY A TREE THAT CAN DOUBLE AS A SCULPTURE by planting a curly-limbed willow. Twisted branches and curling leaves make interesting focal points on small willows such as 'Golden Curls' and 'Scarlet Curls.'

A curly-limbed willow tree makes a unique addition to the landscape.

345 PREVENT SUMMER SPIDER MITE ATTACKS on your evergreens by spraying susceptible plants with a hose every day during hot, dry weather. If you're out watering the garden, turn the hose on the evergreen foliage as well. Water helps to dislodge spider mites and discourage their multiplication, a great nontoxic preventative.

346 ADD AN UPRIGHT ACCENT IN NARROW SPACES (such as courtyard gardens) with special, extra-slender trees. Some examples are 'Columnaris' European hornbeam, 'Dawyck' European beech, 'Princeton Sentry' ginkgo, and 'Columnaris' Swiss stone pine.

A narrow tree fits nicely into a small garden space or corner.

347 **ADD SPICE TO THE LANDSCAPE** by growing peacocks, which are trees with uniquely colored foliage held all season long. Some of the choices that you might consider are red-leaved Japanese maples, golden-leaved box elders and tulip trees, or purple-leaved Norway maples and beech trees.

Some trees with colorful foliage are commonly available at garden centers and nurseries. Others can be found at specialty nurseries.

348 **INCLUDE SOME SHADE TREES WITH BOLD FALL COLOR** for an exciting finish to the growing season. As autumn approaches, trees begin breaking down green chlorophyll and storing the components away for winter. This reveals underlying leaf coloration, which was there all along but hidden beneath the green pigments.

Among the best trees for fall color are maples, birches, sourwood, ginkgo, tulip tree,

A bright burst of color is one of autumn's special delights.

red oak, linden, and white ash such as 'Autumn Applause,' all of which are outstanding when nights are cool and days are sunny.

CHAPTER 22

CONTAINERS

Containers are an excellent way to learn about gardening because they're easy to plant and give great results quickly. They also provide color to highlight patios, steps, garden gates, or anywhere else you find to be a little drab. In addition, pots are the best places to show off rare and exotic plants.

Containers eliminate much of the guesswork in gardening. There is no need to tolerate difficult soil or make do with marginal sites. You can start with any potting mix, picking the perfect blend for the plants you want to grow. You can set the pot where it will have the ideal amount of sun or shade. You provide water when nature comes up short, and you schedule the fertilization. There is nothing left to chance, assuming of course that you take the time to tend the potted plant.

In return, containers become living flower arrangements. With lively color schemes, varied textures, and handsome containers, potted plants grow, flower, and flourish close at hand where they are easily enjoyed.

349 **PLANT ANNUALS IN A BIG BAG OF POTTING SOIL** for a quick, easy balcony garden. This method, commonly used in England, is still a novelty here and will make a great conversation piece:

❧ Lay the bag flat on the ground where you want a mini garden. Punch a few small drainage holes in the bottom.

❧ You can cut one large opening in the top side for several plants, letting them intermingle in a decorative planting scheme. Or make several individual planting holes for a working garden of annual vegetables and herbs.

❧ The plastic wrapper will help to keep the soil inside moist. But when it does begin to dry out, or needs water-soluble fertilizer as a plant pick-me-up, carefully drizzle water or water-soluble fertilizer inside to moisten the entire bag.

350 USE CARE WHEN PLANTING IN DECORATIVE CONTAINERS.

Lovely bark, wicker, wood, and even fine pottery pots and urns make handsome containers. But some of them have one big drawback—they can be damaged by water.

MATERIALS FOR CONTAINERS

Plastic	Stone
Clay	Cement
Ceramic	Cedar
Fiberglass	Redwood
Brass	Compressed fibers
Bronze	Compressed peat
Tin	moss

Regardless, you can still use them for plants, but only as an ornamental cover over a working pot below. Here is the trick:

- Plant in a plastic pot that has no drainage holes or that sits on a plastic saucer, which will prevent moisture spills.
- The pot, and saucer if used, must be smaller than the decorative container.
- Put a layer of plastic inside the container, then set the potted plant on top.
- Cover the top of the pots with sheet moss or other natural fibers to hide the mechanics below.

This combination will be temporary at best and require careful watering so the plant roots won't be drowned or dried. Once every couple of months, remove the potted plant and water thoroughly, draining off the excess moisture to wash out salts that will build up in the soil.

351 **STERILIZE OLD POTS** with a 10 percent bleach solution before using them for other plants. Saving old pots from flowers, vegetables, poinsettias, even shrubs transplanted into the yard is a great way to economize. But you have to be certain to eliminate any disease spores that may have come, like extra baggage, with the previous occupant.

Begin by washing out excess soil, bits of roots, and other debris with warm soapy water. Mix 1 part household bleach with 9 parts water and use the solution to wipe out the pot. Rinse again, and the pot is ready to plant.

352 **CREATE YOUR OWN CUSTOM POTTING SOIL.** Use a peat-moss-based potting mix as the foundation. (It works well for houseplants, seedlings, and many other plants as is.) Peat-based mixes won't compress like true soil, which is a big advantage in pots. But they are low on nutrients and liable to dry out quickly, complications that can be minimized with special potting blends.

- To make a richer mix for annual flowers or for perennials like daylilies, you can blend 2 parts peat mix with 1 part compost.
- For a more fertile, moisture-retentive soil for tomatoes or lettuce, blend 1 part peat mix, 1 part garden soil, and 1 part compost.
- For a lighter mix for propagating cuttings or growing succulents or cacti, add 1 part coarse sand or perlite to 1 part peat mix.

353 **PREMIX A WHEELBARROW FULL OF POTTING BLEND** (see Hint 352). If you have plenty of houseplants that need repotting, or you like to put more than just a few pots or window boxes of summer flowers outdoors, this will save you time and effort. And if you buy the peat mix and extras in large, economy-sized bags, it also will save you money.

354 **PREMOISTEN PEAT-BASED MIXES** in a large tub or wheelbarrow. Prewetting peat moss, which soaks up a surprisingly large amount of water, ensures there will be enough moisture left over to supply new plantings.

Premoistening is easily done with a garden hose. Sprinkle in a generous amount of water, and work the moisture into the peat mix with a trowel (or a hoe if you are making large batches). Continue to add more water until the peat clumps together in a moist ball. Then it is ready to go in a pot.

355 **PLACE A CIRCLE OF FINE MESH SCREEN OVER POT DRAINAGE HOLES** instead of using pebbles or pot shards. The screen will help to hold the soil in place until the roots fill out and claim every particle. But it's still a good idea to water outdoors, in the sink, or over a pot saucer so a little oozing dampness or soil won't damage anything.

The problem with covering drainage holes with pot shards (the clay chunks left after a pot is broken) and pebbles is that they can shift to clog up the drainage holes. With no place for excess water to go, plant roots may soak in saturated soil, a condition few plants emerge from alive.

356 **USE WATER-HOLDING GELS** to reduce the need for watering, especially when planting in quick-drying, peat-based mixes. These gels—actually polymers—look like crystals when dry and safely sealed in their package. But once you add water, you'll be surprised to see them swell up into a large mass of quivering gelatin look-alikes. You can blend the gel into potting mixes, following blending instructions on the package.

Water-holding gels keep plants moister longer than water alone.

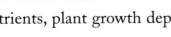

357

USE WINDOW BOXES to brighten your house with flowers and add height to surrounding gardens.

🖛 Elegant window boxes can feature flowers that match the color of nearby curtains, carpets, shrubs, or shutters.

🖛 Some cascading ivy, vinca vine, or vining petunias will soften the geometric outlines of the window box.

🖛 Grow herbs such as thyme, basil, and parsley in a kitchen window box.

358 **SET A NARROW PERFORATED PVC PIPE** in the center of a strawberry pot or large container before filling in around it with potting mix. When you need to water your plants, run the hose gently into the pipe, and the water will ooze out from top to bottom, inside to outside, giving every plant an even share.

359 **USE SLOW-RELEASE FERTILIZERS** to keep plants growing and blooming all season. Because peat-based mixes contain little or no natural nutrients, plant growth depends on a regular

Keep a watertight saucer, either clay or plastic, under flowerpots.

supply of fertilizer. Slow-release fertilizers keep working for several months to a year, depending on the formulation.

360

SEAL THE BOTTOMS OF CLAY SAUCERS WITH POLYURETHANE to keep them water-tight. Then they will be safe to use on floors and carpets. Or, instead of buying clay saucers, you can buy watertight plastic saucers made to look like clay. When one is sitting beneath a pot, it's hard to tell the difference.

361

KEEP A SUCCESSION OF NEW FLOWERS BLOOMING in pots throughout the seasons, so your home and yard will never be short on color.

- In spring, enjoy cool-season flowers like forced bulbs (see Hint 259), primroses, and pansies.
- In summer, grow tender perennials and annuals like impatiens and begonias.
- In fall, enjoy late bloomers like asters and mums.

FOLIAGE PLANTS FOR CONTAINERS

These plants look great when they're mixed with flowering plants in pots.

Caladiums	Hostas
Croton	Scented geraniums
Ferns	Artemisias
Asparagus fern	Spider plants
Rex begonias	Ivies

362  **PUT CLAY AND PLASTIC POTS IN THE GARAGE** before cold winter weather arrives. This will help keep them from cracking and chipping when the weather turns bitterly cold.

363 **WRAP HEAVY URNS AND POTS** that are too bulky to carry indoors in plastic for winter protection. Do this on a dry autumn day, securing the plastic across the top, bottom, and sides of the pots to prevent moisture from getting inside. Moisture expands when it freezes. This causes terra-cotta, ceramic, and even synthetic stone and concrete containers to chip and break.

364 **STORE POTS UNDER TARP** for protection in mild climates. This will save space in your garage or basement and keep the pots handy for when you need them in the spring.

365 **LOOK FOR SELF-WATERING PLANTERS** if you aren't home enough to keep potted plants from drying out (or if you forget to water every day or two). Self-watering planters have a water reservoir in the bottom that's connected to the pot by a water-absorbing wick. When the soil begins to get dry, the wick pulls up more water from the reservoir.

PLANT HARDINESS ZONE MAP

A plant hardiness zone map helps determine which plants will thrive in a particular region, based on the frost date of each area. This hardiness zone map is a summarized version of the U.S. Department of Agriculture Plant Hardiness Zone Map, which divides North America into 10 zones depending on their average minimum winter temperatures. Our map is separated into three regions: Zones 1 through 3, in yellow, represent the coldest areas; Zones 4 through 7, in green, represent moderate temperatures; and Zones 8 through 10, in red, represent the warmest regions.

Zone maps provide general guidelines. Additional factors such as altitude, exposure to wind, and the amount of available sunlight must also be taken into account. The temperatures given for each region are averages, and any particular winter may be warmer or colder than this figure. It should also be noted that plants recommended for one zone might do just as well in the southern part of the adjoining colder zone or in the neighboring warmer zone.

Though a zone map provides only rough guidelines, it is still a very helpful tool in determining which plants are likely to survive in your garden and which ones are not.

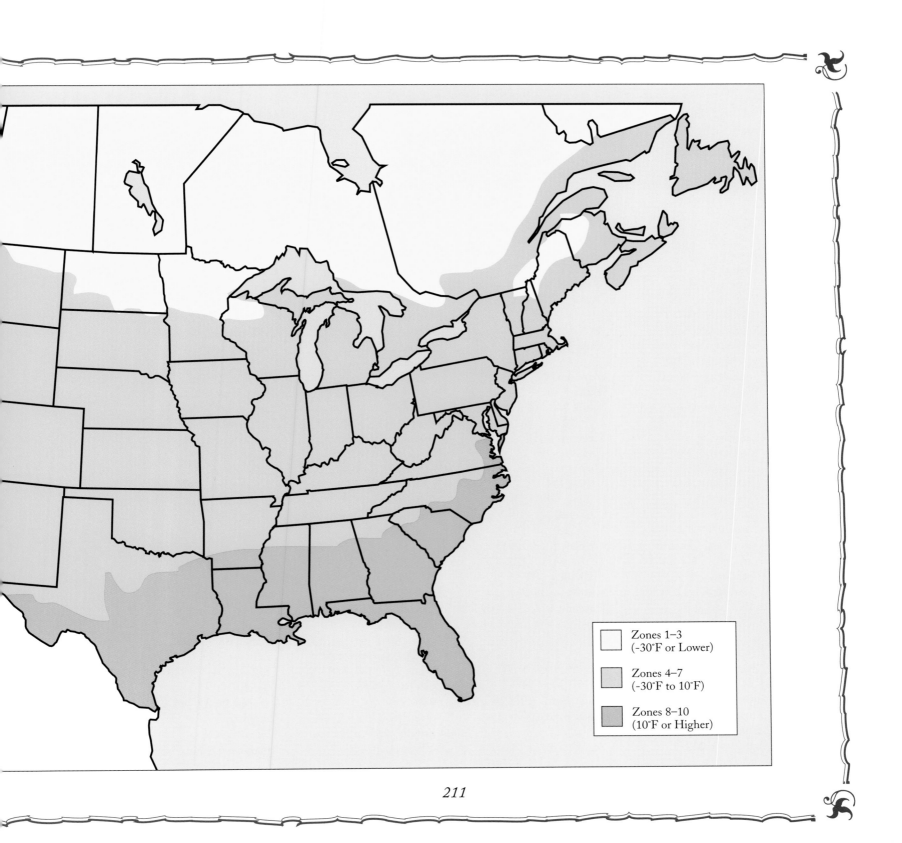

Zones 1–3
(-30°F or Lower)

Zones 4–7
(-30°F to 10°F)

Zones 8–10
(10°F or Higher)

INDEX

A

Abelia, 182
Aerating, 107
Agapanthus, 163
Ageratum, 134
Alstroemeria, 131
Alyssum, 134
Amelanchiers, 188
Anemones, 149–50
Annuals
    container gardening,
        138, 202–3, 208
    disease-resistant
      cultivars, 83
    drying, 138
    fertilizing, 135–36
    fragrant, 132
    in garden design, 93
    pinching back, 136–37
    pruning, 135, 136
    rooting, 137
    seedlings, 133, 134
    self-seeding, 139
Aphids, 87, 130
Apple maggots, 129–30
Apples, 125, 129–30
Arbors, 98
Arborvitaes, 184, 185,
    199
Artemisia, 57, 151
Arugula, 110
Ashes, 199, 201
Asparagus, 112–13

Asters, 56, 72, 79–80, 138,
    152–53
Astilbes, 79, 149–50
Azaleas, 81

B

Baby's breath, 141, 146
Balsam, 139
Bamboo, 99
Barrenwort, 57
Basil, 84, 123, 124,
    207
Bearberry, 151
Beauty bush, 182
Beds
    hot, 111
    preparation, 21–24
    raised, 24, 110–11,
      118
    vegetable, 110–11
Bee balm, 57, 122, 123
    dividing, 79–80
    mildew diseases, 146
Beeches, 199, 200, 201
Begonias, 80, 131, 134,
    137
Berries, 83, 130
Birches, 193, 201
Black spot, 178
Blackberries, 127–28
Black-eyed Susan vine,
    171
Blanketflower, 143

Blazing stars, 72
Bleeding hearts, 145
Blueberries, 129–30
Bluegrass, 102
Bog gardens, 60, 150
Bolting, 115
Boltonia, 151, 152
Borders, 95
Box elders, 201
Boxwoods, 49–50, 184,
    185
Broccoli, 110, 119
Browallia, 134, 136–37
Brussels sprouts, 119
Bugleweed, 142
Bulbs, 36, 208
    choosing, 156
    fertilizing, 159
    foliage, 162–63
    in garden design, 93
    planting, 157–60
    rodent-resistant, 159
    spent stems, 161, 163
    spring-flowering,
      155–56
    summer-flowering, 155
    tender, 163–64, 165
Burlap, 172, 184, 189–90
Bush basil, 178–79
Butterflies, 124
Butterfly bushes, 49–50
Butterfly weed, 148, 152
Buttonbushes, 182

C

Cabbage, 110, 119
Cacti, 25
Cages, 167
Caladiums, 155, 163
California poppies, 139
Candle-pruning, 48
Cannas, 155
Cardinal climbers, 171
Caterpillars, 130
Catmint, 153
Cattails, 60
Chain trees, 188–89
Chamomile, 178–79
Cherry trees, 188
Chili peppers, 112
Chrysanthemums,
    152–53
Clay soil, 16, 20, 21,
    190
Cockscomb, 138, 139
Cold frames, 111
Cold treatments, 71
Coleus, 134, 136–37
Columbines, 141, 143
Companion planting
    annuals, 117
    herbs, 120, 178–79
    perennials, 152
    trees, 188–89, 191
Compost
    blends, 64
    making, 52, 60, 61–63

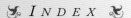

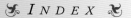

INDEX

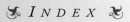

INDEX

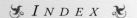

COMPANY MAN

Also by Joseph Finder

COMPANY MAN

Joseph Finder

ORION

First published in Great Britain in 2005 by Orion Books
an imprint of The Orion Publishing Group
Orion House, 5 Upper St Martin's Lane, London WC2H 9EA

1 3 5 7 9 10 8 6 4 2

A CIP catalogue record for this book
is available from the British Library

ISBN 0 75286 887 X (hardback)
ISBN 0 75286 888 8 (trade paperback)

Printed and bound in Great Britain by Clays Ltd, St Ives plc

www.orionbooks.co.uk

For my parents, Morris and Natalie Finder

And in loving memory of my in-laws,
Michel and Josephine Souda

That is the thankless position of the father in the family—
the provider for all, and the enemy of all.

—*August Strindberg, 1886*

PART ONE
SECURITY

1

The office of the chief executive officer of the Stratton Corporation wasn't really an office at all. At a quick glance you'd call it a cubicle, but at the Stratton Corporation—which *made* the elegant silver-mesh fabric panels that served as the walls around the CEO's brushed-steel Stratton Ergon desk— "cubicle" was a dirty word. You didn't work in a cubicle in the middle of a cube farm; you multitasked at your "home base" in an "open-plan system."

Nicholas Conover, Stratton's CEO, leaned back in his top-of-the-line leather Stratton Symbiosis chair, trying to concentrate on the stream of figures spewing from the mouth of his chief financial officer, Scott McNally, a small, nerdy, self-deprecating guy who had a spooky affinity for numbers. Scott was sardonic and quick-witted, in a dark, sharp-edged way. He was also one of the smartest men Nick had ever met. But there was nothing Nick hated more than budget meetings.

"Am I boring you, Nick?"

"You gotta ask?"

Scott was standing by the giant plasma screen, touching it with the stylus to advance the PowerPoint slides. He was not much more than five feet tall, over a foot shorter than Nick. He was prone to nervous twitches, anxious shrugs, and his fingernails were all bitten to the quick. He was also rapidly going bald, though he wasn't even out of his thirties; his dome was fringed with wild curly hair. He had plenty of money, but he always seemed to wear the same blue button-down Oxford shirt, fraying at the collar, that he'd worn since Wharton. His brown eyes darted around as he spoke, sunken in deep lilac hollows.

As he rattled on about the layoffs and how much they were going to cost this year versus how much they'd save the next, he fidgeted, with his free hand, with what remained of his straggly hair.

Nick's desk was kept fastidiously clear by his terrific assistant, Marjorie Dykstra. The only things on it were his computer (wireless keyboard and mouse, no pesky rat's nest of wires, a flat-panel screen), a red model truck with the Stratton logo painted on the side, and framed pictures of his kids. He kept sneaking glances at the photos, hoping Scott would think he was just staring into space and concentrating on the interminable presentation.

What's the bottom line, dude? he wanted to say. *Are the guys in Boston going to be happy or not?*

But Scott kept droning on and on about cost savings, about outplacement costs, about metrics, about employees as "units," as bar graphs on a PowerPoint slide. "Current average employee age is 47.789 years, with a standard deviation of 6.92," Scott said. He noticed Nick's glazed expression as he touched the screen with the aluminum stylus, and a half smile tugged at the corner of his mouth. "But hey, age is just a number, right?"

"Is there any good news here?"

"Ahh, it's only money." Scott paused. "That was a joke."

Nick stared at the little display of silver frames. Since Laura's death last year he cared about two things only: his job and his kids. Julia was ten, and she beamed with her thousand-watt smile in her school picture, her curly chestnut hair unruly, her enormous, liquid brown eyes sparkling, her big new teeth a little crooked, a smile so unself-conscious and dazzling she seemed to be bursting out of the photo. Lucas was sixteen, dark-haired like his little sister, and unnervingly handsome; he had his mother's cornflower-blue eyes, an angular jawline. A high school heartthrob. Lucas smiled for the camera, a smile that Nick hadn't actually seen in person since the accident.

There was just one photo of all four of them, sitting on the porch of the old house, Laura seated in the middle, everyone touching her, hands on her shoulder or her waist, the center of the family. The gaping hole, now. Her amused, twinkling blue eyes looked right at the camera, her expression frank and poised, seemingly tickled by some private joke. And of course Barney, their overweight, lumbering Golden/Lab mix, sat on his haunches in front of everyone, smiling his dog smile. Barney was in all the family pictures, even in last Christmas's family photo, the one with Lucas glowering like Charles Manson.

"Todd Muldaur's going to have a shit fit," Nick said, lifting his eyes to meet Scott's. Muldaur was a general partner in Fairfield Equity Partners in Boston, the private-equity firm that now owned the Stratton Corporation. Todd, not to put too fine a point on it, was Nick's boss.

"That's about the size of it," Scott agreed. He turned his head suddenly, and a second later Nick heard the shouts too.

"What the hell—?" Scott said. A deep male voice, somewhere nearby, yelling. A woman's voice, sounded like Marge's.

"You don't have an *appointment*, sir!" Marge was shouting, her voice high and frightened. An answering rumble, the words indistinct. "He isn't here, anyway, and if you don't leave right this *instant*, sir, I'm going to have to call Security."

A hulking figure crashed into one of the silver panels that outlined Nick's workstation, almost tipping it over. A bearded giant in his late thirties wearing a checked flannel shirt, unbuttoned, over a black Harley-Davidson T-shirt: barrel-chested, powerful-looking. The guy looked vaguely familiar. A factory worker? Someone who'd recently been laid off?

Immediately behind him followed Marge, her arms flailing. "You *cannot* come in here!" she shrilled. "Get out of here immediately, or I'll call Security."

The giant's foghorn voice boomed: "Well, whaddaya know, there he is. Boss man himself. The slasher is in."

Nick felt a cold fear wash over him as he realized that the budget meeting might turn out to be the high point of his day.

The guy, probably a worker just laid off in the most recent round of cuts, was staring, wild-eyed.

Nick flashed on news stories he'd read about crazed employees—"disgruntled workers," they were always called—who'd been let go, and then showed up at work and started picking people off.

"I just remembered a phone conference I'm late for," Scott McNally muttered as he squeezed past the intruder. "If you'll excuse me."

Nick got up slowly, raised himself to his full six-two. The crazy bearded guy was considerably bigger.

"What can I do for you?" Nick asked politely, calmly, the way you might try to lull a rabid Doberman pinscher.

"What can you do for me? That's fucking hilarious. There's nothing more you can do for me, or *to* me, asshole."

Marge, hovering directly behind him, her hands flailing, said: "Nick, I'll call Security."

Nick put up his hand to tell her to hold off. "I'm sure there's no need," he said.

Marge squinted at him to indicate her strong disagreement, but she nodded, backed away warily.

The bearded man took a step forward, puffing up his massive chest, but Nick didn't budge. There was something primal going on here: the interloper was a baboon baring his canines, screaming and strutting to scare off a predator. He smelled of rancid sweat and cigar smoke.

Nick fought the strong temptation to deck the guy but reminded himself that, as CEO of Stratton, he couldn't exactly do stuff like that. Plus, if this was one of the five thousand Stratton workers who'd been laid off within the last two years, he had a right to be angry. The thing to do was to talk the guy down, let him vent, let the air out of the balloon slowly.

Nick pointed to an empty chair, but the bearded man refused to sit. "What's your name?" Nick said, softening his voice a bit.

"Old Man Devries woulda never had to ask," the man retorted. "He knew everyone's name."

Nick shrugged. That was the myth, anyway. Folksy, paternal Milton Devries—Nick's predecessor—had been CEO of Stratton for almost four decades. The old man had been beloved, but there was no way he knew ten thousand names.

"I'm not as good with names as the old man was," Nick said. "So help me out here."

"Louis Goss."

Nick extended his hand to shake, but Goss didn't take it. Instead, Goss pointed a stubby forefinger at him. "When you sat down at your fancy computer at your fancy desk and made the decision to fire half the guys in the chair factory, did you even fucking *think* about who these people are?"

"More than you know," Nick said. "Listen, I'm sorry you lost your job—"

"I'm not here because I lost my job—see, I got seniority. I'm here to tell you that you deserve to lose yours. You think just because you waltz through this plant once a month that you know anything about these guys? These are human beings, buddy. Four hundred and fifty men and women who get up at four in the morning to do the early shift so they can feed their families and pay their rent or their mortgages and take care of their sick kids or their dying parents, okay? Do you realize that because of you some of these guys are going to lose their *houses?*"

Nick closed his eyes briefly. "Louis, are you just going to talk at me, or do you want to hear me out?"

"I'm here to give you a little free advice, Nick."

"I find you get what you pay for."

The man ignored him. "You better think seriously about whether you really want to go through with these layoffs. Because if you don't call them off by tomorrow morning, this place is going to grind to a halt."

"What are you trying to say?"

"I got half, maybe three-quarters of the factory floor with me on this. More, once we start. We're all sicking out tomorrow, Nick. And we're staying sick until my buddies get their jobs back." Goss was smiling with tobacco-darkened teeth, enjoying his moment. "You do the right thing, we do the right thing. Everyone's happy."

Nick stared at Goss. How much of this was bluster, how much on the level? A wildcat strike could paralyze the company, especially if it spread to the other plants.

"Why don't you think this over when you're driving home tonight in your Mercedes to your gated community?" Goss went on. "Ask yourself if you feel like taking your company down with you."

It's a Chevy Suburban, not a Mercedes, Nick wanted to say, but then he was struck by that phrase, "gated community." How did Goss know where he lived? There'd been nothing in the newspaper about that, though of course people talked . . . Was this a veiled threat?

Goss smiled, a mirthless, leering grin, saw the reaction on Nick's face. "Yeah, that's right. I know where you live."

Nick felt his rage flare up like a lit match tossed into a pool of gasoline. He sprang out of his seat, lunged forward, his face a few inches from Louis Goss's face. "What the hell are you trying to say?" It took all his self-restraint to keep from grabbing the collar of the guy's flannel shirt and twisting it tight around his fat neck. Up close he realized that Goss's bulk was all flab, not muscle.

Goss flinched, seemed to shrink back a bit, intimidated.

"You think everyone doesn't know you live in a fucking huge mansion in a gated community?" Goss said. "You think anyone else in this company can afford to live like that?"

Nick's anger subsided as quickly as it had surged. He felt a damp sort of relief; he'd misunderstood. The threat that Louis had actually made seemed suddenly tame by comparison. He leaned even closer, poked a finger against Goss's chest, jabbing the little white hyphen between "Harley" and "Davidson."

"Let me ask *you* something, Louis. Do you remember the 'town meeting' at the chair plant two years ago? When I told you guys the company was in a shitload of trouble and layoffs seemed likely but I wanted to avoid them if possible? You weren't sick that day, were you?"

"I was there," Goss muttered.

"Remember I asked if you'd all be willing to cut your hours back so everyone could stay on the job? Remember what everyone said?"

Goss was silent, looking off to one side, avoiding Nick's direct stare.

"You all said no, you couldn't do that. A pay cut was out of the question."

"Easy for you to—"

"And I asked whether you'd all be willing to cut back on your health plan, with your daycare and your health-club memberships. Now, how many people raised their hands to say yeah, okay, we'll cut back? Any recollection?"

Goss shook his head slowly, resentfully.

"Zero. Not a single goddamned hand went up. Nobody wanted to lose a goddamned hour of work; nobody wanted to lose a single perk." He could hear the blood rushing through his ears, felt a flush of indignation. "You think I slashed five thousand jobs, buddy? Well, the reality is, I *saved* five thousand jobs. Because the boys in Boston who own this company now don't fuck around. They're looking at our biggest competitor and seeing that the other guys aren't bending metal, they're not making their furniture in Michigan anymore. Everything's made in China now, Louis. *That's* why they can undercut us on price. You think the boys in Boston don't remind me of that every single goddamned chance they get?"

"I got no idea," Louis Goss muttered, shuffling his feet. It was all he could muster.

"So go right ahead, Louis. Have your strike. And they'll bring in a new CEO who'll make me look like Mister Rogers. Someone who'll shut down all of our plants the second he walks in this building. Then you wanna keep your job, Louis? I suggest you learn fucking *Mandarin*."

Louis was silent for a few seconds, and when he spoke, it was in a small, sullen voice. "You're going to fire me, aren't you?"

"You?" Nick snorted. "You're not worth the severance package. Now, get the fuck back on the line and get the hell out of my . . . work space."

A few seconds after Louis Goss had lumbered away, Marge appeared again. "You need to go home, Nick," she said. "Now."

"Home?"

"It's the police. There's a problem."

2

Nick backed his Chevy Suburban out of his space too fast, not bothering to check whether anyone was behind him, and careened through the parking lot that encircled the headquarters building. Even at the height of the workday, it stood half-empty as it had for the last two years, since the layoffs began. Gallows humor abounded among the employees these days, Nick knew. The upside of losing half the workforce was, you could always find a parking space.

His nerves felt stretched taught. Acres of empty black asphalt, surrounded by a great black field of charred buffalo grass, the remains of a prescribed fire. Buffalo grass never needed mowing, but every few years it had to be burned to the ground. The air smelled like a Weber grill.

Black against black against the black of the road, a desolate landscape. He wondered whether driving by the vast swath of scorched earth every day, staring at the charred field through the office windows, left a dark carbon smudge on your psyche.

You need to go home. Now.

When you have kids, they're the first thing you think of. Even a guy like Nick, hardly a worrywart, you get a call from the cops and your imagination takes flight in a bad direction.

But both kids were all right, the cops had assured Marjorie. Julia was on her way back from school, and Lucas—well, Lucas had been in classes today

and was doing whatever the hell he did after school these days, which was another issue entirely.

That wasn't it.

Yes, it was another break-in, they'd said, but this time he really needed to
come by. What the hell could that mean?

Over the past year or so, Nick had gotten used to the periodic calls from
the alarm company or the police. The burglar alarm would go off in the middle of the day. There'd been a break-in. The alarm company would verify
that the alarm was genuine by calling home or Nick's office and requesting
a code. If no authorized user said it was a false alarm, the company would
immediately dispatch the Fenwick police. A couple of cops would then drive
by the house, check it out.

Inevitably it happened when no one was there—the crew working on
the kitchen were taking one of their frequent days off; the kids were at school;
the housekeeper, Marta, was out shopping or maybe picking up Julia.

Nothing was ever stolen. The intruder would force a window or one
of the French doors, get inside, and leave a little message.

Literally, a message: words spray-painted in Day-Glo orange, all capital
letters formed with the precision of an architect or mechanical engineer: NO
HIDING PLACE.

Three words, one on top of another.

Was there any doubt it was a deranged laid-off employee? The graffiti de-
faced the walls of the living room, the dining room they never used, the
freshly plastered walls of the kitchen. In the beginning it had scared the shit
out of him.

The real message, of course, was that they weren't safe. They could be
gotten to.

The first graffiti had appeared on the heavy, ornate ash-wood front door,
which Laura had deliberated over for weeks with the architect, a door that
had cost a ridiculous three thousand dollars, a fucking *door*, for God's sake.
Nick had made his feelings known but hadn't objected, because it was obviously important to her, for some reason. He'd been perfectly content with the
flimsy paneled front door that came with the house they'd just bought. He
didn't want to change anything about the house except maybe to shrink it to

half its size. There was a saying that was popular at Stratton, which Old Man Devries was fond of repeating: the whale that spouts gets the harpoon. Sometimes he thought about having one of those bronze-looking estate wall plaques made for him by Frontgate, the kind you see on stone entrance pillars in front of McMansions, saying in raised copper letters, SPOUTING WHALE HOUSE.

But to Laura, the front door was symbolic: it was where you welcomed friends and family, and it was where you kept out those who weren't welcome. So it had to be both beautiful and substantial. "It's the *front door,* Nick," she'd insisted. "The first thing people see. That's the *one* place you don't cheap out."

Maybe, on some level, she thought a three-inch-thick front door would make them safer. Buying this insanely big house in the Fenwicke Estates: that was her idea too. She wanted the safety of the gated community. It took only a couple of anonymous threatening phone calls, as soon as the layoffs were announced.

"If you're a target, we're all targets," she said. There was a lot of anger out there, directed at him. He wasn't going to argue with her. He had a family to protect.

Now, with her gone, it felt as if he'd absorbed her neurosis, as if it had penetrated his bones. He felt, sometimes, that his family, what remained of it, was as fragile as an egg.

He also knew that the security of their gated community was little more than an illusion. It was a show, an elaborate charade, the fancy gatehouse and the guards, the private security, the high black iron fence with the spearhead finials.

The Suburban screeched to a stop before the ornately scrolled cast-iron gate beside the brick gatehouse built to resemble a miniature castle. A brass plaque on one of the piers said FENWICKE ESTATES.

That little "e" at the end of Fenwick—he'd always found it pretentious to the point of being irritating. Plus, he was so over the irony here, this posh enclosed neighborhood equipped with the priciest security you could get—the tall wrought-iron perimeter fence with the fiber-optic sensing cable concealed inside the top rail, the pan-tilt-zoom CCTV surveillance cameras, the motion-sensor intruder alarms—where you couldn't stop the loonies from scrambling in through the dense surrounding woods and climbing over the fence.

"Another break-in, Mr. Conover," said Jorge, the day guard. Nice guy, couldn't be nicer. The security guards were all professional in demeanor, all wore sharp uniforms.

Nick nodded grimly, waited for the motor-driven gate to open, ridiculously slow. The high-pitched electronic warning beep was annoying. Everything beeped these days: trucks backing up, dishwashers and clothes dryers, microwaves. It really could drive you crazy.

"Police are there now, you know," said Jorge. "Three cruisers, sir."

"Any idea what it is?"

"No, sir, I don't, I'm sorry."

The damned gate took forever to open. It was ridiculous. In the evening sometimes there was a line of cars waiting to get in. Something had to be done about it. For Christ's sake, what if his house caught fire—would the fire department trucks have to sit here while his house turned to toast?

He raced the engine in annoyance. Jorge shrugged a sheepish apology.

The second the gate was open far enough for the car to get through, he gunned it—the Suburban's pickup never ceased to amaze him—and barreled over the tiger-teeth tire-shredders that enforced one-way traffic, across the wide circular court paved in antique brick in a geometric pattern by old-world Italian stonemasons shipped over from Sicily, past the SPEED LIMIT 20 sign at twice that at least.

The brick pavement turned into glass-smooth macadam road, no street sign. He raced past the old-growth elms and firs, the mailboxes the size of doghouses, none of the houses visible. You had to be invited over to see what your neighbor's house looked like. And there sure as hell weren't any block parties here in Fenwicke Estates.

When he saw police squad cars parked on the street and at the entrance to his driveway, he felt something small and cold and hard forming at the base of his stomach, a little icicle of fear.

A uniformed policeman halted him a few hundred feet from the house, halfway up the drive. Nick jumped out and slammed the car door in one smooth, swift motion.

The cop was short and squat, powerful-looking, seemed to be perspiring heavily despite the cool weather. His badge said MANZI. A walkie-talkie hitched to his belt squawked unceasingly.

"You Mr. Conover?" He stood directly in front of Nick's path, blocking his way. Nick felt a flash of annoyance. My house, my driveway, my burglar alarm: get the fuck out of my way.

"Yeah, that's me, what's going on?" Nick tried to keep the irritation, and the anxiety, out of his voice.

"Ask you some questions?" Dappled sunlight filtered through the tall birches that lined the asphalt lane, played on the cop's inscrutable face.

Nick shrugged. "Sure—what is it, the graffiti again?"

"What time did you leave the house this morning, sir?"

"Around seven-thirty, but the kids are normally out of there by eight, eight-fifteen at the latest."

"What about your wife?"

Nick gazed at the cop steadily. Most of the cops had to know who he was at least. He wondered if this guy was just trying to yank his chain. "I'm a single parent."

A pause. "Nice house."

"Thank you." Nick could sense the resentment, the envy rising off the man like swamp gas. "What happened?"

"House is okay, sir. It's brand-new, looks like. Not even finished yet, huh?"

"We're just having some work done," Nick said impatiently.

"I see. The workers, they're here every day?"

"I wish. Not yesterday or today."

"Your alarm company lists a work number for you at the Stratton Corporation," Officer Manzi said. He was looking down at an aluminum clipboard, his black eyes small and deeply inset like raisins in a butterscotch pudding. "You work there."

"Right."

"What do you do at Stratton?" There was a beat before the policeman looked up and let his eyes meet Nick's: the guy knew damned well what he did there.

"I'm the CEO."

Manzi nodded as if everything now made sense. "I see. You've had a number of break-ins over the last several months, is that correct, Mr. Conover?"

"Five or six times now."

"What kind of security system you have here, sir?"

"Burglar alarm on the doors and some of the windows and French doors. Basic system. Nothing too elaborate."

"Home like this, that's not much of a system. No cameras, right?"

"Well, we live in this, you know, gated community."

"Yes, sir, I can see that. Lot of good it does, keeping out the wing nuts."

"Point taken." Nick almost smiled.

"Sounds like the burglar alarm isn't on very often, sir, that right?"

"Officer, why so many cars here today for a routine—"

"Mind if I ask the questions?" Officer Manzi said. The guy seemed to be enjoying his authority, pushing around the boss man from Stratton. Let him, Nick thought. Let him have his fun. But—

Nick heard a car approaching, turned and saw the blue Chrysler Town and Country, Marta behind the wheel. He felt that little chemical surge of pleasure he always got when he saw his daughter, the way he used to feel with Lucas too, until that got complicated. The minivan pulled up alongside Nick and the engine was switched off. A car door opened and slammed, and Julia shouted, "What are *you* doing home, Daddy?"

She ran toward him, wearing a light-blue hooded Stratton sweatshirt and jeans, black sneakers. She wore some slight variant of the outfit every day, a sweatshirt or an athletic jersey. When Nick went to the same elementary school, more than thirty years before, you weren't allowed to wear jeans, and sweatshirts weren't considered appropriate school attire. But he didn't have time in the mornings to argue with her, and he was inclined to go easy on his little girl, given what she had to be going through since the death of her mother.

She hugged him tight around his abdomen. He no longer hoisted her up, since at almost five feet and ninety-something pounds, it wasn't so easy. In the last year she'd gotten tall and leggy, almost gangly, though there was still a pocket of baby fat at her tummy. She was starting to develop physically, little breast buds emerging, which Nick couldn't deal with. It was a constant reminder of his inadequacy as a parent: who the hell was going to talk to her, get her through adolescence?

The hug went on for several seconds until Nick released her, another thing that had changed since Laura was gone. His daughter's hugs: she didn't want to let him go.

Now she looked up at him, her meltingly beautiful brown eyes lively. "How come there's all these police?"

"They want to talk to me, baby doll. No big deal. Where's your backpack?"

"In the car. Did that crazy guy get in the house again and write bad stuff?"

Nick nodded, stroked her glossy brown hair. "What are you doing home now? Don't you have piano?"

She gave him a look of amused contempt. "That's not till four."

"I thought it was three."

"Mrs. Guarini changed it, like, *months* ago, don't you remember?"

He shook his head. "Oh, right. I forgot. Well, listen, I have to talk to this policeman here. Marta, you guys stay here until the police say it's okay to go in the house, okay?"

Marta Burrell was from Barbados, a mocha-skinned woman of thirty-eight, tall and slender as a fashion model with an air of sultry indifference, or maybe arrogance, her default mode. Her jeans were a little too tight, and she customarily wore high heels, and she was vocal about her disapproval of Julia's daily uniform. She expressed disapproval of just about everything in the household. She was ferociously devoted to the kids, though, and was able to make both of them do things Nick couldn't. Marta had been a superb nanny when the kids were little, was an excellent cook, and an indifferent housekeeper.

"Sure, Nick," she said. She reached for Julia, but the girl scampered off.

"You were saying," Nick said to the cop.

Manzi looked up, fixed Nick with a blank look, bordering on impertinence, but there was a gleam in his eyes; he seemed to be restraining a smile. "Do you have any enemies, Mr. Conover?"

"Only about five thousand people in town."

The policeman's eyebrows shot up. "Excuse me."

"We laid off half our workforce recently, as I'm sure you know. More than five thousand employees."

"Ah, yes," the cop said. "You're not a popular man around here, are you?"

"You could say that."

It wasn't that long ago, Nick reflected, that everyone loved him. People he didn't know in high school started sucking up to him. *Forbes* magazine even did a profile. After all, Nick was the youthful blue-collar guy, the son of a guy who'd spent a life bending metal in the chair factory—business reporters ate that stuff up. Maybe Nick was never going to be beloved at the company like Old Man Devries, but for a while at least he'd been popular, admired, *liked*. A local hero in the small town of Fenwick, Michigan, sort of, a guy you'd point out at the Shop 'n Save and maybe, if you felt bold, walk up to and introduce yourself in the frozen-foods section.

But that was before—before the first layoffs were announced, two years ago, after Stratton's new owners had laid down the law at the quarterly board meeting in Fenwick. There was no choice. The Stratton Corporation was going down the crapper if they didn't cut costs, and fast. That meant losing half its workforce, five thousand people in a town of maybe forty thousand. It was the most painful thing he'd ever done, something he'd never imagined having to do. There'd been a series of smaller layoffs since the first ones were announced, two years ago. It was like Chinese water torture. The *Fenwick Free Press*, which used to publish puff pieces about Stratton, now ran banner headlines: THREE HUNDRED MORE STRATTON WORKERS FACE THE AXE. CANCER VICTIM SUFFERS LOSS OF STRATTON BENEFITS. The local columnists routinely referred to him as "the Slasher."

Nick Conover, local boy made good, had become the most hated man in town.

"Guy like you ought to have better security than that. You get the security you pay for, you know."

Nick was about to reply when he heard his daughter scream.

3

He ran toward the source of the screaming and found Julia beside the pool. Her cries came in great ragged gulps. She knelt on the bluestone coping, her hands thrashing in the water, her small back torquing back and forth. Marta stood nearby, helpless and aghast, a hand to her mouth.

Then Nick saw what had made Julia scream, and he felt sick.

A dark shape floated in cranberry red water, splayed and distended, surrounded by slick white entrails. The blood was concentrated in a dark cloud around the carcass; the water got lighter, pinkish as it got farther away from the furry brown mass.

The corpse wasn't immediately recognizable as Barney, their old Lab/Golden Retriever. It took a second glance, a struggle with disbelief. On the bluestone not far from where Julia knelt, keening, was a blood-slick, carbon-steel Henckels knife from their kitchen set.

Many things immediately made sense, now: the unusual police presence, the questioning, even the absence of Barney's usual barked greeting when Nick arrived.

A couple of policemen were busy taking pictures, talking to one another, their low conversations punctuated by static blasts from their radios. They seemed to be chatting casually, as if nothing unusual had happened. Business as usual to them. No one was expressing sympathy or concern. Nick felt a flash of rage, but the main thing now was to comfort his daughter.

He rushed to her, sank to his knees, put a hand on her back. "Baby," he said. "Baby."

She turned, flung her arms around his neck, let out a wail. Her gasping breath was hot and moist. He held her tight as if he could squeeze the trauma out of her little body, make everything normal again, make her feel safe.

"Oh, baby, I'm so sorry." Her gasps were like spasms, hiccups. He held her even tighter. The copious flow of her tears pooled in the hollow of his neck. He could feel it soak his shirt.

Ten minutes later, when Marta had taken Julia inside, Nick spoke to Officer Manzi. He made no effort this time to contain his fury. "What the *fuck* are you guys going to do about this?" Nick thundered. "What the hell are you waiting for? These break-ins have been going on for months already, and you haven't done a damned thing about it."

"Excuse me, sir," Manzi said blandly.

"You haven't assigned a detective to the case, you haven't done any investigation, you haven't gone through the lists of laid-off Stratton employees. You've had months to stop this fucking madman. What are you waiting for? Does this lunatic have to murder one of my *kids* before you take it seriously?"

Manzi's detachment—did Nick detect a smug sort of amusement, was that possible?—was infuriating. "Well, sir, as I said, you might want to think about upgrading your security—"

"*My* security? What about you guys? Isn't this your goddamned *job*?"

"You said it yourself, sir—you laid off five thousand Stratton employees. That's going to create more enemies than we can possibly protect you against. You should really upgrade your security system."

"Yeah, and what are *you* going to do? How are *you* going to protect my family?"

"I'll be honest with you, sir. Stalking cases are some of our hardest."

"Meaning you pretty much can't do shit, is that right?"

Manzi shrugged. "You said it. I didn't."

4

After the police left, Nick tried for a long while to console his daughter. He called to cancel her piano lesson, then sat with her, talking a bit, mostly hugging. When she seemed stable, Nick left her in Marta's care and returned to the office for a largely unproductive afternoon.

By the time he returned home, Julia was asleep and Marta was in the family room, watching a movie about a baby who talks with Bruce Willis's voice.

"Where's Julia?" Nick asked.

"She's asleep," Marta said sadly. "She was okay by the time she went to bed. But she cried a lot, Nick."

Nick shook his head. "That poor baby. This is going to be hardest on her, I think. Barney was Laura's dog, really. To Julia, Barney . . ." He fell silent. "Is Lucas upstairs?"

"He called from a friend's house, said they're working on their history projects."

"Yeah, right. Working on a nickel bag, more like it. Which friend?"

"I think Ziegler? Um, listen—Nick? I'm kind of nervous being alone in the house—after today, I mean."

"I can't blame you. You lock the doors and windows, right?"

"I did, but this crazy person . . ."

"I know. I'm going to have a new system put in right away so you can put on the alarm while you're inside." Stratton's corporate security director had told Nick he'd drop by later, see what he could do. Anything for the boss. They'd gone too long with a rudimentary security system; it was time to put in something state-of-the-art, with cameras and motion detectors and all that. "You can go to sleep if you want."

"I want to see the rest of this movie."

"Sure."

Nick went upstairs and down the hall to Julia's bedroom, quietly opening the door and making his way through the darkness by memory. Enough moonlight filtered through the gaps in the curtains that, once his eyes adjusted, he could make out his daughter's sleeping body. Julia slept under, and with, an assortment of favorite blankets, each of which she'd given names to, as well as a rotating selection of stuffed animals and Beanie Babies from her vast menagerie. Tonight she was clutching Winnie the Pooh, who'd been given to her when she was a few days old, now frayed and matted and stained.

Her choice of sleeping partner was a pretty reliable indicator of her mental state: Elmo when she was feeling sprightly; Curious George when she was feeling mischievous; her little Beanie Baby koala, Eucalyptus, when she wanted to nurture someone needier than herself. But Pooh always meant she was feeling especially fragile and in need of the ultimate comfort of her longest-serving pal. For several months after her mommy's death, she slept with Pooh every night. Recently, she'd traded in Pooh for some of the other guys, which was a sign that she was starting to feel a little stronger.

Tonight, though, Pooh was back in her bed.

He touched her sweaty curls, breathed in the sweet baby-shampoo aroma mixed with the slightly sour smell of perspiration, and kissed her damp forehead. She murmured but did not stir.

A door opened and closed somewhere in the house, followed immediately by the thud of something being dropped to the floor. Nick was instantly alert. Heavy, bounding footsteps on the carpeted stairs told him it was Lucas.

Nick navigated a path through the minefield of books and toys and closed the door quietly behind him. The long hall was dark, but a stripe of yellow light glared through the crack under Lucas's bedroom door.

Nick knocked, waited, then knocked again.

"Yeah?"

The depth and timbre of his son's voice always startled him. That and the surly edge to it, in the last year. Nick opened the door and found Lucas lying back on his bed, boots still on, iPod earbuds in his ears.

"Where've you been?" Nick asked.

Lucas glanced at him, then found something in the middle distance that was more interesting. "Where's Barney?"

Nick paused. "I asked you where you've been, Luke. It's a school night."

"Ziggy's."

"You didn't ask me if you could go over there."

"You weren't around to ask."

"If you want to go over to a friend's house, you've got to clear it in advance with me or Marta."

Lucas shrugged in tacit acknowledgment. His eyes were red and glassy, and now Nick was fairly certain he'd been getting high. This was an alarming new development, but he hadn't yet confronted his son about it. He'd been putting it off simply because it was one more mountain to climb, a showdown that would require unwavering strength he didn't have. There was so much going on at work, and there was Julia, who was frankly a hell of a lot easier to console, and then there was his own sadness, which sapped his ability to be a good and understanding dad.

He looked at Lucas, could hear the tinny, percussive hiss coming from the earphones. He wondered what kind of crappy music Lucas was listening to now. He caught a whiff of stale smoke in the room, which smelled like regular cigarettes, though he wasn't sure.

There was a baffling disconnect between Lucas on the inside and Lucas on the outside. Externally, Lucas was a mature sixteen, a tall and handsome man. His almost feminine prettiness had taken on a sharp-featured masculinity. His eyebrows, above blue eyes with long lashes, were dark and thick. The Lucas inside, though, was five or six: petulant, easily wounded, expert at finding insult in the most unexpected places, capable of holding grudges to the end of time.

"You're not smoking, are you?"

Lucas cast his father a look of withering contempt. "Ever hear of second-hand smoke? I was around people who were smoking."

"Ziggy doesn't smoke." Kenny Ziegler was a big, strapping blond kid, a swimmer who was Lucas's best friend from when he was still on the swim team. But ever since Lucas had quit swimming, six months or so ago, he hadn't been hanging out with Ziggy nearly as much. Nick doubted that Lucas had actually spent the afternoon and evening at Ziggy's house. Somewhere else: some other friend, probably.

Lucas's stare was unwavering. His music squealed and hissed.

"You got homework?" Nick persisted.

"I don't need you to monitor me, Nick." Nick. That was something else new, calling his father by his first name. Some of Lucas's friends had always called their own parents by their first names, but Nick and Laura had always insisted on the traditional "Mom" and "Dad." Lucas was just trying to push his buttons. He'd been calling him Nick for the last month or so.

"Can you please take those earphones out when I'm talking to you?"

"I can hear you just fine," Lucas said. "Where's Barney?"

"Take off the earphones, Luke."

Lucas yanked them out of his ears by the dangling wire, let them drop on his chest, the tinny sound now louder and more distinct.

"Something happened to Barney. Something pretty bad."

"What are you talking about?"

"We found him . . . Someone killed him, Luke."

Lucas whipped his legs around until he was perched on the edge of the bed, looking as if he were about to launch himself toward Nick.

"*Killed* him?"

"We found him in the pool today—some nut . . ." Nick couldn't continue, couldn't relive the gruesome scene.

"This is the same guy who keeps breaking in, isn't it? The spray-paint graffiti guy."

"Looks that way."

"It's because of *you!*" Lucas's eyes widened, gleaming with tears. "All those people you fired, the way everyone in town hates you."

Nick didn't know how to answer.

"Like half the kids in school, their parents got laid off by you. It's fucking embarrassing."

"Lucas, listen to me—"

Lucas gave him a ferocious look, eyes bulging, teeth bared, as if Nick was the one who'd killed Barney. "Why don't you get the fuck out of my room," he said, his voice cracking.

Nick's reaction surprised himself. If he'd talked that way to his father, he'd have had the shit beaten out of him. But instead of flying into a fury, he was instead overcome by calm, patient sorrow—his heart ached for the kid, for what he'd had to go through. "Lucas," Nick said, so softly it was almost a whisper, "don't you ever talk to me like that again." He turned around and quietly closed the door behind him. His heart wasn't in it.

Standing in the hallway just outside her adored older brother's room was Julia, tears streaming down her face.

5

It wasn't long after Nick had finally gotten Julia back to sleep—picking her up, hugging her, snuggling with her in her bed—that there was a quick rap on the front door.

Eddie Rinaldi, Stratton's corporate security director, was wearing a tan fleece jacket and a pair of jeans and smelled like beer and cigarettes. Nick wondered whether Eddie had just come over from his usual hangout, Victor's, on Division.

"Shit, man," Eddie said. "That sucks, about the dog."

Eddie was a tall, lanky guy, edgy and intense. His frizzy brown hair was run through with gray. He had pitted cheeks and forehead, the legacy of a nasty case of acne in high school. He had gray eyes, flared nostrils, a weak mouth.

They'd been high school teammates—Eddie was the right wing on the same hockey team on which Nick, the captain, played center—though they'd never been especially close. Nick was the star, of the team and of the high school, the big man on campus, the good-looking guy all the girls wanted to go out with. Eddie, not a bad hockey player, was a natural cut-up, half-crazy, and with a face full of zits he wasn't exactly dating the prom queen. The joke about Eddie among some on the team was that he'd been left on the Tilt-A-Whirl a bit too long as a baby. That wasn't quite fair; he was a goofball who just scraped by in school, but he had a native cunning. He also looked up to Nick, almost hero-worshiped him, though his idolatry always seemed tinged with a little jealousy. After high school, when Nick went to Michigan State, in East Lansing, Eddie went to the police academy in Fraser and lucked out, got a job with the Grand Rapids PD, where after almost two decades he hit a bad patch. As he'd explained to Nick, he'd been accused of brutalizing a suspect—a bullshit charge, but there it was—banished to a desk job, busted down the ranks until the publicity blew over, or so he was assured by the police chief. But he knew his career was as good as done for.

Nick, by then CEO of Stratton, stepped in and saved his ass, offering Eddie a job he was maybe underqualified for, assistant director of corporate security, in charge of background checks, pilferage investigations, that sort of thing. Just as Nick had assured the longtime security director, a white-haired sergeant who'd retired from the Fenwick force, Eddie had poured himself into the job, deeply grateful to Nick and eager to redeem himself.

Two years later, when the security director took early retirement, Eddie moved into the top job. Sometimes Nick thought it was like the old hockey days: Nick, the star, the power forward as they called him, with his hundred-mile-an-hour slap shot, taking the face-offs, making a pass through nine sticks as if he were threading a needle; and Eddie, grinning wildly as he did wild stunts like kicking an opponent's skates out from under him, spearing guys in the gut, carving some other guy's face with his stick, skating up and down the wing with a jittery juking craziness.

"Thanks for coming over," Nick said.

"First I want to see the kitchen."

Nick shrugged, led him down the hall. He switched on the light and peeled back one of the heavy plastic sheets, taped to the doorjamb, which served as a dust barrier between the kitchen and the rest of the house.

Nick stepped through, followed by Eddie, who gave a low whistle, taking in the glass-fronted cabinets, the Wolf commercial range. He set down the little nylon gym bag he'd been carrying. "Jeez Louise, this gotta cost a fortune."

"It's ridiculous."

He switched one of the burners on. It *tick-ticked* and then ignited, a powerful roar of blue flame coming out. "Man, serious gas pressure. And you don't even cook."

"Had to bring in a new line for that. Tore up the lawn, had to reseed and everything."

"Shit, how many sinks you got?"

"I think they call that one a prep sink, and that one's for dishes."

"The dishwasher's gonna go in there?"

"Yeah." Fisher & Paykel, was that it? Another result of Laura's star-searches for the best appliances ever. *It's two drawers*, she'd told him, *so you can run smaller loads*. Okay, whatever.

Eddie tugged at a handle, releasing a slab of rock maple. "This a knife drawer?"

"Built-in cutting board."

"Sweet. Don't tell me you picked all this shit out."

"Laura designed the whole thing, picked out every appliance, the color scheme, the cabinets, everything."

"Tough to cook without a kitchen counter, you know."

"That's coming."

"Where do you keep the booze?"

Nick touched the front of a cabinet. It popped open, revealing an array of liquor bottles.

"Neat trick."

"Magnetic touch-latch. Also Laura's idea. Scotch?"

"Sure."

"Rocks, right?" Nick held a tumbler against the automatic icemaker on the door of the Sub-Zero and watched as the cubes *chink-chink-chinked* against the glass. Then he poured a healthy slug of Johnny Walker, handed it to Eddie, and led the way out of the kitchen.

Eddie took a long sip, then gave a contented sigh. "Hey, Johnny, Daddy's home. What are you drinking, buddy?"

"Better not. I've been taking a pill to sleep, not supposed to mix it with alcohol."

They left the kitchen, entered the dark back corridor, illuminated only by the orange glow from the switch plates. Nick switched on the lamp on the hall table, another of the millions of little details about this house that reminded him of Laura every single day. She'd spent months looking for the perfect alabaster lamp until she found it one day in an antiques store on the Upper East Side of Manhattan when she'd accompanied him on a business trip. The shop dealt only with the trade, decorators and interior designers, but she'd sweet-talked her way in, then spotted the lamp. The base was carved of alabaster quarried in Volterra, Italy, she'd explained, when Nick asked why it had cost so freaking much. To Nick it just looked like white rock.

"Aw, don't take pills, man. You know what you need to help you sleep?"

"Let me guess." The lights in his study came on automatically as they entered, pinpoints in the ceiling and little floods that washed the hand-plastered walls, the huge Sony flat-panel TV mounted on the facing wall, the French doors that opened onto the freshly seeded lawn.

"That's right, Nicky. Pussy. Look at this place. Incredible."

"Laura."

Eddie sank into one of the butter-soft leather Symbiosis chairs, took a swig of his Scotch, and placed it noisily down on the slate-topped side table. Nick sat in the one next to him.

"So I picked up this chick Saturday night at Victor's, right? I mean, I must've had my beer goggles on, because when I woke the next morning she—well, she had a great personality, know what I'm saying? I mean, the bitch must have fell off the ugly tree and hit every branch on the way down." He gave a dry, wheezing cackle.

"But you got a good night's sleep."

"Actually no, I was shit-faced, man. Point is, Nick, you gotta get out there and start dating. Get back on the trail of tail. But man, watch out, there's a lot of skanks out there."

"I don't feel like it yet."

Eddie tried to soften his voice, though it came out more as an insinuating rasp. "She died a year ago, Nicky. That's a long time."

"Not if you're married seventeen years."

"Hey, I'm not talking about getting *married* again. I'm the *last* one to tell you to get married. Look at me—I don't buy, I lease. Trade 'em in regularly for the latest model."

"Can we talk about my security system? It's late, and I've had a long day."

"All right, all right. My systems guy's a total fucking wizard. He put in my home system."

Nick's brows shot up.

"I mean, I paid for it out of my own pocket, come on. If he can get the equipment, I'll have him put one in tomorrow."

"Cameras and everything?"

"Shit. We're talking IP-based cameras at the perimeter and at all points of entry and egress, cameras inside, overt and covert."

"What's IP?"

"Internet-something. Means you can get the signal over the Internet. You can monitor your house from your computer at work—it's amazing shit."

"Back up to tape?"

"No tape. All the cameras record to a hard drive. Maybe put in motion sensors to save on disk space. We can do remote pan-and-tilt, real-time full-color streaming video at seven and a half frames per second or something. The technology's totally different these days."

"This going to keep my stalker out?"

"Put it this way, once he sees these robot cameras swiveling at him as he approaches the house, he'll turn and run, unless he's a total whack job. And at the very least, we get a bunch of high-quality images of him next time he tries to break in. Speaking of which, I saw some serious cameras around the guard booth down the road. Looks like you got cameras all around the perimeter fence, not just at the entrance. We mighta got lucky, got a picture of him. I'll talk to the security guys down there first thing in the morning."

"You don't think the cops already did that?"

Eddie made a *pfft* sound. "Those guys aren't going to do shit for you. They'll do the bare minimum, or less."

Nick nodded. "I think you're right."

"I know I'm right. They all hate your fucking guts. You're Nick the Slasher. You laid off their dads and their brothers and sisters and wives. I bet they love seeing you get some serious payback."

Nick exhaled noisily. "What do you mean, 'unless he's a total whack job'?"

"That's the thing about stalkers, man. They don't necessarily obey the rules of sanity. Only one thing can give you total peace of mind if he comes around again." He unzipped the black nylon gym bag and took out a small oil-cloth bundle. He unwrapped it, revealing a blunt matte-black semi-automatic pistol, squarish and compact, ugly. Its plastic frame was scratched, the slide nicked. "Smith and Wesson Sigma .380," he announced.

"I don't want that," Nick said.

"I wouldn't rule anything out, I were you. Anyone who'd do that to your dog might well go after your kids, and you gonna tell me you're not going to protect your family? That's not the Nick *I* know."

6

Nick slipped into the dark theater—the FutureLab, they called it—and took a seat at the back. The Film was still playing on the giant curved movie screen, a high-gain, rear-projection video screen that took up an entire curved front wall. The darkness of the theater was soothing to his bleary morning eyes.

Jangly techno music emanated in surround sound from dozens of speakers built into the walls, ceiling, and floor. Watching this beauty reel, you were careening through the Kalahari Desert, down a narrow street in Prague, flying over the Grand Canyon, close enough to the walls to be scraped by the jagged rocks. You were whizzing through molecules of DNA and emerging in a City of the Future, the images kaleidoscopic, futuristic. "In an interlinked world," a mellifluous baritone confided, "knowledge reigns supreme." The Film was about the future of work and life and technology; it was totally abstract and cerebral and very trippy. Not a stick of furniture was anywhere to be seen.

Only some customers were shown The Film. Some visitors, particularly Silicon Valley types, were blown away by it and, when the lights came up, wanted to chatter on and on about the "seamless integration" between office furniture and technology, about the Workplace of the Future, ready to sign on the dotted line right then and there.

Others found it pretentious and annoying, didn't get it at all. Like this morning's audience, a delegation of nine high-level executives from the Atlas McKenzie Group. It was one of the world's largest financial services companies, had its spindly tendrils in everything from banking to credit cards to insurance, in more than a hundred countries and territories. Nick watched them squirm in their seats, whispering to each other. They included the Senior VP of Real Estate and the VP for Facilities Management and assorted minions. They'd been flown up from Chicago the day before on the Stratton corporate jet, been given the full-out tour by Stratton's Guest Experience Team. Nick had had lunch with them, shown them around the executive offices himself, given them his standard pitch about the flattening of the corporate pyramidal hierarchy and how the work environment was moving from individual to the collaborative community, all that stuff.

Atlas McKenzie was building an immense office tower in Toronto. A million square feet, a third of which would be their new corporate headquarters, which they wanted outfitted from scratch. That meant at least ten thousand workstations, at least fifty million bucks up front, and then there was the ten-year maintenance contract. If Stratton got the deal, it would be a huge win. Beyond huge. Unbelievable. Then there were all the Atlas McKenzie offices around the world, which could well be standardized on Stratton—Nick couldn't even calculate how much that could mean.

All right, so The Film was flopping. They might as well have been watching some subtitled art house film set in a small Bulgarian village.

At least yesterday afternoon they'd been totally jazzed by the Workplace of the Future exhibit. Visitors always were, without exception. You couldn't help but be. It was a fully functional mock-up of a workstation, eight by ten, that looked a lot more like a network news anchor set than some cubicle out of Dilbertland. The visitors were given ID tags to wear that contained an embedded chip, which communicated with an electronic sensor so that when you entered the space, the overhead lights changed from blue to green. That way, co-workers could tell from way across the floor that you were at your desk. As soon as you sat down, an electronic message was flashed to your team members—in this case, the laptops provided to the visitors—telling them you were in. Amazing what Stratton's engineers came up with, he'd often marveled. In front of the worker's desk in the Workplace of the Future was a six-foot-long wraparound computer monitor, superhigh resolution, on which appeared a page of text, a videoconference window, and a PowerPoint slide. Clients saw this and coveted it, the way some guys drool over Lamborghinis.

They were running about ten minutes behind, so Nick had to sit through The Talk. The screen faded to black, and slowly, slowly, the lights in the Lab came up. Standing at the brushed-aluminum podium was Stratton's Senior Vice President for Workplace Research, a very tall, slender woman in her late thirties with long, straight blond hair cut into severe bangs and giant horn-rim glasses. She was Victoria Zander—never Vicky or Tori, only Victoria. She was dressed dramatically, in all black. She could have been a beatnik from the fifties, a pal of Jack Kerouac's on the road.

Victoria spoke in a mellifluous soprano. She said, "Your corporate headquarters is one of the most powerful branding tools you have. It's your opportunity to tell your employees and your visitors a story about *you*—who you are, what you stand for. It's your *brandscape*. We call this the *narrative office*." As she talked, she jotted down key phrases—"smart workplace" and "heartbeat space" and "Knowledge Age"—on a digital whiteboard set into the wall in front of her, and her notes, zapped instantly into computer text, appeared on the laptops in front of the folks from Atlas McKenzie. She said, "Our model is *wagons around the campfire*. We live our private lives in our own wagon but come together at suppertime."

Even after hearing it a dozen times, Nick didn't understand all of her patter, but that was okay; he figured that no one else did either. Certainly not these guys from Chicago, who were probably rolling their eyes inwardly but didn't want to admit their lack of sophistication. Victoria's loopy little graduate seminar was intimidating and probably soared over their heads too.

What these guys understood was modular wiring infrastructure and preassembled components and data cables built into access floors. That was where they lived. They didn't want to hear about brandscapes.

He waited patiently for her to finish, increasingly aware of the visitors' restlessness. All he had to do was a quick meet-and-greet, make sure everyone was happy, chat them up a bit.

Nick didn't actually get involved in selling since he became CEO, not in any real hands-on way. That was handled on the national accounts level. He just helped close the deal, nudged things along, assured the really big customers that the guy at the top cared. It was remarkable how far a little face time with the CEO went with customers.

He was normally good at this, the firm handshake and the clap on the back, the no-bullshit straight answer that everyone always found so refreshing. This morning, though, he felt a steady pulse of anxiety, a dull stomachache. Maybe it was a rebound reaction to the Ambien he'd taken last night, that tiny sliver of a pill that lulled him to sleep. Maybe it was the three cups of coffee instead of his usual two. Or maybe it was the fact that Stratton really, *really* needed this deal.

After Victoria finished her presentation, the lights came up, and the two lead guys from Atlas McKenzie went right up to him. One, the Senior VP of Real Estate, was a slight, whey-faced man of around fifty with full, almost female lips, long lashes, a permanently bland expression. He didn't speak much. His colleague, the VP for Facilities Management, was a stubby man, all torso, with a heavy five-o'clock shadow, a beetle brow, obviously dyed jet-black hair. He reminded Nick of Richard Nixon.

"And I thought you guys just did chairs and filing cabinets," said Nixon, flashing bright white teeth with a prominent center gap.

"Far from it," Nick chuckled. They knew better; Stratton had been courting them for months, making their business case, running a long series of off-site meetings that Nick had thankfully been spared. "Listen, if you need to check your e-mail or your voice mail or whatever, we've got a wireless campsite down the hall."

The whey-faced man, whose name was Hardwick, sidled up to Nick and said silkily, "I hope you don't mind a rather direct question."

"Of course not." The delicate-featured, blank-faced Hardwick was a killer, a genuine corporate assassin; he could have been an apparatchik out of the old Soviet Politburo.

Hardwick unzipped a Gucci leather portfolio and pulled out a clipping. Nick recognized it; it was an article from *Business Week* headlined, "Has Midas Lost His Touch?" There was a picture of the legendary Willard Osgood, the crusty old founder of Fairfield Equity Partners—the man who'd bought Stratton—with his Coke-bottle glasses and leathery face. The article focused mostly on "the millions in pretax losses incurred by Stratton, once the fastest growing office-furniture company in the U.S." It talked about Osgood's "vaunted Midas touch for picking quality companies and growing them steadily over the long term" and asked, "What happened? Will Osgood stand idly by while one of his investments falls off a cliff? Not likely, say insiders."

Hardwick held the clipping up for a few seconds. "Is Stratton in trouble?" he asked, fixing Nick with a watery stare.

"Absolutely not," Nick replied. "Have we had a couple of lousy quarters? Hell, yeah—but so have Steelcase and Herman Miller and all the other players. We've been through two years of layoffs, as you know, and the severance costs are a bear. But we're doing what we've got to do to stay healthy in the long term."

Hardwick's voice was almost inaudible. "I understand that. But you're not a family-run company like you used to be. You're not running the whole show. I'm sure Willard Osgood's breathing down your neck."

"Osgood and his people pretty much leave us alone," Nick said. "They figure we know what we're doing—that's why they acquired us." His mouth was dry. "You know, they always like to give their companies enough rope."

Hardwick blinked, lizardlike. "We're not just buying a hell of a lot of workstations from you folks, Nick. We're buying a ten-year service contract. Are you going to be around a year or two from now?"

Nick placed a hand on Hardwick's bony shoulder. "Stratton's been around for almost seventy-five years," he said, "and I can assure you, it's going to be here long after you and I are gone."

Hardwick gave a wan smile. "I wasn't asking about Stratton. I'm asking if *you're* going to be around."

"Count on it," Nick said. He gave Hardwick's shoulder a squeeze as, out of the corner of his eye, he saw Eddie Rinaldi leaning against the wall by the entrance to the Lab, arms folded.

"Excuse me for a second," Nick said. Eddie rarely dropped by, and when he did it was always something important. Plus, Nick didn't mind taking a break in this awkward exchange.

He went up to Eddie. "What's up?"

"I got something for you. Something you better take a look at."

"Can it wait?"

"It's about your stalker. You tell me if you want to wait."

7

Eddie sat down in front of Nick's computer as if it were his own and pecked at the keyboard with two fingers. He was surprisingly adept for someone who'd never learned how to type. As he navigated through the corporate intranet to the Corporate Security area, he said, "The boys in the guard booth at your little concentration camp were more than happy to help out, of course."

"You're talking about Fenwicke Estates." Eddie smelled of cigarettes and Brut, the cologne he'd worn back in high school. Nick didn't even know they still made Brut.

"Now, *they've* got a nice setup there—high-definition, high-res Sony digital video cams positioned at the entrance and exit. Backlight compensation. Thirty frames a second. The cops didn't even ask to look at their hard-disk recorder, know that?"

"Like you said."

"Shit, they didn't even do the bare minimum, for appearances' sake. Okay." A color photo appeared on the monitor of a lanky, bespectacled figure. Eddie clicked the mouse a few times, zooming in on the figure. He was a man of around sixty with a deeply creased face, a small, tight mouth, close-cropped gray hair, eyes grotesquely magnified by the lenses of heavy-framed black glasses. Nick's heart began to thud. A few more mouse clicks, and the man's grim face took up most of the screen. The resolution wasn't bad. The man's face was clearly visible.

"Recognize him?" Eddie said.

"No."

"Well, he knows who you are."

"No doubt. What, did he just walk through? Some security."

"Climbed the fence in the wooded section, actually. Cameras there get triggered by motion sensors. No alarms there—they'd get way too many false alarms with all the animals and shit—but cameras up the wazoo."

"Great. Who is he?"

"His name is Andrew Stadler."

Nick shrugged. He'd never heard the name.

"I narrowed it down by laid-off male employees in their fifties or older, especially with outplacement irregularities. Man, I spent most of the morning looking at mug shots. My eyes are crossing. But hey, that's why I get the big bucks, right?"

Eddie double-clicked the mouse, and another photo appeared on a split screen beside the surveillance image. It was the same man, a little younger: the same heavy black glasses with the ogling eyes, the same slit of a mouth. Under this photograph was the name ANDREW M. STADLER and a social-security number, a date of birth, a Stratton employee number, a date of hire.

Nick asked, "Laid off?"

"Yes and no. They sat him down for the layoff meeting and he quit. You know, said, 'After all I've done for this company?' and 'Fuck you,' and like that."

Nick shook his head. "Never even seen the guy before."

"Spend a lot of time at the model shop?"

The model shop was where a small crew of workers—metal-benders, solderers, woodworkers—built prototypes of new Stratton products, in editions of one or two or three, from specs drawn up by the designers. The model-shop employees tended to be odd sorts, Nick had always thought. They'd all done time on the factory floor, bending metal, and they were good with their hands. They also tended to be loners and perfectionists.

"Andrew Stadler," Nick said, listening to the sound of the name, scanning the data on the man's file. "He was with the company thirty-five, thirty-six years."

"Yep. Started as an assembler on the old vertical-file-cabinet line, became a welder. Then he became a specialist level two—worked by himself in
the chair plant repairing the returns. Refused to work on any of the progressive build lines because, he said, he hated listening to other people's music.
Kept getting into fights with his floor supervisor. They learned to leave him
alone and let him do his work. When there was an opening in the model shop
five years ago, he put in for it, and they were glad to get rid of him." With another couple of clicks, Eddie brought up Stadler's employee reviews. Nick
leaned closer to read the small type. "What's this about hospitalization?"

Eddie swiveled around in Nick's chair and looked up, his half-wild eyes
staring. "He's a fucking nutcase, buddy. A brainiac and a maniac. The guy's
been in and out of the locked ward at County Medical."

"Jesus. For what?"

"Schizophrenia. Every couple of years he stops taking his meds."

Nick let his breath out slowly.

"Okay, Nick, now here's the scary part. I put in a call to the Fenwick PD.
Something like fifteen years ago, Stadler was questioned in the possible murder of an entire family that lived across the street."

Nick felt a sudden chill. "What does that mean?"

"Family called Stroup, neighbors, used to hire this guy to do repairs, odd
jobs. Mister Fix-It—guy's a mechanical genius, could fix anything. Maybe
they got into some kinda fight, maybe they looked at him wrong, who knows,
but one night there's a gas leak in their basement, something sets it off, whole
house blows."

"Jesus."

"Never proven if the whole thing was an accident or this wacko did it,
but the cops suspected he did. Never could prove it, though. Had to let him
go—no evidence. Just strong suspicion. Nick, this guy Stadler is one dangerous motherfucker. And I'll tell you something else you're not going to want to
hear. This fruitcake's got a gun."

"What?"

"There's an old safety inspection certificate in his name—found it in the
county records. Like twenty years old. And no record of sale, which means
he's still got it."

"Jesus. Get a restraining order."

Eddie made a soft, dismissive *pfft* sound. "Come on, man, TROs are bullshit. Piece of paper."

"But if he tries to go on my property again—"

"You can get him arrested for *trespassing,* man. Not for stalking. Big fucking deal. You think that's going to stop a goddamned psychopath? Guy who eviscerated your goddamned dog? Guy who hears voices, wears a tinfoil hat?"

"Jesus Christ, Eddie. We got a time-stamped image of this nut climbing the fence right around the time my dog got killed. The cops got a knife that might have prints on it. They got enough to charge the guy with my dog's death."

"Yeah, and what have they done, right? They haven't done shit."

"So how do we make them take action?"

"I don't know, man. Got to apply some serious pressure. But they're going to be busy covering their big fat asses, so they're not exactly going to snap to. I say we scare the shit out of this loon first. Once the police get involved in any real way, we gotta keep hands off Stadler. But in the meantime, we got to make sure you and your family are safe."

Nick considered for a moment. "All right. But don't do anything that'll compromise me in any way. So no getting rough with him. I just want the fucker locked up somewhere."

"Fine with me. I'll track the guy down. Meantime, my man Freddie's going over to your house this afternoon to get started on the new system. I'm having him put a rush on it."

Nick glanced at his watch. He had to head over to the monthly meeting of the Compensation Committee. "Great."

"And hey, if all else fails, remember my little loaner."

Nick lowered his voice, aware that Marjorie was at her desk on the other side of the partition and might be able to hear their voices. "I don't have a permit, Eddie."

Eddie gave a slow shake of his head. "Permit? Come on, man. You know how long it takes to go through the hoops, do all the paperwork? You can't wait that long. Look, carrying an unlicensed weapon is a misdemeanor, okay? A hundred-buck fine. And that's if you get caught. Which you won't, because you won't have to use it. Isn't that worth it to protect your family from that sick fuck? A hundred bucks?"

"All right. Get out of here—I need to check my e-mail, and then I've got three meetings stacked up."

Eddie rose. "Man, you got some fancy computer equipment up here. I could use some monitors like this for my department."

"Not up to me," Nick said. "I'm just a figurehead."

8

Scott McNally lived in a decent-sized, but perfectly ordinary, house in the Forest Hills section of Fenwick where many of the Stratton execs lived. A successful accountant could have lived here. It was a generic white colonial with green shutters, a two-car garage, a rec room, a finished basement. It was decorated generically too. Everything—the dining room set, the couches and chairs and rugs—seemed to have been bought all at once, at the same mid-priced home-furnishings store. Obviously Eden, Scott's trophy wife, didn't share Laura's interest in design.

Nick and Laura had talked about Scott's house once. He admired the fact that Scott, who was loaded from his McKinsey days, didn't try to show it off like so many financial types. Money to Scott wasn't something you spent. It was like frequent-flyer miles you never use. Still, Nick couldn't put his finger on what felt funny about Scott's house until Laura pointed out that it looked somehow *temporary*, like those short-term furnished corporate apartments.

As soon as they arrived, the kids dispersed, Julia to the bedroom of one of Scott's twin twelve-year-old daughters, and Lucas to the rec room to sit by himself and watch TV. Scott was manning the immense, stainless-steel charcoal grill, the only remotely expensive thing he seemed to own. He was wearing a black barbecue apron with a yellow hazard sign on the front of it that said DANGER MEN COOKING, and a matching DANGER MEN COOKING baseball cap.

"How's it going?" Nick said as they stood in the smoke.

"Can't complain," Scott said. "Who'd listen?"

"Think that grill's big enough?"

"A cooking surface of eight hundred and eighty square inches, big enough to burn sixty-four burgers at once. Because you just never know." He shook his head. "That's the last time I let Eden go shopping at Home Depot."

"How *is* Eden these days?"

"The same, only more so. She's become a real fitness nut. If it were up to her, we'd be feasting on texturized tofu, spirulina, and barley green juice. Her latest obsession is this Advanced Pilates course she's taking. I don't quite get how that works. Does it keep getting more advanced? Can you do graduate work in Pilates, end up with a doctorate?"

"Well, she looks great."

"Just don't call her arm candy. She'd rather be thought of as arm tempeh." Scott checked that all the knobs were set to high. "You know, I'm always kind of embarrassed when you come over. It's like the feudal lord leaving his castle to go visit the peasants in their hovels. We should be roasting a boar, really. Maybe a stag." He looked at Nick. "What would you like to drink? A flagon of mead, my liege?"

"A beer would do it."

Scott turned and began shouting to his portly nine-year-old son, who was sitting by himself on the back porch making immense bubbles using a strange gadget, a long pole with a cloth strap dangling off it. "Spencer! Spencer, will you get over here, please?"

"Aww!" Spencer whined.

"Right now!" Scott shouted. Lowering his voice a bit, he said, "Eden can't wait until he's old enough to send to Andover."

"Not you, though."

"I barely notice the kid," he said with a shrug. If Nick didn't know Scott better, he wouldn't realize Scott was kidding, doing his usual shtick. When his son was within speaking range, he said, "Spencer, could you please get Mr. Conover one of those brown bottles of beer?" To Nick he said, "You'll love this beer. It's a Belgian Abbey ale that's brewed in upstate New York."

"Got any Miller?"

"Ah, the Champagne of Beers. What I'd like to find is the beer of champagnes. I think Eden bought some Grolsch, if that'll work."

"Sure."

"Spencer, look for the green bottles that have the funny metal tops with the rubber stoppers on them, got it?"

"Dad, it's not supposed to be good for you to eat barbecued meats." Spencer folded his arms across his chest. "Do you know that barbecuing at high heat can create polycyclic aromatic hydrocarbons, which are known to be mutagens?"

Nick stared at the kid. How the hell do you learn to *pronounce* that stuff?

"Now, that's where you're wrong, son," said Scott. "They *used* to think that aromatic hydrocarbons were bad. Now they know that they're the best thing for you. What do they teach you in school, anyway?"

Spencer looked stymied, but only momentarily. "Don't say I didn't warn you if you get cancer later in life."

"I'll be dead by then, son."

"But Dad—"

"Okay, kid, so here's your burger," Scott said blithely, holding up one of the raw patties. "Go fetch yourself a bun and some ketchup, okay? So instead of cancer, you'll get salmonella and *E. coli* bacteria. Mad cow too, if you're really lucky."

Spencer seemed to get his father's sense of humor but wouldn't let on. "But I thought *E. coli* naturally colonizes the human intestine," he said.

"You don't stop, do you? Go play in traffic. But first get Mr. Conover his beer."

The boy trudged reluctantly away.

Scott chuckled. "Kids these days."

"Impressive," was all Nick could think to say.

"I'm sorry you don't want to try this Belgian ale," Scott said. "I discovered it at that dude ranch in Arizona I went to last month with my old college buddies, remember?"

"You didn't exactly rave about the place."

"Ever smell a horse up close? Anyway, I liked the beer."

"So, Spencer's a little scary, huh?"

"I guess. We first had an inkling of that when he was three and he started composing haiku using the letters from his alphabet soup."

"I don't think you appreciate how cooperative he is. If I'd asked Luke to go fetch me a beer he would have ripped my face off."

"Tough age. By the time Spencer turns sixteen we'll probably see him just once a year, at Christmas. But yeah, he's usually well behaved, and he's into math just like his dad. Of course, later, when he turns into Jeff Dahmer, we'll discover the dissected remains of dogs and cats in the backyard." He started to chuckle, and then his face fell. "Oh, shit, Nick, I forgot about your dog. I'm sorry."

"Don't worry about it."

"I can't believe I said that."

"You might want to turn the burgers. They're burning."

"Oh, right." He wrestled with a big metal spatula. "Nick, the cops have any idea who did it?"

Nick hesitated, then shook his head. "They're guessing it's a downsized employee. But I could've told 'em that."

"That narrows it down to five thousand and sixty-seven. You don't have a security system?"

"Not good enough, obviously. I mean, we're in a gated community."

"Jesus, that could happen to us too."

"Thanks for being so sensitive."

"No, I mean—sorry, but as the CFO I'm just as responsible as you are for the layoffs, and—God, you must be spooked as shit."

"Of course I am. But most of all I'm fucking pissed off."

"The cops aren't going to do anything, are they?"

"They all know someone we laid off. Alarm goes off at my house, they're not going to get off their stools at Dunkin' Donuts."

Spencer ran across the lawn with a bottle of beer in one hand and a glass in the other. "Here you go, Mr. Conover," he said, handing the beer and glass to Nick.

"Thanks, Spencer." Nick set down the glass and struggled with the complicated top of the Grolsch. He'd actually never had a bottle of the stuff outside of a bar, where they poured it for you.

Spencer circled his pudgy little arms around his dad's waist. Scott reached out his free hand and grabbed his son back, made a grunting sound.

"Hey, sweetie," he said. His face was red from the heat, and he blinked the smoke out of his eyes.

"Hey, Dad."

Nick smiled. So Spencer was a little kid, too, not just a *Jeopardy* champ.

"Shit," Scott said, as one of his burgers slipped through the grate and into the fire.

"Do this often?"

"It's my only hobby. Understand, my idea of a good time is filling out my tax return using Roman numerals." He fiddled some more with the metal spatula. "Shit," he said again, as another burger dropped into the flames. "You like well done?"

9

The architect who was doing the renovations to the Conovers' kitchen was a stodgy but affable man named Jeremiah Claflin. He wore round black glasses of the sort that some of the famous architects affected—that Japanese guy, that Swiss guy, Nick forgot their names if he ever knew them—and his white hair contrasted pleasantly with his ruddy face and curled over his shirt collar. Laura had interviewed him and several other architects from Fenwick and the surrounding towns as intensively as she'd interviewed nanny candidates years ago. It was important to her that the architect she hired not only had a portfolio of projects she admired, but also wasn't too stubborn, too much of an *artiste* that he wouldn't do exactly what she wanted.

Nick got along with Claflin, as he got along with just about everyone, but he realized early on that the architect found Nick frustrating. Sure, he was pleased to be working on the house that belonged to Stratton's CEO— that gave him certain bragging rights—and since Laura had chosen nothing but the most high-end, most ridiculously expensive appliances and cabinets and all that, Claflin was making a boatload of money for not that much design work. But Nick wasn't all that interested in the fussy little details that Laura had had such patience for, and there sure as hell were a million fussy little details. The decisions never seemed to end. Did he want the kitchen counters to have a full bullnose or half bullnose or an ogee edge? How much of an overhang? How tall did he want the backsplash to be? A self-rimming sink or an undermount? What about the height of the countertop? Jesus, Nick had a company to run.

Claflin was forever faxing him drawings and lists of questions. Nick would inevitably tell the architect to just do whatever Laura had told him to do. He really didn't give a damn about what the kitchen looked like. What he cared about—was obsessed about, really—was that it be done precisely the way Laura wanted. The renovations had been Laura's last big project, pretty much all she thought about, talked about, in the months before the accident. Nick suspected that part of the reason she'd poured so much of herself into it was that the kids were getting older, and being a mom was no longer a full-time job. After Lucas was born, she'd quit her job teaching art history at St. Thomas More College. She tried to get her teaching position back when the kids were older, but she couldn't. She'd been mommy-tracked. She missed teaching, missed the intellectual engagement.

Laura was by far the smarter one in the marriage. Nick had gone to Michigan State on a full-boat hockey scholarship, busted his hump to get C's and B's, while Laura had breezed through Swarthmore *summa cum laude*. It was like she had a deep well of creative energy inside her that needed to be tapped or she'd go crazy, and the renovations filled a need for her.

But there was more to it: Laura had wanted to knock down the sterile old kitchen, which looked like no one ever used it, and turn it into a hearth, a great room where the whole family could gather. Laura, who was an excellent cook, could make dinner while the kids did their homework or hung out around the kitchen island. The whole family could be together comfortably.

The least Nick could do to honor her was to make sure the damned kitchen was done the way she wanted.

Their marriage had been far from perfect—hell, they'd been arguing the night she was killed, as he'd never forget—but Nick had learned you choose your battles. You made unspoken deals sometimes, ceded turf. Laura, who'd grown up in a shambling Victorian on the Hill, a pediatrician's kid, wanted to live a certain way, namely better than the way in which she'd been brought up. She wanted the elegance and style she never had growing up in a house that was always in some state of chaos and disrepair. She subscribed to *Architectural Digest* and *Elle Décor* and half a dozen other magazines that all looked the same, and she was always tearing out photos and two-page spreads and adding them to a steadily thickening file folder that she might as well have labeled DREAM HOUSE. To Nick, having a house with more than two bedrooms and a backyard and a kitchen you didn't eat in already bordered on unimaginable luxury.

Claflin was waiting for him in the kitchen when he arrived, twenty minutes late. From the family room Nick could hear Julia and her best friend, Emily, playing a computer game called *The Sims* in which they created their own creepily real-looking human beings and bent them to their will. Julia and Emily were shrieking with laughter over something.

"Busy day?" Claflin asked. His tone was jovial, but his eyes betrayed annoyance at being kept waiting.

Nick apologized as he shook the architect's hand, and then his eye was immediately caught by something. The countertops were in. He went up to the island and realized that, even to his untrained eye, something looked wrong.

"I see they've put a new alarm system in," Claflin said. "Fast work."

Nick nodded. He'd noticed the white touch pads on the wall as he entered. "The island," he said. "That's not what Laura wanted."

She'd designed a big island in the center of the kitchen around which the whole family could gather, sitting on stools, while she made dinner. But you sure as hell couldn't sit at this thing. It had walls of black granite that came up about two feet, no overhang, no place for stools.

Claflin beamed. "None of your guests will have to see the cooking mess from the dining table," he said. "Yet it works perfectly as a food-prep station. Clever, don't you think?"

Nick hesitated. "You can't sit at it," he said.

"True," Claflin conceded, his smile fading, "but there's no unsightly mess. That open-kitchen thing, that's the big problem with this great-room design that no one talks about. You have this stunning kitchen with all the best appliances, and this big farmhouse table where your guests eat their dinner, and what do they end up looking at? A mess of dirty pots and pans on the counters and island. This solves that problem."

"But the kids can't sit around it."

"Believe me, that's trivial compared to—"

"Laura wanted everyone to be able to sit around the kitchen island. She wanted to be able to see the kids hanging out here, doing their homework or reading or talking or whatever while she was making dinner."

"Nick," Claflin said slowly, "you don't cook, right? And Laura's—well, she's . . ."

"Laura wanted this big, open, hang-out kitchen," Nick said. "That's what she wanted, and that's what we're going to have."

Claflin looked at him for a few seconds. "Nick, I faxed you the specs, and you signed off on them."

"I probably didn't even look at them. I told you we're doing everything exactly according to Laura's wishes."

"This has already been cut. We can't . . . send it *back*. You own it."

"I really don't give a shit," Nick said. "You get the stone guy back here and have him recut it the way Laura wanted."

"Nick, there's a logic to this design that—"

"Just do it." Nick's voice was arctic. "Are we clear?"

10

As soon as Claflin left, Julia entered the kitchen. She was wearing a gray sweatshirt emblazoned with the arch-shaped logo of the Michigan Wolverines. Her friend was still sitting at the computer in the family room, busily tyrannizing the lives of her Sims family like some high-tech Hitler.

"Daddy, are you the president of Stratton?"

"President and CEO, baby, don't you know that? Give me a hug."

She ran to him as if she'd been waiting for permission, threw her arms around him. Nick leaned over and gave her a kiss on her forehead, thought: *She's just figuring this out?*

"Emily says you fired half the people in Fenwick."

Emily looked up from the computer screen, stole a furtive glance at Nick.

"We had to lay a lot of really good people off," Nick said. "To save the company."

"She says you fired her uncle."

Ah, so that was it. Nick shook his head. "I didn't know that. I'm sorry to hear it, Emily."

Emily gave him an imperious, condescending look, almost withering, quite remarkable for a ten-year-old girl. "Uncle John's been unemployed for almost two years. He says he gave everything to Stratton and you ruined his life."

Nick wanted to respond—*it wasn't me, and anyway we provided extensive outplacement counseling, you know*—but once you start debating with ten-year-olds you might as well hang it up. He was saved by the honk of a car horn. "Okay, Em, you'd better get going. You don't want to keep your mom waiting."

Emily's mom drove a brand-new gold Lexus LX 470 roughly half as long as a city block. She wore a white Fred Perry tennis shirt, white shorts, a Fenwick Country Club windbreaker, expensive-looking white tennis shoes. She had great, tanned legs, short auburn hair coiffed in a high-fashion cut, a giant glittering diamond engagement ring. Her husband was a plastic surgeon who was rumored to be having an affair with his receptionist, and if even Nick, who was completely out of the gossip stream, had heard it, it was probably true.

"Hello, Nick." Her cigarette-husky voice was chilly and bone-dry.

"Hi, Jacqueline. Emily should be out in a second. I had to tear her away from the computer."

Jacqueline smiled in an artful semblance of sociability. Nick knew her only enough to say hi: maintaining friendships among the school parents had been Laura's job. Not that long ago, Jacqueline Renfro would light up when she saw him at school plays and parents' nights, as if he were a long-lost friend. But people didn't suck up to him so much anymore.

"How's Jim?" he said.

"Oh, you know," she said airily. "When people lose their jobs they don't get Botox quite as often."

"Emily mentioned that her uncle got laid off from Stratton. Is he your brother or Jim's?"

She paused, then said sternly, "Mine, but Emily shouldn't have said that. Honestly, she has no manners. I'll talk to her."

"No, no—she was saying what was on her mind. Where'd your brother work?"

"I don't—" she faltered, then she called out, "Emily, what is *taking* you so long?"

They stood in awkward silence for a moment until her daughter emerged from the house, struggling under the weight of a backpack the size of a Sherpa's.

Julia didn't look up from the computer monitor as Nick approached and asked, "Where's your brother?"

"I don't know."

"You finish your homework?"

Julia didn't answer.

"You heard me, right?"

"What?" What was it with the selective hearing? He could whisper "Krispy Kreme" in the kitchen and she'd come bounding.

"Your homework. We're eating dinner in half an hour—it's Marta's night off. Turn off the computer."

"But I'm in the middle—"

"Save it and shut down. Come on, sweetie."

He went to the foot of the stairs and shouted up for Lucas. No reply. The house was so unnecessarily big, though, that sound didn't carry far. Nick went upstairs, past Laura's study, its door unopened since her death, to Lucas's room.

He knocked. The door, slightly ajar, opened inward a few inches. He pushed it open the rest of the way, called, "Luke?" No answer; no Lucas here. His desk lamp was on, a textbook open. He walked over to see which textbook it was, inadvertently bumping against the desk. The iMac's flat panel screen came out of sleep mode, displaying a profusion of colorful flesh-tone photographs. Nick looked again and saw naked bodies in various sexual contortions. He came closer to get a closer look.

The entire screen was taken up with pop-up windows of slutty-looking women with huge boobs in garish shades of pink and orange. "Real Amateur Pussy," one window read, the word "real" flashing red like a neon sign.

Nick's first reaction was a very male one: he looked even closer, intrigued, felt a stirring he hadn't felt in months. Immediately after, though, he felt disgusted at the tawdriness of the images—who were these girls who were willing to do this stuff for all the heavy-breathing Internet world to see? And then the realization washed over him that this was Lucas's computer, that his son was looking at all this stuff. If Laura had discovered this, she would have freaked out, called him at work, demanded that he come home at once and have a Talk with his son.

Whereas Nick didn't know what to think, how to react. He was at a loss. The kid was sixteen, and developmentally a fairly advanced sixteen at that. Of course he was interested in sex. Nick remembered when he and a buddy, around the same age, had found a matted, waterlogged *Playboy* in the woods. They'd dried it out carefully, pored over it as if it were the Dead Sea Scrolls, hid it in Nick's garage. Looking back on it now, it was amazing how different smut was in those days, how innocent, though it sure didn't seem it at the time. The photos in *Playboy* were so heavily airbrushed that it was something of a shock when Nick first got an up-close glimpse of his first real-life tits not long afterward, in the finished basement of his first real girlfriend, Jody Catalfano. Jody, the cutest girl in the class, had been after him for months, was ready long before he was. Her breasts were far smaller than the voluptuous babes in *Playboy*, her nipples larger and darker with a few stray hairs around the edges of the aureoles.

But this stuff, garish and flashing, was way too *real*, somehow. It was more blatant, more perverted than anything from Nick's fevered adolescence. And here it was, a couple of mouse clicks away. It wasn't half-buried under dead leaves in the woods, didn't require conservation efforts or concealment in an empty Pennzoil box in a garage. On some level it was almost sickening. And what if Julia had wandered in here and seen it?

He picked up Lucas's desk phone and called his son's cell.

Lucas answered after five rings, fumbling with the phone a long time. "Yeah?" In the background was loud music, raucous voices.

"Luke, where the hell are you?"

A pause. "What's up?"

"What's *up*? It's suppertime."

"I ate already."

"We have dinner together, remember?" This "dinner together" thing had become one of Nick's recent obsessions, particularly since Laura was gone. He sometimes felt that if he didn't insist on it, the remains of his family could all fly away by centrifugal force.

Another pause. "Where are you, Luke?"

"All right," Lucas said and hung up.

An hour later, Lucas still wasn't home. Julia was hungry, so the two of them sat down to dinner at the small round table that had been temporarily placed in one corner of the kitchen, away from most of the construction. Marta had set the table for the three of them before going out for the evening. In the warm oven was a roast chicken, tented with foil. Nick brought the chicken and rice and broccoli to the table, remembering to put trivets under the chicken pan so he didn't scorch the table. He expected a fight over the broccoli, and he got it. Julia would accept only rice and a chicken drumstick, and Nick was too wiped out to argue.

"I like Mommy's better," Julia said. "This is too dry."

"It's been in the oven for a couple of hours."

"Mommy made the best fried chicken."

"She sure did, baby," Nick said. "Eat."

"Where's Luke?"

"He's on his way back." *Taking his damned time of it too*, Nick thought.

Julia stared at the chicken leg on her plate as if it were a giant cockroach. Finally, she said, "I don't like it here."

Nick thought for a moment, unsure how to respond. "Like it where?"

"Here," she said unhelpfully.

"This house?"

"We don't have any neighbors."

"We do, but . . ."

"We don't know any of them. It's not a neighborhood. It's just . . . houses and trees."

"People do keep to themselves here," he conceded. "But your mommy wanted us to move here because she thought it would be safer than our last house."

"Well, it's not. Barney . . ." She stopped, her eyes welling up with tears, resting her chin in her hands.

"But we will be now, with this new security system in."

"Nothing like that ever happened in our old house," she pointed out.

The front door opened, setting off a high alert tone, and a few seconds later Lucas trundled noisily into the kitchen, threw his backpack down on the floor. He seemed to get taller and broader by the day. He wore a dark blue Old Navy sweatshirt, baggy cargo pants with the waistband of his boxer shorts showing, and some white scarflike thing under his backwards baseball cap.

"What's that on your head?" Nick asked anyway.

"Do-rag, why?"

"That like a hip-hop thing?"

Lucas shook his head, rolled his eyes. "I'm not hungry," he said. "I'm going upstairs."

"Sit with us anyway, Luke," Julia pleaded. "Come on."

"I've got a lot of homework," Lucas said as he left the kitchen without turning back.

11

Nick followed his son upstairs. "We have to have a talk," he said.

Lucas groaned. "What now?" When he reached the open door to his room, he said, "You been in here?"

"Sit down, Luke."

Lucas noticed the computer monitor facing the door, and he leaped toward it, spun it away. "I don't want you going in my room."

"Sit down."

Lucas sat on the edge of his bed, hunched over with his elbows propped on his knees, his chin resting on his hands, a gesture that Julia had recently started imitating. He stared malevolently.

"You're not allowed to go to porn sites," Nick said.

Lucas blinked. His angry blue eyes were crystal clear, innocent and pure. He was trying to grow something under his chin, Nick noticed. For a moment Lucas seemed to be debating whether to own up to the evidence so prominently on display. Then he said: "There's nothing there I don't know about, Nick. I'm sixteen."

"Cut out the 'Nick' stuff."

"Okay, *Dad*," he said with a surly twist. "Hey, at least I'm not going to snuff or torture sites. You should see the shit that's out there."

"You do that again and your Internet access gets cut off, understand?"

"You can't do that. I need e-mail for school. It's required."

"Then I'll leave you with just AOL with whatever those controls are."

"You can't *do* that! I got to do research on the Internet."

"I'll bet. Where were you this afternoon?"

"Friend's."

"Sounded like a bar or something."

Lucas stared as if he weren't going to dignify this with a response.

"What happened to Ziggy?"

"Ziggy's an asshole."

"He's your best friend."

"Look, you don't know him, all right?"

"Then who are these new kids you're hanging out with?"

"Just friends."

"What are their names?"

"Why do you care?"

Nick bit his lip, thought for a moment. "I want you to go back to Underberg." Lucas had seen a counselor for four months after Laura's death until he quit, complaining that Underberg was "full of shit."

"I'm not going back there. No way."

"You've got to talk to someone. You won't talk to me."

"About what?"

"For God's sake, Lucas, you've just been through one of the most traumatic things a kid can go through. Of course you're having a hard time. You think it's any easier on your sister, or on me?"

"Forget it," Lucas said, raising his voice sharply. "Don't even go there."

"What's that supposed to mean?"

Lucas shot him a pitying look. "I got homework," he said, getting up from the bed and walking over to his desk.

Nick poured himself a Scotch on the rocks, sat in the family room and watched TV for a while, but nothing held his interest. He started feeling a mild, pleasant buzz. Around midnight he went up to his room. Both Julia's and Lucas's lights were off. The newly installed alarm touch pad in his bedroom glowed green, announced READY in black letters. *Ready for what?* he

SECURITY

59

thought. The installer had called him and given him the ten-minute low-down that afternoon. If a door was open somewhere, it would say something like FAULT—LIVING ROOM DOOR. If someone moved downstairs it would say, FAULT—MOTION SENSOR, FAMILY ROOM or whatever.

He brushed his teeth, stripped down to his shorts, and climbed into the king-size bed. Next to Laura's side of the bed was the same stack of books that had been there since the night of the accident. Marta dusted them off but knew enough not to put them away. The effect was as if she were away on a business trip and might come back in, keys jingling, at any moment. One of the books, Nick always noticed with a pang, was an old course catalog from St. Thomas More College that had a listing for her art history class. She used to look at it sometimes at night, regretful.

The sheets were cool and smooth. He rolled over something lumpy: one of Julia's Beanie Babies. He smiled, tossed it out of the way. Lately she'd taken to leaving a different Beanie Baby in his bed each night, a little game of hers. He guessed it was her way of sleeping with Daddy, by proxy, since she hadn't been allowed to sleep in the parental bed for some time.

He closed his eyes, but his mind raced. The Scotch hadn't helped at all. A jerky, low-quality movie kept playing in his mind: The cop saying, *Do you have any enemies, Mr. Conover?* Julia's hot, wet tears soaking his shirt by the side of the pool.

Fifteen, twenty minutes later he gave up, switched on the bathroom light, and fished out an Ambien from the brown plastic pharmacy bottle and dry-swallowed it.

He turned on the bedside lamp and read for a while. Nick wasn't a reader, never read fiction, only enjoyed biographies but didn't have time to read anything anymore. He hated reading those books on business management that so many of his Leadership Team kept on their shelves.

After a while he began feeling drowsy, finally, and turned off the light.

He had no idea how much later it was when he was awakened by a rapid beeping tone. Eddie's installers had set the system to go off only in his bedroom or his study, and not too loud, when he was in the house.

He sat up, his heart pounding, his head filled with sludge. For a moment he didn't know where he was or what that strange insistent beeping was.

When he realized where it was coming from, he leaped out of bed and squinted at the green touch pad's LED.

It was flashing: ALARM***PERIMETER***ALARM.

Keeping his footsteps light, in order not to wake the kids, he went downstairs to investigate.

12

Nick padded barefoot downstairs, the house dark and silent. He glanced at one of the new touch pads at the foot of the stairs. It too was flashing: ***ALARM***PERIMETER***.

His brain felt viscous and slow. It was an effort to think clearly. Only the rapid beating of his heart, the adrenaline-fueled anxiety, kept him moving forward.

He paused for a moment, considering which way to go.

Then a light came on *inside* the house, flooding him with panic. He walked quickly toward the light—his study?—until he remembered that the software that ran the cameras had been programmed to detect pixel changes, shifts in light or movement. Not only did the cameras start recording when there was a change in light, but the software was connected to a relay that automatically switched on a couple of inside lights, to scare off potential intruders by making them think someone in the house had been awakened, even if no one was home.

He slowed his pace but kept going, trying to think. The motion-sensor software worked by zones. That meant that whoever or whatever was there was on the side of the lawn nearest his study. Eddie's guy had set up the system so that the alarm company wasn't alerted unless the house itself was broken into, since a large animal moving across the lawn was enough to set off the perimeter alarm. Otherwise there'd be too many false alarms. But if something did cross the lawn, the cameras started and the lights went on.

A deer. Probably that was all it was.

Still, he had to be sure.

He kept going through the family room, down the hall to his study. The lights were on.

He slowed as he entered the study, the sludge in his head starting to clear. No one was here, of course. The only sound was the faint hum from his computer. He looked at the French doors and the darkness beyond. Nothing there; nothing outside. A false alarm.

The room went dark, startling him momentarily, until he remembered that the lights were also programmed to go off after two minutes. He walked through the study, approaching the glass panes of the French doors, staring out.

He could see nothing.

Nothing out there but watery moonlight glinting on the trees and shrubbery.

He glanced back at the illuminated face of his desk clock. Ten minutes after two. The kids were asleep upstairs, Marta presumably back from her night out and asleep in her bedroom in the wing off the kitchen. He glanced back out through the windowpanes, checking again.

After a few seconds he turned to leave the study.

The lawn outside lit up. The floodlights came on, jolting Nick. He spun back around, looked outside, saw a figure approaching from a stand of trees.

He moved closer to the glass, squinted. A man in some kind of trench coat that flapped as he walked. He was crossing the lawn slowly, headed directly toward Nick.

Nick went to the touch pad and deactivated the alarm system. Then he reached for the French doors' lever handle, thought for a moment, and went to his desk. He took the key from the middle drawer and unlocked the bottom one, slid it open, took out the pistol.

He removed it from its oilcloth.

Blood rushed through his head; he could hear it in his ears.

Despite assuring him he'd never have to use the thing, Eddie had left it loaded. Now Nick gripped the weapon, pulled back the slide to chamber the first round, as Eddie had instructed, let the slide go.

He turned slowly, the weapon at his side, careful to keep his finger away from the trigger. With his left hand he turned the handle and opened the French doors. He stepped outside, the soil of the newly seeded lawn cold against his bare feet.

"Stop right there," he called.

The man kept advancing. Now Nick could make out his heavy black eyeglasses, his ogling eyes, his brush-cut gray hair, his bent figure. The man, his name was Andrew Stadler, walked straight ahead, heedlessly.

Nick raised the gun, barked: *"Freeze!"*

Under the flapping trench coat, Stadler wore white pants, a white shirt. He was muttering to himself, all the while staring at Nick as he came closer and closer.

He's a fucking nutcase, buddy . . .

The guy kept coming, goggling eyes staring as if he didn't even see the gun, or if he did, he didn't give a shit.

Eddie's words. *A maniac. The guy's been in and out of the locked ward at County Medical.*

"Don't you fucking take another step!" Nick shouted.

Now the man's mutterings were starting to become distinct. The man raised his hand, pointed a finger at Nick, his expression malevolent, enraged. "Never safe," the man croaked. He smiled, his hands fluttering to his sides, to his coat pockets. The smile was like a twitch: it came and disappeared several times in succession, no logic to it.

Stadler was questioned in the possible murder of an entire family that lived across the street.

"One more step, and I shoot!" Nick shouted, raising the weapon with both hands, aiming at the center of the lunatic's body.

"You're never going to be safe," the man in white said, one hand fumbling in his pocket, now *rushing* toward Nick, toward the open door.

Nick squeezed the trigger, and everything seemed to happen all at once. There was a popping sound, loud but not nearly as loud as he'd expected. The pistol bucked in his hands, flew backward at him. An empty shell casing flew off to one side. Nick could smell gunpowder, sulfuric and acrid.

The maniac stumbled, sank to his knees. A dark blotch appeared on his white shirt, a corona of blood. The bullet had entered his upper chest. Nick watched, his pulse racing, still gripping the pistol in both hands, leveling it at the man until he could be sure the man was down.

Suddenly, with surprisingly agility, the madman sprang to his feet with a throaty growl, shouting, "No!" in an aggrieved, almost offended voice. He propelled himself toward Nick, said, *"Never—safe!"*

The man was less than six feet away now, and Nick fired, aiming higher this time, wild with fear and resolve. He was able to stabilize the weapon better now, felt a spray of powder sting his face, and he saw the man tumble backward and to one side, mouth open, but this time he did not break his fall. He landed on his side, legs splayed at a funny angle, expelling a guttural, animallike sound.

Nick froze, watched in silence for a few seconds.

His ears rang. Gripping the weapon in both hands, he stepped to one side to see the man's face. The lunatic's mouth was gaping, blood seeping over his lips, his chin. The black glasses had fallen off somewhere; now the eyes, much smaller without the magnification of the lenses, stared straight ahead.

The man exhaled with a rattling noise and was silent.

Nick stood, dazed, flooded with adrenaline, even more terrified at this moment than he had been a minute earlier. He pointed the pistol, almost accusingly, at the man and walked slowly up to him. Nick thrust out his right foot, nudged the man's chest, testing.

The man rolled backward, his mouth open, a mouthful of silver fillings glinting, the eyes now staring into the night sky, blood seeping. The high metallic ringing in Nick's ears had begun to subside, and everything was strangely, eerily silent. From very far away, Nick thought he could hear a faint rustling of leaves. A dog now barked, far in the distance, then stopped.

The man's chest was not moving; he was not breathing. Nick leaned over him, the pistol now dangling in his left hand by his side. He placed his right forefinger on the man's throat and felt no pulse. This was no surprise; the staring eyes had already announced that the maniac lay dead.

He's dead, Nick thought. I've killed him.

I've killed a man.

He was suffused with terror. I killed this guy. Another voice in his head began to plead, defensive and frightened as a little boy.

I had to. I had no choice. I had no fucking choice.

I had to stop him.

Maybe he's just unconscious, Nick thought desperately. He felt the man's throat again, couldn't find the pulse. He grabbed one of the man's rough, dry hands, pressed against the inside of his wrist, felt nothing.

He let go of the hand. It dropped to the ground.

He poked again at the man's chest with his toes, but he knew the truth.

The man was dead.

The crazy man, this stalker, this man who would have dismembered my children the way he butchered my dog, lay dead on the freshly seeded lawn, surrounded by tiny sprouts of grass that poked out sparsely from the moist black earth.

Oh, Jesus God, Nick thought. I've just killed a man.

He stood up but felt his knees give way. He sank to the ground, felt tears running down his cheeks. Tears of relief? Of terror? Not, certainly not, of despair or of sadness.

Oh, please, Jesus, he thought. What do I do now?

What do I do now?

For a minute, maybe two, he remained on his knees, sunken in the soft ground. It was as if he were in a church, a place he hadn't been in decades, praying. That was what it felt like. He was praying on the soft, hydroseeded lawn, his back turned to the crumpled body. For a few seconds he wondered if he was going to lose consciousness, pass out on the soil. He waited for a sound, the sound of someone in the house, awakened by the gunshots, running out to see what had happened. The kids couldn't see this, mustn't be allowed to see it.

But not a sound. No one had awakened, not even Marta. Gathering his strength, he rose, dropping the weapon to the ground, moving back toward the study as if in a trance. The lights came on: the motion sensor software again.

He could barely stand. He sank into his desk chair, folding his arms on the desk, resting his head on his arms. His mind was racing, but to no purpose; he was not thinking clear thoughts. His brains felt scrambled.

He was terrified.

What do I do now?

Who can help me? Who do I call?

He lifted the handset on his desk phone, pressed the number nine.

Nine-one-one. The police.

No, I can't. Not yet. He hung up.

Must think. What do I tell them? Everything depends on this. Was it self-defense pure and simple?

The police, who despised him so much, would be looking to hang him. Once they showed up, they'd be asking all sorts of questions, and one wrong answer might put him in prison for years. Nick knew that, given how groggy and out of it he was, he might well be railroaded by the cops.

He needed help.

He picked up the handset again, punched the cell number of the one person who would know what to do now.

Dear God, he thought as the phone rang.

Help me.

Eddie's voice was sleep-thickened, clipped. "Yeah?"

"Eddie, it's Nick."

"Nick—Jesus, it's fucking—"

"Eddie, I need you to come over to my house. Right now." He swallowed. A cool breeze swept through the room from the open doors, making him shiver.

"Now? Nick, are you out of your—"

"Now, Eddie. Oh, God. Right now."

"What the hell is it?"

"The stalker," Nick said. His mouth was dry, and the words stuck in his throat.

"He's *there*?" For a few seconds, Nick couldn't answer. Eddie went on, "Christ, Nick, what *is* it? My God, don't tell me he got to your *kids*!"

"I—I gotta call nine-one-one, but—I need to know what to *tell* them, and—"

"What the fuck *happened*, Nick?" Eddie barked.

"I killed him," Nick heard himself say softly. He paused to think of how to explain it, blinked a few times, then fell silent. What was there to say, really? Eddie had to have figured it out.

"*Shit*, Nick—"

"When I call the cops, they're going to—"

"Nick, you listen to me," Eddie interrupted. "Do *not* pick up the phone again. I'll be there in ten minutes."

The phone slipped from Nick's hand as if his fingers were greased. He felt a sob welling up.

Please, dear God, Nick thought. Make this go away.

13

Standing in the shadowed recesses of the front porch, Nick sipped from a mug of instant coffee and waited. Apart from physical sensations—the chill of the night air, the warmth of the mug against his palms, the gusts of wind— he felt nothing. He was beyond numb. He was a husk, an empty body standing on a porch at night while above him hovered Nick Conover, watching in disbelief. This hadn't happened. This was a nightmare that, even as he experienced it in real time, he told himself was merely a bad dream that he'd awaken from, soon enough, but not before he moved through the twisting, steadily more awful script. At the same time he understood that it wasn't a dream. Any minute now, Eddie's car would pull into the driveway and Nick, by telling another person, seeking his advice, would make it real.

As if on cue, Eddie's Pontiac GTO coasted quietly up the driveway, headlights extinguished. Eddie got out, shut the door quietly, jogged up to Nick. He was wearing sweatpants and a tan Carhartt jacket.

"Nicky, tell me exactly what happened?" Eddie's face was creased, unfamiliarly, with concern. His shoulders were hunched. His breath stank of stale booze; he looked like he'd been asleep.

Nick chewed the inside of his cheek, looking away.

Eddie twisted his head to one side. "All right. Where is he?"

"Okay," Eddie said. "Okay."

His hands made strange, resolute chopping motions in the air. "Okay." He stood over the crumpled body. The floodlights at his back cast a long, spindly shadow.

"Do you think anyone heard?" His first question. A strange one, it seemed to Nick. Not "what happened?"

Nick shook his head. He spoke in a low voice, hoping Eddie would do the same. "Marta or the kids would have gotten up if they did."

"Neighbors?"

"Hard to say. The security guys down at the booth normally drive up if they think there's a problem."

"No lights went on at any of the neighbors' houses?"

"Look for yourself. Our nearest neighbor is hundreds of feet away. Trees and everything between us. I can't see them, they can't see me."

Eddie nodded. "The Smith and Wesson's a .380. Makes kind of a loud popping noise." He leaned over to peer more closely at Stadler. "Did he enter the house?"

"No."

Eddie nodded again. Nick couldn't tell from his expression whether that was good or not.

"He see you?"

"Sure. I was standing right here."

"You told him to stop."

"Of course. Eddie, what the hell am I—"

"You did the right thing." His voice was low, soothing. "You had no fucking choice."

"He kept on going. He wouldn't stop."

"He would have attacked your kids if you didn't stop him."

"I know."

Eddie let out a long, slow breath, a little quaver in it. "Shit, man."

"What?"

"Shit."

"It was self-defense," Nick said.

Eddie drew closer to Stadler's corpse. "How many shots?"

"I think two."

"Chest and the head. The mouth."

Nick noticed that the bleeding had stopped. It looked black in the artificial light. The man's skin was white and waxen, his eyes staring.

"You must have a tarp here, all the construction."

"A tarp?"

"Canvas. Or plastic, better."

"A tarp?"

"A tarpaulin, Nick. You know. A big heavy plastic sheet. Or contractor bags if you have them. You must have those around."

"What for?"

"The hell do you think? Any idea how hard it is to carry a dead body?"

Nick felt a spasm of fear in his abdomen. "We got to call the cops, Eddie."

Eddie looked at Nick incredulously. "You are fucking kidding me. You think you even have a choice here?"

"What the hell else are we going to do?"

"Then what'd you call me for, Nick?"

"I—" He had a point, of course. "This is bad, Eddie. Really bad."

"You just used my fucking gun. To kill a guy, okay? Are you hearing me? My gun. We really don't have a choice."

14

Nick stared, didn't know what to say, went back into the study, Eddie right behind him. Nick sat in one of the side chairs, rubbed the heels of his hands into his eyes.

"It was self-defense," he repeated.

"Maybe."

"Maybe? What are you talking about, maybe? This guy was dangerous."

"Did he have a gun?"

"No. But how the hell could I have known that?"

"You couldn't," Eddie conceded. "Maybe you saw something glint, a knife or a gun or something, you couldn't be sure."

"I saw him reach in his pocket. You told me the guy has a gun—I figured he was reaching for a weapon."

Eddie nodded, turned grimly toward the doors, and stepped back into the inky blackness. He returned a minute or so later, some objects in his cupped hands. He dumped them onto the coffee table. "Wallet, key ring. No knife, no gun, no nothing on the guy."

"I didn't fucking *know* that," Nick said. "He kept saying, 'You're not safe.'"

"Nick, of *course* you didn't know. Jesus, I mean, you were dealing with a fucking psycho, a guy's gotta do what a guy's gotta do. That's not it."

"The truth is, you lent me your gun as protection," Nick said. "Temporarily. You said it's a misdemeanor."

Eddie slammed his fist into his palm. "You still don't fucking get it, do you? You killed the dude outside the house, not inside."

"He was trying to get in, believe me."

"*I* know that. You're allowed to use physical force to terminate attempted commission of criminal trespass." The words sounded unnatural, halting, coming out of his mouth, as if he'd memorized them during his cop days. "But not deadly physical force. That's the premises law. See, Nick, the law says deadly physical force can only be used in the face of deadly physical force."

"But given the guy's record—"

"I'm not saying you wouldn't have a chance of beating this. But what the hell you think's going to happen to you, huh?"

Nick finished his mug of coffee. The caffeine only went so far in counteracting the sleeping pill; it was adrenaline and fear that were keeping him functioning. "I'm the CEO of a major corporation, Eddie. I'm a respected member of the community."

"You're fucking Nick the Slasher!" Eddie hissed. "What the fuck do you think's going to happen to you? And to your family? Think about it. You think the cops are going to cut you any slack?"

"The law's the law."

"Shit! Don't talk to me about the law, Nick. I know the law. I know how it gets twisted and bent if the cops want it to. I've done it, okay?"

"Not all cops," Nick said.

Eddie flashed him a look of barely concealed hostility. "Put it to you this way. The locals'll have no choice but to charge you, right?"

"Maybe."

"For absolute fucking sure. And when it comes to trial—and it will, you can be sure of that—yeah, you might beat it. Maybe. After ten months of a *nightmare*. Yeah, you could get lucky, get a reasonable prosecutor, but even they're going to face all sorts of pressure to string up Nick the Slasher. You're going to be facing a jury of twelve people who all hate your guts—man, the thought of locking you up . . . I mean, in a town this size, there isn't going to be a juror in the pool who doesn't know someone, a friend or a relative, that you fired, right? You saw what that jury did to Martha Stewart for a little insider trading. You fucking murdered an old man, are you with me yet? A sick old man."

"The bottom line is, I'm innocent." Nick was feeling ill again, thought he might throw up, looked around for his metal wastebasket in case he did.

"You don't get to say what the bottom line is, okay?"

"But it was fucking *self-defense!*"

"Hey, don't argue with *me*! I'm on *your* side. But it's homicide, Nick. Manslaughter at a minimum. You say it's self-defense, but you got no witnesses, you got no injuries, and you got a dead guy who was unarmed. I don't care how much money you spend on a lawyer—you get tried here, in Fenwick. And what the hell you think's going to happen to your kids during this goddamned media circus, huh? You have any fucking *idea* what this is going to do to them? You think it's hard for them, dealing with Laura and the layoffs and everything? Imagine you on trial for murder. A fucking lynch mob, Nick. You want to put your kids through that?"

Nick didn't reply. He felt frozen in the chair, completely at a loss.

"They're probably going to send you away, Nick. Five, ten years if you're lucky. Sentence like that, you're going to miss your kids' childhood. And they grow up with a jailbird father. They don't have a mom, Nick. All they got is you. You gonna play Russian roulette with your kids, Nick?"

Eddie's stare was unrelenting, furious.

Finally, Nick spoke. "What are you suggesting?"

PART TWO
TRACE EVIDENCE

15

Audrey Rhimes's pager shrilled in the semidarkness.

She jolted awake, out of a blissful dream of her childhood, a warm summer day, going down a Slip 'N Slide that went on and on and on, in her family's steeply canted backyard. Ordinarily 6:30 A.M. wasn't early at all, but her shift had ended at midnight, and after that came the usual unpleasantness with Leon, so she'd gotten maybe four hours of sleep.

She felt raw, vulnerable like a freshly hatched chick.

Audrey was a woman who liked routine, schedule, regularity. This was a personality trait that didn't go well with her job as a detective with the Fenwick Police Major Case Team. Calls could come at any time of day or night. Though she could no longer remember why, this was a job she'd wanted, a job she fought for. She was not just the only African-American member of the Major Case unit but the only woman—the real difficulty, it turned out.

Leon groaned, rolled over, buried his head beneath a pillow.

She slipped out of bed and moved silently through the dim bedroom, narrowly avoiding a cluster of empty beer cans that Leon had left there. From the kitchen phone she called Dispatch.

A body discovered in a Dumpster on the five hundred block of Hastings. A section of town where all of the town's vice seemed to be concentrated, all the prostitution and drugs and violence and shootings. A dead body there could mean any of a number of things, including drugs or gangs, but the odds were that it meant very little. Was this hard-hearted of her? She preferred not to think so. At first she'd been shocked at the reactions of the survivors, even the mothers, who seemed to be almost resigned to losing a son. They'd already lost their sons. Few of them pleaded their sons' innocence. They knew better.

When Audrey learned who'd be picking her up this morning, whom she'd been partnered with on this case—the loathsome Roy Bugbee—she felt her body go rigid with annoyance. More than annoyance, she had to admit to herself. Something stronger. This was not a worthy feeling, not a generous impulse.

Silently, as she dressed—she kept a clean outfit in the parlor closet—she recited one of her favorite verses of scripture, from Romans 15: "Now the God of patience and consolation grant you to be likeminded one toward another, according to Christ Jesus." She loved this line, even as she realized she didn't yet fully understand it. But she knew it meant that the Lord first teaches us what is true consolation and true patience, and then He instills this in our hearts. Reciting this to herself got her through Leon's recent sulking fits, his drinking problem, lent her a much-needed serenity. Her goal had been to re-read the entire Bible by year's end, but the irregularity of her schedule made that impossible.

Roy Bugbee was a fellow detective in Major Cases who had an unaccountable loathing toward her. He didn't know her. He knew only her outward appearance, her sex, and the color of her skin. His words cut her, though never as deeply as Leon's.

She gathered her equipment, her Sig-Sauer and her handcuffs, rights cards and IBO request forms and her PT, her handheld radio. While she waited, she sat in Leon's favorite chair, the worn rust BarcaLounger, and opened her old leather-bound King James Bible, her mother's, but there was barely time to find her place before Detective Bugbee pulled up in his city car.

He was slovenly. The car, which he was lucky enough to have at his disposal—she hadn't been given one—was littered with pop cans and Styrofoam Quarter Pounder boxes. It smelled of old French fries and cigarette smoke.

He didn't say hello or good morning. Audrey said good morning to him,

however, determined to rise above his pettiness. She sat in uncomfortable silence, amid the squalor, observing the scattering of ketchup packets on the
floor around her feet and hoping that none of them was on the seat beneath
her plum business suit. It would never come out.

After a few minutes he spoke as he flicked the turn signal at a red light.
"You got lucky, huh?" Bugbee's blond hair was slicked back in a pompadour.
His eyebrows were so pale they were almost invisible.

"Pardon me?"

His laugh was raucous. "I don't mean with your husband. If Owens
wasn't drunk on his ass when Dispatch called, you'da been assigned to him.
But lucky you, you get me."

"Mm hm," she said, her tone pleasant. When she first arrived at Major
Cases, only two of the men would talk to her, Owens being one of them.
The others acted as if she wasn't even there. She'd say, "Good morning,"
and they wouldn't answer. There was no women's bathroom, of course—not
for one woman—so she had to share the men's. One of the guys kept uri-
nating right on the toilet seat just to make it unpleasant for her. Her fellow
detectives thought it was hilarious. She'd heard it was Bugbee, and she believed it. He'd done "practical jokes" on her she didn't like to think about.
Finally she'd had to resort to using the bathroom downstairs in the warrant
unit.

"Body found in a Dumpster on Hastings," Bugbee continued. "Wrapped
up like a burrito in Hefty bags."

"How long has it been there?"

"No idea. You better not go blow your cookies on me."

"I'll do my best. Who found it, one of the homeless looking for food?"

"Trash guy. You lose it like you did with that little black girl, you'll get
yanked off the case, I'll see to it."

Little Tiffany Akins, seven years old, had died in her arms a few months
earlier. They'd got her father cuffed, but her mother and her mother's
boyfriend had already died of their gunshot wounds by the time Major Cases
showed up. Audrey could not keep herself from weeping. The beautiful little
girl, wearing SpongeBob pajamas, could have been her own child if she'd
been able to have kids. She didn't understand what kind of father would be

so blinded by rage and jealousy that he'd kill not only his estranged wife and her lover but his own daughter too.

She recited to herself: *Now the God of patience and consolation grant you to be likeminded one toward another . . .*

"I'll do my best, Roy," Audrey said.

16

The crime scene was a small blacktopped parking lot behind a ratty little diner called Lucky's. A yellow streamer of evidence tape secured the area, barricaded off a small gathering of the usuals. It was remarkable, Audrey thought, and not a little sad, that this unknown vagrant was getting in death the kind of attention that he surely never got when it could have made a difference. A man wanders through the streets alone and unnoticed and despairing. Now, with the life gone out of his body, a crowd gathers to pay him the respect he'd never received in life.

No TV cameras here, though. No Newschannel Six truck. Maybe not even a reporter from the *Fenwick Free Press*. No one wanted to come down to the five hundred block of Hastings at six in the morning to report on the discovery of some vagrant's body.

Roy Bugbee parked the city car on the street between two patrol cars. They got out without exchanging another word. She noticed the white van belonging to the Identification Bureau Office, meaning that the crime-scene techs were already there. Not the Medical Examiner yet. The uniformed first officer, who'd notified Dispatch, was swanning around self-importantly, warding off neighborhood gawkers, clearly enjoying the biggest thing that had happened to him all week. Maybe all month. He approached Audrey and Bugbee with a clipboard and demanded that they sign in.

Her eye was caught by a flash of light, then another. The IBO evidence tech on the scene was Bert Koopmans. She liked Koopmans. He was smart and thorough, obsessive-compulsive like the best crime-scene techs, but without being arrogant or difficult. Her kind of cop. Something of a gun nut, maintained his own personal Web site on firearms and forensics. He was a lean man in his fifties with a receding hairline and thick Polar Gray spectacles. He was snapping pictures, switching between Polaroid and digital and 35mm and video like some crazed paparazzi.

Her boss, Sergeant Jack Noyce, the head of the Major Case Team, was talking on his Nextel phone. He saw Audrey and Bugbee duck under the yellow tape, held up a finger to ask them to wait. Noyce was a round-faced, stout man with melancholy eyes, gentle and sweet natured. He'd been the one who'd talked her into putting in for Major Cases. He said he wanted a woman on the squad. Never had he admitted it might have been a mistake. He was her steadfast defender, and she did him the favor of never going to him with the petty insults of her colleagues. From time to time he'd hear about something and would take her aside, promise to talk to them. He never did, though. Noyce preferred to avoid confrontation, and who could blame him, really?

He ended the call and said, "Unknown older white male, sixties maybe, gunshot wounds to the head and chest. Waste Management guy spotted it after he loaded the Dumpster on his frontloader. First pickup too. What a way to start your day."

"Before or after he tipped the trash into the hopper, boss?" asked Audrey.

"He noticed it before. Left the contents intact, stopped a patrol car."

"Coulda been a lot worse," Bugbee said. "Coulda put it through the compactor, huh?" He chortled, winked at his boss. "'Stead of a burrito we'd have a quesadilla. Ever see a body like that, Audrey? You'd really blow lunch."

"You make a very good point there, Roy," Noyce said, smiling thinly. Audrey had always suspected that her boss shared her dislike of Roy Bugbee but was too polite to let on.

Bugbee put a comradely hand on Noyce's shoulder as he strutted past.

"I'm sorry about that," Noyce said under his breath.

Audrey didn't entirely understand what he was sorry about. "He's got a unique sense of humor," she said, taking a stab.

"Owens was intoxicated, according to Dispatch. Bugbee was next on the call list. I wouldn't have partnered you two, but . . ." He shrugged, his voice trailing off.

Noyce waved at someone. Audrey turned to look. Curtis Decker, the body mover, was getting out of his old black Ford Econoline van. Decker, a small man of ghostly pallor, had a funeral home in Fenwick and was also the town's conveyance specialist. He'd been transferring bodies from crime scenes to the morgue at Boswell Medical Center for twenty-seven years. Decker lighted a cigarette, leaned back against his van, chatting idly to his assistant, waiting his turn.

Noyce's phone chirped. He picked it up, said, "Noyce," and Audrey silently excused herself.

Bert Koopmans was painstakingly brushing powder on the rim of the battered dark-blue Dumpster. Without turning his head from his work, he said, "Morning, Aud."

"Good morning, Bert." As she drew closer to the Dumpster, she caught a whiff of a ripe stench, which mingled with the odor of bacon that wafted from the open service entrance door.

The asphalt was littered with cigarette butts. This was where the busboys and short-order cooks smoked. There were a few jagged shards from a brown beer bottle. She knew there wasn't likely to be any evidence here, no shell casings or anything, since the body had been dumped.

"Partnered with Bugbee on this, I see."

"Mm-hmm."

"The Lord trieth the righteous."

She smiled, her eyes straying to the body in the Dumpster, wrapped tightly in black trash bags. It did look a little like a take-out burrito. The bundle lay atop a foul mound of slimy lettuce heads and banana peels, a discarded submarine sandwich, next to a giant empty tin of Kaola Golden Solid Vegetable Griddle Shortening.

"Was it right on top like that?" she asked.

"No. Buried under a bunch of trash."

"I assume you haven't found anything, shell casings or whatever."

"I didn't really look that hard. There's eight cubic yards of garbage in there. I figure that's a job for the uniformed guys."

"You already print the bags?"

"Huh," Koopmans said. "Hadn't thought of it." Meaning: Of course, what do you think?

"So what's your take, smart guy?"

"On what?"

"You unwrap that package up there, Bert?"

"First thing I did."

"And? A mugging? Did you find a wallet or anything?"

Koopmans finished dusting a patch, carefully replaced his brush in the kit. "Just this." He held up a plastic sandwich bag.

"Crack cocaine," she said.

"Off-white chunky material in a baggie, to be precise."

"Which looks like crack. Like eighty dollars' worth."

He shrugged.

"A white guy in this part of town," she said, "has to be a drug deal."

"If the deal went bad, how come he got to keep the crack?"

"Good question."

"Where's your partner?"

She turned, saw Bugbee smoking, laughing raucously with one of the uniforms. "Hard at work interviewing witnesses, looks like. Bert, you'll get this stuff tested, right?"

"Standard procedure."

"How long does it take to get back results?"

"Few weeks, given the MSP's work load." The Michigan State Police lab did all the drug testing.

"You happen to have one of those field test kits with you?"

"Somewhere, sure."

"Can I have a pair of gloves? I left mine in the car."

Koopmans reached into a nylon rucksack beside him and pulled out a blue cardboard box, from which he yanked a pair of latex gloves. She snapped them on. "Could you hand me that baggie?"

Koopmans gave her a questioning look but handed over the bag of crack. It was one of those Ziploc kinds. She pulled it open, removed one of the individually wrapped chunks—five or six in there, she noticed—and peeled off the plastic wrap.

"Don't start doing my work," Koopmans said. "Leads to worse things.

Pretty soon you'll be squinting into a microscope and bitching about detectives."

With one gloved index finger she scraped at an edge of the off-white rock. Strange, she thought. A little too round-looking, too perfect a formation. Only one side was jagged. Then she touched her forefinger to her tongue.

"What the hell are you doing?" Koopmans said, alarmed.

"Thought so," she said. "Didn't numb my tongue like it's supposed to. This isn't crack. These are lemon drops."

Koopmans gave a slow smile. "Still need me to get the test kit?"

"That's okay. Could you help me up the side of this Dumpster, Bert? Of all the days I picked to wear my good shoes."

17

Another ordinary morning at the office. Arrive at the Stratton parking lot at seven-thirty. Check e-mail, voice mail. Return a few calls, leave voice mails for people who won't be in their offices for at least another hour.

You have killed a man.

Just another ordinary day. Business as usual.

The day before, Sunday, he'd even fantasized about going to church, to confession, which he hadn't done since he was a kid. He'd never do it, he knew, but in his mind he rehearsed his confession, imagined the dark confessional booth, that musty cedar-vanilla smell, the scuffling footsteps outside. "Forgive me, Father, for I have sinned," he says. "It has been thirty-three years since my last confession. I have committed these sins. I have taken the Lord's name in vain. I have gazed lustfully upon other women. I have lost patience with my kids. And, oh yeah, I killed a man." What would Father Garrison say about that? What would his own father have made of it?

He heard Marge's voice, intercepting the early morning calls like the pro she was. "He *is* in the office, yes, but I'm afraid he's in conference just now . . ."

How much had he slept in the past two days? He was in one of those weird, wobbly all-nighter states poised between calm and despair, and despite the coffee he'd had, he felt a sudden surge of weariness. He would have been tempted to close his office door and lay his head on his desk, except there was no door.

And it wasn't an office, really, at all. Certainly not what he used to imagine a CEO's office would look like. Which wasn't to say he'd ever spent much time thinking about being CEO of Stratton, or CEO of anything for that matter. As a kid, sitting at supper at his parents' Formica kitchen table, inhaling the acrid must of machine oil that emanated from his dad's hair and skin even after his father had taken his post-shift shower, Nick used to imagine one day working alongside Dad on the Stratton shop floor, bending metal at the brake machine. His father's gnarled stubby fingers, with the crescents of black grime still lodged under his fingernails, fascinated him. These were the fingers of a man who knew how to fix anything, could open a Mason jar that had been rusted shut, could build a fort out of spare lumber, nestled securely in the oak in their tiny backyard, that was the envy of all the neighbor kids. They were the hands of a worker, a guy who came home from the factory exhausted but then went right to work again, after his shower, around the house, tumbler of whiskey in one hand: fixing the dripping sink, a wobbly table leg, a lamp whose socket had a short. Dad liked fixing things that were broken, liked restoring order, getting things to work right. But more than anything, he liked being left alone. Working around the house was his way to get what he really wanted: a cone of silence around him, his thoughts kept to himself, not having to talk to his wife or son. Nick Conover only realized this about his dad much later when he saw it in himself.

He never thought one day he'd be running the company his father spoke of, the rare times he did speak, with such awe and disgruntlement. They barely knew anyone who *didn't* work for Stratton. All the neighbor kids, all the grown-ups his parents ever saw or talked about, they all worked at Stratton. Dad always groused about fat old Arch Campbell, the nasty round-shouldered factory manager who tyrannized the day shift. Complaining about Stratton was like complaining about the weather: you were stuck with whatever you got. It was the big annoying extended family you could never escape from.

When he was around fourteen or fifteen, Nick's junior-high class took the obligatory tour of Stratton—as if any of the kids needed a close look at the company that dominated their parents' supper conversations, the company whose logo was sewn in red on their white baseball caps, on team uniforms, emblazoned in neon over the arched entrance to the high school stadium. Walking through the chair factory, cavernous and thundering, deafeningly loud, might have been fun if most of the kids hadn't already been taken there at one time or another by their dads. Instead, it was the headquarters building that fascinated the rambunctious eighth-graders, finally intimidated them into a respectful awed silence.

At the climax of the tour they were crowded into the anteroom of the immense office suite of the president and chief executive officer, Milton Devries. This was the inner sanctum, the beating heart of the company that they realized, even as kids, ruled their lives. It was like being taken into King Tut's tomb; it was that alien, that fascinating, that intimidating. There, Devries's frightening mastiff-faced secretary, Mildred Birkerts, gave them a grudging little memorized talk, punctuated by the occasional dyspeptic scowl, about the vital function of the chief executive officer at Stratton. Craning his neck, Nick caught an illicit glimpse of Devries's desk, an acre of burnished mahogany, bare except for a gold desk set and a perfectly neat pile of papers. Devries wasn't there: that would have been too much. He saw huge windows, a leafy private balcony.

When, years later, Milton Devries died, Nick—who'd become the old man's favorite vice president—was summoned by Milton's widow, Dorothy, to her dark mansion on Michigan Avenue, where she told him he was the next CEO. Her family owned Stratton, so she could do that.

With great discomfort, Nick had moved into the old man's Mussolini-size office, with the floor-to-ceiling windows, the Oriental rugs, the immense mahogany desk, the outer office where *his* executive assistant, Marjorie Dykstra, would guard his privacy. It was like living in a mausoleum. Of course, by then, Stratton had changed. Now everyone wanted to stuff as many employees as possible into a building, and Stratton had gone to the open-plan system, that fancy term for cubicles and all the furnishings that went with them. No one really liked the cube farm, but at least Stratton's designs were elegant, cool, and friendly, 120-degree angles, the panels not too tall, all the computer cables and electrical wires and stuff hidden in the floors and panels.

One day a visitor looked around Nick's office and made a crack. He was head of worldwide purchasing for IBM, a harried-looking guy with a sharp tongue, who'd surveyed Nick's mahogany chamber and muttered dryly, "Oh, *I* see—you get the fancy digs while everyone *else* gets the 'open plan.'"

The next day Nick had ordered the executive floor completely remodeled, switched to the open plan too, over the howls of protest from his entire executive management team. They'd busted their humps for years to finally land the big office with the private balcony and now they were all getting *cubicles*? This was a joke, right? You couldn't do this.

But he did. Of course, everyone on the fifth floor got the best of the best, the elegant, high-end Ambience Office System with its silver mesh fabric panels on brushed aluminum frames, sound-absorbing panel walls, and the top-of-the-line leather Stratton Symbiosis chairs, the harp-back beauties that had pretty much taken the place of the Aeron chair in fancy offices around the world, much coveted, just added to the permanent collection of the Museum of Modern Art.

Eventually people got used to the new arrangement. The complaints stopped. It got a little easier when *Fortune* did a big spread on the Stratton executive offices, on how they were walking the walk as well as talking the talk. It got easier still when delegations of design-school students started coming to gape at the executive offices, marvel at how *edgy* they were.

The new offices were pretty damned cool, it was true. If you had to work in cubicles, this was the best damned cube farm money could buy. So now, Nick had often reflected, you had guys sitting in cubicles thinking about . . . cubicles.

Of course, there really wasn't any privacy anymore. Everyone knew where you were, when you went out to lunch or to work out, who you were meeting with. If you yelled at someone on the phone, everyone heard it.

The bottom line was, when Steve Jobs from Apple Computer came in for a meeting, or Warren Buffett flew in from Omaha, they could see that the top executives of Stratton weren't hypocrites. They ate the same dog food they were selling. That was the best sales pitch of all.

So now Nick Conover's office was a "workstation" or a "home base." The new arrangement was less grandiose, suited him more. It wasn't a big sacrifice. Most days he liked it a lot more anyway.

Only this wasn't one of them.

"Nick, are you all right?"

Marjorie had come over to make sure he had the stapled agenda for

Nick's 8:30 meeting of his Executive Management Team. She was dressed elegantly, as always; she was wearing a lavender suit, the short string of pearls he'd bought as a gift for her a few years before. She wafted a faint cloud of Shalimar.

"Me? Oh, I'm fine, Marge, thanks."

She wasn't moving. She stood there, cocked her head. "You don't look it. Have you been sleeping?"

Rough couple of nights, he almost said. Immediately he could hear her repeating back the words in a courtroom. *He said he'd had a couple of rough nights, but he didn't elaborate.* "Ah, Lucas is driving me crazy," he said.

A knowing smile. She'd raised two boys and a girl pretty much by herself and rightly considered herself an expert. "Poor kid's in a tough place."

"Yeah, called adolescence."

"Anything you want to talk about?"

"I'd love to, later on," Nick said, knowing that would never happen; he'd make sure of it.

"Right, the EMT meeting. You all set for that, Nick?"

"I'm all set."

Was it possible to look like a murderer? Was it visible on his face? It was stupid, it made no sense, but in his dazed, scrambled egg–brain state, he worried about it. In the EMT meeting, he barely spoke, because he could barely concentrate. He remembered the time when the family was camping in Taos, and a snake got into their cabin. Laura and the kids screamed, and she begged Nick to get a shovel and kill the vile thing. But he couldn't. He couldn't bring himself to do it. It wasn't a venomous snake—it was a Western coachwhip—but Laura and the kids kept demanding that he get the shovel. Finally he reached down, picked it up, and threw it, twisting and wriggling, out into the desert.

Couldn't kill a snake, he thought.

Some irony in that.

He strode out of the room as soon as the meeting was over, avoiding the usual post-meeting entanglements.

Back at his desk, he went on the Stratton intranet and checked Eddie Rinaldi's online Meeting Maker to see what his schedule was. They hadn't talked since Eddie had driven away with the body in the trunk of his car.

Every time the phone rang, all Saturday and Sunday, he flinched a little, dreading that it might be Eddie. But Eddie never called, and he never called Eddie. He assumed everything had gone okay, but now he wanted the assurance of knowing. He thought about e-mailing Eddie to tell him he wanted to talk, but then decided against it. E-mails, instant messages, voice mails— they were all recorded somewhere. They were all evidence.

18

The only reason Audrey attended autopsies was that she had no choice. It was department policy. The Medical Examiner's office required that at least one detective on a case be present. She told herself she didn't see the need, since she knew she could ask the pathologist anything she wanted, anything that wasn't in the path report.

In truth, of course, it made perfect sense to have a detective there. There were all sorts of things you found out at an autopsy that didn't appear in the sterile lines of a report. Even so, they were the part of her job she most disliked. The dissection of bodies made her queasy. She was always afraid she might have to vomit, though she hadn't done so since her first one, and that was a terribly burned female.

But that wasn't what she hated most about autopsies. She found them deeply depressing. This was where you saw the human body devoid of its spirit, its soul, a carapace of flesh meted out in grams and liters. To her, on the other hand, homicide cases were about setting things right. Solving the crime didn't always heal the wounds of the victim's family—often it didn't— but it was her way of restoring some kind of moral order to a deeply messed-up world. She'd taped a sign to her computer at work, a quote from one Vernon Geberth, whose name was well known to all homicide investigators, the author of a classic text, *Practical Homicide Investigation*. It said, "Remember: We work for God." She believed this. She felt deeply that, as much as she was troubled by her work—and she was, most of the time—she really was doing God's work here on earth. She was looking for the one lost sheep. But autopsies required a detachment she preferred not to have.

So she uneasily entered this white-tiled room that stank of bleach and formaldehyde and disinfectant, while her partner got to make phone calls and do interviews, though she wondered just how hard Roy Bugbee was working to solve this case of what he called "a shitbird crackhead." Not too hard, she figured.

The morgue and autopsy room were located in the basement of Boswell Medical Center, concealed behind a door marked PATHOLOGY CONFERENCE ROOM. Everything about this place gave her the heebie-jeebies, from the stainless-steel gurney on which the victim's nude body had been placed, head a few inches higher than the feet to facilitate drainage of bodily fluids, to the handheld Stryker bone saw on the steel shelf, the garbage disposals in the stainless-steel sink, the organ tray whose plastic drainage tube, once clear, was now discolored brown.

The assistant medical examiner, one of three attached to the department, was a young doctor named Jordan Metzler, strikingly handsome and he knew it well. He had a head of dark curly hair, great brown eyes, a strong nose, full lips, a dazzling smile. Everyone knew he wasn't long for this job, or this town: he'd recently been offered a job in pathology at Mass General, in Boston. In a matter of months he'd be sitting at some fancy restaurant on Beacon Hill, regaling a beautiful nurse with tales of this backwater town in Michigan where he'd been stuck the last couple of years.

"Audrey's in the *house!*" he crowed as she entered. "'S'up, Detective?"

What was it with white guys who felt compelled to use black slang when African-Americans were around? Did they think it made them seem cool, instead of ridiculous? Did they think that made black folks connect with them better? Did Metzler even notice that she didn't talk that way?

She smiled sweetly. "Dr. Metzler," she said.

He found her attractive; Audrey could tell by the way he grinned at her. Her antennae still worked, even after eight years of marriage to Leon. Like most women, she was adept at reading males; sometimes she was convinced she knew them better than they knew themselves. Eight years of marriage to Leon hadn't knocked the self-esteem out of her, not even the terrible last couple of years. She knew that men had always been drawn to her, because of her looks. She didn't consider herself beautiful, far from it, but she knew she was pretty. She took care of herself, she exercised, she never went without makeup and she was adept at choosing the right lipstick for her skin tone. She liked to think that it was her deep abiding faith that kept her looking good, but she had seen enough women of equally deep abiding faith at church, women whose looks only God could love, to know better.

"Have you found any bullets?" she asked.

"Well, we've got two in there, X-ray shows. No exit wounds. I'll get 'em. You don't have an ID on this one yet, do you?"

She found herself avoiding looking at the body, the wrinkled flesh and the yellow-brown toenails, which meant she had to keep looking at Metzler, and she didn't want to send him the wrong signals. Not a horn-dog like him.

"Maybe we'll get lucky and score a hit on AFIS," she said. The crime scene techs had just finished fingerprinting the victim, having collected whatever trace evidence they could find on the body, scraping and clipping the fingernails and all that. Since the body was unidentified, they'd run the prints right away through the Michigan Automated Fingerprint Identification System in Lansing.

She asked, "Evidence of habitual drug use?"

"You mean needle marks or something? No, nothing like that. We'll see what tox finds on the blood."

"Look like a homeless guy to you?"

He jutted his jaw, frowned. "Not based on his clothes, which didn't smell unusually bad. Or grooming or dental care or hygiene. I'd guess no. In fact, the guy's pretty clean. I mean, he could take better care of his cuticles, but he looks more like a house case than a police case." That was what the pathologists called the autopsies they did on hospital patients, whose bodies were always clean and well scrubbed when they got here.

"Any signs of struggle?"

"None apparent."

"The mouth looks sort of bashed in," she said, forcing herself to look. "Broken teeth and all. Is it possible he got hit with, say, the butt of the gun?"

Metzler looked amused by her hypothesis. "Possible? Anything's *possible*." He probably sensed that he'd come off as too arrogant, so he softened his tone. "The teeth are chipped and cracked, not pushed in. That's consistent with a bullet. And there's no trauma to the lips—no swelling or bruising you'd find if there was a blunt-force injury. Also, there's the little matter of the bullet hole in his palate."

"I see." She let him enjoy his moment of superiority. The fragile male ego needed to be flattered. She had no problem with that; she'd been doing that all of her adult life. "Doctor, what do you estimate as the time of death? We found the body at six—"

"Call me Jordan." Another dazzling smile. He was working it. "We can't tell. It's in full rigor at this point."

"At the crime scene you said there was no rigor mortis, and since rigor doesn't really start setting in until three, four hours after death, I figured—"

"Nah, Audrey, there's too many other factors—physique, environment, cause of death, whether the guy was running or not. Doesn't really tell you anything."

"What about the body temperature?" she pointed out, careful to sound tentative. She wanted answers from the pathologist; she had no interest in showing him up.

"What about it?"

"Well, at the scene, didn't you take a body temperature reading of ninety-two? That means it dropped around six degrees, right? If the body temperature drops one point five to two degrees per hour after death, I estimate the victim had been killed three or four hours before the body was found. Does that sound about right to you?"

"In a perfect world, sure." Dr. Metzler smiled, but this time it was the look a parent might give a five-year-old asking if the moon was made of green cheese. "It's just not an accurate science. There are too many variables."

"I see."

"You seem more versed in forensics than a lot of the cops who come in here."

"It's an important part of my job, that's all."

"If you're interested, I'd be willing to teach you a little, help you out. No sense me having all this information in my head if I can't share it with someone who so clearly wants to learn."

She nodded, smiled politely. The burdens of being so smart, she wanted to say.

"I wonder whether they really appreciate you on the Major Case Team." He pretended to adjust the perforated stainless-steel tubing around the perimeter of the examination table, which washed the fluids off the body during the autopsy.

"I've never felt unappreciated," she lied. For the first time she noticed the toe tag on the body's left foot. It said "Unknown John Doe #6." Wasn't that, what was the word? A "John Doe" *was* unknown, wasn't it?

"Somehow I doubt your beauty helps you in your line of work."

"That's very kind of you, Doctor," she said, casting around desperately for a question in order to change the subject, but her mind had gone blank.

"Not kind at all. Accurate. You're a fine-looking woman, Audrey. Beauty *and* brains—not a bad combination at all."

"Why, you sound just like my husband," she said lightly. He'd never actually said anything remotely like that, but she wanted the pathologist to get the message without hammering him over the head about it, and that was the first thing she thought of.

"I saw your ring, Audrey," he said, giving her a smile that seemed more than playful.

The man was cutting up a dead body, for heaven's sake. This wasn't exactly a singles bar.

"You're too kind," she said. "Doctor, do the gunshot wounds give you any sense of the distance from the shooter?"

Metzler smiled to himself awkwardly as he studied the body on the table before him. He took a steel scalpel from the metal shelf attached to the table and, with maybe a little too much force, carved a large Y-shaped incision from the shoulders all the way down to the pubic bone. He was clearly trying his best to accept defeat gracefully. "There's no stippling, no powder burns, no tattooing, no soot," he said. His voice had changed; now he was all business.

"So they're not contact wounds?"

"Neither contact nor intermediate range." He began trimming back the skin and the muscle and tissue below.

"So what does that tell us distancewise?"

He was silent for a good thirty seconds as he worked. Then he said, "Actually, Detective, that tells us nothing except that the muzzle was more than three feet from the wound. Certainly not without determining the caliber of the bullet, the type of ammo, and then test-firing the gun. It could have been fired from three feet away, or a hundred feet. You can't tell."

The glistening rib cage exposed, he positioned the round jagged-toothed blade above the bone and flicked the switch to start it. Above the high-pitched mechanical whine, he said, "You might want to stand back, Detective. This can get a little messy."

19

As badly as he wanted to, Nick couldn't easily cancel the weekly number-crunching lunch with Scott McNally, not with the big quarterly board meeting coming up. He felt feverish, clammy, nauseated. He felt, unusually for him, antisocial. His normal ebullience had been tamped down. He felt the beginnings of a raging headache, and he hadn't had a headache in years. He felt hung over, his stomach roiling. Coffee upset his stomach now, even though he needed it to stay awake and alert.

A chef from the corporate cafeteria had set out lunch for the two of them at the small round table adjacent to his home base. It was the usual—an eggplant Parmesan sub and a salad for Scott, a tuna sandwich and a cup of tomato soup for Nick. Folded linen napkins, glasses of ice water and a glass pitcher, Diet Cokes for both of them. Nick normally just ate a sandwich at his desk unless he had to do a working lunch. And until Laura's death, she always packed his lunch—a tuna fish sandwich, a bag of Fritos, carrot sticks—and put it in his briefcase. It was a little tradition that went back to their earliest days, when they had no money, and he'd gotten used to it. It was one of those little things Laura liked to do for him, even when she was teaching college and barely had time in the morning before class to make his lunch. She always put a little mash note in the paper lunch bag, which always made him smile when he came upon it, like the prize in a Crackerjacks box. There'd been times when he'd been having an informal lunch with Scott or another of his executives and one of Laura's notes had fluttered out, to Nick's embarrassment and secret pride. He'd saved every single one of her notes, without telling her. After her death, he'd come very close to throwing them away or burning them or something, because it was just too excruciating to have them around. But he couldn't bring himself to do that. So a neat pile of yellow Post-it notes in Laura's beautiful handwriting lay in the bottom drawer of his desk at work, secured with a rubber band. Sometimes he'd been tempted to take them out and look through them, but in the end, he couldn't. It was too painful.

"You look wiped out," Scott said, tucking right in to his sub. "You getting sick?"

Nick shook his head, took a careful sip of ice water, its coldness making him shiver. "I'm fine."

"Well, this ought to help," Scott said. "I know how you feel about the numbers. You might want to grab a pillow." He produced a couple of Velo-bound documents, slid one in front of Nick, next to his lunch plate.

Nick glanced at it. Income statement, cash-flow statement, and balance sheet.

"Check it out," Scott said. "Man, I love the way they toast the bun. Grill it, maybe, I don't know." He took a slug of Diet Coke. "You're not eating?"

"Not hungry."

Nick skimmed through the statements without interest while Scott examined the Diet Coke can. "I hear the artificial sweetener in this stuff can cause mood disorders in rats," he said.

Nick grunted, not listening.

"Ever seen a depressed rat?" Scott went on. "Curled up in a ball and everything? Some days they just don't feel the maze is worth it, you know?" He took a large bite of his sub.

"What's Stratton Asia Ventures?" Nick asked.

"You read footnotes. Very good. It's a subsidiary corporation I've formed to invest in Stratton's Asia Pacific ops. We needed a local subsidiary for permitting and to take advantage of certain tax treaties with the U.S."

"Nice. Legal?"

"Picky, picky," Scott said. "Of course legal. Clever doesn't mean illegal, Nick."

Nick looked up. "I don't get it," he said. "Our earnings are *up*?"

Scott nodded, chewing his huge mouthful, made some grunting noises indicating he wanted to speak but couldn't. Then he said, mouth still half full of food, "So it appears."

"I thought—Jesus, Scott, you told me we were in the toilet."

Scott shrugged, gave an impish smile. "That's why you've got me around. You know I always come to play. I'm bringing my A game, huh?"

"Your 'A game'? Scott, did you ever play a competitive sport in your life?"

Scott tilted his head to one side. "What are you talking about? I was point guard on the Stuyvesant math team."

"Wait a second." Nick went back to the beginning of the booklet, began reading over the numbers more closely. "All right, hold on. You're telling me our *international* business is up twelve percent? What gives?"

"Read the numbers. The numbers don't lie. It's all there in black and white."

"I just talked with George Colesandro in London last week, and he was pissing and moaning all over the place. You telling me he was reading the numbers wrong? Guy's got a fucking microprocessor for a brain."

Scott shook his head. "Stratton UK reports in pounds, and the pound's way up against the dollar," he said with his Cheshire-cat smile. "Gotta use the latest exchange rate, right?"

"So this is all hocus-pocus. Foreign exchange crap." Nick's nerve endings were raw, and it felt good somehow to think about something besides Friday night. At the same time, though, what Scott seemed to be doing was unbelievable. It was smarmy. "We're not up at all—we're down. You're—you're juggling the numbers."

"According to GAAP, we're supposed to use the correct exchange rates." GAAP stood for Generally Accepted Accounting Principles, but bland and jargony as it sounded, it had the force of law.

"Look, Scott, it's not apples to apples. I mean, you're using a different exchange rate than the one you used last quarter. You're just making it *look* like we did better." Nick rubbed his eyes. "You did the same thing in Asia Pacific?"

"Everywhere, sure." Scott's eyes were narrowed, apprehensive.

"Scott, this is fucking *illegal*." Nick slammed the booklet down on the table. "What are you trying to do to me?"

"To *you*? This isn't *about* you." Red-faced, Scott was looking down at the table as he spoke. "First of all, there's nothing illegal about it. Call it pushing the envelope a little, maybe. But let me tell you something. If I don't pretty these numbers up a little, our friends from Boston are going to come down on you like Nazi storm troopers. They are going to parachute in and tear this place up. I'm telling you this is a perfectly legitimate way to spin the numbers."

"You're—you're putting lipstick on a pig, Scott."

"Well, a little lip *gloss*, maybe. Look, when company comes over for dinner, you clean house, right? Before you sell your car, you take it to the car wash. None of the board members are going to look this close."

"So you're saying we can get *away* with it," Nick said.

Scott shrugged again. "What I'm saying, Nick, is that everyone's job is at risk here, okay? Including yours and mine. This way, at least, we buy ourselves a little time."

"No. Uh-uh," Nick said, drumming his fingertips on the clear plastic cover. "We give it to 'em straight. You got me?"

Scott's face flushed, as if he were embarrassed or angry, or both. He was clearly straining hard to sound calm, like it was taking enormous effort to keep from raising his voice to his boss. "Gosh, and I was hoping to have a corporate tax loophole named after me," he said after a pause.

Nick nodded, dispensed a grudging smile. He thought of Hutch, the old CFO. Henry Hutchens was a brilliant accountant, in his green-eyeshade, bean-counting way—no one knew the intricacies of the good old-fashioned balance sheet the way he did—but he knew little about structured finance and derivatives and all the shiny new financial instruments you had to use these days to stay afloat.

Hutch would never have done anything like this. Then again, he probably wouldn't have known how.

"You told me we're having dinner tonight with Todd Muldaur, remember?"

"Eight o'clock," Nick said. He was dreading it. Todd had called just a few days ago to mention he was passing through Fenwick, as if anyone ever "passed through" Fenwick, and wanted to have dinner. It couldn't be a good thing.

"Well, I told him I'd get him the updated financials before dinner."

"Fine, but let's make sure we're on rock-solid foundations here, okay?"

"In accounting?" Scott shook his head. "No such thing. It's like that story about the famous scientist who's giving a lecture on astronomy, and afterward an old lady comes up to him and tells him he's got it all wrong—the world is really a big flat plate resting on the back of a giant turtle. And the scientist says, 'But what's *that* turtle standing on?' And the old lady says, 'You're very clever, young man, very clever, but it's no use—it's turtles all the way down.'"

"Is that meant to be reassuring?"

Scott shrugged.

"I want you to give Todd the real, unvarnished numbers, no matter how shitty they look."

"Okay," Scott said, looking down at the table. "You're the boss."

20

Audrey's desk phone was ringing as she approached her cubicle. She glanced at the caller ID and was glad she did, because it was a call she didn't want to take.

She recognized the phone number. The woman called her every week, regular as clockwork, had done so for so many weeks Audrey had lost count. Once a week since the woman's son was found murdered.

The woman, whose name was Ethel Dorsey, was a sweet Christian woman, an African-American lady who'd raised four sons on her own and was justifiably proud of that, convinced herself she'd done a good job, had no idea that three of her boys were deep into the life of gangs and drugs and cheap guns. When her son Tyrone was found shot to death on Hastings, Audrey recognized right away that it was drug-related. And like a lot of drug-related murders, it went unsolved. Sometimes people talked. Sometimes they didn't. Audrey had an open file, one less clearance. Ethel Dorsey had one less son. But here was the thing: Audrey simply couldn't bring herself to tell poor devout Ethel Dorsey the truth, that her Tyrone had been killed in some bad drug deal. Audrey remembered Ethel's moist eyes, her warm direct gaze, during the interviews. The woman reminded Audrey of her grandmother. "He's a good boy," she kept saying. Audrey couldn't break it to her that her son had not only been murdered, but he'd been a small-time dealer. For what? Why did the woman need to have her illusions shattered?

So Ethel Dorsey called once a week and asked, politely and apologetically, was there any progress on Tyrone? And Audrey had to tell her the truth: No, I'm sorry, nothing yet. But we haven't given up. We're still working, ma'am.

Audrey couldn't bear it. Because she realized that they'd probably never find Tyrone Dorsey's killer, and even if they did, it would bring no peace to Ethel Dorsey. Yet even a lowlife drug dealer was someone's son. Everyone matters, or else no one matters. Jesus told of the shepherd who kept search- ing for the one lost lamb, leaving his flock behind. For this purpose, Christ said, I was born.

Today she couldn't even bring herself to pick up the phone and talk to the woman. She looked at the photo of Tyrone she'd taped to the side wall of the cubicle, alongside the pictures of all the other victims whose cases she was working or had worked. As she waited for the phone to stop ringing, she noticed a folded square of paper that had been placed on top of the brown ac- cordion file at the center of her desk. "UNKNOWN WHITE MALE #03486," the file had been labeled in her neat capital letters.

The white square of paper, folded a little unevenly into a makeshift card. On the front a black-and-white image of some generic church, a cheesy graphic that looked like clip art downloaded off the Internet. Below it, in Gothic lettering done on someone's computer, the words "Jesus Loves You."

She opened it, knowing more or less what she'd find. Inside it said, "But Everyone Else Thinks Your an Asshole."

She crumpled up Roy Bugbee's inane little prank, misspelling and all, and tossed it into the metal wastebasket. She glanced, for the five-hundred- thousandth time, at the index card taped to her computer monitor, the card starting to go sepia at the edges, her lettering neat and fervent: "Remember: We work for God." She wondered who Roy Bugbee thought he worked for.

Bugbee sauntered in an hour or so later, and they sat in an empty interview room.

"Strikeout on AFIS," he announced, almost proudly. "Nada."

So the old man's prints didn't match any of the fingerprint records in Lansing, neither the Tenprint Database nor the unsolved ones in the Latent

Database. No real surprise there. The victim's prints would only be in AFIS if he'd been arrested for something.

She said, "The rounds that were fired were .380s, according to Bert Koopmans. Brass-jacketed."

"Oh, that's helpful," said Bugbee, deadpan. "Narrows it down to about a thousand possible weapons."

"Well, not really." Audrey ignored his sarcasm, proceeded on the assumption that Roy just didn't know what he was talking about. "Once the MSP in Grand Rapids takes a look at it, they'll winnow it down a whole lot more for us." The Forensic Science Lab of the Michigan State Police, in Grand Rapids, handled the firearms investigations for the police in this part of the state. Their examiners were good, trained in identifying weapons and ammunition using all sorts of tools, including IBIS, the Integrated Ballistics Identification System database, which was managed by the Bureau of Alcohol, Tobacco, and Firearms.

"That shouldn't take more than six months," said Bugbee.

"Actually, I was hoping that when you drive it over there, you could press them to speed it up."

"Me?" Bugbee laughed. "I think *you* ought to drive to Grand Rapids, Audrey. Pretty woman like you, bat your little eyes at them, ask 'em to put it on the top of the heap."

She breathed in. "I'll drive it over there," she said. "Now, what about informants?"

"None of the snitches know a damned thing about some old guy trying to buy crack down the dog pound," he said grudgingly, as if it annoyed him to part with the information. Why that section of town was called the "dog pound" Audrey didn't remember if she ever knew. It just was.

"But the crack in the guy's pocket was fake."

"Yeah, yeah," Bugbee said with a wave of his hand. "Oldest trick in the book. White guy, easy mark, goes down to the dog pound to buy rock, and some zoomer sells him flex made outta candle wax and baking soda."

"Horehound lemon drops broken up, actually." So Bert Koopmans had told her.

"Whatever, don't make no difference. White guy argues with the zoomer who says, who needs this shit? and wastes the guy. Takes his wallet while he's at it and takes off. Open and shut."

"And leaves the lemon drops."

Bugbee gave a "lay off" shrug. He leaned back in the steel chair until his head was resting against the wall.

"And then instead of leaving the body in an alley somewhere, he goes to the trouble of wrapping it in garbage bags and then lifting it into a Dumpster, which isn't easy."

"Coulda been two guys."

"Wearing surgical gloves."

"Hmm?" He looked annoyed.

"The lab found traces of surgical-grade cornstarch on the trash bags consistent with the use of latex gloves."

Bugbee probed a seam in the sheetrock wall with a lazy forefinger. "Probably the lab's."

"I think they're more careful than that," she said, thinking: *Come on, Roy, did you even think this one through? Are you working this case?* She felt a pulse of annoyance, then willed herself back to serenity. "I kind of doubt many crackheads have surgical gloves lying around."

Bugbee exhaled showily. "Is Noyce in this room?"

"Excuse me?"

"I said, I don't see Sergeant Noyce standing here, so if you're trying to show off, no one's watching, okay?"

Audrey swallowed, heard her inner voice begin, *Now the God of patience and consolation grant you . . .* and then she interrupted that inward sensible voice and spoke in a voice even softer than usual: "Roy, I'm not here to impress you. I'm here to do my job."

Bugbee brought his chair forward, sat up straight, gave her a sleepy-eyed look.

She could hear her heart thudding. "Now, I know you don't like me, for whatever reason, but I'm not going to apologize to you for being who I am and what I am. I'm afraid you're just going to have to deal with it. I don't judge you, and you shouldn't judge me. You don't sign my paycheck on Fridays. If you want off of this case, talk to Noyce. Otherwise, let's both try to be professionals, okay?"

Bugbee looked as if he was debating shoving the table at her or getting up and slamming the door. A couple of seconds of silence passed. Then he said, "You don't judge me, huh? Christers like you, that's all you do. You're always ticking off everyone's little infractions like some hall monitor at school. It's all about feeling superior, isn't it, Audrey? Like you got the Big Guy on your side. All that praying you do, it's about sucking up to the Big Boss in the Sky. Ass-kissing your way to heaven, right?"

"That's enough, Roy," she said.

A pounding on the door, and it swung open. Sergeant Noyce stood there, squaring his shoulders, looking from one to the other. "May I ask you two something?" he said. "Did either one of you check the missing persons database?"

"I called Family Services this morning," Audrey said, "but they had nothing."

"You've got to keep checking, you know," Noyce said. "These things sometimes take a day or more to get posted."

"You got a possibility?" Bugbee asked.

"It's a lead, a pretty decent one," Noyce replied. "I'd say it's worth a look."

21

Nick called Eddie, didn't IM him, still feeling paranoid about what kind of records were stored on the corporate server.

They met at the southwest building entrance, outside of the Security offices, Eddie's idea. Eddie didn't want to talk inside the building. What did that mean, Nick wondered, if his own security chief didn't feel safe talking in there?

They walked along the paved path that encircled one of the parking lots. The air had a faint manure smell, from all the surrounding farms, mixed with the charred scent of the burnt buffalo grass.

"What's up?" Eddie said, lighting up a Marlboro. "Dude, you look worried."

"Who, me?" Nick said, grimacing. "What's to worry about?"

"Come on. Everything's under control."

Nick looked around, made sure no one was walking remotely near. "What'd you do with . . . him?"

"You don't want to know."

Nick was silent, listened to the scuff of Eddie's shoes on the pavement. "No, I do. I want to know."

"Nick, believe me, it's better this way."

"Did you get rid of the gun, or do you still have it, or what?"

Eddie shook his head. "The less you know, the better."

"All right, listen. I've been thinking a lot about it, and I think—I've got to go to the cops. There's just no other way. What happened was legally defensible. It'll be a goddamned mess, but with a smart enough attorney, I think I can tough it out."

Eddie gave a low, dry chuckle. "Oh, no, you don't," he said. "You can't put that toothpaste back in the tube."

"Meaning what?"

"Friday night you wanted it to go away. I made it go away." He seemed to be straining to keep his tone civil. "At this point, we've got a serious cover-up, involving both of us."

"A cover-up devised in a panic —"

"Look, Nick," Eddie said. "I don't swim in your toilet, you don't pee in my pool, understand?"

"Huh?"

"I don't tell you how to run Stratton. You don't tell me about crime and cops and all that shit. This is my area of expertise."

"I'm not telling you what to do," Nick said. "I'm telling you what *I'm* going to do."

"Any decision you make involves me too," Eddie said. "And I vote no. Which means you don't do a damned thing. What's done can't be undone. It's just too fucking late."

22

They pulled up in front of a modest house on West Sixteenth in Steepletown, Audrey feeling that jellyfish wriggling in her belly, the thing she always felt when she first met a survivor of a homicide. The spill of raw grief, disbelief, fathomless pain—she could hardly stand it. You had to distance yourself from all that, or you'd go crazy, Noyce had warned her early on. We all do. What looks to the outside world like cynicism, hardness, that's what it is. Protective insulation. You'll learn it.

She never did.

The investigative work, even the routine stuff that phone-it-in types like Roy Bugbee had no patience for, she enjoyed. Not this. Not feeling the hot spray of another human being's agony up close and being unable, fundamentally, to do anything about it. I'll find your dad's murderer, I'll track down the kids who killed your daughter, I'll uncover the guy who popped your father in the 7-Eleven—that was the most she could promise, and it helped, but it didn't heal.

So a missing persons report had been called in to the police by a woman whose father had never come home Friday night. The physical description—age, height, weight, clothing—matched the murder victim found in the Dumpster on Hastings. Audrey knew this was it. The Family Services Division had called the daughter, which was the protocol, to say in their most diplomatic, tender way—they were good at this—that a body had been found, and there was a chance, just a chance, that it was her father, would she be so kind as to come down to the police morgue at Boswell Medical Center and help them identify a body, rule it out?

The aluminum screen door slammed, the woman coming toward them, even before Audrey was out of the Crown Vic. She was a small woman, even tiny, and from twenty feet she looked like a little girl. She wore a white T-shirt, faded and paint-splotched jeans, a ragged jeans jacket. Her brown hair was cut in a spiky sort of hairdo that Audrey associated with punk rockers and artists. Her hands flopped from side to side as she walked, making her look a little like some neglected rag doll.

"You must be from the police," she said. Her brown eyes were large and moist. Up close she was actually quite beautiful and even more fragile. She looked to be in her mid- to late twenties. She had that glazed look of disbelief that Audrey had seen dozens of times in the faces of victim's families. Her voice was deeper than Audrey had expected, its timbre oddly soothing.

"I'm Audrey Rhimes." She extended a hand, beamed a look of compassion. "That's my partner, Roy Bugbee."

Roy, standing beside the open driver's side door, did not come around to shake the daughter's hand, probably figuring that it would be overkill. He gave a quick wave, a tight smile. Move your butt over here, Audrey thought. The man had no manners, no compassion. He didn't even have the ability to fake it.

"Cassie Stadler." Her palm was warm and damp, and her eye makeup was smudged. She got into the backseat of the cruiser. Bugbee drove.

The object here was to low-key it, to reduce the woman's anxiety if at all possible. She's being driven over to the city morgue to identify a body that might be her father's, for God's sake; probably nothing could diminish her anxiety. Cassie Stadler probably knew just as surely as Audrey knew. But Audrey kept speaking, turning around to face the passenger, who sat in the middle of the back seat, staring glassily ahead.

"Tell me about your father," she said. "Does he tend to go out at night?" She hoped the present tense would just slip in there unobserved, silently reassuring.

"No, not really," Cassie Stadler said, and fell silent.

"Does he get disoriented from time to time?"

She blinked. "What? I'm sorry. Disoriented? Yes, I guess he does, sometimes. His . . . his condition."

Audrey waited for more. But Bugbee, heedless, broke in, his voice booming. "Did your father go down to the Hastings Street area often, to your knowledge?"

A series of expressions flashed in this lovely woman's dark eyes, a slide show: puzzlement, hurt, annoyance, sorrow. Audrey, embarrassed, averted her gaze and turned back around in her seat, facing forward.

"It's him, isn't it?" was all the daughter finally said. "My daddy."

They pulled into the hospital parking garage in silence. Audrey had never done one of these before. Identifying a body in the morgue — it was not at all common, thank God, no matter what you saw on TV. There were no sliding drawers at the morgue either, none of those hokey gothic touches. But death was gruesome, unavoidably so.

The body lay on a steel gurney covered with a green surgical sheet, the room sterile and air-conditioned to a chill and smelling of formalin. Jordan Metzler, polite if distant, pulled back the green cloth as matter-of-factly as if he were turning down a bed, exposing the head and neck.

Beneath that spiky mane, Cassie Stadler's perfect little doll face crumpled, and no one had to say anything.

23

Audrey found an empty room in the hospital basement where the three of them could talk. It was an employees' lounge: a collection of chairs upholstered in different institutional fabrics, a short couch, a coffee machine that looked as if no one ever used it, a TV. She and Bugbee moved chairs into a cluster. A couple of open soda cans were clustered on an end table. She found an almost-empty box of Kleenex. Cassie Stadler's narrow shoulders bobbed; she sobbed silently, with all her body. Bugbee, who'd obviously learned how to distance, sat impatiently with a clipboard on his lap. Audrey couldn't take it anymore, put her arms around the woman, murmuring, "Oh, it's so hard, I know it."

Cassie took in great gulps of air, her head bent. Eventually she looked up, saw the Kleenex box and pulled out a few tissues, blew her nose.

"I'm sorry," she said. "I didn't think . . ."

"Don't apologize, sweetheart," Audrey said. "What a terrible time for you."

Cassie took out a pack of cigarettes and shook one out. "Okay if I smoke?"

Audrey nodded, gave Bugbee a sidelong glance. Smoking wasn't allowed in here, but she wasn't going to make a point of it, not with this poor woman at this time, and fortunately neither was Bugbee, who nodded as well.

Cassie took out a cheap plastic lighter and lit up, then exhaled a cloud of smoke. "He was shot in—in the mouth?"

A funeral home would have done some reconstruction, skillfully applied makeup. The face would have looked artificial in that way that all dead bodies look at funeral homes, but at least she'd have been spared the brutal sight.

"That's right," Bugbee said. He didn't elaborate, didn't say twice, didn't say Stadler had also been shot in the chest. He was following standard procedure, which was to give out as little information as possible, in case a withheld detail could help them, down the line, confirm the killer.

"God!" she erupted. "Why? Who'd *do* that to my daddy?" She took another puff, took an empty Coke can off the end table and tapped out the ash into its small opening.

"That's what we want to find out," Audrey said. *Daddy*: it stabbed her, hearing that from a grown woman. She thought of her own daddy, remembered his smell of tobacco and sweat and Vitalis. "We need your help. I know this is a painful time, and you probably don't want to talk at all, but anything you can think of will help."

"Miss Stadler," asked Bugbee, "was your father a drug user?"

"Drugs?" She looked puzzled. "What kind of drugs?"

"Such as crack?"

"Crack? My *dad*? Never."

"You'd be surprised at who uses drugs like crack cocaine," Audrey put in hastily. "People you'd never ever think of as users, people from all walks of life. Prominent citizens even."

"My dad didn't even know about that world. He was a simple guy."

"But it's possible he kept things from you," Audrey persisted.

"Sure, possible, but I mean—crack? I'd have noticed," Cassie said, expelling smoke through her nostrils like the twin plumes of a fire-breathing dragon. "I've been living with him for almost a year, I'd have seen something."

"Maybe not," Bugbee said.

"Look, I don't do drugs myself, but I sure know people who do. I mean, I'm an artist, I live in Chicago, it's not unheard of, you know? Dad had none of the signs. He—it's absurd, really."

"You're originally from here?" Audrey asked.

"I was born here, but my parents divorced when I was a kid, and I went to live with my mom in Chicago. I come . . . came back here to visit Dad pretty often."

"What made you come back to stay?"

"He called me and told me he'd just quit his job at Stratton, and I was worried about him. He's not well, and my mom passed away four or five years ago, and I knew he needed someone to take care of him. I was afraid he couldn't cope."

"When Detective Bugbee asked you about drugs just now, you hesitated," Audrey said. "Was he on any kind of medication?"

She nodded, passed a hand over her eyes. "A number of meds including Risperdal, an antipsychotic."

"Psychotic?" Bugbee blurted out. "Was he psychotic?"

Audrey briefly closed her eyes. The guy never failed to do or say the wrong thing.

Cassie turned slowly to look at Bugbee as she snubbed out the cigarette on the top of the Coke can, then dropped it through the opening. "He suffered from schizophrenia," she said absently. "He suffered from it for most of my life." She turned to Audrey. "But it was more or less under control."

"Did he ever disappear for stretches of time?" asked Audrey.

"No, not really. He'd go out for walks once in a while. I was glad when he got out of the house. This last year has been hard for him."

"What did he do at Stratton?" Bugbee asked.

"He was a model builder."

"What's that mean?"

"He worked in their model shop making prototypes of products they were working on, the latest chairs or desks or whatever."

"He quit, didn't get laid off?" Bugbee said.

"They were about to lay him off, but he just sort of blew up and quit before they could do it."

"When did you last see him?" Audrey asked.

"At supper Friday night. I—I'd just made supper for us, and he usually watches TV after supper. I went to the room I've been using as a studio and painted."

"You're an artist?"

"Sort of. Not as serious as I used to be, but I still paint. I never got a gallery or anything. I support myself by teaching Kripalu yoga."

"Here?"

"In Chicago I did. I haven't worked since I got to Fenwick."

"Did you see him before you went to sleep?" Audrey asked.

"No," she said sadly. "I fell asleep on the couch in there—I do that fairly often, when a painting's not working and I want to think about it, sometimes I just fall asleep and wake up in the morning. That's what happened Saturday morning—I got up and had breakfast, and when he wasn't down by ten I started to worry about him, so I went to his room, but he was gone. I—will you excuse me? I'm thirsty—I need—"

"What can we get you, honey?" said Audrey.

"Anything, just—I'm so thirsty."

"Water? Pop?"

"Something with sugar in it." She smiled apologetically. "I need a hit of sugar. Sprite, Seven-Up, anything. Just no caffeine. It makes me crazy."

"Roy," Audrey said, "there's a vending machine down the hall—could you . . . ?"

Bugbee's eyebrows went up, a nasty smile curling the corners of his mouth. He looked like he was about to say something unpleasant. But she wanted a little time alone with this woman. She had a feeling Cassie would open up more easily with her alone.

"Sure," Roy said after a long pause. "Happy to."

When the door closed, Audrey cleared her throat to speak, but Cassie spoke first.

"He has it in for you, doesn't he?"

Good God, was it that obvious? "Detective Bugbee?" Audrey said, feigning surprise.

Cassie nodded. "It's like he can barely contain his contempt for you."

"Detective Bugbee and I have a very good working relationship."

"I'm surprised you put up with him."

Audrey smiled. "I'd prefer to talk about your father."

"Of course. I'm sorry. I just—noticed." She was weeping again, wiping a hand across her eyes. "Detective, I—I have no idea in the world who might have killed my daddy. Or why. But I have a feeling that if anyone can find out, you can."

Audrey felt tears come into her eyes. "I'll do my best," she said. "That's all I can promise."

24

Terra was the finest restaurant in Fenwick, the place you went to celebrate special occasions like birthdays, promotions, a visit of a special old friend. It had the slightly forbidding air of an expensive place where it was assumed you didn't go often. Men were expected to wear ties. There was a maitre d' and a sommelier who wore a big silver taste-vin on a ribbon around his neck like an Olympic medal. The waiters ground pepper for you in a mill the size of a Louisville Slugger. The tablecloths were heavily starched white linen. The menu was immense, leather-bound, and required two hands. The wine list itself, a separate leather-bound folio, was twenty pages long. Nick had taken Laura here for her birthday, a few weeks before the accident; it was her favorite place. She loved their signature dessert, a molten chocolate cake that oozed chocolate like lava when you spooned into it. Nick found Terra stuffy and nervous-making, but the food was always great. From time to time he'd take important clients here.

Dinner tonight was with his most important client: his boss, the managing partner from Fairfield Equity Partners in Boston. Nick hadn't particularly liked Todd Muldaur when he first met him, in the company of Fairfield's founder, Willard Osgood. But Osgood always placed one of his deputies in charge of the companies his firm owned, and Todd was the man he picked.

Not long after Dorothy Devries had tapped Nick as her husband's successor as CEO, she'd summoned Nick back to her old dark mansion to announce that the family was facing a huge tax bill and had to sell. It was up to

Nick to find the ideal buyer. There was no shortage of interested bidders. The Stratton Corporation had no debt, steady profits, a major market share, and a famous name. But plenty of the buyout firms wanted to buy Stratton, gussy it up, then turn it around for a quick sale to someone else. Spin it off, maybe take it public—who the hell knew what those rape-and-pillage folks might do. Then the call came from the famous Willard Osgood, who had a reputation for buying companies and holding on to them forever, letting them run themselves. Willard Osgood: "the man with the Midas Touch," as *Fortune* magazine called him. The perfect solution. Osgood even flew in to Fenwick—well, he flew in to Grand Rapids in his private jet and then was driven out to Fenwick in a plain old Chrysler sedan—and came a-courtin' on the widow Devries and Nick. He charmed the pants off Dorothy Devries (she was partial to pantsuits, actually), and won over Nick as well. Willard Osgood was as plainspoken and unpretentious in person as he was in all his interviews. He was a lifelong Republican, an archconservative, just like Dorothy. He told her his favorite holding period was forever. Rule number one, he said, is never lose money; rule number two is never forget rule number one. He really won her over when he said it's better to buy a great company at a fair price than a fair company at a great price.

The deputy he brought with him, Todd Muldaur, a straw-haired Yale football jock who'd done time at the big management-consulting firm McKinsey, didn't say too much, but there was something about him Nick didn't like. He didn't like Todd's swagger. But hey, it was Osgood who ran the show, Nick figured. Not Muldaur.

Of course, now it was Todd who presided over the quarterly board meetings, Todd who read the monthly financial reports and asked all the questions, Todd who had to sign off on the major decisions. After that first meeting with Willard Osgood, Nick never saw the old guy again.

Nick arrived a few minutes early. Scott McNally was already at the table, nursing a Diet Coke. He'd changed out of his frayed blue button-down shirt into a crisp blue-and-white broad-striped one, a red tie, a good dark suit. Nick was wearing his best suit too, which Laura had picked out for him at Brooks Brothers in Grand Rapids.

"Muldaur give you any sense of what he's here for?" Nick asked as he sat down. This was just about the last place he wanted to be, eating at a fancy restaurant when he had no appetite, being social with some strutting asshole when he just wanted to be home in bed.

"No idea. He didn't say."

"He told me he wanted to 'touch base' in advance of the board meeting."

"Gotta be the updated financials I just sent him. They can't be happy about our numbers either."

"Still, no need for a personal visit."

Scott lowered his head, muttered, "He just walked in." Nick looked up, saw the big blond man coming their way. Both he and Scott stood.

Scott stepped around the table, went up to Muldaur, gave him a hearty two-handed shake. "Hey, bud!"

"Scotty! My man!"

Muldaur extended his beefy hand to Nick and gave him one of those unnecessarily crushing handshakes, grabbing his fingers just below the knuckles in such a way that Nick couldn't shake back. Nick hated that. "Nice to see you," Todd said.

Todd Muldaur had a big square jaw, a button nose, and turquoise eyes that were bluer than they'd been last time Nick had seen him, in a glass-walled conference room at Fairfield's offices on Federal Street in Boston. Had to be colored contacts. He had the lean, drawn face of a guy who ate a lot of protein, worked out regularly. He wore a dove-gray suit that looked expensive. "So, this must be the one good restaurant in town, huh?"

"Nothing but the best for our friends from Boston," Nick said affably as they sat down.

Todd took the big white linen napkin, unfolded it, and put it in his lap. "Gotta be good," he said sardonically. "The American Automobile Association gives this place its 'prestigious Four Diamond Award,' it says out front."

Nick smiled and imagined punching Todd's face out. He noticed a couple being seated a few tables over and recognized them. The man had been a senior manager at Stratton until last year, when his division had been shut down in the layoffs. The guy was in his fifties, with two kids in college, and despite the best efforts of the outplacement service Stratton had hired, hadn't been able to find another job.

That familiar sinking feeling came over him. Nick excused himself, and went over to say hello.

It was the man's wife who saw him first. Her eyes widened briefly. She turned away, said something quickly to her husband, then stood up, but not to greet him.

"Bill," Nick said.

Now the man rose without saying anything, and he and his wife turned and walked out of the dining room. For a few seconds, Nick stood there, his face burning. He wondered why he subjected himself to this kind of snub. It happened often enough for him to know better. Maybe, on some level, he felt he deserved it.

By the time he returned to his table, Todd and Scott were deep in conversation about the good old days at McKinsey. Nick hoped that neither man had seen what had just happened.

It had been Todd who'd insisted that Stratton replace their old CFO, Henry "Hutch" Hutchens, with Scott McNally. Nick had gone along quite happily, but it annoyed him sometimes that Scott was so friendly with Muldaur.

"Whatever happened to that guy Nolan Bennis?" Scott was saying. "Remember him?" He smiled at Nick. "Another McKinseyite. You wouldn't believe this dweeb." He turned back to Todd. "Remember that Shedd Island retreat?" He explained to Nick: "McKinsey always used to rent out this really posh hotel on this superexclusive island off the coast of South Carolina, for a retreat with top clients. So this guy Nolan Bennis is out there on the tennis court with some Carbide guys, and I swear to God, he's wearing black socks and penny loafers. Couldn't play for shit. Really stank up the place. We heard about that for months—what an embarrassment. I mean, the guy was a total loser. You couldn't take him out in public. He still at McKinsey?"

"You obviously didn't see the latest *Forbes* Four Hundred," Todd said.

"What are you talking about?" Scott said, a quizzical look on his face.

"Nolan Bennis is the CEO of ValueMetrics. Worth four billion dollars now. He bought the Shedd Island hotel a couple of years ago, along with about five hundred acres on the island."

"I always thought that guy would go places," Scott said.

"Gotta love this menu," Todd said. "Duck breast with raspberry coulis. I mean, how 1995 can you get? I'm getting nostalgic here."

The waitress approached their table. "May I tell you about our specials tonight?" she said. The woman looked familiar to Nick, though he couldn't quite place her. She glanced at Nick, looked away quickly. She knew him too. Not another one.

"We have a Chilean sea bass with roasted cauliflower, pancetta, and tangerine juice for twenty-nine dollars. There's a pistachio-crusted rack of lamb with celery root puree and wild mushrooms. And the catch of the day is a seared tuna—"

"Let me guess," Todd broke in. "It's 'sushi quality,' and it's served rare in the center."

"That's *right*!" she said.

"Where have I heard that before?"

"You look familiar," Nick said, feeling bad for the woman.

Her eyes flitted to him and then away. "Yes, Mr. Conover. I used to work for Stratton, in Travel."

"I'm sorry to hear that. You doing okay?"

She hesitated. "Waitressing pays less than half what I was making at Stratton, sir," she answered tightly.

"It's been tough all around," Nick said.

"I'll give you gentlemen a few more minutes to decide," she said, and moved quickly away.

"Is she going to spit in our salads?" Todd said.

"You guys don't need me to tell you we got a real problem here," Todd said.

"No question," Scott agreed quickly.

Nick nodded, waited.

"A bad quarter or two, blame it on a lousy economy," Todd said. "But it keeps happening, it begins to look like a death spiral. And we can't afford that."

"I understand your concern," Nick said, "and believe me, I share it. I want to assure you that we've got things under control. We've got a major customer coming in tomorrow—I mean *major*—and it looks good for signing them up. That contract alone will turn things around."

"Hey, we can always hope lightning strikes," Todd said. "Maybe you'll get lucky. But let me tell you something. Corporations may be based on continuity, but capital markets are all about *creative destruction*. If you're unwilling to change, you'll be drawn into that big slide toward mediocrity. As CEO, you've got to overcome the organizational inertia. Unclog those corporate arteries. Free the flow of fresh ideas. Even the best boats need rocking, man. That's the magic of capitalism. That's what Joseph Schumpeter said years ago."

"Didn't he used to play for the Bruins?" Nick said, deadpan.

"There's the quick, and there's the dead, Nick," Todd said.

"Well, I don't know about 'creative destruction,'" Nick said, "but I know we're all basically in sync. That's why we sold the company to Fairfield. You guys are value investors with the long view—that's the only reason I was able to convince Dorothy Devries to sell to you. I always remember what Willard said to Dorothy and me, in the parlor of her house on Michigan Avenue— 'We want to be your partner, your sounding board. We don't want to run the business—we want you to run the business. We may have to go through some pain together, but we're all in this for the long haul.'"

Todd smiled slyly. He got what Nick was doing, invoking the words of the ultimate boss like Holy Scripture. "That sounds just like Willard. But you gotta understand something—the old man's been spending an awful lot of time fly-fishing in the Florida Keys these days. Guy loves fly-fishing—last year or so, he seems to think a lot more about tarpon and bonefish than P and Ls."

"He's retiring?"

"Not yet, but soon. All but. Which means he leaves the heavy lifting to us, the poor suckers who have to go to work every day and do the dirty work while he's standing in the bow of his Hell's Bay, casting his line. The world has changed, Nick. Used to be all the big institutional investors would write us a twenty-million-dollar check, maybe a hundred-million-dollar check, and let us do our job. At the end of six years, ten years, they cash out, everyone's happy. Not anymore. Now they're all looking over our shoulders, calling all the time. They don't want to see one of our major investments turn sour. They want to see results yesterday."

"They ought to go to your Web site," Nick said. Fairfield Equity Partners actually had an animated Flash movie on its Web site, the Aesop's fable of the tortoise and the hare, made to look like a storybook. It was beyond corn-ball. "Tell 'em to check out the tortoise-and-the-hare story. Remind 'em about the long view."

"These days, the tortoise gets made into turtle soup, buddy," Todd said.

Scott laughed a bit too loud.

"Don't worry," Nick said, "that's not on the menu."

Todd didn't smile. "The kind of companies we like are healthy compa-nies that are growing. We don't believe in catching a falling knife."

"We're not a falling knife, Todd," Nick said calmly. "We're going through some adjustments, but we're on the right path."

"Nick, the quarterly board meeting is in a couple of days, and I want to make sure the board sees a comprehensive plan to turn things around. I'm talking plant consolidation, selling off real estate, whatever. Creative de-struction. I don't want the board losing confidence in you."

"Are you implying what I think you're implying?"

Todd cracked a victorious smile. "Hell no, Nick! Don't take me the wrong way! When we bought Stratton, we weren't just buying some outdated factories in East Bumfuck, Michigan, with equipment out of 1954. We were buying a *team*. That means you. We want you to hang in there. We just need you to start thinking different. A balls-out, warp-speed effort to come up with a way to change the trend line."

Scott nodded sagely, chewing his lower lip, twirling a few strands of his hair behind his right ear. "I get what you're saying, and I think I've got some interesting ideas."

"What I like to hear. I mean, hell, there's no reason for you to have all your components made in the U.S. when you can get 'em at half the price from China, you know?"

"Actually," Nick said, "we've considered and rejected that, Todd, because—"

Scott broke in, "I think it's worth taking up again."

Nick gave him a black look.

"I knew I could count on you guys. Well, who's up for dessert? Let me guess—the dessert trend that swept Manhattan in 1998 has finally made it to Fenwick: molten chocolate cake?"

After they said goodbye to Todd and watched him drive away in his rented Lincoln Town Car, Nick turned to Scott. "Whose side are you on, anyway?"

"What are you talking about? You've got to keep the boss happy."

"I'm your boss, Scott. Not Todd Muldaur. Remember that."

Scott hesitated, seemingly debating whether to argue. "Anyway, who says there's sides? We're all in this together, Nick."

"There's always sides," Nick said quietly. "Inside or outside. Are you with me?"

"Of course, Nick. Jesus. Of course I'm on your side, what do you think?"

25

Leon was watching TV and drinking a beer. That was pretty much all he did these days, when he wasn't sleeping. Audrey looked at her husband, slouched in the middle of the couch, wearing pajama bottoms and a white T-shirt that was too tight over his ever-expanding beer gut. The thirty or forty pounds he'd put on in the past year or so made him look ten years older. Once she would have said he was the hardest-working man she'd ever met, never missed a day of work on the line, never complaining. Now, with his work life taken away from him, he was lost. Without work, he retreated into a life of sloth; there was no in-between for him.

She went over to the couch and kissed him. He hadn't shaved, hadn't bathed either. He didn't turn his head to kiss her; he received her kiss, his eyes not even moving from the screen. After a while, Audrey standing there, hands on her hips, smiling, he said, "Hey, Shorty," in his whiskey-and-cigarettes voice. "Home late."

Shorty: his term of endearment almost since they'd started going out. He was well over six feet, she was barely five, and they did look funny walking together.

"I called and left you a message," she said. "You must have been in conference." He knew she meant asleep. That was how she dealt with Leon's newfound lifestyle. The idea of his sitting around watching TV and sleeping during the day, when they had a mortgage to pay—it was infuriating to her. She knew she wasn't being entirely reasonable about it. The poor guy had been laid off from his job, and there wasn't a company for hundreds of miles around that was looking to hire an electrostatic powder-coating technician. Still, half the town had been laid off, and plenty of people had managed to get jobs working for Home Depot or bagging groceries at the Food Town. The pay was lousy, but it was better than nothing, and certainly better than sleeping on the couch all day.

He didn't answer. Leon had deep-set eyes, a large head, a powerful build, and once, not that long ago, he would have been considered a fine-looking man. Now he looked beaten down, defeated.

"You . . . get my message about dinner?" Meaning, of course, that she wanted him to make dinner. Nothing complicated. There was frozen hamburger he could defrost in the microwave. A package of romaine hearts he could wash for salad. Whatever. But she smelled nothing, no food cooking, and she knew the answer before he spoke.

"I ate already."

"Oh. Okay." She'd left him a message around four, as soon as she knew she'd be staying late, way before he ever ate supper. She suppressed her annoyance, went into the kitchen. The small counter was stacked so high—dirty plates, glasses, coffee mugs, beer bottles—that you couldn't even see the swirly rose Formica surface. How, she marveled, could one person create such a mess in a day? Why did he refuse to clean up after himself? Did he expect her to be breadwinner and wife and housekeeper all at the same time? In the plastic trash bucket was a discarded Hungry Man box and plastic compartmented tray, crusted with tomato sauce goo. She reached down, felt it. It was still warm. He'd just eaten. Not hours ago. He'd been hungry and just made himself dinner, didn't make anything for her even though she'd asked him to. Well, exactly *because* she'd asked him to, probably.

Returning to the living room, she stood there, waiting to get his attention, but he kept watching the baseball game. She cleared her throat. Nothing.

She said, "Leon, honey, can I talk to you for a second?"

"Sure."

"Could you look at me?"

He muted the TV, finally, and turned.

"Baby, I thought you were going to make us both supper."

"I didn't know when you were getting back."

"But I said . . ." She bit her lip. She was not going to yell at him. She was not going to be the one to start the quarreling, not this time. She softened her voice a bit. "I asked you to make dinner for us, right?"

"I figured you'd eat whenever you got home, Shorty. Don't want to make something's gonna get cold."

She nodded. Paused. By now she knew the script by heart. But our deal, our agreement, was that you make dinner, clean up, you know I can't do everything. And he says, How come you can't do what you did before? You had time to do that stuff before. And she says, I need help, Leon, that's the point. I get home exhausted. And he says, How do you think I feel, sitting here like a good-for-nothing piece of shit? At least you got a job.

That worked for a long time, that guilt thing. But then he began to take it to another level, talking about how cooking and cleaning, that was woman's work, and how come all of a sudden he's expected to do woman's work, was this all because he wasn't bringing home a paycheck? And by now she wants to scream, woman's work? Woman's work? What makes this woman's work? And can't you at least pick up after yourself? And so it would go, tedious and mind-numbing and pointless.

"Okay," she said.

She was working six cases, three of them active, one a homicide. You couldn't really focus on more than one at a time; tonight was Andrew Stadler. She placed the accordion file on the couch next to her, and while Leon watched the Tigers and drank himself into a stupor, she read over the files. She liked to read case files just before she went to sleep. She believed that her unconscious kept working on things, poking and prodding, turning things over with its gimlet eye, saw things more clearly than she did awake.

How Andrew Stadler's body ended up in a Dumpster on the five hundred block of Hastings baffled her. So did the fake crack. His diagnosed schizophrenia—did that fit in anywhere? Obviously she'd have to talk to his boss at Stratton, and the Employee Relations director too. See if there'd been any indication of drug use.

She was tempted to ask Leon about Stratton, about the model shop, if he knew anything about it. Maybe he'd even run across Stadler in the factory some time, or knew someone who knew him. She was, in fact, just about to say something when she turned to look at him, saw his glazed eyes, his defeated face, and decided not to. Any little thing she mentioned about the job these days was like probing a bad tooth for him. It reminded him of how she had a job she was involved in, and how he didn't.

Not worth the pain, she decided.

When the game was over, he went to bed, and she followed. As she brushed her teeth and washed her face, she debated whether to put on her usual long T-shirt or a teddy. They hadn't had sex in more than six months, and not because she didn't want it. He'd lost all interest. But she needed it, needed to regain that physical closeness. Otherwise . . .

By the time she got into bed, Leon was snoring.

She slipped in beside him, clicked off her bedside lamp, and was soon asleep.

She dreamed of Tiffany Akins, dying in her arms. The little girl in the SpongeBob pajamas. The girl who could have been her own. Who could have been herself. She dreamed of her father, of that moment when Cassie Stadler called her father Daddy.

And then her gimlet-eyed subconscious kicked something upstairs, and her eyes came open. She sat up slowly.

It was all too clean. An *absence* of evidence.

Not just the daubs of pharmaceutical-grade starch on the plastic bags wrapped around the body. This indicated that the body had been moved by someone wearing surgical gloves, someone who was careful about not leaving fingerprints. That in itself revealed a degree of caution not often found in drug murder cases. But neither was there any particulate matter on the body, no fibers, none of the normal trace evidence you always found on the body of a victim. Even the treads on the victim's shoes, where you always found dirt, had been brushed clean.

She remembered, too, how clean the body was at the autopsy. She remembered the pathologist saying, "He looks more like a house case than a police case."

That was it; that was the anomaly. The body had been fastidiously cleaned, gone over by an expert. By someone who *knew* what the police looked for.

Andrew Stadler's body hadn't been disposed of by some crack dealer in a panic. It had been carefully, methodically placed in a Dumpster by someone who knew what he was doing.

It took her a long time to fall back asleep.

26

"This stuff tastes like twigs," Julia said.

Nick couldn't stop himself from laughing out loud. The front of the box had a photograph of two smiling people, a little Asian girl and a blond Nordic-looking boy. They weren't smiling about the cereal, that was for sure.

"It's good for you," he said.

"How come I always have to have healthy cereal? Everyone else in my class gets to have whatever they want for breakfast."

"I doubt that."

"Paige gets to have Froot Loops or Cap'n Crunch or Apple Jacks every morning."

"Paige . . ." Normally the parental responses came quickly to him, auto-pilot, but this morning he wasn't thinking very clearly. He worried about taking the sleeping pill so many days in a row. It was probably addictive. He wondered whether Julia or Lucas or Marta had heard anything two nights before. "Paige doesn't do well in school because she doesn't start off her day with a healthy breakfast." Sometimes he couldn't believe the crap he said aloud, the shameless propaganda. When he was a kid, he ate whatever the hell he wanted for break-fast, sugary shit like Quisp and Quake and Cocoa Puffs, and he did just fine in school. He didn't know, actually, if all kids were forced to eat healthy breakfasts by their parents these days, or it was just Laura who'd insisted on it. Whatever, he observed the Law of Healthy Breakfast as if it were the Constitution.

"Paige is in my math group," Julia countered.

"Good for her. I don't care if she eats chocolate cake for breakfast." The TV had been set up on a table in this temporary corner of the kitchen. The *Today* show was on, but right now there was a local commercial for Pajot Ford, always an annoying ad. John Pajot, the owner, was also the pitchman—hell, he paid for the ads, he could star in them if he wanted to—and he always did them wearing a hunting outfit. He made puns about saving "bucks" and "racking up" savings.

"Where's your brother?" he asked.

She shrugged, staring balefully at the cereal. It actually did look like stuff gathered from the ground in a forest. "Asleep, probably."

"All right, just have some yogurt, then."

"But I don't like the kind we have. It doesn't taste good."

"It's what we have. That's your choice. Yogurt or . . . twigs."

"But I like strawberry."

"I'll ask Marta to get more strawberry. In the meantime we have vanilla. It's good." Marta was doing laundry. He'd have to remember to ask her to add strawberry yogurt to her shopping list. Also some healthy cereal that didn't taste like twigs.

"No, it's not. It's the organic kind. Their vanilla tastes funny."

"It's that or string cheese, take your choice."

Julia sighed with bottomless frustration. "String cheese," she said sullenly.

The local news segment came on, and the anchorman, a lean-faced, slick-looking guy with shoe-polish black hair, said something about "found brutally murdered."

"Where's the remote?" asked Nick. When Julia was in hearing range, he normally muted any TV stories about murders or gruesome crimes or child molestation. She reached for it between the carton of organic one-percent milk and the sugar bowl, handed it to her father. He grabbed it, searched for the tiny mute button—why didn't they make the damned mute button bigger, and a different color?—but as he was about to press it, he saw the graphic on the screen. A photograph of a horribly familiar face, the words "Andrew Stadler." He froze, stared, his heart pounding.

He heard: "Dumpster behind Lucky's Restaurant on Hastings Street."

He heard: "Thirty-six years at the Stratton Company until he was laid off last March."

"What's the matter, Daddy?" Julia asked.

He heard something about funeral arrangements. "Hmm? Oh, nothing. One of our Stratton employees died, baby. Come on, get yourself some string cheese."

"Was he old?" she asked, getting up.

"Yeah," Nick said. "He was old."

Marge was already at her desk when he arrived, sipping coffee from a Stratton mug and reading a novel by Jane Austen. She flipped the paperback closed apologetically. "Oh, good morning," she said. "Sorry, I was hoping to finish this before my book group meets tonight."

"Don't let me stop you."

A copy of the *Fenwick Free Press* had been placed on his desk next to his keyboard. A front-page headline read: "Longtime Stratton Employee a Probable Homicide." Marjorie must have placed it there, folded so that the Stadler article faced up.

He hadn't bothered to look at the paper this morning before leaving the house; it had been too hectic. Luke hadn't gotten up, so Nick had gone to his room to awaken him. From under his mound of blankets and sheet, Luke had said he had study hour first period and was going to sleep in. Instead of arguing, Nick simply closed Luke's bedroom door.

Now he picked up the article and read it closely. Once again his heart was drumming. Not much here in the way of details. ". . . body discovered in a Dumpster behind a restaurant on Hastings Street." Nothing about it being wrapped in plastic; Nick wondered whether Eddie had, for some reason, removed the trash bags. "Apparently shot several times," though it didn't say where the man had been shot. Surely the police hadn't released to the paper everything they knew about the case. As nerve-wracking as it was to read, Nick found it oddly reassuring. The details formed a convincing picture of an unemployed man who'd been murdered in a rough part of town, probably having been involved in some street crime. There was a photo of Stadler taken at least twenty years ago: the same glasses, the same tight mouth. You'd read the article, shake your head sadly over how the loss of a job had caused an already troubled man to spiral into drugs or crime or something, and you'd move on to the sports.

Nick's eyes filled with tears. This is the man I killed. A man who left behind one child—"a daughter, Cassie, twenty-nine, of Chicago"—and an ex-wife who'd died four years earlier. A modest, quiet-living man, worked in a Stratton factory for his entire adult life.

He was suddenly aware of Marge standing there, looking worriedly at him. She'd said something.

"Excuse me?"

"I said, it's sad, isn't it?"

"Terribly sad," Nick said.

"The funeral's this afternoon. You have a telcon with Sales, but that can be rescheduled."

He nodded, realizing what she was saying. Nick usually attended the funerals of all Stratton employees, just as old man Devries had done. It was a tradition, a ceremonial obligation of the CEO in this company town.

He'd have to go to Andrew Stadler's funeral. He didn't really have a choice.

27

"You're not helping me any," Audrey said.

Bert Koopmans, the evidence tech, turned at the sink where he was washing his hands. There was something birdlike about the way he inclined his head, gawked at her. He was tall, almost spindly, with small close-set eyes that always looked startled.

"Not my job," he said, dry but not unfriendly. "What's the problem?"

She hesitated. "Well, you really didn't find anything on the body, when it comes right down to it."

"What body are we talking about?"

"Stadler."

"Who?"

"The guy in the Dumpster. Down on Hastings."

"The tortilla."

"Burrito, really."

He allowed a hint of a smile. "You got everything I got."

"Did the body strike you as too . . . clean?"

"Clean? You talking hygiene? I mean, the guy's fingernails were filthy."

"That's not what I mean, Bert." She thought a minute. "The dirt under his fingernails—that got tagged, right?"

"No, I lost it," Bert said, flashing her a look. "You forget who you're talking to? Like this was one of Wayne's cases?" Not all the techs were as meticulous, as obsessive-compulsive as Koopmans. He walked over to a black file cabinet, pulled it open, selected a folder. He scanned a sheet of paper. "Pubic hairs, head hairs, fingernails left hand, fingernails right hand. Fibers from shoe left, fibers from shoe right. Unidentified substance under fingernails right hand, unidentified substance under fingernails left hand. Want me to keep going?"

"No, thanks. What's the unidentified substance?"

Another look. "If I knew what it was, think I'd call it unidentified?"

"Are we talking skin or blood or dirt?"

"You try my patience, Detective. Skin and blood, these are substances I've seen before, believe it or not."

"Dirt you've seen before too."

He shrugged one shoulder. "But dirt isn't dirt. It's . . . stuff. It's anything. I made a note that it had a kind of greenish hue to it."

"Green paint? If Stadler scraped his fingernails against the side of a house, say . . . ?"

"Paint I would have recognized." He handed her the chain-of-custody sheet. "Here. Why don't you take a walk down to Property and get the shit. We can both take a look."

The guy who ran the Property room was a clock-puncher named Arthur something, a flabby white man with a toothbrush mustache who wore coveralls. She pushed the buzzer, and he took his time coming around to the window. She handed him the pink copy of the Property Receipt, explaining that she only wanted item number fifteen. All the evidence—the pulled head hair, pulled pubic hair, the two vials of blood—was kept in a big refrigerator. Arthur returned a few minutes later and could not have looked more bored. As he went through the ritual of scanning the bar code label on the five-by-seven evidence envelope marked "Nail Clippings From Autopsy," then the bar code on the wall chart to capture her name and number, Audrey heard Roy Bugbee's voice.

"That looks like the Stadler case," Bugbee said.

She nodded. "You working Jamal Wilson?"

Bugbee ignored her question. As the property guy slid the envelope under the window, Bugbee snatched it before Audrey could get to it. "Nail clippings, eh?"

"Just some more trace evidence I'm running past IBO again."

"Why do I get the crazy feeling we're not partnering on this, Audrey?"

"There's no end of things I'd appreciate your help on," she said uneasily.

"Right," Bugbee said. "You going over to IBO right now?"

Koopmans, who seemed surprised to see Roy Bugbee, placed two sheets of copy paper on the counter in the long narrow lab room where they fumed for fingerprints. He slit the bottom of each little envelope with a disposable scalpel and tapped out the contents onto the paper.

"Like I said, green dirt," Koopmans said. He and Audrey both wore surgical masks so that their breath wouldn't blow away the dirt. Bugbee did not.

Audrey peered closely. "Would it help to put it under a binocular microscope?"

"Happy to. But I've already done it, and there's nothing more to see." He sifted the tiny pile with a wooden applicator. "Sand, some kind of fine green powder, some fragments of what looks like pellets, maybe. Take it over to the state lab, if you want, but they're just going to tell you what I've just said. And it'll take 'em six weeks to tell you."

"Christ," said Bugbee, "you don't need a microscope for this shit."

"Oh, is that right," said Koopmans, giving Audrey a quick look.

"You don't have a lawn, obviously," Bugbee said. "That's hydroseed."

"Hydroseed," said Koopmans.

"Which is what, exactly?" Audrey asked.

"It's grass seed and, I don't know, ground-up newspaper and shit they spray. To start a new lawn. Hate the shit, myself—full of weed seed. I call it 'hydroweed.'"

"But it's green," Audrey said.

"That's the dye powder," Koopmans said. "And the pellets—that's the mulch." He pulled at his chin with his thumb and forefinger.

"Well, you saw the Stadler home," Audrey said. "I didn't see any hydroseed, did you?"

"Naw," said Bugbee, cocky. "A shitty lawn. All crabgrass and broadleaf weeds. Guys notice stuff like that."

"If you're lawn-obsessed," Koopmans said. "Is it possible your guy had some part-time job doing landscaping work or something?"

"No," Audrey said. "He could barely hold on to his job at Stratton. No, I suspect he got that stuff under his fingernails from wherever he went. Maybe—probably—the night he was killed."

28

The Mount Pleasant Cemetery was not the biggest burial ground in Fenwick Township, nor especially well tended. It sat on a high bluff above a busy highway and seemed forlorn, even for a cemetery. Nick had never been here before. Then again, he hated cemeteries and avoided them whenever possible. When he had to attend a funeral, he went to the church or funeral home and missed this part. Laura's death had made burials harder, not easier.

But he was late. He'd missed the service at the funeral home, having been unable to reschedule a major teleconference with the CEOs of Steelcase and Herman Miller to discuss a lobbying effort against an idiotic bill before Congress.

He parked his Suburban along a curb near where a ceremony was going on. There was a small clutch of people in dark clothing, maybe ten or twelve people in all. There was a pastor, a black woman, an elderly couple, five or six guys who might have worked with Stadler, a pretty young woman who had to be the man's daughter. She was petite, with big eyes and short, sort of chopped-looking punk hair. The paper had said she was twenty-nine and lived in Chicago.

Nick approached tentatively, heard the pastor, standing beside the casket, say: "Bless this grave that the body of our brother Andrew may sleep here in peace until You awaken him to glory, when he will see You face to face and know the splendor of the eternal God, who lives and reigns, now and forever." The roaring traffic obliterated some of his words.

A couple of the mourners turned to look at him. The Stratton guys recognized him, their eyes lingering a moment longer. Nick thought he saw surprise, maybe a flash or two of indignation, though he wasn't sure. The beautiful daughter looked dazed, like a deer caught in the headlights. Near her stood the black woman, who was quite attractive as well. She looked at Nick, her glance piercing, tears running down her cheeks. Nick wondered who she was. There weren't that many blacks in town.

He wasn't prepared for the sight of the burnished mahogany casket, sitting atop the lowering device, Nick remembered from Laura's burial, which was hidden behind drapes of green crushed velvet. It jolted him. Somehow it was even more brutal, that tall, rounded mahogany coffin, than seeing Andrew Stadler's dead body crumpled on his lawn. It was more final, more *real*. This was a man with a family—a daughter, at least—and friends. He might have been a dangerous, unmedicated schizophrenic—but he was somebody's daddy too. This lovely young woman with the spiky hair and porcelain skin. Tears sprang to Nick's eyes. He was embarrassed.

The black woman glanced at him again. Who was she?

The Stratton guys looked at him again, no doubt noticing his tears and inwardly rolling their eyes at the hypocrisy. Slasher Nick weeping at the grave of a guy he laid off, they had to be thinking.

When it was over, and the coffin was lowered smoothly and silently into the grave, the mourners began tossing clods of earth and flowers onto the coffin. Some of them embraced the daughter, clutching her hand, murmuring condolences. When the moment seemed right, he approached her.

"Ms. Stadler, I'm Nick Conover. I'm the—"

"I know who you are," she replied coolly. She had the tiniest stud on the right side of her nose, a glint of light.

"I didn't know your father personally, but I wanted to tell you how sorry I am. He was a valued employee."

"So valued that you fired him." She spoke in a quiet tone, but her bitterness was obvious.

"The layoffs have been difficult for all of us. So many deserving people lost their jobs."

She sighed as if the subject wasn't worth discussing any further. "Yeah, well, everything started to fall apart for my dad when he got forced out."

He'd steeled himself against anger, given how often he met former Stratton employees, but this he wasn't quite prepared for, not here in a cemetery, from a woman who was burying her father. "It's a terrible thing he had to go through." He noticed the black woman watching the exchange with interest, though she was far enough away that she might not have been able to hear what they were saying.

Stadler's daughter smiled ruefully. "Let's get one thing straight, Mr. Conover. As far as I'm concerned, you killed my dad."

29

Leon's oldest sister, LaTonya, was a very large woman with an imperious way about her, adamant in all her opinions, though maybe you had to be to raise six kids. Audrey liked being around her—she was everything Audrey wasn't, bawdy where Audrey was respectful, profane where Audrey was polite, stubborn where Audrey was compliant. Things might not have been so good with Leon, but that didn't affect their friendship. Sisterhood was stronger. LaTonya didn't have much respect for her younger brother anyway, it seemed.

Fairly often Audrey baby-sat the three younger Saunders kids. Most of the time she enjoyed it. They were good kids, a twelve-year-old girl and two boys, nine and eleven. No doubt they ran roughshod over her, took advantage of her good nature, got away with stuff their drill-sergeant mother would never let them. But that, she figured, was what aunts were for. It didn't escape her, either, that LaTonya herself took advantage of Audrey, asking her to sit way more than she should, because LaTonya understood what was never said aloud, that her kids were the only kids Audrey would ever have.

LaTonya arrived home an hour later this evening than she'd said she would. She was taking a motivational training seminar at the Days Inn on Winsted Avenue, learning to start a home business. Her husband, Paul, managed the service department of a GMC dealership and usually worked late, didn't get home until eight. Audrey didn't mind, really. She'd just come off a long shift, which included attending the Andrew Stadler funeral, and would rather spend a few hours with her niece and nephews than at home with Leon, to be honest. Or thinking about poor Cassie Stadler. You had to take a break sometimes.

LaTonya was lugging a huge cardboard box heaped with white plastic bottles. Her moon-shaped face was beaded with sweat. "This here," she announced as the screen door slammed behind her, "is going to liberate us from debt."

"What is it?" Audrey asked. Camille was practicing her piano in the den by now and the two boys were watching TV.

"Hey, what's this? What the *hell* is *this*?" LaTonya hollered at her sons as she dropped the box on the kitchen table. "I don't care how much of a pushover your Auntie Audrey is, we have a rule about the TV. Turn that goddamned set off, and get to your homework, right now!"

"But Audrey said we could!" protested Thomas, the younger son. Matthew, experienced enough to know never to argue with their mother, scampered upstairs.

"I don't give a shit what Audrey said, you know the rules!" she thundered. She turned to Audrey, her voice softening. "It's weight-loss supplements. In a year or two, I'm not going to *need* Paul's salary. Not that there's much of that."

"Weight-loss supplements?"

"Thermogenic," LaTonya said. It was clear she had just learned the word. "Burns the fat off. Stokes up your metabolism. Blocks carbs too. And it's all natural."

"Sistah, you got to be careful with those make-money-at-home schemes," Audrey said. It was funny, when she was around LaTonya she found herself talking black, the rhythms of her speech changing. She was acutely aware that LaTonya considered Audrey saditty, or conceited.

"Careful?" LaTonya gasped. "This is the wellness industry we're talking about. In five years it's going to be a *trillion*-dollar industry, and I'm getting on the elevator at the ground floor." She opened a new box of Ritz crackers, offered it to Audrey, who shook her head. LaTonya tore open the wax paper on one of the cracker rolls and grabbed a handful.

"LaTonya, can I talk to you for a second?"

"Mmmph?" LaTonya replied through a mouthful of cracker.

"It's the way you talk to your kids. The language. I don't think children should hear that kind of language, particularly from a parent."

LaTonya's eyes widened in indignation. She put her hands on her hips. She chewed, swallowed, then said, "Audrey, baby, I love you, but they're my kids, you understand? Not yours. Mine."

"But still," Audrey said, regretting she'd said anything, wanting to take it back.

"Honey, these little buggers respect strong words. If you had kids, you'd understand." LaTonya saw the wounded look in Audrey's face. "I'm—I'm sorry, I didn't mean it the way it came out."

"That's okay," Audrey said with a dismissive shake of the head. "I shouldn't have said anything."

LaTonya was holding up one of the big white plastic bottles. "*This* you need," she said.

"*I* need?"

"For your no-good, lazy-ass husband. My brother. Least he can do while he's sitting on his butt is take some of these thermogenic supplements. Twenty-four ninety-five. You can afford it. Tell you what: I'll give you my discount. Sixteen fifty. Can't do better than that."

30

Audrey didn't much like the security director of the Stratton Corporation, an ex-cop named Edward Rinaldi. For one thing, there was his initial unwillingness to meet her, which she found peculiar. She was investigating the death of a Stratton employee, after all. How packed could his schedule really be? On the phone, after she'd told him what she wanted, he'd said he was "raked."

Then there was his reputation, which was a little hinky. She always did her homework, of course, and before coming to Stratton headquarters, she called around, figuring that the security director of the biggest company in town had to be known to at least the uniform division of the police. She learned that he was a local boy, went to high school with Nicholas Conover, Stratton's CEO. That he'd joined the force in Grand Rapids. His dealings with the Fenwick police were limited to pilferage cases and vandalism at Stratton. "That guy?" a veteran patrol cop named Vogel told her. "He never woulda made it here. We'd have kicked him out on his ass."

"How come?"

"Smartass. Got his own rule book, know what I'm saying."

"I don't think I do, no."

"I don't want to spread rumors. Ask around in GR."

"I will, but you've dealt with him yourself, haven't you?"

"Ah, he was all over us on some vandalism deal at the CEO's house like it was our fault, instead of some whacked laid-off employee."

"All over you how?"

"He wanted the priors on this employee."

"Who?"

Vogel seemed surprised. "What're you talking, your guy, of course, right? That Stadler guy, isn't that why you called me?"

Suddenly Edward Rinaldi was becoming more interesting.

When she called Grand Rapids, she had a harder time finding someone who'd talk to her about Edward Rinaldi, until a lieutenant there named Pettigrew confided that Rinaldi was not missed. "Put it this way," the lieutenant said cagily, "he lived pretty good."

"Meaning what?"

"Meaning his income wasn't necessarily limited to his salary."

"We talking bribes, Lieutenant?"

"Could be, but that's not what I mean. I'm just saying that not all the evidence from drug busts made it to the property room."

"He was a user?"

The lieutenant chuckled. "Not so far as I know. He seemed a lot more interested in the shoeboxes full of cash. But he was booted out without a formal IA investigation, so that's just rumor."

It was enough to make her wary of the man.

But most of all she didn't like Rinaldi's manner—the evasiveness, the shiftiness in his eyes, the quick and inappropriate grins, the intensity of his stare. There was something vulgar, something scammy about the man.

"Where's your partner?" he asked after they'd chatted a few minutes. "Don't you guys always work in teams?"

"Often." He and Bugbee would have hit it off just fine, she thought. Cut from the same bolt of polyester fabric.

"You're Detective Rhimes? As in LeAnn Rimes?"

"Spelled differently," she said. "Did Andrew Stadler vandalize your CEO's house, Mr. Rinaldi?" she asked, coming straight to the point.

Rinaldi looked away too quickly, searched the ceiling as if wracking his brain, furrowed his brow. "I have no idea, Detective."

"You wanted to know his priors, Mr. Rinaldi. You must have had some suspicion."

Now he looked straight at her. "I like to do a thorough job. I investigate all possibilities. Same as I'm sure you do."

"I'm sorry, I don't quite understand. You did suspect Mr. Stadler, or you didn't?"

"Look, Detective. My boss's house gets vandalized in a particularly sick and twisted way, first thing I'm gonna do is go through the rolls of people who got the ax here, right? Anyone who made any threats during their out-placement interviews, all that. I find out that one guy who got laid off has a mental history, I'm gonna look a little more closely. Make sense?"

"Absolutely. So what did you find when you looked closely?"

"What'd I find?"

"Right. Did he make any threats during his outplacement?"

"Wouldn't surprise me. People do, you know. People lose it, time like that."

"Not according to his boss at the model shop, the fellow who conducted the outplacement interview along with someone from HR. He said Stadler quit, but he wasn't violent."

Rinaldi guffawed. "You trying to trap me or something, Detective? Forget it. I'm telling you this guy was in and out of the loony bin."

"He was diagnosed with schizophrenia, is that right?"

"What do you want from me? You want to know if this guy Stadler was the sick fuck who went to my boss's home and killed his dog, I have no idea."

"Did you talk to him?"

Rinaldi waved his hand. "Nah."

"Did you ask the police to investigate him?"

"For what? Get the poor guy in trouble, for what?"

"You just said it wouldn't surprise you if he made threats during his out-placement interview."

Rinaldi spun his fancy chair around and looked at his computer screen, squinted his eyes. "Who's the head of Major Cases now? Is it Noyce?"

"Sergeant Noyce, that's right."

"Say hi for me. Nice guy. Good cop."

"I will." Was he threatening to pull strings? Wouldn't work if he did, she thought. Sergeant Noyce barely knew him. She'd asked her boss about Ri-naldi. "But as to my question, Mr. Rinaldi—you never talked to Stadler, never pointed him out as a potential suspect in the incident at Mr. Conover's home?"

Rinaldi shook his head again, gave a thoughtful frown. "I had no reason to think he was the one," he said reasonably.

"So that situation is unresolved, what happened at Mr. Conover's home?"

"You tell me. Fenwick PD doesn't seem optimistic about solving it."

"Did you ever meet Andrew Stadler or talk with him?"

"Nope."

"Or Mr. Conover? Did he ever meet with Stadler or talk with him?"

"I doubt it. The CEO of a company this size doesn't usually meet most of his employees, except maybe in group settings."

"Then it was very kind of him to attend Mr. Stadler's funeral."

"Did he? Well, that sounds like Nick."

"How so?"

"He's very considerate about his employees. Probably goes to all funerals of Stratton workers. Town like this, he's a public figure, you know. Part of his job."

"I see." She thought for a moment. "But you must have run names by Mr. Conover, names of laid-off employees, to see if any of them rang a bell."

"I usually don't bother him at that level, Detective. Not unless I have a firm lead. I let him do his job, and I do mine. No, I wish I could help you. The guy worked for Stratton for, what, like thirty-five years. I just hate to see a loyal employee come to an end like that."

31

"Yo," Scott said, appearing from behind Marge's side of the divider panel next to Nick's desk. "Looking for some exciting reading? The board books are ready."

Nick looked up from his screen, a testy e-mail exchange with his general counsel, Stephanie Alstrom, about some tedious and endless battle with the Environmental Protection Agency over the emissions of certain volatile organic compounds in an adhesive used in the manufacture of one of the Stratton chairs that they'd discontinued anyway.

"Fiction or nonfiction?" he said.

"Nonfiction, unfortunately. Sorry it's so last minute, but I had to redo all the numbers the way you wanted."

"Sorry to be so unreasonable," Nick said sardonically. "But I'm the guy on the hot seat."

"Muldaur and Eilers are arriving at the Grand Fenwick this afternoon," Scott said, "and I told them I'd get the board books over there before dinner tonight so they could look 'em over. You know those guys—there's going to be questions, the second they see you. Just so long as you're ready to face them."

The board of directors always had dinner in town the night before the quarterly board meeting. Dorothy Devries, the founder's daughter and the only member of the Devries family on the board, usually hosted them at the Fenwick Country Club, which she more or less owned. It was always a stiff and awkward occasion, with no overt business transacted.

"Ah, Scott, I'm going to have to miss it tonight." He stood up, feeling rubbed raw, his headache full blown now.

"You're—you're kidding me."

"It's the fourth-grade school play tonight—they're doing *The Wizard of Oz*, and Julia's got a big part. I really can't miss it."

"Please tell me you're joking, Nick. The *fourth-grade play?*"

"I missed her school play last year, and I've missed the art exhibit and just about every school assembly. I can't miss this too."

"You can't get someone to videotape it?"

"Videotape it? What kind of dad are you?"

"Absentee and proud of it. My kids respect me more for being distant and unavailable."

"Now. Wait 'til they get into therapy. Anyway, you know as well as I do that nothing ever gets done at those dinners."

"It's called schmoozing. A Yiddish word that means saving your job."

"They're going to fire me because I didn't have dinner with them? If they do, Scott, they're just looking for an excuse anyway."

Scott shook his head. "Okay," he said, looking down at the floor. "You're the boss. But if you ask me—"

"Thanks, Scott. But I didn't ask you."

32

Audrey sat at her desk, staring at her little gallery of photographs, and then phoned the Michigan State Police crime lab in Grand Rapids.

Yesterday she'd driven almost two hours to Grand Rapids and handed the bullets, in their little brown paper evidence envelopes, to a crime lab tech who looked barely old enough to be shaving. Trooper Halverson had been polite but all business. He asked her if there were any shell casings, as if she'd maybe forgotten. She told him they hadn't recovered any, found herself actually apologizing to the boy. She asked how long it would take, and he said their caseload was huge, they were badly understaffed, their backlog was running a good three or four months. Luckily, Sergeant Noyce knew one of the Ramp Rangers, as they called the Michigan highway patrolmen, and when she reminded him of that—subtly, delicately—Trooper Halverson had said he'd try to get right to it.

On the phone, Trooper Halverson sounded even younger. He didn't remember her name, but when she read off the lab file number, he pulled it up on the computer.

"Yes, Detective," he said, tentative. "Um, well, let's see here. Okay. They're .380, brass-jacketed, like you said. The rifling looks to be six left. Gosh, you guys didn't turn up any casings?"

"The body was dumped. So, as I said, unfortunately, no."

"It's just that if you had a casing we could really learn a whole lot more," he said. He spoke as if she were holding the cartridge casings back and maybe just needed a little persuasion to hand them over. "The casings tend to take imprints so much better than the bullets."

"No such luck," she said. She waited patiently while he went through the measurements and specs from his microscope exam. "So, um, based on the land and groove widths, the GRC database spits out like twenty different possible models that might've been the weapon in question." The GRC, she recalled, was the General Rifling Characteristics database, put out by the FBI every year or so on a CD.

"Twenty," she said, disappointed. "That doesn't narrow it down too much."

"Mostly Colts and Davis Industries. A lot of street guns look like this. So I'd say you're looking for a Colt .380, a Davis .380, or a Smith and Wesson."

"There's no way to narrow it down any more? What about the ammunition?"

"Yes, ma'am, these are hollow-point brass-jacketed bullets. There are some indications that they're Remington Golden Sabers, but don't hold me to it. That's problematic."

"Okay."

"And also—well, I probably shouldn't say this."

"Yes?"

"No, I'm just saying. Personal observation here. The land width is between .0252 and .054. The groove measurement is between .124 and .128. So it's pretty tight. That tells me the weapon that fired it is a pretty decent one, not just some Saturday night special. So I'm thinking maybe it's the Smith and Wesson, because they're a good manufacturer."

"How many possible Smith and Wesson models are we talking about?"

"Well, Smith and Wesson doesn't make any .380s any more. The only one they ever made was the baby Sigma."

"Baby Sigma? That's the name of the gun?"

"No, ma'am. I mean, you know, they have a product line called the Sigma, and for a couple of years—like the mid-to-late nineties—the bottom end of the Sigma line was a .380 pocket pistol that people sometimes called the 'baby' Sigma."

She wrote down "S&W Sigma .380."

"Okay, good," she said, "so we're looking for a Smith and Wesson Sigma .380."

"No, ma'am. I didn't say that. No suspect weapons should be overlooked."

"Of course, Trooper Halverson." The troops were supercareful about what they told you, because they knew that everything had to stand up in a court of law, everything had to be carefully documented, and there couldn't be any guesswork. "When do you think you might know more?"

"Well, after our IBIS technician enters it."

She didn't want to ask how long that would take. "Well, anything you can do to put wings on this, Trooper, would be much appreciated."

33

The brand-new Fenwick Elementary School auditorium was fancier than a lot of college theaters: plush stadium seating, great acoustics, professional sound system and lighting. It was called the Devries Theater, a gift from Dorothy Stratton Devries, in honor of her late husband.

When Nick had gone to Fenwick Elementary, there hadn't even been an auditorium. School assemblies had been held in the gym, all the kids sitting on the splintery wooden bleachers. Now it seemed like the fourth-grade class was doing its annual play in a Broadway theater.

Looking around, Nick was glad he'd come. All the parents were here, grandparents too. Even parents who rarely came to any of their kids' school events, like Emily Renfro's plastic-surgeon dad, Jim. Jacqueline Renfro was a class mom or something, but her husband was usually too busy doing face-lifts or screwing his receptionist to show up. A number of the parents had mini videocams, ready to film the production on compact digital tape that no one would ever bother to watch.

He was late as usual. Everywhere he went, he seemed to arrive late these days. Marta had dropped Julia off an hour ago so she and the rest of the fourth-graders could get into their handmade costumes, which they'd been working on in art class for months. Julia was excited about tonight because she got to play the Wicked Witch of the West—her choice, a role she'd auditioned for and then pleaded for. Not for her Dorothy, which all the other girls wanted. Nick's little tomboy had no interest in playing a wimpy character wearing a braided wig and a gingham dress. She knew that the witch part was the scene-stealer. He liked that about her.

She didn't expect him to be here. He'd already told her a couple of times that he had a work dinner he had to go to and couldn't get out of. She was disappointed, but resigned. So she'd be all the more excited when she saw her daddy here. In truth, of course, Nick considered sitting through the school play, one of those unpleasant parental obligations like changing a poopy diaper, or going to "The Lion King On Ice" (or *anything* on ice, for that matter), or watching the *Teletubbies* or *The Wiggles* and not letting on how creepy they were.

The back sections of the theater had been cordoned off, and there didn't seem to be any available seats in the front. He peered around, saw a few spaces here and there, a sea of averted glances, a few unfriendly faces. Maybe he was being a little paranoid. Guilt burned on his face as visibly as a scarlet letter. He was convinced people knew what he'd done just by looking at him.

But that wasn't it, of course. They hated him for other reasons, for being Slasher Nick, for being the local hero who'd turned on them. He saw the Renfros, caught their icy glares before they looked away. Finally he saw one friendly face, a buddy of his from high school days whose son was in Julia's class.

"Hey, Bobby," he said, sitting down in the seat Bob Casey had freed up by moving his jacket. Casey, a bald, red-faced guy with an enormous beer gut, was a stockbroker who'd tried to hit Nick up for business several times. He was a wisenheimer whose chief claim to fame since high school was his ability to memorize long stretches of dialogue from Monty Python or any of the National Lampoon or Airplane movies.

"There he is," Casey said heartily. "Big night, huh?"

"Oh, yeah. How's Gracie?"

"Doin' good. Doin' good."

A long, uncomfortable silence followed. Then Bob Casey said, "Ever see anything like this theater? We never had anything like this."

"We were lucky to use the gym."

"Luxury!" Casey said in his Monty Python voice. "Luxury! We had to walk thirty miles to school every morning in a blizzard—uphill, both ways. And we loved it!"

Nick smiled, amused but unable to laugh.

Casey noticed Nick's subdued response and said, "So, you've had a hard year, huh?"

"Not as hard as a lot of people here."

"Hey, come on, Nick. You lost your wife."

"Yeah, well."

"How's the house?"

"Almost done."

"It's been almost done for a year, right?" he gibed. "Kids okay? Julia seems to be doing good."

"She's great."

"I hear Luke's having a hard time of it."

Nick wondered how much Bob Casey knew about Luke's troubles—probably more than Nick did himself. "Well, you know. Sixteen, right?"

"Tough age. Plus, only one parent and all that."

The production was about what you'd expect for a fourth-grade play—an Emerald City set they'd all painted themselves, the talking apple tree made out of painted corrugated cardboard. The music teacher playing sloppily on the Yamaha digital piano. Julia, as the Witch, froze up, kept forgetting her lines. You could almost hear the parents in the audience *thinking* them out loud for her—"Poppies!" and "I'll get you, my pretty!"

When it was over, Jacqueline Renfro seemed to go out of her way to find Nick and say, "Poor Julia." She shook her head. "It can't be easy for her."

Nick furrowed his brow.

"Well, only one parent, and you hardly ever there."

"I'm there as much as I can," he replied.

Jacqueline shrugged, having made her point, and moved on. But her husband, Jim, lagged behind. He wore a brown tweed jacket and a blue button-down shirt, looking like he was still a Princeton undergrad. He pointed a finger at Nick and winked. "Can't imagine how I'd get by without Jackie," he said in a confiding tone. "I don't know how you get by. Still, Julia's a great kid—you're very lucky."

"Thanks."

Jim Renfro was smiling too hard. "Of course, the thing about family is, when they get to be too much, you can't exactly downsize them." A cheery, self-satisfied wink. "Am I right?"

Any number of responses occurred to Nick—too many. None of them nonviolent. He had this strange feeling of a lid coming off, the bleed valves blowing.

At that point, Julia came running up, still wearing her pointed black construction-paper hat and her green face makeup. "You came!" she said.

He threw his arms around her. "I couldn't miss this."

"How was I?" she asked. There wasn't a drop of concern in her voice, no awareness that she'd messed up. She was bursting with pride. He loved this little girl.

"You were great," he said.

34

In the car on the way home, Nick's cell phone went off, a weird synthesized, symphonic fanfare that he'd never bothered to reprogram.

He glanced at the caller ID, saw that it was Eddie Rinaldi. He picked it up from the cradle, not wanting Julia to hear whatever Eddie had to say over the speakers. She was sitting in the backseat of the Suburban, poring over the *Wizard of Oz* program in the darkness. She still had the green zinc-oxide face makeup on, and Nick could see a bedtime struggle ahead when he made her clean it off.

"Hey, Eddie," he said.

"There you are. You had the phone off?"

"I was watching Julia's school play."

"Okay," he said. Eddie, who had no kids, no plans to have any, and no interest in them, never asked about his kids beyond the bare minimum required. "I was thinking of dropping by."

"Can't it wait?"

A pause. "I think not. We should talk. Only take five minutes, maybe."

"There a problem?" Nick was suddenly on edge.

"No, no. No problem. Just, we should talk."

Eddie sprawled in the easy chair in Nick's study, legs splayed wide as if he owned the place.

"A homicide detective came to talk to me," he said casually.

Nick felt his insides go cold. He leaned forward in his desk chair. Here they sat, just a few feet from where it had happened. "What the fuck?" he said.

Eddie shrugged, no big deal. "Standard operating procedure. Routine shit."

"*Routine?*"

"She's just covering all the bases. Got to, sloppy if she didn't."

"It's a woman." Nick focused on the anomaly, avoiding the main issue: *a homicide detective was on the case, already?*

"Negro lady." Eddie could have put it much more crudely. His racism was no secret to anyone, but maybe he'd learned over the years that it wasn't socially acceptable, not even around his old buddies. Or maybe he didn't want to antagonize Nick at the moment.

"I didn't know the Fenwick police had any."

"I didn't either."

A long silence in which Nick could hear the ticking of the clock. A silver clock, engraved FENWICK CITIZEN OF THE YEAR, awarded to him three years ago. When everything was going great. "What'd she want?"

"What do you think? She wanted to ask about Stadler."

"What *about* Stadler?"

"You know, what you'd expect. Did he make any threats, whatever."

Eddie was being evasive, and Nick didn't like it. Something didn't sit right. "Why was she talking to you?"

"Hey, man, I'm the security director, remember?"

"No. There has to be some more specific reason she went to talk to you. What are you leaving out, Eddie?"

"Leaving out? I'm leaving nothing out, buddy. I mean, look, she knew I asked some guys on the job about Stadler."

So that was it. By doing his background check on Stadler, he'd in effect tipped his hand to the police. "Shit."

"Come on. I never talked to the guy."

"No," Nick said, one hand cupping his chin. "You call the cops, asking about some downsized employee who slaughtered your boss's dog, then the guy turns up dead a couple days later. This doesn't look good."

Eddie shook his head, rolling his eyes in contempt. "Like this is, what, the Mafia or something? Get real. The guy goes off the deep end, doing sick shit, matter of time before he pisses off the wrong guy."

"Yeah."

"In the dog pound, I mean, come on. Look, they got nothing tying Stadler to me — or to you."

"Then what was she asking about?"

"Ah, she wanted to know if you'd ever talked to Stadler, had any contact with the guy. Told her you probably didn't even know who the guy was. Pretty much true."

Nick inhaled slowly, tried to calm himself, held his breath. "And if I did? What's the assumption here, that I went after the guy, *killed* him?" Nick heard the aggrieved tone in his own voice, as if he were actually starting to believe himself innocent.

"Nah, she's just looking for scraps. Anyway, don't worry, I handled her fine. Believe me, she left knowing she's barking up the wrong tree."

"How do you know?"

"I can tell, come on. Get serious here, Nick. The CEO of Stratton murdered one of his employees? I don't *think* so. No one's going to believe that for a second."

Nick was silent for a long while. "I hope so."

"I just wanted to keep you in the loop. In case she comes to talk to you."

Nick, his chest tightening, said, "She said she was going to?"

"No, but she might. Wouldn't surprise me."

"I'd never even heard the name," Nick said. "Right? You tell her otherwise?"

"Exactly. Told her you're a busy guy, I do my job, you don't get involved."

"Right."

"So you figured maybe some downsized employee went wacko, killed your dog, but you called the cops, figured they'd handle it, you had no idea who it mighta been."

"Right."

"Guy turns up dead, mighta been the same guy, mighta been different, you have no idea. Like that."

Nick nodded, rehearsing the answer in his mind, turning it over and over, poking at the soft spots. "There's nothing tying me to this thing?" he said after a few moments.

A long silence. Eddie replied with a kind of smoldering indignation. "I did my job, Nick, you clear?"

"I don't doubt it. I'm asking you to think like a cop. Like a homicide cop."

"That's how I think, man. Like a cop."

"No prints, nothing like that, on the . . . body? Fibers, DNA, whatever?"

"Nick, I told you, we're not going to talk about this."

"We are now. I want to know."

"The body was clean, Nick," Eddie said. "Okay? Clean as a whistle. Clean as I could get it in the time we had."

"What about the gun?"

"What about it?"

"What'd you do with it? You don't still have it, do you?"

"Like I'm a stupid fuck? Come on, man."

"Then where is it?"

Eddie let out a puff of air, made a sound like *pah*. "Bottom of the river, you really want to know." Fenwick, like so many towns in Michigan, was built on the shores of one of the many waterways leading into Lake Michigan.

"Shell casings too?"

"Yup."

"And if it turns up?"

"You realize how unlikely that is?"

"I'm saying."

"Even if they do find it, they got no way to connect it to me."

"Why not? It's your gun."

"It's a goddamned drop gun, Nick."

"A what?"

"A throw-down. A piece I picked up at a scene in GR. Some crack dealer, who the hell knows where he got it. Point is, there's no record anywhere. No paperwork, no purchase permit, nothing. Clean."

Nick had heard of cops picking up guns they found at crime scenes, keeping them, but he knew you weren't supposed to do that, and it made him nervous to hear Eddie admit to it. If he did that, what else did he do?

"You sure," Nick said.

"Sure as shit."

"What about the security cameras?"

Eddie nodded. "Hey, I'm a pro, right? Took care of that too."

"How?"

"Why do you need to know?"

"I need to know. My own fucking security cameras recorded me killing the guy."

Eddie closed his eyes, shook his head in irritation. "I reformatted the hard drive on the digital video recorder. That night's gone. Never happened. System started recording next day—makes sense, right? Since we just put it in the day before."

"Not a trace?"

"Nada. Hey, don't worry about it. The lady comes to talk to you, you co-operate, tell her everything you know, which is a big fat zero, right?" Eddie gave his dry cackle.

"Right. I know she talked to you?"

Eddie shrugged. "Play it either way. Let's say, no, I didn't get around to it. Got nothing to do with you, right?"

"Right."

Eddie got up. "Nothing to worry about, man. Get some sleep. You look like shit."

"Thanks." Nick got up, to walk Eddie out, then thought of something. "Eddie," he said. "That night. You said it was your gun, tied everything to you, right? That's why I didn't have a choice."

Eddie's eyes were dead. "Yeah?"

"Now you tell me the gun was clean. No connection to you at all. I don't get it."

A long silence.

"Can't take chances, Nicky," Eddie finally said. "Never take chances."

Nick walked Eddie out of his study, heard footfalls on the carpeting. Saw a jeans-clad leg, a sneaker, disappear up the stairs.

Lucas.

Just getting home? Was it possible that he'd overheard their conversation? Nah, he'd have had to have stood outside the study door, listening. Lucas didn't do that, the main reason being that he had no interest in what his dad was up to.

Still.

Nick wondered, a tiny wriggle of worry.

35

Driving to work the next morning, Nick was in a foul mood. The news that a homicide detective was poking around the corporation had sent him spiraling into a tense, sleepless night. He thrashed around in the big bed, got up repeatedly, obsessed about that night.

What Happened That Night—that was how he thought of it now. The memory had receded to attenuated, kaleidoscopic images: Stadler's leering face, the gunfire, the body sprawled on the ground, Eddie's face, carrying the body wrapped in black trash bags.

He was out of pills, which was just as well; any more of them, he figured, and he was headed for the Betty Ford clinic. He tried to think about work stuff, anything but that night. But that just meant the board meeting in the morning. Board meetings always made him tense, but this time he knew that the shit was about to rain down.

On the way into work he stopped at a light next to a gleaming silver S-Class Mercedes. He turned to admire it and saw that the driver was Stratton's VP of sales, Ken Coleman. Nick rolled down his passenger's side window, tapped on his horn until he got Coleman's attention. When Coleman—forty-one, a good seventy pounds overweight, a bad hairpiece—rolled down his window, his face lit up.

"Hey, Nick! Looking pretty slick."

"Board meeting. New car, Kenny?"

Coleman's grin got even wider. "Got it yesterday. You like?"

"Must list for a hundred grand, right?"

Coleman, always hyper, nodded fast, up and down and up and down like some bobble-head doll. "Over. Fully loaded. Like, AMG sports package and, I mean, heated *steering wheel,* you know?" The top sales guys at Stratton made more than Nick did. He didn't resent it; someone had to do the soul-destroying shit they did.

The light turned green, but Nick didn't move. "Buy or lease?" he asked.

"Well, lease. I always lease, you know?"

"Good. Because it's going back to the dealer."

Coleman cocked his bobble head, a movement like a terrier, almost comic. "What?"

Behind him, someone honked a horn. Nick ignored it. "We laid off five thousand workers, Ken. Half the company. To cut costs, save Stratton. Pretty much wiped out the town. So I don't want a member of my executive management team driving around town in a fucking hundred-thousand-dollar Mercedes, understand?"

Coleman stared in disbelief.

Nick went on, "You take that back to the dealership by close of business today and tell 'em you want a fucking Subaru or something. But I don't want to see you behind that heated steering wheel again, you understand?"

Nick gunned the engine and took off.

The five members of the board of directors of the Stratton Corporation, and their guests, were gathered in the anteroom to the boardroom. Coffee was being served from vacuum carafes, and not the institutional food-service blend that was served in the Stratton employee cafeteria, either. It was brewed from Sulawesi Peaberry beans fresh-roasted by Town Grounds, Fenwick's best coffee place. Todd Muldaur had complained about the coffee at the first board meeting after the buyout, poked fun at the Bunn-O-Matic. Nick thought Todd was being ridiculous, but he ordered the change. That, and little cold bottles of Evian water, melon slices, raspberries and strawberries, fancy pastries trucked in from a famous bakery in Ann Arbor.

Todd Muldaur, in another of his expensive suits, was at the tail end of a joke when Nick arrived, holding forth to Scott, the other guy from Fairfield

Partners, Davis Eilers, and someone Nick had never seen before. "I told him the best way to see Fenwick is in your rearview mirror," Todd was saying. Eilers and the other guy laughed raucously. Scott, who'd noticed Nick's approach, just smiled politely.

Davis Eilers was the other deal partner, a guy who had a lot of operational experience. He'd done his time at McKinsey like Todd and Scott, only he'd played football at Dartmouth, not Yale. He later ran a number of companies, sort of a CEO-for-hire.

Todd turned, saw Nick. "There he is." He tipped his cup at Nick. "Great coffee!" he said expansively and gave a wink. "Sorry to miss you last night. Busy being a dad, huh?"

Nick shook Todd's hand, then Scott's, then Eilers's. "Yeah, couldn't get out of it. My daughter's school play, you know, and given—"

"Hey, you got your priorities straight," Todd said with an excess of sincerity. "I respect that."

Nick wanted to toss the cup of hot Sulawesi Peaberry in the guy's face, but he just looked straight in Todd's too-blue eyes and smiled appreciatively.

"Nick, I want you to meet our new board member, Dan Finegold." A tall, handsome guy, athletic-looking. A thatch of dark brown hair starting to silver over. What was it with Fairfield Equity Partners? It was a fucking frat.

Dan Finegold's handshake was a crusher.

"Don't tell me Yale football too," Nick said cordially. Thinking: *our new board member? Like, were they going to tell me? Just spring it on me?*

"Yale baseball, actually," said Todd, clapping both men on their shoulders, bringing them together. "Dan was a legendary pitcher."

"Legendary, my ass," said Finegold.

"Hey, man, you *were*," Todd said. He looked at Nick. "Dan's got twenty years' experience in the office-supply space, with all the scar tissue. I'm sure you know OfficeSource—that was his baby. When Willard bought it, he grabbed Dan for Fairfield."

"You like Boston?" Nick asked. He couldn't think of anything else to say. He couldn't say what he was really thinking, which was: Why are you here, and who invited you onto the board, and what's really going on here? Fairfield had the right to put whomever they wanted on the board, but it wasn't exactly cool for them to just show up with a new board member in tow. They hadn't done it before. It wasn't a good precedent, or maybe that was the point.

"It's great. Especially for a foodie like me. Lot of happening restaurants in Boston these days."

"Dan's part owner of an artisanal brewery in upstate New York," said Todd. "They make the best Belgian beer outside of Belgium. Abbey ale, right?"

"That's right."

"Welcome to the board," Nick said. "I'm sure your expertise in Belgian beer's going to come in handy." Something about Belgian beer and Abbey ale sounded familiar, but he couldn't place it.

Todd took Nick by the elbow as they walked to the boardroom. He spoke in a low voice. "Bummer about Atlas McKenzie."

"Huh?"

"Scott told me last night."

"What are you talking about?"

Todd gave him a quick, curious glance. "The deal," he said under his breath. "How it fell through."

"*What?*" What the hell was he talking about? The Atlas McKenzie deal was all but inked. This made no sense!

"Don't worry, it's not going to come up this morning. But still, a *major* bummer, huh?" In a louder voice, he called out, "Mrs. Devries!"

Todd turned away and strode up to Dorothy Devries, who had just entered the boardroom. Todd clasped her small hand in both of his large ones and waited until she turned her cheek toward him before he kissed it.

Dorothy was wearing a Nancy Reagan burgundy pants suit with white piping around the lapels. Her white hair was a perfect cumulus cloud with just a hint of blue rinse in it, which brought out the steely blue of her eyes. Fairfield Partners had left Dorothy Stratton Devries a small piece of the company and a seat on the board, which was a condition of hers that Willard Osgood had no quibble with. It looked good to have the founder's family still connected to Stratton. It told the world that Fairfield still respected the old ways. Of course, Dorothy had no power. She was there for window dressing, mostly. Fairfield owned ninety percent of Stratton, controlled the board, ran the show. Dorothy, a sharp cookie, understood that, but she also understood that, outside the boardroom at least, she still possessed some moral authority.

Her dad, Harold Stratton, had been a machinist for the Wabash Railroad, a tinsmith's apprentice, a steeplejack. He worked as a machinist at Steelcase, in Grand Rapids, before he started his own company with money provided by his rich father-in-law. His big innovation had been to develop a better roller suspension for metal file cabinets—progressive roller bearings in a suspension-file drawer. His only son had died in childhood, leaving Dorothy, but women didn't run companies in those days, so eventually he turned it over to Dorothy's husband, Milton Devries. She'd spent her later years in her big, dark mansion in East Fenwick as the town matriarch, a social arbiter as fearsome as only a small-town society queen can be. She was on every board in town, chairwoman of most of them. Even though she liked Nick, and made him the CEO, she still looked down on him as being from a lower social class. Nick's dad, after all, had worked on the shop floor. Never mind that Dorothy was but one generation away from having machinist's grease on her own fingers.

Nick, reeling from Todd's casual revelation, saw Scott sitting down at his customary place at the oval mahogany board table. As Nick approached him, put a hand on his shoulder, he heard Todd saying, "Dorothy, I'd like you to meet Dan Finegold."

"Hey," Nick whispered, standing immediately behind Scott, "what's this about Atlas McKenzie?"

Scott craned his neck around, eyes wide. "Yeah, I just got the call on my cell at dinner last night—Todd happened to be there, you know . . ." His voice trailed off. Nick remained silent. Scott went on: "They went with Steelcase—you know, that joint venture Steelcase has with Gale and Wentworth—"

"They called *you?*"

"I guess I was on Hardwick's speed-dial, all those negotiations at the end—"

"You get bad news, you tell me first, understand?"

Nick could see Scott's pale face flush instantly. "I—of course, Nick, it was just that Todd was right there, you know, and—"

"We'll talk later," Nick said, giving Scott a shoulder squeeze too hard to be merely companionable.

He heard Dorothy Devries's brittle laugh from across the room, and he took his place at the head of the table.

The Stratton boardroom was the most conservative place in the head-quarters—the immense mahogany table with places for fifteen, even though there hadn't been fifteen board members since the takeover; the top-of-the-line black leather Stratton Symbiosis chairs, the slim monitors at each place that could be raised and lowered with the touch of a button. It looked like a boardroom in any big corporation in the world.

Nick cleared his throat, looked around at the board, and knew he was not among friends anymore. "Well, why don't we get started with the CFO's report?" he said.

36

Something about the way Scott went through his depressing presentation—his dry, monotone, doom-and-gloom voice-over to the PowerPoint slides projected on the little plasma screens in front of everyone—was almost defiant, Nick thought. As if he knew full well he was hurling carrion to the hyenas.

Of course, they didn't need his little dog-and-pony show, since they'd all gotten the charts in their black loose-leaf board books, FedExed to everyone yesterday, or couriered over to their hotel. But it was a board ritual, it had to go into the minutes, and besides, you couldn't assume that any of them had actually read through the materials.

Nick knew, however, that Todd Muldaur had read the financials closely, the instant he got them in Boston, the way some guys grab the sports section and devour the baseball box scores. Todd probably didn't wait even for the printouts; he'd surely gone through the Adobe PDF files and Excel spreadsheets as soon as Scott had e-mailed them.

Because his questions sounded awfully rehearsed. They weren't even questions, really. They were frontal assaults.

"I don't believe what I'm seeing here," he said. He looked around at the other board members—Dorothy, Davis Eilers, Dan Finegold—and the two "invited guests" who always attended the first half of the board meeting: Scott, and the Stratton general counsel who was here in her capacity as board secretary. Stephanie Alstrom was a small, serious woman with prematurely gray hair and a small, pruned mouth that seldom smiled. There was something juiceless, almost desiccated about Stephanie. Scott had once described her as a "raisin of anxiety," and the description had stuck in Nick's mind.

"This is a train wreck," Todd went on.

"Todd, there's no question these numbers look bad," Nick tried to put in.

"*Look* bad?" Todd shot back. "They *are* bad."

"My point is, this has been a challenging quarter—hell, a challenging year—for the entire sector," Nick said. "Office furniture is economically sensitive, we all know that. Companies stop buying stuff practically overnight when the economy slows."

Todd was staring at him, rattling Nick momentarily. "I mean, look, new office installations have plummeted, business startups and expansions have slowed to almost nothing," Nick went on. "Last couple of years, there's been serious overcapacity in the office furniture sector, and that, combined with weaker demand across the board, has put serious downward pressure on prices and profit margins."

"Nick," Todd said. "When I hear the word 'sector,' I reach for my barf bag."

Nick smiled involuntarily. "It's the reality," he said. He folded his arms, felt something crinkle in one of the breast pockets of his suit.

"If I may quote Willard Osgood," Todd went on, "'Explanations aren't excuses.' There's an *explanation* for everything."

"Uh, in all fairness to Nick," Scott put in, "he's just seeing these numbers for the first time."

"*What?*" said Todd. "Today? You mean, *I* saw these numbers before the CEO?" He turned to Nick. "You got something more important on your mind? Like, your daughter's *ballet recital* or something?"

Nick gave Scott a furious look. Yeah, it's the first time seeing the *real* numbers, he thought. Not the fudged ones you wanted to fob off on them. Nick was sorely tempted to let loose, but who knew where that might lead? Nervously, he fished inside the breast pocket of his suit and found a scrap of paper, pulled it out. It was a yellow Post-it note. Laura's handwriting: "Love you, babe. You're the best." A little heart and three X's. Tears immediately sprang to his eyes. He so rarely wore this suit that he must not have had it dry-cleaned last time he wore it, before Laura's death. He slipped the note carefully back where he'd found it.

"Come on, now, Todd," said Davis Eilers. "We're all dads here." Noticing Dorothy, he said, "Or moms." He ignored Stephanie Alstrom, who had no kids and wasn't married and seemed to shrink into herself as she tapped away at her laptop.

Calm, Nick told himself, blinking away the tears. *Stay calm.* The room revolved slowly around him. "Scott means the final figures, Todd, but believe me, there's no surprise here. I take heart from the fact that our profit margins are still positive."

"No surprise?" Todd said. "No *surprise*? Let me tell you something, I don't really care how the rest of the sector's doing. We didn't buy Stratton because you're like everyone else, because you're *average*. We bought you because you were marquee. Same reason we use Stratton chairs and work panels and all that in our own offices in Boston, when we could have bought anything. Because you were the best in your space. Not just good enough. As Willard's so fond of saying, ' "Good enough" is *not* good enough.' "

"We're still the best," Nick said. "Bear in mind that we did our layoffs early—at your insistence, let me remind you. Everyone else waited. We got ahead of the curve."

"Fine, but you're still not delivering on your plan."

"To be fair," Scott pointed out, "Nick's plan didn't assume the economy was going to get worse."

"Scott," Todd said in a deadly quiet voice, "Nick's the CEO. He should have anticipated turns in the economy. Look, Nick, we always like to give our CEOs a lot of rope." He gave Nick a steady blue stare. What did that mean, anyway? Give a man enough rope and he'll hang himself—was that it? "We don't want to run your business—we want *you* to run your business," Todd went on. "But not if you're going to run it into the ground. At the end of the day, you work for us. That means that your job is to protect our investors' capital."

"And the way to protect your capital," Nick said, straining to remain civil, "is to invest in the business now, during the downturn. Now's the time to invest in new technology. That way, when the economy comes back, we kick butt." He looked at Dorothy. "Sorry." She didn't respond, her icy blue eyes focused on the middle distance.

Todd, leafing through his board book, looked up. "Like spending thirty million dollars in the last three years in development costs for a new *chair*?"

"A bargain," Nick said. "Design and retooling costs, twenty-six patents, two separate design teams. And that's actually less than Steelcase spent on their Leap chair, which turned out to be a great investment. Or Herman Miller spent on developing the Aeron chair. I mean, don't forget, product design and development is a core value at Stratton." Todd was silent for a moment. *Score one for the defense.* Before he could reply, Nick went on: "Now, if you want to continue this discussion, I'd like to move that we go into executive session." The motion was seconded and approved by voice vote. This was the point when Scott, as an invited guest but not a board member, normally got up to leave. Nick caught his eye, but Scott's expression was opaque, unreadable. He wasn't gathering his things, wasn't getting up.

"Listen, Nick, we're going to ask Scott to stay," Todd said.

"Really?" was all Nick could think to say. "That's—that's not the protocol."

Now Davis Eilers, who'd barely said a word, spoke up. "Nick, we've decided that it's time that Scott join the board formally. We really feel that Scott's become an important enough part of the management team that we'd like his official participation on the board. We think he can add a lot of value."

Nick, stunned, swallowed hard as he racked his brain for something to say. He tried to catch Scott's eye again, but Scott was avoiding his glance. He nodded, thought. The Dan Finegold thing was outrageous. But now, adding Scott as a board member without even telling him in advance, let alone pretending to seek his opinion? He wanted to call them on it, bring it all out into the open, but all he said was, "Well, he can certainly add value."

"Thanks for understanding," Eilers said.

"Uh, Nick, we're going to be making a few changes going forward," Todd said.

As opposed to what? Nick thought. *Going backward?* He said, "Oh?"

"We think this board should be meeting every month instead of quarterly."

Nick nodded. "That's a lot of travel to Fenwick," he said.

"Well, we can alternate between Boston and Fenwick," Todd said. "And we'll be looking to see the financials weekly instead of monthly."

"I'm sure that can be arranged," Nick said slowly. "As long as Scott doesn't mind." Scott was examining his board book closely and didn't look up.

"Nick," said Davis Eilers, "we've also been thinking that, if and when you decide to fire any of your direct reports—any of the executive managers—that's going to require board approval."

"Well, that's not what my contract says." He could feel his face start to prickle.

"No, but it's an amendment we'd be in favor of. Sort of making sure we're all on the same page, personnelwise. Like they say, the only constant is change."

"You guys are hiring me to do the best job I can," Nick said. "Enough rope, like you always say. And you just said you want me to run the company—you don't want to run it yourself."

"Of course," Eilers said.

Todd said, "We just don't want any surprises. You know, keep things running smoothly." He'd adopted a reasonable tone, no longer combative. He knew he'd won. "We've got an almost-two-billion-dollar company to run. That's a big job for anyone, even someone who's paying full attention. Hey, it's like football, you know? You may be the quarterback, but you're not going to have a winning team without linesmen and receivers and running backs—and coaches. Think of us as your coaches, right?"

Nick gave a slow, faint smile. "Coaches," he said. "Right."

When the board meeting came to an end an hour and a half later, Nick was the first to leave the room. He needed to get the hell out of there before he lost it. That wouldn't be good. I'm not going to quit, he told himself. Make them fire me. Quit and you get nothing. Get fired without cause, and the payoff was considerable. Five million bucks. That was in the contract he'd negotiated when he sold to Fairfield, when the idea of getting fired seemed like science fiction. He was a rock star then; they'd never dump him.

As he left, he noticed two people seated just outside the boardroom, a thuggy-looking blond man in a bad suit and a well-dressed, attractive black woman.

The woman Rinaldi had told him about.

The homicide detective.

The woman he'd seen at Stadler's funeral.

"Mr. Conover," she called out. "Could we talk to you for a few minutes?"

PART THREE
GUILT

37

Nick took them into one of the conference rooms. Talking at his home base was out of the question, given the way anyone, including Marjorie, could listen in.

He took the lead. He sat at the head of the table. The moment the two homicide detectives sat, he began speaking. He adopted a calm, authoritative tone, brisk but cordial. He was the head of a major corporation with a million things going on, and these two cops were here without an appointment, without even giving him the courtesy of a heads-up call. Yet he didn't want to diminish the importance of what they were doing. They were investigating the murder of a Stratton employee. He wanted them to feel that he took this seriously. It was a delicate balancing act.

He was scared shitless. He didn't like the fact that they'd just shown up at his workplace. There was something aggressive, almost accusatory about that. He wanted to let them know, through his tone and his attitude, that he didn't appreciate this, while at the same time communicating his respect for their mission.

"Detectives," he said, "I can spare maybe five minutes. You've caught me on my busiest day."

"Thanks for seeing us," said the black woman. The blond man blinked a few times, like a Komodo dragon admiring a delicious-looking goat, but said nothing. Nick could tell that he was going to be trouble. The black woman was sweetly apologetic, an obvious pushover. The blond man—Busbee? Bugbee?—was the one to watch.

"I wish you'd called my office and made an appointment. I'd be happy to talk to you at greater length another time."

"This shouldn't take that long," said the blond man.

"Tell me what I can do for you," Nick said.

"Mr. Conover, as you know, an employee of the Stratton Company was found dead last week," said the black woman. She was quite pretty, and there was something serene about her.

"Yes," Nick said. "Andrew Stadler. A terrible tragedy."

"Did you know Mr. Stadler?" she went on.

Nick shook his head. "No, unfortunately. We have five thousand employees—as many as ten thousand two years ago, before we had to let so many people go—and I can't possibly get to know everyone. Though I wish I could." He smiled wistfully.

"Yet you went to his funeral," she pointed out.

"Of course."

"You always go to the funerals of Stratton employees?" said the blond detective.

"Not always. When I can, though. I don't always feel welcome, not anymore. But I feel it's the least I can do."

"You never met Mr. Stadler, is that right?" the black woman said.

"Right."

"You were aware of his . . . situation, though, isn't that right?" she continued.

"His situation?"

"His personal troubles."

"I heard later that he'd been hospitalized, but plenty of people have mental illness and aren't violent."

"Oh?" the black detective said quickly. "How did you know he'd been hospitalized? Did you see his personnel file?"

"Didn't I read it in the newspaper?"

"There wasn't anything in the paper about that," said the blond man.

"Must've been," Nick said. There *had* been something in the paper, hadn't there? "Said something about a 'troubled emotional history' or something, right?"

"Nothing about hospitalization," the blond man said firmly.

"Someone must have mentioned it to me, then."

"Your corporate security director, Edward Rinaldi?"

"Possibly. But I don't recall."

"I see," the black woman said, jotting something down.

"Mr. Conover, did Edward Rinaldi tell you he thought Andrew Stadler was the guy who killed your dog?" the blond cop asked.

Nick squinted, as if trying to recall. He remembered asking Eddie about this.

Told her you didn't even know who the guy was. Pretty much true.

"*I never even heard the name,*" Nick had said. "*Right? You tell her otherwise?*"

"*Exactly. Told her you're a busy guy, I do my job, you don't get involved.*"

"Eddie didn't mention any names to me," Nick said.

"Is that right?" the woman said, sounding surprised.

Nick nodded. "To be honest, it's been a rough year. I'm the head of a company that's had to let half its employees go. There's a lot of anger out there, understandably."

"You're not the most popular man in town," she suggested.

"That's putting it mildly. I've gotten angry letters from downsized employees, really heartbreaking letters."

"Threats?" she asked.

"Could be, but I wouldn't know about them."

"How could you not know about threats?" the male cop said.

"I'm not the first to open my mail here. If I get a threatening letter, it goes right to Security—I never see it."

"You don't want to know?" he said. "Me, I'd want to know."

"Not me. Not unless I need to know for some reason. The less I know, the better."

"Really?" said the blond man.

"Really. I don't like to go around feeling paranoid. There's no point in it."

"Did Mr. Rinaldi tell you why he was looking into Mr. Stadler's background?" the black woman persisted.

"No. I didn't even know he was."

"He didn't tell you later he'd been looking into Stadler?" she persisted.

"Nope. He never told me anything about Stadler. I mean, I had no idea—*have* no idea—what Eddie was looking into. He does his job and I do mine."

"Mr. Rinaldi never even mentioned Stadler's name to you?" the woman said.

"Not that I recall, no."

"I'm confused," she said. "I thought you just said Mr. Rinaldi might have told you about Andrew Stadler's hospitalization. Which would sort of require him to mention Stadler's name, right?"

Nick felt the tiniest trickle of sweat run slowly down his earlobe. "After the news of Stadler's death came out, Eddie may have mentioned his name to me in passing. But I really don't recall."

"Hmm," the woman said. A few seconds of silence went by.

Nick ignored the sweat trickle, not wanting to call attention to it by brushing it away.

"Mr. Conover," said the blond man, "your house has been broken into a bunch of times in the last year, right? Since the layoffs began?"

"Several times, yes."

"By the same person?"

"It's hard to say. But I'd guess yeah, the same person."

"There was graffiti and such?"

"Graffiti spray-painted inside my house, on the walls."

"What kind of graffiti?" the black detective asked.

" 'No hiding place.' "

"That's what they wrote?"

"Right."

"Did you receive any death threats?"

"No. Ever since the layoffs started, two years ago, I've gotten occasional threatening phone calls, but nothing quite that specific."

"Well, your family dog was killed," said the blond detective. "That's sort of a death threat, wouldn't you say?"

Nick considered for a moment. "Possibly. Whatever it was, it was a sick, depraved thing to do." He worried that he'd just gone too far: had be just betrayed his anger? Yet how else would he be expected to react? He noticed that the black woman wrote something down in her notebook.

"The Fenwick police have any idea who did this?" the guy said.

"No idea."

"Does Mr. Rinaldi get involved in your personal security, outside the corporation?" the black detective asked.

"Informally, yeah," Nick said. "Sometimes. After this last incident, I asked him to put in a new security system."

"So you must have discussed the incident with him," she said.

Nick hesitated, a beat too long. What did Eddie tell them, exactly? Did Eddie tell them he came over to the house after Barney was slaughtered? He wished he'd talked to Eddie longer, found out everything he'd said. Shit. "A bit. I asked his advice, sure." He waited for the inevitable next question—inevitable to him, at least: did Eddie Rinaldi come to his house after Barney had been discovered in the pool? And what was the right answer?

Instead, the black detective said, "Mr. Conover, how long ago did you move into Fenwicke Estates?"

"About a year ago."

"After all the layoffs were announced?" she went on.

"About a year after."

"Why?"

Nick paused. "My wife insisted."

"Why was that?"

"She was concerned."

"About what?"

"That our family might be threatened."

"What made her so concerned?"

"Instinct, mostly. She knew there were a few people who might want to do us harm."

"So you did hear about threats," the black woman said. "But you just said you didn't know about any—you didn't *want* to know about them."

Nick folded his hands on the table. He was feeling increasingly frantic, trapped like some cornered animal, and he knew the only way to respond was to sound both reasonable and blunt. "Did I hear about specific threats? No. Did I hear that there *were* threats—that a few isolated fringe cases might have it in for me and my family? Sure. People talk. Rumors spread. I wasn't going to wait to see if there was any basis in these rumors. And I can tell you my wife sure as hell wasn't going to wait."

The two detectives seemed to accept his answer. "Before you moved to your new house, Mr. Conover, did you have any break-ins?"

"Not till we moved to Fenwicke Estates."

The blond detective smiled. "Guess the . . . *gated community* . . . didn't give you much protection, huh?" He put a surly spin on the words "gated community," made no attempt to conceal a note of smugness.

"Just takes longer to get in and out of," Nick admitted.

The blond guy chuckled, shook his head. "Costs a lot more, though, I bet."

"There you go."

"But you can afford it."

Nick shrugged. "Wasn't my idea to move there. It was my wife's."

"Your wife," said the black woman. "She—she passed away last year, isn't that right?"

"That's right."

"Nothing suspicious about her death, was there?"

A pause. "No, nothing suspicious," Nick said slowly. "She was killed in a car accident."

"You were driving?" she asked.

"She was driving."

"Nothing—was alcohol involved?"

"The other driver, yeah," Nick said. "A semi. He'd been drinking."

"But not you."

"No," he said. "Not me." He compressed his lips, then looked at his watch. "I'm afraid—"

The blond guy stood up. "Thanks for taking the time."

But the black woman remained seated. "Just a couple more things, sir?"

"Can we continue this some other time?" Nick said.

"Just—just another minute, if you don't mind. We don't want to leave any stone unturned. Do you own any guns, Mr. Conover?"

"Guns?" Nick shook his head. He hoped his face hadn't reddened.

"No handguns at all?"

"Nope. Sorry."

"Thank you. And last Tuesday night, where were you?"

"At home. I haven't traveled anywhere in ten days or so."

"What time did you go to sleep, do you remember?"

"Last Tuesday?"

"A week ago."

Nick thought a moment. "I went out for dinner Wednesday night. Tuesday I was at home."

"Do you remember what time you went to sleep?"

"I can't—well, I'm normally asleep by eleven, eleven-thirty."

"So you'd say by eleven-thirty you were in bed?"

"That sounds about right." She was smart, Nick realized. Smarter, he saw now, than the blond guy, who was all posture and attitude.

"Sleep through the night?"

"Sure." *Jesus*, he thought. What was she implying?

"Okay, great," she said. She got up. "That's all we need. We appreciate your taking the time to talk to us."

Nick rose, shook their hands. "Anytime," he said. "Just next time, give me some notice."

"We will," the black woman said. She stopped, appeared to hesitate. "I'm sorry to take up your time, Mr. Conover. But you know, our victims aren't just victims—they're human beings. Whatever their problems, whatever their difficulties, a man is dead. Someone who mattered to someone. We're all beloved by someone, you know."

"I'd like to think so," Nick said.

38

As soon as Nick showed the two homicide cops to the elevator, he returned to the boardroom, hoping to catch Todd Muldaur, but the room was empty. Todd and the others had left. He returned to his office area—hell, his *cubicle*—taking an indirect route, past Scott's area.

"Afternoon, Gloria," he said to Scott's admin, a small, hypercompetent woman with a broad face and blond hair cut in bangs. "Scott in?"

"Good afternoon, Mr. Conover. Scott's right—"

"Hey, Nick," Scott said, emerging from behind his panel. "Man, that was a rough ride today, huh?"

"Tell me about it," Nick said blandly. He kept on going, toward Scott's desk, to the round table where Scott held his conferences.

"That put root canals in a whole new perspective," Scott said. He began lifting piles of papers off the round table, moving them to a credenza next to his desk. "So what'd you think of that new guy, Finegold?"

"Seems nice enough," Nick said guardedly, standing at the table, waiting for Scott to finish clearing away the papers.

"That guy's rolling in it, you know. I mean, totally loaded. You know he hired that boy band 'N Sync to play at his daughter's bat mitzvah a couple of years back, when they were still hot?"

"He's a hot spare," Nick said.

"A what?"

"A hot spare. Disk drive fails, you swap it with a spare, all ready to go. Plug-'n'-play. Ready to go."

"Dan? Oh—no, I'm sure they're just trying to strengthen the bench. Is that the right sports term? He's a great guy, actually—tell you a funny story, when he was at—"

"I had to learn about Atlas McKenzie from *Todd*?" Nick broke in. "What the hell's up with that?"

Scott's face colored; he examined the tabletop. "I told you, I got the call from Hardwick on my way over to dinner," he said. "I tried you on your cell, but I guess it was off."

"You didn't leave a message."

"Well, it's—it wasn't the sort of thing you want to leave in a voice mail, you know—"

"And you didn't e-mail me? You didn't call me this morning before the board meeting? You let me find out from *Todd* fucking *Muldaur*?"

Scott's hands flew up, palms out. "I didn't have a chance—"

"And you didn't have a *chance* to tell me they wanted to put you on the board?" Nick said.

Scott stared at the white Formica tabletop as if he'd just seen something alarming there. "I didn't," he began, falteringly.

"*Don't* tell me you didn't know that was going to happen. Why the hell didn't you mention it to me? You couldn't reach me on my cell, that it?"

"It—it wasn't my place, Nick," Scott said. He looked up at last, face gone burgundy, eyes watering. His voice was meek but his expression was fierce.

"Not your place? The fuck are you telling me? You knew they were going to put you on the board and it wasn't your place to tell me that? You kept their little secret, embarrassed me in front of the board?"

"Hey, come on, Nick, calm down," Scott said. "All right? It was complicated—I mean, maybe I should have said something, in retrospect, but Todd wanted me to keep it—Nick, you should take it up with Todd."

Nick got up. "Yeah," he said. "I just might do that."

Don't fuck with me, he thought. Almost said it, but at the last second something stopped him.

———

As he returned to his desk, Marge stopped him, holding up an envelope.

"This just came in from HR," she said. "That check you requested."

"Thanks," he said, taking the envelope as he resumed walking.

"Nick," she said.

He stopped, turned around.

"That check—for Cassie Stadler?"

"Yeah?"

"That's a lot of money. It's for her dad's severance pay, isn't it? Which he lost when he quit?"

Nick nodded.

"The company isn't obligated to pay that, right?"

"No, it's not."

"But it's the right thing to do. It's—that's nice, Nick." There were tears in her eyes.

Nick nodded again, returned to his desk. He immediately picked up his handset and called Todd Muldaur's cell phone. It rang three times, four, and just as Nick was about to hang up, Todd's voice came on. "This is Todd."

It sounded like a prerecorded voice-mail message, so Nick waited a second before saying, "Todd, it's Nick Conover."

"Oh, hey, Nick, there you are. You bolted before I had a chance to say goodbye, dude."

"Todd, are you trying to squeeze me out?"

A beat. "What makes you say that?"

"Come on, man. What happened in there, in the board meeting. Bring in Finegold, your hot spare, putting Scott on the board without giving me a heads-up. The monthly board meetings, the weekly financials. Changing the rules of the game like that. Taking away my ability to change my team the way I see fit. What, you think I'm an idiot?"

"Nick, we don't need to squeeze you out," Todd said, his voice gone steely. "If we wanted you gone, you'd be gone."

"Not without a pretty damned huge payday."

"A rounding error at Fairfield Partners, buddy."

"Five million bucks is a rounding error to you guys?"

"Nick, I meant what I said. We want to bring more to the table. Strengthen the team."

"You don't trust me to run the company, you should just come out with it."

Todd said something, but the signal started to break up ". . . the way," he was saying.

"Say again?" Nick said. "I lost you there."

"I said, we trust you, Nick. We just don't want you getting in the way."

"In the *way?*"

"We need to make sure you're responsive, Nick. That's all. We want to make sure you're on board."

"Oh, *I'm* on board," Nick said, deliberately ambiguous, insinuating. He didn't know what that was supposed to mean, exactly, except that he hoped it sounded vaguely threatening.

"Excellent," Todd said. His voice got all crackly again as the signal weakened. A fragment: ". . . to hear."

"Say again?" Nick said.

"Man, do you guys have, like, one cell tower out here in cow town? I swear, the reception *sucks.* All right, I better go. I'm losing you." Then the line went dead.

For a long time, Nick stared at the long blue Stratton check he'd had the treasurer's office cut for Cassie Stadler: a payoff, pure and simple. Andrew Stadler had quit before being laid off; legally, he wasn't entitled to any severance. But what was legal, and what the courts might decide—if Cassie Stadler decided to press the issue—were two separate things. Better to preempt, he'd decided. Be generous. Show her that her father's employer meant well, that Stratton was willing to go above and beyond what it was required to do.

That was all there was to it, he told himself.

Keep the woman happy. No one wanted a lawsuit.

And he remembered what that black woman detective had said as she left. "We're all beloved by someone," she'd said. She had a point. As crazy, as deranged as Andrew Stadler was, he'd been loved by his daughter.

He hit the intercom button. "Marge," he said. "I need you to call Cassie Stadler for me."

"I believe she's living in her father's house," came Marge's voice over the speakerphone.

"Right. Tell her I want to stop by. I have something for her."

39

Sergeant Jack Noyce pulled Audrey into his glass-walled office, which was not much bigger than Audrey's cubicle. He had it outfitted with an expensive-looking sound system, though, a top-of-the-line DVD player and speakers. Noyce loved his audio equipment, and he loved music. Sometimes Audrey would see him with his headphones on, enjoying music, or listening to the speakers with the office door closed.

As head of the Major Case Team, he had all sorts of administrative responsibilities and more than a dozen cops to supervise, and he spent much of his day in meetings. Music—Keith Jarrett, Bill Evans, Art Tatum, Charlie Mingus, Thelonious Monk, all the jazz piano greats—seemed to be his only escape.

A piece was playing quietly on Noyce's stereo, a beautiful and soulful rendition of the ballad "You Go to My Head," a pianist doing the melody.

"Tommy Flanagan?" Audrey said.

Noyce nodded. "You close your eyes, and you're back in the Village Vanguard."

"It's lovely."

"Audrey, you haven't said anything about Bugbee." His sad eyes, behind thick aviator-framed glasses, shone with concern.

"It's okay," she said.

"You'd tell me if it wasn't, right?"

She laughed. "Only if I couldn't take it anymore."

"The practical jokes seem to have stopped."

"Maybe he got tired of them."

"Or maybe he's learned to respect you."

"You give him way too much credit," she said with a laugh.

"And you're the one who's supposed to believe in the possibility of redemption. Listen, Audrey—you guys went over to Stratton?"

"Now don't tell me he's filling you in on every step we take."

"No. I got a call from the security director at Stratton."

"Rinaldi."

"Right. You talked to him, and then you both went over to talk to Nicholas Conover."

"What'd he call you for?"

"He says you just showed up and waited for Conover outside a board meeting? That true?"

She felt a prickle of defensiveness. "That was my decision. I wanted to avoid any prepared answers, any coordination."

"I'm not following." Noyce took off his glasses and began rubbing at them with a little cleaning cloth.

"I'd already talked to Rinaldi, and something didn't sit right with me. I can't explain it."

"You don't need to. Gut instinct."

"Right."

"Which ninety percent of the time doesn't pan out. But hey." He smiled. "You take what you get."

"I didn't want Rinaldi talking to his boss and getting his story straight."

"So you just ambushed the CEO outside the boardroom?" Noyce laughed quietly.

"I just thought if we set up a meeting with him in advance, he'd call his security director and say, what's this about?"

"Still not following. You telling me you think the CEO of Stratton's got something to do with this case?"

She shook her head. "No, of course not. But there may be some connection. A couple of days before Stadler's death, there was an incident at Nicholas Conover's house. Someone slaughtered the family dog and dumped it in the swimming pool."

Noyce winced. "My God. Was it Stadler?"

"We don't know. But this was just the latest of a long series of incidents at the Conover house since they moved in, about a year ago. Up till now it's been graffiti, nothing stolen, no violence. But each time, our uniformed division was notified—and we haven't done a thing. They didn't even print the knife that was used to kill the dog. From what I hear, there wasn't a lot of motivation to do anything about it, given the way people feel about Conover."

"Well, yeah, but that's not right."

"So just before Stadler's death, Rinaldi got in touch with our uniformed division to ask about this guy Andrew Stadler and find out if he had any priors."

"And were there any?"

"A long time ago Stadler was questioned in connection to the death of a neighbor family, but nothing ever came of it."

"What got Rinaldi interested in Andrew Stadler?"

"Rinaldi said he went through the list of people they laid off—and it's a long list, like five thousand people—to see who might have exhibited signs of violence."

"Stadler did?"

"Rinaldi was evasive on that point. When I interviewed Stadler's supervisor, at the model shop where he worked, the guy said Stadler wasn't violent at all. Though he did quit in anger, which meant he lost the severance package. But Rinaldi said he found that Stadler had a history of mental illness."

"So he suspected Stadler of being Conover's stalker."

"He denies it, but that's the feeling I got."

"So you think Conover or Rinaldi had something to do with Stadler's murder?"

"I don't know. But I do wonder about this Rinaldi fellow."

"Oh, I know about Rinaldi."

"He said you're friends, you two."

Noyce chuckled. "Did he, now."

"He didn't exactly play by the rules on the GRPD. He was squeezed out on suspicions of holding onto cash in a drug bust."

"How do you know that?" Noyce was suddenly intrigued.

"I called Grand Rapids, asked around until I found someone who knew him."

Noyce frowned, shook his head. "I'd rather you didn't call GR."

"Why not?"

"People talk. Rumors spread like wildfire. Things could get back to Rinaldi, and I don't want him knowing that we've been asking around about him. That way we're more likely to catch him in a lie."

"Okay, makes sense."

"You saying you like Rinaldi for the Stadler homicide?"

"That's not what I'm saying. Edward Rinaldi's an ex-cop, and a guy like that may know people, you know?"

"Who might have done a hit on some loony ex-employee?" Noyce replaced his glasses, raised one brow.

"Far-fetched, right?"

"Just a little."

"But no more unlikely than a crack-related murder involving a guy who doesn't fit the profile of a crackhead, had no crack in his bloodstream, and had fake crack in his pocket. A setup, in other words."

"You make a good point."

"Also, no fingerprints anywhere on the plastic wrapped over the body. Traces of talc indicating that surgical gloves were used to move the body. It's all very strange. I'd like to get Rinaldi's phone records."

Noyce gave a long sigh. "Man, you're opening a can of worms with Stratton."

"What about Rinaldi's personal phone records—home, cell, whatever?"

"Easier."

"Could you sign off on that?"

Noyce bit his lip. "Sure. I'll do it. You got an instinct, I like to go with it. But Audrey, listen. The Stratton Corporation has a lot of enemies in this town."

"Tell me about it."

"That's why I want to be fair. I don't want it to look like we're going after them arbitrarily, trying to embarrass them. Bowing to public pressure, pandering. Nothing like that. I want us to play fair, but just as important, I want the *appearance* of fairness, okay?"

"Of course."

"Just so long as we're on the same page here."

40

Cassie Stadler's house was on West Sixteenth Street, in the part of Fenwick still known as Steepletown because of all the churches that used to be there. It was an area Nick knew well; he'd grown up here, in a tiny brown split-level with a little scrubby lawn, a chain-link fence keeping out the neighbors. When Nick was a kid, Steepletown was blue-collar, most of the men factory workers employed at Stratton. Mostly Polish Catholic, too, though the Conovers were neither Polish nor members of Sacred Heart. This was a place where people kept their money in mattresses.

He was overcome by a strange, wistful nostalgia driving through these streets. It all looked and smelled so familiar, the American Legion hall, the bowling alley, the pool hall. The triple-deckers, the aluminum siding, Corky's Bottled Liquors. Even the cars were still big and American. Unlike the rest of Fenwick, which had gone upscale and fancy, vegan and latte, with all the galleries and the SUVs and the BMWs, something uncomfortable and ill fitting about it, like a little girl playing dress up in her mother's high heels. Just before he parked the car at the curb in front of the house, a song came on the radio: Billy Joel's "She's Always a Woman." One of Laura's favorites. She'd taught herself to play it on the piano, not badly at all. She'd sing it in the shower—"*Oh, she takes care of herself . . .*"—badly, off-key, in a thin, wobbly voice. Hearing it caused a lump to rise in Nick's throat. He switched the radio off, couldn't take it, and had to sit there in the car for a few minutes before he got out.

He rang the doorbell: six melodious tones sounding like a carillon. The door opened, a small figure emerging from the gloom behind the dusty screen door.

What the hell am I doing? he thought. Jesus, this is insane. The daughter of the man I killed.

Everyone is beloved by someone, the cop had said.

This is that someone.

"Mr. Conover," she said. She wore a black T-shirt and worn jeans. She was slim, even tinier than he remembered from the funeral, and her expression was hard, wary.

"May I come in for a second?"

Her eyes were red-rimmed, raccoon smudges beneath. "Why?"

"I have something for you."

She stared some more, then shrugged. "Okay." The bare minimum of politeness, nothing more. She pushed open the screen door.

Nick entered a small, dark foyer that smelled of mildew and damp carpeting. Mail lay in heaps on a trestle table. There were a few homey touches—a painting in an ornate gold frame, a bad seascape, looked like a reproduction. A vase of dried flowers. A lamp with a fringed shade. A sampler in a severe black frame, done in needlepoint or whatever, that said LET ME LIVE IN THE HOUSE BY THE SIDE OF THE ROAD AND BE A FRIEND TO MAN, over a stitched image of a house that looked a good deal nicer than the one it hung in. It seemed as if nothing had been moved, or dusted, in a decade. He caught a glimpse of a small kitchen, a big old white round-shouldered refrigerator.

She backed up a few steps, standing in a cone of light from a torchiere. "What's this all about?"

Nick produced the envelope from his jacket pocket and handed it to her. She took it, gave a puzzled look, examined the envelope as if she'd never seen one before. Then she slid out the pale blue check. When she saw the amount, she betrayed no surprise, no reaction at all. "I don't get it."

"The least we can do," Nick said.

"What's it for?"

"The severance pay your father should have gotten."

Realization dawned in her eyes. "My dad quit."

"He was a troubled man."

She flashed a smile, bright white teeth, that in another context would have been sexy. Now it seemed just unsettling. "This is so interesting," she said. Her voice was velvety smooth, pleasingly deep. There was something about her mouth, the way it curled up at the ends even when she wasn't smiling, giving her a kind of knowing look.

"Hmm?"

"This," she said.

"The check? I don't understand."

"No. You. What you're doing here."

"Oh?"

"It's like you're making a payoff."

"A payoff? No. Your father should have been counseled better at his outplacement interview. We shouldn't have let him walk out without the same severance package everyone else got, whether he quit or not. He was angry, and rightly so. But he was a longtime employee who deserved better than that."

"It's a hell of a lot of money."

"He worked for Stratton for thirty-six years. It's what he was entitled to. Maybe not legally, but morally."

"It's guilt money. *Schuldgeld*, in German, right?" Those corners of her mouth turned all the way up in a canny smile. Closer to a smirk, maybe. "The word guilt has the same root as the German word for money, *Geld*."

"I wouldn't know." He felt his insides clutch tight. "I just didn't think you should be left high and dry."

"God, I don't know how you can stand doing what you do."

She has the right to go after me, Nick thought. *Let her. Let her rant, do her whole anti-corporate thing. Trash Stratton, and me. Make her feel better. Maybe that's why you're here: masochism.*

"Ah, right," he said. " 'Slasher Nick' and all that."

"I mean, it can't be easy. Being hated by just about everyone in town."

"Part of my job," he said.

"Must be nice to have one."

"Sometimes yes, sometimes no."

"Life must have been a lot easier a couple of years ago when everyone loved you, I bet. You must have felt you were really in the groove, hitting on all cylinders. Then all of a sudden you're the bad guy."

"It's not a popularity contest." *The hell was this?*

A mysterious smile. "A man like you wants to be liked. *Needs* to be liked."

"I should be going."

"I'm making you uncomfortable," she said. "You're not the introspective type." A beat. "Why are you really here? Don't trust the messenger service?"

Nick shook his head vaguely. "I'm not sure. Maybe I feel really bad for you. I lost my wife last year. I know how hard this can be."

When she looked up at him, there seemed to be a kind of pain in the depths of her hazel eyes. "Kids?"

"Two. Girl and a boy."

"How old?"

"Julia's ten. Lucas is sixteen."

"God, to lose your mother at that age. I guess there's always enough pain to go around at the banquet of life. Plenty of seconds, right?" She sounded as if the wind had suddenly gone out of her.

"I've got to get back. I'm sorry if it bothered you, me coming by like this."

Suddenly she sank to the floor, collapsing into a seated position on the wall-to-wall carpet, canting to one side. Her legs folded up under her. She supported herself with one arm. "Jesus," she said.

"You okay?" Nick came up to her, leaned over.

Her other hand was against her forehead. Her eyes were closed. Her translucent skin was ashen.

"Jesus, I'm sorry. All the blood just left my head, and I . . ."

"What can I get you?"

She shook her head. "I just need to sit down. Light-headed."

"Glass of water or something?" He kneeled beside her. She looked like she was on the verge of toppling over, passing out. "Food, maybe?"

She shook her head again. "I'm fine."

"I don't think so. Stay there, I'll get you something."

"I'm not going anywhere," she said, her eyes unfocused. "Forget it, don't worry about it. I'm fine."

Nick got up, went into the kitchen. Dirty dishes were piled up in the sink and on the counter next to it, a bunch of Chinese takeout cartons. He looked around, found the electric stove, a kettle sitting on one burner. He picked it up, felt it was empty. He filled it in the sink, shoving aside some of the stacked plates to make room for the kettle. It took him a couple of seconds to figure out which knob on the stove turned on which burner. The burner took a long time to go from black to orange.

"You like Szechuan Garden?" he called out.

Silence.

"You okay?" he said.

"It's pretty gross, actually," she said after another pause, voice weak. "There's like two, maybe three Chinese restaurants in this whole town, one worse than the next." Another pause. "There's more than that on my *block* in Chicago."

"Looks like you get a lot of takeout from there anyway."

"I can walk to it. I haven't felt much like cooking, since . . ."

She was standing at the threshold to the kitchen, entered slowly and un-steadily. She sank down in one of the kitchen chairs, chrome with a red vinyl seat back, the table red Formica with a cracked ice pattern and chrome band-ing around the edge.

The teakettle was making a hollow roaring sound. Nick opened the re-frigerator—"Frigidaire" on the front in that great old squat script, raised metal lettering, reminding Nick of the refrigerator in his childhood home—and found it pretty much empty. A quart of skim milk, an opened bottle of Australian chardonnay with a cork in it; a carton of eggs, half gone.

He found a rind of Parmesan cheese, a salvageable bunch of scallions.

"You got a grater?"

"You serious?"

41

He set the omelet on the table before her, a fork and a paper napkin, a mug of tea. The mug, he noticed too late, had the old 1970s Stratton logo on one side.

She dug into it, eating ravenously.

"When's the last time you ate today?" Nick asked.

"Right now," she said. "I forgot to eat."

"Forgot?"

"I've had other things on my mind. Hey, this isn't bad."

"Thank you."

"I wouldn't have figured you for a chef."

"That's about the extent of my cooking ability."

"I feel way better already. Thank you. I thought I was going to pass out."

"You're welcome. I saw some salami in there, but I thought you might be a vegan or something."

"Vegans don't eat eggs," she said. "Yum. God, you know, there's some kinds of ribbon worms that actually eat themselves if they don't find any food."

"Glad I got here in time."

"The head of Stratton makes a mean omelet. Wait till the newspapers get hold of that."

"So how did you end up in Chicago?"

"Long story. I grew up here. But my mom grew tired of my dad's crazi-

ness, when I was like nine or ten. That was before he was diagnosed as schizophrenic. She moved to the Windy City and left me here with Dad. A couple of years later, I went to live with her and her new husband. Hey, this is my
house, and I'm not being much of a hostess."

She got up, went over to one of the lower cabinets, opened the door. It
held a collection of dusty bottles, vermouth and Bailey's Irish Cream and
such. "Let me guess—you're a Scotch kinda guy."

"I've got to get home to the kids."

"Oh," she said. "Right. Sure." Something waiflike and needy in her face
got to him. He'd told Marta an hour or so; another hour wouldn't be a big
deal.

"But maybe a little Scotch would be okay."

She seemed to light up, leaned over and pulled out a bottle of Jameson's.
"Irish, not Scotch—okay?"

"Fine with me."

She pulled out a cut-glass tumbler from the same cabinet. "Whoo boy,"
she said, blowing a cloud of dust out of it. She held it under the running tap
in the sink. "I'm going to say rocks."

"Hmm?"

"Ice cubes. You drink your whiskey on the rocks." She went to the antique Frigidaire, opened the freezer, took out the kind of ice tray Nick hadn't
seen in decades, aluminum with the lever you pull up to break the ice into
cubes. She yanked back the handle, making a scrunching sound that
sounded like his childhood. Reminded him of his dad, who liked his Scotch
on the rocks, every night and too much of it.

She plopped a handful of jagged cubes into the glass, glugged in a few
inches of whiskey, came over and handed it to him. She looked directly into
his eyes, the first time she'd done that. Her eyes were big and gray-green and
lucid, and Nick felt a tug in his groin. He immediately felt a flush of shame.
Jesus, he thought.

"Thanks," he said. The glass had FAMOUS GROUSE etched into it. It was
the kind of thing you get at a liquor store packed with the bottle, a promo-
tional deal.

"How about you?"

"I hate whiskey," she said. The kettle began whistling shrilly. She pulled it off the burner, found a carton of teabags in a drawer, and poured herself a mug of herbal tea.

"How does it feel being home?" The whiskey had a pleasant bite to it, and he felt its effect immediately. He didn't recall when he'd last eaten anything himself, actually.

"Strange," she said, sitting down at the table. "Brings a lot of things back. Some good things, some not good things." She looked at him. "I don't expect you to understand."

"Try me."

"Do you know what it's like to have a parent with severe mental illness? The whole point is, you're a child, so you don't grasp what's going on."

"Right. How could you?"

Cassie closed her eyes, and it was as if she were in some other place. "So you're his beloved daughter, and he hugs you like nobody can hug you and he puts his forehead to yours and you feel so safe, and so loved, and everything's right with the world. And then, one day, he's different—except, as far as he's concerned, *you're* different."

"Because of the disease."

"He looks at you and you're a stranger to him. You're not his beloved daughter now. Maybe you resemble her, but he's not fooled, he knows you've been replaced by someone or something else. He looks at you and he sees a Fembot, you know? And you say, 'Daddy!' You're three or four or five and you throw your arms open, waiting for your super-special hug. And he says, 'Who are you? Who are you *really*?' and he says, 'Get away! Get away! Get away!'" Her mimicry was uncanny; Nick was beginning to glimpse the nightmare she had endured. "You realize that he's *terrified* of you. And it's different from anything you've ever experienced. Because it isn't what happens when, you know, you misbehave, and Mommy or Daddy turns red and you get yelled at. Every kid knows what that's like. They're mad. But you know they still love you, and they're still aware of your *existence*. They don't think you're an alien. They're not frightened of you. It's different when a parent has schizophrenia. It steals over them, and suddenly you don't exist to them any longer. You're not a daughter anymore. Just some impostor. Just some intruder. Some . . . outsider. Someone who doesn't belong." She smiled sadly.

"He was ill."

"He was ill," Cassie repeated. "But a child doesn't understand that. A child *can't* understand it. Even if anybody had explained to me, I probably wouldn't have understood." She sniffed, her eyes flooded with tears. She frowned, turned away, wiped her eyes with her T-shirt, exposing her flat belly, a tiny pouting navel. Nick tried not to look.

"Nobody ever told you what was going on?"

"When I was maybe thirteen, I finally figured it out. My mother didn't want to deal, and her way of not dealing meant you didn't talk about it. Which is pretty crazy, too, when you think about it."

"I can't imagine what you had to go through." And he couldn't—not what she'd had to go through, nor what her father's death was causing her to relive. He ached to do something for her.

"No, you can't imagine. But it messes with your head. I mean, it messed with mine."

She tucked her chin in close to her chest, ran her fingers through her spiky hair, and when she looked up, her cheeks were wet. "You don't need this," she said, her voice thick with tears. "I think you should go."

"Cassie," he said. It came out in a whisper, sounded far more intimate than he'd intended.

For a while, her breaths came in short little puffs. When she spoke again, her voice was strained. "You need to be there for your kids," she said. "There's nothing more important than family, okay?"

"Not much of a family these days."

"Don't say that," Cassie said. She looked up at him, eyes fierce. "You don't *fucking* talk that way, *ever*." Something had flared up inside her, like a whole book of matches, and then subsided almost as quickly. But who could blame the woman, having so recently put her father in the ground? And then he remembered why.

"Sorry," he said. "It hasn't been easy for the kids, and I'm not exactly doing my job."

"How'd she die?" Her voice was soft. "Their mother."

He took another sip. A quick scene played in his head, jittery, badly spliced film. The pebbles of glass strewn throughout Laura's hair. The spiderwebbed windshield. "I don't like to talk about it."

"Oh, I'm sorry."

"Don't apologize. Natural question."

"No, you're—crying."

He realized that he was, and as he turned his face, embarrassed, cursing the booze, she got up from her chair, came up to him. She put a small warm hand on his face, leaned close to him, and put her lips on his.

Startled, he backed away, but she moved in closer, pressed her lips against his, harder, her other hand pressed against his chest.

He turned his head away. "Cassie, I've got to get home."

Cassie smiled uncomfortably. "Go," she said. "Your kids are waiting."

"It's the babysitter, actually. She hates it when I come home later than I promised."

"Your daughter—what's her name, again?"

"Julia."

"Julia. Sweet name. Go home to Julia and Luke. They need you. Go back to your gated community."

"How'd you know?"

"People talk. It's perfect."

"What?"

"You living in a gated community."

"I'm not really the gated-community type."

"Oh, I think you are," she said. "More than you know."

42

LaTonya's twelve-year-old daughter, Camille, was practicing piano in the next room, which made it hard for Audrey to concentrate on what her sister-in-law was saying. LaTonya was speaking in a low voice, uncharacteristically for her, while she removed a sweet-potato casserole from the oven.

"Let me tell you," LaTonya said, "if Paul didn't have a steady income, I don't know how we'd get by with three kids still in the house."

Audrey, who'd noticed the kitchen piled high with cartons of thermogenic fat-burning supplements, said, "But what about the vitamins?"

"Shit!" LaTonya shouted, dropping the casserole to the open oven door. "These damned oven mitts have a hole in them—what the hell good are they?"

Thomas, who was nine, ran in from the dining room where he and Matthew, eleven, were allegedly setting the table, though mostly just clattering the dishes and giggling. "You okay, Mom?"

"I'm fine," LaTonya said, picking up the casserole again and putting it on the stovetop. "You get back out there and finish setting the table, and you tell Matthew to go tell your father and Uncle Leon to get off their lazy butts and come in to dinner." She turned to Audrey, a disgusted look on her face. "Once again, I'm ahead of the curve."

"How so?"

"These thermogenic supplements. Fenwick is a backward, fearful community," she said gravely. "They do *not* want to try new things."

"And now you're stuck with all these bottles."

"If they think I'm paying for them, they've got another think coming. I'm going to ask you to read the small print on my agreement, because I don't think they can get away with it."

"Sure," Audrey said without enthusiasm. The last thing she wanted to do was get involved in extricating LaTonya from another mess she'd created. "You know, the money isn't the worst part," Audrey said. "I mean, it's not easy, but we can get by."

"Not having kids," LaTonya pointed out.

"Right. It's dealing with Leon."

"What the *hell* does he do all day?" LaTonya demanded, one hand on her left hip, waggling the other hand to cool it off.

"He watches a lot of TV and he drinks," Audrey said.

"You see, I knew this would happen. We spoiled him growing up. The baby of the family. Anything he wanted, he got. My momma and me, we waited on him hand and foot, and now you're paying the price. You hear what I hear?"

"I don't hear anything."

"Exactly." She shouted, earsplittingly loud, "Camille, you've got twenty more minutes of practicing, so don't stop now!"

An anguished, garbled protest came from the next room.

"And you don't get any supper until you're done, so *move* it!" She glowered at Audrey. "Honestly, I don't know what's wrong with her ownself. She pays me no mind at all."

Dinner was meat loaf, macaroni and cheese, collards, and sweet-potato casserole, everything heavy and greasy but delicious. Leon sat next to his sister at one end of the table, LaTonya's husband at the other, the two squirming boys on one side facing Audrey and Camille's empty place.

The sound of the piano came from the living room, sporadic, sullen. Brahms, Audrey recognized. A pretty piece. A waltz, maybe? Her niece was struggling with it.

Thomas squawked with laughter over something, and Matthew said, "Fuck you!"

LaTonya exploded: "Don't you *ever* use language like that in this house, you hear me?"

The two boys fell instantly silent. Matthew, looking like a whipped puppy, said, "Yes, ma'am."

"That's right," LaTonya said.

Audrey caught the younger boy's eye and gave him a mildly disapproving look that was still, she hoped, filled with aunty love.

Leon was stuffing his face meanwhile. He said, "I wish I could eat supper here every night, LaTonya."

She beamed, then caught herself. "Is there any reason you can't get yourself a job?"

"Doing what?" Leon said, dropping his fork dramatically. "Operating an electrostatic spray gun at the Seven-Eleven, maybe?"

"Doing something," LaTonya said.

"Doing something?" Leon said. "Like what? Like what do you think a guy with my skills can do here?"

"Your skills," LaTonya scoffed.

"How do you think it feels getting laid off?" Leon said, his voice rising. "Do you have any idea? How do you think I feel about myself?"

"I'll tell you how I feel about you sitting around doing absolutely nothing," LaTonya said. She cocked her head. "Camille," she shouted, "what are you doing?"

Another muffled cry.

"We're all eating in here," LaTonya yelled. "We're likely to finish dinner without you, rate you're practicing."

Camille screamed back, "I can't stand it!"

"You can yell all you want," LaTonya bellowed. "Won't make any difference. You're not getting over on me."

"Let me talk to her," Audrey said. She excused herself from the table, went into the next room.

Camille was weeping at the piano, her head resting on her elbows atop the keys. Audrey sat down at the bench next to her. She stroked her niece's hair, lingering on the kitchen, that kinky hair at the nape of her neck. "What is it, honey?"

"I can't stand it," Camille said. She sat up. Her face was streaked with tears. She looked genuinely upset; it was no act. "I don't understand this. This is torture."

Audrey looked at the sheet music. Brahms's Waltz in A Minor. "What don't you get, baby?"

Camille touched the music with a pudgy, tear-damp finger, making a tiny pucker.

"The trill, is that it?"

"I guess."

Audrey nudged Camille over a bit and played a few measures. "Like that?"

"Yeah, but I can't do that."

"Try this." Audrey played the trill slowly. "Down an octave."

Camille placed her fingers on the keyboard and tried.

"Like this," Audrey said, playing again.

Camille imitated her. Close enough. "That's it, baby. You got it. Try it again."

Camille played it, got it right.

"Now go back a couple of measures. To here. Let me hear it."

Camille played the first two lines of the second page.

"Boy, are you a fast learner," Audrey marveled. "You don't even need me anymore."

Camille smiled faintly.

"When's your recital?"

"Next week."

"What are you doing besides this?"

"Little Prelude."

"Beethoven?"

Camille nodded.

"Can I come?"

Camille smiled again, this time a happy grin. "You think you have time?"

"I'll make time, baby. I'd love to. Now, hurry up and finish. I'm getting lonely at the table without you."

———

Paul looked up as Audrey entered the dining room. He was a pigeon-chested man with sunken cheeks, a recessive gene but a sweet-natured guy. Camille was back at the Brahms, strong and enthusiastic. "I don't know what you threatened her with, but sounds like it worked," he said.

"She probably pulled out her handcuffs," said LaTonya.

"Probably her gun," Leon mumbled. He seemed to have calmed down in the meantime, retreated back into his old, monosyllabic self.

"No," Audrey said, sitting down. "She just needed a little help figuring something out."

"I want an ice cream sundae for dessert," the younger boy said.

"I'll be the judge of that," said LaTonya. "Right now it's looking awful grim for you."

"How come?"

"You got more than half your meat loaf left. Now Audrey, what are you working on these days?"

"It's not dinner-table conversation," Audrey said.

"I don't mean the gory details."

"I'm afraid it's all gory details," Audrey said.

"She's working on that murder of the Stratton worker got murdered down on Hastings," Leon said.

Audrey was amazed he even knew what she was working on. "People aren't supposed to know what I'm doing," she told him.

"We're all family here," said LaTonya.

"Right, but still," said Audrey.

"No one's going to say anything, my seddity sister," LaTonya said. "You think we know anybody? This guy fell off the edge, that right? Get into crack and other poisons like that?" She cast an evil eye at her two sons.

"I met the guy," Leon said.

"Who?" said Audrey. "Andrew Stadler?"

Leon nodded. "Sure. He kept to himself, but I talked to him in the break room once or twice." Leon reached for the macaroni and cheese and shoveled a huge lump onto his plate, a third helping. "Couldn't meet a nicer guy."

"A troubled man," Audrey said.

"Troubled?" said Leon. "I don't know. Gentle as a lamb, I'll tell you that."

"Really?" said Audrey.

"Gentle as a lamb," Leon said again.

"I'm done," Camille announced, entering the room and sitting down next to Audrey. She found Audrey's hand under the table and gave it a little secret squeeze. Audrey's heart fluttered for a moment.

"Took you long enough," said LaTonya. "I hope you learned your lesson."

"You sounded great," Audrey said.

43

Nick got in a little earlier than usual, got a cup of coffee from the executive lounge, and checked his e-mail. As usual, his inbox was cluttered with offers for Viagra and penis enlargement and low-interest mortgages, the subject headings inventively misspelled. The putative wives and sons of various deceased African heads of state urgently sought his assistance in transferring millions of dollars out of their country.

He thought about this woman, Cassie Stadler. She was not only seriously attractive, but she was unlike any woman he'd ever met before. And she—who, of course, had no idea what he'd done—was clearly as attracted to him as he was to her.

No message from the Atlas McKenzie guys—the mammoth deal that had unaccountably fallen through—but that didn't surprise him. He was going to have to confront them on it, find out what the reason was, see if there was a way to sweet-talk them back on board.

Marjorie wasn't in yet, so Nick placed the calls himself. It was 7:10 A.M. The Atlas McKenzie guys were usually in by then. Ten digits away. Not a lot of work to press those ten digits on the telephone keypad. How many calories did this take? Nick imagined a tiny scrap of the twiggy cereal Julia wouldn't eat: *that* many calories. Why wouldn't he place his own calls?

The woman on the other line was really sorry. Mr. Hardwick was still in conference. Nick imagined Hardwick making throat-cut, I'm-not-in gestures.

There it was. *That* was a reason not to place your own calls. To spare yourself the humiliation of dissembling secretaries. The smile in the voice that accompanied the singsongy formula *I'm sorry*. The micro–power trip of putting one over on a CEO. Fun for the whole family. He wondered whether the waitress at Terra really had spit in his arugula salad. She'd brightened a little when she brought it out, hadn't she?

Nick felt a little acid come up his gullet as he stared at the silver-mesh fabric panels in front of him. There were certain things that money and position protected you from. There were certain things that it didn't. When his driver's license needed renewing a couple of years ago, he didn't stand in line at the DMV, the way he once had to. The CEO of a major corporation didn't wait in line at the DMV. Some young staffer from the corporate counsel's office did, and it got taken care of. Nick couldn't remember the last time he'd waited in line for a taxi at an airport. Senior execs had cars; you looked for the guy holding a sign that said CONOVER. And senior execs of major corporations didn't haul their own baggage. That got taken care of, too, even when Nick was flying commercial. But when the weather was bad, it was bad for you too. When your car was stuck in traffic, it didn't matter what your company's valuation was; traffic was traffic. Those things were the Levelers. The things that reminded you that you lived in the same world and were going to end up in the same place as everybody else. You thought you were a master of the universe, but you were just lording it over a little box of dirt, the tyrant of a terrarium. Having a kid who hated you—that had to be a leveler too. And so was sickness.

And so was death.

Next he tried MacFarland—that was the name of the Nixon look-alike. But his assistant apologized: Mr. MacFarland was traveling. "I'll be sure to let him know that you called," MacFarland's assistant told him, with the bright artificiality of someone from a casting director's office. Don't call us; we'll call you.

Twenty minutes later came the faint settling-in noises, the heavy vanilla smell of Shalimar: Marjorie was in.

Nick got up, stretched, stepped around the partition. "How's the novel coming?" He tried to remember the title. "*Manchester Abbey*, was it?"

She smiled. "We did *Northanger Abbey* a few weeks ago. This week is *Mansfield Park*."

"Got it," Nick said.

"I think Jane Austen wrote *Northanger Abbey* first, but it didn't come out until after her death," Marjorie said, turning on her computer. She said distantly, "Amazing what comes out after people die."

Nick felt as if someone had touched his neck with an ice cube. His smile faded.

"*Persuasion* did too," she went on. "And *Billy Budd*, which we read last year. I didn't know you had such an interest, Nick. You ought to come to our book club."

"Let me know when you decide to do the Chevrolet Suburban Owner's Manual—that's what *I* call a book," he said. "Listen, I'm expecting a call from those Atlas McKenzie guys. Hardwick, MacFarland. Let me know when they're on the line. Wherever I am, I'll take the call."

Nick spent the next couple of hours in conference rooms, two back-to-back, bun-numbing meetings. There was the supply-chain-management team, whose seven members had reached an important conclusion: Stratton needed to diversify its suppliers of metallic paint. They were bubbling with excitement as they reviewed the considerations they had taken into account, like they'd discovered penicillin. Then there was the industrial-safety team, which always had more lawyers than engineers, more concerned about lawsuits than limbs. Nobody came to spring him. No message from Marjorie.

He gave Marjorie a questioning look as he made his way back to his desk.

"The Atlas McKenzie people—they were supposed to get back this morning?" she asked.

Nick sighed. "I'm beginning to feel like I'm getting the bum's rush. I phoned first thing today, you know, and they said Hardwick's in conference, MacFarland's on the road, they'll get back to me." Then again, they were supposed to return his call from yesterday too. Apparently they had other priorities.

"You think they're trying to dodge you."

"Could be."

"Want to get them on line?" Marjorie looked sunny but sly. It was a good look.

"Yup."

"Let me have a go."

Nick took a few more steps toward his desk as Marjorie made a couple of phone calls. He couldn't hear everything. "That's right," she was saying. "United Airlines. We've located the lost baggage, and he gave us a cell number to call him at. James MacFarland, yes. He seemed frantic. But the clerk must have written it down wrong . . ."

A minute later, an intercom tone told Nick to pick up his Line 1.

"Jim MacFarland?" Nick said as he answered the phone.

Cautiously: "Yes?"

"Nick Conover here."

"Nick. Hey." Friendly, but with a tremor of unease.

Nick wanted to say, *Do you realize the amount of money and man-hours we've spent designing your goddamn prototypes? And you can't be bothered to return my calls?* Instead he tried to sound breezy. "Just wanted to touch base," he said. "About where things stood."

"Yeah," MacFarland said. "Yeah. I meant to give you a call about that. About the current thinking."

"Lay it on me."

A deep breath. "Thing is, Nick—well, we hadn't realized that Stratton's on the block. Which kind of changes the picture for us."

"On the block? Meaning what?" Nick struggled to keep his voice calm. At the start of his career, Nick figured that being the boss meant not having to kiss ass. A nice thought, anyway. Turned out there was always somebody whose ass you had to kiss. The commander in chief of the free world had to suck up to farmers in Iowa. *It's good to be the boss*—wasn't that what they said? But every boss had a boss. Turtles all the way down. Asses all the way up.

That was how it felt sometimes, anyway. That was how it felt just now.

"It's just that Hardwick's always real concerned about stability when it comes to sourcing and support," MacFarland was saying. "We hadn't realized things were in flux that way. It's not like you had a big 'For Sale' sign over the front door, right?"

Nick was dumbfounded. "Stratton's not for sale," he said simply.

There was a moment of silence on the other end. "Huh." Not the sound of agreement. "Look, Nick, you didn't hear this from me. We use the same law firm in Hong Kong that Fairfield Partners does. And, you know, people talk."

"That's *bullshit*," Nick said.

"What it is, is water under the bridge."

"Come on. I'm the CEO of the company. If Stratton was being sold, you'd think I'd know, right?"

"You said it." The chilling thing was that MacFarland sounded kindly, sympathetic, like an oncologist breaking the news of a bad diagnosis to a favorite patient.

44

Marjorie poked her head around at ten thirty.

"Remember, you've got a lunch at half past with Roderick Douglass, the Chamber of Commerce guy," she said. "He'll be wanting to hit you up again. Then there's the meeting with the business development execs right after."

Nick swiveled around and looked out the window. "Right, thanks," he said, distracted.

It was a beautiful day. The sky was blue, deepened a little by the tint of the glass. There was enough of a breeze to flutter the leaves of the trees. A jet was making its way across the sky, its double contrails quickly turning into smudgy fluff.

It was also the seventh day in a row that Andrew Stadler hadn't been alive to see.

Nick shivered, as if a gust of cool air had somehow made it through the building's glass membrane. Cassie Stadler's fragile, china-doll face now filled his mind. *What did I do to you?* He remembered the look of infinite hurt in her eyes, and he found himself dialing her number before he was even conscious of having decided to.

"Hello." Cassie's voice, deep and sleepy-sounding.

"It's Nick Conover," he said. "Hope I'm not calling you too early."

"Me? No—it's—what time is it?"

"I woke you up. I'm sorry. It's ten thirty. Go back to sleep."

"No," she said hastily. "I'm glad you called. Listen, about yesterday—"

"Cassie, I'm just calling to make sure you're okay. When I left, you didn't look so great."

"Thanks."

"You know what I mean."

"I—it helped, talking to you. Really helped."

"I'm glad."

"Would you like to come over for lunch?"

"You mean today?"

"Oh, God, that's ridiculous, I can't believe I just said that. You're this big CEO, you've probably got lunch meetings scheduled every day until you're sixty-five."

"Not at all," he said. "My lunch meeting just canceled, in fact. Which means a sandwich at my desk. So, yeah, I'd love to get out of the office, sure."

"Really? Hey, great. Oh—just one little thing."

"You don't have any food in your refrigerator."

"Sad but true. What kind of host am I?"

"I'll pick something up. See you at noon."

When he hung up, he stopped by his assistant's desk. "Marge," he said, "could you cancel my lunch meetings?"

"Both of them?"

"Right."

Marjorie smiled. "Going to play hooky? It's a beautiful day."

"Hooky? Does that sound like me?"

"Hope springs eternal."

"Nah," he said. "I just need to run a couple of errands."

45

The house on West Sixteenth, in Steepletown, was even smaller than he remembered it. A dollhouse, a miniature, almost.

Two stories. White sidings that could have been aluminum or vinyl, you'd have to tap to be sure. Black shutters that weren't big enough to pretend to be shutters.

Nick, holding a couple of brown bags from the Family Fare supermarket he'd stopped at on the way over, rang the bell, heard the carillon tones.

It was almost half a minute before Cassie came to the door. She was in a black knitted top and black stretchy pants. Her face was pale, and sad, and perfect. She was wearing glossy orange lipstick, which was a little strange, but it looked right on her. She also looked better, more rested, than she had yesterday.

"Hey, you actually came." Cassie opened the door, and walked him past the vase with the dried flowers and the framed embroidered sampler to the small living room. He could hear "One Is the Loneliest Number" come from the small speakers of a portable CD player. Not the old Three Dog Night version. A modern cover. A woman with a voice like clove cigarettes. Cassie switched it off.

Nick unloaded the stuff he'd bought—bread, eggs, juice, milk, bottled water, fruit, a couple of bottles of iced tea. "Toss whatever you don't like," he said. Then he unwrapped a couple of sandwiches, placing them ceremoniously on paper plates. "Turkey or roast beef?"

She looked doubtfully at the roast beef. "Too bloody," she said. "I like my meat burned to a crisp, basically."

"I'll have it," Nick said. "You have the turkey."

They ate together in silence. He folded up the Boar's Head delicatessen wrappers into neat squares, a form of fidgeting. She finished most of her iced tea and toyed with the cap. It was a little awkward, and Nick wondered why she'd invited him over. He tried to think of something to say, but before he could, she said, "Hey, you never know what you're going to learn from a bottle cap. It says here, 'Real Fact'—the last letter added to the English-language alphabet was the 'J.'"

Nick tried to think of something to say, but before he could, she went on: "Aren't you supposed to be running a Fortune Five Hundred company or something?"

"We're not a public company. Anyway, I had a boring lunch I canceled."

"Now I feel guilty."

"Not at all. I was happy to have an excuse to miss it."

"You know, you really surprised me yesterday."

"Why?"

"It wasn't very 'Nick the Slasher.' I guess people are never what you expect. Like they say, still waters—"

"Get clogged with algae?"

"Something like that. You know how it is—you see someone who seems so desperate, and you just have to reach out and help."

"You don't seem desperate."

"I'm talking about you."

Nick reddened. "Excuse me?"

She got up and put the kettle on. Standing at the stove, she said, "We've both suffered a loss. It's like Rilke says—when we lose something, it circles around us. 'It draws around us its unbroken curve.'"

"Huh. I used to have a Spirograph set when I was a kid."

"I guess I figured you for the typical company man. Until I met you. But you know what I think now?" Her gaze was calm but intent. "I think you're actually a real family man."

He cleared his throat. "Yeah, well, tell that to my son. Tell that to Lucas."

"It's a bad age for a boy to lose his mom," Cassie said quietly. She took a teapot down from a cabinet, then some mugs.

"Like there's a good one?"

"The kid probably needs you badly."

"I don't think that's how he sees it," Nick said, a little bitterly.

Cassie looked away. "You're saying that because he's isolated and he's angry, and he turns on you. Am I right? Because you're safe. But you'll get through it. You love each other. You're a family."

"We were."

"You know how lucky your kids are?"

"Yeah, well."

She turned to face him. "I'll bet being a CEO is sort of like being head of a family too."

"Yeah," Nick said acerbically. "Maybe one of those Eskimo families. The kind that puts Grandma on the ice floe when she's not bringing in the whale blubber anymore."

"I bet the layoffs were hard on you."

"Harder on the people who got laid off."

"My dad had a lot of problems, but I think having a job helped him keep it together. Then when he found out they don't want him anymore, he fell apart."

Nick felt as if there was a metal strap around his chest and it was steadily tightening. He nodded.

"I was mad at Stratton," Cassie said. "Mad at you, is the truth. Maybe because I'm a girl, I take these things too personally. But it might have had a bad effect on him. Someone with a thought disorder, it's hard to know."

"Cassie," Nick started, but whatever he was going to say died in his throat.

"That was before I met you, though. You didn't want to do this. The people in Boston made you. Because, end of the day, Stratton is a business."

"Right."

"But it's never just a business to you, is it? See, I just realized something. Being a Stratton employee in the past couple of years must have been like being the daughter of a schizophrenic. One day you're a beloved family member, the next you're a unit, a cost center, something to be slashed." She leaned against the counter, her arms folded.

"I'm sorry about your dad," Nick said. "More sorry than I can tell you." *With more to be sorry about than I can tell you.*

"My daddy . . ." Cassie's voice was hushed, halting. "He didn't—he didn't want to be the way he was. It would just take over him. He wanted to be a good father like you. He wanted . . ." Cassie's breathing started to become ragged, and Nick realized that she was weeping. Her face was red, bowed, and she put a hand over her eyes. Tears rolled copiously down her cheeks.

Nick got up suddenly, his chair scraping against the linoleum floor, and put his arms around her.

"Oh, Cassie," he said softly. "I'm sorry."

She was tiny, birdlike, and her shoulders were narrow and bony. She made a sound like she was hiccupping. She smelled like something spicy and New-Agey—patchouli, was that it? Nick was ashamed to realize he was getting aroused.

"I'm sorry," he said again.

"Stop saying that." Cassie looked up at him and smiled wanly through her tears. "It's got nothing to do with you."

Nick remembered a time when he was trying to fix a lamp socket he'd thought was switched off. An eerie, hair-erecting, tingling feeling had swept through his arm, and it had taken him a second to identify the sensation as house current that was leaking through the screwdriver. He felt something like that now, guilt washing through his body like an electrical flux. He didn't know how to respond.

But Cassie said, "I think you're a good man, Nicholas Conover."

"You don't know me," he said.

"I know you better than you think," she said, and he felt her arms squeezing against his back, pulling him toward her. Then she seemed to be standing on tiptoes, her face close to his, her lips pressing against his.

The moment for refusing, for backing out, came and went. Nick's response was almost reflexive. This time he kissed her back, her tears sticky against his face, and his hands moved downward from her shoulders.

"Mmm," she said.

The teakettle started whistling.

For a long time afterward, she lay on top of him in the slick of their perspiration, her mouth pressed against his chest. He could feel her heartbeat, fast as a bird's, slowing gradually. He stroked her hair, nuzzled her porcelain neck, smelling her hair, a conditioner or whatever. He felt her breasts against his stomach.

"I don't know what to say," Nick began.

"Then keep silent." She smiled, lifted herself up on her elbows until she was sitting upright on him. She lightly scratched her fingernails across his upper chest, tangling them in his chest hair.

Nick shifted his butt against the coarse-textured couch in the living room. He rocked upward, enfolded her in an embrace, leaned forward until he was sitting up too.

"Strong guy," she said.

Her breasts were small and round, the nipples pink and still erect like little upturned thumbs. Her waist was tiny. She reached across him to the table next to the couch, and as she did, her breasts brushed against his face. He gave them a quick kiss. She retrieved a pack of Marlboros and a Bic lighter, took one out of the pack and waved it at him, offering.

"No, thanks," Nick said.

She shrugged, lighted the cigarette, took in a lungful of air and spewed out a thin stream of smoke.

" 'Let me live in a house by the side of the road and be a friend to man,' " Nick quoted.

"Yep."

"Needlepoint by Grandma?"

"Mom got it in some junk store. She liked what it said."

"So how long has it been since you left this place?"

"I just turned twenty-nine. Left when I was around twelve. So, a long time. But I came back to visit Dad a bunch of times."

"School in Chicago, then."

"You're trying to piece together the Cassie Stadler saga? Good luck."

"Just wondering."

"My mom remarried when I was eleven. An orthodontist. Had a couple of kids of his own, my age, a little older. Let's just say it wasn't the Brady Bunch. Dr. Reese didn't exactly take to me. Neither did the little Reese's pieces, Bret and Justin. Finally shipped me off to Lake Forest Academy, basically to get me out of the way."

"Must have been tough on you."

She inhaled, held a lungful of smoke for several seconds. Then, as she let it out, she said, "Yes and no. In some ways, they did me a favor. I actually flourished at the academy. I was a precocious kid. Got a Headmaster scholarship, graduated top of the class. Should have seen me when I was seventeen. A real promising young citizen. Not the head case you see before you."

"You don't seem like a head case to me."

"Because I don't drool and wear bad glasses?" She crossed her eyes. "Fools them every time."

"You talk about it like it's a big joke."

"Probably it *is* a joke. Some cosmic joke that's just a little over our heads. God's joke. Nothing to do but to smile and nod and try to pretend that we get it."

"You can go pretty far in life doing that," Nick said. He sneaked a glimpse at his wristwatch, saw it was after two already. With a jolt, he realized he had to get back to the office.

She noticed. "Time to go."

"Cassie, I—"

"Just go, Nick. You've got a company to run."

46

Dr. Aaron Landis, the clinical director of mental health services for County Medical, seemed to wear a permanent sneer. Audrey realized, though, that there was something not quite right about the man's face, a crookedness to the mouth, a congenital deformity that made him look that way. His gray hair resembled a Brillo pad, and he had a receding chin that he tried to disguise, not very successfully, with a neatly trimmed gray beard. At first Audrey felt a bit sorry for the psychiatrist because of his homeliness, but her compassion quickly faded.

His office was small and messy, so heaped with books and papers that there was scarcely room for the two of them to sit. The only decoration was a photograph of a plain-looking wife and an even plainer son, and a series of colorful scans of a human brain, purple with yellow-orange highlights, on curling slick paper, thumbtacked along one wall.

"I don't think I understand what you're asking, Detective," he said.

She had been as clear as day. "I'm asking whether Andrew Stadler exhibited violent tendencies."

"You're asking me to breach doctor-patient confidentiality."

"Your patient is dead," she said gently.

"And the confidentiality of his medical records survives his death, Detective. As does physician-patient confidentiality. You know that, or if you don't, you should. The Supreme Court upheld that privilege a decade ago.

More important, it's part of the Hippocratic oath I took when I became a doctor."

"Mr. Stadler was murdered, Doctor. I want to find his killer or killers."

"An effort I certainly applaud. But I don't see how it concerns me."

"You see, there are a number of unanswered questions about his death that might help us determine what really happened. I'm sure you want to help us do our job."

"I'm happy to help in any way I can. Just so long as you don't ask me to violate Mr. Stadler's rights."

"Thank you, Doctor. Then let me restate my question. Speaking generally. Do most schizophrenics tend to be violent?"

The psychiatrist looked upward for a moment, as if consulting the heavens. He exhaled noisily. Then he fixed her with a sorrowful look. "That, Detective, is one of the most pernicious myths about schizophrenia."

"Then maybe you can enlighten me, Doctor."

"Schizophrenia is a chronic recurring psychotic illness that begins in early adulthood, as a rule, and lasts until death. We don't even know if it's a single disease or a syndrome. Myself, I prefer to call it SSD, or schizophrenia spectrum disorder, though I'm in the minority on this. Now, the defining symptoms of schizophrenia are thought disorder, a failure of logic, reality distortion, and hallucinations."

"And paranoia?"

"Often, yes. And a psychosocial disability. So let me ask *you* something, Detective. You see a good deal of violence in your work, I'm sure."

"Yes, I do."

"Is most of it inflicted by schizophrenics?"

"No."

"My point. Most violent crimes are not committed by persons with schizophrenia, and most persons with schizophrenia don't commit violent crimes."

"But there's a—"

"Let me finish, please. The vast majority of patients with schizophrenia have never been violent. They're a hundred times more likely to commit *suicide* than homicide."

"So are you saying that Andrew Stadler was not a violent man?"

"Detective, I admire your persistence, but the backdoor approach won't work either. I will not discuss the particulars of his case. But let me tell you what the real correlation is between schizophrenia and violence: schizophrenia increases the likelihood of being the *victim* of a crime."

"Exactly. Mr. Stadler was the victim of a terrible crime. Which is why I need to know whether he might have provoked his own death by killing an animal, a family pet."

"If I knew that, I wouldn't tell you."

"I'm asking whether he was capable of such an act."

"I won't tell you that either."

"Are you saying that schizophrenics are never violent?"

After a long pause, he said: "Obviously there are the exceptions."

"Was Andrew Stadler one of those exceptions, Doctor?"

"Please, Detective. I won't discuss the particulars of Mr. Stadler's medical records. I don't know how much more clear I can be."

Audrey sighed in exasperation. "Then let me ask you a purely hypothetical question, all right?"

"Purely hypothetical," Dr. Landis repeated.

"Let's take a . . . *hypothetical* case in which an individual repeatedly breaks into a family's house in order to write threatening graffiti. Is able to do so, cleverly and without leaving any evidence, despite the security provided by the gated community in which this family lives. And has even slaughtered the family's pet. What sort of person might do this, would you say?"

"What sort of *hypothetical* individual?" He attempted a smile, which twisted unpleasantly. "Someone, I would say, who's extremely intelligent, high-functioning, capable of higher-order thinking and goal-governed behavior, and yet has pervasive impulse-control problems, marked mood swings, and is highly sensitive to rejection. There may be, say, a great fear of abandonment, derived from difficulties in childhood feeling connected to important persons in one's life. He might have absolutely black-and-white views of others—might tend to idealize people and then suddenly despise them."

"And then?"

"And then he might be subject to sudden and unpredictable rages, brief psychotic episodes, with suicidal impulses."

"What might set him off?"

"A situation of great stress. The loss of someone or something important to him."

"Or the loss of a job?"

"Certainly."

"Can a schizophrenic exhibit this pattern of behavior you're describing?"

Dr. Landis paused for a long moment. "Conceivably. It's not impossible." Then he gave a creepy sort of smile. "But what does all this have to do with Andrew Stadler?"

47

"Grover Herrick," Marjorie said over the intercom the next morning.

Grover Herrick was a senior procurement manager at the U.S. General Services Administration, which did purchasing for federal agencies. He was also the point man for an enormous contract Stratton had negotiated for the Department of Homeland Security. DHS now encompassed the Coast Guard, Customs, Immigration and Naturalization Service, and the Transportation Security Administration—thousands of offices, a hundred and eighty thousand employees, and a major infusion of federal cash. The contract was second in value only to the Atlas McKenzie deal, and had been in the works almost as long.

You didn't keep a GSA procurement manager on hold for long. That was one rule. Another was that anytime Grover Herrick wanted to talk to the CEO, Grover Herrick talked to the CEO. On half a dozen occasions in the past year, Nick fulfilled his duties as Stratton's chief executive by feigning interest as Grover talked about the sailboat he was going to buy as soon as he retired, and pretending to care about the difference between a ketch and a yawl. If Herrick had wanted to talk about hemorrhoids, Nick would have boned up on that topic too.

This time, though, there were no preliminaries.

"Nick," the GSA man said, "Gotta tell you, it looks like we're going with Haworth."

Nick felt gut-punched. It was all he could do not to double over. "You're *kidding*."

"I think you know by now when I'm kidding." There was a pause. "Remember when I told you the story about dropping the Thanksgiving turkey in front of all the guests, and how my wife had the presence of mind to say, 'Never mind, just bring out the other bird'? *That* I was kidding about."

"Fucking *Haworth*?"

"Well, what the hell did you *think* would happen?" Herrick's voice was a squawk of indignation. "You were going to have us ink the deal, move the company to *Shenzhen*, and then what? Have us outfit Homeland Security offices with desks from *China*?"

"What—?" Nick managed to choke out.

"When were you planning on telling us? I can think of some Senators who'd have a ball with that—but politics aside, it's completely against GSA procurement guidelines. Can't happen. Don't pretend you've forgotten about 41 USC 10. You guys oughta have the Buy American Act tattooed on your forehead."

"Wait a minute—who told you Stratton's going offshore?"

"What does it matter? Where there's smoke, there's fire. We liked Stratton. Great American company. I can see the temptation to cash in, put everything on a fast boat to China. Still think it's a mistake, though. My personal opinion."

"What you're saying doesn't make any sense. We're not going anywhere. I don't care what you've heard."

Herrick ignored him. "What was the game plan—inflate revenues with a hefty GSA prepayment, jack up the purchase price, figure the Heathen Chinese wouldn't figure out the game? Strategic vision, huh? I guess that's why you get the big bucks."

"*No*, Grover. This is bullshit."

"I told you before. We really liked you guys. We liked Haworth, too, but the Stratton price points looked better, all in. We just didn't realize your price points came courtesy of cheap Chinese labor."

"Listen to me, Grover." Nick tried to cut him off, to no avail.

"Thing that chafes my ass is, you guys wasted a *hell* of a lot of my time. Got half a mind to bill you for it."

"Grover, *no*."

"Happy sailing, Nick," the GSA man said, and he hung up.

Nick cursed loudly. He wanted to fling the phone across the room—across *a* room—but the Ambience system didn't really lend itself to boss-man theatrics.

Marjorie came over. "Something going on that I should know about?"

"That's pretty much *my* question, Marge," Nick said, struggling to regain his composure.

He walked across the executive floor to Scott's area, taking a back way in order to bypass Gloria, Scott's admin. As he approached, he heard Scott talking on the phone.

"Well, sure," Scott was saying. "We'll give it a try, Todd man, why not?"

Nick advanced until he was in Scott's line of sight.

Scott noticed him now, seemed to flinch just a bit, but instantly recovered: widening his eyes and smiling, raising his chin by way of greeting. "Right," he said, more loudly. "Sounds like a great trip. Gotta go." He hung up and said to Nick, "Hey, my liege, welcome to the low-rent district."

"How's Todd?" Nick said.

"Ah, he's trying to set up a golf trip to Hilton Head."

"I didn't know you golf."

"I don't." He laughed uncomfortably. "Well, badly. But that's why they love having me around. Makes them look like Tiger Woods."

"'They' being Todd and the other Fairfield boys?"

"Todd and his wife and Eden and another couple. Anyway."

"I had an interesting talk with MacFarland at Atlas McKenzie."

"Oh, yeah?" Scott's expression seemed wary.

"Yeah. Learn something new everyday. You know why they decided not to go with us?"

"Gotta be price, what else. Not quality, that's for sure. But you get what you pay for."

"MacFarland seems to think we're on the block. Now, why would he think that?"

Scott spread out his palms.

"Atlas McKenzie uses the same Hong Kong law firm as Fairfield, which is how they heard."

"That's *crazy*."

"Funny thing is, I heard something sort of similar from the guy at GSA just now."

"GSA?" Scott said, swallowing.

"The Homeland Security deal? That just fell apart too."

"Shit."

"And you know why? They need Made-in-America, and they heard a rumor we're going to be offshoring our manufacturing to China. Isn't that the craziest thing?"

Scott, picking up on Nick's bitter sarcasm, sat up straight in his chair and said solemnly, "If Todd and those guys were planning a move like that, don't you think they'd at least mention it to me?"

"Yeah, I do, actually. Have they?"

"Obviously not—I would have told you right away."

"Would you?"

"Of course—Jesus, Nick, I can't believe people listen to stupid rumors like that. I mean, it's no different from those idiotic rumors about the deep-fried chicken head in the box of Chicken McNuggets, or the bonsai kittens, or how the moon walk was a fraud—"

"Scott."

"Look, I'll make some calls, look into it for you, okay? But I'm sure there's nothing to it."

"I hope you're right," Nick said. "I really hope you're right."

48

Eddie didn't stand up when Nick came to his office that afternoon. Just gave him a mock salute, as he leaned back in his Symbiosis chair with his feet on his desk. On the silver-mesh fabric wall behind him was a poster with the words "MEDIOCRITY. It Takes a Lot Less Time and Most People Won't Notice the Difference Until It's Too Late." Above the slogan was a photograph of the Leaning Tower of Pisa. It was one of those wiseass spoofs of corporate workplace propaganda, but Nick sometimes wondered how much irony Eddie really meant.

"I get a promotion?" Eddie asked. "I mean, with you coming down here instead of making me come up."

Nick pulled up a small, wheeled stool. "They call it Management by Walking Around. MBWA."

"Lot to be said for MBSOYA. Management by Sitting on Your Ass."

Nick forced a smile, and told him about what MacFarland and Grover Herrick had said, skipping the incidentals.

"Fuck me," Eddie said. "Gotta be bullshit, right? You talk to Scott McNally about this?"

"He says there's nothing to it. But he knows more than he's telling me. I'm sure of it."

Eddie nodded slowly. "If you're out, I'm out, right?"

"Who said anything about my being out? I just want you to see what Scott's up to, that's all."

Eddie grinned slowly. "You want an assist, I'll fire you the puck and cross-check the assholes. I'll even break the fucking stick over their heads."

"A little e-mail surveillance should do it, Eddie."

"I'll get one of the techs to pull his e-mail records off the server, right? Just get me a few keywords."

"That sounds like a start."

"Oh, sure. Phone records, all that stuff. Easy peasy. But boy, you sure do have a knack for stepping in the shit." Eddie's skin formed webbing around his eyes as he smiled. "Good thing you got a friend who doesn't mind cleaning your shoes."

"You'll let me know if you find anything."

"That's what friends are for."

Nick didn't meet his eyes. "And not a word to anyone."

"Back at ya, buddy."

Nick hesitated for a moment, then wheeled the stool close to Eddie's desk. "Eddie, did you tell the cops you went over to my house after we found my dog?"

Eddie peered at him for a while. "They didn't ask me. I don't volunteer information. That's cop interview lesson number one."

Nick nodded. "They didn't ask me either. Not yet. But in case it comes up, I want to make sure we have a consistent story, okay? I asked you to come over, and you did. Only natural that I'd give you a call. You're my security director."

"Only natural," Eddie repeated. "Makes sense. But you got to calm down, buddy. You worry too much."

49

When he returned to the executive floor, Marjorie stopped him and handed him a slip of paper, a concerned look in her face. "I think you need to return this call right away," she said.

Principal J. Sundquist, she had written in her clear, elegant script, and then the telephone number.

Jerome Sundquist. Twenty-five years ago, he'd been Nick's high school math teacher. Nick remembered him as a rangy guy—a former tennis pro—who bounced around the classroom and was pretty good at keeping up the Math Is Fun act. To his students, he was Mr. Sundquist, not "Jerome" or "Jerry," and though he was reasonably laid back he didn't pretend to be pals with the kids in their chair desks. Nick half-smiled as he remembered those chair desks, with the little steel basket for books under the seat, and a "tablet arm" supported by a continuous piece of steel tube that ran from the back supports to the crossover legs. They were manufactured, back then as they were now, right in town, at Stratton's chair plant, a few miles down the road. Nick hadn't seen the numbers recently, but they listed for about a hundred and fifty, on a unit cost of maybe forty. Basically, it was the same design today.

Jerome Sundquist hadn't changed that much, either. Now he was the school principal, not a young teacher, and allowed himself a little more sententiousness than he used to, but if you were a high school principal that was pretty much part of the job description.

"Nick, glad you called," Jerome Sundquist said, in a tone that was both cordial and distant. "It's about your son."

Fenwick Regional High was a big brick-and-glass complex with a long traffic oval and the kind of juniper-and-mulch landscaping you found at shopping centers and office parks—nothing fancy, but somebody had to keep it up. Nick remembered when he came home after his first semester at Michigan State, remembered how *small* everything seemed. That's how it should have felt when he visited his old high school, but it didn't. The place was *bigger*—lots of add-ons, new structures, new brick facings on the old ones—and somehow plusher than it was in the old days. Plenty of it had to do with how Stratton had grown over the past couple of decades, with a valuation that broke two billion dollars three years ago. Then again, the higher you got, the longer the fall to the bottom. If Stratton collapsed, it would bring a lot of things down with it.

He stepped through the glass double doors and inhaled. As much as the place had changed, it somehow *smelled* the same. That grapefruit-scented disinfectant they still used: maybe they'd ordered a vat in 1970 and were still working through it. Some sort of faint burnt-pea-soup odor wafting from the cafeteria, as ineradicable as cat piss. It was the kind of thing you only noticed when you were away from it. Like the first day of homeroom after summer vacation, when you realized that the air was heavy with hair-styling products and eggy breakfasts and cinnamon Dentyne and underarm deodorant and farts—the smell of Fenwick's future.

But the place had changed dramatically. In the old days everyone came to school on the bus; now the kids were either dropped off in vans or SUVs or drove to school themselves. The old Fenwick Regional had no blacks, or maybe one or two a year; now the social leaders of the school seemed to be black kids who looked like rappers and the white kids who tried to. They'd added a sleek new wing that looked like something out of a private school. In the old days there used to be a smoking area, where longhaired kids in Black Sabbath T-shirts hung out and puffed and jeered at the jocks like Nick. Now smoking was outlawed and the Black Sabbath kids had become Goths with nose rings.

Nick hadn't spent much time in the principal's office when he was a student, but the oatmeal curtains and carpeting looked new, and the multicultural photographs of tennis champs on the court—the Williams sisters, Sania Merza, Martina Hingis, Boris Becker—was very Jerome Sundquist.

Sundquist stepped around from his desk and shook Nick's hand somberly. They sat down together on two camel-colored chairs. Sundquist glanced at a manila file he had left on his desk, but he already knew what was in it.

"Love what you've done with the place," Nick said.

"My office, or the school?"

"Both."

Sundquist smiled. "You'd be surprised how many two-generation families the school has now, which is a nice thing. And obviously the district has been very lucky in a lot of ways. When the parents prosper, the schools prosper. We're all hoping the downturn isn't permanent. I appreciate you've got a lot on your shoulders right now."

Nick shrugged.

"You were a pretty good student, as I recall," Sundquist said.

"Not especially."

Sundquist looked amused, tilted his head. "Okay, maybe 'indifferent' would be closer to the mark. I don't think I ever persuaded you about the glories of polar coordinates. Your interest in trig was more practical. All about what angle you could use to slap a puck between the goalie's legs."

"I remember your trying to sell me on that at the time. Nice try, though."

"But you always did okay on the exams. And, Christ, you were a popular kid. The school's blue-eyed boy. Brought Fenwick Regional to the state semifinals, twice, isn't that right?"

"Semifinals one year. Finals the next."

"That's one area where we haven't kept up. Caldicott has kicked our ass for the past four years."

"Maybe you need a new coach."

"Mallon is supposed to be good. Gets paid more than me, anyway. It's always hard to know when to blame the coach and when to blame the players." Sundquist broke off. "I know how busy you are, so let me get right to the point."

"Luke's been having problems," Nick said with a twinge of defensiveness. "I realize that. I want to do whatever I can."

"Of course," Sundquist said, sounding unconvinced. "Well, as I told you, Lucas is being suspended. A three-day suspension. He was caught smoking, and that's what happens."

So Lucas would have even more time to light up. That was really going to make things better. "I remember when there used to be a smoking area."

"Not anymore. Smoking is forbidden on the entire campus. We've got very tough rules on that. All the kids know it."

Campus was new. When Nick was at school, the school only had *grounds*. Campuses were for colleges.

"Obviously I don't want him smoking at all," Nick put in. "I'm just saying."

"Second offense, Lucas gets thrown out of school. Expelled."

"He's a good kid. It's just been a rough time for him."

Sundquist looked at him hard. "How well do you know your son?"

"What are you saying? He's my kid."

"Nick, I don't want to overstate the situation, but I don't want to understate it, either. It's pretty serious. I spent some time this morning talking to our crisis counselor. We don't think this is just about smoking, okay? You need to appreciate that we have the right to search his locker, and we may do some surprise searches, with the police."

"The police?"

"And if drugs are found, we will let the police prosecute. That's the way we do it these days. I want to warn you about that. Lucas is a troubled kid. Our crisis counselor is very concerned about him. Lucas isn't like you, okay?"

"Not everybody has to be a jock."

"That isn't what I meant," Sundquist said, not elaborating. Another glance back at the manila folder on his desk. "Besides which, his grades are going to hell. He used to be an honor student. With the grades he's been getting, he's not going to stay in that track. You understand what that means?"

"I understand," Nick said. "I do. He needs help."

"He needs help," Sundquist agreed, tight-lipped. "And he hasn't been receiving it."

Nick felt as if he were being graded as a father, and getting an *F*. "Jerry, I just don't see how suspending him or—God forbid—expelling him is the right thing to do. How is that *helping* him?" he asked. Then he wondered how many times those words had been spoken in that office.

"We have these rules for a reason," Sundquist said smoothly, leaning back a little in his chair. "There are almost fifteen hundred kids in this high school, and we have to do what's in the best interests of all of them."

Nick took a deep breath. "It's been hard for him, what happened. I get that he's a troubled kid. Believe me, this is something that's very much on my mind. I just think that he's been hanging out with a bad crowd."

"One way to look at it." Sundquist's gaze was unwavering. "Of course, there's another way to look at it."

"How do you mean?" Nick asked blankly.

"You could say that he *is* the bad crowd."

"Luke."

"What?" He'd picked up his cell phone on the first ring. The deal was that if he failed to answer a call from his father, he'd lose the phone.

"Where are you?"

"Home. Why?"

"What the hell happened at school?"

"What do you mean?"

"What do I *mean*? Three guesses. Mr. Sundquist called me in."

"What'd he tell you?"

"Don't play this game, Luke." Nick tried to stay calm. Talking to Lucas was like dousing a fire with lighter fluid. "You were smoking, and you got caught. Forget about what *I* think about smoking—you know the rules on smoking at school. You just got a three-day suspension."

"So? It's all bullshit anyway."

"Suspension from school is bullshit?"

"Yeah." His voice shook a bit. "Because school is bullshit."

An instant message popped up on his monitor from Marge:

Compensation Committee meeting right now, remember?

"Luke, I'm furious about this," he said. "You and I are going to have a talk about this later."

Yeah, Nick thought. *That's telling him.*

"And, Luke—?"

But Lucas had hung up.

50

No sooner had Audrey returned to the squad room than Bugbee found her. He approached her desk holding a mug of coffee in one hand, a sheaf of papers in the other, looking pleased about something.

"Don't tell me," he said. "The shrink spilled it all about his looney-tunes patient."

Now she understood his self-satisfied look. He was gloating, yes, but it was something more. It was the told-you-so look she'd seen LaTonya give the boys when they got in trouble for doing something she'd told them not to.

"He gave me some useful background on schizophrenia and violence," she said.

"Stuff you could have read in a textbook, I'm figuring. But he wouldn't talk about Stadler, would he? Doctor-patient confidentiality, right?"

"There has to be a way to get access to Stadler's medical records." She couldn't bring herself to tell Bugbee he was right any more directly than that.

"What would Jesus do, Audrey? Get a search warrant."

She ignored the crack. "That won't do it. The most we can get out of a search warrant is dates of admission to the hospital and such. The medical records are still protected. Maybe a Freedom of Information request."

"How many years you got?"

"Right."

"Speaking of search warrants," Bugbee said, waving the sheaf of papers in his left hand, "when were you planning on telling me you requested the phone records of the Stratton security guy?"

"They came in already?"

"Not my point. What'd you want 'em for?"

Bugbee must have picked them up from the fax machine, or maybe he'd seen them in her in-box. "Let me see," she said.

"Why are you so interested in Edward Rinaldi's phone records?"

Audrey gave him a long cold look, the sort of look LaTonya was so skilled at. "Are you holding them back from me, Roy?"

Bugbee handed the papers right over.

Boy, she thought, I'm going to have to take LaTonya Assertiveness Training. She felt a pulse of triumph and wondered whether this was a worthy feeling. She thought not, but she enjoyed it guiltily all the same. "Thank you, Roy. Now, in answer to your question, I wanted them because I'm curious as to whether Rinaldi ever made any phone calls to Andrew Stadler."

"How come?"

"Well, now, think about it. He called our records division to find out if Stadler had any priors, right? Stadler's the *only* former Stratton employee he called about. That tells me he was suspicious of Stadler—that he must have suspected Stadler of being the stalker who kept breaking into Nicholas Conover's home."

"Yeah, and maybe he was right. There haven't been any more break-ins at Conover's house since Stadler's murder."

"None that he's reported," she conceded. "But it's only been a week or so."

"So maybe Stadler was the guy. Maybe Rinaldi was on to something."

"Maybe. Maybe not. Either way, it wouldn't surprise me if the security director called Stadler and warned him to stay away from Nicholas Conover's house. You know, said, 'We know it's you, and if you do anything again you'll regret it.'"

The computer-generated phone record faxed over by Rinaldi's cellphone provider was dense and thick, maybe ten or twenty pages long. She gave it a quick glance, saw that most of the information she'd requested was there, but not all. Dates and times of all telephone calls he'd placed and received—all those seemed to be there. But only some of the phone numbers also listed names. Some did not.

"I assume you already looked through this," Audrey said.

"Quick scan, yeah. Guy has a pretty active social life, looks like. Lot of women's names there."

"Did you come across Andrew Stadler's name?"

Bugbee shook his head.

"You looked closely at the day and night when the murder took place?"

Bugbee gave her his deadeye look. "Phone numbers don't all have names."

"I noticed that. There doesn't seem to be a logic to it."

"I figure if a number's unlisted, the name doesn't pop up automatically."

"Makes sense," she said. She hesitated, tempted to be as stingy with praise as Bugbee always was. But wasn't it written in Proverbs somewhere that a word fitly spoken is like apples of gold in settings of silver? "I think you're right. Very good point."

Bugbee shrugged, a gesture not of modesty but of dismissiveness, his way of letting her know that clever thinking was second nature to him. "That means a hell of a lot of cross-referencing," he said.

"Would you be able to take a crack at that?"

Bugbee snorted. "Yeah, like I got free time."

"Well, someone's got to."

A beat of silence: a standoff. "Did you get any more on that hydroseed stuff?"

Bugbee gave a lazy smile, pulled from his pants pocket a crumpled pink lab request sheet. "It's Penn Mulch."

"Penn mulch? What's that?"

"Penn Mulch is a proprietary formula marketed by the Lebanon Seaboard Corporation in Pennsylvania, a fertilizer and lawn products company." He was reading from notes prepared by someone else, probably a lab tech. "The distinctive characteristic is small, regular pellets half an inch long by an eighth of an inch wide. Looks kinda like hamster shit. Cellulose pellets made up of freeze-dried recycled newspaper, one-three-one starter fertilizer, and super-absorbent polymer crystals. And green dye."

"And grass seed."

"Not part of the Penn Mulch. The lawn company mixes in the grass seed with the mulch and a tackifier and makes a kind of slurry they can spray on the ground. Kind of like a pea soup, only thinner. The grass seed in this case is a mixture of Kentucky Bluegrass and Creeping Red Fescue, with a little Saturn Perennial Ryegrass and Buccaneer Perennial Ryegrass thrown in."

"Nice work," she said. "But that doesn't really mean much to me—is this a pretty common formula for hydroseed?"

"The grass seed, that varies a lot. There's like nine hundred different varieties to choose from. Some of it's cheap shit."

"The lawn companies don't all use the same mix, then?"

"Nah. The shit they use along the highway, the contractor mix, you don't want to use on your lawn. The better the mulch, the better results you get."

"The Penn Mulch—"

"Expensive. Way better than the crap they normally use—ground-up wood mulch or newspaper, comes in fifty-pound bags. This is pricey stuff. Doubt it's very common. It's what you might use on some rich guy's lawn— rich guy who knows the difference, I mean."

"So we need to find out what lawn companies in the area use Penn Mulch."

"That's a lot of phone calls."

"How many lawn companies in Fenwick? Two or three, maybe?"

"Not my point," Bugbee said. "So you find the one company that sometimes uses Penn Mulch in its hydroseed mix. Then what?"

"Then you find out whose lawns they used Penn Mulch on. If you're saying it's so expensive, there can't be all that many."

"So what do you get? Our dead guy walked over someone's lawn that had Penn Mulch on it. So?"

"I don't imagine there are too many fancy lawns down in the dog pound, Roy," she said. "Do you?"

51

During the drive from the high school back to Stratton, Nick found himself thinking about Cassie Stadler.

She was not only gorgeous—he'd had more than his share of gorgeous women over the years, especially during college, when Laura had wanted them to "take a break" and "see other people"—but she was so smart it was scary, eerily perceptive. She seemed to understand him fully, to see through him, almost. She knew him better than he knew himself.

And he couldn't deny the physical attraction: for the first time in over a year he'd had sex, and he felt like a sexual being again. This was a sensation he'd almost forgotten about. The pump had been primed. He felt horny. He thought about yesterday afternoon and got hard.

Then he remembered who she was, how he'd come to know her, and his mood collapsed. The guilt came surging back, worse than ever.

A voice in his head: *Are you kidding me? You're screwing the daughter of the man you murdered?*

What's wrong with you?

He didn't understand what he was doing. If he allowed himself to get close to her . . . Well, what if she found out, somehow? Could he keep up this crazy balancing act?

What the hell am I doing?

But he badly wanted to see her again. That was the craziest thing of all.

It was late afternoon by now, and he didn't have to return to the office.

He pulled over to the side of the road and fished a scrap of paper out of his jacket pocket. On it he'd scrawled Cassie Stadler's phone number. Impulsively—without heeding that chiding voice in his head—he called her on his cell.

"Hello," he said when she answered. His voice sounded small. "It's Nick."

A beat. "Nick," she said, and stopped.

"I just wanted to . . ." His voice actually cracked. Just wanted to—what? Turn back the clock? Reverse what happened That Night? Make everything *all better?* And since that wasn't possible, then what? He just wanted to talk to her. That was the truth. "I was just calling . . ."

"I know," she said quickly.

"You okay?"

"Are *you?*"

"I'd like to see you," he said.

"Nick," she said. "You should stay away from me. I'm trouble. Really."

Nick almost smiled. Cassie didn't know what trouble was. *You think you're trouble? You should see me when I've got a Smith & Wesson in my hands.* Acid splashed the back of his throat.

"I don't think so," Nick said.

"Don't you think you've done enough?"

He felt something like an electric jolt. Hadn't he done enough? That was one way of looking at it. "Excuse me?"

"Not that I didn't appreciate it. I did. *All* of it. But we need to leave it there. You've got a company to run. A family to hold together. I don't fit into that."

"I'm just leaving an appointment," he said. "I can be there in about five minutes."

"Hey," Cassie said, opening the dusty screen door. Carpenter-style jeans, white T-shirt, flecks of paint. Then she smiled, a smile that crinkled her eyes. She looked better, sounded better. "I didn't think you'd come back."

"Why?"

"Well, you know, buyer's remorse. Regret over what you'd done. The usual male stuff."

"Maybe I'm not your usual male."

"I'm getting that idea. Bring me anything today?"

Nick shrugged. "Sorry. There's a bottle of windshield-wiper fluid in the trunk."

"Forget it," Cassie said. "That stuff always gives me a hangover."

"Might have a can of WD-40 around, too."

"Now that's more promising. I'm really digging the idea of having the CEO of Stratton as my personal grocery boy."

"Point of pride with me. Nick Conover buys a mean turkey sandwich."

"But should I take it personally that you got me nonfat yogurt?" She brought him inside. "Let me make you some of the tea you bought."

She disappeared into the kitchen for a moment. She had a CD on, a woman singing something about, "I'm brave but I'm chicken shit."

When she came back, Nick said, "You look good."

"I'm beginning to feel more like myself again," she said. "You caught me at a low point the other day. I'm sure you know how it goes."

"Well, you look a lot better."

"And you look like shit," she said, matter of fact.

"Well," Nick said. "Long day."

She stretched herself out on the nubby brown sofa, with the gold thread woven through the upholstery like something out of the 1950s.

"Long day, or long story?"

"Trust me, you don't want to hear a grown man bitch and moan about troubles at the shop."

"Trust me, I could use the distraction."

Nick leaned back in the ancient green La-Z-Boy. After a few moments, he began to tell her about the Rumor, leaving out a few details. He didn't mention Scott by name, didn't go into Scott's disloyalty. That was too painful a subject right now.

Cassie hugged her knees, gathering herself into some tight yoga-like ball, and listened intently as he explained.

"And if that weren't enough, I get a call from Lucas's school," he went on. He stopped. He wasn't accustomed to talking about his life that way. Not since Laura's death. Somehow he'd gotten out of practice.

"Tell me," she said.

He did, telling her, too, about how he'd called Lucas at home, confronted him, and how Luke had hung up. When he finally checked his watch, he realized he'd been talking for more than five minutes.

"I never understood that," Cassie said.

"Understood what?"

"Kid gets suspended for three days, meaning what? They don't have to go to school for three days? They stay home?"

"Right."

"And get into more trouble? That's supposed to be a punishment? I mean, a baseball player gets suspended for five games for fighting with the umpire, that's a punishment. But telling a kid he can't go to school, which he hates, for three days?"

"Maybe it's like social humiliation."

"For a teenager? Isn't that more like a badge of honor?"

Nick shrugged. "Wouldn't have been for me."

"No, you were probably Mr. Perfect."

"No way. I got into the usual trouble. I was just careful about it. I didn't want to get kicked off the hockey team. Hey, where's that tea?" he asked.

"That stove takes forever. Electric, and underpowered. Dad wouldn't allow gas in the house. One of his many 'things.' But we won't go there." She craned her head, listening. "I'm sure it's ready now."

"Just that all this talking makes a man thirsty," Nick said.

Cassie came back with two steaming mugs. "English Breakfast," she said. "Though I saw that you also bought me a box of Blue Moon Kava Kava and Chamomile mix. I'm guessing that's not Nick Conover's usual cup."

"Maybe not."

"Why do I get the feeling you've got me figured for some sort of New Age nut?" She shrugged. "Possibly because I am one. How can I deny it? You make chairs, I teach *asanas*. Hey, when it comes down to it, we're both in the sitting industry, right?"

"So you're not going to tell me about my aura."

"You can take the girl out of Carnegie Mellon—and believe me, they did." A smile hovered around her lips. "But you can't take the Carnegie Mellon out of the girl. Never really got into chakras and shit. There's a lot of my dad in me. I've got an empirical streak a mile wide."

"And I took you for a nineteen waist."

"Thanks." She took a careful sip of her tea. "So you've got problems. You'll deal, because that's the kind of person you are. When life gives you lemons, you make Lemon Pledge."

"I was expecting something more Zen, somehow."

"I see you haven't touched your English Breakfast. So what kind of tea do you like?"

"Any kind. So long as it's coffee."

She found a bottle of Four Roses bourbon on a low table beside the sofa, handed it to him. "Put a slug of this in it. It'll cut the tannins."

He sloshed a little into his cup. It definitely improved the taste.

Cassie was looking at him with cat eyes. "So are you here for me or for you?"

"Both."

She nodded, amused. "You're my caseworker?"

"Come on," Nick said. "You're not exactly a charity case."

"I'm doing okay."

"Well, I want you to know that if you're ever not doing okay, you've got me here to help."

"This is starting to sound like adios."

"No. Not at all."

"Good." She got up, tugged at the cord on the venetian blinds, closing them and darkening the room. "That's a relief."

He came up to her from behind, slipped his hands under her knit top, and felt the silky warmth of her belly.

"Why don't we go upstairs?" Nick said.

"We don't go upstairs," she said at once.

"We don't, huh. Okay." Slowly he began moving his hands upward until he found her breasts, teased her nipples as he kissed and licked the back of her neck.

"Yeah," she said throatily.

Still with her back to his, she brought her hands around to his butt and squeezed each cheek, hard.

He entered her from behind this time.

"Jesus," he said, and she looked up at him, her eyes gleaming.

It took him several minutes to catch his breath.

"Wow," he said. "Thank you."

"My pleasure."

"Well, mine, I think."

She took a sip of tea, curled up next to him on the sofa. She began singing along with the CD, which must have been set on repeat mode, something about "best friend with benefits."

"You've got a nice voice."

"Sang in the church choir. Mom was a real holy roller, used to drag me there. It was the only thing that got me through. So, boss man, you can't give up the fight, you know." An odd sort of vehemence had entered Cassie's voice. "You've got to play the game balls out, with all your heart. *Everything* matters."

"That's the way I always played hockey. Gave it my all—you have to."

"Always kept your head up while you skated?"

He smiled. She obviously got hockey too. "Oh yeah. Put your head down for a second, and you're signed, sealed, and delivered. The game's fast."

"You been keeping your head up at Stratton?"

"Not enough," he admitted.

"I suspect people maybe underestimate you sometimes, because they sense you're eager to be liked. My guess is that people who push you too far live to regret it."

"Maybe." Memories swirled in Nick's head, dark ones that he didn't want to reexamine.

"You've already surprised a lot of people, is my bet. Dorothy Devries— she's cooled toward you in the past several years. Am I right?"

Nick blinked. It wasn't a conscious realization he'd had, but it was true. "Yes," he said. "How did you know?"

Cassie looked away. "Don't take this the wrong way. But when Old Man Devries's widow appoints a successor, there are a lot of things going on in her head. One thing she's *not* looking to do is to bring in someone who's going to show up her beloved Milton. A reliable hand on the tiller, sure. The kind of reliable guy about whom you could say, 'He's no Milton Devries, of course, but who is?' They could have poached some hotshot from the competition — I bet that would have been the usual thing. But it wasn't what she wanted. You were meant to be Milton's mini-me. Then you came in, and you kicked ass. You weren't Milton's protégé anymore. And even if she benefited from that financially, the whole Nick Conover show had to bother her too."

Nick just shook his head.

"You don't believe me, do you?"

"The trouble is," Nick said slowly, "I do believe you. What you say never really occurred to me before, and it's sure not doing anything for my ego, but when I listen to you talk, I'm thinking, Yeah, that's probably what went down. The old lady wasn't expecting what she got. Truth is, I wasn't either. I got in there, made three or four critical hires, let them do their thing. It could have played differently. I'm not that smart, but I know what I don't know. What I'm good at, maybe, is bringing in smarts."

"And so long as they're loyal to you, you're going to be okay. But if they aren't family-first people, you could have problems."

"Family-first?"

"The Stratton family."

"You really are the woman with X-ray eyes," Nick said. "You see right through people." Suddenly he shivered. How much *did* she see? Did she see the blood on his hands? He swallowed hard. It wasn't a good time to start losing it.

"You know what they say."

"Who?"

"They. Anaïs Nin, maybe, I forget. 'We don't see things as they are. We see things as *we* are.'"

"Not sure I get that."

"And the hardest people to see, sometimes, are the people we love. Like your son."

"A complete mystery to me these days."

"What time did you say your kids would be home?"

"Less than an hour."

"I'd like to meet them," she said.

"Uh, I'm not sure that's a good idea," Nick said.

Cassie got to her feet, ran her fingers through her hair. "Jesus, what am I saying, it's a *terrible* idea," she said. The change in her was abrupt, startling. "What was I thinking? I'm not part of your life. I don't make *sense* in your life. Listen, I'd probably be ashamed of me too." She tugged at her paint-flecked jeans. "So let's leave things here. After all, we'll always have Steeple-town. Goodbye, Nick. Have a good life."

"Cassie," Nick said. "That's not what I meant."

Cassie was silent. When Nick turned to look at her, her eyes were wells of sorrow. He felt a wave of guilt, and longing.

"Would you like to come by for dinner?" he asked.

52

Cassie was subdued as the Chevy Suburban waited in a queue in front of the Fenwicke Estates gatehouse. Nick suppressed the urge to drum his fingers on the steering wheel.

"Evening, Jorge," Nick said, as they slowly passed the gatehouse.

Cassie leaned over so she could see him. "Hi, Jorge, I'm Cassie." She smiled and gave him a little wave.

"Evening," Jorge said, more animatedly than usual.

Okay, Nick thought. Chalk one up for the girl's humanity. She noticed the guys in uniform. So long as it wasn't the start of some big worker's solidarity trip, that was probably a good sign.

He wondered how the kids would react to his bringing a woman home. More than wondered: he was, he had to admit, nervous about it. She was the first woman he'd been involved with in any way since Laura's death, and he had no idea how they'd react. Lucas, he could safely predict, would be hostile. Hostility was his default mode. Julia? Now, that was a question. There was the Freudian thing where the girl wants Daddy all to herself, and there was that powerful strain of unthinking loyalty to her mom: how dare Daddy date someone other than Mommy.

It could be ugly. But the one who'd really suffer the brunt of it was Cassie. He felt bad for her, for what she was about to experience. As he drove to the house, he began to regret his impulsive invitation. He should have introduced her to the kids more gradually.

As they approached the driveway to the house, Cassie gave a low whistle.

"Sweet," she said. "Wouldn't have guessed it was your style, I have to admit."

"Maybe it isn't," Nick admitted, but he felt self-conscious about saying it. Like he was putting the blame on Laura.

She squinted at the yellow Dumpster that was stationed underneath a basketball hoop. "Construction?"

"Always."

"*Portoncini dei morti*," she said.

"You're in America now," Nick said lightly. "About time you learned to speak English."

"I take it you've never been to Gubbio."

"If they don't manufacture casters there, I've probably never been."

"It's in Umbria. Amazing place. I spent a whole year there—painting, busking, you name it. Great place, but spooky too. You go through the old part of town, and you start to notice that a lot of the houses have these areas that look oddly bricked up. Turns out that they had this old custom, like a sacrament. They bricked up the doorway where a dead person was taken out of a house. They're called *portoncini dei morti*. Doors of the dead. Ghost doors."

"Must have kept a lot of masons busy," Nick said. *It's the front door, Nick. That's the one place you don't cheap out.* Doors of the dead.

"This was Laura's house, wasn't it?" Cassie asked.

That wasn't how Nick would have put it, but it was more or less true. It was Laura's house.

"Sort of," he said.

Marta was at the door when they came in. "I told you we'd be having company," Nick said. "Well, she's the company."

Marta didn't shake Cassie's hand, he noticed, just said, "Nice to meet you," and none too cordially. Same expression she reserved for telephone solicitors.

"Where's Julia?" Nick asked Marta.

"Watching TV in the family room. Emily just left a little while ago."

"And Luke?"

"In his room. On the computer, maybe. He said he can't stay for dinner."

"Oh, that right? Well, he's *going* to stay for dinner," Nick said, icily. Christ. The whole suspension thing—they would have to have a Very Serious Talk. Which probably meant a Perfect Storm of an argument.

Just not tonight.

Nick took Cassie over to the family room, where Julia was engrossed in *Slime Time Live* on Nickelodeon.

"Hey, baby," Nick said. "I want you to meet my friend Cassie."

"Hi," Julia said, and turned back to the show. Not rude, but not exactly friendly. A little cool, maybe.

"Cassie is going to be joining us for dinner."

Julia turned around again. "Okay," she said, warily. To Cassie, she said, "We usually don't have company for dinner."

Then she turned back to the flickering screen. Someone was getting doused with green slime.

"Don't worry," Cassie said. "I eat like a bird."

Julia nodded.

"Two and half times my body weight in earthworms," Cassie said.

Julia giggled.

"Are you a baseball fan?" Cassie asked.

"Yeah, I guess," Julia said. "You mean my jersey?"

"I *love* the Tigers," Cassie said.

Julia shrugged dismissively. "The girls in school keep calling me 'tomboy' because I wear it all the time."

"They're just jealous of your jersey," Nick put in, but Julia wasn't listening.

"You ever been to Comerica Park?" Cassie asked her.

Julia shook her head.

"Oh, it's amazing. You'd love it. We've got to go there some time."

"Really?" Julia said.

"Definitely. And listen—I got called 'tomboy' when I was a kid too," said Cassie. "Just 'cause I wasn't into Barbie."

"Really? I *hate* Barbie," Julia said.

"Barbie's kind of creepy," Cassie agreed. "I was never into dolls."

"Me neither."

"But I'll bet you have stuffed animals to keep you company, right?"

"Beanie Babies, mostly."

"Do you collect them?"

"Sort of." Julia was now looking at Cassie with interest. "They're very valuable, you know. But only if you don't use them and stuff."

"You mean like, never take the label off, and put them on the shelf?"

Julia nodded, this time more animatedly.

"I don't get that," Cassie said. "The whole point of Beanie Babies is to play with them, right? Do you have a lot, or just a couple of them?"

"I don't know. I guess a lot. You want to see my collection?"

"Really? I'd love to."

"Not now," said Nick. "Later. Right now it's suppertime, and we're having company."

"Okay," Julia said. Then she yelled, "Luke, supper! We have company."

As Nick took Cassie back to the front hall, she said, "She's a sweetie, isn't she?"

"A regular Ma Barker is what she is," Nick said. "For sweetness and light, we've got Lucas Conover." He took her upstairs, gestured toward the hallway. There was no need to specify which was Lucas's room. From beneath the closed door, thrash music pulsed, an avalanche of noise with someone shouting at the top of his lungs over a thudding bass beat. Something about *outta my mind*, something about *ashes to ashes*, something about *all pain, no gain*. A lot of incomprehensible screaming in between.

"As you can tell, he's a huge Lawrence Welk fan," Nick said. He decided against knocking on the door. Let Marta get him downstairs. Lucas responded better to her anyway.

"How do you know so much about Beanie Babies?" Nick asked.

"My knowledge of Beanie Babies is limited to what I read in *Newsweek*. Am I busted?"

"You sure got Julia believing you're a Beanie Babies expert."

"Hey, whatever works, right? Though I get a feeling your son isn't into Beanie Babies."

"He's a hard case, my son," Nick said, not wanting to dwell on it. "I'm going to change, meet you downstairs in a few."

When he came back down, Cassie and Julia were deep in conversation in the family room. "And there was blood everywhere," Julia was saying in a hushed, serious voice.

"Oh no," Cassie breathed.

"And it was Barney." Julia's eyes were moist.

"My God."

"And Daddy said he would protect us. He said he'd do whatever he had to do."

Nick cleared his throat; it wasn't a conversation he wanted to encourage. "Hey girls," he called. "Suppertime."

"I've just been hearing about what happened to Barney," Cassie said, looking up. "Sounds horrible."

"It was rough," Nick said. "For all of us." He tried to sound a little brusque, to let Cassie know he didn't want the conversation to continue.

Luckily, Marta emerged from the kitchen just then and announced that dinner was ready.

"All right," Nick said. "Let's go, girls. Marta, would you go upstairs and ask Sid Vicious to join us?"

As Marta went upstairs, Julia asked, "Who's Sid Vicious?"

"*You* know the Sex Pistols?" Cassie said to Nick, smiling.

"I think I saw part of some movie about them before I walked out," Nick said. "I'm not a total geek, you know, no matter what my son thinks."

"But who's Sid Vicious?" Julia asked again.

Lucas's heavy footsteps thundered as if a crate of bowling balls had been upended at the top of the stairs. At the landing he looked around, taking in Cassie's presence with an unblinking stare.

"Luke, I'd like you to meet my friend Cassie Stadler," Nick said.

"Cassie *Stadler*?"

The way he said it made Nick's blood run cold.

"That's right," he said quietly. "She'll be joining us for dinner."

"I have to go out," Lucas said.

"You have to stay here."

"I have a homework project I need to do with some kids in class."

Nick refrained from rolling his eyes. A science experiment, no doubt, designed to study the effect of *Cannabis sativa* on the psychophysiology of the American sixteen-year-old. "It isn't up for discussion," he said. "Sit."

"I like your music," Cassie said to him.

Lucas looked at her with something just shy of hostility. "Yeah?" His tone of voice made it short for: *Yeah, what of it?*

"If you call that music," Nick said, feeling protective of Cassie. He gave her an apologetic shrug. "And when he isn't listening to this kind of noise, it's that gangsta rap stuff."

"Gangsta rap stuff." Cassie's mimicry was perfect, and devastating.

Lucas half snorted, half chortled.

"You'd prefer it if he listened to the Mamas and the Papas?" she asked. "Like some kind of Stepford son?"

Hey, no fair, Nick wanted to say. "*I* didn't even listen to the Mamas and the Papas," he said.

Cassie wasn't paying attention. She was focused on Lucas. "I'm curious. How long have you been into Slasher?"

"A few months," Lucas said, surprised.

"Not a lot of people your age even know about Slasher. I bet you have all their albums."

"Got downloads of some stuff they haven't released yet, and some bootleg demos, too."

"Slasher would be a rock band," Nick said, feeling obscurely excluded. "Tell me if I'm warm."

" 'Slasher' is what they call Dad, you know," Lucas said, pleased.

"I've heard. Anyway, Slasher's cool, but John Horrigan's kind of a jerk, I gotta tell you," Cassie said, taking a step toward Lucas.

Lucas's eyes widened. "You *know* him? No fucking way." An entirely different Lucas was making an appearance.

She nodded. "You heard about how he fell off the stage in Saratoga, during the Sudden Death tour? Well, he had some problems with his neck and back after that. Nothing helped. So I used to teach this yoga class in Chicago, where he's based. One day he shows up, and it's the first thing that really helps. Then he's asking me for extra sessions. And then . . ." She walked closer to Lucas and put her hand on his arm as she murmured the rest.

Lucas giggled, blushing.

"I can't believe it," he said. "Horrigan *rocks*. So . . ." He glanced at Nick, at Julia, and lowered his voice. "What was he like?"

"Selfish," Cassie said. "First I thought, bad technique. But then I realized it was just selfishness. Finally I just stopped returning his phone calls. Great guitar player, though."

"Horrigan rocks."

"What do you mean 'selfish'?" Julia demanded, with a ten-year-old's unerring instinct for inappropriate subjects.

"We're just talking about who gets their guitar licks in," Cassie said.

Lucas began to quake with silent laughter.

Julia started to laugh, too, for no particular reason. Then Nick, too, began to laugh, and for the life of him he couldn't say why. Except that he couldn't remember when Lucas had last laughed.

Marta brought a platter of pork chops to the table, some sort of chili and cilantro thing on top. "More in the kitchen if anyone wants," she said, sounding slightly peevish, or maybe just a little out of sorts.

"Everything smells delicious, Marta," Nick said.

"And there's salad." She pointed to two covered ceramic bowls. "And there's rice and there's ratatouille."

"That's great, Marta," said Cassie. "I think we're going to be okay."

"I didn't make a dessert, but there's ice cream," Marta added darkly. "And some fruit. Some bananas."

"I make one hell of a banana flambé," said Cassie. "Any takers?"

"Knock yourself out," Lucas said, and grinned.

Perfect white teeth, clear blue eyes, almost perfect complexion. A beautiful kid. Nick felt a surge of paternal pride. *Three-day suspension.* They'd have to have The Talk. Just not now. It hung over him like a sword.

"All you need are bananas, some butter, brown sugar, and rum."

"We've got all that," Nick said.

"Oh, and a light. For a blaze of glory." Cassie turned to Lucas. "Got a lighter, kiddo?"

53

After driving Cassie home, Nick returned to find Lucas in his room, lying back on his bed, earbuds in. Nick signaled to him to take them off. To his surprise, Lucas did without complaint, and he spoke first: "So, she's cool."

"Good. I'm glad you like her." Nick sat in the only chair in the room that wasn't piled with books and papers and discarded clothes. He took a breath, plunged in. The normal force field of hostility seemed to be down, or maybe just diminished. That was good; that would make it easier.

"Luke, buddy, you and I have to talk."

Lucas watched him, blinking, said nothing.

"I told you Mr. Sundquist called me in for a conference today."

"So?"

"You understand how serious this is, this suspension."

"It's a three-day vacation."

"That's what I was afraid I'd hear. No, Luke. It goes on your record. When you apply to colleges, they see that."

"Like you care?"

"Oh, now, come on. Of course I care."

"You don't even know what I'm studying in school, do you?"

"I didn't know you were studying anything," Nick cracked without thinking.

"That's a *big* help, Dad. You basically spend all your time at work, and now you're trying to pretend like you're interested in how I do in school?" It was amazing how Lucas could take those pure, innocent eyes and focus them like a laser beam into one cold, hard blue ray of hatred.

"Yeah, well, I'm worried about what's happening to you."

"What's happening to me," Lucas repeated mockingly.

"This is all about Mom, isn't it?" He regretted saying it as soon as it came out. That was way too blunt. But how else to say it?

"Excuse me?" Lucas said, incredulous.

"Look, ever since Mom's death, you've totally changed. I know it, and you know it."

"That's deep, Nick. Really deep. Coming from you, that's really great."

"What's that supposed to mean?"

"Well, look at you. You went right back to work, no problem."

"I have a job, Luke."

"Moving right on, huh, Nick?"

"Don't *ever* talk to me that way," Nick said.

"Get the hell out of my room. I don't need this shit from you."

"I'm not leaving until you hear me out," Nick said.

"Fine," Lucas said, getting up from the bed and walking out of his room. "Sit there and blab all you want."

Nick followed his son into the hall. "You come back here," he said.

"I don't need this shit."

"I said, get *back* here. We're not done talking."

"Hey, you've made your point, okay. I'm *sorry* I'm such a *disappointment* to you." Lucas raced down the stairs, taking them two steps at a time.

Nick ran after him. "You don't walk away from me when I'm talking to you," he shouted. He caught up with him just as Lucas reached the front door, put his hand on his son's shoulder.

Luke swiveled, swatted Nick's hand off. "Get your fucking hands off me!" he screamed, turning the big brass knob and shoving the door open.

"You get back here," Nick shouted after him, standing in the doorway. "This cannot go on!"

But Lucas was running down the stone path into the darkness. "I'm sick of this fucking house, and I'm sick of you!" came his son's voice, echoing.

"Where do you think you're going?" Nick yelled back. "You get back here right now!"

He thought about taking off after his son, but what would be the point, really? He was overcome with a sense of futility and desperation. He stood there on the threshold until the sound of Lucas's footsteps faded to silence.

Julia was there at the bottom of the stairs when he turned around. She was weeping.

He went up to her, gave her a tight squeeze, and said, "He'll be okay, baby. *We'll* be okay. Now you go to bed."

In the shower a little later, Nick cursed himself for how badly he'd handled the whole thing, how ham-handed he'd been, how emotionally obtuse. There had to be ways of reaching Lucas, even if he didn't know them. It was like a foreign country where the language sounds nothing like your own, the street signs are unreadable, you're alone and lost. As the needles of water stung his neck and back, he looked at the row of shampoos and conditioners in the tiled inset: Laura's stuff, all of it. He hadn't bothered to remove it. Couldn't *bring* himself to remove it, really.

He soaped himself up, got soap in his eyes, which made his eyes smart so that when his eyes started stinging and watering, he couldn't tell if it was the soap or the tears.

He put on a T-shirt, pajama bottoms, and got into bed just as he heard the front door open, the alert tone go off. Luke had returned.

He switched off the bedside lamp. As always, he slept on the side of the bed that had always been his, wondered when, if ever, he'd start sleeping in the middle of the bed.

His bedroom door opened, and he thought for a split second that it might be Lucas, here to apologize. But it wasn't, of course.

Julia stood there, her lanky shape and curly hair silhouetted by the night-light in the hall.

"I can't sleep," she said.

"Come here."

She ran to Nick, scrambled into the bed. "Daddy," she said very softly. "Can I sleep in your bed? Just for tonight."

He brushed back the curls, saw the tear-streaked face. "Sure, baby. But just for tonight."

54

Leon slept late, of course, so it was no problem for Audrey to be up long before him Saturday morning. She enjoyed the quiet of the morning, the solitude, being in her own head. She made herself a pot of hazelnut coffee—the kind Leon hated, but she'd make regular coffee when he got up—and read the morning papers.

The weekends used to be their little island of intimacy, before—before he lost his job, before she started working overtime hours in order to be gone as much as possible. They'd sleep late on Saturday, snuggle, make love. They'd make brunch together, read the papers together, sometimes even make love again. Take a nap together. Then go out and enjoy the weekend, shopping or going for walks. Sundays he'd sleep until she returned from church, and then they'd maybe go out for brunch or make something at home, and they'd make love too.

Those days were like ancient Mesopotamia. She'd almost forgotten what they felt like, they'd receded so into the distant shrouded past.

This Saturday morning, after she'd had her coffee, she considered getting out her case files and working. But a glimmering of ancient Mesopotamia arose in her mind.

Someone had to break the gridlock, she told herself. They were both frozen. Neither wanted to make the first move to try to change things.

She debated internally, the way she debated most things large or small. *How many times are you going to keep trying?* she asked herself. *How often are you going to butt your head against a brick wall before you realize it feels better to stop?* The other voice—the wiser, more generous voice—said: *But he's the damaged one. He's the hurt one. You need to take the lead.*

This morning—maybe it was the still beauty of the morning, maybe it was the deliciousness of the coffee, maybe it was the time alone—she decided to take the lead.

She walked quietly through the dark bedroom, careful not to wake him. She slid open her bottom dresser drawer and pulled out the pale apricot silk teddy she'd bought from the Victoria's Secret catalog, never worn.

She closed the bedroom door and went down the hall to the bathroom, where she took a nice hot shower, using the loofah. She applied lotion all over—her skin tended to get ashy if she didn't—and then put on makeup, something she never did unless she was going out. She daubed perfume on in all the right secret places—Opium, the only perfume that Leon had ever complimented her on.

Wearing just her teddy, and feeling a bit silly at first, she went into the kitchen and made brunch. French toast, bacon, even some cantaloupe balls. His favorite breakfast: he liked French toast even more than eggs Benedict. A fresh pot of coffee, the kind he liked. A white porcelain creamer, in the shape of a cow, filled with half-and-half.

Then she arranged everything carefully on a bed tray—it took her a while to find it in the overhead storage in the little pantry, and then she'd had to wash off the accumulated dust—and went in to wake up Leon.

Since he'd been in a sour mood for most of the last year, she was pleasantly surprised at his sweet smile upon seeing her and the breakfast she'd placed on the bed.

"Hey, Shorty," he rasped. "What's all this?"

"Brunch, baby."

"French toast. It's not my birthday, is it?"

She climbed into the bed and kissed him. "I just felt like it, that's all."

He took a sip of coffee, made a contented noise. "I got to go take a whiz." The breakfast tray tottered dangerously as he tried to extricate himself from the bed.

She could hear the sound of his urine splashing noisily in the toilet bowl, the toilet flushing, then she could hear him brushing his teeth, something he didn't normally do before breakfast. A good sign. Even though he was getting as big as his sister, he remained a very sexy man.

He came back into the bed; she moved the tray to allow him to get in without upsetting it. He kissed her again, to her surprise. She shifted her body, angled it toward him, a hand on his upper arm, ready—but then he pulled away and took another sip of coffee.

"You forgot the syrup," he said.

She touched the white porcelain gravy boat.

He tipped it over the stack of French toast, dousing it liberally, then took the knife and fork and cut a tall wedge. She'd even dusted it with powdered sugar, which he liked.

"Mmm-mmm. You warmed it."

Audrey smiled, pleased. Didn't they always say the way to a man's heart is through his stomach? Maybe this was all it took to break through the ice floes that had accumulated in their marriage.

After he'd wolfed down half the stack of French toast and all but two of the bacon strips, he turned to her. "How come you're not eating?"

"I ate some in the kitchen."

He nodded, devoured another piece of bacon, took another swig of coffee. "I thought you were working today."

"I'm taking the day off."

"How come?"

"Well, I thought we could spend some time together."

He turned his attention back to the French toast. "Hmph."

"You feel like going for a walk later, maybe?" she asked.

After a moment, he said, "I thought we needed the money."

"One day's not going to send us to the poorhouse. We could go for a drive out in the country."

Another silence, and then he spoke through a mouthful of cantaloupe. "Just don't be telling me about getting a job as a night watchman."

She was annoyed but didn't let on. "We don't have to talk about that stuff now, honey."

"All right."

Her cell phone rang. She hesitated. Not just that it was a flow-breaker, but it was an unwelcome reminder of the job she had and he didn't. She knew it couldn't be a personal call. It rang again.

"I'll make it quick," she said, reaching for the cell phone on her nightstand.

Leon cast her a warning look.

It was Roy Bugbee. This was unusual, a call from Bugbee on a Saturday morning. He wasn't friendly, but neither was he as rude as usual. "The phone records," he said.

"One second." She walked out of the bedroom so as not to subject Leon to her conversation. "Rinaldi's cell phone records?"

"One of the numbers kept coming up a lot, no ID, so I looked it up in Bresser's." He was referring to one of the reverse phone directories. She was impressed at Bugbee's initiative, relieved that he'd finally agreed to take this job on. Maybe he wasn't completely beyond redemption.

Bugbee had paused, waiting for her to say something, or maybe for dramatic effect, so she said, "Great idea."

"Right. And three guesses who called Rinaldi at 2:07 in the morning, the day Stadler got plugged."

"Stadler," she ventured.

"No," Bugbee said. "Nicholas Conover."

"Two in the morning? The same morning when Stadler's body was found, you mean."

"Uh huh."

"But . . . but Conover told me he slept through the night."

"Hmph. Guess not, huh?"

"No," Audrey said, feeling a little tingle of excitement. "I guess not." Another awkward pause. "Is that it?"

"Is that *it*?" Bugbee scoffed. "You got something better on a Saturday morning?"

"No, I mean—nice job," she said. "Well done."

She ended the call and returned to the bedroom, but Leon was no longer in bed. He was sitting in the chair, dressed, tying his sneakers.

"What are you doing?" she said.

Leon stood up, and as he walked out of the bedroom, he passed the bed

and flung out a hand at the breakfast tray, flipping it onto the floor. The cantaloupe balls went skittering across the carpet, the French toast flopping
down in a neat pile, the maple syrup puddle sitting atop the gray wool. The
coffee spill soaked right in, as did the half-and-half. Audrey couldn't keep
from letting out a squawk of surprise.

She followed him out, crying, "Leon, baby, I'm sorry—I didn't . . ." But
didn't *what*? The call was important, wasn't it?

"You'll make it quick, huh," Leon said bitterly as he clomped down the
hall. "Sure you will. You got business to do, you're gonna do it no matter
what we're doing. You got your priorities straight, don't you?"

She felt sad and almost despondent. "No, Leon, that's not fair," she said.
"I couldn't have been on the phone for more than a minute. I'm sorry—"

But the screen door slammed, and he was gone.

Audrey was alone in the house now, feeling lonely and a tad anxious. She
had no idea where Leon had stormed off to, just that he'd taken his car.

She called Bugbee back, reaching him on his cell.

He didn't sound happy to hear from her, but then he never did. "You said
Conover called Rinaldi at 2:07 on Wednesday morning. Was that the only
call that night?"

"That morning," Bugbee corrected her. She could hear traffic noise in
the background. He was probably in his car now.

"Were there any other calls that night or that morning between Conover
and Rinaldi?"

"No."

"That means Rinaldi didn't call Conover first, wake him up or something. Conover wasn't calling Rinaldi back, in other words."

"Right. Put it this way: Rinaldi didn't call Conover from either his home
phone or his cell phone. It's conceivable he called Conover from a pay-
phone, but you'd have to get Conover's phone records for that."

"Yes. I think we should talk to both of these gentlemen again."

"I'd say so. Hold on, I'm losing you." A few seconds went by, a half a
minute, and he was back on. "Yeah, put the squeeze on 'em both. I'd say we
got 'em there with an inconsistency."

"I'd like to talk to them tomorrow."

"Tomorrow's Sunday—don't you have church or something?"

"Sunday afternoon."

"I'm golfing."

"Well, I'm going to see if I can't talk to Nicholas Conover tomorrow afternoon."

"On Sunday?"

"I figure he can't be too busy at work if it's a Sunday."

"But that's family time."

"Stadler had a family too. Now the thing is, Roy, I think we should talk to these gentlemen simultaneously. And we ought to call them at the last minute before we go over. I really don't want one calling the other to get their stories straight."

"Right, but like I said, I'm golfing tomorrow."

"I'm flexible as to the time tomorrow," she said. "You tell me what works best for you. I'm usually out of church by eleven."

"Christ. Well, I'd rather do Conover. I want to take down the fucker. You can talk to Rinaldi."

"My sense, talking to Rinaldi, is that he might respond better to a male detective."

"I don't really give a shit what makes him comfortable."

"It's not a matter of comfort," Audrey said. "It's a matter of what's going to work best, what will help us extract the information we want most effectively."

Bugbee raised his voice a few decibels. "You want to get information out of Nicholas Conover, you gotta play him hard. And that calls for me. My style. Not yours. You're a pushover, and he can tell."

"Oh, I'm less of a pushover than you might think, Roy," she said.

55

Cassie was already seated at a booth when Nick arrived at the Town Grounds, Fenwick's upscale coffee house. The national craze for good coffee had even come to Fenwick, a Maxwell-House-in-the-can kind of place if ever there was one, but Starbucks had stayed clear so far. The result was this small, sort of neo-hippy joint that roasted their own coffee, did a healthy take-out business in beans, and served coffee in little glass French presses.

She was drinking a cup of herbal tea—a Celestial Seasonings Cranberry Apple Zinger packet was crumpled next to the teapot—and looked tired, gloomy. The smudges under her eyes were back.

"Am I late?" Nick asked.

A quick shake of the head. "No, why?"

"You look pissed off."

"You obviously don't know me well enough yet," she said. "You'll learn to recognize pissed off. This isn't pissed off. This is tired."

"Well, that dinner wasn't so bad, was it?"

"Your kids are great."

"You really hit it off with them. I think Julia loved having another woman around."

"It's a pretty male household, with you two Conover men exuding all that testosterone."

"The thing is, you know, Julia's at this age where—well, I don't know who's going to talk to her about periods and tampons, all that girl stuff. She doesn't want to hear it from me. Like I know anything about it anyway."

"Her nanny, maybe? Marta, right?"

"I guess. But it's not the same thing as a mom. There's Laura's sister, Aunt Abby, but we barely see her anymore since Laura's death. And Luke spends most of his time hating me. One big happy family." He told her about the big fight, Lucas storming out of the house.

"You talk about him like he's the bad seed."

"Sometimes I think he is."

"Since Laura's death."

Nick nodded.

"How'd that happen?"

Nick shook his head. "I don't want to get into that, you mind?"

"Hey, fine. What do I care?"

Nick looked at her. "Come on, don't get offended. It's just a sort of heavy topic for a Sunday morning, okay?" He took a breath. "We were driving to a swim meet and we hit an icy path and skidded." He studied the tabletop. "And blah blah blah."

"You were driving," she said softly.

"Laura was, actually."

"So you don't blame yourself for it?"

"Oh, I do. I totally do."

"But you know it's not rational."

"Who's talking rational?"

"Whose swim meet?"

"Luke's. Can we talk about something else, please?"

"So he gets to blame you and also share in the guilt, right?"

"You got it. It's a mess."

"He's a good kid, deep down. Lot of attitude, like most sixteen-year-old boys. Hard shell, but soft nougat center."

"How come I never get to see the nougat center?"

"Because you're his dad, and you're safe."

"Well, maybe you can talk to him about the evils of smoking."

"Yeah, right," she said, chuckling. She took a pack of Marlboros from her jeans jacket and tapped one out. "I think I'm not the best person to do that. Kinda like your Sid Vicious giving 'Just Say No' lectures on heroin." She took out her orange plastic Bic lighter and lit the cigarette, pulling the saucer toward her to use as an ashtray.

"I thought people who do yoga don't smoke," Nick said.

She flicked him a glare.

"Isn't yoga all about breath?"

"Come on," she said.

"Sorry."

"Can I ask you something?" she said offhandedly.

"Sure."

"Julia told me about your dog." Nick felt his guts constrict, but he said nothing. "God," she went on. "That's so incredible. I mean, how did you feel when that happened?"

"How did I feel?" He didn't know how to respond. How would anyone feel? He shook his head, faltered for a bit. "I was frightened for my kids, I guess, most of all. I was terrified they might be next."

"But you must have been furious too. I mean, God, someone who'd do something like that to your family!" She tilted her head as she peered at him, her eyes keen. "I'd want to kill him."

Why was she asking this?

He felt a wave of cold wash over him. "No," he said, "it wasn't anger so much as—as this protective instinct. That's what I felt most of all."

She nodded. "Sure. That's right. The normal dad reaction. Gotta protect the kids."

"Right. Got a new alarm system, told all the kids to be extra careful. But there's only so much you can do." His cell phone rang.

He apologized, and picked it up. "Nick Conover," he said.

"Mr. Conover, this is Detective Rhimes?"

He paused for a few seconds. "Oh, yes. Hi—"

He wondered whether Cassie could hear the police detective's voice.

Cassie smoked, idly studying a hand-lettered "This Is a Smoke-Free Zone!" sign on a little chalkboard, pink Day-Glo chalk.

"I'm terribly sorry to bother you on a Sunday, but if there's any way you could spare a little time, I'd like to come by and talk for a little bit."

"Well, sure, I suppose. What's up?"

"There's a couple of little details I'm confused about, I thought you might be able to clear up for me. I know Sunday is family time, but if you wouldn't mind . . ."

"Sure," Nick said. "What time do you have in mind?"

"Is half an hour from now convenient for you?"

Nick hesitated. "I think that would be okay," he said.

When he ended the call, he said, "Cassie, listen—I'm sorry, but—"

"Family calls," she said.

He nodded. "Afraid so. I'll make it up to you."

She put a hand on his forearm. "Hey, don't worry about it. Family's always number one."

As soon as he'd dropped her off, he dialed Eddie's cell.

56

Driving up to the fancy iron gate with the brass plaque that said FENWICKE ESTATES, Audrey was distinctly aware that she was entering another world. She had changed out of her church clothes into something more casual, and now she felt underdressed. Her Honda Accord was definitely underdressed. The guard at the gatehouse looked her over with disapproval as he took her name and picked up his phone to call Conover. She doubted it was the color of her skin. More likely the color of the rust on her front left quarter panel.

She noticed all the security cameras. One, mounted to the gatehouse, took her picture. Another was positioned to capture her license plate at the rear of her car. There was a proximity-card reader by the guard's window too: people who lived in Fenwicke Estates probably had to wave a card at the sensor to be admitted. The security was impressive. But what must it be like to live like this, she wondered? In a place like Fenwick, where the crimes were mostly localized in the bad part of town, why would you want to live this way? Then she remembered what Conover had said about his wife's concern that the family might be threatened by employees laid off from Stratton.

When she drove up to the house, she drew breath.

This was a mansion, there was no other word for it. The place was immense, made of stone and brick, beautiful. She'd never seen a house like this in real life, outside of the movies. It sat in the middle of a huge green field of a lawn, with specimen trees and flowers everywhere. As she walked up the stone path to the house, she glanced again at the lawn and noticed that the blades of grass were small and slender and sparse. Up close she could see that the lawn had recently been seeded.

The lawn.

She pretended to trip on one of the paving stones, fell to her knees, breaking her fall with one hand. When she got back on her feet, she slipped a good healthy pinch of soil into her purse just as the front door opened and Nicholas Conover came out.

"You okay?" he said, walking down the front steps toward her.

"Just clumsy. My husband's always saying to me, 'Walk much?'"

"Well, you're not the first to trip on those stones. Gotta do something about that path."

He was wearing faded jeans, a navy blue polo shirt, white running shoes. She hadn't noticed before how tall he was and trim and powerful looking. He looked like an athlete, or a former athlete. She remembered reading that he'd been a hockey star at the high school.

"I'm so sorry to disturb you at home on a Sunday."

"Don't worry about it," Conover said. "It's probably just as well. My schedule during the week's pretty jammed. Plus, anything I can do to help you out, I want to do. You're doing important work."

"I appreciate it. This is such a beautiful home."

"Thanks. Come on in. Can I get you some coffee?"

"No, thanks."

"Lemonade? My daughter makes the best lemonade."

"That right?"

"Right from frozen concentrate. Yep."

"That sounds tempting, but I'll pass." Before they got to the front steps, she turned around and said, "That really has to be the most beautiful lawn I've ever seen."

"Now, that's what a guy likes to hear."

"Oh, right. Men and their lawns. But seriously, it looks like a putting green."

"And I don't even golf. My greatest failing as a CEO."

"Is it—do you mind if I ask, because my husband, Leon, is always complaining about the state of our lawn—did you put down sod?"

"No, just seed."

"Regular grass seed, or what's that stuff called—where you spray it?"

"Hydroseed. Yep, that's what we did."

"Well, I've got to tell Leon. He's always calling it hydro*weeding* because he says you get way too many weeds in the grass, but this looks just perfect to me."

"That Leon sounds like a real card."

"Oh, he is," Audrey said, feeling a prickle. "That he is."

The front door looked like something out of Versailles, ornately carved wood in a honey color. A quiet high-pitched tone sounded when Conover opened the door: an alarm system. He led her through an enormous foyer, high vaulted ceilings, really breathtaking. So this is how rich people live, she thought. Imagine being able to afford a house like this. She tried not to gawk, but it was hard.

She heard the sound of someone playing a piano and thought of Camille. "Is that one of yours?" she asked.

"My daughter," he said. "Believe me, it doesn't happen often, her practicing. It's like a total eclipse of the sun."

They walked by the room where a young girl was practicing, a lanky dark-haired girl around Camille's age wearing a baseball shirt. The girl was playing the first prelude from Bach's *Well-Tempered Clavier,* one of Audrey's favorite pieces. She played it haltingly, mechanically, clearly not yet grasping how fluid it had to be. Audrey caught a quick flash of a baby grand piano, a Steinway. She remembered how long LaTonya and Paul had scrimped to buy the battered old upright, which never stayed in tune. Imagine owning a Steinway, she thought.

She was briefly tempted to stop and listen, but Conover kept going down the hall, and she kept up. As they entered an elegant sitting room with Persian rugs and big comfortable-looking easy chairs, she said, "Oh, they never like practicing."

"Tell me about it," Conover said, sinking into one of the chairs. "You pretty much have to put a—" he began, then started again. "They fight you on everything at this age. You have kids, Detective?"

She sat in the chair alongside his, not the one directly opposite, preferring to avoid the body language of confrontation. "No, I'm afraid we haven't been blessed with children," she said. What was he about to say—You have to put a gun to their heads? What was interesting was not the figure of speech but that he'd caught himself.

Interesting.

She casually glanced at an arrangement of family photographs in silver frames on a low table between them, and she felt a pang of jealousy. She saw Conover and his late wife, a son, and a daughter, Conover with his two children and the family dog. An extremely handsome family.

This house, these children—she was overcome by envy, which shamed her.

Envy and wrath shorten the life, it said in Ecclesiastes. Somewhere else it said that envy is the rottenness of the bones—was it Proverbs? Who is able to stand before envy? Who indeed? *Behold, these are the ungodly, who prosper in the world; they increase in riches.* That was in Psalms, she was quite sure. *Surely thou didst set them in slippery places: thou castedst them down into destruction.*

Her entire house could fit into a couple of these rooms.

She would never have children.

She was sitting next to the man who was responsible for laying Leon off.

She took out her notebook and said, "Well, I just wanted to clear up a few things from our last conversation."

"Sure." Conover leaned back in his chair, arms folded back, stretching. "How can I help you?"

"If we can go back to last Tuesday evening, ten days ago."

Conover looked puzzled.

"The night that Andrew Stadler was murdered."

He nodded his head. "Okay. Right."

She consulted her pad, as if she had the notes from their last interview right in front of her. She'd already transcribed them and put them into a folder in one of the Stadler file boxes. "We talked about where you were that night," she prompted, "when your memory was maybe a little fresher. You said you were at home, asleep by eleven or eleven thirty. You said you slept through the night."

"Okay."

"You don't remember getting up that night."

He furrowed his brow. "I suppose it's possible I got up to pee."

"But you didn't make a phone call."

"When?"

"In the middle of the night. After you went to sleep."

"Not that I recall," he said, smiling, leaning forward. "If I'm making calls in my sleep, I've got even bigger problems than I'm aware of."

She smiled too. "Mr. Conover, at 2:07 A.M. that night you placed a call to your security director, Edward Rinaldi. Do you remember that?"

Conover didn't seem to react. He seemed to be examining the pattern on the Oriental rug. "We're talking after midnight, early on Wednesday?"

"That's right."

"Then I must have my days wrong."

"I'm sorry?"

"One of those nights I remember the alarm went off. I've got it set to make a sound in my bedroom so it doesn't wake up the whole house."

"The alarm went off," Audrey said. That was checkable, of course.

"Something set it off, and I went downstairs to check it out. It was nothing, as far as I could see, but I was a little anxious. You can understand, I'm sure, with what had just happened."

She nodded, compressed her lips, jotted a note. Didn't meet his eyes.

"Eddie, Stratton's security director, had just had one of his guys put in this fancy new alarm system, and I wasn't sure if this was a false alarm or something I should be concerned about."

"You didn't call the alarm company?"

"My first thought was to call Eddie—I asked him to come out to the house and check it out."

She looked up. "You couldn't check it out yourself?"

"Oh, I did. But I wanted to make sure there wasn't something faulty in the system. I didn't want to call the cops for what was sure to be a false alarm. I wanted Eddie to check it out."

"At two in the morning?"

"He wasn't happy about it." Conover grinned again. "But given what I've been through, we both agreed it was better safe than sorry."

"Yet you told me you slept through the night."

"Obviously I got the days mixed up. My apologies." He didn't sound at all defensive. He sounded quite casual. Matter-of-fact. "Tell you something else, I've been taking this pill to help me sleep, and it kind of makes the nights sort of blurry for me."

"Amnesia?"

"No, nothing like that. I don't think Ambien causes amnesia like some of those other sleeping pills, Halcion or whatever. It's just that when I pass out, I'm zonked."

"I see."

He'd just altered his story significantly, but in a completely believable way. Or was she being too suspicious? Maybe he really had mixed up the days. People did it all the time. If that night hadn't been unusual or remarkable for him—if, that is, he hadn't witnessed Andrew Stadler's murder that night, or been aware of it whether before or after the fact—then there was no reason for him to have any special, fixed memory of what he'd done. Or not done.

"And did Mr. Rinaldi come over?"

Conover nodded. "Maybe half an hour later. He walked around the yard, didn't find anything. Checked the system. He thought maybe a large animal had set it off, like a deer or something."

"Not an intruder."

"Not that he could see. I mean, it's possible someone was out there, walking around on my property, near the house. But I didn't see anyone when I got up, and by the time Eddie got here, he didn't see anything either."

"You said you took Ambien to go to sleep that night?"

"Right."

"So you must have been pretty groggy when the alarm went off."

"I'll say."

"So there might have been someone, or something, that you just didn't notice. Being groggy and all."

"Definitely possible."

"Did anyone else in the house wake up at the time?"

"No. The kids were asleep, and Marta—she's the nanny and housekeeper—she didn't get up either. Like I said, the alarm was set to sound in my bedroom, and not too loud. And the house is pretty soundproof."

"Mr. Conover, you said your security director had 'just' put in the new alarm system. How long ago?"

"Two weeks ago. Not even."

"After the incident with the dog?"

"You got it. If I could have had Eddie put in a moat and a drawbridge, I'd have done that too. I don't ever want my kids to be endangered."

"Certainly." She'd noticed the cameras around the house when she'd arrived. "If you'd had a system like this earlier, you might have been able to prevent the break-ins."

"Maybe," Conover said.

"But you live in this gated community. There seems to be a lot of security when you come in—the guard, the access control, the cameras in front and all around the perimeter fence."

"Which does a pretty good job of keeping out unauthorized vehicles. Problem is, there's nothing that stops someone from just climbing the fence out of sight of the guardhouse and getting in that way. The cameras'll pick them up, but there's no motion sensor around the fence—no alarm goes off."

"That's a serious security flaw."

"Tell me about it. That's why Eddie wanted to beef up the system at the house."

But now another thought appeared at the back of her thoughts, and she tugged at it like a stray thread.

The security system.

The cameras.

Nothing that stops someone from just climbing the fence.

If Stadler had climbed the fence that surrounded Fenwicke Estates and walked to Conover's house in the middle of the night, walked across the lawn, setting off the brand-new motion sensors, wouldn't that have been captured by Conover's own video cameras?

And if so, wouldn't there be a recording somewhere? Probably not videotape: no one used that anymore. Probably recorded onto a hard drive somewhere in the house, right? She wondered about that. She didn't really know much about how these newfangled security systems worked.

She'd have to take a closer look.

"You know, I've changed my mind about that coffee," Audrey said.

57

Audrey did not arrive home until a little after seven, feeling a knot in her stomach as she turned the key in the front door. She'd told him that she'd be home for dinner, though she hadn't said what time that would be. It took so little to set Leon off.

But he wasn't home.

Several nights in a row he hadn't been home until late, almost ten o'clock. What was he doing? Did he go out drinking? Yet recently he didn't seem to be drunk when he got home. She couldn't smell liquor on his breath.

She had another suspicion, though it made her sick to think about it. It explained why Leon was no longer interested in having sex with her.

He was getting it somewhere else. He was, she feared, having an affair, and lately he was being brazen about it, not even attempting to cover it up.

Leon was at home all day while she was at work, which gave him plenty of opportunity to cheat without her ever finding out. But going out, coming home at nine, ten o'clock without so much as an excuse—that was a thumb in her eye. That was blatant.

Sure enough, at a few minutes after ten she heard the jingling of the keys in the lock, and Leon walked in, went right to the kitchen, ran water into a glass. He didn't even say hello.

"Leon," she called out.

But he didn't answer.

And she knew. You didn't have to be a detective. It was that obvious. She knew, and it was like a punch to her solar plexus.

Nick sat in his study, trying to go over some paperwork. He'd been calling Eddie, at home and on his cell, but no answer. On his fourth try, Eddie answered with an annoyed "What?"

"Eddie, she was just here," Nick said.

"Fenwick's own Cleopatra Jones? She don't have no superpowers, Nick. She's just sweating you. They tried the same shit on me today—the other one came by, Bugbee, asked me a shitload of questions, but I could see they got nothing."

"She asked me about the call I made to you that night."

"What'd you tell her?"

"Well, I—see, I'd told her I slept through the night that night."

"*Shit.*"

"No, listen. That's what I said at first, but then when she said she knew I'd made a call to you on your cell phone, I told her I must have mixed up the nights. I said the alarm went off that night, so I called you to ask you to check it out." Nick waited for Eddie's response with rising dread. "My God, Eddie, did you tell the other cop something different? I mean, I figured the alarm going off, that's a matter of record—"

"No, you did the right thing. I said pretty much the same once I saw what he had. But man, I was shitting bricks you might try to wing it, say something else. Good job."

"We've got to coordinate a little more closely, Eddie. Make sure we don't say different things."

"Right."

"And something else. She was admiring the alarm system."

"She's got good taste." He lowered his voice. "And so does the superfreak who's naked in my bed. Who was just admiring my dick. Which is why I gotta go."

"Especially the cameras. Especially the *cameras*, Eddie."

"Yeah?"

"Are you *positive* there's no way to retrieve the part of the tape you erased?"

"It's not tape, it's digital," Eddie snapped. "Anyway, I told you, you have nothing to worry about. What's gone is gone. Why are we fucking *having* this conversation? I just spent ten minutes preheating the oven—now I got to stick in my French bread before it cools down, you get what I'm saying?"

"The hard drive is totally clean, right? They can't bring it back?"

An exasperated sigh. "Stop being such a *girl*, okay?"

Nick felt a surge of anger he knew better than to vent. "I sure as hell hope you know what you're doing," he said stonily.

"Nick, you're doing it again. You're peeing in my pool. Oh, by the way. That work you wanted me to do on Scott McNally?"

"Yeah?"

"Remember last month when he was away for a week?"

"I remember. Some sort of dude ranch in Arizona. Grapevine Canyon, was it? He said it was like *City Slickers* without the laughs."

"*City Slickers,* he said? *Crouching* fucking *Tiger*'s more like it. He's a sneak, but a cheapskate numbers guy like him can't pass up the corporate travel rates, right? So this pencil dick puts in for a Stratton discount when he buys his ticket to Hong Kong. I got the receipts from the girls in the travel office. Unfucking*believable*."

"Hong Kong?"

Eddie nodded. "Hong Kong and then Shenzhen. Which is this huge industrial area near Hong Kong, shitload of factories, on the mainland."

"I know about Shenzhen."

"That mean anything to you?"

"It means he's lying to me," Nick replied. *It also means that all these rumors are right. Where there's smoke there's fire, as the GSA guy said.*

"Sounds to me like you got trouble everywhere you go," Eddie said. "Big trouble."

58

Audrey was surprised to find Bugbee in this early, sitting in his cubicle on the phone. She approached and heard him talking to a lawn company, asking about hydroseeding. Well, she thought, what do you know? He really is working this case.

He wore his customary sport coat, a pale green with a windowpane plaid, a pale blue shirt, red tie. In repose, he was not a bad-looking man, even if he dressed like a used-car salesman. He saw her standing nearby, kept talking without acknowledging her presence. She held up a finger. After a little while he gave her a brusque nod.

She waited until he got off the phone, then wordlessly showed him the little clear-plastic eye-cream vial.

He looked at the pinch of dirt, said suspiciously, "What's that?"

"I took it from Conover's lawn yesterday." She paused. "His lawn was recently hydroseeded."

Bugbee stared, the realization dawning. "That's not admissible," he said. "Poison fruit."

"I know. But worth taking a look at. To my eye it looks like the same stuff from under Stadler's fingernails."

"It's been, what, like two weeks since the murder. It's probably disintegrated a lot since then. The mulch pellets are supposed to break down."

"It's been a dry couple of weeks. The only water probably came from his irrigation system. More interesting, I managed to get a look at his security system while he was making coffee for me." She handed him a While You Were Out message slip on which she'd written some notes. "Pretty fancy. Sixteen cameras. Here's the name of the alarm monitoring company he uses. And the makes and models of the equipment, including the digital video recorder."

"You want me to talk to one of the techs," he said. She noticed that for the first time he didn't argue with her.

"I think we should go over there and take a look at the recorder. And while we're at it, check for blood and prints, inside and outside the house."

Bugbee nodded. "You're thinking the whole thing went down in or near Conover's house, and the surveillance cameras recorded it."

"We can't ignore the possibility."

"They'd be stupid to forget about that little detail."

"We've both seen a lot of stupidity. People forget. Also, it's not like the old days when you could just take out a videotape and get rid of it. It's got to be a lot harder to erase a digital surveillance recording. You've got to know what you're doing."

"Eddie Rinaldi knows what he's doing."

"Maybe."

"Of course he does," Bugbee said. "Are you thinking Conover did it?"

"I'm thinking Eddie did it." Now that he was a suspect, she noticed, he'd gone from Rinaldi to Eddie. "I think Conover saw or heard Stadler outside his house. Maybe the alarm went off, maybe not—"

"The alarm company would probably have a record of that."

"Okay, but either way, Conover calls Eddie, tells him this guy's trying to get into his house. Eddie comes over, confronts Stadler, then kills him."

"And gets rid of the body."

"He's an ex-cop. He's smart enough, or experienced enough, to make sure he doesn't leave any trace evidence on the body—"

"Except the fingernails."

"It's the middle of the night, two in the morning, it's late and it's dark and they're both panicking. They overlook some things. Subtleties like that."

"One of them moves the body down to Hastings."

"Eddie, I'm guessing."

Bugbee thought a moment. "The gatehouse at Fenwicke Estates probably has records of who left when. We can see if Conover drove out of there some time after Eddie drove in. Or if it was just Eddie."

"Which would tell you what?"

"If the shooting happened inside or outside Conover's house, they had to move the body down to the Dumpster on Hastings. Which they're going to do in a car. If both Conover and Rinaldi left Fenwicke Estates some time after two, then it could have been either one of them. But if only Eddie left, then it's Eddie who moved it."

"Exactly." A moment of silence passed. "There are cameras everywhere around the community."

Bugbee smiled. "If so, we got 'em."

"That's not what I'm saying. If we can get the surveillance tapes, we can confirm when Eddie entered and exited, sure."

"Or Eddie and Conover."

"Okay. But more important, we can see if *Stadler* came over. If Andrew Stadler entered. Then we've got Stadler's whereabouts pinned down."

Bugbee nodded. "Yeah." Another pause. "Which means that Eddie has an unlicensed .380."

"Why unlicensed?"

"Because I went through the safety inspection certificate files at the county sheriff's department. He's got paperwork for a Ruger, a Glock, a hunting rifle, couple of shotguns. But no .380. So if he's got one, he doesn't have any paper on it."

"I've been pushing the state crime lab," Audrey said. "I want to see if they can use their database to match the rounds we found in Stadler's body with any other no-gun case anywhere."

Bugbee looked impressed, but he just nodded.

"In any case, we're going to need a search warrant to see what weapons Rinaldi has."

"Not going to be a problem getting one."

"Fine. If we find a .380 and we get a match . . ." She was starting to enjoy the genuine back-and-forth, even if Bugbee was still prickly and defensive.

"You're dreaming. He can't be that stupid."

"We can always hope. What did he say about the phone call?"

"He was pretty slick. Said, yeah, he got a call from Conover that night, the alarm went off at Conover's house and could he check it out. Said he was a little pissed off, but he went over there to check it out. You know, the shit you do to keep your boss happy. It was like no big deal. Did Conover put his foot in it?"

"No. He—well, it felt like he sort of evolved his story."

"Evolved?"

"He didn't revise his story right away. I reminded him that he'd said he slept through the night, and then I asked him about the phone call he made at two in the morning, and he owned right up to it. He said he must have got the days mixed up."

"Happens. You believe him?"

"I don't know."

"He sound rehearsed?"

"It was hard to tell. Either he was telling the truth, or he'd done his homework."

"Usually you can tell."

"Usually. But I couldn't."

"So maybe he's a good liar."

"Or he's telling the truth. The way I see it, he's telling *part* of the truth. He called Eddie, Eddie came over—and that's where the true part ends. Did Eddie say if he found anything when he looked around Conover's yard?"

"Yeah. He said he found nothing."

"That much they got straight," Audrey said.

"Maybe too straight."

"I don't know what that means. Straight is straight. You know what? I say we ought to move quickly on this. The gun, the tape recorder—this is all stuff that they could do something about if they haven't already. Toss the gun, delete the tape, whatever. Now that we've talked to them both separately, at the same time, they're both going to be suspicious. If they're going to destroy evidence, now is the time they're going to do it."

Bugbee nodded. "Talk to Noyce, put in for the warrants anyway in case we need them. I'll make a couple of calls. Can you clear your schedule today?"

"Happy to."

"Oh, I called that Stadler chick for a follow-up."

"And?"

"She doesn't know shit about what her father did on the night he was killed. Says he never said anything about Conover."

"You think she's telling you the truth?"

"I got no reason to think otherwise. My instinct tells me, yeah, she's on the level."

Audrey nodded. "Me too."

A few minutes later, Bugbee came up to Audrey's cubicle with a cat-that-ate-the-canary smile. "Wouldn't you just know Nicholas Conover would use a company called Elite Professional Lawn Care? Sixteen days ago they hydroseeded the property around a house belonging to the CEO of the Stratton Corporation. The guy remembered it well—the architect, guy named Claflin, specified Penn Mulch. Said they had to put in a new gas line or something, tore up the old grass, and his client decided to put in a whole new lawn, replace the crappy old one. Lawn guy, he said it's a waste of money to put stuff like that in the slurry, but he's not going to argue. Not with a customer who has the big bucks, you know?"

59

Scott McNally tended to get into work around the same time as Nick did, around seven thirty. Normally, they and the other early arrivers sat at their desks working and doing e-mail, tended not to socialize, took advantage of the quiet time to get work done uninterrupted.

But this morning, Nick took a stroll across the floor to the other side and approached Scott's cubicle quietly. He felt a pulse of fury every time he thought about how Scott had lied to him about going to that dude ranch in Arizona, had instead made a secret trip to mainland China. That coupled with what he'd learned from the Atlas McKenzie and the Homeland Security guys—these goddamned rumors that Stratton was quietly negotiating to "move the company to China," whatever that meant exactly.

It was time to rattle Scott's cage, find out what he was doing.

"Got any interesting vacation ideas?" Nick asked abruptly.

Scott looked up, startled. "Me? Come on, my idea of a great vacation is a Trekkie convention." He caught the look on Nick's face and laughed nervously. "I mean, well, Eden loves Parrot Cay in the Turks and Caicos."

"Actually, I was thinking some place further east. Like Shenzhen, maybe? Where do you like to stay when you visit Shenzhen, Scott?"

Scott reddened. He looked down at his desk—it was almost a reflex, Nick noticed—and said, "I'll go anywhere for a good mu shu pork."

"Why, Scott?"

Scott didn't answer right away.

"We both know how hard Muldaur's been pushing for us to move manu-facturing to Asia," Nick said. "That what you're doing for him? Checking out Chinese factories behind my back?"

Scott looked up from his desk, looking pained. "Look, Nick, right now Stratton is like a puppy with diarrhea, okay? Cute to look at, but no one wants to get too close. I'm not doing any of us any good if I don't scout out these possibilities."

"Possibilities?"

"I realize you find it upsetting. I can't blame you. But one day, when you look at the numbers and you finally say, 'Scott, what are our options here?' I've got to be able to tell you what they are."

"Let me get this straight," Nick said. "You made some sort of secret-agent trip to China to scout out factories, then *lied* about it to me?"

Scott closed his eyes and nodded, compressing his lips. "I'm sorry," he said very quietly. "It wasn't my idea. Todd insisted on it. He just felt it was too much of a sore point with you—that you'd do everything you could to block any kind of overtures to China."

"What kind of 'overtures' are you talking about? I want specifics."

"Nick, I really hate being caught in the middle like this."

"I asked you a question."

"I know. And it's really not my place to say any more than I have already. So let's just leave it right there, okay?"

Nick stared. Scott wasn't even feigning deference anymore. Nick felt his anger growing greater by the second. It was all he could do not to reach over and grab Scott by the scrawny neck, lift him up, and hurl him against the silver-mesh fabric panel.

Nick turned to leave without saying another word.

"Oh, and Nick?"

Nick turned back, looked at him blankly.

"The Nan Hai is the place."

"Huh?"

"The place to stay in Shenzhen. The Nan Hai Hotel. Great views, great restaurant—I think you'll like it."

A voice squawked out of Scott's intercom. "Scott, it's Marjorie?"

"Oh, hey, Marge. Looking for Nick? He's right here."

"Nick," Marge said. "Call for you."

Nick picked up Scott's handset to speak to her privately. "There a problem?"

"It's someone from the police."

"My burglar alarm again."

"No, it's . . . it's something else. Nothing urgent, and your kids are fine, but it sounds important."

Scott gave him a curious look as Nick hurried away.

60

"This is Nick Conover."

Audrey was astonished, actually, when Nicholas Conover picked up the phone so quickly. She was expecting the usual runaround, the game of telephone tag that powerful men so often liked to play.

"Mr. Conover, this is Detective Rhimes. I'm sorry to bother you again."

The slightest beat of silence.

"No bother at all," he said. "What can I do for you?"

"Well, now, I was wondering if we might be able to look around your house."

"Look around . . . ?"

"We were thinking it would help us a great deal in establishing Andrew Stadler's whereabouts that night. That morning." She hoped the shift to "we" was subtle enough. "If indeed it was Andrew Stadler who went to your house that night, he might have been scared off by all the new security measures. The cameras and the lights and what have you."

"It's possible." Conover's voice sounded a bit less friendly now.

"So if we're able to nail down whether he did go to your house—whether it really was him who came by and not, say, a deer—that'll be a big help in mapping his last hours. Really narrow things down for us."

She could hear Conover inhale.

"When you're talking 'look around,' what do you mean, exactly?"

"A search. You know, the usual."

"Not sure I know what that means." Was there the slightest strain in his voice? Certainly something had shifted, changed. He was no longer putting out friendly vibes. He'd gone neutral.

"We come over with our techs, collect evidence, take pictures, whatever."

They both knew what she meant. No matter how she spun it, how she dressed it up, it was still a crime-scene search, and Conover surely understood that. It was a funny sort of dance now. A performance, almost.

"You talking about searching my yard?"

"Well, yes. That and your premises as well."

"My house."

"That's right."

"But—but no one entered my house."

She was ready for that. "Well, see, if Andrew Stadler really is the stalker who's repeatedly broken into your house over the last year, we might find evidence of that inside. Am I wrong in concluding that no one from the Fenwick police ever took fingerprints after the previous incidents?"

"That's right."

She shook her head, closed her eyes. "The less said about that, the better."

"When are you talking about doing this? This week some time?"

"Actually, given how things are progressing in this investigation," she said, "we'd like to do it today."

Another pause, this one even longer.

"Tell you what," Conover said at last. "Let me call you right back. What's the best number to reach you at?"

She wondered what he was going to do now—consult an attorney? His security director? One way or the other, whether he gave permission or not, she was going to search his premises.

If he refused—if she needed to get a search warrant—she'd be able to get one in about an hour. She'd already talked to one of the prosecutors, woke him up at home this morning, in fact, which didn't endear her to him. Once the prosecutor's head cleared, he'd said that there were sufficient grounds to grant a warrant. A district court judge would sign it, no problem.

But Audrey didn't want to get a search warrant. She didn't want to play hardball. Not yet. That was escalation, and if and when she needed to step things up, she could always do it. Better to low-key things. Keep up the pretense—the *shared* pretense, she was quite sure—that Nicholas Conover was being cooperative just because he was a good citizen, wanted to see justice done, wanted to get to the bottom of this. Because the moment he shifted to opposition and antagonism, she'd be all over him.

If he refused, four patrol units would be on their way over to his house in a matter of minutes to secure the premises and the curtilage, or the surrounding area, make sure no one took anything out. Then she'd be there an hour later with a search warrant and a crime-scene team.

She didn't want to go down that road yet. But she always had to be aware of the legalities. The prosecutor had rendered his judgment that she *could* get a warrant if she wanted to, yes. Instead, Audrey wanted to conduct what they called a consent search. That meant that Conover would sign a standard Consent to Search form.

It was a little tricky, though. If Conover signed it and his signature was witnessed, that established that he'd given his knowing, intelligent, and voluntary consent to a search. But there'd been cases, she knew, where a suspect with a clever lawyer had managed to get the results of a search thrown out at trial, insisting that they'd been coerced, or they didn't totally understand, or whatever. Audrey was determined not to commit that gaffe. So she was following the prosecutor's advice: Get Conover to sign the waiver, date it, get two witnesses, and you're fine. And if he refuses, we'll get you a warrant.

Half an hour later he called back, sounding confident once again. "Sure, Detective, I have no problem with that."

"Thank you, Mr. Conover. Now, I'm going to need you to sign a consent form allowing us to search your premises. You know, cross every *T* and so on."

"No problem."

"Would you like to be there for the search? It's up to you, certainly, but I know how busy you are."

"I think it's a good idea, don't you?"

"I think it's a good idea, yes."

"Listen, Detective. One thing. I don't mind you guys searching my property, looking for whatever you want, but I really don't want the neighborhood crawling with cops, you know? There going to be a bunch of patrol cars with lights and sirens and all that?"

Audrey chuckled. "It won't be as bad as all that."

"Can you do this using whatever you call them, unmarked vehicles?"

"For the most part, yes. There will be an evidence van and such, but we'll try to be subtle about it."

"As much as a police search can be subtle, right? Subtle as a brick to the head."

They shared a polite, uneasy laugh.

"One more thing," Conover said. "This is a small town, and we both know how people talk. I really hope this is all kept discreet."

"Discreet?"

"Out of the public eye. I really can't afford to have people hearing about how the police have been talking to me and searching my house in connection with this terrible murder. You know, I'm just saying I want to make sure my name stays out of it."

"Your name stays out of it," she repeated, thinking: *What are you saying exactly?*

"Look, you know, I'm the CEO of a major corporation in a town where not everybody loves me, right? Last thing I want is for rumors to start spreading— for people to be making stuff up about how Nick Conover's being looked into. Right?"

"Sure." She felt that prickle again, like an eruption of goose bumps.

"I mean, hey, we both know I'm not a suspect. But you get rumors and all that."

"Right."

"You know, it's like they say. A lie's halfway around the world before the truth has a chance to get its pants on, right?"

"I like that," she said. Here was another thing that made her uneasy. When an innocent person is being investigated for a homicide, he almost always squawks about it to his friends, protests, gets indignant. An innocent person in the klieg lights wants the support of his friends, so he invariably tells everyone about the outrage of the police suspecting him.

Nick Conover didn't want people to know that the police were interested in him.

This was not the reaction of an innocent man.

PART FOUR
CRIME SCENE

61

Early that morning, the day after Detective Rhimes had come over to the house to talk, Nick had awakened damp with sweat.

The T-shirt he'd slept in was wet around the neck. His pillow, even, was soaked, the wet feathers and down giving off that barnyard smell. His pulse was racing the way it used to during a particularly fierce scrimmage.

He'd just been jolted out of a dream that was way too real. It was one of those movielike dreams that feel vivid and fully imagined, not like his normal fleeting fragments of scenes and images. This one had a plot to it, a terrible, inexorable story in which he felt trapped.

Everyone *knew*.

They knew what he'd done That Night. They knew about Stadler. It was common knowledge, everywhere he went, walking through the halls of Stratton, the factory floor, the supermarket, the kids' schools. Everyone knew he'd killed a man, but he continued to insist, to pretend—it made no sense, he didn't know why—that he was innocent. It was almost a ritual acted out between him and everyone else: they knew, and he knew they knew, and yet he continued to maintain his innocence.

Okay, but then the dream took a sharp left turn into the gothic, like one of those scary movies about teenagers and homicidal maniacs, but also like a story by Edgar Allan Poe he'd read in high school about a telltale heart.

He came home one day, found the house crawling with cops. Not the house he and the kids lived in now, not Laura's mansion in Fenwicke Estates, but the dark, little brown-shingled, split-level ranch in Steepletown he'd grown up in. The house was a lot bigger though. Lots of hallways and empty rooms, room for the police to spread out and search, and he was powerless to stop them.

Hey, he tried to say but he couldn't speak, you're not playing by the rules. I pretend I'm innocent, and so do you. Remember? That's how it works.

Detective Audrey Rhimes was there and a dozen other faceless police investigators, and they were fanning out across the eerily large house, searching for clues. Someone had tipped them off. He heard one of the cops say the tip came from Laura. Laura was there too, taking an afternoon nap, but he woke her up to yell at her and she looked wounded but then there was a shout and he went to find out what was up.

It was the basement. Not the basement of the Fenwicke Estates house, with its hardwood floors and all the systems, the Weil-McLain gas-fired boiler and water heater and all that, neatly enclosed behind slatted bifold doors. But the basement of his childhood house, dark and damp and musty, concrete-floored.

Someone had found a pool of bodily fluids.

Not blood, but something else. It reeked. A spill of decomposition that had somehow seeped out from the basement wall.

One of the cops summoned a bunch of the other guys, and they broke through the concrete walls, and they found it there, the curled-up, decomposed body of Andrew Stadler, and Nick saw it, an electric jolt running through his body. They'd found it, and the game of pretenses was over because they'd found the proof, a body walled up in his basement, decomposing, rotting, leaching telltale fluids. The body so carefully and artfully concealed had signaled its location by festering and decaying and putrefying, leaking the black gravy of death.

A good ten hours after he'd awakened in a puddle of his own flop sweat, Nick pulled into the driveway and saw a fleet of police vehicles, cruisers, and unmarked sedans and vans, and it was as if he'd never woken up. So much for low-key. They couldn't have been much more obvious if they'd arrived with sirens screaming. Luckily the neighbors couldn't see the cars from the road, but the police must have caused a commotion arriving at the gates.

It was just before five o'clock. He saw Detective Rhimes standing on the porch waiting for him, wearing a peach-colored business suit.

He switched off the Suburban's engine and sat there for a moment in silence. Once he got out of the car, he was sure, nothing would be the same. Before and after. The engine block ticked as it cooled off, and the late afternoon sun was the color of burnt umber, the trees casting long shadows, clouds beginning to gather.

He noticed activity on the green carpet of lawn around the side of the house where his study was. A couple of people, a man and a woman—police techs?—were grazing slowly like sheep, heads down, looking closely for something. The woman was a squat fireplug with a wide ass, wearing a denim shirt and brand-new-looking dark blue jeans. The other one was a tall gawky guy with thick glasses, a camera around his neck.

This was real now. Not a nightmare. He wondered how they knew to look in the area nearest his study.

He tried to slow his heartbeat. Breathe in, breathe out, think placid thoughts.

Think of the first time he and Laura had gone to Maui, seventeen years ago, pre-kids, a Pleistocene era of his life. That perfect crescent of white sand beach in the sheltered cove, the absurdly blue crystal-clear water, the coconut palms rustling. A time when he felt more than just relaxed; he'd felt a deep inner serenity, Laura's fingers interlaced with his, the Hawaiian sun beating down on him and warming him to his core.

Detective Rhimes cocked her head, saw him sitting in the car. Probably deciding whether to walk up to the Suburban or wait for him there.

They were looking for spent cartridges. He had a gut feeling.

But Eddie had retrieved them all, didn't he?

Nick had been such a wreck that night, so dazed and so out of it. Eddie had asked him how many shots he'd fired, and Nick had answered two. That was right, wasn't it? The thing was such a blur that it was possible it was three. But Nick had said two, and Eddie had found two shell casings on the grass close to the French doors.

Had there been a third shot?

Had Eddie stopped when he found two, leaving one there that waited to be found by the gawky man and the fireplug woman, those experts in locating spent cartridge casings?

The lawn hadn't been mowed, of course, because the grass was too new. The fast-talking guy from the lawn company had told him to wait a good three weeks before he let his gardener mow.

So a chunk of metal that might otherwise have been thrown up into the blades of Hugo's wide walk-behind Gravely could well be lying there, glinting in the late-afternoon sun, just waiting for the wide-ass chick to bend over and snatch it up in her gloved hand.

He took another breath, did his best to compose himself, and got out of the Suburban.

"I'm terribly sorry to intrude on you this way," Detective Rhimes said. She looked genuinely apologetic. "You're very kind to let us look around. It's such a big help to our investigation."

"That's all right," Nick said. Strange, he thought, that she was keeping up the pretense. They both knew he was a suspect. He heard the rattling squawk of a crow circling overhead.

"I know you're a very busy man."

"You're busy too. We're all busy. I just want to do everything I can to help." His mouth went dry, choking off his last couple of words, and he wondered if she'd picked up on that. He swallowed, wondered if she noticed that too.

"Thank you so much," she said.

"Where's your charming partner?"

"He's busy on something else," she said.

Nick noticed the gawky guy walking across the lawn to them, holding something aloft.

He went light headed.

The guy was holding a large pair of forceps, and as he drew closer Nick could see a small brown something gripped at the end of the forceps. When the tech showed it to Detective Rhimes, without saying a word, Nick saw that it was a cigarette butt.

Detective Rhimes nodded as the man dropped the cigarette butt into a paper evidence bag, then turned back to Nick. She went on speaking as if they hadn't been interrupted.

Was Stadler smoking that night? Or had that been dropped there by one of the contractor's guys, taking a cigarette break outside the house, knowing they weren't allowed to smoke inside? He'd found some discarded Marlboro butts out there not so long ago, just before the loam was hydroseeded, picked them up with annoyance, made a mental note to say something to the contractor about the guys tossing their smokes around his lawn. Back when he had the luxury to be annoyed about such trivialities.

"I hope you don't mind that we got started a little early," Detective Rhimes said. "Your housekeeper refused to let my team in until you arrived, and I wanted to respect her wishes."

Nick nodded. "That's kind of you." He noticed that the woman articulated her words too clearly, her enunciation almost exaggerated, hypercorrect. There was something formal and off-putting about her manner that contrasted jarringly with her shyness and reserve, a glimmering of uncertainty, a vein of sweetness. Nick prided himself on his ability to read people pretty well, but this woman he didn't quite get. He didn't know what to make of her. Yesterday he'd tried to charm her, but he knew that hadn't worked.

"We're going to need to get a set of your fingerprints," she said.

"Sure. Of course."

"Also, we're going to need to take prints from everyone who lives in the house—the housekeeper, your children."

"My children? Is that really necessary?"

"These are only what we call elimination prints."

"My kids will freak out."

"Oh, they might think it's fun," she said. A sweet smile. "Kids often find it a novelty."

Nick shrugged. They entered the house, the high alert tone sounding quietly. The place different now: hushed, tense, like it was bracing itself for something. He heard the sound of running feet.

Julia.

"Daddy," his daughter said, face creased with concern, "what's going on?"

62

He sat down with the kids in the family room, the two of them on the couch that faced the enormous TV, Nick in the big side chair that Lucas normally staked out, which Nick thought of as his Archie Bunker chair. The Dad chair. He couldn't remember when they'd all watched TV together last, but back when they did, Lucas always grabbed the Archie Bunker chair, to his silent annoyance.

On a trestle table next to the TV set Nick noticed the little shrine that Julia and Lucas had made to Barney: a collection of photographs of their beloved dog, his collar and tags. His favorite toys, including a bedraggled stuffed lamb—his own pet—that he slept with and carried everywhere in his slobbering mouth. There was a letter Julia had written to him in different colored markers, which began: "Barney—we miss you SO MUCH!!!" Julia had explained that the shrine was Cassie's idea.

Lucas sat on the couch in huge baggy jeans, his legs splayed wide. The waistband of his boxer shorts was showing. He wore a black T-shirt with the word AMERIKAN in white letters on the front. Nick had no idea what that referred to. The laces on his Timberland boots were untied. He was wearing that rag on his head again. My own in-house, upper-middle-class, gated-community gangsta, Nick thought.

Lucas, staring off into the distance, said, "You gonna tell us what's up with the five-oh?"

"The police, you mean."

Lucas was looking out the bay window, watching the cops on the lawn.

"The police are here because of that guy who we think kept coming by and writing things inside our house," Nick said.

" 'No Hiding Place,' " recited Julia.

"Right. All that. He was a man who had something wrong with his head." She said in a small voice, "Is he the man who killed Barney?"

"We're not sure, but we think so."

"Cassie's dad," Lucas said. "Andrew Stadler."

"Right." Cassie's dad.

"He was fucked up," Lucas said.

"Watch your mouth around your sister."

"I've heard that word before, Dad," said Julia.

"No doubt. I just don't want either one of you using language like that."

Lucas, smirking, shook his head with amused contempt.

"So this man, Andrew Stadler, he died a couple of weeks ago," Nick went on, "and the police think he might have tried to come by our house the night he was killed, on his way to wherever he was going."

"They think you did it," Lucas said. A triumphant smile.

Nick's insides seized. Maybe he *had* heard, that night when Eddie came over. Or did he just put two and two together?

"*Hey!*" said Julia, outraged.

"Actually, Luke, what they're doing here is trying to trace his whereabouts."

"Then how come they're gathering evidence? I can see 'em out my window. They dug up some dirt from the lawn and put it in a little container thing, and they keep walking back and forth on the lawn like they're scoping for something."

Nick nodded, breathing in and out. They were gathering dirt? What did that mean? Had they found dirt on Stadler's body? He remembered that Eddie had brushed Stadler's shoes clean.

Could they have found dirt on Stadler's body that connected him with the house? Could they even do something like that? This was the awful thing: Nick had no idea of what the police were actually capable of, how advanced their forensic science was, or how backward.

"Luke," he said calmly, "they're looking for anything that can tell them whether the guy came by here that night or not." Nick knew he was treading water here. His kids were too bright. They'd watched too many TV shows and movies. They knew about cops and murders and suspects.

"Why do they care?" asked Julia.

"Simple," he said. "They need to nail down what he did that night, see if he really was here instead of somewhere else, so they can figure out where he might have gone after that, when he was killed."

"Wouldn't that be on the cameras?" Lucas asked.

"Could be," Nick said. "I don't remember when the new security system was put in and when exactly the guy was killed."

"I do," Lucas said right back. "They put the cameras in the day before Stadler was killed." How the hell did he know that, *remember* that?

"Well, if you're right, then yes, they might find something on the cameras. I have no idea. Anyway, the police want to get your fingerprints while they're here."

"Cool," said Lucas.

"How come? They don't think *we* killed the man, right?" said Julia, looking worried.

Nick laughed convincingly. "Don't worry about that. When they check for fingerprints inside and outside the house, they're going to find our fingerprints—yours and mine and Marta's—"

"And probably Emily's too," said Julia.

"Right."

"And probably that guy Digga, right, Luke?"

Luke rolled his eyes, looked away.

"Who's Digga?" Nick asked.

Lucas didn't answer, still shaking his head.

"He's this guy who wears a do-rag just like Luke and plays really loud music when you're not here and always smells like smoke. He stinks."

"When does he come over?" said Nick.

"Like once or twice," Lucas said. "Jesus Christ. This is totally wack. He's a friend of mine, all right? Am I allowed to have friends, or is this, like, a prison where you're not allowed to have visitors? You happy, Julia? Fuckin' tattletale."

"Hey!" Nick said.

Julia, so unused to being yelled at by her older brother, ran out of the room crying.

"Uh, Mr. Conover?"

Detective Rhimes, standing tentatively at the door to the family room.

"Yes?"

"Could I see you for a minute?"

63

"We found something on your lawn," she said.

"Oh?"

She'd taken him out into the hall, far enough away from the kids that they couldn't hear.

"A mangled piece of metal."

Nick shrugged, as if to say, so? Is that supposed to mean something to me?

"It may be a bullet fragment, maybe a piece of shell casing."

"From a gun?" His breath stopped. Outwardly he tried to project an image of nonchalance, but interested, as someone in his position should be. Someone who was innocent, who wanted the cops to find the killer.

"It's hard to say. I'm no expert."

"Can I take a look?" he said, and he immediately regretted saying it. Mustn't betray too much interest. Must get the balance right.

She shook her head. "The techs have it. I just wanted to ask you—it may seem a silly question—but you've said you don't own a gun, right?"

"That's right."

"So obviously you've never fired a gun on your property, I'm sure. But has anyone you know fired a gun in your yard, to your knowledge?"

He attempted a dismissive laugh, though it sounded hollow. "No target practice allowed here," he said.

"So, no one's ever fired a gun outside your house, to your knowledge."

"Nope. Not as far as I know."

"Never."

"Never." A cool trickle of sweat traced a path along the back of one ear and down his neck, where it was absorbed by the collar of his shirt.

She nodded again, slowly. "Interesting."

"The techs—are they sure it's from a bullet or whatever?"

"Well, you know, I doubt *I* could tell the difference between a bottle cap and a—a Remington Golden Saber .380 cartridge," she said. Nick couldn't stop himself from flinching, and he hoped she hadn't noticed. "But the crime scene techs, they're awfully good at what they do, and I have to defer to them on that. They tell me it sure looks like a fragment from a projectile."

"Strange," Nick said. He tried to look puzzled in a sort of neutral, disinterested way, not letting the way he was really feeling leak out—terrified and trembling and nauseated.

Eddie had assured him he'd collected everything, all the shell casings, and checked for any other trace evidence that might be on the lawn. Then again, he could easily have missed a small piece of lead or brass or whatever it was, a flying piece of metal that had lodged itself into the earth, say. That would be easy to miss.

After all, Nick had noticed the smell of liquor on Eddie's breath that night. He'd probably been sleeping it off when Nick called. Didn't have all his faculties about him. Maybe he hadn't been so thorough.

Detective Rhimes seemed about to say something more when Nick noticed someone walking by, carrying a black rectangular metal object sealed in a clear plastic bag. The fireplug woman, the evidence tech with the wide ass in the new jeans, was holding what Nick recognized at once as the digital video recorder that was hooked up to the security cameras. They must have taken it from the closet where the installer had put the alarm system.

"Hey, what's that?" Nick called out. The woman, whose nametag on her denim shirt said Trento, stopped, looked at Detective Rhimes.

The detective said, "That's the recording unit from your security system."

"I need that," Nick said.

"I understand. We'll make sure this is turned around just as quickly as possible."

Nick shook his head in apparent frustration. He hoped, prayed that the little shimmy of terror moving through his body wasn't obvious. Eddie had wiped the disk clean, he'd said. Reformatted it. Nothing was there from that night.

Nick could only imagine what the camera image would look like. The lurching of a man in a too-big flapping overcoat suddenly illuminated by the outside lights. The flailing hands. The way the man had crumpled to the ground. Or did one of the cameras capture the act itself, Nick holding the pistol, his face contorted with fear and anger, pulling the trigger? The gun bucking up and back, the smoke cloud. The murder itself.

But that was all gone.

Eddie had assured him of that. Eddie, whose breath had stunk of booze. Who was always cocky but never thoughtful and thorough, certainly not in the rink. Who'd always acted hastily, impulsively.

Who might have missed something.

Done it wrong. Failed to reformat it properly.

Might have fucked up.

"Also, Mr. Conover, we're going to need the keys to both of your cars, if you don't mind."

"My cars?"

"The Chevy Suburban that you drive, and the minivan. We'll want to dust for prints and so on."

"How come?"

"In case Stadler tried to get in, steal one of the cars, whatever."

Nick nodded, logy and dazed, reached into his pants pocket for his key ring. As he did so, he noticed a swarm of activity in his study, straight down the hall. "I'm going to need to check my e-mail," he said.

Detective Rhimes cocked her head. "I'm sorry?"

"My study. I need to get in there. I have work to do."

"I'm sorry, Mr. Conover, but this might take a while."

"How long are we talking?"

"Hard to say. The evidence techs move in mysterious ways." She smiled, her face lighting up, really lovely. "Oh, one quick question, if you don't mind?"

"Sure."

"About your security director—Mr. Rinaldi?"

"What about him?"

"Oh," she said with a quiet laugh, "I suppose it's like 'who will guard the guards' or something, but I'm sure you did a background check on him before you hired him to be your security director."

"Of course," Nick said. A background check was precisely what he hadn't done. Eddie was an old friend. Well, a buddy, maybe. Whatever that meant.

"What do you know about his police career?" she asked.

There was a yellow tape across the entrance to his study. It said, "Crime Scene—Do Not Cross."

Crime scene, he thought.

You don't know.

Two evidence techs in there, wearing rubber gloves. One was dusting the doors, door frames, light switch plates, the desk, the wood frame and glass panes of the French doors, with fluorescent orange powder. The other was vacuuming the carpet with a strange-looking handheld vacuum cleaner, a black barrel, long straight nozzle.

Nick watched for a moment, cleared his throat to get their attention, and said, "You don't need to do that. We've got a housekeeper."

A lame joke, pathetic even. Offensive, probably. *They* didn't have housekeepers.

The tech with the vacuum cleaner gave him a hard look.

Nick let it slide. They were dusting for fingerprints, but there was no way they were going to find anything incriminating. Stadler wasn't inside the house on the night of his murder. He'd dropped to the ground, easily twenty feet from the French doors.

That wasn't what bothered him.

What bothered him was why they seemed to be focusing on the study. There were lots of other rooms in the house where Stadler might plausibly have gotten in. Why the study?

Did they *know* something?

"Mr. Conover, do you have a key to this drawer?"

A confident baritone. One of the techs was pointing at the locked drawer where he'd kept the gun Eddie had given him.

He felt his entire body seize up.

"Key's right in the top middle drawer," Nick said mildly. "Real high security."

He flashed on the box of cartridges in the drawer next to the gun. A green and gold cardboard box, the words REMINGTON and GOLDEN SABER in white lettering.

Eddie had taken them away, right?

When he took the gun?

Nick didn't remember anymore. That night was such a blur.

Please God oh please God let them be gone the bullets make them gone.

He waited. Holding his breath, while the tech opened the big middle desk drawer, located the key at once, knelt down to unlock the bottom drawer.

The back of his shirt collar was seriously damp now. Downright wet.

My life is in this anonymous guy's hands right now. He has the power to lock me away forever.

There's no death penalty in Michigan, he found himself thinking. He'd never thought about it before, never had a reason to think about it. No death penalty.

Life in prison, though.

That was in the balance.

The drawer slid open, the tech bent over.

A second went by, two, then three.

The vacuum cleaner was turned off.

Nick felt like vomiting. He stood there on the other side of the yellow crime-scene tape like some casual sightseer, a tourist, and he waited.

The tech got to his feet. Nothing in his hands.

Maybe the drawer was empty.

If one stray bullet had rolled to the back of the drawer . . .

No, the tech would have taken out his camera and taken a picture if he'd found something.

The drawer had to be empty.

Nick felt relief. Temporary, maybe. Momentary.

He stood there watching the tech, the one who'd been vacuuming, take out a plastic bottle with a pistol grip and begin spraying a section of the hand-plastered walls around the light switch.

Decora rocker switch, Nick thought. Laura had replaced all the light switches in the house with Decora rocker switches, which she insisted were much more elegant. Nick had no opinion on Decora rockers. He'd never really thought much about light switches before.

The guy started spraying the bottom of the French doors, then the carpet.

He heard the two techs murmuring, heard the one with the plastic bottle say something like, "Miss my Luminol."

The other one said something in a low voice, something about a daylight search, and then the first one said, "But Christ, this LCV shit is messy."

Nick didn't know what they were talking about. He felt stupid standing there on the threshold of his own study, gawking and eavesdropping.

The first one said, "stain's gonna be degraded."

The second one said something about "DNA match."

Nick swallowed hard. "Stain" had to mean blood. They were looking for bloodstains on the door handles, on the door, on the carpet. Bloodstains that weren't visible to the naked eye, which had maybe been wiped away but not well enough.

Well, at least I'm safe on that, Nick thought. Stadler never entered the house.

But his brain was not cooperating. It kicked up a thought that made the adrenaline surge, made him break out in sweat once again.

Stadler had bled, fairly profusely.

The black puddle of blood.

Nick had walked up to him, kicked at the body with his bare feet. Maybe even stood in the blood, who knows, he couldn't remember.

Then walked back into the house.

Onto the carpet. To call Eddie.

He'd never *noticed* any bloodstains on the carpet, and neither did Eddie, but how much did it take? What scintilla of evidence, carried into the study on the soles of his bare feet from the puddle beside Stadler's body? Mere droplets perhaps, invisible to the naked eye, smeared onto the wall-to-wall carpet unseen, soaking into the woolen fibers, waiting to announce their presence?

The tech who wasn't spraying the carpet turned around to look at Nick's desk, noticed Nick still standing there.

Quickly Nick said something, just so they wouldn't think he was watching in terrified fascination, as he was. "Is that stuff gonna come off my carpet?"

The tech who was spraying shrugged.

"And what about all that powder?" Nick went on, fake-indignant. "How the hell am I going to get that out?"

The tech with the spray bottle turned around, blinked a few times, a lazy, malevolent grin on his face. "You got a housekeeper," he said.

64

"Eddie." Nick, calling from his study, scared out of his mind.

"What?" He sounded annoyed.

"They were here today."

"I know. Here too. It's bullshit. They're trying to put a scare into you."

"Yeah, well, it worked. They found something."

A pause. "Huh?"

"They found a metal fragment. They think it might be a piece of a shell casing."

"*What*? They recovered a shell casing?"

"No, a piece of one."

"I don't get it." Eddie's swaggering confidence had evaporated. "I recovered both shells, and I don't remember any fragmentation. You said you fired two rounds, right?"

"I think so."

"You *think* so? Now you *think* so?"

"I was freaked out, Eddie. Everything was a blur."

"You told me you fired two rounds, so when I found two shells, I stopped looking. I coulda spent all night on that fucking lawn walking around with the flashlight."

"You think they really might have a piece of ammunition?" Nick said, a quaver in his voice.

"The *fuck* do I know?" Eddie said. "Shit. Tell you this, I gotta start digging into this lady detective. See what skeletons she has in her closet."

"I think she's a good Christian, Eddie."

"Great. Maybe I'll find something real good."

And he hung up the phone.

"We got shit, is what we got," said Bugbee.

"The search warrant," Audrey began.

"Was as broad as I could make it. Not just .380s, but any firearms of any description. On top of the usual. No blood or fibers in Rinaldi's car anywhere."

"We didn't expect he took the body home with him."

"Obviously not."

"Any .380s?"

Bugbee shook his head. "But here's the weird thing. Guy's got a couple of those wall-mounted locking handgun racks, right? Found it in a closet behind some clothes, bolted onto the wall. Each one holds three guns, but two of them are missing."

"Missing, or not there? Maybe he only has four."

Bugbee smiled, held up a finger. "Ah, that's the thing. There's two guns in one, two in the other, and you can see from the dust patterns that there used to be two more. They've been removed."

Audrey nodded. "Two."

"I'm saying one is the murder weapon."

"And the other?"

"Just a guess. But maybe there's a reason he didn't want us to find that one too. Two unregistered handguns."

Audrey turned to go back to her cubicle when a thought occurred to her. "You didn't warn him you were doing the search?"

"Come on."

"Then how'd he know you were coming? How'd he know to remove the guns?"

"Now you get it."

"Conover knew we were coming to search his house," Audrey said. "I'm sure he told Rinaldi, and Rinaldi knew it was only a matter of time before we searched his house too."

Bugbee considered for a few seconds.

"Maybe that's all it is," he conceded.

An e-mail popped up on Audrey's computer from Kevin Lenehan in Forensic Services, asking her to come by.

The techs in the Forensic Services Unit all went to crime scenes, but some of them had their specialties, too. If you wanted to get a fingerprint off the sticky side of a piece of duct tape, you went to Koopmans. If you wanted a serial number restoration, you took it to Brian. If you wanted a court exhibit, an aerial map, a scene diagram rendered in a hurry, you went to Koopmans or Julie or Brigid.

Kevin Lenehan was the tech most often entrusted with, or perhaps saddled with, retrieving information from computers or video capture work. That meant that while his co-workers got jammed with all the street calls, he had to waste vast amounts of time watching shadowy, indistinct video images of robberies taken by store surveillance cameras. Or poring over the video from the in-car cameras that went on automatically when an officer flipped on his overheads and sirens.

He was scrawny, late twenties, had a wispy goatee and long greasy hair that was either light brown or dark blond, though it was hard to tell, because Audrey had never seen him with his hair recently washed.

The rectangular black metal box that housed the digital video recorder from Conover's security system was on his workbench, connected to a computer monitor.

"Hey, Audrey," he said. "Heard about your little bluff."

"Bluff?" Audrey said innocently.

"The bullet fragment thing. Brigid told me. Never knew you had it in you."

She smiled modestly. "You do what it takes. How's this coming?"

"I'm kinda not clear on what you wanted," Kevin said. "You're looking for a homicide, right? But nothing like that here."

It was too easy, Audrey thought. "So what is on there?"

"Like three weeks of the moon moving behind the clouds. Lights going off and on. Coupla deer. Cars going in and out of the driveway. Dad, kids, whatever. Am I looking for something in particular?"

"A murder would be nice," she said.

"Sorry to disappoint you."

"If the cameras recorded it, it's going to be on there, right?" She pointed at the box.

"Right. This bad boy's a Maxtor hundred-and-twenty gig drive connected to sixteen cameras, set to record at seven-point-five frames per second."

"Could it be missing anything?"

"Missing how?"

"I don't know, erased or something?"

"Not far's I can tell."

"Isn't three weeks a long time to record on a hard drive that size?"

Lenehan looked at her differently, with more respect. "Yeah, in fact, it is. If this baby was in a twenty-four-hour store, it would recycle after three days. But it's residential, and it's got motion technology, so it doesn't use up much disk space."

"Meaning that the camera starts when there's a movement that sets off the motion detector and gets the cameras rolling?"

"Sort of. It's all done by software here. Not external motion sensors. The software is continually sampling the picture, and whenever a certain number of pixels change, it starts the recording process."

"It recycles when the disk gets full?"

"Right. First in, first out."

"Could it have recycled over the part I'm interested in?"

"You're interested in the early morning hours of the sixteenth, you said, and that's all there."

"I'm interested in anything from the evening of the fifteenth to, say, five in the morning on the sixteenth. But the alarm went off at two in the morning, so I'm most interested in two in the morning. Well, 2:07, to be exact. An eleven-minute period."

Kevin swiveled around on his metal stool to look at the monitor. "Sorry.

Just misses it. The recording starts Wednesday the sixteenth. Three-eighteen A.M."

"You mean Tuesday the fifteenth, right? That's when it was put in. Some time on the afternoon of the fifteenth."

"Hey, whatever, but the recording starts Wednesday the sixteenth. Three-eighteen in the morning. About an hour after the time you're interested in."

"Shoot. I don't get it."

He spun back around. "Can't help you there."

"You sure the eleven-minute segment couldn't have just been erased?"

Kevin paused. "No sign of that. It just started at—"

"Could someone have recycled it?"

"Manually? Sure. Have to be someone who knows the system, knows what he's doing, of course."

Eddie Rinaldi, she thought. "Then it would have recorded over the part I'm interested in?"

"Right. Records over the oldest part first."

"Do you have the ability to bring it back?"

"Like, unerase it? Maybe someone does. That's kind of beyond what I know how to do. The State, maybe?"

"The State would mean six months at least."

"At least. And who knows if they can do it? I don't even know if it can be done."

"Kevin, do you think it's worth looking at again?"

"For what, though?"

"See if you can figure anything else about it. Such as whether you can find any traces. Anything that proves the recording was recycled over or deleted or whatever."

Kevin waggled his head from one side to the other. "Take a fair amount of time."

"But you're good. And you're fast."

"And I'm also way behind on my other work. I've got a boatload of vid-caps to do for Sergeant Noyce and Detective Johnson."

"That serial robber case."

"Yeah. Plus Noyce wants me to watch like two days worth of tape from a store robbery, looking for a guy in a black Raiders jacket with white Nike Air shoes."

"Sounds like fun."

"Eye-crossing fun. He wants it done—"

"Yesterday. Oh yes, I know Jack."

"I mean, you want to talk to Noyce, get him to move you up in the queue, go ahead. But I gotta do what they tell me to do, you know?"

65

The next morning was jam-packed with complicated, if tedious, paperwork, which Nick was actually grateful for. It kept his mind off what was happening, kept him from obsessing over what the cops might have found in the house. And that fragment of a shell casing had ruined his sleep last night. He'd tossed and turned, alternating between blank terror and a steady, pulsing anxiety.

There was a bunch of stuff from the corporate counsel's office outlining the patent lawsuit they wanted to file against one of Stratton's chief competitors, Knoll. Stephanie Alstrom's staff insisted that Knoll had basically ripped off a patented Stratton design for an ergonomic keyboard tray.

Stratton filed dozens of these complaints every year; Knoll probably did too. Kept the corporate attorneys employed. The legal department salivated at the prospect of litigation; Nick preferred arbitration, pretty much down the line. It kept the out-of-pocket costs down, and even if Stratton won the ruling, Knoll would have already figured out a workaround that would pass legal muster. Go after Knoll in a public courtroom, and you blow all confidentiality— your secrets are laid out there for every other competitor to rip off. Then there'd be subpoenas all over the place; Stratton would have to hand over all sorts of secret design documents. Forget it. Plus, in Nick's experience, the awarded damages rarely added up to much once you subtracted your legal expenses. He scrawled *ARB* on the top sheet.

After an hour of sitting at his home base, going over this sort of crap,

Nick's shoulders were already starting to ache. The truth was, home base wasn't feeling especially homey these days. His eyes settled on one of the family photographs. Laura, the kids, Barney. Two down, three to go, he thought. The curse of the House of Conover.

He remembered a line he'd seen quoted somewhere: Maybe this world is another planet's hell. There had to be a bunch of corollaries to that. He had made someone else's world a hell, and someone had made his world a hell. Supply-chain management for human suffering.

An instant-message from Marjorie popped up, even though she was sitting not ten feet away, on the other side of the panel. She didn't want to break his concentration—she knew how fragile it tended to be.

```
The usual for lunch today, right?
```

Oh, right. Nick remembered: the regular weekly lunch with Scott. Which was just about the last thing he felt like doing.

He wanted to confront Scott, tell him to get the fuck out and go back home to McKinsey. But he couldn't, not yet. Not until he got to the bottom of what exactly was going on. And the truth was, he no longer had the power to fire Scott if he wanted to. Which right now he very much did.

He typed:

```
OK, thanks.
```

He noticed that there was an e-mail in his in-box from Cassie; he could tell from the subject line.

He hadn't given her his e-mail address, hadn't gotten an e-mail from her before, and he hesitated before clicking on it:

```
From: ChakraGrrl@hotmail.com
To: Nconover@Strattoninc.com
Subject: From Cassie
Nick—Where's my grocery delivery boy been? Free for lunch
today? Come over between 12:30 and 1? I'll supply the
sandwiches.
C.
```

He felt his spirits lift at once, and he hit Reply:

```
I'm there.
```

"Marge," he said into the intercom, "change in plans. Tell Scott I'm not going to be able to make lunch today, okay?"

"Okay. Want me to give a reason?"

Nick paused. "No."

On the way to the elevator he passed Scott, who was coming out of the men's room. "Got your message," Scott said. "Everything okay?"

"Everything's fine. Just got really hectic all of a sudden."

"You'll do anything to avoid talking numbers," Scott said with a grin.

"You got me figured out," Nick said, grinning right back as he headed for the elevator bank. A couple of women from Payroll got in on the floor below, smiled shyly at him. One of them said, "Hey, Mr. Conover."

He said, "Hey, Wanda. Hey, Barb." They both seemed surprised, and pleased, that he knew their names. But Nick made it a point to know as many Stratton employees by name as possible; he knew how good it was for morale. *And there's fewer and fewer of them all the time*, he thought mordantly. *Makes it easier.*

When the elevator stopped at the third floor, Eddie got in, said, "It's the big dog."

Something awfully disrespectful about that, especially in front of other employees. "Eddie," Nick said.

"Had a feeling you were headed out to, uh, 'lunch,'" Eddie said. The way he dropped little quotation marks around the word "lunch" was unnerving. *Does he know where I'm going? How could he?* And then Nick remembered that he'd asked Eddie to start looking closely at Scott's e-mail. He wondered whether Eddie had taken that as an opportunity to look at Nick's e-mail too. If true, that would be outrageous—but how the hell could he prevent Eddie from doing it? He was the goddamned security director.

Nick just gave him a stony look, which would be missed by Wanda and Barb from Payroll.

"I'll walk you to your car," Eddie said. He was carrying an umbrella.

Nick nodded.

They walked together, silently, through the main lobby, past the waterfall that some feng shui expert had insisted they put there to repair a "blocked energy feeling" at the entrance. Nick had thought that was complete and utter bullshit, but he went along with it anyway, the way he'd always avoided stepping on cracks in the sidewalk so as not to break his mother's back. Anyway, the waterfall looked good there, that was the main thing.

Nick could see through the big glass doors that it was raining. That explained the umbrella, but had Eddie planned to go out for lunch, or did he "happen" to run into Nick in the elevator—by design? Nick wondered but said nothing. He considered, too, asking Eddie about what Detective Rhimes had told him—that Eddie had left the Grand Rapids police force "under a cloud of suspicion." But he didn't know why she'd told him that. Was she trying to put a wedge between the two men? If so, that was a clever way to do it. If Eddie had lied to him about why he'd left police work, what else might he have lied about?

He'd ask Eddie. Not yet, though.

Outside, Eddie opened the big golf umbrella and held it up for Nick. When they'd walked a good distance away from the building, Eddie said, "Foxy Brown better watch her ass."

"I don't know what you're talking about."

"Come on, man. Cleopatra Jones. Sheba baby."

"I'm in a hurry, Eddie. It's been fun free-associating with you."

Eddie gripped Nick's shoulder. "Your black lady detective, man. The one who's trying to roast our nuts over the fire." The rain thrummed loudly on the umbrella. "The Negro lady who's got it in for you because you fucking *laid off her husband*," he said ferociously, drawing out the words.

"You're kidding me."

"Think I'd joke about something like that? About something that should get her fucking thrown off the case?"

"Who's her husband?"

"Some fucking nobody, man, worked on the shop floor spraying paint or whatever. Point is, Stratton laid him off, and now his wife's coming to collect your scalp." He shook his head. "And I say that ain't right."

"She shouldn't be investigating us," Nick said. "That's outrageous."

"That's what I say. Bitch gets disqualified."

"How do we do that?"

"Leave it to me." His smile was almost a leer. "Meanwhile, I got some interesting stuff on your man Scott."

Nick looked at him questioningly.

"You asked me to poke into his e-mail and shit."

"What'd you get?"

"You know what Scott's been doing just about every weekend for the last two months?"

"Burning hamburgers," Nick said. "I was just over there last Saturday."

"Not last Saturday, but almost every other weekend. He's been flying to Boston. Think he's visiting his sick aunt Gertrude?"

"He's getting the corporate discount through the travel office," Nick said.

Eddie nodded. "I guess he figures you don't look at travel expenses—not your job."

"I do have a company to run. Run into the ground, some would say."

"Plus a shitload of phone calls back and forth between him and that guy Todd Muldaur at Fairfield Equity Partners. Kinda doubt it's all social chitchat, right?"

"Any idea what they're talking about?"

"Nah, that's just phone records. Voice mails I can hack into, but Scotty-boy's a good camper. Deletes all voice mails when he's done listening to them. Him and Todd-O e-mail each other, but it's all kinda generic stuff like you'd expect—you know, here's the monthly numbers, or shit like that. Scotty must know e-mails aren't safe. Maybe that's why, when he's got something he wants to keep quiet, he uses encryption."

"*Encryption?*"

"You got it. My techs intercepted a couple dozen encrypted documents coming and going between Scotty and Todd-O."

Nick couldn't think of any possible reason why Scott would be sending or receiving encrypted documents. Then again, he couldn't think of a reason why Scott would make a secret trip to China either.

"What are they about?"

"Don't know yet, seeing as how they're encrypted. But my guys are crackerjacks. They'll get 'em open for me. Let you know the second they do."

"Okay." They'd reached Nick's Suburban, and he pressed the remote to unlock it.

"Cool. Enjoy your"—Eddie cleared his throat—"lunch."

"You implying something, Eddie?"

"No umbrella or raincoat?" Eddie said. "Don't you have a nice view out of your office? You musta seen it was raining."

"I was too busy working."

"Well, you don't want to go out without protection," Eddie said with a wink. "Not where you're going."

And he walked off.

66

When he arrived at Cassie's, the rain had turned into a full-fledged downpour. He parked in her driveway and raced to the front door, rang the bell, stood there getting soaked. No answer; he rang again.

No answer. He rang a third time, looked at his watch. It was 12:40, so he was on time. She'd said between 12:30 and 1:00. Of course, that was ambiguous; maybe she'd wanted him to specify a time.

Drenched, shivering from the cold rain, he knocked on the door and then rang again. He'd have to change his clothes back at the office, where he kept a spare set. It wasn't exactly cool for the CEO of Stratton to walk around headquarters looking like a drowned rat.

Finally he turned the knob and was surprised when it opened. He went in, called, "Cassie?"

No answer.

He walked into the kitchen. "Cassie, it's Nick. You here?"

Nothing.

He went to the living room, but she wasn't there either. In the back of his mind he worried. She seemed a little fragile, and her father had just died, and who the hell knew what she might do to herself?

"Cassie," he shouted, louder still. She wasn't downstairs. The blinds were drawn in the living room. He opened a slat and looked out, but she wasn't out there either.

Nervous, he went upstairs, calling her name. The second floor was even darker and dingier than the downstairs. No wonder she didn't want him going up here. Two doors on either side of a short hallway, and two at both ends. None of the doors was closed. He started at the room at the far end of the hall. It was a bedroom, furnished with not much more than a full-size bed and a dresser. The bed was made. The room had the look and smell of vacancy, as if no one had been in here for a long time. He assumed it was Andrew Stadler's room. He left and went into the room at the other end of the hall, where a sloppily unmade bed, a discarded pair of jeans turned inside out on the floor, and the odor of patchouli and cigarettes told him it was Cassie's.

"Cassie," he called again as he tried another other room. It smelled strongly of paint, and he knew even before he entered that this was the room Cassie was using as her studio. Sure enough, there was a half-finished canvas on an easel, a weird-looking picture, a woman surrounded by bright strokes of orange and yellow. Other canvases leaned against the walls, and all of them seemed to be variations on the same bizarre image of a black-haired young woman, naked, her mouth contorted in a scream. It looked a little like that famous painting by Edvard Munch, *The Scream*. In each one, the woman was surrounded by concentric strokes of yellow and orange, like a sunset, or maybe fire. They were disturbing paintings, actually, but she was pretty good, Nick thought, even if he didn't know much about art.

Well, she wasn't here either, which meant that something really was wrong, or they'd somehow gotten their signals crossed in the couple of hours since he'd sent his e-mail. Maybe she'd changed her mind, or had to go out, and had e-mailed back to tell him that, and the e-mail never arrived. That happened.

He tried the last door, but this was a bathroom. He took a much-needed piss, then took a bath towel and began blotting his shirt and pants. He put the towel back on the rod, and then, before he left, he took a peek in the mirror-fronted medicine cabinet, hating himself for snooping.

Apart from the usual cosmetics and women's products, he found a couple of brown plastic pharmacy bottles labeled Zyprexa and lithium. He knew lithium was for manic-depressives, but he didn't know what the other one was. He saw Andrew Stadler's name printed on the labels.

Her dad's meds, he thought. Still hasn't thrown them out.

"They're not all his, you know."

Cassie's voice made him jump. He reddened instantly.

"That lithium—that's mine," she said. "I hate it. Makes me fat and gives me acne. It's like being a teenager all over again." She waved an unopened pack of cigarettes at him, and he realized at once where she'd been.

"Cassie—Jesus, I'm sorry." He didn't even try to pretend he was looking for an Advil or something. "I feel like such a shit. I didn't mean to snoop. I mean, I *was* snooping, but I shouldn't have—"

"Would you snoop around to find out whether it's raining? It's pretty much staring you in the face. I mean, when you meet a person who was valedictorian of her high school, eight hundreds on her SATs, got into every college she applied to, and she's basically doing fuck-all in the world, well, you've got to wonder. How come she isn't pulling down six figures at Corning or working on signal-transduction pathways at Albert Einstein College of Medicine?"

"Listen, Cassie . . ."

Cassie made a circular gesture at her temple with her forefinger, the sign for crazy. "You just got to assume that this girl is a few clowns short of a circus."

"Don't talk that way."

"Would you feel better if I put on a white coat and talked about catecholamine levels in the medial forebrain of the hypothalamus? Put my science education to work? Is that less offensive? It isn't any more informative."

"I don't think you're crazy."

"Crazy is as crazy does," Cassie said in a cornpone Forrest Gump voice.

"Come on, Cassie."

"Let's go downstairs."

Sitting together on the nubby brown couch in the living room, Cassie kept talking. "Full scholarship to Carnegie Mellon. I wanted to go to MIT, but my stepdad didn't want to spend a red cent on me, and even with financial aid it was going to be a stretch. Freshman year was tough. Not the course work so much as the classmates. My sorority house burns down freshman year, and half the girls are killed. Blew me away. I mean, I came back here and didn't want to leave my room. Never went back to college."

"You were traumatized."

"I also got addicted to cocaine and Valium, you name it. I was self-medicating, of course. Took me a few years before I figured out I had 'bipolar tendencies.' Was hospitalized for six months with depression. But the meds they put me on worked pretty well."

"Better living through chemistry, I guess."

"Yeah. By then, of course, I'd wandered off the Path."

"The Path? That some religious thing?"

"The Path, Nick. The Path. You went to Michigan State, studied business, got a job at the Vatican of Office Furniture, and you were pretty much set so long as you kept working hard and kept your nose clean and didn't piss too many people off."

"I get it. And you . . . ?"

"I got off the Path. Or I lost my way. Maybe I was in the woods and a big gust of wind came and blew leaves all over the path and I just headed off in the wrong direction. Maybe birds ate the damn bread-crumb trail. I'm not saying my life lacks a purpose. It's just that maybe the purpose is to provide a cautionary tale for everyone else."

"I don't think the world is that unforgiving," Nick said.

"People like you never do," Cassie said.

"It's never too late."

Cassie stepped over to him, pressed herself against his chest. "Isn't it pretty to think so," she murmured.

67

Noyce called Audrey into his office and asked her to sit down.

"I got a call from the security director at Stratton," he said.

"He can't have been happy."

"He was ripshit, Audrey. About both him and Conover."

"I can't speak for Roy, but I know my team was as careful as can be. We didn't trash the place."

"I don't think Bugbee was as careful."

"That doesn't surprise me. Mine was a consent search. Roy had a warrant."

"And Roy is Roy. Listen." He leaned forward, rested his elbows on a bare patch of desk, rested his chin on his hands. "Rinaldi hit me with something we have to take seriously."

"They're threatening us with legal action," Audrey said, half-kidding.

"He knows about Leon."

"About Leon."

"I'm surprised, frankly, it took him this long. But he obviously did some looking into you, and Leon's name came up."

"You knew Leon was laid off from Stratton. I didn't keep that from you."

"Of course not. But I didn't really weigh that as carefully as I should have. It didn't occur to me, frankly."

"Everyone in this town's got someone in their family who's been laid off by Stratton."

"Just about."

"You start taking everyone off this case who has any connection to Stratton, and pretty soon there'd be no one left. I mean lab techs and crime scene—"

"This is always something we have to be hypersensitive about."

"Jack, I was assigned to this case randomly. My name came up on the board. I didn't request it."

"I know."

"And when I started it, there was no connection to the Stratton Corporation."

"Granted, but—"

"Let me finish. Leon's situation has nothing to do with this. I'm following the leads here. I'm not on any witch hunt. You know that."

"*I* know it, Aud. Of course I know that. But if and when this comes to trial, I don't want anything fucking it up. If I go to the prosecutor, he's going to say he doesn't want you involved—this has to be clean and pristine. And he'll be right. Any DA is going to worry that this'll look like payback on your part."

She sat up straight in the uncomfortable chair, looked at her boss directly. "Are you taking me off the case?"

He sighed. "I'm not taking you off the case. That's not it. I mean, maybe I should. The Stratton security guy is demanding it. But the fact is, you're one of our best."

"That's not true, and you know it. My clearance rate is pretty darned mediocre."

He laughed. "Your modesty is refreshing. I wish everyone around here had some of that. No, your clearance rate could be higher, but that's because you're still getting your chops. You tend to use a microscope when binoculars are what you want."

"Pardon me?"

"You do waste time, sometimes, looking superclose at evidence that doesn't lead anywhere. Going up blind alleys, barking up the wrong trees, all that. I think that gets better with experience. The more cases you do, the more developed your instinct gets. You learn what's worth following up and what isn't."

She nodded.

"You know I'm your biggest fan."

"I know it," she said, feeling a surge of affection toward the man that was almost love. Maybe it was love.

"I pushed you to apply for the job, and I pushed you through. You know how many hoops you had to jump through."

An abashed smile. She remembered how many interviews she'd had to do. Just when she thought she'd clinched it, someone else asked to interview her. Noyce had steered it all the way. "The race thing," she said.

"The woman thing. That was really it. But look, a lot of people are waiting for you to fail."

"I don't see it that way."

"I do, and believe me, I know. A good number of people around here are waiting for you to trip and fall flat on your face. And I don't want that to happen."

"I don't either."

"Go back to the Leon issue for a second. Whether you say it's an issue or not. We're all susceptible to being driven by unconscious biases. Protective instincts. I know you, and you have a lot of love in your heart, and you hate seeing what your husband's going through. You hate seeing him hurt in any way." Audrey started to object, but Noyce said, "Hear me out. My turn, okay?"

"Okay."

"You've got a forest of facts, of evidence and clues. You've got to find a path through that forest. I mean, the stuff about the hydroseed—that's damned good police work."

"Thank you."

"But we don't know, do we, what that means? Did Stadler walk around Nicholas Conover's premises? Sure. No one's disputing that. Did he crawl around the property on his hands and knees, get dirt under his fingernails? Sure, why not. But does that mean Conover did it?"

"It's a piece of the puzzle."

"But is the puzzle one of those easy twenty-piece wooden jigsaws that little kids do? Or is it one of those impossible thousand-piece jobs my wife likes to do? That's the thing. A hunch and some hydroseed isn't enough."

"The body was too clean," she said. "Most of the trace evidence was removed by someone who knew what he was doing."

"Maybe."

"Rinaldi's an ex-homicide detective."

"Don't have to be a cop to know about trace evidence."

"We caught Conover in a lie," she went on. "He said he slept through the night, the night Stadler was killed. But at two in the morning he called Rinaldi. That's in the phone records."

"They give different stories?"

"Well, when I asked Conover about it, he said maybe he got the day wrong, maybe that was the night his alarm went off and he called Rinaldi to check it out, since Rinaldi's staff put it in."

"Well, so maybe he did get the day wrong."

"The bottom line," Audrey said, exasperated, "is that they knew Stadler was stalking Conover. He butchered the family dog. Then he turns up dead. It just can't be a coincidence."

"You sound certain of it."

"It's my instinct."

"Your instinct, Aud?—don't take this the wrong way—but your instinct isn't exactly developed yet."

She nodded again, hoping her irritation didn't show in her face.

"The bullet fragments," he said. "At Conover's house. What was that all about?"

She hesitated. "We didn't find any bullet fragments."

"That's not what you told Conover. You said you found a piece of metal. You said it was a fragment from a projectile." Rinaldi must have told him this. How else could he know?

"I didn't say that."

"No, but you let him think that, didn't you?"

"Yes," she confessed.

"That was a little show you put on for Conover, wasn't it?" he said sadly. "That was all a bluff, designed to get Conover to break down and admit it. Am I right?"

She nodded, hotly embarrassed. "I hardly think I'm the first homicide detective to try a bluff."

"No, you're not. Far from it. I've done my share, believe me. But we're dealing with the CEO of the Stratton Corporation. That means we're under the klieg lights here. Everything you do, everything *we* do, is going to be scrutinized."

"I understand. But you know, if my little bluff pushes him closer to an admission, it'll be worth it."

Noyce sighed. "Audrey. Okay, so the crack on Stadler's body was really lemon drops. Whether the guy got swindled or the thing was a setup, we just don't know. But you got a schizo guy wandering around the dog pound in the middle of the night, it's not so surprising he gets shot, right?"

"None of the informants knew anything about it."

"Stuff goes on down there, our informants only know one little slice of it."

"But boss—"

"I don't want to be a backseat driver on this one, but before you go off trying to sweat the CEO and the security director of a major corporation for conspiracy to murder some crazy guy—two men who have an awful lot to lose—you want to make sure you're not being seduced by a great story. I mean, your theory is sure a heck of a lot sexier than some drug killing. But this case mustn't be about entertainment value. It's got to be about hard-nosed police work. Right?"

"Right."

"For your own sake. And ours."

"I understand."

"I can't help you if you don't keep me fully informed, okay? From now on, I want you to keep me in the loop. Help me help you. I don't want you getting burned on this."

68

Eddie lived in a small condominium complex called Pebble Creek. It had been built about half a dozen years ago, and consisted of four five-story buildings—stained wood, red brick, big windows—set on a big square of grass and gravel. Each of the condos had its own white-trellised balcony, where residents had put out things like folding chairs and trees in pots. It was a look Nick had heard described as neo-Prairie. No creek anywhere, but plenty of pebbles around the parking lot. There were homey-looking office parks that looked like this—the Conovers' pediatric dentist was located in one—and some people might have found Pebble Creek a little officey-looking for a home. Eddie wouldn't have been one of them.

"Be it ever so humble," Eddie said as he let Nick in. He was wearing black jeans and a gray knit shirt that was furred from one too many tumbles in the dryer. "Welcome to the Edward J. Rinaldi fuck pad."

Nick had never visited Eddie at his home before, but he wasn't surprised at what he saw. A lot of glass, a lot of chrome. Blue-gray carpeting. Black lacquered furniture and booze cabinet, big mirrors on the wall behind it. The biggest things in the room were two big flat Magnapan speakers, in silver, standing at either side of a black sofa like shoji screens. Everything more or less matched. In the bedroom, Eddie showed off an immense waterbed that he said got so much use he'd had to replace the liner three times already.

"So what do you know?" Eddie said, walking Nick into the area of his living room he no doubt called his "entertainment center," though maybe he had a more colorful name for it.

"Well," Nick said, "I know that 'J' was the last letter added to the alphabet."

"No shit? How did they get by without it? Jacking off. Jheri Curl. Jism. Jesus. Jock straps. You got all the basics of civilization right there." Eddie opened the drinks cabinet, twisted open a bottle of Scotch. "Not to mention J & B. And Jameson's. What'll you have?"

"I'm okay," Nick said.

"Yeah," Eddie said, settling into a chair covered in fake silver-gray suede, and putting his feet on the glass coffee table, next to a couple of books titled *Beyer on Speed* and *Play Poker Like the Pros*. "I think maybe you are."

"What makes you say that?" Nick sat on the adjoining sofa, which was covered in the same fake suede.

"'Cause, Nicky, I got something for you. Figured you wouldn't mind coming over to my place to look at a couple of e-mails our boy Scotty deleted a couple of weeks ago. I guess he figures if you delete something it's gone, poof. Doesn't realize all e-mail's archived on the server. So who's Martin Lai?"

"Martin Lai. He's our manager for Asia Pacific, out of Hong Kong. In charge of accounting. Truly the deadliest, most stultifyingly dull guy you're ever going to meet. Human ether."

"Well, check it out." He handed Nick a couple of pages.

To: SMcNally@Strattoninc.com
From: MLai@Strattoninc.com
Scott,
Can you please confirm for me that the USD $10 million that was wired out of Stratton Asia Ventures LLC this morning to a numbered account, no attached name, was done at your behest? The SWIFT code indicates that the funds went to the Seng Fung Bank-Macau. This entirely depletes the fund's assets. Please reply soonest.
Thank you,
Martin Lai

```
Managing Director, Accounting
Stratton Inc., Hong Kong.
```

And then, Scott's immediate reply:

```
To: MLai@Strattoninc.com
From: SMcNally@Strattoninc.com
This is fine — just part of the usual process of repatri-
ation of funds in order to avoid tax payments. Thanks for
keeping an eye out, but all is OK.
—Scott
```

When Nick looked up, he said, "Ten million bucks? What's it for?"

"I don't know, but it looks to me like Scotty-Boy's being a little reckless. Playing fast and loose, huh?"

"It does, doesn't it."

"Not like you."

"Huh?"

"*You're* not being reckless at all, right?"

"What's that supposed to mean?"

"What *you're* doing, man, is a fuck of a lot stupider than whatever Scott McNally's up to. You better check yourself before you wreck yourself, bro, or we're both going to the slammer. And don't think I'm going to take the rap for you."

"What the hell are you talking about?"

Eddie's gaze bore down on him relentlessly. "You want to explain what the fuck you're doing layin' pipe with Stadler's daughter?"

Nick was speechless for a moment. "Are you *spying* on me, Eddie? That's how you knew where I was going that day, in the rain, isn't it? You have no business monitoring my e-mail or my phone lines—"

"It's like we're on a road trip together, Nick. We gotta be taking the same turns. You need to be watching the speed limit, observing all traffic signs. And right here, see, there's no Merge sign. Sign says DO NOT ENTER. Are you hearing me? Because it's real important that you do." Eddie locked eyes with him. "Do you realize how unbelievably fucking *reckless* you're being?"

"It's totally none of your business, Eddie."

Eddie stretched, raised his arms and put his hands behind his head. Under his arms, sweat stains blackened his gray shirt. "See, that's where you're wrong, buddy. It's very much my business. Because if this keeps up, we could both be making license plates in the shithouse, and I promise you, that's not going to happen."

"This is out of bounds. You lay off her."

"I wish you'd lay off her too. You tell me you're getting rim jobs from the local Brownie troop, I could give a shit. You tell me you're setting up a crystal-meth lab in your basement, I could give a flying fuck. But this thing involves the two of us. You let that piece of ass into your life—for whatever freaky, fucked-up reasons of your own—and you are jeopardizing both of us. What the fuck do you *think* she's after?"

"I don't know what you're talking about."

"News flash," Eddie said in a low voice. "You wasted her old man."

The blood left Nick's face. He was groping for words, but none came.

"You really don't get it, do you? Cops think you might've had something to do with it. Let's say the cops talk to her, maybe let on their suspicions, let it slip, see if she knows anything, right? So this little girl figures she gets close to you— I'm just spitballing here—and maybe she finds something out. Something that could help bring you down. Who the hell knows what? Maybe her thing isn't really getting into your pants. Maybe it's about getting into your *head*."

"That's bullshit. I don't believe it," Nick said. It felt as if his guts had furled into a small hard ball.

That time at Town Grounds.

God, someone who'd do something like that to your family.

I'd want to kill him.

"Believe it," Eddie said. "Entertain the goddamn possibility." He drained his glass, exhaled with a loud alcohol wheeze. "The ass you save could be your own."

"I'm not going to sit here and listen to this," Nick said, his face burning. He stood up, went to the door, but stopped halfway there and turned back around. "You know, Eddie, I'm not so sure you're in any position to be giving lectures about recklessness."

Eddie was staring at him defiantly, an ugly grin on his face.

Nick went on, "I don't think you really leveled with me about why you left the Grand Rapids police."

Eddie's eyes narrowed to slits. "I already told you about that bullshit charge."

"You didn't tell me you were drummed out for pilfering."

"Oh, Christ. Sounds like the kinda thing Cleopatra Jones might have told you. You going to believe her, or me?"

Nick pursed his lips. "I don't know, Eddie. I'm beginning to think I believe her."

"Yeah," Eddie said acidly. "You would, wouldn't you."

"You didn't say it wasn't true."

"Did I cut corners? Sure. But that's it. You can't believe everything you hear. People talk some crazy shit."

69

Audrey's desk phone rang, and she checked the caller ID to make sure it wasn't poor Mrs. Dorsey again. But it was a 616 area code, which meant Grand Rapids, and so she picked it up.

A woman was calling from the Michigan State Police crime lab who identified herself as an IBIS technician named Susan Calloway. She was soft-spoken but authoritative-sounding, her voice arid, devoid of any warmth or personality. She gave the case number she was calling about—it was the Stadler homicide—and said, "The reason I'm calling, Detective, is that I believe you asked us to see if we could match the bullet in your case with any others, correct?"

"That's correct."

"Well, it seems we got a warm hit on IBIS."

Audrey knew a fair amount about the Integrated Ballistics Identification System. She knew it was a computerized database of archived digital images of fired bullets and cartridges that linked police and FBI crime labs across the country. It was sort of like AFIS, the fingerprint-matching network, only the fingerprints here were photographs of bullets and casings.

"A warm hit?" Audrey said. That term she hadn't heard before, though.

"I mean a possible hit," the woman said, her bland voice betraying the tiniest hint of annoyance. "To me, it looks quite similar to a bullet recovered in a no-gun case in Grand Rapids about five, six years ago. Six years ago, to be precise."

"What kind of case?"

"The file class is 0900-01."

That was the Michigan state police offense code for a homicide. So the gun used to kill Stadler had been used six years earlier in another homicide, in Grand Rapids. That could be significant—or it could mean almost nothing. Guns were bought and sold on the black market all the time.

"Really? What do we know about the case?"

"Not much, Detective, I'm sorry to say. I have only the submitting agency's case number, which won't do you much good. But I've already called over there and asked them to bring over the bullet in question so I can do the comparison."

"Thank you."

"And as to the question you're probably about to ask—how long will this take?—the answer is, as soon as I get the bullet from the GR PD."

"Well, I wasn't going to ask that," Audrey said. She thought: only because it would rankle if I *did* ask. If you had no juice with these firearms examiners, you'd better be as sweet as pie. "But I appreciate the information."

Interesting, she thought. Very interesting.

She took a stroll across the squad room and over to Forensic Services, where she found Kevin Lenehan slumped over his desk, arms folded, a dim shadowy tape playing on a TV monitor, numbers racing across the top of the screen.

She put a hand on his shoulder, and he jolted awake.

"Hey," she said, "you don't want to miss the guy in the Nike Air sneakers and the Raiders jacket."

"I hate my life," he said.

"You're too good for this kind of work," she said.

"Tell that to my manager."

"Where is she?"

"Maternity leave. Noyce's my manager these days. Aren't you tight with him?"

"I wouldn't say that. Kevin, listen. Could you take another look at my recorder? I mean, unofficially and off the books and all that?"

"When? In my voluminous spare time?"

"I'll owe you one."

"No offense, but that doesn't really work on me."

"Then how about out of the goodness of your heart?"

"Not much there," he said.

"Kevin."

He blinked. "Let's say, hypothetically now, that I had ten minutes for a coffee break that I decided to spend chasing the great white whale out of a personal obsession. What would I be looking for anyway?"

70

"I just tried Fairfield," Marge said over the intercom, "but Todd's assistant said he's out of the office for the day, so I left a message."

"Can you try his cell? You have the number, right?"

"Of course."

Of course she did. She never lost a phone number, never misplaced an address, could pull up a name from her file in a matter of seconds without fail. God, she was the best.

There was a certain etiquette to making phone calls, which she appreciated. If she called Todd's office and he was there, she'd put Nick on before Todd picked up. That was how it worked. Nick had always hated the telephone brinksmanship, where someone's assistant would call Marge, be put through to Nick, and then the assistant would say, "I have Mr. Smith," and Nick would say, "Okay, thanks," and then Mr. Smith would get on, as if he were too busy even to suffer a few seconds of being on hold. It was demeaning. Nick had devised his own way around that. He'd instructed Marge to tell the assistant, "Put Mr. Smith on, please, and I'll get Mr. Conover." That usually worked. So when Marge placed calls for him, he didn't like to play Mr. Smith's game. Todd picked up his own cell phone, of course—who didn't?— so Nick dialed the call himself.

Todd answered right away.

"Todd, it's Nick Conover."

"Oh, hey, man." No background noise. Nick wondered whether Todd actually was in his office anyway.

"Todd, we've got some funny things going on around here, and we need to talk."

"Hey, that's what I'm here for." Like he was a shrink or something.

"Two massive deals just fell through because they each, separately, heard that we're planning to shift all manufacturing to China."

"Yeah?"

"Any truth to it?"

"I can't be responsible for gossip, Nick."

"Of course. But I'm asking you now, flat out—man to man—if it's true." Man to toad, he thought. Man to weasel. "If you guys are even exploring the idea."

"Well, you know how I feel about this, and I've let you know. I think we're eroding our profit margins by continuing to operate these old factories in Michigan like it's nineteen fifty-nine or something. The world's changed. It's a global economy."

"Right," Nick said. "We've been through all that, and I've made it clear that the day Stratton stops making its own stuff is the day we're no longer Stratton. I'm not going to be the guy who shuts down our factories."

"I hear you," Todd said testily.

"I've already laid off half the company as you guys asked me to. It was the most painful thing I've ever done. But turning Stratton into some kind of virtual company, a little sales office with all the manufacturing done eight thousand miles away—that's not going to happen on *my* watch."

"I hear you," Todd said again. "What are you calling for?"

"Let me repeat the question, because I don't think I heard your answer. Is there any truth to these reports that you guys are negotiating to move our manufacturing offshore, Todd?"

"No," he said quickly.

"Not even preliminary talks?"

"No."

Nick didn't know what else to say. Either he was telling the truth, or he was lying, and if he was willing to lie so baldly, well, what the hell could

Nick do about it anyway? He thought about mentioning all the back-and-forth e-mail between Todd and Scott, the encrypted documents—but he didn't want Todd to know he was having his security director keep a close watch. He didn't want to shut one of the few windows he had into what was really going on.

"Then maybe you can explain to me why you've got Scott going to China on some secret mission, like Henry fucking *Kissinger*, without even telling me."

A few seconds of silence. "News to me," Todd finally said. "Ask him."

"Scott said he went to China to explore the options. He didn't do that for you? Because if he did, I want you to understand something. That's not the way it works around here, Todd."

"He doesn't report to me, Nick."

"Exactly. I don't want to be undermined."

"I don't want that either."

"The job's tough enough without having to worry about whether my chief financial officer's taking secret flights to the Orient on Cathay Pacific."

Todd chuckled politely. "It's a tough job, and it takes a lot out of you." The timbre of his voice suddenly changed, as if he'd just thought of something. "You know, I understand your family's been through some rough times, death of your wife, all that. If you need to spend more time with them, we're here to help. You want to take a little sabbatical, a little break, might be a good thing. You could probably *use* a vacation. Be good for you."

"I'm fine, Todd," Nick said. *Not so easy, Todd.* "Going to work every-day—that's what keeps me going."

"Good to hear it," Todd said. "Good to hear it."

71

Bugbee was gobbling Cheetos out of a small vending machine bag. His fingers—which Audrey had noticed were usually immaculate, the nails neatly clipped—were stained orange.

"Makes sense," he said through a mouthful of Cheetos. "Rinaldi picked up a piece in Grand Rapids when he was working there."

"Or here. Those guns travel."

"Maybe. So where'd he toss it?"

"Any of a million possibilities." She was hungry, and he wasn't offering her any, the jerk.

"I forget who the poor slobs were searched the Dumpster, but nothing there."

"There's probably hundreds of Dumpsters in town," Audrey pointed out. "And the dump. And sewer grates, and the lake and the ponds and the rivers. We're never going to find the gun."

"Sad but true," Bugbee said. He crumpled up the empty bag, tossed the wad at the metal trash can against the wall, but the bag unballed in the air and landed on the floor. "Shit."

"Did you have a chance to talk to the alarm company?"

He nodded. "Fenwick Alarm's just an office downtown. I don't know what the hell they do—they install, but not in this case. They don't even do the monitoring themselves. That's done by a joint called Central Michigan Monitoring, out of Lansing. They keep all the electronic records."

"And?"

"Nada. Just confirms what we already know. That Wednesday morning one of the perimeter alarms at Conover's house got triggered. Alert lasted eleven minutes. Big fucking deal. You got the hard drive—that ought to give up what the cameras recorded, right?"

She explained what she knew about Conover's digital video recording system. "I've asked Lenehan to look again. But Noyce has him doing all kinds of other things ahead of us."

"Why does that not surprise me?"

"Speaking of cameras, one of us should check out whatever they have at Fenwicke Estates security for that night."

Bugbee shook his head. "Did already. They use a central station downtown. Nothing special—Stadler climbs a perimeter fence, that's it."

"Too bad."

"I say we poly the guy. Both of those assholes."

"That's a tough one. It may be early. We may want to wait until we have more. I know that's what Noyce would say."

"Screw Noyce. This is our case, not his. You notice the way he's been breathing down our necks?"

"Some."

"He must smell something big about to pop."

She didn't know how much to say. "I think it's more that he wants to make sure we don't slip up."

"Slip up? Like we're rookies?"

Audrey shrugged. "It's a big case."

Bugbee said, with a crooked grin, "No shit."

Audrey responded with a rueful smile as she turned to go back to her cubicle.

"That thing about the shell casing or bullet fragment or whatever," Bugbee said.

She turned. "What shell casing?"

"That bluff?"

"Yes?"

"Not bad," Bugbee said.

72

Nick was beyond weary. All the shit that was going on with Todd and Scott, all the crap he didn't understand: it was draining. And that on top of Eddie and his warnings about Cassie: check yourself before you wreck yourself. And: What do you think she's after? Could there be something to what Eddie was saying?

Was it possible, he'd begun to wonder, that, on some subconscious level, he *wanted* to be found out?

And worst of all, so awful he couldn't stand to think about it, was this fragment of a shell casing the police had discovered on his lawn.

He'd always prided himself on his ability to endure pressure that would crush most other guys. Maybe it was the hockey training, the way you learned to find the serene place inside you and go there when things got tough. He never used to panic. Laura, always on the high-strung side, never got that. She thought he didn't care, didn't get it. And he'd just shrug and reply blandly, "What's the use in panicking? Not going to help."

But since the murder, everything had changed. His hard shell had cracked or turned porous. Or maybe all the stress of the last few weeks was additive, the worries heaped onto his back until his muscles trembled and spasmed. Any second now he'd collapse to the ground.

But he couldn't, not yet.

Because whatever Todd and Scott were up to—all this maneuvering, the secret trips and the phone calls and the encrypted document—it had ignited a fuse in him that crackled and sparked.

You want to take a little sabbatical, a little break, might be a good thing.

Like Todd gave a shit about his emotional well-being.

Todd wanted him to take time off. Not resign: that was interesting. If Todd and the boys at Fairfield wanted to get rid of him, they'd have fired him long ago. So why hadn't they? Was it really the huge payday, the five million bucks they'd have to pay to fire him without cause, that was stopping them? Given how many billions Fairfield had under management?

He tapped at his keyboard and pulled up the corporate directory, clicked on MARTIN LAI. A photo popped up—a fat-faced, phlegmatic-looking guy—along with his direct reports, his e-mail, his phone number.

He glanced at his watch. Thirteen-hour time difference in Hong Kong. Nine-thirty in the morning here meant ten-thirty at night there. He picked up the phone and dialed Martin Lai's home number. It rang and rang, and then a recorded message came on in Chinese, followed by a few perfunctory words in heavily accented English. "Martin," he said, "this is Nick Conover. I need to speak to you right away." He left the usual array of phone numbers.

Then he spoke into the intercom and asked Marge to locate Martin Lai's cell phone number, which wasn't on the Stratton intranet. A minute later, a long number popped up on his screen.

He called it and got a recorded voice again, and he left the same message. He checked Lai's Meeting Maker, his online corporate schedule, and the man appeared not to be away from Stratton's Hong Kong office.

Todd's words kept coming back to him: *You want to take a little sabbatical, a little break, might be a good thing.*

What the hell were Todd Muldaur and Fairfield Equity Partners up to, really? Who, he wondered, might know?

The answer came to him so swiftly that he wondered why he hadn't thought of it before. A "cousin" in the extended Fairfield family, that was who.

He opened his middle desk drawer and found a dog-eared business card that said KENDALL RESTAURANT GROUP, and underneath it, RONNIE KENDALL, CEO.

Ronnie Kendall was a sharp entrepreneur, a quick-witted bantam with an impenetrable Texan accent. He'd started the Kendall Restaurant Group with a little Tex-Mex place in Dallas and turned it into a thriving chain and eventually a prosperous restaurant holding company. It was mostly a chain of Tex-Mex restaurants popular in the Southwest, but his company also owned a cheesecake chain, a barbecued-chicken chain that wasn't doing so well, a lousy Japanese-food chain where chefs dressed like samurai sliced and flipped your food right at your table, and a "good times" bar-and-grill chain known for its baby back ribs and gargantuan frozen margaritas. Ten years ago he'd sold to Willard Osgood.

Nick had met him at some business conference in Tokyo, and they'd hit it off. Ronnie Kendall turned out to be a big hockey fan and had followed Nick's college career at Michigan State, amazingly. Nick had confessed he'd eaten at the Japanese restaurant chain that Kendall's group owned and didn't much like it, and Kendall had shot right back, "You kidding? Every time I set foot in there I get diarrhea. Never eat there, but people *love* it. Go figure."

Nick was put on hold several times before Ronnie Kendall picked up, sounding exuberant as always, speaking a mile a minute. Nick made the mistake of asking how business was, and Ronnie launched into a manic monologue about how the barbecued-chicken chain was expanding in Georgia and South Carolina, and then he somehow shifted into a rant on the low-carb craze. "Man, am I glad that fad is over, huh? That was *killing* us! The low-carb cheesecake never went over, and the low-carb diet Margaritas— *forget* it! And then just when we signed up our new celebrity endorser"—he mentioned the name of a famous football player—"and we'd even taped a bunch of fifteen- and thirty-second spots, then out of the blue he gets hit with a *rape* charge!"

"Ronnie," Nick finally broke in, "how well do you know Todd Muldaur?"

Ronnie cackled. "I *hate* the slick bastard and he loves me just the same. But I stay out of his way, and he stays out of mine. He and his MBA buddies were trying to muck around in my business, got so bad I called Willard himself and said, you put a choke collar on your little poodles or I'm gone. I quit. I'm too old and too rich, I don't need it. Willard must have taken Todd to the woodshed, because he started backing off. 'Course, he had his hands full, what with the chip meltdown."

"Chip meltdown?"

"Isn't that what you call them things? Microchips or whatever? Semi-conductors, right?"

"Yeah?"

"You read the *Journal*, right? The semiconductor industry bubble, the way all those private-equity guys overinvested in chips, then the bubble burst?" He cackled again. "Gotta love it, the way all those guys took a bath."

"Hold on, Ronnie. Fairfield Equity Partners overinvested in microchips?"

"Not the whole of Fairfield, just the funds our boy Todd runs. He made a massive bet on the chip business. Put all his chips on chips, right?"

Nick didn't join Ronnie's laughter. "I thought there's some kind of limit to how much they can invest in one particular sector."

"Todd's an arrogant guy, you know that, right? You can smell it on him. He figured when the semiconductor stocks started sinking, he'd pick up a bunch of companies cheap, turn a big fat profit. Well, he's sure gettin' his. His funds are sucking wind. Willard Osgood has got to be madder 'n a wet hen. If Todd's funds collapse, the whole mother ship goes down."

"Really?"

"I imagine Todd Muldaur should be makin' nice to you these days. I know Stratton's going through some hard times, but at least you're solvent. Compared to some of his other investments, you're a cash cow. He could take you guys public, make some real money. Of course, given how long that takes, it might be too late for him."

"That would take a year at least."

"At least. Why, they talking about spinning you guys off?"

"No. Nothing about that."

"Well, Fairfield needs what they call a liquidity event, and real soon."

"Meaning they need cash."

"You got it."

"Yeah, well, they're up to something," Nick said. "Really pushing hard to cut costs."

"Forget that. You know what I always say, when your house is on fire, you don't hold a garage sale."

"Come again?"

"I mean, Todd's so deep in the shit that he's probably desperate to make a quick buck, sell Stratton quick-and-dirty just to save his ass. I were you, I'd watch Todd's moves *real* close."

The instant he hung up, another call came in, this one from Eddie.

"The small conference room on your floor," Eddie said without preface. "Right now."

73

Ever since they'd had it out at Eddie's condo, there had been an acute chill in their already frosty relationship. Eddie no longer joked around as much. He avoided Nick's eyes. He often seemed to be seething.

But when he entered the conference room, he looked as though he had a secret he couldn't wait to share. It was a look Nick hadn't seen in a while.

Eddie closed the conference room door and said, "The piece of shell casing?"

Nick's voice caught in his throat. He was unable to speak.

"It's bullshit," Eddie said.

"*What?*"

"The cops never found any fragment of a shell casing on your lawn."

"Are you sure?"

"Positive."

"What was it, then?"

"It was bullshit. A pressure tactic. There never was any metal scrap."

"They *lied* about it?"

"I wouldn't get on my high horse if I were you, Nick."

"You're certain? How do you know this for sure?"

"I told you. I got sources. It's a fake out, dude. Don't you recognize a fake out when you see one?"

Nick shrugged. "I don't know."

"Come on, man. Remember when we were playing Hillsdale in the finals, our senior year, and you made that great deke to your backhand at the blue line before you fired a rocket behind Mallory, sent the game into overtime?"

"Yeah, I remember," Nick said. "I also remember that we lost."

74

Nick put his briefcase down in the front hall. Its antique, reclaimed pumpkin-pine flooring—the strip oak that had been there didn't make the cut, as far as Laura was concerned—glowed in the amber light that spilled from soffits overhead. Without thinking about it, he expected to hear the *click click click* of Barney's dog toenails on the wood, the jangle of his collar, and the absence of that happy sound saddened him.

It was almost eight o'clock. The marketing strategy committee meeting had run almost two hours late; he'd called home during a break and told Marta to make dinner for the kids. She'd said that Julia was over at her friend Jessica's, so it would just be Lucas.

He heard voices from upstairs. Did Lucas have a friend over? Nick walked upstairs, and the murmur resolved into conversation.

It was Cassie's voice, he realized with surprise. Cassie and Lucas. What was she doing here? The staircase was solidly mortised, no squeaks and creaks like the old house, or like the house he'd grown up in. They hadn't heard him come up. He felt a prickling sensation as he paused at the top landing and listened. Lucas's door was open for a change.

"They should have assigned this in physics class," Lucas was complaining. "Why would a poet know how the world's going to end anyway?"

"You think the poem is really about how the world is going to end?" Cassie's husky voice.

He was relieved. Cassie was helping Lucas with his homework, that was all.

"Fire or ice. That's how the world will end. It's what he's saying."

"Desire and hate," Cassie said. "The human heart can be a molten thing, and it can be sheathed in ice. Don't think outer space. Think inner space. Don't think *the* world. Think *your* world. Frost can be an incredibly dark poet, but he's also a poet of intimacy. So what's he saying here?"

"Thin line between love and hate, basically."

"But love and desire aren't the same, are they? There's the love of family, but we don't call that desire. Because desire is about an absence, right? To desire something is to want it, and you always want the thing you don't have."

"I guess."

"Think about Silas, in the last poem they gave you. He's about to die, and he comes home."

"Except it's not his home."

"In that one, Warren says 'home is the place where, when you have to go there, they have to take you in.' One of the most famous lines Frost ever wrote. Is that love or desire? How does *his* world end?"

Nick, feeling self-conscious, took a few steps down the hall toward his bedroom. Cassie's voice receded to a singsong murmur, asking something, and Lucas's adolescent baritone rose in impatience. "Some say this, some say that. You feel, like, make up your friggin' mind already."

Nick stopped again to listen.

Cassie laughed. "What's the *rhythm* telling you? The poem's lines mainly have four beats, right? But not the last lines, about hate: 'Is also great.' Two stressed syllables. 'And would suffice.' Clear and simple. Like it's funneling to a point. About the ice of hatred, how potent that is, right?"

"Mad props to my dawg Bobby Frost," Lucas said. "He could flow, no doubt. But he starts with fire."

"A lot of things start with fire, Luke. The crucial question is how they end."

Nick debated whether he should join them. He wouldn't have hesitated in the old days, but Lucas was different now. What was going on was a good thing, yet probably a fragile thing too. Lucas wouldn't let him help with his homework anymore, and now that he was in the eleventh grade, Nick wasn't much use anyway. But Cassie had somehow figured out a way to talk to him, and she knew that stuff—she was a natural. A goddamn valedictorian.

Finally, Nick walked past Lucas's bedroom, which let them know he was home, and made his way to his own room. Removed his clothes, brushed his teeth, took a quick shower. When he came out again, Lucas was alone in his room, sitting at his computer, working.

"Hey, Luke," he said.

Lucas glanced up with his usual look of annoyance.

Nick wanted to say something like, Did Cassie help? I'm glad you're focusing on work. But he held back. Any such comment might be resented, taken as intrusive. "Where's Cassie?" he said.

Lucas shrugged. "Downstairs, I guess."

He went downstairs to look for Cassie, but she wasn't in the family room or the kitchen, none of the usual places. He called her name, but there was no answer.

Well, she has the right to snoop around my house, he thought. After she caught me going through her medicine cabinet.

But she wouldn't do that, would she?

He passed through the kitchen to the back hallway, switched on the alabaster lamp, kept going to his study.

Unlikely she'd be in there.

The door to his study was open, as it almost always was, and the lights were on. Cassie was seated behind his desk.

His heart thumped. He walked faster, the carpet muffling his footsteps so his approach was silent. Not that he was intending to sneak up on her, though.

Several of the desk drawers were ajar, he saw.

All but the bottom one, which he kept locked. They were open just a bit, as if they'd been open and then shut hastily.

And he knew he hadn't done it. He rarely used the desk drawers, and when he did, he was meticulous about closing them all the way, otherwise the desk looked sloppy.

She was sitting back in his black leather Symbiosis chair, writing on a yellow legal pad.

"Cassie."

She jumped, let out a shriek. "Oh, my God! Don't ever do that!" She put a hand across her breasts.

"Sorry," he said.

"Oh—God. I was in my own world. No, I should apologize—I shouldn't be in here. I guess I'm just a low-boundaries gal."

"That's okay," he said, trying to sound as if he meant it.

She seemed instantly aware of the drawers that had been left slightly ajar and began pushing them all the way closed. "I was looking for a pad and a pen," she said. "I hope you don't mind."

"No," he said. "It's fine."

"I had this idea, and I had to write it down right away—that happens to me."

"Idea?"

"Just—just something I want to write. Someday, if I ever get my shit together."

"Fiction?"

"Oh, no. Nonfiction. Too much fiction in my life. I hope you don't mind my coming over tonight. I did call, you know, but Marta said you were at work, and Lucas and I got to talking, and he said he was busting his head over some poem. Which turns out to be one of the poems I actually know something about. So I . . ."

"Hey," Nick said. "You're doing God's work. I'm afraid my arrival broke things up."

"He's going to write the first few paragraphs of his poetry term paper. See where it's heading."

"You're good with him," Nick said. *You're amazing,* is what he thought.

Maybe that's all it was. She came over to help him figure out some Robert Frost poem.

"You ever teach?"

"I told you," Cassie said. "I've pretty much done everything." The pinpoint ceiling lights caught her hair, made it sparkle. She looked waiflike, still, but her skin wasn't so transparent. She looked healthier. The dark smudges beneath her eyes were gone. "'He thinks if he could teach him that, he'd be / Some good perhaps to someone in the world.'"

"Come again?"

Cassie shook her head. "It's just a line from *Death of a Hired Man*. It's a poem about home. About family, really."

"And the true meaning of Christmas?"

"You Conovers," she said. "What am I going to do with you?"

"I have a few ideas," Nick said, attempting a leer. "God, you're good at everything, aren't you?"

"Coming from *you*? The alpha male? Jock of all trades?"

"I wish. I may be the most math-challenged CEO in the country."

"Is there a sport you can't do?"

He thought a moment. "Never learned to ride a horse."

"Horseshoes?"

"That's not a sport."

"Archery, I bet."

"I'm okay."

"Shooting?"

He went dead inside. After a split second, he gave a small shake of his head, looking perplexed. For a second his eyes went out of focus.

"You know," she said. "Target shooting, whatever it's called. On the range."

"Nope," he said, hearing the studied casualness in his voice as if from a distance. He lowered himself onto a rush-seated Windsor chair that invariably threatened to leave splinters in his backside. Laura had banished his favorite old leather club chair when they moved. Frat house furniture, she called it. He rubbed his eyes, trying to conceal the flush of terror. "Sorry, I'm just wiped out. Long day."

"Want to talk about it?"

"Not now. Sorry. I mean, thanks, but another time. I'd rather talk about anything else than work."

"Can I make you dinner?"

"You cook?"

"No," she admitted with a quick laugh. "You've had one of my three specialties. But I'm sure Marta left something for you in that haunted kitchen of yours."

"Haunted?"

"Oh yeah. I met your contractor right when I got here, and I got the low-down from him."

"Like why it's taking his guys forever to put in a kitchen counter?"

"Don't blame them. You're driving them crazy, is what I hear. He can't get signoffs when they need them. Things like that."

"Too many goddamn decisions. I don't really have the time for it. And I don't want to get it wrong."

" 'Wrong' defined as what?"

Nick was quiet for a moment. "Laura had very definite ideas of what she wanted."

"And you want everything to be just the way she'd planned. Like it's your memorial to her."

"Please don't do the shrink thing."

"But maybe you're afraid to finish it too, because when it's over, something else is over too."

"Cassie, can we change the subject?"

"So it's like Penelope, in the *Odyssey*. She weaves a shroud during the day, and unravels it at night. That way it's never finished. She staves off the suitors, and honors the departed Odysseus."

"I don't even know what you're talking about." Nick took a deep breath.

"I think you do."

"Except, you know, it's reached a point where I really do want the damn thing finished already. It was her big project, and, okay, maybe as long as it was underway, it was like she was still at work. Which doesn't make any sense, but still. Thing is, now I just want the plastic draft sheets out of here, and I want the Dumpster gone, and the trucks, and all that. I want this to be a goddamn *home*. Not a project. Not a thing in process. Just a place where the Conovers live." A beat. "Whatever's left of them."

"I get it," she said. "So why don't you take me out to dinner somewhere." A smile hovered around her lips. "A date."

75

They walked through the Grand Fenwick Hotel parking lot holding hands. It was a cool, cloudless night, and the stars twinkled. Cassie stopped for a moment before they reached the porte cochere and looked up.

"You know, when I was six or seven, my best friend, Marcy Stroup, told me that every star was really the soul of someone who'd died."

Nick grunted.

"I didn't believe it either. Then in school we learned that each star is actually a ball of fire, and some of them probably have solar systems of their own. I remember when they taught us in school about how stars die, how in just a few thousandths of a second a star's core would collapse and the whole star would blow up—a great supernova followed by nothingness. And I started to cry. Right there at my desk in sixth grade. Crazy, huh? That night I was talking to my Daddy about it, and he said that was just the way of the universe. That people die, and stars die too—they have to, to make room for new ones."

"Huh."

"Daddy said if no one ever died, there'd be no room on the planet for the babies being born. He said if nothing ever came to an end, nothing could ever begin. He said it was the same way in the heavens—that sometimes a world has to come to an end so that new ones can be born." She squeezed his hand. "Come on, I'm hungry."

The lobby of the Grand Fenwick was carpeted in what was meant to suggest an old-fashioned English broadloom, with lots of oversized leather furniture arranged in clubby "conversation pits," like a dozen living rooms stitched together. Velvet ropes on stanchions partitioned the restaurant from the lobby. The menu offered fifties favorites like duck à l'orange and salmon hollandaise, but mainly what it offered were steaks, for old-school types who knew the names for the different cuts: Delmonico, porterhouse, Kansas City strip. The place smelled like cigars, and not especially expensive ones; the smoke had seeped into everything like dressing on a salad.

"They have fish," Nick said, apologetically, as they were led to a corner table.

"Now why would you say that? You think girls don't eat red meat?"

"That's right, I forgot—you do. So long as it isn't actually red."

"Exactly."

Cassie ordered a rib steak well done, Nick a medium-rare sirloin. Both of them ordered salads.

After Nick ate his salad, he looked at Cassie. "Brainstorm. I always order a salad. But I just realized something: I don't particularly like salad."

"Not exactly the solution to Fermat's last theorem," Cassie said, "but we can work with this. You don't like salad. Same deal as with tea."

"Right. I drink tea. Laura would make it and I'd drink it. Same deal. I order salads. But you know, I never liked tea, and I never liked salad."

"You just realized this."

"Yeah. It was always true. I just wasn't conscious of it, somehow. Like . . . Chinese food. I don't really like it. I don't hate it. I just don't have any liking for it."

"You're on a roll, now. What else."

"What else? Okay. Eggplants. Who the hell decided that eggplants were edible? Nontoxic, I get. But is everything that's nontoxic a food? If I were some cave man, and I weren't starving, and I bit into an eggplant, cooked or not, I wouldn't say, wow, a new taste sensation—I've discovered a foodstuff. I'd say, well, this definitely won't kill you. Don't bother to dip your arrowhead in it. It's like—I don't know—maple leaves. You could probably eat them, but why would you?"

Cassie looked at him.

"You're the one who was complaining I was a stranger to myself," Nick said, tugging on the table linen absently.

"That wasn't really what I meant."

"Gotta start somewhere."

She laughed. He felt her hand stroking his thigh under the tablecloth. Affectionately, not sexually. "Forget eggplant. Give yourself credit—you know what's most precious to you. Not everyone does. Your kids. Your family. They're everything to you, aren't they?"

Nick nodded. There was a lump of sadness in his throat. "When I was playing hockey, I could convince myself that the harder I worked, the harder I trained, the harder I *played*, the better I'd do. It was true, or true enough. True of a lot of things. You work harder, and you do better. In hockey, they talk about playing with a lot of 'heart'—giving it your all. Not true of family, though. Not true of being a father. The harder I try to get through to Lucas, the harder he fights me. You got through the force field. I can't."

"That's because you always argue with him, Nick. You're always trying to make a case, and he doesn't want to hear it."

"The way he looks at me, I think he couldn't care less whether I lived or died."

"That's not what's going on here. Has Lucas ever talked to you about Laura's death?"

"Never. The Conover men don't really do *feelings*, okay?" Nick looked around the darkened room, and was surprised to see Scott McNally being seated a few tables away. Their eyes met, and Scott waved a hand. He was with a tall, gangly man with a narrow face and a prominent chin. Nick saw Scott talking to his dinner companion hurriedly, gesturing toward him. It looked like Scott was deciding whether to do the dessert visit, or to get it over with, and had decided that it would be better to get it over with. The two men stood up and came over to Nick's table.

"Fancy seeing you here," Scott said, patting Nick's shoulder. "I had no idea this was one of your hangouts."

"It's not," Nick said. "Scott, I'd like you to meet my friend Cassie."

"Pleasure to meet you, Cassie," Scott said. "And this is Randall Enright." He paused. "Randall's just helping me understand some of the legal aspects of financial restructuring. Boring technical stuff. Unless you're me, of course, in which case it's like *Conan the Barbarian* with spreadsheets."

"Nice to meet you, Randall," said Nick.

"Pleased to meet you," the tall man said pleasantly. His suit jacket was unbuttoned, and he put his glasses in his breast pocket before shaking hands.

"We get that contract with the Fisher Group analyzed?" Nick said.

"Not sure that's something we want to rush into, actually," said Scott.

"Sooner the better, I'd say."

"Well," said Scott, fidgeting with a lock of hair above his left ear, glancing away. "You're the boss."

"Enjoy Fenwick," Cassie said to the lawyer. "When are you heading back to Chicago?"

The tall man exchanged a glance with Scott. "Not until tomorrow," he said.

"Enjoy your dinner," Nick said, with a hint of dismissal.

Soon, heavy white plates arrived with their steaks, each accompanied by a scoop of pureed spinach and a potato. Nick looked at Cassie. "How did you know he was heading back to Chicago?"

"The Hart, Schaffner & Marx label inside his jacket. The obvious fact that he's got to be some sort of hot-shot lawyer if he's having a working dinner with your CFO." She saw the question in his eyes and said, "He put his glasses away because they were reading glasses. And they hadn't been given their menus yet. We're definitely looking at a working dinner."

"I see."

"And Scott wasn't happy about introducing him. He did it strategically, but the fact is, he chose to have dinner here for the same reason you did. Because it's a perfectly okay place where you don't expect to see anyone you know."

Nick grinned, unable to deny it.

"And then there's the 'you're the boss' stuff. Resent-o-rama. A line like that always comes with an asterisk. 'You're the boss.' Asterisk says, 'For now.'"

"You're being a little melodramatic. Don't you think you might be over-interpreting?"

"Don't you think you might not be seeing what's right in front of your face?"

"You may have a point," Nick admitted. He told her about Scott's secret trip to China, the way he tried to cover it up with a lie about going to a dude ranch in Arizona.

"There you go," she said with a shrug. "He's fucking with you."

"Sure seems that way."

"But you like him, don't you?"

"Yeah. Or maybe it's more accurate to say, I did. He's funny, he's a whiz with numbers. We're friends."

"That's your problem—it's blinding you. Your alleged 'friendship' with Scott didn't exactly keep him from stabbing you in the back, did it?"

"True."

"He's not scared of you."

"Should he be?"

"Most definitely. Scared of you, not of what's-his-name, the Yale guy from Boston."

"Todd Muldaur. Todd's really calling the shots, and Scott knows it. Truth is, I'm surprised by him. I brought him in here, I would have expected a modicum of loyalty."

"You're a problem for Scott. A speed bump. An impediment. He's decided you're part of the problem, not part of the solution. His deal is all about Scott Incorporated."

"I'm not sure you're right, there—there's actually nothing greedy or materialistic about him."

"People like Scott McNally—it's not about making a life, or attaining a certain level of comfort. You told me he wears the same shirts he's probably worn since he was a student, right?"

"So whatever he's about, it's not exactly money. I get it."

"Wrong. You *don't* get it. He's a type. People like him don't care about enjoying the things money can buy. They're not into rare Bordeaux or Lamborghini muscle cars. At the same time, they're incredibly competitive. And here's the thing. *Money is how they keep score.*"

Nick thought about Michael Milken, Sam Walton, those other billionaire-next-door types. They lived in little split-level ranch houses and were completely fixated on adding to their Scrooge McDuck vaults, day after day. He remembered hearing about how Warren Buffett lived like a miser in the same little suburban house in Omaha he bought for thirty thousand bucks in 1958. He thought about Scott's nothing-special house and how much money he had. Maybe she was right.

"Scott McNally has his mind on winning this round, so he can play in the big-stakes games," Cassie went on.

"They teach this after the lotus position or before?"

"Okay, then let me just ask you this. What do you think Scott McNally wants to be when he grows up?"

"What do you mean?"

"Does he want to be selling chairs and filing cabinets, or does he want to be a financial engineer at Fairfield Partners? Which is more his style?"

"Point taken."

"In which case, it's fair to ask yourself, who's he really working for?"

Nick gave a crooked smile.

She stood up. "I'll be right back."

Nick watched as she made her way to the ladies room, admiring the curve of her butt. She wasn't there long. On her way back, she walked past Scott's table, and stopped there briefly. She said something to the lawyer, then sat down next to him for a moment. She was laughing, as if he'd said something witty. A few moments later, he saw the lawyer hand her something. Cassie was laughing again as she stood up and returned to her seat.

"What was that about?" Nick asked.

Cassie handed him the lawyer's business card. "Just check him out, okay?"

"That was quick work." Nick glanced at the card and read, "Abbotsford Gruendig."

"Just being neighborly," Cassie said.

"By the way, I *can* see what's in front of my face," Nick said. "You're in front of my face. I see you quite well, and I like what I see."

"But as I said, we don't see things as they are. We see things as we are."

"Does the same go for you?"

"Goes for all of us. We lie to ourselves because it's the only way we can get through the day. Time comes, though, when the lies get tired and quit."

"What's that supposed to mean?"

Cassie looked at him steadily, searchingly. "Tell me the truth, Nick. What's the real reason the police were at your house?"

76

For a moment, he was at a loss for words.

He hadn't told her about the police searching the house and yard, which was a pretty damn huge thing not to have told her about. Especially given the connection to her father. Both Lucas and Julia knew the police had been searching for traces of Andrew Stadler. They just didn't know the real reason.

"Lucas told you," Nick said neutrally. He tried to keep his pulse steady, his breathing regular. He took a forkful of steak for which he had no appetite.

"It freaked him out."

"Yeah, well, he seemed to think it was a hoot. Cassie, I should have said something to you about it, but I knew how it would upset you. I didn't want to bring up your dad—"

"I understand," she said. "I understand. And I appreciate it." She was toying with a spoon. "They actually think my *father* was the stalker?"

"It's just one possibility," Nick said. "I think they're really groping." He swallowed hard. "Hell, they probably even wonder if I had something to do with it." The last words came out in a rush, not the way he had heard himself say it in his mind.

"With his death," Cassie said carefully.

Nick grunted.

"And is it possible that you did?"

Nick couldn't speak right away. He didn't look at her, couldn't. "What do you mean?"

She set down the spoon, placed it carefully alongside the knife. "If you thought he might have been the one doing all that crazy stuff, maybe you could have intervened, somehow. Helped him to get help." She broke off. "But then, these are the questions I ask myself. Why didn't I *make* him get help? Why didn't I intervene? I keep asking myself whether there was something I could have done that would have changed things. Stratton's supposed to have all these great mental health programs, but suddenly he wasn't eligible for them anymore—that's a real Catch-22, isn't it? Because of a mental illness, you quit and lose your right to treatment for your mental illness. That isn't right."

Warily: "It's not right."

"And because of these decisions—decisions you and I and God knows how many other people made—my daddy's dead." Cassie was weeping now, tears spilling down both cheeks.

"Cassie," Nick said. He took her hand in his, and fell silent. Her hand looked pale and small in his. Then a thought came to him, and he felt as if he had swallowed ice. His hand, the hand with which he tried to comfort her, was the hand that had held the gun.

"But you want to know something?" Cassie said haltingly. "When I got the news about—you know—"

"I know."

"I felt like I'd run into a brick wall. But, Nick, I felt something else too. I felt *relieved*. Do you understand?"

"Relieved." He repeated the word numbly.

"All the hospitalizations, all the relapses, all the agony he'd endured. Pain that's not physical but every bit as real. He didn't like the place he was in—the world that, more and more, he *had* to live in. It wasn't your world or my world, it was his world, Nick, and it was a cold and scary place."

"It had to have been hell, for both of you."

"And then one day he disappears. Then he's dead. *Killed*—shot dead, God knows why. But it was almost like an act of mercy. Do you ever think that things happen for a reason?"

"I think some things happen for a reason," Nick said slowly. "But not everything. I don't think Laura died for any particular reason. It just happened. To her. To us. Like a piano that just falls out of the sky and flattens you."

"Shit happens, you're saying." Cassie palmed away the tears on her face. "But that's never the whole story. Shit happens, and it changes your life, and then what do you do? Do you just go on as if nothing happened? Or do you face it?"

"I choose option A."

"Yeah. I see that." Cassie rumpled her spiky hair with a hand. "There's a parable of Schopenhauer's, it's called *'Die Stachelschweine'*—the porcupines. You've got these porcupines, and it's winter, and so they huddle together for warmth—but when they get too close, of course, they hurt each other."

"Allegory alert," Nick said.

"You got it. Too far, and they freeze to death. Too near, and they bleed. We're all like that. Same with you and Lucas."

"Yeah, well, he's a porcupine, all right."

"Got to hand it to you Conover men," Cassie said. "You're as well defended as a medieval castle. Got your moat, got your boiling oil over the gate, got your castle keep. 'Bring it on,' right? Hope you got plenty of provisions in the larder."

"All right, babe. Since you see so much more clearly than I do, let me ask you something. How much do you think I have to worry about my son?"

"Well, some. He's a stoner, as you know. Probably gets high a couple of times a day. Which can do a number on your ability to concentrate."

"A *couple* of times a day? You sure?"

"Oh please. He's got two bottles of Visine on his dresser. He's got Febreze fabric spray in his closet."

Nick looked blank.

"Fabric freshener. You spritz it on your clothing to remove the smell of the herb. Then he's got these Dutch Master leavings in his wastebasket. For making a blunt, okay? This is all Pothead 101 stuff."

"Christ," said Nick. "He's sixteen years old."

"And he's going to be seventeen. And then eighteen. And that's going to be rough too."

"A year ago you wouldn't have recognized him. He was this totally straight, popular athlete."

"Just like his dad."

"Yeah, well. My mom didn't die when I was fifteen."

"What makes it worse is if you can't talk about it."

"He's a kid. It's hard for him to talk about stuff like that."

Cassie looked at him.

"What?"

"I wasn't just talking about Lucas," she said quietly. "I was talking about you."

A deep breath. "You like metaphors? Here's one. You know the cartoon coyote that's always racing off the edge of the cliff?"

"Yes, Nick. Wile E. Coyote. An odd role model for the CEO of Acme Industries, I'd have thought."

"And he's in midair, but his legs are still pumping and he's moving along fine. But then—he looks down, and he sinks like a stone. Moral of the story? *Never fucking look down.*"

"Beautiful," Cassie said, her voice as astringent as witch hazel. "Just beautiful." Her eyes flashed. "Have you noticed that Lucas can't even *look* at you? And you can barely look at him. Now why is that?"

"If you bring up those Black Forest porcupines again, I'm out of here."

"He's lost his mom, and he desperately needs to bond with his father. But you're not around, and when you are, you're not *there*. You're not exactly verbally expressive, right? He needs you to be the healer, but you can't do it— you don't know how. And the more isolated he feels, the more he turns on you, and the angrier you get."

"The armchair psychologist," Nick said. "Another one of your imaginative 'readings.' Nice guess, though."

"No," she said. "Not a guess. He pretty much told me."

"He *told* you? I can't even imagine that."

"He was stoned, Nick. He was stoned, and he started to cry, and it came out."

"He was *stoned*? In your presence?"

"Lit up a nice fat doobie," Cassie said, with a half-smile. "We shared it. And we had a long talk. I wish you could have heard him. He has a lot on his mind. A lot he hasn't been able to say to you. A lot you need to hear."

"You smoked marijuana with my *son*?"

"Yes."

"That is *incredibly* irresponsible. How could you do that?"

"Whoa, Daddy, you're missing the big picture here."

"Lucas has a problem with this shit. You were supposed to help him. Not encourage him, goddammit. He looks up to you!"

"I told him to lay off the weed, at least on school nights. I think he's going to."

"Goddammit! You haven't got a clue, have you? I don't care what kind of a fucked-up childhood you had. This is my *son* you're dealing with. A sixteen-year-old boy with a drug problem. What part of this isn't registering?"

"Nick, be careful," she said, in a low, husky voice. Her face was turning a deep red, but her expression remained oddly fixed, a stone mask. "We had a very open and honest conversation, Luke and I. He told me all kinds of things." Now she turned to look at him with hooded eyes.

Nick was torn between fury and fear, wanting to lay into her for what she'd done, getting high with Lucas—and yet frightened of what she might have found out from Lucas.

Lucas, who might—or might not—have heard shots one night.

Who might—or might not—have overheard his father and Eddie discussing what had really happened that night.

"Like what?" he managed to say.

"All *kinds* of things," she whispered darkly.

Nick closed his eyes, waited for his heart to stop hammering. When he opened them again, she was gone.

77

Audrey's e-mail icon was bouncing, and she saw it was Kevin Lenehan, the electronics tech.

She walked right over there, almost ran.

"What's the best restaurant in town, would you say?" Kevin said.

"I don't know. Terra, maybe? I've never been there."

"How about Taco Gordito?"

"Why do you ask?"

"Because you owe me dinner. I told you the recording on this baby started at three-eighteen in the morning on Wednesday the sixteenth, right? After the sequence you're so interested in?"

"What'd you find?"

"The hard drive's partitioned into two sections, right? One for the digital images, the other for the software that drives the thing." He turned to his computer monitor, moved the mouse around and clicked on something. "Very cool system, by the way. Internet-based."

"Meaning?"

"Your guy had the ability to monitor his cameras from his office."

"What does that tell you?"

"Nothing. I'm just saying. Anyway, look at this."

"That doesn't mean anything to me. It's a long list of numbers."

"Not a techie, huh? Your husband has to program the VCR for you?"

"He can't either."

"Same with me. No one can. So, look. This is the log of all recorded content."

"Is that the fifteenth?"

"You got it. This log says that the recording actually started on Tuesday the fifteenth at four minutes after noon, right? Not like fifteen hours later."

"So you found more video?"

"I wish. No, you're not following me. Someone must have gone in and reformatted the section of the hard drive where the recordings are made, then started the whole machine over, recycled it, so it just *looked* like it started from scratch at three-whatever in the morning on Wednesday. But the log here tells us that the system was initiated fifteen hours earlier. I mean, it's saying there's recorded content going back to like noon that day. Only, when you click on the files, it says 'file not found.'"

"Deleted?"

"You got it."

Audrey stared at the screen. "You're sure of this."

"Am I sure the box started recording at noon the day before? Yeah, sure as shit."

"No. Sure you can't retrieve the recording."

"It's, like, so gone."

"That's too bad."

"Hey, you look, like, disappointed. I thought you'd be thrilled. You want proof part of the video was erased, you got it right here."

"You ever read the book *Fortunately* when you were a kid?"

"My mom plopped me down in front of *One Life to Live* and *General Hospital*. Everything I learned about life I learned from soap operas. That's why I'm single."

"I must have read it a thousand times. There's a boy named Ned, and he's invited to a surprise party, but unfortunately the party's a thousand miles away. Fortunately a friend lends him an airplane, but unfortunately the motor explodes."

"Ouch. I hate when that happens."

"Fortunately there's a parachute in the airplane."

"But unfortunately he's horribly burned over ninety percent of his body and he's unable to open the chute? See how my mind works."

"This case is like that. Fortunately, unfortunately."

"That pretty much describes my sex life," Kevin said. "Fortunately the girl goes home with Kevin. Unfortunately she turns out to be a radical feminist lesbian who only wants him to teach her how to use Photoshop."

"Thanks, Kevin," Audrey got up from the stool. "Lunch at Taco Gordito's on me."

"Dinner," Kevin said firmly. "That's the deal."

78

Nick's cell phone rang just as he was pulling into the parking lot, almost half an hour later than usual this morning.

It was Victoria Zander, the Senior Vice President for Workplace Research, calling from Milan. "Nick," she said, "I'm at the *Salone Internazionale del Mobile* in Milan, and I'm so upset I can barely speak."

"Okay, Victoria, take a deep breath and tell me what's up."

"Will you please explain to me what's going on with Dashboard?"

Dashboard was one of the big new projects Victoria was developing, a portfolio of flexible, modular glass walls and partitions—very cool, beautifully designed, and something Victoria was really high on. Nick was high on it for business reasons: there was nothing else like it out there, and it was sure to hit a sweet spot.

"What do you mean, 'What's going on'?"

"After all the time and money we've put in on this, and—it just makes no *sense*! 'All major capital expenditures on hold'—what do you *mean* by that? And not even giving me the courtesy of advance notice?"

"Victoria—"

"I don't see how I can continue working for Stratton. I really don't. You know, Herman Miller has been after me for two years, and frankly I think that's a far better home for—"

"Victoria, hold on. Cool your jets, will you? Now, who told you we're shelving Dashboard?"

"You guys did! I just got the e-mail from Scott."

What e-mail? Nick almost asked, but instead he said, "Victoria, there's some kind of glitch. I'll call you right back."

He clicked off, slammed the car door, and went to look for Scott.

"He's not here, Nick," Gloria said. "He had an appointment."

"An appointment where?" Nick demanded.

She hesitated. "He didn't say."

"Get him on his cell, please. Right now."

Gloria hesitated again. "I'm sorry, Nick, but his cell phone doesn't work inside the plant. That's where he is."

"The *plant*? Which one?"

"The chair factory. He's—well, he's giving someone a tour."

As far as Nick knew, Scott had been inside the factories maybe twice before. "Who?"

"Nick, I—please."

"He asked you not to say anything."

Gloria closed her eyes, nodded. "I'm really sorry. It's a difficult position."

Difficult position? I'm the goddamned CEO, he thought.

"Don't worry about it," he said kindly.

Nick hadn't visited the chair plant in almost three months. There was a time when he'd visit monthly, sometimes more, just to check out how things were running, ask questions, listen to complaints, see how much inventory backlog was on hand. He'd check the quality boards at each station too, mostly to set an example, figuring that if he paid attention to the quality charts, the plant manager would too, and so would everyone below him.

He visited the plant just like Old Man Devries used to do, only when the old man did it, they weren't called Gemba walks, as they were now. That term had been introduced by Scott, along with Kaizen and a bunch of other Japanese words that Nick didn't remember, and that sounded to him like types of sushi.

It was the layoffs that made walking the plants an unpleasant chore. He could sense the hostility when he came through. It wasn't lost on him, or anybody else, that Old Man Devries's job had been to build plants, and his was to tear them down.

But he knew it was something he should probably start doing again, both here and in the other manufacturing complex about ten miles down the road. He'd go back to the monthly walks, he vowed.

If he had the chance.

If the factories were still here.

He noticed the big white sign on the front of the red brick building that said DAYS SINCE LAST ACCIDENT, and next to it a black LED panel with the red digital numerals 322. Someone had crossed out ACCIDENT and scrawled over it, with a heavy black marker, LAYOFFS.

He went in the visitors' entrance and caught the old familiar smell of welding and soldering, of hot metal. It took him back to visits to his father at work, of dog-day summers in high school and college spent working on the line.

The plump girl who sat at the battered old desk and handed out safety glasses, greeted visitors, and answered the phone, did a double take. "Good *morning*, Mr. Conover."

"Morning, Beth." Beth-something-Italian. He signed the log, noticed Scott had signed in about twenty minutes earlier along with someone else whose signature was illegible.

"Boy, both you *and* Mr. McNally in the space of an hour. Something going on I should know about?"

"No, in fact, I'm looking for Mr. McNally—any idea where he is?"

"No, sir. He had a visitor with him, though."

"Catch the other guy's name?"

"No, sir." She looked ashamed, as if she hadn't been doing her job. But Nick couldn't blame her for not checking the ID of the CFO's guest too carefully.

"Did Scott say where they were going?"

"No, sir. Sounded like Mr. McNally was giving a tour."

"Brad take them around?" Brad Kennedy was the plant manager, who gave tours only to the VIPs.

"No, sir. Want me to call Brad for you?"

"That's okay, Beth." He put on a pair of dorky-looking safety glasses.

He'd forgotten how deafening the place was. A million square feet of clattering, pounding, thudding metal. As he entered the main floor, keeping to the "green mile," as it was called—the green-painted border where you'd be safe from the Hi-Lo electric lift trucks that barreled down the aisles at heedless speeds—he could feel the floor shake. That meant the thousand-ton press, which stamped out the bases of the Symbiosis Chair control panel, was operating. The amazing thing was that the thousand-ton press was all the way across the factory floor, clear on the other end, and you could still feel it go.

The place filled him with pride. This was the real heart of Stratton—not the glitzy headquarters building with its silver-fabric cubicles and flat-panel monitors and all the backstabbing. The company's heartbeat was the regular thud of the thousand-ton behemoth, which sent vibrations up your spine as you passed through. It was here, where you still found some of those antique, dangerous, hydraulic-powered machines that could bend steel three-quarters of an inch thick, the exact same one on which his father had worked, bending steel, a seething monster that could take your hand off if you weren't careful. His dad had in fact lost the tip of his ring finger to the old green workhorse once, which caused him more embarrassment than anger, because he knew it was his fault. He must have felt that the brake machine, after all those years of a close working relationship, had been disappointed in him.

As he walked, he looked for Scott, and the more he looked, the angrier he got. The idea that Scott, who worked for him, a guy he'd hired, would dare shelve projects, block funding, change vendors without consulting him—that was insubordination of the most egregious sort.

Four hundred hourly workers in this plant, and another hundred or so salaried employees, all turning out chairs for the Armani-clad butts of investment bankers and hedge-fund managers, the Prada-clad rumps of art directors.

He was always impressed by how clean the factory floor was kept, free of oil spills, each area clearly marked with hanging signs. Each section had its own safety board, marked green for a safe day, yellow for a day with a minor injury, red for an injury requiring hospitalization. Good thing, he thought grimly, he didn't have one of those hanging in his house. What was the color for death?

He was looking for two men in business suits. They shouldn't be hard to find here, among the guys (and a few women) in jeans and T-shirts and hard hats.

Periodic messages flashed on the TV monitors, a steady stream of propaganda and morale-building. THE STRATTON FAMILY CARES ABOUT YOUR FAMILY—TALK TO YOUR BENEFITS ADVISER. And: THE NEXT INSPECTOR IS OUR CUSTOMER. And then: STRATTON SALUTES JIM VEENSTRA—FENWICK PLANT— 25 YEARS OF SERVICE.

A radio was blasting out Fleetwood Mac's "Shadows" from the progressive-build station where the Symbiosis chairs were assembled. Nick had borrowed the process from Ford and pretty much forced it on the workers, who resisted any further dumbing-down of their jobs. They liked building the whole chair themselves, and who could blame them? They liked the old piecework incentives. Now, one chair was assembled every fifty-four seconds as a light cycled from green to amber to red, signaling the workers to finish up. This plant turned out ten thousand Symbiosis chairs a week.

He jogged past the in-line washer that cleaned the oil off the chair-control covers and then sent them clattering down into an orange supply tub. He couldn't help slowing a bit to admire the robotic machine, a recent acquisition, that took sized and straightened wire stock, made five perfect bends, and then cut it, all in twelve seconds. In front of a press that made tubes out of eight-foot steel coils for the stacking chairs, a guy wearing green earplugs was asleep, obviously on break.

The floor supervisor, Tommy Pratt, saw him, threw him a wave, came hurrying up. Nick couldn't politely avoid the guy.

"Hey! Mr. Conover!" Tommy Pratt was a small man who looked like he'd been compacted from a larger man: everything about him seemed *dense*. Even his hair was dense, a helmet of tight brown curls. "Haven't seen you down here in a while."

"Couldn't stay away," Nick said, raising his voice to be heard above the din. "You seen Scott McNally?"

Pratt nodded, pointed toward the far end of the floor.

"Thanks," Nick shouted back. He gestured with his chin at an orange tub stacked high with black chair casters. An unusual sight—Scott's new inventory-control system made sure there was never a backlog. Keeping too much inventory on hand was a cardinal sin against the religion of Lean Manufacturing. "What's this?" he said.

"Yeah, Mr. Conover—we've been having a problem with, like, every other lot of those casters. You know, they're vended parts—"

"Seriously? That's a first. I'll have someone call Lenny at Peerless—no, in fact, I'll call Lenny myself." Peerless, in St. Joseph, Michigan, had been manufacturing chair casters for Stratton since forever. Nick vaguely remembered getting a couple of phone messages from Lenny Bloch, the CEO of Peerless. "Uh, no, sir," Pratt said. "We switched to another vendor last month. Chinese company, I think."

"Huh?"

"The bitch of it is, sir, with Peerless, if we ever got a bad batch, which hardly ever happened by the way, he'd just truck us a new lot overnight. Now we gotta deal with container ships, you know, takes forever."

"Who switched vendors?"

"Well, I think Brad said it was Ted Hollander who insisted on it. Brad put up a fight, but you know, the word came down, we're cutting costs and all that."

Ted Hollander was vice president for control and procurement, and one of Scott McNally's direct reports. Nick clenched his jaw.

"I'll get back to you on that," he said in a voice of corporate cordiality. "When I tell the guys to look at cost containment, some of them go a little overboard." Nick turned to go, but Pratt touched his elbow. "Uh, Mr. Conover, one more thing. I hope I'm not driving you away here—I don't want you to think all we're ever gonna do is bitch at you, you know?"

"What is it?"

"The damned Slear Line. We had to shut it down twice since the shift started this morning. It's really bottlenecking things."

"It's older than I am."

"That's just it. The service guy keeps telling us we gotta replace it. I know that's a load of dough, but I don't think we have a choice."

"I trust your judgment," Nick said blandly.

Pratt gave him a quizzical look; he'd been expecting an argument. "I'm not complaining. I'm just saying, we can't put it off that much longer."

"I'm sure you know what you're doing."

"Because we couldn't get the requisition approved," Pratt said. "Your people said it wasn't a good time right now. Something about putting major capital expenditures on hold."

"What do you mean, 'my people'?"

"We put the request through last month. Word came down from Hollander a couple of weeks ago."

"There's no freeze on major expenditures, okay? We're in this for the long haul." Nick shook his head. "Some people do tend to get a little overzealous. Excuse me."

Two men in suits and safety glasses were walking through the "supermarket," the area where parts were stored in aisles. They were walking quickly, and one of them—Scott—was waving a hand at something as they left the floor. Nick wondered what he was saying to the other man, whom he recognized from last night.

The attorney from Chicago who was supposedly advising Scott on structuring deals. The man whom Scott, who hadn't been on the shop floor in more than a year, was showing around in such a low-profile, almost secretive way.

There was, of course, no reason in the world for a financial engineer to tour one of Stratton's factories. Nick thought about trying to catch up with them, but he decided not to bother.

No need to be lied to again.

79

There wasn't any e-mail from Cassie. Not that he expected any, but he was sort of hoping there'd be something. He realized he owed her an apology, so he typed:

```
Where'd my little porcupine go?
—N
```

Then he adjusted the angle on the flat-panel monitor, opened his browser and went to Google. He typed in Randall Enright's name, and the name of his law firm, from the card Cassie had gotten from him last night.

Abbotsford Gruendig had offices in London, Chicago, Los Angeles, Tokyo, and Hong Kong, among other places. "With over two thousand lawyers in 25 offices around the world, Abbotsford Gruendig provides worldwide service to national and multinational corporations, institutions and governments," the firm's home page boasted.

He typed in Randall Enright's name. It appeared, as part of a list of names, on a page headed with the rubric MERGERS & ACQUISITIONS and then more boilerplate:

Our corporate lawyers are leaders in M&A, focusing on multijurisdictional transactions. They can advise on licence requirements and regulatory compliance and provide local legal services in over twenty jurisdictions. Our clients include many larger corporations in the telecommunications, defence and manufacturing sectors.

Blah blah blah. More legal gobbledygook.

But it told him that Scott sure as hell wasn't getting up to speed on new accounting regulations.

He was up to something completely different.

Stephanie Alstrom, Stratton's corporate counsel, wore a navy blue suit with a white blouse and a big heavy gold chain necklace that was probably intended to make her look more authoritative. Instead, the necklace and matching earrings diminished her, made her look tiny. Her gray hair was close-cropped, her mouth heavily lined, the bags under her eyes pronounced. She was in her fifties but looked twenty years older. Maybe that was what decades of practicing corporate law could do to you.

"Sit down," Nick said. "Thanks for dropping by."

"Sure." She looked worried, but then again, she always looked worried. "You wanted to know about Abbotsford Gruendig?"

Nick nodded.

"I'm not sure what you wanted to know, exactly, but it's a big international law firm, offices all over the world. A merger of an old-line British firm and a German one."

"And that guy Randall Enright?"

"M and A lawyer, speaks fluent Mandarin. A real hotshot. China law specialist, spent years in their Hong Kong office until his wife forced them to move back to the States. Mind if I ask why the sudden interest?"

"The name came up, that's all. Now, what do you know about Stratton Asia Ventures?"

She wrinkled her brow. "Not much. A subsidiary corporation Scott set up. He never ran it by my office."

"Is that unusual?"

"We review all sorts of contracts, but we don't go after people and insist on it. I assumed he was using local counsel in Hong Kong."

"Check this out, would you?" Nick handed her the e-mail from Scott to Martin Lai in Hong Kong, which Scott had tried to delete.

"Ten million dollars wired to an account in Macau," Nick said as she looked it over. "What does that tell you?"

She looked at Nick, looked down quickly. "I don't know what you're asking me."

"Can you think of a circumstance in which ten million dollars would be wired to a numbered account in Macau?"

She flushed. "I don't want to be casting aspersions. I really don't want to guess."

"I'm asking you to, Steph."

"Between you and me?"

"Please. Not to be repeated to anyone."

After a moment's hesitation, she said, "One of two things. Macau is one of those money-laundering havens. The banks there are used for hidden accounts by the Chinese leaders, same way deposed third-world dictators use the Caymans."

"Interesting. Are you thinking what I'm thinking?"

She was clearly uncomfortable. "Embezzlement—or a bribe. But this is only speculation on my part, Nick."

"I understand."

"And not to be repeated."

"You're afraid of Scott, aren't you?"

Stephanie looked down at the table, her eyes darting back and forth, and she said nothing.

"He works for me," Nick said.

"On paper, I guess," she said.

"Excuse me?" Her remark felt to Nick like a blow to his solar plexus. It felt like the wind had been knocked out of him.

"The org chart says he's under you, Nick," she said hastily. "That's all I mean."

80

"Got something for you," Eddie said over the phone.

"I'll meet you in the small conference room on my floor in ten minutes," Nick said.

Eddie hesitated. "Actually, why don't you come down to my office?"

"How come?"

"Maybe I'm tired of taking the elevator up there."

The only thing worse than this kind of idiotic, petty game, Nick thought, was responding to it. "Fine," he said curtly, and hung up.

"You know how much e-mail Scotty blasts out?" Eddie said, leaning back in his chair. It was a new chair, Nick noticed, one of a premium, super-limited run of Symbiosis chairs upholstered in butter-soft Gucci leather. "He's like a one-man spam generator or something."

"Sorry to put you out," Nick said. He also noticed that Eddie had a new computer with the largest flat-panel monitor he'd ever seen.

"Guy's a Levitra addict, first off. Gets it over the Internet. I guess he doesn't want his doc to know — small town and all that."

"I really don't care."

"He also buys sex tapes. Like *How to Be a Better Lover. Enhance Your Performance. Sex for Life.*"

"Goddammit," Nick said, "that's his business, and I don't want to hear about it. I'm only interested in *our* business."

"Our business," Eddie said. He sat upright, reached over for a thick manila folder, and set it down in front of Nick with a thud. "Here's something that's very much our business. Do you even know the first fucking thing about Cassie Stadler?"

"We're back to that?" Nick snapped. "You stay out of my goddamned e-mails, or—"

Eddie looked up suddenly, his eyes locked with Nick's. "Or what?"

Nick shook his head, didn't reply.

"That's right. We're joined at the hip now, big guy. I got job security, you understand?"

Nick's heart thrummed, and he bit his lower lip.

"Now," Eddie said, a lilt to his voice. "I'm not reading your fucking e-mails. I don't need to. You forget I can watch your house on my computer."

"Watch my *house*?" Nick shook his head. "Huh?"

Eddie shrugged. "Your security cameras transmit over the Internet to the company server, you know that. I can see who's coming and going. And I can see this babe coming and going a *lot*."

"You do not have permission to spy on me, you hear me?"

"Couple of weeks ago you were begging for my help. Someday soon you'll thank me. You know this chick spent eight months in a psycho ward?"

"Yeah," Nick said. "Only it was six months, and it wasn't a 'psycho ward.' She was hospitalized for depression after a bunch of college friends of hers were killed in an accident. So what?"

"You know that for the last six years, there's no record of any FICA payments on this broad? Meaning that she didn't have a job? Don't you think that's strange?"

"I'm not hiring her to be vice president of human resources. In fact, I'm not hiring her at all. She's been a yoga teacher. How many yoga teachers make regular social-security payments, anyway?"

"I'm not done yet. Get this: 'Cassie' isn't even her real name."

Nick furrowed his brow.

Eddie smiled. "Helen. Her name is Helen Stadler. Cassie—that's not on her birth certificate. Not a legal name change. Totally made up."

"So what? What's your point?"

"I got a feeling about her," Eddie said. "Something about her ain't correct. We talked about this already, but let me say it again: I don't care how sweet the snatch. It ain't worth the risk."

"All I asked you to do was to find out what Scott McNally was up to."

After a few seconds of sullen silence, Eddie handed Nick another folder.

"So, those encrypted documents my guys found?"

"Yeah?"

"My guys cracked 'em all. It's really just one document, bunch of different drafts, went back and forth between Scotty and some lawyer in Chicago."

"Randall Enright."

Eddie cocked his head. "That's right."

"What is it?"

"Fuck if I know. Legal bullshit."

Nick started to page through the documents. Many of them were labeled DRAFT ONLY and REDLINE. The sheets were dense with legal jargon and stippled with numbers, the demon spawn of a lawyer and an accountant.

"Maybe he's selling company secrets," Eddie said.

Nick shook his head. "Not our Scott. Huh-uh. He's not selling company secrets."

"No?"

"No," Nick said, once again short of breath. "He's selling the company."

81

"Why do you trust me?" said Stephanie Alstrom. They met in one of the smaller conference rooms on her floor. There was just no damned privacy in this company, Nick realized. Everyone knew who was meeting with whom; everyone could listen in.

"What do you mean?"

"Scott's stabbing you in the back, and you hired him too."

"Instinct, I guess. Why, are you working against me too?"

"No," she smiled. Nick had never seen her smile before, and it wrinkled her face strangely. "I just guess I should feel flattered."

"Well," Nick said, "my instinct has failed me before. But you can't be distrustful of everyone."

"Good point," she said, putting on a pair of half-glasses. "So, you know what you've got here, right?"

"A Definitive Purchase Agreement," Nick said. He'd looked over hundreds of contracts like this in his career, and even though the legalese froze his brain, he'd learned to hack his way through the dense underbrush to uncover the key points. "Fairfield Equity Partners is selling us to some Hong Kong–based firm called Pacific Rim Investors."

Stephanie shook her head slowly. "That's not what I pick up from this. It's strange. For one thing, there's not a single mention in the list of assets of any factories or plants or employees. Which, if they were planning to keep any of it, they'd have to list. And then, in the Representations and Warranties section, it says the buyer's on the hook for any costs, liabilities, et cetera, associated with shutting down U.S. facilities or firing all employees. So, it's pretty clear. Pacific Rim is buying only Stratton's name. And getting rid of everything else."

Nick stared. "They don't need our factories. They've got plenty in Shenzhen. But all this money for a *name*?"

"Stratton means class. An old reliable American name that's synonymous with elegance and solidity. Plus, they get our distribution channels. Think about it—they can make everything over there at a fraction of the price, slap a Stratton nameplate on it, sell it for a premium. No American firm would have made a deal like this."

"Who are they, this Pacific Rim Investors?"

"No idea, but I'll find out for you. Looks like Randall Enright wasn't working for Fairfield after all—he represents the buyer. Pacific Rim."

Nick nodded. Now he understood why Scott had given Enright the factory tour. Enright was in Fenwick to do due diligence on behalf of a Hong Kong–based firm that couldn't come to visit because they wanted to keep everything very quiet.

She said, "The least they could do is tell you."

"They knew I'd go ballistic."

"That must be why they put Scott on the board. Asians always demand to meet with the top brass. If Todd Muldaur thought firing you would help, he'd have done it already."

"Exactly."

"It freaks potential buyers out if a CEO gets fired right before a sale. Everyone's antennae go up. Plus, a lot of the key relationships are yours. The smarter move was to hermetically seal you off. As they did."

"I used to think Todd Muldaur was an idiot, but now I know better. He's just a prick. Can you explain this side agreement to me?"

Her pruned mouth turned down in a scowl. "I've never seen anything like it. It looks like some kind of deal-sweetener. From what I can tell, it's a way to speed up the deal, make it happen fast. But that's just a guess. You might want to talk to someone who knows."

"Like who? Scott's the only one I know who understands the really devious stuff."

"He's good, but he's not the only one," Stephanie said. "Does Hutch still speak to you?"

82

Nick had begun to dread going out in public.

Not "public" as in going to work, though that still took a fair amount of effort, putting on his Nick Conover, CEO act, confident and friendly and outgoing, when a toxic spill of anxiety threatened to ooze out through his pores. But whether it was school functions or shopping or taking clients out to restaurants, it was getting harder and harder to keep the mask fastened securely.

What was once just uncomfortable, even painful—seeing people the company had laid off, exchanging polite if tense words with them, or just generally feeling like a pariah in this town—was now close to intolerable. Everywhere he went, everyone he ran into, he felt as if a neon sign was hanging around his neck, its gaudy orange tubes flashing the word MURDERER.

Even tonight, when he was just another spectator at Julia's piano recital. Her long-dreaded, long-awaited piano recital. It was being held in one of the old town performance theaters, Aftermath Hall, a mildew-smelling old place that had been built in the nineteen thirties, a Steinway grand on a yellow wooden stage, red velvet curtain, matching red velvet upholstered seats with uncomfortable wooden backs.

The kids in their little coats and ties or their dresses streaked across the lobby, propelled by nervous energy. A couple of little African-American boys in jackets and ties with their older sister, in a white dress with a bow: unusual in Fenwick, given how few blacks there were.

He was startled to find Laura's sister there. Abby was a couple of years older than Laura, had two kids as well, married a guy with a trust fund and no personality. He claimed to be a novelist, but mostly he played tennis and golf. Abby had the same clear blue eyes as Laura, had the same swan neck. Instead of Laura's corkscrew brown curls, though, her brown hair was straight and glossy and fell to her shoulders. She was more reserved, had a more regal bearing, was less approachable. Nick didn't especially like her. The feeling was probably mutual.

"Hey," he said, touching her elbow. "Nice of you to come. Julia's going to be thrilled."

"It was sweet of Julia to call me."

"She did?"

"You seem surprised. You didn't tell her to?"

"I can't tell her to do anything, you know that. How's the family?"

"We're fine. Kids doing okay?"

He shrugged. "Sometimes yes, sometimes no. They miss you a lot."

"Do they. Not you, though." Then she softened it a bit with a smile that didn't look very sincere.

"Come on. We all do. How come we haven't seen you?"

"Oh," she breathed, "it's been crazy."

"Crazy how?"

She blinked, looked uncomfortable. Finally she said, "Look, Nick, it's hard for me. Since . . ."

"Hey, it's okay," Nick put in hastily. "I'm just saying, don't be a stranger."

"No, Nick," Abby said, inclining her head, lowering her voice, her eyes gleaming with something bad. "It's just that—every time I look at you." She looked down, then back up at him. "Every time I look at you it makes me sick."

Nick felt as if he'd just been kicked in the throat.

Little kids, big kids running past, dressed up, taut with the pre-performance jitters. Someone playing a swatch of complicated music on the Steinway, sounding like a professional you might hear at Carnegie Hall.

Laura's nude body on the folding wheeled table after the embalming, Nick weeping and slobbering as he dressed her, his request, honored by the funeral director with some reluctance. Nick unable to look at her waxen face, a plausible imitation of her once glowing skin, the neck and cheek he'd nuzzled against so many times.

"You think the accident was my fault, that it?"

"I really see no sense in talking about it," she said, looking at the floor. "Where's Julia?"

"Probably waiting her turn at the piano." Nick felt a hand on his shoulder, turned, and was stunned to see Cassie. His heart lifted.

She stood on her tiptoes, gave him a quick peck on the lips.

"Cass—Jesus, I had no idea—"

"Wouldn't miss it for the world."

"Did Julia order you to show up too?"

"She *told* me about it, which is a different thing. I'd say a daughter's piano recital falls in the category of a family obligation, don't you think?"

"I'm—wow."

"Come on, I'm practically family. Plus, I'm a big classical piano fan, don't you know that about me?"

"Why do I doubt that?"

She put her lips to his ear and whispered, her hot breath getting him excited: "I owe you an apology."

Then she was gone, before Nick had a chance to introduce her.

"Who's the new girlfriend?" Abby's voice, abrupt and harsh and brittle, an undertone of ridicule.

Nick froze. "Her name's . . . Cassie. I mean, she's—"

I mean, she's what? Not a girlfriend? Just a fuck? Oh, she's the daughter of the guy I murdered, ain't that a funny coincidence? Tell that to Craig, your alleged-writer husband. Give him something to write about.

"She's beautiful." Abby's arched brows, lowered lids, glimmering with contempt.

He nodded, supremely uncomfortable.

"She doesn't exactly seem like the Nick Conover type, though. Is she an . . . artist or something?"

"She does some painting. Teaches yoga."

"Glad you're dating again." Abby could not have sounded more inauthentic.

"Yeah, well . . ."

"Hey, it's been a year, right?" she said brightly, something cold and hard and lilting in her voice. "You're allowed to date." She smiled, victorious, not even bothering to hide it.

Nick couldn't think of anything to say.

LaTonya was lecturing some poor soul as Audrey approached, wagging her forefinger, her long coral-colored nails—a self-adhesive French manicure kit she'd been hounding Audrey to try—looking like dangerous instruments. She was dressed in an avocado muumuu with big jangly earrings. "That's right," she was saying. "I can make a hundred and fifty dollars an hour easy, taking these online surveys. Sitting at home in my pajamas. I get paid for expressing my *opinions*!"

When she saw Audrey, she lit up. "And I figured you'd be working," she said, enfolding Audrey in an immense bosomy hug.

"Don't tell me Leon's here too." LaTonya seemed to have forgotten about her sales pitch, freeing the victim to drift off.

"I don't know where Leon is," Audrey confessed. "He wasn't at home when I stopped in."

"Mmm *hmm*," LaTonya hummed significantly. "The one thing I *know* he's not doing is working."

"Do you know something you're not telling me?" Audrey said, embarrassed by the desperation she'd let show.

"About Leon? You think he tells me anything?"

"LaTonya, sister," Audrey said, moving in close, "I'm worried about him."

"You do too much worrying about that man. He don't deserve it."

"That's not what I mean. He's—well, he's gone too much."

"Thank your lucky stars for that."

"We—we haven't had much of a private life in a very long time," Audrey forced herself to say.

LaTonya waggled her head. "I don't think I want to know the gory details about my brother, you know?"

"No, I'm . . . Something's going on, LaTonya, you understand what I'm saying, don't you?"

"His drinking getting even worse?"

"It isn't that, I don't think. He's just been disappearing a lot."

"Think that bastard is cheating on you, that it?"

Tears sprang to Audrey's eyes. She compressed her lips, nodded.

"You want me to have a talk with him? I'll slice his fucking balls off."

"I'll handle it, LaTonya."

"You don't hesitate to call me in, hear? Lazy bastard don't know what a good thing he has in you."

83

Audrey's heart broke when Nicholas Conover's daughter played the first prelude from the *Well-Tempered Clavier*. It wasn't just that the girl hadn't played all that well—a number of note fumbles, her technique not very polished, her performance mechanical. Camille had all but stolen the show with the Brahms waltz, had played perfectly and with heart, making Audrey burst with pride. It was what was about to happen to Julia Conover. This little girl, awkward in her dress, had lost her mother, something that should never happen to a child. And now she was about to lose her father.

In just a couple of days her father would be arrested, charged with murder. The only time she'd ever see her remaining parent would be during supervised jail visits, her daddy wearing an orange jumpsuit, behind a bulletproof window. Her life would be upended by a public murder trial; she'd never stop hearing the vicious gossip, she'd cry herself to sleep, and who would tuck her in at night? A paid babysitter? It was too awful to think about.

And then her daddy would be sent away to prison. This beautiful little girl, who wasn't much of a pianist but radiated sweetness and naïveté: her life was about to change forever. Andrew Stadler may have been the murder victim, but this little girl was a victim too, and it filled Audrey with sorrow and foreboding.

As the teacher, Mrs. Guarini, thanked the audience for coming and invited everyone to stay for refreshments, Audrey turned around and saw Nicholas Conover.

He was holding up a video camera. Next to him sat a beautiful young woman, and next to her Conover's handsome son, Lucas. Audrey did a double take, recognizing the woman, who just then put her hand on Conover's neck, stroking it familiarly.

It was Cassie Stadler.

Andrew Stadler's daughter.

Her mind spun crazily. She didn't know what to think, what to make of it.

Nicholas Conover, having an affair with the daughter of the man he'd murdered.

She felt as if a whole row of doors had just been flung open.

84

It had to happen, since the two of them got into work at about the same time.

Nick and Scott had been avoiding each other studiously. Even at meetings where both of them were present, they were publicly cordial yet no longer exchanged small talk, before or after.

But they could hardly avoid each other right now. Nick stood at the elevator bank, waiting, just as Scott approached.

Nick was the first to speak: " 'Morning, Scott."

" 'Morning, Nick."

A long stretch of silence.

Fortunately, someone else came up to them, a woman who worked in Accounts Receivable. She greeted Scott, who was her boss, then shyly said, "Hi" in Nick's general direction.

The three of them rode up in silence, everyone watching the numbers change. The woman got off on three.

Nick turned to Scott. "So you've been busy," he said. It came out more fiercely than he intended.

Scott shrugged. "Just the usual."

"The usual include killing new projects like Dashboard?"

A beat, and then: "I tabled it, actually."

"I didn't know new product development was in your job description."

Scott looked momentarily uncertain, as if he were considering ducking the question, but then he said, "Any expenditures of that magnitude concern me."

The elevator dinged as it reached the executive floor.

"Well," Scott said with visible relief, "to be continued, I'm sure."

Nick reached over to the elevator control panel and pressed the emergency stop button, which immediately stopped the doors from opening and also set off an alarm bell that sounded distantly in the elevator shaft.

"What the hell are you—"

"Whose side are you on, Scott?" Nick asked with ferocious calm, crowding Scott into the corner of the elevator. "You think I don't know what's going on?"

Nick braced himself for the usual wisecracking evasions. Scott's face went a deep plum color, his eyes growing, but Nick saw anger in his face, not fear.

He's not scared of you, Cassie had observed.

"There aren't any sides here, Nick. It's not like shirts versus skins."

"I want you to listen to me closely. You are not to kill or 'table' projects, change vendors, or in fact make any changes whatsoever without consulting me, are we clear?"

"Not that simple," Scott replied levelly, a tic starting in his left eye. "I make decisions all day long—"

The elevator emergency alarm kept ringing.

Nick dropped his voice to a near-whisper. "Who do you think you're working for? Any decision you make, any order you give, that's not in your designated area of responsibility will be countermanded—by me. Publicly, if need be. You see, Scott, like it or not, you work for me," Nick said. "Not for Todd Muldaur, not for Willard Osgood, but for me. Understand?"

Scott stared, his left eye wincing madly. Finally he said, "The real question is, who do you think *you're* working for? We both work for our stakeholders. It's pretty simple. Your problem is that you've never really understood that. You talk about managing this company as if you own the place. But I've got news for you. You don't own the place, and neither do I. You think you're a better man than me because you got all teary-eyed when the layoffs came? You talk about the 'Stratton Family,' but guess what, Nick. It's not a family. It's a business. You're a great face to parade in front of the Wall Street analysts. But just because you look good in tights doesn't make you a superhero."

"That's enough, Scott."

"Fairfield gave you the car keys, Nick. They didn't give you the car."

Nick took a deep breath. "There's only one driver."

The tic in Scott's eye was coming more rapidly now. Nick could see a vein pulsing at his temple. "In case you haven't figured it out," Scott said, "things have changed around here. You can't fire me." He tried to reach around for the emergency stop button to get the elevator doors open. But Nick swiveled his body in one quick motion to block Scott's hand.

"You're right," he said. "I can't fire you. But let me be really clear: so long as I'm here, you are not to conduct any discussions regarding the sale of this company."

A thin smile crept across Scott's face as he kept staring. Several seconds ticked by. The only sound was the ring of the elevator alarm. "Fine," he said freezingly. "You're the boss." But his tone called to mind Cassie's interpretation of Scott's refrain: those unspoken words *for now*.

85

He returned to his desk shaken and began to go through his e-mail. More Nigerians who sought to share their plundered millions. More offers to add inches, or borrow money, or acquire painkillers.

He called Henry Hutchens and made an appointment for coffee or an early lunch tomorrow. Then he tried Martin Lai in Hong Kong, at home, where it was around nine in the evening.

This time, Martin Lai answered. "Oh—Mr. Conover, yes, thank you, thank you," he said, a cataract of nerves. "I'm very sorry I didn't call you back—I was on a trip, sir."

Nick knew that wasn't true. Had Lai, surprised to get a call from the CEO, checked in with Scott, who told him not to reply? "Martin, I need your help with something important."

"Yes, sir. Of course, sir."

"What can you tell me about a ten-million-dollar transfer of funds out of Stratton Asia Ventures to a numbered account in Macau?"

"Sir, I don't know anything about that," Lai answered, too quickly.

"Meaning you don't know why the transfer was made?"

"No, sir, this is the first I hear of it."

He was covering up. Scott must have gotten to him.

"Martin, this financial irregularity has been called to my attention, and it's something I'm quite concerned about. I thought I'd see if you know anything before the formal investigation is launched by Compliance."

"No, sir," Lai said. "I never heard of it before."

As he stared at the computer screen, Marjorie's voice came over the intercom, and at the same instant, an instant message popped up.

"Nick," she said, "it's the high school again."

Nick groaned.

The message was from Stephanie Alstrom:

```
Nick—info for you—talk soon?
```

"Is it Sundquist again?" he said to Marjorie, as he typed:

```
come by my office now.
```

"I'm afraid it is," Marjorie said. "And this time—well, it sounds awfully serious."

"Oh, God," he said. "Can you put me through?"

Stephanie Alstrom was getting out of the elevator just as Nick was about to get in. He gestured for her to stay in the cabin, and once the doors closed, he said, "I'm in a rush. Personal business. What do you have, Steph?"

"Pacific Rim Investors," she said. "Apparently it's a consortium whose silent partner—their anonymous sugar daddy—is an arm of the P.L.A.—the People's Liberation Army of China."

"Why the hell would the Chinese *army* want to buy Stratton?"

"Capitalism, pure and simple. They've bought up thousands of foreign corporations, usually through shell companies to avoid the political backlash. I wonder if Willard Osgood knows it. He's somewhere to the right of Attila the Hun."

"I wonder," Nick said. "But no one's a bigger archconservative than Dorothy Devries. And you can bet *she* has no idea."

86

"Nick, I know you're an extremely busy man," Jerome Sundquist said, leading him past the framed photos of multicultural tennis champs, "but if anyone owes you an apology, it's your son." He spoke loudly so Lucas could hear.

Lucas sat in one of the camel-upholstered side chairs, looking small, shoulders hunched, furled into himself. He was wearing a gray T-shirt under a plaid shirt and track pants that were zippered above the knee so you could turn them into shorts, not that Lucas ever did.

He didn't look up when Nick entered.

Nick stood there in his raincoat—this time he was prepared for the lousy weather, even brought an umbrella—and said, "You did it again, didn't you."

Lucas didn't reply.

"Tell your father, Lucas," Sundquist said as he took a seat behind his overly large desk. Nick wondered, fleetingly, why it was that people with the biggest desks and the biggest offices were often not all that powerful, in the scheme of things.

Then he reminded himself that Jerry Sundquist might only run a high school in a small town in Michigan, but right now he was as powerful in the lives of the Conovers as Willard Osgood.

Lucas cast the principal a bloodshot glare and looked back down at his feet. Had he been crying?

"Well, if he doesn't have the courage to tell you, I will," Sundquist said, leaning back in his chair. He actually seemed to be enjoying this moment,

Nick thought. "I told you that the second time he was caught smoking he'd be expelled."

"Understood," Nick said.

"And I think I also told you that if we found drugs, we'd let the police prosecute."

"Drugs?"

"The school board voted unanimously a few years ago that any student using, distributing, or even possessing marijuana on school property will be suspended, arrested, and face an expulsion hearing."

"Arrested," Nick said, suddenly feeling a chill, as if he'd just stepped into a meat locker. Lucas wasn't crying. He was high.

"We notify the police and let them prosecute. And I have to tell you, Michigan tends to be tough on minors in possession of marijuana. The two-thousand-dollar fine is probably insignificant to you, Nick, but I've seen judges give minors anything from probation to forty-five days in prison, as much as a year."

"Jerry—"

"Under Michigan law, we're required to notify the local police, do you know that? MCL three-eighty, thirteen oh eight. We don't have a choice about it."

Nick nodded, put a hand on his forehead and began massaging away the headache. My God, he thought. Expulsion? There wasn't another high school for forty miles. And what private school would take Lucas, given his record? How would Laura have handled this? She was so much better at difficult situations than he was. "Jerry, I'd like us to talk. You and me. Without Luke."

Sundquist didn't have to do anything more than raise his chin at Lucas, who quickly got up, as if shot from a cannon. "Wait in the faculty lounge," he said to Lucas's back.

"I'm sorry, Nick. I hate to do this to you."

"Jerry," Nick said, leaning forward in his chair. For a moment, he lost his train of thought. Suddenly he wasn't a prominent parent, the president and chief executive officer of the biggest company in town. He was a high school kid pleading with the principal. "I'm as angry about this as you are. More so, probably. And we've got to let him know it's totally unacceptable. But it's his first time."

"Somehow I doubt it's his first time using marijuana," Sundquist said with a sidelong glance. "But in any case, we have a zero-tolerance policy. Our options are severely limited here."

"It's not a gun, and he's not exactly a dealer. We're talking about one marijuana cigarette, right?"

Sundquist nodded. "That's all it takes these days."

"Jerry, you've got to consider what the kid has been going through in the last year, with Laura's death." There was a note of pleading in his voice that embarrassed Nick.

The principal looked unmoved. In fact, he looked almost pleased. Nick felt the anger in him rise, but he knew anger would be the worst response in this situation.

Nick took a deep breath. "Jerry, I'm asking for your mercy. If there's anything I can do for the high school, the school system. Anything Stratton can do."

"Are you offering a *payoff*?" Sundquist said, biting off the words.

"Of course not," Nick said, although both men knew that was exactly what he was talking about. An extra deep discount on furniture could save the high school hundreds of thousands of dollars a year.

Sundquist closed his eyes, shook his head sadly. "That's beneath you, Nick. What kind of lesson do you think it's going to teach your son if he gets special treatment because of who his dad is?"

"What we talk about stays between us," Nick said. He couldn't believe that he'd just offered the high school principal a bribe. Was anything lower? Bribes—that was the coin of Scott McNally's realm, Todd Muldaur's realm. Not his.

Jerome Sundquist was looking at him with a new expression now, one of disappointment and maybe even contempt. "I'm going to pretend I didn't hear it, Nick. But I'm willing to show some leniency on the grounds of his mother's death. I do have to notify the police that we're willing to handle the incident ourselves, and generally they leave it to our discretion. I'm giving Lucas a five-day suspension and assigning him to crisis counseling during that time and for the rest of the school year. But the next time, I go right to the police."

Nick stood up, walked up to Sundquist's desk and put out his hand to shake. "Thanks, Jerry," he said. "I think it's the right decision, and I appreciate it."

But Sundquist wouldn't shake his hand.

Ten minutes later Nick and Lucas walked out together through the glass doors of the high school. The rain was really coming down now—it was monsoon season, had to be—and Nick held up his umbrella for Lucas, who shunned it, striding ahead through the rain, head up as if he wanted to get soaked.

Lucas seemed to hesitate before getting into the front seat, as if contemplating making a run for it. As the car nosed through the parking lot and onto Grandview Avenue, the silence was electric with tension.

Lucas wasn't high anymore. He was low, and he was silent, but it wasn't a neutral silence. It was a defiant silence, like that of a prisoner of war determined to reveal nothing more than his name, rank, and serial number.

Nick's own silence was the silence of someone who had plenty to say but was afraid of what would happen if he began to speak.

Lucas's hand snaked around to the radio dial and turned on some alternative rock station, blasting it.

Nick immediately switched it off. "You proud of yourself?"

Lucas said nothing, just stared fixedly ahead as the windshield wipers flipped back and forth in a lulling rhythm.

"You know something? This would have broken your mother's heart. You should be relieved she isn't around to see this."

More silence. This time Nick waited for a reply. He was about to go on when Lucas said, in a hollow voice, "I guess you made sure of that."

"And what's that supposed to mean?"

Lucas didn't respond.

"What the *fuck* is that supposed to mean?" Nick realized he was shouting. He could see a spray of his own spittle on the windshield. He pulled the car over, braked to an abrupt stop, and turned to face Lucas.

"What do *you* think?" Lucas said in a low, wobbly voice, not meeting his eyes.

Nick stared, disbelieving. "What are you trying to say?" he whispered, summoning all the calm he could muster.

"Forget it," Lucas said, making a little buzz-off gesture with his left hand.

"What are you trying to say?"

"I wouldn't know, Dad. I wasn't there."

"What's gotten into you, Lucas?" The windshield wipers ticked back and forth, back and forth, and he could hear the regular clicking of the turn signal that hadn't gone off. He reached over, switched off the signal. The rain sheeted the car's windows, making it feel like the two of them were inside a cabin in a terrible storm, but it wasn't a safe place. "Look, Luke, you don't have Mom anymore. You just have me. You wish it were otherwise. So do I. But we've got to make the best of a bad situation."

"It wasn't me who made that situation."

"No one 'made' that situation," Nick said.

"You killed Mom," he said, so quietly that for a moment Nick wasn't sure Lucas had actually spoken the words.

Nick felt like someone had grabbed his heart and squeezed. "I can't deal with this right now. I can't deal with *you*."

You Conover men. Better defended than a medieval castle.

"Fine with me."

"No," Nick said. "No. Scratch that." He was breathing hard, as if he had just done an eight-hundred-meter sprint. "Okay, listen to me. What happened to your mother that night—God knows we've talked about it . . ."

"No, Dad." Lucas's voice was shaky but resolute. "We've never talked about it. You *refer* to it. You don't talk about it. That's the house rule. We don't talk about it. *You* don't. You talk about what a fuck-up I am. *That's* what you talk about."

The windows had begun to fog up. Nick closed his eyes. "About your mother. There isn't a day that goes by when I don't wonder whether there was anything I could have done—anything at all—that might have made a difference."

"You never said . . ." Lucas's eyes were wet and his voice was thick, muffled.

"The truck came out of nowhere," Nick began, but then he stopped. It was too painful. "Luke, what happened happened. And it wasn't about me and it wasn't about you."

Lucas was quiet for a moment. "Fucking swim meet."

"Lucas, don't try to make sense of it. Don't try to connect the dots, as if there was some kind of logic to it all. It just *happened*."

"I didn't visit her." Lucas's words were slurred, whether from the pot or from emotion, Nick couldn't tell, and didn't care. "In the hospital. Afterward."

"She was in a coma. She was already gone, Luke."

"Maybe she could have heard me." His voice had gotten thin and reedy.

"She knew you loved her, Luke. She didn't need reminding. I don't think she wanted you to remember her like that, anyway. She wouldn't have been sore that you weren't there. She would have been glad. I really believe that. You were always attuned to her feelings. Like there was some radio frequency only the two of you could hear. You know something, Luke? I think maybe you were the only one of us who did what she would have wanted."

Lucas buried his face in his hands. When he spoke again, his voice sounded as if it were coming from a long way off. "Why do you hate me so much? Is it 'cause I look like her, and you can't deal with that?"

"Lucas," Nick said. He was determined to hold it together. "I want you to listen to me. I need you to hear this." He squeezed his eyes shut. "There is nothing in my life more precious to me than you are." His voice was hoarse, and he got the words out with difficulty, but he got them out. "I love you more than my life."

He put his arms around his son, who at first stiffened and squirmed, and then, suddenly, put his own arms around Nick and clasped him tightly, the way he did when Lucas was a little boy.

Nick felt the rhythmic convulsions of grief, the staccato expulsions of breath, and it took him a moment before he realized that Lucas wasn't the only one who was weeping.

87

The phone rang, and Audrey picked it up without thinking.

"Is this Detective Rhimes?" A sweet, female voice, the words slow and careful.

Her heart sank. "Yes it is," Audrey said, although she was sorely tempted to say, No, I'm afraid Detective Rhimes is on vacation.

"Detective, this is Ethel Dorsey."

"Yes, Mrs. Dorsey," she said, softening her voice. "How are you doing?"

"I'm doing as well as could be expected with my Tyrone gone and all. But I thank the good Lord I still have my three wonderful sons."

"There's so much we can't understand, Mrs. Dorsey," Audrey said. "But the Scriptures tell us that those who sow in tears will reap with songs of joy."

"I know he records our tears and collects them all in his bottle."

"He does. That he does."

"God is good."

"All the time," Audrey said, her response a reflex.

"Detective, I'm so sorry to disturb you, but I was wondering if you've made any progress on my Tyrone's case."

"No, I'm sorry. Nothing yet. We keep plugging away, though." The lie made her ashamed.

"Please don't give up, Detective."

"Of course not, Mrs. Dorsey." She hadn't given the case more than a fleeting thought in the last several weeks. She was thankful that Mrs. Dorsey worshipped in another church, the next town over.

"I know you're doing your best."

"Yes, I am."

"May the Lord keep you strong, Detective."

"You too, Mrs. Dorsey. You too."

She hung up filled with sorrow, ashamed beyond ashamed, and the phone rang again immediately.

It was Susan Calloway, the bland-voiced woman from the state police lab in Grand Rapids. The firearms examiner in charge of the IBIS database. She sounded a little different, and Audrey realized that what she was hearing was excitement, in the woman's tamped-down, squelched way.

"Well, I do think we have something for you," the woman said.

"You have a match."

"I'm sorry this has taken so long—"

"Oh, not at all—"

"But the Grand Rapids PD certainly took their time. I mean, all I was asking them to do was to check the bullets out of Property and drive them all of seventeen blocks over to Fuller. You'd think I'd asked for a human sacrifice or something."

Audrey chuckled politely. "But you got a match," she prompted. The technician sounded positively giddy.

"Of course, the real problem was that it wasn't anyone's case anymore. I mean, it was from six years ago, and both detectives are gone, they tell me. There's always an excuse."

"Tell me about it," Audrey laughed.

"In any case, the bullets they brought over matched the ones in your case. They're copper-jacketed Rainiers, so the ammunition is different. But the striation markings are identical."

"So it's a positive match."

"It's a positive match, yes."

"The weapon—?"

"I can't tell you that for absolute certain. But I'd say it's a safe guess it's a

Smith and Wesson .380. That's not legally admissible, though." The woman read off the Grand Rapids PD report number for the bullet.

"So Grand Rapids should have all the information I need," Audrey said.

"Well, I don't know how much more they'll have than I already told you. "Both detectives on the case are off the force, as I say."

"Even so, those names would be a help."

"Oh, well, if that's all you want, I have *that*. The submitting detective, anyway. Right here in the comments box." The technician went silent, and Audrey was about to prompt her for the name, when the woman spoke again, and Audrey went cold.

"Says here it was submitted by a Detective Edward J. Rinaldi," the technician said. "But they say he's retired from the force, so that's probably not going to be much use to you. Sorry about that."

PART FIVE
NO HIDING PLACE

88

Mulligans—never an apostrophe—was a diner on Bainbridge Road in Fenwick famous for its Bolognese sauce, the subject of a yellowed framed article from the *Fenwick Free Press* on the wall as you entered. The headline was typical of the paper's dopey, punning style: "A Meaty Subject." This was the place Nick used to go at three in the morning, after the junior and senior proms. Frank Mulligan was long gone. It was now owned by a guy who'd been a few years ahead of Nick and Eddie in high school, Johnny Frechette, who'd done three years in Ionia for drug trafficking.

Nick hadn't been here in years, and he noticed that the place had a staleness to it. The Formica tables had a faint cloth pattern, faded to white in the areas where mugs and plates had banged and scraped against it. They were serving breakfast now, and the place smelled of coffee and maple syrup and bacon, all blended into a single aroma: Eau du Diner.

Eddie seemed to know the waitresses here. Probably he came here for breakfast a lot. They were seated in a corner, away from the window. Aside from a few people eating at the counter, the place was empty.

"You look like shit," Eddie said.

"Thanks," Nick said irritably. "You too."

"Well, you're not going to want to hear this."

Nick held his breath. "What is it?"

"They ID'd the gun."

The blood drained from Nick's face. "You said you tossed it."

"I did."

"Then how could that be?"

The two fell silent as an overperfumed waitress arrived with a Silex carafe, and sloshed coffee into their thick white mugs.

"They got all kinds of tricky ballistics shit these days," Eddie said.

"I don't get what you're telling me." Nick took a hurried sip of his black coffee, scalding his tongue. Maybe he didn't *want* to understand what Eddie seemed to be getting at.

"They matched the bullets with the gun."

"They matched the bullets with *what?*" Nick was aware that his voice was a bit too loud, and he lowered it at once. "There's *no gun*, right? You said it's *gone!*"

"Yeah, well, apparently they don't need a gun anymore." Eddie popped open a couple of little half-and-half containers and tipped them into his mug, stirring until it turned an unappealing gray. "All's they need is bullets, 'cause of the big new computer database, I forget what it's called. They must have matched up the bullets in Stadler's body with the ones from the scene years ago where I got the piece—how the hell do I know? My source didn't get into details."

"Who's your source?"

Eddie ducked his head to the side. "Forget it."

"You know this for a fact? You're one-hundred-percent certain?"

"It's a fact. Suck it up."

"Jesus Christ, Eddie, you said everything was cool!" Nick's voice cracked. "You said the gun wasn't registered to you. You—you said you picked it up at a crime scene, and there was no record of it anywhere."

Eddie's normally confident expression had given way, disconcertingly, to a pallid, sweaty discomfort. "That's what I thought. Sometimes shit gets out of your control, buddy boy."

"I don't believe this," Nick said, his voice hoarse. "I don't fucking believe it. What the hell do we do now?"

Eddie set down his coffee mug and gave Nick a stone-cold look. "We do absolutely nothing. We say nothing, admit nothing, we don't say a fucking word. Are you getting this?"

"But if they—they know the gun I used was one you took—"

"They're going to try to connect the dots, but they don't have it nailed down. Maybe they can prove the ammo that killed Stadler came from that gun, but they can't prove I took it. Everything they got is circumstantial. They got *nada* when they searched your house—that whole thing was a scare tactic. They got no witnesses, and they got a lot of little forensic shit, and now they got this gun, but in the end it's all circumstantial. So all they can do now is scare you into talking, see. This is why I'm telling you about it. I want you to be prepared. I don't want those jokers springing this on you and having you crumble, okay? You got to be a rock." Eddie took a sip of coffee without moving his eyes from Nick's.

"They can't just arrest us? Maybe they don't need us to talk."

"No. If neither one of us says a damned thing, they're not going to arrest."

"*You* wouldn't say anything, would you?" Nick whispered. "*You're* not going to say anything, right?"

Eddie smiled a slow smile, and Nick got a shivery feeling. There was something almost sociopathic about Eddie, something dead in his eyes. "Now you're starting to understand," he said. "See, at the end of the day, Nick, they don't give a shit about me. I'm just some small-time corporate security guy, a nobody. You're the CEO everyone in this town despises. They're not interested in putting my puny antlers on the wall. You're the monster buck they're hunting. You're the fucking *twelve-point rack*, okay?"

Nick nodded slowly. The room was turning slowly around him.

"The only way this thing unravels," Eddie said, "is if you talk. Maybe you decide to play 'Let's Make a Deal' with the cops. Try to strike your own separate deal—good for you, bad for me. This would be a huge, *huge* fucking mistake, Nick. Because I will hear about it. You have even the most preliminary, exploratory conversation with those jokers, and I will hear about it in a matter of *seconds*, Nick—count on it. Believe me, I'm wired into that place. And my lawyer will be in the DA's office so fast it'll make your head spin, with an offer they will fucking jump at."

"Your . . . *lawyer?*" Nick croaked.

"See, Nick, let's be clear what they got me for. It's called 'obstruction,' and it's no big deal. First offenders get maybe six months, if any time at all, but not me. Not when I agree to tell the whole story, testify truthfully in the grand jury and at the trial. They get a *murderer*, see. And what do *I* get out of it? A walk. Not even probation. It's a sure thing, Nick."

"But you wouldn't do that, would you?" Nick said. He heard his own voice, and it seemed to be coming from very far away. "You'd never do that, right?"

"Only if you change the rules of the game, bud. Only if you talk. Though I gotta tell you, I shoulda done this on day one. Why I ever came over to help you that night, I don't know. Goodness of my heart, I guess. Help an old buddy who's in deep shit. I shoulda said, sorry, not me, amigo, and just stayed in bed. Look what I get for being a nice guy. Very least, I should have shopped you long ago. Rolled over, made a deal. I don't know why I didn't. Anyway, what's done is done, but let's be crystal clear, I am *not* going down for this. You try to make a deal, you talk, and at that point I'm gonna do what's in my own best interests."

Nick couldn't catch his breath. "I'm not going to talk," he said.

Eddie gave him a sidelong glance, and he smiled as if he were enjoying this. "All you gotta do, Nicky, is hold it together, and we're going to be just fine, you and me. Keep your fucking mouth shut, don't panic, and we'll ride this out."

The waitress was back, wielding her glass carafe. "Freshen your coffee?" she said.

Neither Eddie nor Nick responded at first, and then Nick said slowly, not looking at her, "I think we're okay."

"That's right," Eddie said. "We're okay. We're just fine."

89

The Fenwick Racquet Club wasn't a place where much tennis was played, as far as Nick could tell. But for Henry Hutchens—Hutch, as he was always known—it had evidently become a home away from home. Hutch had been Stratton's chief financial officer back when the position was called, less grandly, controller. He had served Old Man Devries for a quarter of a century, and when Nick took over, he helped prepare the financial statements for the sale to Fairfield. Did a good job of it too. His manner was unfailingly courtly, maybe a little formal. And when Nick had come to his office—that's how he did it, in Hutch's office, not his own—and told him that Fairfield wanted to replace him with one of their own, he didn't utter a word of protest.

Nick had told him the truth about Fairfield. Still, they both knew that if Nick had seriously objected, Fairfield would have backed down. Nick hadn't. Hutch was a highly competent old-school controller. But Fairfield was loaded up with high-powered financial engineers, ready to lecture you on the advantages of activity-based costing and economic-value-added accounting systems. They viewed Hutch as a green-eyeshades guy; he didn't use words like "strategic." Scott McNally was someone the people at Fairfield were comfortable with, and he was someone who could help Nick take Stratton to the next level. *The next level*—there was a time when Nick couldn't get enough of that phrase; now the cliché had the stink of yesterday's breakfast.

"Long time between drinks, Nick," Hutch said as Nick joined him at a table inside the clubhouse. He lifted a martini glass, and smiled crookedly, but didn't stand. "Join me?"

Hutch had the kind of ruddy complexion that looked like good health from a distance. Up close, Nick could see the alcohol-inflamed capillaries. Even his sweat seemed juniper-scented.

"It's a little early for me," Nick said. Christ, it wasn't even noon yet.

"Well, of *course*," Hutch said, with his Thurston Howell III purr. "You're a working man. With an *office* to go to. And lots of employees who *depend* on you." He drained the last drops of his drink, and signaled to the waiter for another.

"For the moment, anyway."

Hutch clasped his hands together. "You must be riding high, though. Layoffs—everyone talks about the layoffs! They must be *ecstatic* in Boston. To think that my own humble self was to be the first of so many on the gallows. It's kind of an honor, really."

Nick blanched. "The company owes you a lot, Hutch. I've always been grateful to you, personally."

"Oh please. Not everyone has the privilege of selling the rope to one's own hangman." Another drink was placed before him. "Thank you, Vinnie," Hutch murmured. The waiter, a sixtyish man whose neck strained against the club-required red bowtie, nodded pleasantly.

"A tomato juice would be great," Nick told him.

"You surprised a great many people, you know," Hutch went on. He popped the cocktail olive into his mouth and chewed thoughtfully. "Have to keep my strength up," he added with a wink.

"What happened has been hard for everyone. A lot of good people have been hurt. I'm very aware of that."

"You misunderstand," Hutch said. "I didn't mean about the layoffs. I just meant that not everyone took you to be CEO material. A solid company man, absolutely. But not quite cut out for the corner office."

"Well." Nick looked around, taking in the fieldstone fireplace, the white tablecloths, the red patterned wall-to-wall carpet. "I guess Old Man Devries—"

"It had nothing to do with Milton," Hutch said sharply. "If he'd wanted to, Milton could have named you president, or chief operating officer. One of those next-in-line positions. That's the custom with a corporate heir apparent. He did not choose to do so."

"Fair enough," Nick said, trying not to bridle.

"He was *fond* of you. We all were. But when the issue came up, well . . ." Hutch peered into the watery depths of his cocktail. "Milton considered you a little callow. Too much of a big-man-on-campus type. Someone too concerned with being popular to be a real leader." He looked up. "Thought you didn't have the killer instinct. Now *there's* one heck of an irony."

Nick's face was hot. "Being that you're such a connoisseur of irony, you might enjoy this one." He unzipped his black leather portfolio and presented Hutch with the contract that Eddie had taken from Scott's e-mail.

"What is this?"

"You tell me." *If you're not too drunk to make sense of it,* Nick thought.

Hutch reached for his reading glasses, convex lenses with wire frames, and started paging through the document. A few times he tapped on the pages and gave a dry chuckle. "My, my," he finally said. "I take it this isn't your masterwork."

"Not mine."

"Milton! Thou shouldst be living at this hour: Stratton hath need of thee." Hutch put his reading glasses away, and made tsk-tsking sounds. "Pacific Rim Investors," he said, and then: "I can't even pronounce this name— is it Malaysian? Good Lord." He looked up, bleary-eyed. "So much for the match made in Heaven. Looks like your white knights came riding in from Boston only to sell Stratton down the Yangtze River."

Nick explained what Stephanie Alstrom had told him about the real owner being the Chinese P.L.A.

"Oh, that's rich," Hutch said happily. "That's really a thing of beauty. Though it's not exactly sporting to put one over on the Communists like that these days, is it?"

"Put one over?"

"If these balance sheets are authentic, then Stratton's doing marvelously well. But I have a suspicion they're as phony as a glass apple."

Lipstick on a pig, Nick thought.

"If I had access to your most recent P and L statements, *and* if I weren't three sheets to the wind, *and* if I actually *cared,* I could give you a breakdown of this document that was so clear even *you* could understand it." He took a swallow of his drink. "But even in my current condition, I can tell you that somebody's been coloring outside the lines. For one thing, you're taking your reserves against losses from your last profitable year and using it to cover over the new tide of red ink. That's 'cookie jar' accounting, and we both know about that company that got caught doing it not so long ago and had to pay three billion dollars in damages to make it all better. It's not nice to fool with your accrued liability."

"What good is that?" Nick said. "Once the new owners find out the truth, they'll hit Fairfield with a huge lawsuit."

"Ah, but you see, that's the beauty part, my boy. They can't sue."

"Why not?"

"There's a clever non-litigation clause here," Hutch said, tapping the paper. "Once the deal goes through, no lawsuits are permitted over any representations and warranties made herein, ya de ya de ya."

"Why in the world would the buyers agree to that?"

"I think the answer is manifest," Hutch said, looking up again. "It's in the side agreement. Guaranteeing a seven-figure payout to someone, no doubt a Chinese government official with the ability to speed through the acquisition."

"A bribe."

"You put it so *harshly*, son. The Chinese have a wonderful tradition of giving red envelopes of *hong bao*—good-luck money—to start off the lunar new year right."

"Ten million dollars is a lot of good-luck money for one man."

"Indeed. But to grease a deal like this through the Chinese bureaucracy without endless quibbling—well, that's quite a bargain, isn't it?"

"It's early for Chinese New Year, isn't it?"

"Now you're catching on. Unless you can think of some other reason why Stratton would be routing him his money to a numbered account in Macau. From where, I'll wager, it was immediately transferred to another account at the Bank of Commerce of Labuan."

"Labuan?"

"Labuan is an island off the coast of Malaysia. A speck of sand, and a great big offshore financial services industry. The bankers of Labuan make the Swiss seem *gabby*. Basically, it's where Chinese kleptocrats like to sock away their ill-gotten gains."

"I had no idea."

"I'm sure they were *counting* on that. Good boys and girls don't know about Labuan. And they certainly don't wire money there."

"Christ," Nick said. "How many people are in on this thing?"

"Impossible to say, though it only takes two countersigners to execute it. One corporate officer—that would be your charming young CFO—and a managing partner from Fairfield. It does seem a little low-rent, the whole thing, but I suppose these are two young men in a hurry. There are a *lot* of people in a hurry these days. Sure you won't join me in a drink?"

"Still waiting for my tomato juice," Nick said. "Seems to be taking an awfully long time."

"Oh dear," Hutch said in a low voice. "I should have realized. Doubt it's ever going to come, Vinnie being your waiter and all. I guess you must be used to this sort of thing."

"What are you saying?"

Hutch glanced at the waiter and shrugged elaborately. "It's just that you laid off his brother."

90

Audrey tracked down Bugbee on his cell phone at the Burger Shack, the place he liked to go for lunch. He could barely hear her. In the background was a cacophony of laughter and clinking plates and bad rock music.

"When are you coming back?" she said several times.

"I'm on lunch."

"I can tell that. But this is important."

"What?"

"You'd better get over here."

"I said it can wait."

"No, it can't," she said.

"I'm at the Burger Shack for the next—"

"See you there," she said, and she hung up before he could object.

Bugbee quickly got over his pique at having his lunch with the guys—three uniformed officers, all around his age—interrupted.

He excused himself, and he and Audrey found an empty booth.

"That's it," he said when Audrey told him about the weapon match. "We got 'em."

"It's still tenuous," she said. "It's circumstantial."

He glared. There was a large splotch of ketchup on his hideous tie, which only improved its appearance. "The *fuck* are you waiting for—Nick

Conover's diary with a special entry for that night saying I plugged the guy, me and Eddie?"

"We're connecting dots that I don't know if the prosecutor's going to let us connect."

"Connecting *what* fucking dots?" he spat out.

She briefly considered asking him to cut out the potty-mouth stuff, but now was not the time. "We know this suggests that Eddie Rinaldi and Nick Conover were behind it."

"Tell me something I don't know—"

"Will you shut up for a second, please?" It was worth saying just to see Bugbee's stunned expression. "The gun that was used to kill Stadler was also used on a no-gun case that Eddie Rinaldi worked six years ago. But does that prove Rinaldi pocketed the gun back in Grand Rapids? The case is still full of holes."

"Yeah? I don't think so, and neither do you."

"Our opinion isn't the same thing as what's going to convince the DA to prosecute. Especially in a capital case involving the CEO of a huge corporation and one of his top officers."

"Tell you something—once we hook our boy Eddie up to a polygraph, he'll crack."

"He doesn't have to submit to a polygraph."

"If he's facing a first-degree murder charge and life without parole, believe me, he'll take it." He leaned back in the booth, savoring the moment. "This is beautiful. Shit, this is beautiful." He smiled, and she realized that this was the first time she'd seen him give a genuine smile of pleasure. It looked wrong on his face, didn't come naturally, looked like a disturbance in the natural order of things. His cheeks creased deeply like heavily starched fabric.

"Conover won't take a polygraph," Audrey said. "Let's face it, we still don't know which one of them the shooter is," Audrey said.

"Fuck it. Charge 'em both with first-degree murder, and sort it out later. Whoever comes to the window first gets the deal, that's how it works."

"I don't know if we're even going to get to that point, if we'll get a prosecutor to write out a warrant."

"So you go prosecutor-shopping. Come on. You know how the game works."

"Noyce really frowns on that."

"Screw Noyce. This is our case, I told you. Not his."

"Still," she said. "I don't know. I don't want to mess this up."

Bugbee started counting on his left hand, starting with his thumb. "We got the soil match, we got the fucking erased surveillance tape, we got Conover's alarm going off at two A.M., followed by the desperate cell phone call, we got Schizo Man with a history of attacks on the suspect, and now we got a gun match." He held up five fingers triumphantly. "The fuck else you want? I say we run with it."

"I want to pass this by Noyce first."

"You want to run to Daddy?" He shook his head. "Haven't you figured out that Noyce isn't our friend?"

"Why do you say that?"

"Take a look. The closer we get to Stratton's CEO, the harder Noyce's been fighting us, right? He doesn't want us taking on the big kahuna. Wouldn't surprise me if he's in Stratton's pocket."

"Come on."

"I'm fucking serious. Something's off about the way that guy's taking their side."

"He's got to be cautious on a case this big."

"This is way beyond cautious. You notice how when I searched Rinaldi's condo, total surprise, and all of a sudden a couple of guns are missing from his rack, like someone gave him a heads-up?"

"Or maybe he dumped them after he or Conover murdered Stadler," Audrey said. "Or Conover called him, told him a team was coming to search Conover's house, and Eddie races home and disposes of the evidence."

"Yeah, any of those are possible. Theoretically. Then you notice how Noyce is trying to make life difficult for you, jam up your schedule with other shit so you don't have time to do this right? Look, Audrey, I don't trust the guy."

"He's my friend, Roy," she said softly.

"Oh, is he?" Bugbee said. "I wouldn't be so sure of that."

She didn't reply.

91

Dorothy Devries's mansion on Michigan Avenue in East Fenwick didn't seem quite as big as Nick remembered it, but was possibly even darker. Outside, the gables and peaked eaves stopped just shy of Addams Family gothic. Inside, wooden floors were stained to a chocolate hue and partly covered with blood red Orientals. The furniture was either a dark mahogany or covered in a dark damask. She kept the curtains drawn, and he remembered her once saying something about how sunlight could bleach the fabrics. The moon glow of her pale skin was the brightest thing in the house.

"Did you say you wanted tea?" she asked, squinting at him. She sat almost motionless in a burgundy-clad Queen Anne's chair. There was a chandelier above them, which she kept pointedly unlit.

"No thanks," he said.

"But I've interrupted you," she said. "Please go on."

"Well, the basic situation is what I've described. You and I worked hard on the sale to Fairfield, and we did that because we wanted to preserve your father's legacy. And your husband's."

"Legacy," she repeated. In the gloom, he wasn't sure whether her dress was charcoal gray or navy. "That's a pretty word."

"And a pretty big accomplishment," he said. She seemed to brighten. "Harold Stratton created a company that did what it did as well as—or better than—any other, and he did it right here in Fenwick. And then your husband put Fenwick on the map, as far as corporate America was concerned."

Dorothy had had a glossy vanity biography of her husband, Milton, privately printed, copies distributed widely. Nick knew she always responded to the most unctuous praise of her father's historical significance. "So the prospect of seeing Stratton bundled in brown paper and shipped to the Far East— well, I think he'd be appalled. I know I am. It isn't right. It's not right for Fenwick, and it's not right for Stratton."

Mrs. Devries blinked. "But you're telling me all this for a reason."

"Well, sure."

"I'm all ears, Nicholas." She used his full name as if he were a grade student, and a little small for all three syllables.

"You're part owner of the company. You sit on the board. I thought if I could enlist your support, we might be able to present the case together to the others. That way, they'd see it wasn't just about a manager trying to save his job. Because this deal—well, frankly, it would be a disaster. The Chinese aren't interested in our manufacturing facilities. They've got their own. They're going to gut Stratton, run a fire sale of the shop machines, and pass out walking papers to the remaining employees."

"That puts things rather starkly."

"It's a stark situation."

"Well, you do have a flair for the dramatic. That isn't a criticism. But then you haven't come here to consult, have you?"

"Sure I have."

"Because I didn't hear you ask me my opinion. I heard you telling me yours."

"I just thought I should fill you in," Nick said, perplexed. "See what you thought." A pause. "I'm interested in getting your . . . help and guidance."

A watery smile. "Is that right," she said.

Nick looked at her, and his face started to prickle. *Had she already known before I came here?*

"I must say I'm a little taken aback to hear you make an argument that's based on sentiment, as opposed to dollars and sense. Because, you see, I don't recall your seeking my help or guidance when you decided to discontinue the Stratton Ultra line. Which was, of course, one of my husband's proudest *legacies*." In a quiet voice, she added, "Pretty word."

Nick said nothing.

"And I don't recall your seeking my help or guidance when you decided to lay off five thousand workers, dragging the Stratton name through the mud," she went on. "And after Milton worked *so* hard to make it a byword for what was *best* about Fenwick. That was part of his legacy, too, Nicholas."

"Dorothy, you voted to approve the layoffs."

"Oh, as if I could stop that train in its tracks! But please don't misunderstand me. I'm not complaining. We sold the firm. Almost all of it belongs to Fairfield Partners. And so we must be *very* businesslike about the whole thing."

"With all respect, Dorothy, aren't you bothered by the idea of Stratton being owned by—by the Chinese government? The Communist Chinese?"

Dorothy Devries shot him a wintry look. "Please. Coming from *you*? Business is business. My family made good money when we sold to Fairfield, and we stand to make quite a bit more when they sell it to this consortium."

"But for God's sake—?" He saw something in her face. "You knew all about it, didn't you?"

She refused to reply. "Nicholas, I didn't give you Milton's job in order for you to dismantle his company, believe it or not. But you did. You cheesed it up with all that Office of the Future eyewash. You got rid of what was real, what was solid, and replaced it with gilt and papier mâchè. Milton would have been appalled. Though I suppose I really can't judge you without judging myself, can I? *I'm* the one who gave you the keys to the corner office."

"Yes," Nick said, finally. "And why did you?"

Dorothy sat silent for a while. "As you might imagine," she said with a drawn smile, "I've often asked myself the same thing."

92

Audrey had promised to keep Noyce in the loop, that was the thing. Strictly speaking, she knew she had the right to go right to the prosecutor's office and request an arrest warrant for Conover and Rinaldi without even telling Noyce. She knew that. But it wasn't right to exclude him. It was a matter of courtesy to keep Noyce updated. She'd told him about the gun match as soon as she found out, and there was no reason to start keeping him in the dark now. It would infuriate him, but worse, it would hurt his feelings, and she wasn't about to do that.

Music was playing softly in Noyce's office as she entered. Audrey recognized Duke Ellington's "Mood Indigo," a trumpet solo.

"Is that Louis?" she asked.

Noyce nodded, absorbed. "Ellington and Armstrong recorded this in one take. Unbelievable."

"Sure is."

"The Duke was great at composing under deadline pressure, you know. The night before a recording date, he's waiting for his mother to finish cooking dinner, and he goes to his piano, and in fifteen minutes he knocks off a piece he calls 'Dreamy Blues.' Next night his band plays it over the radio, broadcasting from the Cotton Club. Later he renames it 'Mood Indigo.'" Noyce shook his head, waited for the song to end, and then clicked off the CD player. "What can I do you for?"

"I think we've got enough to arrest Conover and Rinaldi."

Noyce's eyes widened as she explained, then just as quickly narrowed. "Audrey, let me take you out for ice cream."

"I'm trying not to eat—"

"Well, you can watch. I've been thinking about one of those chocolate-dipped strawberry sundaes at the Dairy Queen."

Noyce tucked into a boat-sized dish of soft-serve vanilla ice cream smothered in syrupy strawberries, while Audrey tried to avert her eyes, because it looked too good, and her will was weak when it came to desserts, especially in the midafternoon.

"You don't want your butt out there for false arrest, Aud," he said, a strawberry smear at the side of his mouth. "You realizing who you're dealing with, don't you?"

"You think Nicholas Conover's all that powerful?"

"He's a wealthy and powerful guy, but more to the point, he now works for a holding company in Boston that's going to be intent on protecting their investment. And if that means suing the police department in the town of Fenwick, Michigan, they've got the resources to do it. That means they sue you. And us."

"That could work the other way too," she pointed out. Her stomach was growling, and her mouth kept filling with saliva. "The holding company could get nervous about having a CEO charged with first-degree murder and jettison him."

Noyce didn't look up from his ice cream. "You willing to take that chance?"

"If I have a genuine belief that Conover and Rinaldi were involved in a homicide, and I got a prosecutor to back me up on it, how is that false arrest?"

"It just means more of us in the soup. Plus, I can tell you, you're not going to get a prosecutor to write a warrant unless he's sure he can win the case. And I worry that we're still thin on the ground here."

"But look at what we've got, Jack—"

He looked up. "Well, let's take a look at it, Aud. What's your most damaging lead? The gun? So you've got Rinaldi on some case in Grand Rapids, and the same gun in that one turns up here."

"Which is no coincidence. Rinaldi had a reputation as a bad cop."

"Now, you've got to be careful there. That's hearsay. Cops are always gossiping, stabbing each other in the back, you know that better than anyone." He sighed. "No one's going to let you run with that. If you want to say he took the gun, fine—but you don't have any proof of that."

"No, but—"

"Look at it through the eyes of a defense attorney. The same gun used in Grand Rapids turned up here? Well, you think that's the first time a gun was used in Grand Rapids and here? Where do you think our drug dealers get their guns? Flint, Lansing, Detroit, Grand Rapids. They've got to come from somewhere."

Audrey fell silent, watching him spoon the soft-serve, careful to catch a dollop of strawberry goo in each spoonful.

"Far more likely, in fact," Noyce went on, "is that some shitbird in Fenwick bought a piece from some other shitbird in GR. Pardon my French, Audrey."

"But the hydroseed stuff—the soil match—"

"That's an awfully slender reed to hang a first-degree murder on, don't you think?"

She felt increasingly desperate. "The cell phone call Conover lied about—"

"Again, maybe he really did get the day wrong. Audrey, I'm just being devil's advocate here, okay?"

"But Conover's own security system—the video for that night was erased, and we can *prove* it."

"You can prove it was erased, or you can prove the tape recycled? There's quite a difference."

Noyce had clearly been talking to Kevin Lenehan. "You have a point," she conceded.

"Then there's the fact that both you and Bugbee canvassed Conover's neighbors, and not one of them heard a shot that night."

"Jack, you know how far apart the houses are in Fenwicke Estates? Plus, a three-eighty isn't all that loud."

"Audrey. You've got no blood, no weapon, no footprints, no witnesses. What *do* you have?"

"Motive and opportunity. A stalker with a history of violence and a handgun who was stalking the CEO of Stratton—"

"Unarmed, as far as we know."

"Even worse for Conover if Stadler was unarmed."

"And you yourself told me the guy had no prior history of violence. 'Gentle as a lamb,' wasn't that the phrase you used? Audrey, listen. If you had a solid case against these guys, no one would be happier than me. I'd love to take 'em down for this murder, you kidding me? But I don't want us to fuck it up. I don't want us to go off half-cocked."

"I *know* we have a case here," she said.

"You know what you are? You're an optimist, down deep."

"I don't know about that."

"Anyone who loves God the way you do's got to be an optimist. But you see, here's the sad truth. The longer you stay in this job, the harder it is to stay an optimist. Witnesses recant and the guilty go free and cases don't get solved. Pessimism, cynicism—that's the natural order. Audrey, did I ever tell you about the case I had when I was just starting out? Woman shot in the head standing in her front parlor, shifty cheating husband, we kept catching him lying about his alibis, which kept changing. The more we looked at him, the more we were convinced he was the shooter."

"He wasn't," she said, impatient.

"You know why he kept lying about his alibi? Turned out he was in the sack with his sister-in-law at the time. This guy wouldn't own up to the fact that he was cheating on his wife even when he was faced with a first-degree murder charge. He didn't crack until just before the trial was scheduled, the bastard. And you know what it was killed the wife? Just a random, stray bullet through her open window, a street shooting gone bad. Wasn't her lucky day. Or maybe that's what you get for living in a bad neighborhood. What seemed so obvious to us turned out not to be true when we really dug into it."

"I get it, Jack," she said, watching him scrape the boat clean, pleased to see that his last spoonful contained equal portions of ice cream and strawberry. "But we've dug into it."

"A crazy guy's found in a Dumpster in the dog pound, with fake crack on him—I'm sorry, but you've got to go with a crack murder as your central hypothesis. Not some white-collar CEO with so much to lose. You know the old saying—in Texas, when you hear approaching hoofbeats, you don't think zebra. You gotta think horses. And I think you're going after a zebra here."

"That's not—"

"Oh, I know it would be a hell of a lot more intriguing to spot a zebra than a horse, but you've always got to consider the likelihoods. Because ultimately your time is limited. Who's that woman who calls you every week?"

"Ethel Dorsey?"

"Tyrone's her son, probably killed in a drug deal, right? How much time have you been putting in on that case?"

"I haven't really had much time recently."

"No, you haven't. And if I know you, I'll bet you feel that you're letting Ethel Dorsey down."

"I—" she faltered.

"You're good, and you have the potential to be great. You can make a real difference. But think of how many other cases are clamoring for your attention. There's only so many hours in the day, right?"

"I understand." She was shaken; what he said made sense.

"There's another case I want you to get involved in. Not instead of this one, but in addition to it. One that will really, I think, give you an opportunity to shine. Instead of just getting bogged down in this dog-pound murder. Now, Jensen's got the Hernandez robbery trial on Monday, but he's going on vacation, so I'd like you to handle it."

"Isn't Phelps the secondary on that? I only did one follow-up interview."

"Phelps is on personal leave. I need you on this. And the prosecutor wants a pretrial conference on Friday."

"Friday? That's—that's in two days!"

"You can do it. I know you can."

She was befuddled and most of all depressed now. "You know," she said in a small voice, "that looks good, what you had. What do I ask for?"

93

Marta came to the front hall, holding a dish towel in wet hands. No doubt she'd heard the little double beep of the alarm system when he opened the door. Somewhere in the background were peals of girlish laughter.

"Something wrong?" Nick asked her.

Marta shook her head. "Everything's fine," she said huffily, her tone implying the exact opposite.

"Is it Luke?"

Marta stiffened. "Miss Stadler invited herself over."

"Oh," Nick said. "That's fine."

Marta shrugged unhappily. It wasn't fine with *her*.

"Is there a problem, then?" Nick asked. What was with this Mrs. Danvers act, anyway?

"It's just getting hard to keep track of who's in the family and who isn't, these days."

It was an invitation to a heavy conversation; Nick silently declined.

In the family room he found Cassie, in an oversized Stratton T-shirt and black jeans, sitting with Julia, who was wearing an outfit Nick hadn't seen before, a turquoise velour tracksuit. Very J. Lo. The word "Juicy" ran across her butt.

He stood at the threshold and watched, unnoticed.

"There's nothing dirty about it," Cassie was saying.

"Dirty pillows!" Julia said, in silly mode. "Dirty pillows!"

"You get older, your body changes. Boys seem less yucky. You start to feel more private about your body. Everyone goes through it. It's as natural as granola."

Julia giggled at that, somehow anxious and pleased at the same time. "I hate granola," she said.

"The main thing is, don't feel it's something you can't talk about. Don't feel it's some weird, shameful thing, okay? Tits aren't the end of the world. Zits, on the other hand . . ."

Another burst of giggles, less nervous and more high-spirited.

They were having The Talk. Relief washed over him, mixed with a little jealousy over the intimacy Cassie and Julia seemed to have developed. He'd mentioned to Cassie how much he was dreading the prospect of having the girl-stuff talk with his daughter: in his hands, it would probably have ended in some grisly level of mutual embarrassment. Marta, despite her tight jeans, was prim and embarrassed about talking about sex and had let Nick know that she most emphatically didn't consider it her place to tell Julia about things like periods.

Cassie, though, was talking about it as if it were no big deal, and somehow *making* it no big deal. Something about her low, commonsensical voice was keeping everything real, down-to-earth, and comfortable. Or at least as comfortable as it could be for a giddy, giggly ten-year-old.

"Lot of things change, lot of things don't," Cassie told Julia. "Just remember, whatever happens to you, you're always going to be your daddy's little girl."

Nick cleared his throat, then said to Julia, "Hey, baby."

"Daddy!" She got up and received his hug.

"Where's your brother?"

"He's upstairs working."

"Good to hear. And where'd you get this outfit?"

"Cassie bought it for me."

"She did, huh?" A velour tracksuit? It even exposed her tummy. She was ten years old, for Christ's sake.

Cassie looked up, shrugged sheepishly. "*All* the fifth-graders consider me their fashion guru," she said.

———

When Julia had left to go to her room, Nick looked at Cassie and shrugged. "Thanks, by the way. I gather you were talking about girl stuff with her. Not easy for her old man to do."

"She's a sweet pea, Nick. The main thing is that she knows you're always going to be her daddy, and you're always going to love her."

"Stay for dinner?"

"I can't," she said.

"Plans?"

"No. I just—you know, what's that they say about guests and fish? They start stinking after—I forget how many days."

"You think Julia considers you a guest? Or Luke?"

She couldn't hide her smile. "You understand, don't you?"

"Stay. Plus, I could use your take on what's going on at work."

"You've come to the right place," she said. "The wisdom tooth of Fenwick, Michigan."

He told her about his meeting with Dorothy Devries.

"Well, she's not calling the shots anymore," Cassie said. "You said Todd Muldaur is."

"That's the problem."

"The question I always like to ask is: Who's your daddy?"

"Yeah. You and Shaft."

"So who's Todd Muldaur's daddy?"

A shrug. "Willard Osgood is the chairman of Fairfield Partners. But it sounds like he's become an absentee father."

"Willard Osgood—the guy with the thick glasses and all that folksy investment advice, right? I read that profile in *Fortune* you showed me. He's the one you've got to go to."

"For what? I don't see the upside."

"Correct me if I'm wrong, but doesn't Osgood really think of himself as a father figure? What you're describing doesn't sound like his style."

"True," Nick said. "But times change. The face of the future is probably Todd Muldaur."

"See, that doesn't add up to me. The way it's all been kept under wraps—that's not just about keeping the details away from you. Is it possible they're trying to keep the details away from Daddy too?"

"Hmph. I hadn't thought of that."

"But it's possible, right?"

"It's possible, yes."

"So maybe you should go right to Osgood."

"And what if you're wrong? What if he knows everything that's going on?"

"Consider your options right now. The real question is, What if I'm right?"

94

Audrey's e-mail icon was bouncing. It was a message from Kevin Lenehan in Forensic Services. She opened it immediately, then practically ran to Forensic Services.

"Guess what?" he said.

"You got it. The video."

"No fucking way. I told you, that's so gone."

"Then what?"

"This is cool. I noticed this code on here. It backs up to an FTP server on a preset schedule."

"Can you explain that?"

"Sure. Certain archivable events, ranging from alarm inputs to motion-detector inputs, get automatically sent to an FTP server using the IP address that's preprogrammed in here."

"Kevin," she said, mildly exasperated, "that really wasn't much of an explanation, now, was it?"

"The eleven minutes of video you're looking for? That we thought got totally erased? Well, it got erased on the box, here. But it also got sent over the Internet to Stratton's LAN—sorry, the company's computers. There's a backup copy at Stratton. That clear enough?"

Audrey smiled. "Can you get into the Stratton computers from here—on the Internet or something?"

"If I was that good, do you think I'd have a job like this?"

She shrugged.

"But get me into Stratton and I'll know where to look."

95

It was an hour drive to the Gerald R. Ford International Airport, then a five-hour flight to Logan Airport, a bustling place that seemed as populous as all of Fenwick. Nick made his way past a Legal Seafoods restaurant, a W. H. Smith bookstore, and a Brookstone gadget center before he reached the escalator to Ground Transportation. Among a flock of livery drivers, he caught the eye of an olive-skinned man in a blue blazer and gray slacks who was holding a card that read NICHOLAS CONVER. Close enough.

Fairfield Partners was the anchor tenant of a vast glass- and granite-faced building on Federal Street, in the heart of downtown Boston. Willard Osgood's offices were on the thirty-seventh and thirty-eighth floors. The reception area was all dove-gray velvet and tropical woods, and Nick expected he'd be given plenty of time to study its details, cooling his heels in preparation for his audience with the Great Man. To his surprise, though, the strawberry blond receptionist told him to go right in. Nick wondered whether he was late. His watch told him that he was a few minutes early if anything.

As he walked through the glass door, Nick was immediately met by another blond woman, this one with red plastic-framed glasses. "Mr. Conover," she said. "Your flight okay?"

"It was," Nick said.

"Can I get you anything? Water, a soda, coffee?"

"I'm fine," Nick said, striding to keep up with her power walk.

"I'm sorry Todd's on the road. I'm sure he would have loved to say hi if he knew you were coming in."

I'm sure he would have, Nick thought. "Well, you might want to check with Mr. Osgood before you tell Todd or anyone else that I was here."

"Yes, sir," she said quickly. "Of course."

The offices of Fairfield Equity Partners were soaring and glass-walled, two floors combined into one. Along the walls, he noticed framed magazine covers featuring Willard Osgood—holding a fishing reel on the cover of *Field & Stream*, wearing a blue suit and yellow tie on *Forbes*. Osgood's square, bespectacled face and pleased-yet-concerned expression were always identical, as if the head had been Photoshopped onto different models.

Finally, she gestured toward a tan leather sofa in what looked like a vast waiting area, and said, "Have a seat. I'll leave you here."

Nick craned his head around, took in the large glass desk and various fishing trophies on the wall. It took a moment before he figured out he was in Willard Osgood's own office. He looked out of the windows on two sides and could see the Boston harbor in the distance, then some scrubby little islands beyond that.

Moments later, Willard Osgood himself strode in: the square, weathered face, the Coke-bottle glasses—he could have been peeled off one of those magazine covers. Nick stood up and realized that Osgood probably had an inch or two on him.

"Nick Conover," Osgood said in a booming voice, giving him a friendly bump on the shoulder. "I hope you noticed what kind of chair I've got at my desk." He pointed to the Stratton Symbiosis chair.

Nick grinned. "You liked it so much you bought the company."

Osgood raised a shaggy eyebrow. "Did I make the right decision?"

"Hope you still like the chair. It's still a good company."

"Then what the hell are you doing here in Beantown?"

"I'm here to ask your help solving a problem."

Osgood's expression vacillated between amusement and perplexity. "Let me put that Stratton chair into service," he said after a moment, walking over to his desk. Nick took a chair in front of it. "I always think better on my butt."

Nick started right in. "As I recall, when you came to Fenwick, you told us that your favorite holding period is forever."

"Ah," Osgood said, seeming to understand. He blinked a few times, folded his hands on the desk, and then cleared his throat. "Nick, I think I also told you that my rule number one is, never lose money."

Osgood knew Todd was selling the company, Nick now realized. So maybe Cassie was wrong. Did he know *everything*, though? "Which is a lesson that Todd Muldaur seems to have forgotten, if he ever learned it," Nick said.

"Todd's had a rough year," Osgood came right back, sounding a little annoyed. "There are some mighty good explanations for that, though."

"Yeah, well, 'explanations aren't excuses,' as you also like to say."

Osgood smiled, exposing a blinding row of porcelain veneers. "I see the gospel spreads."

"But I can't help but wonder whether one of the explanations is that no one's watching the shop. That's what Todd seems to indicate, anyway. He says you've taken to spending a lot of time away from the office. That maybe you've gotten more interested in fly-fishing than in profit margins."

Osgood's smile almost reached his eyes. "I hope you don't believe that."

"I don't know what to think."

"What my lieutenants really mean by that, of course, is that my day has passed. They like to think that, because it means their day has arrived." Osgood leaned back in his chair, but of course the Stratton Symbiosis chair, being ergonomic, wouldn't let him tip all the way back like the older chairs would. "Tell you a story, but don't repeat it, okay?"

Nick nodded.

"Couple years ago I took Todd down to Islamorada, Florida, for the annual migration of the tarpon. 'Course, he showed up with his brand-new Sage rod and his Abel reel, and he's got a leather belt on, with a bonefish on the buckle." He gave a hearty guffaw. "He's a confident fellow—told me he'd done a lot of fly-fishing at some fancy lodge in Alaska, kind of place with gourmet meals and a sauna and the guide does everything for you except wipe your ass. So I graciously allowed him the bow and watched him flail for hours. Poor guy missed shot after shot, got more and more frustrated, his line kept getting wrapped, the flies hitting him on the backside." He blinked a few times. "Finally I decided I'd had enough fun. I stood up, stripped out ninety feet of line. Soon as I spotted a school of fish approaching, I delivered the fly.

The fish ate, and six and a half feet of silver king went airborne. You with me? One school of fish—one shot—one cast—and one fish brought to the side of the boat."

"Okay," Nick said, enjoying the tale but wondering what the point was.

"See, I don't think Todd realized that the secret isn't how pricey your equipment or how nice your Ex Officio slacks are. All that counts is *bow time*—just doing it over and over and over again. Takes years of practice. No substitute for it."

"How do you cook tarpon?"

"Oh, heavens, no, you don't eat it. That's the beauty part. You release it. It's all about the fight."

"Huh," Nick said. "Doesn't sound like my kind of sport."

"From what I understand, hockey's all about the fight too. And you don't even get a fish to show for it."

"I guess that's one way of looking at it."

"But anyway, you're right. Todd's made some mistakes. A couple of bold gambles."

"I believe the phrase 'sucking wind' might be more accurate."

Osgood wasn't amused. "I'm well aware of what's happening," he said brittlely.

"Are you? I wonder." Nick leaned over and removed a file folder from his briefcase, then slid the folder across the desk. Osgood opened it, tipped his glasses up onto his forehead, and examined the documents. Nick noticed that the horizontal creases on Osgood's forehead were equally spaced and straight, almost as if drawn with a ruler.

Osgood looked up for a moment. "I wish he hadn't done things this way."

"What way?"

"Keeping you out of the loop. It's not the way I prefer. I like to be a straight shooter. Now I see why you've come to talk to me. I understand why you're upset."

"Oh, no," Nick said quickly. "I totally understand why he didn't want me to know. Hell, he knew how opposed I was—am—to a sale like this. Even though I don't have the power to stop it, he was probably afraid I'd kick up a fuss, maybe even take it public. Better to just do the deal without me knowing, he figured, so that by the time I figured it out, it would be a fait accompli. It would be too late."

"Something like that. But as I say, that's not my way."

"Todd needed a quick infusion of cash to help bail out the firm, after all his bad bets on semiconductors. And an IPO takes forever. I get it."

"I told Todd you're a reasonable man, Nick. He should have just leveled with you."

"Maybe he should have leveled with *you*. Like telling you who the fairy godmother behind 'Pacific Rim Investors' really is. Though he probably figured that you, with your political beliefs, wouldn't want to hear where the money comes from." Nick paused. "The P.L.A."

Osgood blinked owlishly.

"That's the People's Liberation Army," Nick explained. "The Communist Chinese army."

"I know who they are," Osgood said curtly. "Wouldn't have gotten to where I am without doing my homework."

"You knew this?" Nick said.

"Good Lord, of *course* I knew it. There's nothing illegal about it, my friend."

"The Communist Chinese," Nick persisted, hoping the incantation might jangle the old right-winger.

"Oh, for heaven's sake, this is *office furniture*. Not Patriot missiles or nuclear weapons or something. Desks and chairs and file cabinets. I hardly call that selling our enemy the rope they're going to hang us with."

"But have you actually looked at the numbers on Stratton that Todd provided Pacific Rim Investors?"

Osgood pushed the folder away from him. "I don't micromanage. I don't look over my partners' shoulders. Nick, we're both busy men—"

"You might want to. See, the balance sheet Todd gave them is a fraud. Prepared by my CFO, Scott McNally, who knows a thing or two about how to put lipstick on a pig."

Another flash of the porcelain Chiclets. "Nick, maybe you've been in the Midwest a bit too long, but that Jimmy Stewart, *Mr. Smith Goes to Washington* bit's not going to play here."

"I'm not talking morality, Willard. I'm talking illegality."

Osgood waved Nick away with an impatient hand. "There's all kinds of ways of doing the books. Anyway, we've got a no-litigate clause, even if they do get buyer's remorse."

"You know about that too," Nick said dully.

Osgood's stare seemed to drill right through him. "Conover, you're wasting your time and mine, trying to backtrack over everything. Horse is out of the barn. Gripe session's over. Now, this it? We done here?" Osgood rose, pressing a button on his intercom. "Rosemary, could you show Mr. Conover out, please?"

But Nick remained in his seat. "I'm not done yet," he said.

96

The Information Technology Director at the Stratton Corporation didn't look like the computer type, Audrey thought. She was a tall, matronly woman named Carly Lindgren, who wore her beautiful and very long auburn hair knotted on top of her head. She wore a navy suit over an olive silk shell, a braided gold necklace and matching earrings.

Audrey had gotten an appointment with Mrs. Lindgren with a single phone call, telling her only it was "police business." But once Audrey had presented the search warrant, she could see Mrs. Lindgren rear up like a cornered tigress. She examined it as if searching for flaws, though very few people knew what to look for, and in any case the warrant had been written carefully. It was as broad as Audrey could get the prosecutor to sign off on, even though all she really wanted was any archived video images on the Stratton network that came from Nicholas Conover's home security system.

Mrs. Lindgren kept Audrey and Kevin Lenehan waiting in an outer office while she placed a flurry of panicked calls all the way up her reporting chain—the Chief Information Officer and the Chief Technology Officer, and Audrey lost track of who all, but there really was nothing Mrs. Lindgren could do.

After twenty minutes or so, Kevin was given a chair and a computer in an empty office. Audrey had nothing to do but watch. She looked around, saw a blue poster with white letters that said something about "The Stratton Family," sort of a mission statement. The chairs they sat in were particularly comfortable; she noticed they were Stratton chairs. Nothing like this in Major Cases. Kevin put a CD in the computer and installed a program. He explained to her that it was viewer software he'd downloaded from the Web site of the company that made the digital video recorder in Conover's home. This would allow them to view, and capture, the video images.

"You know where to look?" Audrey asked, worried.

"It was in the settings in the DVR," replied Kevin. "The folder it was written to, the date and time and everything. No *problema*."

Audrey felt a little tremble of anticipation, which she tried to tamp down, tried to reason herself out of. She was sure that the murder of Andrew Stadler would be on this eleven minutes of camera footage. If indeed there was a backup here.

How often in any homicide detective's career could one hope to come across a piece of evidence like that? A digital image of a murder being committed? It was almost too much to hope for. She didn't want to allow herself to hope for it, because the disappointment would be crushing.

"Anything I can do to help, Detective?"

She looked up, saw Eddie Rinaldi standing in the doorway, felt her heart do a flip-flop. From where she sat, that angle, Rinaldi seemed tall and broad and powerful. He wore a dark blazer and a black collarless shirt. He was smiling, and his eyes glittered malevolently.

"Mr. Rinaldi," she said. Even when talking to murder suspects, she tended to be polite, but she refused to be cordial with this man. Something about him she really couldn't stand. Maybe it was his air of knowingness, his cockiness, the feeling she got that he was enjoying the games he was playing with her.

"So you have a search warrant for the company's network, that it?"

"You're welcome to examine it."

"No, no, no. I don't doubt you dotted every *I* and crossed every *T*. You're one thorough lady, I can tell."

"Thank you."

"Maybe thorough's a polite way to say it. Obsessed, maybe? Looks like you're still after my boss's home security tape."

"Oh, we have the recorder in our custody." She considered telling him they knew the tape had been erased, just to see his reaction, but that would be giving him information he shouldn't have.

Kevin muttered, "Almost there."

Rinaldi glanced at Kevin curiously, as if he'd only just noticed him. Then he looked back at Audrey. He couldn't have been more blasé.

"I still don't get what you're hoping to find," Rinaldi said.

"I have a feeling you know," Audrey said.

"You're right. I do."

"Oh?"

"Right. Couple of frames of some crazy old coot hobbling across my boss's lawn in the middle of the night. But what's that going to tell you, come right down to it?"

Audrey leaned over to the computer where Kevin was working. He tilted the monitor toward Audrey, who squinted, didn't see any picture, and then saw the words "ERASED HERE TOO" on a document on the screen.

"Excellent," Audrey said, nodding. "Good work." She reached for the keyboard and typed out the words, "PLAY ALONG WITH ME." Then she said, "Beautiful, Kevin. Can you improve the resolution just a bit?"

"Oh yeah," he said. "Sure. I've got some great digital-imaging firmware that'll eliminate the motion artifacts and reduce the dot crawl. A comb filter oughta separate the chrominance from the luminance. A little line doubling and some deinterlacing, and we got a nice clean image. No problem at all on this guy."

Kevin tapped some more, and the document disappeared before Rinaldi had a chance to look for himself.

But that was the peculiar thing. Eddie Rinaldi never moved from where he stood, never bothered to peer at the monitor. He seemed utterly uninterested.

No, that wasn't it, Audrey realized.

He was utterly confident. He knew what Kevin had just discovered, that the backup video had been deleted on the Stratton LAN, just as it had been deleted from Conover's home security recorder.

And his confidence had just given him away.

97

Nick felt a tiny tremble in his hands. He put them in his lap so Osgood wouldn't see. "Willard, don't get me wrong. I have no interest in taking you on. I'd much rather work together with you on this. You want to save the funds Todd's running, and I want to save the company. We both want to make money."

Osgood slid his glasses back into place and gave Nick a steely stare as he stood behind his desk. He grunted.

"Now, I don't know you," Nick said, "but I can tell you're not a gambler." Nick noticed that the blond woman with the red glasses had slipped into the office to usher him out and was hovering in the background, waiting for her cue. He lowered his voice so that the woman couldn't hear. "So when Scott McNally and Todd Muldaur funnel a ten-million-dollar bribe to a Chinese government official to make sure this deal happens, that's where I think they're crossing a line you don't want to cross."

"What the hell are you talking about?" Osgood put his hands flat on the glass of his desk and leaned forward, intimidatingly.

"They're putting your company at risk, doing that. Word always leaks out. And then your entire firm will be jeopardized." Nick opened his arms wide. "All of this. Everything you've worked your whole life building. And I wonder whether you think it's really worth taking such an enormous risk, when there's another way to get what you want."

"Rosemary," Osgood barked. "Excuse us, please. We'll be another few minutes." When his secretary had left, he sat down again. "What the hell are you talking about, bribe?"

"Stratton Asia Ventures," Nick said.

"I don't know anything about that."

Was he being straight? Or was he being careful? "It's all right there in front of you—the last couple of pages in that pile. How do you think Todd was able to get this deal done in a month instead of a year? Call it a deal-sweetener or a kickback or a bribe—whatever you call it, it's a clear-cut violation of the Foreign Corrupt Practices Act. And it's the kind of legal exposure that you can't afford."

The way Osgood yanked the folder back toward him, Nick realized that this really was news to the man. Osgood shoved his glasses back up on his forehead and hunched over the papers.

A few minutes later, he looked back up. His leathery face seemed to color. He looked thunderstruck. "Jesus," he said. "Looks like you weren't the only one kept out of the loop."

"I had a feeling Todd wasn't telling you everything," Nick said.

"This is *stupid*, is what it is."

"Desperate men sometimes do stupid things. Frankly, on some level I resent it. My company's worth a hell of a lot more than what Pacific Rim Investors is paying for it. There's no need to pay anyone off."

"God*damn* it," Osgood said.

"You may be great with tarpons, Willard, but I think what we're dealing with here is a snakehead."

Osgood seemed to be doing a slow burn. "I think my Yale boy just got hisself in over his head."

"I guess he figured no one was watching the shop . . ."

Osgood's pearly Chiclets looked more like a snarl than a smile. "From time to time, someone thinks they can pull one over on the old man. Maybe they've been reading too many *Parade* magazine profiles of me. But they always realize the error of their ways."

Nick realized then how terrifying Willard Osgood could be once the cornpone mask fell away, a truly formidable opponent.

"A lot of people have been underestimating you too," Osgood said. "I think I may be one of them. So tell me: What do you have in mind?"

98

"Daddy!" Julia ran up to Nick as he entered the house. "You're back!"

"I'm back." He set down his garment bag, lifted her up, felt a slight twinge in his lower back around the lumbar. Yikes. Can't be picking her up anymore like she's an infant. "How's my baby?"

"Good." Julia never said anything else. She was always good. School was always good. Everything was good.

"Where's your brother?"

She shrugged. "Probably in his room? Do you know Marta just left a couple of hours ago for Barbados? She said she's going to visit her family."

"I know. I thought she needed some time off. Her trip to Barbados is a present from all of us. Where's Cassie?" Cassie had happily agreed to come over to watch the kids.

"She's here. She was just teaching me yoga."

"Where is she?"

"In your study, maybe?"

Nick hesitated a moment. That again. But there was nothing to find there. He had to stop being so suspicious.

"She has a surprise for you," Julia said with a mischievous smile, her big brown eyes wide. "But I can't tell you what it is."

"Can I guess?"

"No."

"Not even one guess?"

"No!" she scolded. "It's a *surprise!*"

"Okay. Don't tell me. But I have a surprise for *you.*"

"What is it?"

"How would you like to go to Hawaii?"

"*What?* No *way!*"

"Way. We're leaving tomorrow night."

"But what about school?"

"I'm taking you and Luke out of school for a few days, that's all."

"Hawaii! I don't believe it! Maui?"

"Maui."

"The same place as last time?"

"Same place. I even got us the exact same villa on the beach."

Julia threw her arms around him, squeezing hard. "I want to do snorkeling again," she said, "and take those hula lessons, and I want to make a lei, and this time I want to learn how to windsurf. Aren't I old enough?"

"You're old enough, sure." Laura had been afraid to let her try, last time.

"Luke said he'd show me how. Are you going to scuba dive again?"

"I think I might have forgotten how."

"What about surfing? Can I learn how to surf too?"

Nick laughed. "Are you going to have time for all these lessons?"

"Remember when I found that gecko in our room, and its tail broke off? Oh, wow, this is so *awesome.*"

Nick went to the kitchen to take the shortcut to his study, but he stopped at the threshold.

In place of the usual plastic draft sheets hanging down was some kind of paper barrier. He looked closer. Wrapping paper had been taped across the entrance, floor to ceiling and jamb to jamb. A wide blue ribbon crisscrossed it like a gift. The paper, he noticed, had little pictures of Superman all over it, cape flying.

"Even though you look more like Clark Kent right now." Cassie's voice. Her arms slid around his waist; she kissed the back of his neck.

"What's this?"

He turned, gave her a hug and planted a big kiss on her mouth.

"You'll see. How was Boston?"

"Let's just say your instincts were right."

Cassie nodded. The dark smudges were visible beneath her eyes again. She looked drawn, exhausted. "Well, you'll get things back on track. You'll see. It's not too late."

"We'll see. Can I open my gift?"

She bowed her head, turned up an "after you" palm.

Nick punched a fist through the gift wrap. The kitchen was all lit up, every light on, dazzling. The granite-topped kitchen island was perfect, just as Laura had once sketched it for him.

"Jesus," Nick said. He went in slowly, taking it all in, awed. He ran a hand over the island top. There was an overhang, enabling the whole family to sit around it. Exactly what Laura had wanted.

He felt its edge. "Bullnose?"

"Half bullnose."

He turned to look at Cassie, saw the little pleased smile. "How the hell did you do this?"

"I didn't do it myself, Nick. I mean, I may have inherited my dad's mechanical ability, but I'm not *that* good. What I'm good at is getting what I want." She shrugged modestly. "It really only took them one full day of work. But it took me a lot of begging and pleading to get them here to do it and finish it by the end of the day."

"My God, you're a miracle worker," Nick said.

"Just like to finish what I start, that's all. Or what your wife started." She paused and then said in a small voice, "Nick, are you ever going to be able to talk about her death?"

He closed his eyes for a while before he spoke. He opened his eyes, took a breath. "I can try. Lucas had a swim meet. It was half past seven, but dark, you know? First week of December. It gets dark early. We were driving to Stratford, because the meet was in the high school there. We're on Stratford-Hillsdale Road, which is what truckers sometimes use to connect to the interstate."

Nick closed his eyes again. He was back in the car on that dark night, a nightmare he had relived only in dreams, and then in shards and fragments of time. He spoke in a low, expressionless monotone. "So there's a tractor trailer heading the opposite way, and the guy driving it had had a couple of beers, and the road surface was icy. Laura was driving—she hated to drive at night, but I asked her to, because I had some calls to make on the cell phone. That was me—company man, always working. We were bickering over something, and Laura was upset, and she wasn't paying attention to the road, see. She didn't see the truck drifting into our lane, across those double yellow lines, until it was too late. She—she tried to turn the wheel, but she didn't do it in time. The truck rammed into us."

He opened his eyes. "Funny thing is, it didn't seem like we were hit all that hard," Nick went on. "It wasn't like some horrible collision in the movies where everything goes black. It was a hard bump, like you might feel if you were playing bumper cars. Kind of a hollow crunch. I didn't get whiplash. Never blacked out. Nothing like that. I turn to Laura and I'm yelling, 'Can you believe that guy?' And she doesn't say anything. And I notice how the windshield is all spiderwebbed on her side. And there's some pebbles of glass on her forehead. Something glistening in her hair. But there's no blood, or hardly any. A fleck or two, maybe. She looked fine. Like she'd nodded off."

"There was nothing you could have done," Cassie breathed.

Nick only knew that his eyes were wet because his vision was blurred. "Except there were *hundreds* of things I could have done. Any one of them, and Laura would still be alive. You know, when we were leaving the house that night, Laura was about to make a phone call, and I made her hang up. I told her she was making us late. I told her it was ridiculous that she'd spent fifteen minutes putting on makeup and perfume for a goddamn *swim meet*. I told her that, for once, we weren't going to be late. I told her I wanted to get a good seat in the stands so I could see what the hell was going on. Now, thing is, if she had made that phone call, we wouldn't have been in an accident. If I hadn't been in such a hurry, we would actually have arrived. And I didn't have to make those goddamned phone calls in the car that night, for Christ's sake. Like they couldn't wait till the morning. I could have driven the car—I mean, look, I was the better driver, we both knew that, she *hated* driving. I shouldn't have been arguing with her while she was behind the wheel. Oh, and here's a sweet one. She wanted to take the Suburban. I said it would just be a pain to park. I insisted that we take the sedan. If we'd taken the Suburban, she might have survived the impact. And I'm just starting a long, long list. All kinds of things I could have done differently. The weeks after she died, I became the world's leading expert on this subject. Had 'em all cross-tabulated in my mind. Should have been on *Jeopardy!* Thanks, Alex, I'll take Vehicular Fatalities for a hundred."

Cassie looked wan, ran her fingers through her hair. Nick wondered whether she was even listening to him. "Intracerebral hemorrhage," he went on. "She died in the hospital the next day."

"You're a good person."

"No," Nick said. "But I wish I were."

"You give so much."

"You don't know, Cassie. All right? You don't know what I've *taken*, what I've done. You don't know . . ."

"You've given me a family."

And I've taken yours away. He looked at her for a long time. He felt foolish about how he'd suspected her secret intentions and worried that she'd been trying to dig up the truth about what had happened to her father.

Then again, he obviously wasn't so good at sizing people up, he realized. He'd gotten Osgood wrong in all sorts of ways, and he'd gotten Scott wrong. Todd Muldaur—well, he had Todd's number from the start, so no surprise there. Eddie? He wasn't really surprised, when it came right down to it, that Eddie wouldn't hesitate to kick the skates out from under him.

But Cassie. He hadn't known just what to make of her, and maybe he still didn't know her all that well. Maybe his overpowering guilt and her overpowering seductiveness made it hard for him to see her clearly. She was a little emotionally unstable, that was obvious. Bipolar and having your dad murdered—that was a fairly lethal combination.

And he wondered how she'd react when he came clean.

It made no difference to him whether Eddie would strike some kind of deal with the police or not. He'd leave Eddie to his own smarmy fate.

When he and the kids came back from Hawaii, he was going to tell her the truth. And then he'd tell Detective Rhimes the truth.

And there would be an arrest, he knew that. Because whether a DA decided it was self-defense or not, he had killed a man.

Back in Boston, after his meeting with Willard Osgood, he'd taken a cab over to Ropes & Gray, a big law firm where a friend of his worked as a criminal defense attorney. A really smart guy he knew from Michigan State. Nick had told him what had happened, the whole story.

The lawyer had blanched, of course. He told Nick he was in deep shit, there was no way around it. He said the best Nick could hope for was criminally negligent homicide, that if he were very lucky he might get only a couple of years in prison. But it might well be more—five, seven, even ten years, because there was also the matter of having moved the body—tampering with physical evidence. The lawyer said that if Nick wanted to go through with it, he'd get a local counsel and petition to try the case in Michigan *pro hoc vici*, whatever that meant. He'd arrange for Nick to surrender, and he'd try to negotiate a plea agreement with the DA in Fenwick. And he said he'd ask for a lot of money up front.

Whatever would happen to him, though, was the least of it. What was going to happen to his kids? Would Aunt Abby be willing to take care of them?

This was the worst thing of all, the thing that truly terrified him.

But he knew it was the right thing to do, at long last, however long it had taken him to come to his senses. It was like that dream he'd had recently, the one about the body in the basement wall that gave away its hiding place by oozing the fluids of decay. He couldn't hold the horrible secret inside anymore.

So in a week or so, after his last vacation with the kids, he was going to tell Cassie the truth. He'd already begun to rehearse, in his head, how he'd tell her.

"What is it?" she said.

"I've been doing a lot of thinking, and I've made some decisions."

"Decisions about the company?"

"Not that, no. My life is about other things."

An anxious look came over her. "Is this bad?"

"No," he said, shaking his head.

"Is it bad for us?"

"No. It's not about us, exactly."

" 'Not about us, exactly'—what's that supposed to mean?"

"We'll talk when the time is right. Just not yet."

She placed her hand on his. He took it in his hand, holding it gently. Hers was small and trembling; his was big and steady.

The hand that killed her father.

"Cass, we're off tomorrow," he said. "We're going to Hawaii for a few days. I already got the tickets."

"Hawaii?"

"Maui. Laura loved that place most of all. There's this great resort Laura and I discovered before we had kids. We had our own villa, right on the beach, with its own pool—not that you needed it—and all you could see from it was the Pacific Ocean."

"Sounds amazing."

"Until Laura died, we used to take the family there every year. Our big splurge. Same villa every time, Laura made sure of it. I think of it as a time when we were completely happy, all of us. I remember last time we were there, Laura and I were in bed and she turned to me and she said she wanted to spray a fixative on the whole day and keep it forever."

"God, it sounds beautiful, Nick." A light seemed to flicker in her eyes. She looked almost serene.

"I called the travel agency we'd used, and—it felt like a miracle—they said that exact same villa's available."

"Are you sure you want to return to a place they associate so closely with Laura? It might be better to go somewhere new—you know, create new memories."

"You may be right. I know it won't be the same. It'll be sad in some ways. But it'll be a new start. A good thing—just going there as a family, being to-gether again. And there isn't going to be any pressure to talk, or work through 'issues,' or anything else. We're just going to play on the beach and do stuff and eat pineapple and just *be*. It won't be the same, but it'll be *something*. And it'll be something we can all remember when things change, because they're going to change."

"The kids can miss school, right? No big deal."

"I already called the school, told them I'd be taking Julia and Lucas out of classes for a few days. Hell, I even picked up the tickets at the airport when I got in." He pulled an envelope from his breast pocket, took out the tickets and held them up, fanning them like a winning hand of cards.

Cassie's smile vanished. "Three tickets." She pulled her hand away.

"Just family. Me and the kids. I don't think we've ever done this. Just us three, heading off for a few days somewhere."

"Just family," Cassie repeated in a harsh whisper.

"I think it's important for me to try to reconnect with the kids. I mean, you get along with them better than I do, which is great. But I've let my part in it slip—I've sort of delegated that to you, like I'm CEO of the family or something, and that's not right. I'm their dad, whether I'm any good at it or not, and it's my job to work on making us a family again."

Cassie's face was transfigured, weirdly tight as if every muscle in her face were clenched.

"Oh God, Cassie, I'm sorry," Nick said, flushing, embarrassed by his own obliviousness. "You know how much you mean to us."

Cassie's eyelids fluttered oddly, and he could see the veins in her neck pulsing. It was as if she were struggling to contain herself—or maybe to contain something larger than herself.

He smiled ruefully. "Luke and Julia—they're my direct reports, you know. And I don't know when I'll have the chance again."

"Just family." The sound of one heavy stone scraping against another.

"I think it'll be really good for us, don't you?"

"You want to get away."

"Exactly."

"You want to escape." Her voice was an incantation.

"Pretty much."

"From me."

"What? Jesus, no! You're taking this the wrong way. It isn't about—"

"No." She shook her head slowly. "No. No hiding place. There's no hiding place down there."

Adrenaline surged through Nick's veins. "*What* did you say?"

An odd smile appeared on her face. "Isn't that what the stalker spray-painted in the house? That's what Julia told me."

"Yeah," Nick said. "Those very words."

"I can read the writing on the wall, Nick."

"Come on, Cassie, don't be silly."

"It's like the book of Daniel, isn't it? The king of Babylon throws a big drunken party and all of a sudden he sees a mysterious hand appear and start writing something strange and cryptic on the plaster wall, right? And the king's scared out of his mind and he calls in the prophet Daniel who tells him the message means the king's days are over, Babylon's history, he's going to be killed." Her expression was glassy.

"Okay, you're starting to creep me out."

Suddenly her eyes focused, and she met his gaze. "Maybe I should be grateful. I was wrong, wrong about so many things. It's *humbling*. Humbling to be put right. Just like with the Stroups. But so necessary. Listen, you do what you think is best. You do what's best for family. There's nothing more important than that."

Nick held out his arms. "Cassie, come here."

"I think I'd better go," she said. "I think I've done enough, don't you think?"

"Cassie, please," Nick protested. "I don't get it."

"Because I can do a lot more." Noiselessly, she walked out of the kitchen, her steps so fluid she could have been gliding. "I can do a lot more."

"We'll talk, Cassie," said Nick. "When we get back."

A final glance over her shoulders. "A *lot* more."

99

Early Sunday morning, before church. Audrey sat in the kitchen with her coffee and her buttered toast while Leon slept. She was poring over the bills, wondering how they'd be able to keep up, now that Leon's unemployment benefits were running out. Usually she paid off the entire credit-card balance each month, but she was going to have to start paying only the minimum balance due. She wondered too, whether they should drop to basic cable. She thought they should, though Leon would not be happy about losing the sports channels.

Her cell phone rang. A 616 number: Grand Rapids.

It was a Lieutenant Lawrence Pettigrew of the Grand Rapids police. The man who'd first talked to her about Edward Rinaldi. She'd placed several calls to him over the last few days and had all but given up on him. Noyce had made it clear that he didn't want her asking around in GR about Rinaldi, but she had no choice in the matter.

"How can I help you, Detective?" Pettigrew said. "The kids are waiting for me to take them out for pancakes, so can we make this quick?"

The guy was no fan of Edward Rinaldi, so she knew that asking about Rinaldi again would be like pushing a button and watching the vitriol spew out. But she had no reason to expect that he'd know the specifics of a long-forgotten and, in fact, quite minor, drug case.

He didn't. "Far as I'm concerned, Rinaldi's gone and good riddance," he said. "He wasn't exactly a credit to the uniform."

"Was he fired?"

"Squeezed out might be more accurate. But I were you, I wouldn't be bad-mouthing Eddie Rinaldi over there in Fenwick."

"He's the security director of Stratton, is that what you mean?"

"Yeah, yeah, but that's not what I'm talking about. Didn't you say you're in Major Cases?"

"That's right."

"Hell, you want to know chapter and verse on Eddie Rinaldi, you could ask Jack Noyce. But then again, maybe you shouldn't."

"I don't think Sergeant Noyce knows all that much about Rinaldi."

Pettigrew's laugh was abrupt and percussive. "Noyce knows him like a book, sweetheart. Guarantee it. Jack was Eddie's partner."

Audrey's scalp tightened.

"Sergeant Noyce?" she said, disbelieving.

"Partner in crime, I like to say. Don't take this the wrong way, Detective—what's your name again?"

"Rhimes." Audrey shuddered.

"Like LeAnn Rimes, the singer?" He warbled, off-key, 'How do I *live* . . . without you?'"

"Spelled differently, I believe."

"Quite the babe, though, no matter how you spell it."

"So I hear, yes. Noyce . . . Noyce was known to be dirty, is that what you're telling me?"

"Hell, there's a reason Jack got sent to Siberia, right?"

"Siberia?"

"No offense, sweetheart. But from where I sit, Fenwick is Siberia."

"Noyce was . . . squeezed out too?"

"Peas in a pod, those guys. I got no idea who did more pilfering, but I'd say they both did pretty good. Works better in a team, so they're each willing to look away. Eddie was more into the guns, and Jack was more into the home electronics and the stereo components and what have you, but they both loved the cash."

"They both . . ." she started to say, but she lost the heart to go on.

"Oh, and Detective LeAnn?"

"Audrey." She wanted to vomit, wanted to end the call and throw up and then wrap herself in a blanket and go back to sleep.

"Sweetheart, I were you, I wouldn't use my name with Noyce. Guy's a survivor, and he'll wanna let bygones be bygones, know what I'm saying?"

She thanked him, pushed End, and then did exactly what she knew she would. She rushed to the bathroom and heaved the contents of her stomach, the acid from the coffee scalding her throat. Then she washed her face. All she wanted to do right now was to enrobe herself in the old blue blanket on the living room couch, but it was time for church.

100

The First Abyssinian Church of the New Covenant was a once-grand stone building that had slowly, over the years, gone to seed. The velvet pew cushions, badly in need of replacing, had been repaired in far too many places with duct tape. The place was always cold, summer or winter: something about the stone walls and floor, that plus the fact that the building fund was suffering, and it cost a fortune to heat the cavernous interior adequately.

Attendance was sparse this morning, as it was on most Sundays except Easter and Christmas. There were even a few white faces: a couple of regulars who seemed to find the sustenance here they didn't get in the white congregations. LaTonya's family wasn't here, which was no surprise, since they came only a few times a year. Early in their marriage, Leon used to accompany Audrey here, until he announced it wasn't for him. She didn't even know whether he was sleeping late this morning or doing something else, whatever else he'd been doing.

Leon was only one of the reasons why her heart was heavy today. There was also Noyce. That news had punctured her. She felt betrayed by this man who'd been her friend and supporter and who hid from her his true nature. It sickened her.

But this discovery, as much as it shook her to the core, liberated her at the same time. She no longer had to agonize about betraying him, going behind his back, end-running him. She knew there was no choice, really. Whether Jack Noyce was in the Stratton Corporation's pocket, had been leaking to his old partner details of the investigation — or was simply compromised, trapped, by what Rinaldi knew about him — he had been working to defeat her investigation. She thought back to the many talks she'd had with him about this case, the advice he'd dispensed so freely. The way he'd cautioned her to proceed carefully, telling her she didn't have enough to arrest Conover and Rinaldi. And who would ever know what else he'd done to slow things up, block her progress? What resources had he quietly blocked? Whatever the truth was, she couldn't tell Noyce that she and Bugbee were about to get an arrest warrant for the CEO and the security director of Stratton. Noyce had to be kept in the dark, or he'd surely notify Rinaldi and do everything in his power to halt the arrest.

But here, at least, here she felt at peace and welcome and loved. Everyone said good morning, even people whose names she didn't know, courtly gentlemen and polite young men and lovely young women and hovering mothers and sweet old white-haired women. Maxine Blake was dressed all in white, wearing an ornate hat that looked a little like an upside-down bucket with white tendrils coming out of it and encircling it like rings around a planet. She threw her arms around Audrey, pressing Audrey to her enormous bosom, bringing her into a cloud of perfume and warmth and love. "God is good," Maxine said.

"All the time," Audrey responded.

The service started a good twenty minutes late. "Colored people's time," the joke went. The choir, dressed in their magnificent red-and-white robes, marched down the aisle clapping and singing "It's a Highway to Heaven," and then they were joined by the electric organ and then the trumpet and drum and then Audrey joined in along with most everybody else. She'd always wanted to sing in the choir, but her voice was nothing special — though, as she'd noticed, some of the women in the choir had thin voices and tended to sing out of tune. Some had spectacular voices, it was true. The men mostly sang in a rumbling bass, but the tenor was more off-key than on.

Reverend Jamison started his sermon as he always did, by calling out, "God is good," to which everyone responded: "All the time." He said it again, and everyone responded again. His sermons were always heartfelt, usually inspired, and never went on too long. They weren't particularly original, though. Audrey had heard he got them off the Internet from Baptist Web sites that posted sample sermons and notes. Once, confronted on his lack of originality, Reverend Jamison had said, "I milk a lot of cows, but I churn my own butter." Audrey liked that.

Today he told the story of Joshua and the armies of Israel fighting the good fight, battling five of the kings of Canaan for the conquest of the promised land. About how the kings played right into Joshua's hands by joining the battle together. About how it wasn't the Lord who fought the battle, it was Israel. The five kings tried to hide in a cave, but Joshua ordered the cave sealed up. And after the battle had been won, Joshua brought the kings out of their cave, out of their hiding place, and humiliated them by ordering his princes to place their feet on the kings' necks. Reverend Jamison talked about how there's no hiding place. "We can't hide from God," he declared. "The only hiding place from God is Hell."

That made her think, as it had so many times, about Nicholas Conover and the graffiti that had been repeatedly spray-painted on the interior walls of his house. No hiding place.

That could be frightening, as no doubt Conover found it to be. No hiding place: from what? From a faceless adversary, from a stalker? From his guilt, his sins?

But here in church, "no hiding place" was meant to be a stern yet hopeful admonition.

In his most orotund voice the reverend recited from Proverbs 28: "He that covereth his sins shall not prosper: but whoso confesseth and forsaketh them shall have mercy."

And she thought, because every single one of Reverend Jamison's sermons was devised to mean something to each and everyone in the congregation, about Nicholas Conover. The king hiding in his cave.

But no hiding place. Andrew Stadler had been right, hadn't he?

Reverend Jamison cued the choir, which went right into a lively rendition of "No Hiding Place Down Here." The soloist was Mabel Darnell, a large woman who sang and swayed like Aretha Franklin and Mahalia Jackson put together. The organist, Ike Robinson, was right up front, on display, not hidden the way the organist usually was in the other churches she'd seen. He was a white-haired, dark-skinned man of near eighty with expressive eyes and an endearing smile. He wore a white suit and looked like Count Basie, Audrey had always thought.

"I went to the rock to hide my face," Mabel sang, clapping her hands, "but the rock cried out, 'No hiding place!'"

Count Basie's pudgy fingers ran up and down the keys, syncopating, making swinging jazz out of it, and the rest of the choir joined in at *the rock* and *my face* and *cried out* and *no hiding place no hiding place no hiding place*.

Audrey felt a thrill coursing through her body, a shiver that moved along her spine like an electric current.

And the instant the choir had finished, while the organ chords still resounded, Reverend Jamison's voice boomed out, "My friends, none of us can hide from the Lord. 'And the kings of the earth, and the great men, and the rich men, and the chief captains, and the mighty men, and every bondman, and every free man'"—his voice rose steadily until the sound system squealed with feedback—"'hid themselves in the dens and in the rocks of the mountains.'" Now he dropped to a stage whisper: "'And said to the mountains and rocks, fall on us, and hide us from the face of him that sitteth on the throne, and from the wrath of the Lamb. For the great day of his wrath is come; and who shall be able to stand?'"

He paused to let the congregation know that his sermon had concluded. Then he invited anyone in the congregation who wished to come up to the altar for a moment of personal prayer. Ike Robinson, no longer Count Basie, played softly as a dozen or so people got up from their pews and knelt at the altar rail, and all of a sudden Audrey felt moved to do it too, something she hadn't done since her mother's death. She went up there and knelt between Maxine Blake and her enormous rings-of-Saturn hat and another woman, Sylvia-something, whose husband had just died of complications from liver transplant surgery, leaving her with four small children.

Sylvia-something was going through a terrible, terrible time, and what did Audrey have to complain about, really? Her problems were small ones, but they filled her up, as small problems will until the big ones move in and elbow them aside.

She knew she had allowed her anger at Leon to fester inside her, and she recalled the words from Ephesians 4:26: "Do not let the sun go down while you are still angry, and do not give the devil a foothold." And she knew it was time to let go of that anger and confront him once and for all.

She knew that her hurt and disappointment over Jack Noyce might never heal, but it would not get in the way of her doing the right thing.

She thought of that poor little daughter of Nicholas Conover, fumbling at the piano, that beautiful needy face. That little girl who had just lost her mother and was about to lose her father too.

And that was the most wrenching thing of all, knowing that she was about to orphan that little girl.

She began weeping, her shoulders heaving, the hot tears running down her cheeks, and someone was rubbing her shoulder and consoling her, and she felt loved.

Outside the church, in the gloomy daylight, she took her cell phone out of her purse and called Roy Bugbee.

101

The throaty growl of a car coming up the driveway.

Leon? No, Leon's car didn't sound that way. Out catting, Leon was. And on a Sunday. She felt a swell of resentment, of resolve.

She parted the sheer curtains in the front parlor. Bugbee.

His leering grin. "Finally decided to do it, eh?"

She invited him into the front parlor, where he took Leon's chair and Audrey sat facing him on the couch. Bugbee's foot jostled something, and a couple of brown glass bottles clattered.

He glanced down. "Hitting the sauce, Aud? Pressure getting too much for you?"

"I don't even like the taste of beer," she said, embarrassed. "So what's up?"

"One complication."

"Oh no."

"A good complication. Our friend Eddie's rolling over on Conover."

"What does that mean, exactly?"

"He wants to deal."

"How much did he tell you?"

"Not a fucking thing. Just that he might have some information of interest to us."

"He's got to show us the wares."

"He wants a deal first. I'm betting he's the coconspirator."

She thought a moment. "What if he's the shooter, not Conover?"

"Them's the breaks. If he gives up Conover for aiding and abetting, we got 'em both."

"He knows about the gun match." Another car engine, had to be Leon.

"You tell him? I sure as hell didn't."

She shook her head and told him about the call from Grand Rapids.

"Fucking Noyce," said Bugbee. "What'd I tell you?"

"What did you tell me?"

"I never liked him."

"That's because he doesn't like you."

"Touché. But not my point. Him and Eddie Rinaldi both have something on each other. Now looks like we have something on Noyce."

"I don't play that game," Audrey said firmly.

"Christ," said Bugbee. "The fuck is the point of being a church lady, time like this?"

"How about I put it in terms you might understand? You want to be up front and open with Noyce, I have no problem with that. But I'll bet you he knows that we know."

"You think?"

"He knows I've been talking to Grand Rapids. He knows I dig deep. Anyway, you want to play games with him later, I really don't care. My heart breaks for him, but right now I'm just thinking about this case and how we make it work. My way is to ignore him, work around him, put through this arrest paperwork on the down low so he doesn't have a chance to tell Rinaldi."

Bugbee shrugged, accepting defeat.

"And I'll tell you something else. I don't want to make a deal with Rinaldi."

"That's fucked up," Bugbee protested. "He's our way in."

"You're the one who kept saying we have this case nailed, right? Why do you want to give up so easily?"

"It's not giving up," Bugbee said.

"It's not, huh? I want to charge them both with open murder. That way we have maximum bargaining room. We sort it out later."

"So now *you* think we've got it nailed, that it?"

"Just about. Tomorrow morning first thing, I'm going to talk to Stadler's psychiatrist again."

"A little late for that, don't you think?"

"Not at all. It'll strengthen our hand considerably with the prosecutor's office if he'll agree to testify that Stadler could be deranged, even dangerous. If we get that, we'll get the arrest warrants for sure."

"I thought he already refused to talk to you."

"I'm not giving up."

"You can't force him."

"No, but I can persuade him. Or try, at least."

"You believe it?"

"Believe what?"

"Believe that Stadler was dangerous."

"I don't know what to believe. I think Conover and Rinaldi believed it. If we have the psychiatrist on board, we have motive. The slickest lawyer Nick Conover can find's going to have a steep hill to climb on that one. And then we sure don't need any deal with Eddie, understand?"

"Roll the dice, you mean?"

"Sometimes you have to," she said.

"You don't want to roast Noyce's balls over a campfire like I do, huh?"

She shook her head. "I'm not angry. I'm . . ." She thought. "I'm disappointed. I'm sad."

"You know something, I always thought you Jesus freaks were kidding, on some level. But I think you're serious about all that do-the-right-thing stuff. About being good. Aren't you?"

She laughed. "It's not about being good, Roy. It's about trying to be good. You think Jesus is some . . ." She searched for the word. "Some wimp? No. He was a real hard ass. He had to be."

Bugbee smiled, his eyes crinkling. She tried to read his expression, wasn't sure if she detected the tiniest glint of admiration. "Jesus the hard ass. I like that."

"So when was the last time *you* went to church, Roy?"

"Oh, no. Don't fucking start on me. Let's get one thing clear. That's not going to happen." He paused. "Besides, sounds to me like Jesus's got some work to do in your own household."

Stung, Audrey didn't reply.

"Sorry," Bugbee said after a few seconds. "That was out of bounds."

"That's okay," she said. "You may be right."

102

A chill was in the air, the fall days tinged with the coming winter. The sky was steel gray and ominous, threatening to rain at any moment.

In the living room, however, where Audrey sat reading, it was warm almost to the point of stifling. After Bugbee left, she'd made a fire in the fireplace, the first of the season. The fatwood had caught right away, which pleased her, and now the logs crackled loudly, making her jump from time to time as she lingered over a passage that wouldn't let go.

She opened the Bible to the book of Matthew and wept for the man who'd been her friend. She thought, too, about Leon, about how she'd have it out with him. Now she was all the more determined to somehow rise above anger and recrimination.

Noyce and Leon: they were nothing alike, but both were men with feet of clay. Leon was a lost man, but he was a man she loved. She knew how quick she was to judge others. Maybe it was time to learn forgiveness. That seemed to be the whole point of the parable of the unmerciful servant in the book of Matthew.

A king was owed a great sum of money by one of his servants and was about to sell the servant and his family in order to raise the money. But when the servant pleaded, his master took pity and forgave him his debt. Not long afterward, the servant met a fellow servant of the king's who owed *him* some money, and what did he do? He grabbed the man by the throat and demanded payment. The king summoned the ingrate and said, "You wicked servant! I forgave you all that debt because you besought me; and should not you have had mercy on your fellow servant, as I had mercy on you?"

A key jangled in the front door lock.

Leon. Back from wherever he went without telling her.

"Oh, hey, Shorty," he said as he entered. "You made a fire. That's nice."

She nodded. "You're out and about early."

"Looks like it's about to pour out there."

"Where'd you go, Leon?"

He immediately looked away. "Gotta get out of the house sometimes. Good for me."

"Come sit down in here. We need to talk."

"Uh oh," he said. "Those are words no guy ever wants to hear." But he sat down anyway, in his favorite chair, looking supremely uncomfortable.

"This is not going to continue," she said.

He nodded.

"Well?"

"Well what?" he said.

"I've been doing some reading in the Bible."

"I see that. Old Testament or New?"

"Hmm?"

"As I recall from my churchgoing days, the Old Testament God's a pretty judgmental sort."

"None of us is perfect, baby. And the Bible tells us about when Jesus refused to condemn an adulterer who was about to be stoned to death."

"Where's this going?" Leon said.

"You going to tell me what you're up to?"

"Ah," he said with a low chuckle that began to grow. "Oh, yeah," he said and his chuckle grew into an unrestrained guffaw. "My sister been putting crazy ideas in your head?"

"You going to explain yourself? Or is this going to be the last talk we ever have?"

"Oh, Shorty," Leon said. He got up from his chair and sat down on the couch next to her, snuggling close. She was astonished, but she didn't hug him back, just sat there, stiff and angry and confused. A bottle rolled around under the couch. She reached a hand down and grabbed it. A brown beer bottle. She held it up.

"Is it this, or is it a woman?" she said.

He was laughing, enjoying himself, and she grew steadily more furious. "It's funny to you?"

"You're some detective," he finally said. "That's root beer."

"Oh, so it is," she said, embarrassed.

"I haven't had a drink in seventeen days. You haven't noticed?"

"Is that true?"

"Forgiveness is step nine. I'm nowhere near that."

"Step nine?"

"The eighth step is to make a list of everyone I ever harmed and be willing to make amends to them. I should do that too. You know I was never good about lists."

"You—how come you didn't tell me you're doing AA?"

Now it was his turn to look sheepish. "Maybe I wanted to make sure it would take."

"Oh, baby," she said, tears springing to her eyes. "I'm so proud of you."

"Hey, Shorty, don't go getting all proud yet. I still haven't gotten past step three."

"Which is what?"

"Hell if I know," Leon said. He put a big callused hand on her face, brushed away her tears, and leaned in to kiss her, and this time she kissed him back. She'd almost forgotten what it was like, kissing her husband, but she was remembering now, and it was nice.

The two of them got up and went to the bedroom.

Outside it began to rain, but it was warm in their bed.

In the morning she would get up early and arrange the arrest warrants for Eddie Rinaldi and Nicholas Conover.

103

On her way to the prosecutor's office, Audrey heard Noyce's voice calling to her.

He was standing in the door to his office, waving her in.

She stopped for just a moment.

"Audrey," he said, something different in his voice. "We need to talk."

"I'm in a rush, Jack. I'm sorry."

"What's up?"

"I—I'd rather not say."

His eyebrows shot up. "Audrey?"

"Excuse me, Jack. I'm sorry."

He put out a hand, touched her shoulder. "Audrey," he said, "I don't know exactly what they told you about me, but . . ."

He knew. Of course he knew. She fixed him with a level gaze. "I'm listening," she said.

Noyce took a breath, colored, and then said, "Fuck it. I don't want your pity." He turned and went into his office, and she hurried on.

Dr. Aaron Landis's habitual sneer had become an incredulous scowl. "We've been over this, Detective. You've already asked me to breach Mr. Stadler's confidentiality. If you somehow imagine that your persistence is going to make me reconsider—"

"I'm sure you're aware what the *Principles of Medical Ethics*, published by the American Psychiatric Association, says about confidentiality."

"Oh, please."

"You're permitted to release relevant confidential information about a patient under legal compulsion."

"As I recall, it says 'proper' legal compulsion. Do you have a court order?"

"If that'll make a difference to you, I'll get one. But I'm appealing to you not as a law enforcement officer, but as a human being."

"Not the same thing, I take it."

She ignored this. "Ethically you have the right to testify about Andrew Stadler's history, especially if you have any interest in helping bring his killer to justice."

Landis's eyelids drooped as if he were deep in thought. "What does one have to do with the other?"

"Well, you see, Dr. Landis, we've found Andrew Stadler's killer."

"And who might that be?" His phlegmatic tone, carefully calibrated, didn't quite mask his natural curiosity.

"That I can't tell you until he's charged. But I'm going to ask you to take the stand and testify to the fact that Andrew Stadler was, at times, violent."

"I won't."

"Don't you understand what's at stake, Dr. Landis?"

"I will not testify to that," Landis said.

"If you refuse to speak for this man," Audrey said, "his killer may not find justice. Doesn't that make a difference to you?"

"You want me to testify that he had violent tendencies, and I'm not going to do that. I can't. I can't say what you want me to say—because it's not true."

"What do you mean?"

"I saw no violent inclinations whatever."

"What makes you say that?"

"I didn't tell you a thing."

"Pardon me?"

"You didn't hear any of this from me." He scratched his chin. "Andrew Stadler was a sad, desperately afflicted man. A tormented man. But not a violent man."

"Dr. Landis, the man who killed him held him responsible for a particularly sadistic attack, an evisceration of a dog, a family pet. In fact, a whole series of attacks on the suspect's home. It's the reason, we're convinced, this man killed Stadler."

Landis nodded, a glint of recognition in his eyes. "Yes," he said. "That would make a certain sense."

"It would?"

"If it were true, yes. But I can tell you with a high degree of certainty that Andrew Stadler never did these things."

"Hold on a second. Last time we spoke, you talked about a pattern of sudden rages, brief psychotic episodes—"

"Indeed. I was describing a syndrome we call Borderline Personality Disorder."

"All right, but you said a schizophrenic like Stadler could have this borderline disorder."

"I've seen it, sure. But I wasn't talking about Andrew Stadler."

"Then who *were* you talking about, Doctor?"

He hesitated.

"Doctor, please!"

Ten minutes later, short of breath, Audrey raced out of County Medical, cell phone to her ear.

104

The special board meeting was set to start at 2 P.M., and by a quarter to, most of the invited participants had arrived in the narrow anteroom. Scott had come first, and he didn't dance around the subject. Nick had a stack of unanswered phone messages from him, all from this morning. Marjorie had been instructed to keep him away from Nick's home base.

"Don't leave me in the dark here, Nick," Scott said. Nick noticed he was wearing a brand-new shirt: white, narrow-point collar, looked like Armani, completely different from the frayed Oxford-cloth button-downs he usually wore. "Come on, Nick, I can't read my lines if I don't have a script, okay?"

"I thought we'd be spontaneous."

"Spontaneous," Scott repeated. "Spontaneous combustion. Spontaneous abortion. Spontaneous aortic aneurysm." He shook his head. "I don't like that word 'spontaneous.'"

Nick cocked his head. "We're trying something new, here," he said, deliberately cryptic.

"I just want to help, Nick." There was a sullen look in his lilac-rimmed eyes.

"I'm counting on it," Nick said. "In fact, could you get me a Diet Coke? No ice if it's already cold."

Scott looked like he was about to say something when Davis Eilers—khakis and a white polo shirt beneath a blue blazer—slung an arm around Scott's shoulder and took him away.

"So where's the agenda?" Todd Muldaur asked Nick, as the anteroom started to grow crowded. "Dan, Davis, and I flew here on the Fairfield corporate jet together, and guess what—none of us got an agenda."

"Oh, there's an agenda," Nick said with a smile. "It's just not printed."

"I never heard of that. Special board meeting but no written agenda?" He exchanged glances with Dan Finegold. "Hope this isn't one of those panic moves," he said to Nick with what was meant to be a look of kindly concern in his too-blue eyes.

Finegold gave Nick an upper-bicep squeeze. "Slow and steady, right?"

"How's the brewery?" Nick asked him.

"Couldn't be better," Finegold said. "On the brewing end, at least. Micro's a crowded category right now."

Nick dropped his voice confidingly. "Truth is, Rolling Rock's more my speed. I like a beer I can see through." He scanned the room until he saw Scott McNally, huddled in a corner with Davis Eilers. Nick didn't need to hear them talk to work out that Eilers was trying to get the lowdown from Scott. Scott's response was evident from series of nervous shrugs and headshakes.

Now Todd took Nick by the elbow, and spoke to him in a low, tense voice. "Pretty short notice, don't you think?"

"The chairman of the board has the power to convene an extraordinary session of the board," Nick said blandly.

"But what's the goddamned *agenda?*"

Nick grinned, didn't answer. "Funny, I was remembering what you said about turtles and turtle soup."

Todd shrugged. "Dan and I didn't mind canceling our other appointments, but, hey, there's a Yankees–Red Sox game tonight. We both had to give away our tickets. So I hope it's going to be worth our while, huh?"

"Definitely. Count on it. We weren't able to rustle up that good coffee, though. You'll have to overlook a few things."

"We're getting used to that," said Todd with a grin that snapped shut an instant later. "Just hope you know what you're doing." He craned his head and exchanged a long glance with Scott.

Nick noticed Dorothy Devries making her entrance. She was wearing a royal blue skirt suit, with big clown-suit buttons. Her mouth was pursed and she was fingering her silver brooch with a clawlike hand. Nick waved to her from across the room, a big hearty gesture that she returned with a refrigerator smile.

Nick continued to shake hands, and make welcoming noises, until he noticed that Eddie Rinaldi had entered the room. Eddie sidled up to him with a look of impatience. "Guess what? Your fucking alarm went off again."

Nick groaned. "I can't—can you handle it?"

Eddie nodded. "Gas leak."

"*Gas* leak?"

"Alarm company called, then they called back, said a 'Mrs. Conover' told them she's handling it, but I think I should check it out. Unless you got married without telling me."

Nick, distracted, shook his head. "And Marta's out of the country."

"Your girlfriend?"

"She's not there. The kids should be home by now, though."

Eddie put a hand on Nick's shoulder. "I'll head over there. You don't fuck around with a gas leak." He took an amused look around the room before sidling off.

"Well, why don't we go sit down?" Nick said. His words were addressed to Todd but were loud enough to count as instructions to the room.

A couple of minutes later, everyone had taken a seat around the oversized mahogany table in the boardroom. Scott was playing with his plasma screen, raising it and lowering it nervously, like a kid with a Transformer action figure.

Nick didn't sit at his usual spot at the head of the table. He left that chair empty and took the seat next to it. He nodded at Stephanie Alstrom, who wore her usual look of arid unease. She rested her hands on a thick file folder.

"I want to start with some very good news," Nick said. "Atlas McKenzie is in. They signed this morning."

"Why, that's *tremendous*, Nick," Todd said. "Good going! You talk them off the ledge yourself?"

"Wish I could take the credit," Nick said. "Willard Osgood had to get on the horn himself."

"Really," Todd said, coolly. "That's an unusual tactic."

"He volunteered," Nick said. "I didn't twist his arm."

"Did he? I guess he likes to show that he can land a big one from time to time." Todd's expression hovered between amusement and condescension. "They don't make 'em like that anymore."

"I'll say." Nick pressed an intercom button and spoke to Marjorie. "Marjorie, I think we're all ready here. Could you let our visitor know?" Looking up, he went on, "Now, I didn't convene this extraordinary session to crow about good news. There are some serious issues we've got in front of us, which have to do with the future of this company." He paused for a moment. "A number of you have urged me to take a hard look at manufacturing costs. I've been resistant, and maybe I've been too resistant. Looking forward, now, we have decided to start diversifying our manufacturing base. Stratton is going to contract out the manufacturing for our low-cost Stratton/Basics lines. We're currently in negotiation with a number of overseas manufacturers, including some strong candidates in China. It's a move that will ensure we'll continue to be competitive in the most price-sensitive part of our market."

Dorothy Devries's expression was almost a smirk. Todd and Scott both looked confused, as if they were on a train that had gone one stop past their destination.

"We've reached a different decision about the higher-end lines, which are at the core of our brand identity," Nick went on. "These we'll continue to manufacture right here in Fenwick."

"I'm sorry to step in," Todd said, clearing his throat. "But you're referring to 'we,' and I don't know who you mean by that. Are you talking about your full management team? Because a lot of us are inclined to think that it's too late in the day for half measures."

"I'm aware of this." In a louder voice, he said, "As some of you here know and some of you don't know—and until recently, I was among those who didn't know—certain parties representing Fairfield have been negotiating to sell the Stratton brand to a consortium called Pacific Rim Investors, which controls a large Shenzhen-based manufacturer of office furniture, Shenyang Industries."

Nick didn't know whether he had been expecting gasps or cries of astonishment, but there weren't any. Just the sound of shuffling papers and cleared throats.

Todd looked smug. "May I say a few words?"

"Absolutely," Nick said.

Todd turned slightly, addressing the other members of the board. "First, I want to apologize to the CEO of this company for keeping him out of the loop on the deal. We at Fairfield have been taking a long, hard look at the numbers, and, frankly, we see an opportunity here, one we cannot afford to pass up. Stratton has entered into a crisis phase. Nick Conover—and I want to commend him for his candor—has made it very clear, every step of the way, that there are certain options he just can't accept. Well, we respect his views. And we certainly respect his excellent work on behalf of the company. But this is a case where management cannot be given the final word." A beat. "The greatest praise I can give any manager is to say that he does his work with passion." He turned to face Nick. "That's certainly true of you, Nick. But when a firm reaches a critical inflection point, there are hard choices to be made—and they need to be made with *dis*passion."

He leaned back in his black Stratton chair, looking sleeker by the moment. "That's the thing about being in a crisis zone," he said, hardly bothering to conceal his self-satisfaction. "It's what everyone at McKinsey gets drummed into their heads from day one. The Chinese word for 'crisis' combines the characters for 'danger' and 'opportunity.'"

"No doubt," Nick said breezily. "And the Chinese word for 'outsourcing' combines the characters for 'lost' and 'jobs.'"

"We owe you a lot," Todd said in a lordly tone. "Don't think we're not grateful. I'm sure I speak for *everyone* when I say that we appreciate all you've given to Stratton. It's just that the time has come to move on."

"I know you'd *like* to speak for everyone. But maybe some of us prefer to speak for themselves." Nick stood up, nodding at the tall bespectacled man who had just let himself into the room.

Willard Osgood.

105

The central monitoring station for Fenwicke Estates also serviced three other gated communities in and around Fenwick, including Safe Harbor, Whitewood Farms, and Catamount Acres. It was a low-slung windowless building located in an anonymous area of strip malls and fast-food restaurants. It could have been a warehouse. It was surrounded by chain-link fencing and was unmarked except for a street number. Audrey knew this was for security reasons. Out back were two hulking emergency diesel generators.

When in doubt, get a warrant. You couldn't count on people to be cooperative, even in an emergency, so she'd called in for a search warrant, had it faxed over to the central monitoring station, to the attention of the facility's general manager. Police headquarters had all that information on file.

The assistant operations manager, Bryan Mundy, was a man in a wheelchair who was as cooperative as could be, as it turned out. He was also extremely voluble, which was annoying, but she nodded and smiled pleasantly, silently urging him to hurry. She pretended to be interested, but not too interested.

As he led her through a maze of cubicles where women, mostly, sat in front of computers wearing headsets, he maneuvered his chair deftly and boasted about how they also monitored fire alarms for quite a few businesses and residences in the area. He talked about how they were connected via secure Internet protocol to the many cameras and guard booths they monitored. About how they did live remote viewing of all cameras via a Web browser. Rolling through another area where other people, mostly men, were watching video feed on computer monitors, he talked proudly, and in endless detail, about the digital watermark on the video files that provided authentication using something called an MD5 algorithm that ensured the image had not been altered.

Audrey didn't understand but stored away the fact that Bryan Mundy would be a good resource when the case went to trial.

He told her that he'd considered a job in law enforcement too, but preferred the pay of the private sector.

"Events up to thirty days ago are stored right here," he said as they entered another area, which was crowded with large racks of computer servers and storage media. "You're in luck. Anything older than that gets sent off to secure storage."

She gave him the date she was interested in viewing, and he hooked up the black disk-array box, inside of which were several hard drives containing digital video backups. He located for her the video file from between noon and 6 P.M. on the day that Nicholas Conover's family dog had been killed. She'd gotten the date and time from the uniform division. He showed her how to identify the files by camera number, but she told him she didn't know what camera it was she was looking for. Any camera located along Fenwicke Estates' perimeter fencing whose motion sensing might have been triggered during that time period.

Anyone, she thought, who had slipped into, or out of, Fenwicke Estates in the time surrounding the slaughter of Conover's dog.

"Lot of interest in this disk, huh?" Bryan Mundy said. "Log says that the security director of the Stratton Corporation came in here a while back and made some video caps off of it."

"Do you have a record of which video frames he copied?

Mundy shook his head and poked at his teeth absently with an orange wooden plaque stick. "He said he worked for Nicholas Conover, the CEO of Stratton. Wanted to know if we had any perimeter video near the Conover house, but no dice. Conover's house is apparently a good ways from the fence."

It didn't take her long to find a tall, gawky figure in a flapping coat, wearing heavy-framed glasses, approaching the fence, captured on camera 17.

"That's what he wanted too, the security director."

Yes. That's how he and Conover came to believe it was Stadler who had eviscerated the dog.

But she could see from the way Stadler was craning his neck and squinting, his body language, that he was following someone. He wasn't looking behind, not afraid that he might have been followed. He was definitely *following* someone.

She knew who he was following. Dr. Landis's speculations made a terrible and clear sense.

"Can this rewind slowly?" she asked.

"Doesn't really rewind per se," he said, smacking his lips around the plaque stick.

"How do I view earlier images, then?"

"Like this," he said, and he pointed and double-clicked the mouse. "Let's go back, I don't know, fifteen minutes and go from there."

"You know which cameras you want?"

"No, unfortunately. Any one of them for fifteen minutes before this guy appears."

He set it up for her and sat back as she moved through the images. His curiosity had gotten the better of his politeness; he sat there and watched as if he had nothing better to do.

Fortunately there weren't too many images to go through, since the recording was triggered by motion.

Seven minutes before Andrew Stadler had climbed the fence around Fenwicke Estates, scrambling like he was in hot pursuit, she found another figure. This one was smaller, wearing a leather jacket, moving nimbly and with great purpose.

Dr. Landis's words: *Stadler would go off his meds periodically. His wife was unable to stay married to the man, understandably, and she abandoned her child, then took her away from her father a few years later—a psychic wound from which the child might have recovered had she not had an inherited genetic predisposition.*

As the leather-jacketed figure approached the wrought-iron fence, it turned its face to the camera, almost as if posing. A smile.

The figure's face was now distinct.

Cassie Stadler.

Helen Stadler, Dr. Landis had corrected Audrey.

She changed her name to Cassie some time in adolescence. She thought it was a more interesting name. Maybe she liked the association with Cassandra, the Greek heroine endowed with the gift of prophecy whom no one heeded.

She had been the one who had repeatedly broken into Nicholas Conover's house to spray ominous and threatening graffiti. The timing now made it clear that Cassie had been the one who had killed the Conovers' dog.

Not her father, who had followed her to Conover's house, just as he'd probably followed her many times before.

Knowing that his daughter was disturbed.

Andrew Stadler knew Cassie was afflicted with this disorder, talked about it with Dr. Landis obsessively, blamed himself.

With unsteady hands she picked up her cell phone and called Dr. Landis. His answering machine came on. After the beep, she began speaking.

"Dr. Landis, it's Detective Rhimes, and it's urgent that I speak with you at once."

Dr. Landis picked up the phone.

"You told me Helen Stadler was obsessed with the notion of the family she never had," Audrey said without giving her name. "Families she could never be a part of, families that excluded her."

"Yes, yes," the psychiatrist cut in, "what of it?"

"Dr. Landis, you mentioned a family that lived across the street from the Stadlers where Cass—Helen used to play all the time when she was growing up. A little girl she considered her best friend—she used to spend all of her time over there until they became annoyed and asked her to leave?"

"Yes." Dr. Landis's voice was grave.

"Andrew Stadler was questioned years ago in connection with a tragic house fire across the street in which an entire family, the Stroups, died. He apparently did some repair work for them. Was this—?"

"Yes. Andrew said his daughter had his mechanical ability, and he'd taught her how to fix all sorts of things, and one night after they'd asked her to stop coming over she slipped into their house through the bulkhead doors, opened the gas line, and lit a match on her way out."

"Dear God. She was never charged."

"I was quite sure this was simply a fantasy of Andrew's, a manifestation of his paranoid fixation on his daughter. In any case, who would suspect a twelve-year-old girl? The authorities thought it was Andrew, but his alibi apparently held up under questioning. Something similar happened, you know, at Carnegie Mellon University during Helen's freshman year there. Andrew told me that his daughter belonged to a sorority, and she was quite obsessed with them as a surrogate family of sorts. Much later, he said, he heard about the terrible gas explosion in the sorority house in which eighteen women perished. This was the same night that Helen drove home from Pittsburgh, quite upset that one of her sorority sisters had said something to make her feel rejected."

"I—I have to go, Doctor," she said, ending the call.

Bryan Mundy had rolled up to her in his wheelchair and was signaling to her. "Talk about coincidences," he said. "We were talking about Conover's house, and what do you know? We just got an alert on that system, maybe ten, fifteen minutes ago."

"An alert?"

"No, not a burglar alarm or anything. Combustible gas detector. Probably a gas leak. But the homeowner said she's got it under control."

"She?"

"Mrs. Conover."

"There is no Mrs. Conover," Audrey said, heart knocking.

Mundy shrugged. "That's how she identified herself," he said, but Audrey was already running toward the door.

106

Todd immediately sprang to his feet, followed by Eilers and Finegold. Their faces were wreathed in anxious cordiality.

"Mind if I join you?" Osgood asked gruffly.

"Willard," Todd said, "I had no idea you were coming." He turned to Nick. "You see? The personal touch—some people never lose it."

Osgood ignored him as he took the empty seat at the head of the board table.

"There isn't going to be any sale," Nick said. "The sale is wrong for Stratton, and wrong for Fairfield. We too have looked at the numbers—and by 'we,' I mean Willard and I—and that's our considered assessment."

"May I speak?" Todd said.

"We're talking about an opportunity here," Scott said. "Not something that's going to knock twice."

"An opportunity?" Nick asked. "Or a danger?" He paused, and turned to Stephanie Alstrom. "Stephanie, a few words? I know I haven't given you enough time to prepare a PowerPoint presentation, but maybe you can do it the old-fashioned way."

Stephanie Alstrom started sorting through the stapled sheaths in her file, making three separate stacks next to her. "Here's the principal tort and criminal case law governing the salient issues, starting with federal statutes," she began in her most juiceless tone. "There's the Bribery of Foreign Officials Act of 1999, part No. 43, and the International Anti-Bribery and Fair Competition Act of 1998, and—oh heavens—the antifraud provisions of the securities laws, Section 10(b) of the Securities Exchange Act of 1934 and Rule 10b-5. And, though I haven't read through the case law properly yet, there's Section 13(b)(5) of the Exchange Act and Rule 13b2-1, to deal with." She was sounding increasingly flustered. "And, of course, Sections 13(a) and 13(b)(2)(A) of the Exchange Act, and Rules 12b-20 and 13a too. But also there's—"

"I think we get the picture," Nick said smoothly.

"Pretty much what Dino Panetta told me back in Boston," Osgood rumbled.

"That is ridiculous," Todd said. Blood was returning to his face. Too much blood. "These are completely unfounded allegations that I dispute—"

"Todd?" Osgood's craggy face formed a scowl. "It's one thing if *you* want to go fly-fishing with your private parts for bait, but you do *not* put the partnership at risk. Question I was asking myself last night was, Where did I go wrong? Then this morning, I had the answer. I didn't go wrong. You went wrong. You ignored company policy and made a huge bet on microchips, way more than you should have, and the entire firm almost went belly-up as a result. Then you figured you could save your ass, and ours, by doing a quick-and-dirty sale. A nice big pile of dough, and who cares how you got it. Well, not like this." He struck the table, stressing each word. "Not. Like. This." His eyes flashed behind his Coke-bottle glasses. "Because you've put Fairfield Equity Partners in a potentially ruinous legal situation. We could have brown-suited lawyers from the SEC camped out on Federal Street for the next five years, combing through our files with a jeweler's loupe. You wanted to land a big fish—and you didn't care if you rammed the boat through a goddamned barrier reef to do it."

"I think you're blowing this out of proportion," Todd said, wheedling. "Fairfield is in no danger."

"Damned right," Osgood replied. "Fairfield Equity Partners is completely in the clear."

"Good," Todd said uncertainly.

"That's right," Osgood said. "Because the partnership did the responsible thing. Demonstrated it wasn't party to the misdeeds. As soon as the errant be-

havior came to our attention, we severed our relations with the principals—
former principals, not to put too fine a point on it, and took all possible
measures to separate ourselves from the malefactors. Including the com-
mencement of legal action against Todd Erickson Muldaur. You violated the
gross misconduct clause of your agreement with the Partnership, which
means, as I'm sure you know, that your share reverts to the general equity
fund."

"You're joking," Todd said, blinking as if there was a bit of grit lodged behind one of his blue contact lenses. "I've got all my money invested in Fairfield. You can't just declare—"

"You signed the same agreement we all did. Now we're activating the
provision. Only way to show the feds we're serious. You can contest it—I'm
sure you will. But I think you'll find most high-powered lawyers are going to
want to see a hefty chunk of their fee up front. And we've already filed for a
separate tort claim against you and your coconspirator, Mr. McNally, for a
hundred and ten million dollars. We've requested that the judge place the
funds we're trying to recover in escrow, pending legal resolution, and we've
received indications that he intends to do so."

Scott's face looked like a plaster death mask. He tugged robotically at a
lock of hair at his temple. As Nick listened to Osgood, he found himself staring out the window at the charred buffalo grass. It no longer looked like a
lifeless black carpet anymore, he noticed. The new grass had begun to grow
back. Tiny green blades were now peeking through the black.

"That's insane!" Todd spoke with a squeaky groan, a crowbar pulling out
a long nail. "You can't do that. I will *not* be treated this way, Willard. I'm
owed some basic respect. I am a full-fledged partner at Fairfield, of eight
years standing. I'm not some . . . some goddamn *catfish* you can play catch-
and-release with."

Osgood turned to Nick. "He's got a point. You wouldn't want to mix
him up with a catfish. You see, one's a bottom-feeding, scum-sucking
scavenger . . ."

"And the other's a fish," Nick said. "Got it. And one more bit of business." He looked around the table. "Now that Stratton's future is secure, I'm
hereby submitting my resignation."

Osgood turned to face him, stunned. "*What?* Oh, Christ."

"I'm about to face a legal . . . situation . . . which I don't want to drag my company through."

The men and women around the boardroom table seemed as astonished as Osgood was. Stephanie Alstrom began shaking her head.

But Nick stood up and shook Osgood's hand firmly. "Stratton's been through enough. When we make the announcement, we'll just say that Mr. Conover resigned 'in order to spend more time with his family.'" He gave a little wink. "Which has the added virtue of being true. Now, if you'll excuse me."

He got up and strode confidently out of the room, and for the first time in a long while he felt a palpable sense of relief.

Marjorie was crying as she watched him gather up his framed family pictures. Her phone was ringing nonstop, but she was ignoring it.

"I don't understand," she said. "I think you owe me an explanation."

"You're right. I do." He reached down to the bottom drawer of his desk and pulled out the rubber-banded stack of Post-it notes in Laura's handwriting. "But first, could you find me a box?"

She turned and, as she passed her desk, she picked up the phone. A few seconds later, Marge looked around the partition, looking grim. "Nick, there's some kind of emergency at your house."

"Eddie's handling it."

"Well, the thing is—that was a woman named Cathy or Cassie, calling from your house. I didn't get the name—she was speaking fast, sounding panicked. She said you've got to get over there as fast as you can. I don't have a good feeling about this."

Nick dropped the picture frames onto his desk and broke into a run.

107

On his way to the parking lot he called home, let it ring.

No answer, which was strange. Cassie had just called from there—and what the hell was she doing there anyway? Plus, both kids should have gotten home from school by now to do their last-minute packing, both of them excited about the trip. Even, in his grudging way, Lucas, or so Nick thought.

But the phone rang and rang and the voice mail kept coming on.

Okay, so Lucas often didn't answer the home phone, let the voice mail get it, but Julia always answered. She loved the phone. And Cassie—she'd just called. Weird.

No answer.

Lucas's cell? He didn't remember the number, too many numbers in his head and this one he didn't call all that often. He hit the green call button on his phone, which pulled up the last ten or whatever calls he'd dialed.

There it was, LUCAS CELL. Had Marjorie programmed that in? Probably. He hit SEND as he ran through the parking lot, a couple of employees waving hello but he didn't have time for niceties.

Come on, damn it, answer the fucking phone. Told you if you don't answer the cell, I take it away, that's the deal.

A couple of rings and then his son's recorded voice, adolescent-buzzy in timbre, curt and full of attitude in just a few words.

Hey, it's Luke, what up? Leave a message.

A beep, then a female voice: *Please leave your message after the tone. Press One to send a numeric page—*

Nick ended the call, heart drumming and not from the run. He fumbled for the Suburban's key-fob thing, pressed it to unlock just as he reached the car door.

Roaring out of the parking lot, he tried Eddie's cell.

No answer.

"She's not here," Bugbee said. The cellular signal began to fade . . . "Patrol units, but no Cassie Stadler at her house."

"She's at Conover's," Audrey said. "Gas leak."

"Huh?"

"I'm heading over there now. You too. Right away. Notify the fire department."

"You know she's there?"

"She answered the phone when the alarm monitoring service called. Get over there, Roy. Right now."

"Why?" Bugbee said.

"Just do it. And bring backup." She ended the call so he didn't have a chance to argue.

Gas leak. The Stroups, her neighbors when she was twelve.

She lit a match on the way out.

Her sorority house at Carnegie Mellon when she was a freshman.

Eighteen young women perished.

The families she desperately wanted to be part of. Who all rejected her.

Then Audrey called Nicholas Conover's office at the Stratton Corporation, but she was told he wasn't there.

Tell him it's urgent, she said. It's a matter of safety. His house.

The secretary's voice lost its hard edge. "He's on his way over there, officer."

The alarm company?

Nick didn't even remember the name.

A gas leak? He tried to imagine what that was all about—something goes wrong in the house, the kids smell gas, maybe they're smart about it and get the hell out of the house, that's why the house phone line went unanswered—but what about Lucas's cell?

Say he left it inside in the rush to get out. Sure, that was all.

But Eddie?

Guy lived with a cell phone planted to his ear. Why the hell would he not answer either?

Twelve minutes he could be at the gates of Fenwicke Estates. Assuming he caught the lights right. He gunned it, then slowed just a bit, keeping it no more then ten miles an hour over the speed limit. An overzealous cop could pull him over, slow things way down even if Nick told him it was an emergency. Ask for my license and registration, maybe decide to take his fucking time about it once he caught the name.

He drove the whole way in a mental tunnel of concentration, barely aware of the traffic around him, thinking only of getting to the house. Kept hitting REDIAL for Eddie's cell, but no answer.

A moment of relief as he pulled up to the gatehouse. No emergency vehicles here, no fire trucks or whatever, probably no big deal.

A gas leak is not the same thing as a fire, of course.

Could the kids and Eddie and Cassie all have been overcome by gas fumes, maybe that's why they couldn't answer? He had no idea if natural gas did that.

"Hi, Mr. Conover," said Jorge, behind the bulletproof glass in the booth.

"Emergency, Jorge," Nick called out.

"Your security director, Mr. Rinaldi, he came through here already."

"How long ago?"

"Let me check the log—"

"Forget it. Open the gate, Jorge."

"It's opening, Mr. Conover."

And so it was, glacially slow. Inching open.

"Can you speed it up?" Nick said.

Jorge smiled apologetically, shrugged. "You know this gate, I'm sorry. Also your friend came by."

"My friend?"

"Miss Stadler? She came by too. Hour ago, I think."

Did the kids call Cassie to come over? he wondered. Why didn't they call me? They know how to reach me. More comfortable calling Cassie, that it?

"Goddammit," Nick shouted in frustration. "Speed this fucking thing up."

"I can't do that, Mr. Conover, I'm sorry."

Nick floored it, the Suburban lurching forward, hitting the solid iron bars of the gate, a crunch of metal that he knew wasn't the gate. Even the goddamned Suburban is a fucking tin can, crumples like a wad of aluminum foil. Front-end work. Fuck it.

It didn't budge the gate, which continued its stately pace, oblivious, arrogant, taking its goddamned fucking time.

Jorge's eyes widened. Finally the gate was open just enough, Nick calculated, to get through. He gunned it again, the squeal of metal against metal as the car scraped against the gate but got through, just barely.

SPEED LIMIT 20, the sign said.

Fuck it.

No fire trucks on the street or along the driveway. No police cars either.

Maybe this was nothing. He was overreacting, no emergency at all, no gas leak at all, a false alarm.

No. A false alarm, there would have been an answer, one of the calls he'd made.

Gas leak for real. Eddie came by, got the kids out of there and Cassie too, saved them all, thank God for that traitorous bastard, a bastard but *my* bastard, maybe turned out to be a real friend after all, maybe I owe him an apology.

Eddie's GTO in the driveway, parked behind the van. Cassie's red VW convertible too. It didn't compute. Cassie came over, Eddie too, both of their cars here, the van here too. That meant no one drove the kids away, thus the kids are still here and Eddie and Cassie too, so what the hell, then?

He raced up the stone path to the house, noticed all the windows were closed, the house sealed tight as if they were already out of there, on vacation, and as he approached the front door he smelled rotten eggs.

The gas smell.

It was for real. It was strong too, if he could smell it out here. Very strong. That odorant they add to natural gas so you know if there's a leak.

Front door was locked, which was a little strange if everyone had just run out of there, but he didn't linger on that, totally single-minded. He grabbed his key ring, got the door open.

Dark in here.

He yelled out, "Hello? Anyone here?"

No answer.

The rotten-egg smell was overpowering. More like skunk, maybe. A wall of odor, sharp as a knife, nauseating.

"Hello?"

Faint noises now. Thumping? From upstairs? He couldn't tell, the house was so solid. He entered the kitchen, but no one there either.

Distant bumping sounds, but then footsteps nearby, and Cassie appeared, walking slowly, looking worn out, a wreck.

"Cass," he said. "Thank God you're here. Where are the kids?"

She kept approaching, one hand behind her back, slowly, almost hesitant. Her eyes sleepy, not looking at him, her stare distant.

"Cass?"

"Yeah," she said at last. "Thank God I'm here." Flat, almost affectless.

He heard a high-pitched mechanical beeping coming from somewhere. What the hell was that?

"Where is everyone?"

"They're safe," she said, but something in her tone seemed off, as if she wasn't sure.

"Where's Eddie?"

A beat. "He's . . . safe too." She drew out the words.

He stepped toward her to give her a hug, but she stepped backward, shook her head.

"No," she said.

"Cassie?"

He felt the twang of fear even before his brain could make sense of it.

"You've got to get out of here. We've got to open some windows, call the fire department. Jesus, this is incredibly dangerous, this stuff is unbelievably combustible. Where are Luke and Julia?"

The high beeping was getting faster, higher in pitch, and Nick realized the source was a device on the kitchen counter he'd seen before, a small yellow box with flexible metal tubing coming out of it. What was it, and what was it doing there?

"I'm glad you came home, Nick." Her eyes were smudged, looking like black holes. They darted from side to side. "I knew you would, though. Daddy protects his family. You're a good daddy. Not like my daddy. He never protected me."

"Cassie," he said, "what *is* it? You look so frightened."

She nodded. "I'm terrified."

He felt his skin go cold and goosefleshy. He saw it in her eyes, that same absent look he'd seen before, as if she'd gone somewhere else where no one could reach her. "Cassie," he said in a gentle and firm tone, hollow inside, "where are my children?"

"I'm terrified of *me*, Nick. And you should be too."

With her left hand she reached into the pocket of her denim shirt and pulled out an object that he recognized as Lucas's Zippo lighter. The lighter decorated with a skull crawling with spiders and surrounded by spider webs, a real stoner lighter. She flipped the top off, one-handed, and her thumb touched the flint wheel.

"No!" Nick shouted. "What are you doing, are you *crazy*?"

"Come on, Nick, you *know* I am. Can't you read the writing on the wall?" She began singing softly, "Oh, I ran to the rock to hide my face, the rock cried out 'No hiding place.'"

"Where *are* they, Cassie?"

The electronic beeping, rising all the while in pitch, had now become a steady high squeal, almost ear-piercing. He realized where he'd seen that yellow box before: in the basement, placed there by the gas company serviceman. A combustible gas detector. Supposed to warn you about gas leaks. Beeping got higher and faster as the concentration of gas in the air increased. A steady squeal meant dangerous amounts of gas. Combustible levels. Someone had taken the device upstairs from the basement, and he now knew who.

"I told you, they're safe," she said in a flat voice, and her other hand, the one she'd been keeping behind her back, came around to the front now, gripping the huge carbon-steel Henckels carving knife from the kitchen knife rack.

Heart thumping a million miles a minute now. Oh sweet Jesus, she's out of her mind. Dear God, help me.

"Cassie," he said, moving closer, his arms outspread to give her a hug, but she raised the knife and pointed it at him, and with her left hand she held up the lighter, thumb on the wheel, and said, "Not another step, Nick."

The guard's face appeared behind the tempered glass of the security booth at the entrance to the Fenwicke Estates.

His voice squawked through the intercom. "Yes?"

She flashed her police badge. "Police emergency," she said.

The guard looked at it through the glass and immediately activated the security gate.

"Jesus, Cassie, please *don't*—"

"Oh, I really don't like this part," she said, and at that instant he noticed the red slick on the knife blade, still wet.

108

The high wrought-iron gate began to open, but so slowly, so agonizingly slowly. She drummed her fingers on the steering wheel and finally she said, "Please, speed this up. There's no time to waste."

"Sorry, I can't make it go any faster," the guard said. "That's as fast as it goes. I'm sorry."

"Put the knife down, Cassie," Nick said, all forced calm, voice soft and wheedling.

"When I'm done with my work, Nick. I'm very tired. I just want to finish. It has to end."

"Your work," Nick said numbly. "Please, Cassie. What have you done with them?" Fear rose in him like a flood tide.

Please God no not the kids no oh Jesus Christ no.

"Who?" she said.

No please not that dear God not the kids.

"My . . . family."

"Oh, they're safe, Nick. Like a family should be. Safe. Protected."

"Please, Cassie," he whispered, a catch in his throat, hot tears in his eyes. "Where are my kids?"

"Safe, Nick."

"Cassie, please tell me they're . . ." He stopped, couldn't say *alive*, couldn't allow himself to think the word, even, because its opposite was unendurable.

She cocked her head. "You can't hear them? Banging away? They're locked up nice and safe in the basement. You can hear it, I know you can."

And he could, now that she pointed it out, hear a distant thumping. The basement door? He almost gasped in relief, his knees buckling. She'd locked them in the basement. They were alive down there.

Where the gas was coming from.

"Where's Eddie?" he managed to say.

Oh God please if Eddie's down there he'll get them out, he'll figure out a way, he can bust through a locked door, pick it. Fucking windowless basement. Vent grates are too small to climb out of. But he'll figure it out.

She shook her head. "He's not down there. I never trusted him either." She waggled the lighter, the skull leering at him.

"Don't do it, Cassie. You'll kill us all. Please don't do it, Cassie."

She kept waggling the lighter back and forth, back and forth, her thumb at the flint wheel. "I didn't ask him to come. I told *you* to come. Eddie's not family."

His eyes frantically scanned the kitchen, then stopped when he saw a shape on the lawn outside the kitchen doors. Through the glass of the French doors he recognized Eddie's body.

He saw the blood-darkened front of Eddie's pale shirt.

The contorted position. The unnatural splay of the limbs.

He knew, and it was all he could do to keep from screaming.

Audrey couldn't stand how slowly the gate was opening, almost deliberately so, as if the residents of the Fenwicke Estates were never in a hurry, because haste was unseemly.

Move it! she screamed in her mind.

She gripped the steering wheel, tapping at the gas pedal.

Faster!

She knew what was going to happen, what the poor demented soul was doing, as she'd done before. Somehow Cassie Stadler had gotten into the

Conover house—well, that couldn't have been too hard, right? She and Conover had become intimate; maybe she had a key—and something had happened to set her off, make her feel rejected. Cassie Stadler was a borderline personality, Dr. Landis had said, with a dangerous psychotic component. An obsession with family, with inclusion, and rejection always propelled her into a towering irrational rage.

Cassie Stadler was going to incinerate the Conover home.

Audrey prayed that the children weren't home. It was early in the afternoon—maybe they were still in school. Maybe the house was empty. The worst that could happen, then, was that the house would be destroyed.

Maybe no one was home. She prayed that was so.

"Put down the lighter, baby," Nick said, voice silky, all the fake affection he could summon. "Is this about Maui? Because I didn't invite you?"

Fuck the knife. He'd lunge at her, grab it.

The lighter? All that took was a flick of her Bic. Could happen by accident. That he'd have to be careful of.

"Why should you invite me on a family trip, Nick? I mean, it's just for family, right? I'm not family."

He understood. He realized that he didn't know her, had never known her, that he'd seen in her only what he wanted to see.

She'd said as much, hadn't she? "We don't see things as they are," she'd said once, quoting someone. "We see things as *we* are."

But he knew enough about her to understand what she was saying now.

Audrey could smell the natural gas as soon as she got out of the car.

She saw all the other vehicles in the driveway, two of them belonging to Nicholas Conover, the other she didn't recognize. Not Bugbee's. He was all the way across town. It would take him a while. She hoped he knew to get here fast, sirens and lights on.

Her instinct told her not to go in the front door. She had to obey her instinct, times like this.

She took out the pistol from her shoulder holster under her jacket and began walking across the wide expanse of lawn, so very green, heading toward the back of the house where she could enter unnoticed.

She chose the right side of the house, where she remembered the kitchen was. As she rounded the house she noticed a figure standing in the kitchen, a small slender figure, and she knew it was Cassie Stadler.

And then she saw the body sprawled on the lawn.

Running now, low to the ground, she approached the body.

A terrible bloody mess. Sweet Jesus. It was Edward Rinaldi, and it looked as if he'd been disemboweled.

His eyes open, staring, one hand curled by his abdomen, the other outstretched toward the kitchen. Blood-soaked beige knit shirt crisscrossed with slashes as if from a knife.

Most of his shirt front dark with blood, which pooled on the green lawn.

She dropped to her knees to feel for a pulse.

She wasn't sure.

If there was a pulse, it was so slow she couldn't detect it. Maybe there was a pulse. Maybe not.

She touched his jugular vein and felt nothing, and she knew for certain the man was dead.

Nothing she could do for him. She set down her pistol, took out her cell phone, got Bugbee on the first ring.

"Alert the ME," she said. "And body conveyance."

She was frightened as she'd never been frightened before, and she'd been through some horrific crime scenes. She got up and ran around to the back of the house.

"God, I wasn't even thinking," Nick said, shaking his head. "I was in such a rush to just get the kids out of town, get us on a vacation, I really fucked that up. I mean, I really blew it."

"Don't, Nick," she said, but he saw something flicker in her eyes, as if maybe she wanted to believe.

"No, seriously, I mean, how could it be a true family vacation without you? You've become such an important part of the family, babe, you know that? If I hadn't been so distracted with everything that's been going on at work, I—"

"*Don't*, Nick," she said a little louder, her voice still petulant. "Please."

"We can still be a family, Cass. I'd like that. Wouldn't you like that?"

Her eyes glistened with tears. "Oh, Nick, I've been through this before, you know. I recognize the pattern."

"The pattern?" Heart thwacking, because he saw that faint glint of hopefulness in her eyes go dark like the last winking of a dying fire.

"The first signs. It's always the same. They take you in and make you feel like a part of everything and then something always happens. There's like a line you can never cross. A brick wall. It's like the Stroups."

"The Stroups?"

"One day, no reason, they say I can't keep coming over, I'm spending too much time over there. Lines are drawn. They're family, you're not. Maybe that's the way it has to be. But I know I can't go through it again. It's too much."

"That's where you're wrong, baby," Nick said. "It's not too late. We can still be a family."

"Sometimes a world has to come to an end. So new ones can come into being."

The electronic squeal, steady, earsplitting.

Audrey considered, then rejected, entering through the French doors that led into the kitchen. No. She'd have to approach with some stealth. She raced to the next set of French doors, but they were locked too. Was there no basement entrance, bulkhead doors or whatever?

There didn't seem to be.

A hissing sound drew her to the far side of the house near the pool fence. She saw pipes—gas pipes, she realized. Some kind of metal objects were lying on the ground next to the pipe stand, and a crescent wrench. Valves or something. They'd been removed, and maybe that was why the hissing was so loud, like the flow had been turned up full, maybe.

The gas pipes had to lead into the basement, she knew, because that was always where they went.

Over the hissing she could hear a shout. It was coming from a grate about twenty feet away.

She ran to the grate, put her face against it, the skunky, metallic smell of gas nauseating her. "Hello?" she called out.

"Down here! We're down here!" An adolescent male voice. Conover's son?

"Who is it?" Audrey said.

"Lucas. And my sister. She's got us locked in here."

"Who does?"

"That crazy bitch. Cassie."

"Where's your dad?"

"I don't know—just, shit, will you *help* us? We're going to fucking *die* down here!"

"Stay calm," Audrey said, though calm was the one thing she didn't feel. "Listen, Lucas. Help me out. You can help me, okay?"

"Who're *you*?"

"I'm Detective Rhimes. Listen to me. How's your sister doing?"

"She's—she's scared, what the fuck do you think?"

"Julia, right? Julia, can you hear me?"

A small, frightened voice. "Yes."

"Are you getting enough oxygen?"

"What?"

"Stand over here by this grate, sweetheart. Make sure you get enough air from the outside. You'll be okay."

"Okay," the girl said.

"Now, Lucas, is there a pilot light down there?"

"A pilot light?"

"Are you near the water heater? There's usually a pilot light going on the water heater, and if that ignites the cloud of gas, the whole house is going to blow. You've got to turn it off."

"There's no pilot light." His voice was faint, distant, as if he'd gone to check. "No pilot light. She must have put it out so the gas wouldn't ignite too early."

Smart kid, she thought. "All right. Is there a shutoff for the gas line? It would be on the wall where the gas pipes enter."

"I see it."

"You see the shutoff?"

Footsteps. "No. I don't see a shutoff."

She sighed, tried to think. "Are any of the doors to the house open?"

"I—I don't know, how would I know?" the boy replied.

"I think they're all locked. Is there a key hidden somewhere outside, like under a rock or something?"

She heard a jingling, and a small steel key ring poked up through the slats in the grate. "Use mine," the boy said.

Thumping from the basement, frantic, the noises reassuring because they were alive. Now in the few seconds of stillness Nick could faintly hear Lucas's voice yelling. They were alive. And desperate to get out of there.

"I'm going to call United right now," Nick said. "I'll get you on our flight no matter what it costs. First class if you want it, but you probably want to sit with us in business class." He thought, *Don't pick up the phone, even as a pretense. The phone could ignite the gas.* He remembered reading somewhere about a woman who had a gas leak and she picked up the phone and called 911, and an electric arc from the phone circuit sparked and the house exploded. "The kids would love that. You know they would, baby."

"Please, Nick." She toyed with the lighter, and in her other hand the knife dangled at her side.

He could leap at her, hurl her to the ground, if he did it carefully, chose the right moment.

"I know you now," she said in a monotone. "I can see right through you."

Quietly, quietly, Audrey turned the key in the back-door lock, and then pushed the door open.

A tone sounded. The alarm system's entry alert.

It had just announced her arrival.

The skunk stench was overpowering in here.

She walked slowly, orienting herself. She didn't remember the layout of the house well, but then she could hear voices, female and male, and she knew which way to go.

Was the unhinged woman holding Conover hostage? If she was, then the sound of Audrey entering might attract her attention, unnerve her, maybe make her do something rash. The wrench, the gas pipes—it told Audrey that Cassie Stadler, it had to be her, had opened the pipes in order to fill the house with gas just as she'd done in other houses before.

All she'd have to do would be to strike a match and the house would explode, killing herself and the children in the basement and Audrey too. But why hadn't she done it yet?

Audrey had an idea now.

Cassie Stadler was filling the house with gas, had been for a while. Maybe she was just waiting for the entire house to fill up. So she could get the biggest bang possible.

Yes. That's what she was waiting for.

The children. That was the first thing. She had to free them.

A pounding on a door somewhere nearby told her where to go. A door in the hall. She heard the kids, or maybe it was just Lucas, pounding and pounding.

Swiftly she turned the dead bolt with a loud, satisfying click, and she pulled the door open. The boy tumbled out, sprawled to the floor.

"Hush," Audrey whispered. "Where's your sister?"

"Right here," said Lucas, and the girl came streaking out, weeping, her face red.

"Go!" Audrey whispered. "Both of you." She pointed to the open door. "Run!"

"Where's Dad?" Julia cried. "Where is he?"

"He's all right," Audrey said, not knowing what else to say. She had to get them out of here. "Go!"

Julia took right off, pushed open the screen door and began running across the lawn, but Lucas didn't move. He looked at her.

"Don't fire that gun," he said. "That'll set it off."

"I know," she said.

———

"What was that?" said Cassie.

"What?"

"That sound. The alarm. Someone just came in the house."

"I didn't hear it."

Cassie turned slowly, looked from one entrance to the other, all the while flicking her eyes back to Nick, making sure he didn't advance toward her.

"You know," she said, her eyes trained on him, "it's funny, the way I went through stages of thinking about you. First I saw you as the destroyer of families. You sure destroyed my dad's life when you fired him, so I had to let you know you weren't any safer than anyone else."

"The graffiti," Nick said, realizing. " 'No hiding place.' "

"But then I got to know you a little better, and I thought I'd been wrong, I decided you were a good man. But I know better now. Sometimes you gotta trust your first impressions."

"Put the lighter down, Cassie. You don't want to do this. Let's talk, let's figure things out."

"You know what fooled me? When I saw what a good daddy you were."

"Please, Cassie."

Behind her was the entrance that led to the back hallway. He became aware of a slight change in the light, a shadow. A movement.

A figure slowly approaching.

Nick knew enough not to break eye contact with Cassie. He looked into her red-rimmed eyes, while in his peripheral vision he could make out a woman moving stealthily along the wall, advancing toward the kitchen.

It was the police detective, Audrey Rhimes.

Don't break eye contact. He forced himself to look into Cassie's desperate heavy-lidded eyes, bottomless pools of anguish and madness.

"Not like my daddy. He was scared of me, he followed me everywhere, wouldn't leave me alone, but he'd never do for me what you did for your kids."

"He loved you, Cass, you know that." His voice was shaking a little.

Keep your eyes on Cassie.

Detective Rhimes was advancing ever so slowly.

"You were so scared that night. I could see it from where I was standing, in the woods. I could hear it. The way you told him, 'Freeze,' and, 'One more step, and I shoot!'" She shook her head. "I don't know what they told you about him, but I can just imagine. Schizophrenic, right? You thought *he* was the one who killed your dog. You didn't know he was just trying to hand you a note saying he was innocent, right? You thought he was pulling out a gun. So you did the right thing, the brave thing. You protected your family. You protected your kids. You squeezed the trigger and you shot him down, and you did what a dad should do. You protected your family."

Oh, Christ. I took her father away from her and she knew it all along. Before we met she knew it.

I took her family, and now she's going to take mine.

A terrible chill ran through his body.

She nodded, raised her left hand, the lighter hand, and Nick flinched, but she only rubbed her left forearm against her nose, sniffling. "Yeah, I was there that night, Nick. I was there first. He was following me, always following me. He knew I was paying another visit to your house. I *saw* you, Nick."

Out of the corner of his eye he saw Detective Rhimes inch ahead, closer, closer, but he didn't dare shift his eyes even a millimeter.

"He just kept coming at you and coming at you, didn't he? And no matter how much you told him to stop he kept coming because he really didn't understand." Her voice deepened, in an eerie imitation of her father's voice: "Never—safe! Never—safe!" She shook her head. "I'll never forget the look on your face afterward. I've never seen a man look so frightened. And so sad."

"Cassie, I—God, I'm so, *so* sorry, I don't know what else to say. I'm going to face up to what I've done. I'm going to answer for it."

"Sorry? Oh, don't get me wrong, I'm not *mad*. Don't apologize. It was beautiful, what you did. You were protecting your family."

"Cassie, please . . ."

"Of course you had to do it. Oh, don't I know it. Don't get me wrong, I'm grateful. It was a liberation, you know. It freed me. My daddy was in a prison of his own mind, but I was a prisoner, too, until you freed me. And then I met you and I saw what a strong man you were. A good man, I thought. You needed a wife, and your kids needed a mommy, and we could all be a family."

"We can still be a family."

She shook her head, knife dangling at one side, toying with the lighter in the other. A rueful smile. "No, Nick. I know how these things work. I've been through it time and time again, and I just"—her voice cracked, her face got small and wrinkled, and she began to really cry now—"I just can't go through it again. I'm tired. I can't do it again. Once the door slams shut you can't open it again. It's never the same. Do you understand?"

"I understand," Nick said, moving closer, wearing an expression of gentle empathy.

"Stop, Nick," she said, holding up the lighter warningly as she stepped back. "No closer."

"Things can change, Cassie. In a good way."

Tears were streaming down her face now from her smudged eyes. "No," she said. "It's time," and Nick could hear the rasp of her thumb on the flint wheel.

109

Audrey listened closely as she advanced toward the kitchen. She could hear everything the two said, and it was strange how insignificant, all of a sudden, it was to have Nicholas Conover's guilt confirmed from his own mouth.

She thought of that passage from Matthew, the parable of the unmerciful servant. She thought of the sign taped to her computer monitor that said, "Remember: We work for God."

She understood what she had to do about Nicholas Conover. The weapon that had killed Andrew Stadler had been stolen years earlier by Eddie Rinaldi, who now lay dead on the lawn.

You can't convict a dead man.

Things would be sorted out later.

But for now she had to stop Cassie Stadler.

The problem was that this situation fit no pattern she had ever trained for. She slid along the wall, felt it cold against her cheek. Gripped the smooth paint of the doorframe molding.

Did Conover know she was there?

She thought he did.

She could hear the steady high-pitched tone, and she saw where it was coming from. It was a combustible gas detector, which measured the concentration of gas in the air. The steady tone meant that the gas in the air had reached optimal combustibility—she forgot the exact percentages, but she knew it was a range on either side of ten percent. Cassie Stadler was waiting until the air up here had reached the most dangerous concentration of propane gas, no less and no more.

You must always think several steps ahead, she told herself. What if, as she stole up on Cassie, relying on the element of surprise to take her down barehanded, she startled the woman, causing her to strike the lighter?

That had to be avoided at all costs.

She slid past the hall table, careful not to jar it and thus knock the alabaster lamp to the floor. Finally, she entered the room, and she didn't know what she was going to do next.

She listened hard, and she thought.

The flint didn't spark on her first try. Cassie frowned, tears coursing down her cheeks.

The gas detector shrilled, and meanwhile she sang softly in her lovely, lilting voice: "Oh, the rock cried out, I'm burning too—I want to go to Heaven the same as you."

"Cassie, don't do it."

"This was your decision. You made this happen."

"I made a mistake."

She looked above Nick's shoulder, saw something. "Luke?" she said.

"Cassie," Lucas said, walking across the kitchen straight toward her.

"Luke," Nick said. "Get out of here."

"What are you doing here, Luke?" Cassie said. "I told you and Julia to stay in the basement."

Audrey Rhimes had somehow gotten into the house through the back door; that was the alert tone sounding, she knew to unlock the basement, let the kids out. But where was Julia?

Lucas must have taken the back corridor around, through the family room to the kitchen's other entrance.

"You locked us in," Lucas said, coming right up to her, standing to one side of her. "I know you didn't mean to. But I found the spare key."

What the hell was he doing? "Luke, please," Nick said.

But Lucas was ignoring his father. "Cassie," he said, touching her shoulder, "remember that poem you helped me with—that guy Robert Frost?" He smiled, warm and winning and appealing. "'Hired Hand' or 'Hired Man' or whatever it was called."

Cassie didn't move Lucas's hand off her shoulder, Nick noticed. She turned to look at him, her expression seeming to soften just a bit, he thought.

"Home is the place where, when you have to go there, they have to take you in," Cassie said, her voice hollow.

Lucas nodded.

His eyes slid toward Nick's for just a fraction of a second.

Nick saw it.

Lucas wasn't ignoring him at all. He was *signaling* to his father.

"Remember what you told me?" Lucas said. His luminous blue eyes held hers. "There's nothing more important than family. You said that's what it's all about, finally, in the end. That's what makes us human."

"Lucas," Cassie said, and there was a slight shift in her tone, and at that instant Nick dove at her to knock her to the ground—

—but Cassie spun, snakelike, off to one side, the speed of a jungle animal, all lithe arms and legs. He slammed against her, knocking the knife out of her hand, but she managed to sidestep him. The knife went clattering across the tile.

She sprang to her feet and held the lighter aloft, displaying it for both men to admire, and she said, "You Conover men. What am I going to do with you?" She made a strange grimace. "I think it's time. We have to go now. A world must come to an end."

A sudden movement from behind Cassie.

Must hold her attention.

"Cassie," Nick said. "Look at me."

Her opaque eyes locked with his.

"I'm not hiding anymore, Cass. Look in my eyes and you can see it. I'm not hiding."

Her face was radiant, flushed and gleaming, more beautiful at that moment than Nick had ever seen her before. She was transfigured. A remarkable serenity had settled over her features as she thumbed the flint wheel.

And something flew out of the background and smashed down upon her head, the white alabaster lamp, and as the stone cracked into her skull,

Cassie crumpled to the floor with an *Unnnnh* sound as the lighter skittered under the refrigerator.

An eerie burbling sound escaped her lips.

Audrey Rhimes's face was streaked with sweat. She looked down at the lamp still in her hand, apparently stunned by what she'd just done.

Nick stared in shock. Mixed with the powerful gas smell he could detect the faint scent of Cassie's patchouli perfume.

"*Run!*" she shouted. "Get out of here *now!*"

"Where's Julia?" Nick said as he started toward the exit.

"She's outside somewhere," Lucas said.

"*Go!*" Audrey screamed. "Anything—the slightest spark—can set this gas off. We've all got to get out of here immediately and let the fire department clear the house. *Now!*"

Lucas vaulted ahead of Nick, crashing against the front screen door before he managed to get it open, then held it open for Audrey and his father.

Julia was standing on the front lawn alongside the driveway, a good distance away.

Nick raced to her, grabbed her and hoisted her up to his shoulder, and kept on running, Lucas and Audrey close behind. They all stopped at the edge of the property just as Nick heard the loud wail of sirens.

"Look!" said Lucas, pointing back toward the house, and Nick immediately saw what he was indicating. It was Cassie, standing unsteadily at the window, watching them, a cigarette dangling out of her mouth.

"No!" Nick shouted, but he knew she couldn't hear him and wasn't listening anyway.

There was a blinding flash, and in the next instant, the house erupted in a massive brilliant fireball.

The ground shook, and fire engulfed the house almost instantly, entirely, throwing up a great column of sparks and billowing gray smoke, and seconds later the windows popped and the glass in the French doors shattered as the door frames and the window frames flew into the air, and then the flames began to plume out of every orifice, blackening the stone walls and chimneys, lighting up the clouded sky a terrible orange, and waves of heat came after them, searing their faces as they ran. Julia shrieked, and Nick held her tight, as they all ran down the long driveway.

Nick didn't stop until they had reached the road, when, winded by carrying his daughter, he had to stop. He turned back to look at the house, but all he could see now were the plumes of fire and smoke. The sirens of the fire trucks had gotten no louder, no closer. Nick knew they'd been halted at the security gate.

There would be very little left for the fire department to salvage.

He squeezed Julia harder as he said to Audrey Rhimes, "Before I come in to . . . face charges . . . I'd like to take a little vacation with my kids. Just a few days together. Is that possible, you think?"

Detective Rhimes stared at him. Their eyes locked. Her face was impassive, unreadable.

After what seemed an endless pause, she nodded. "That should be okay."

Nick looked at the blaze for a moment, and then turned to thank her, but she had already started walking down the driveway toward the police car that was just pulling in ahead of a convoy of fire trucks. The blond detective was behind the wheel.

He felt something clutch his elbow, a trembling needy grip, and he saw it was Lucas. Together, dazed and speechless, they watched the inferno for another few minutes. Though the afternoon was overcast and gray, the fire blazed so brightly that it illuminated the sky a dusky orange, the color of sunrise.

EPILOGUE

The first couple of days, Nick did little besides sleep. He went to bed early, got up late, took naps on the beach.

Their "villa," as the resort called it, was right on Ka'anapali Beach. You stepped out the door and onto the sand. At night you could hear the lulling sound of the waves lapping against the shore. Lucas, normally the late sleeper, got up early with Julia to swim or snorkel. He even taught her to surf. By the time the kids returned to the bungalow in the late morning, Nick would just be getting up, drinking his coffee on the lanai. They'd all share a meal, a late breakfast or early lunch, and then the kids would go snorkeling at Pu'u Keka'a, a volcanic reef that the ancient Hawaiians revered as a sacred place where the spirits of the dead leaped from this world to the next.

He and the kids talked some, but rarely about anything serious. They'd lost just about all of their earthly possessions, which seemed not to have sunk in yet. It was funny how they never mentioned it.

Several times he tried to bring himself to talk with them about the legal nightmare he'd face when he got home: the likelihood of a trial and the near-certainty of his going to prison. But he couldn't do it, maybe for the same reason nobody wanted to talk about the day the house burned down. He didn't want to spoil what was sure to be their last vacation together for many years.

It was as if they were all surfing, riding the perfect wave, and for the moment it didn't matter that deep in the water beneath them were big, scary creatures with big, sharp teeth. Because the Conovers were up here, in the

sun, and they all seemed to know without articulating it that the key to staying afloat was not thinking about what might lurk down below.

So they swam and snorkeled, surfed and ate. Nick fell asleep on the
beach too long on the second day and got a painful sunburn on his ears and
forehead.

Nick brought no work—he had no work—and he left his cell phone on
his bedside table, switched off. He lay on the beach reading and thinking and
dozing, wriggling his toes in the powdery gray sand and watching the sun
shimmer over the water.

On the third day, he finally turned his cell phone back on, only to find
dozens of messages from friends and Stratton colleagues who'd heard or read
about what had happened to their house and wanted to make sure Nick and
the kids were okay. Nick listened but answered none of them.

One was from his former assistant, Marge Dykstra, who reported that the
Fenwick newspaper had run several front-page stories about how Fairfield
Equity Partners had been on the verge of selling the Stratton Corporation
to China, shutting down all U.S. operations, and laying off all employees—
until the deal had been blocked by "ex-CEO Nicholas Conover," who'd just
announced his resignation "in order to spend more time with his family."

It was the first good press he, and Stratton, had gotten in a long time.
Marge pointed out that it was the first time in almost three years that his
name had appeared in a headline without the word "slash" next to it.

On the fourth day, Nick was lying on a lounge chair on the lanai, reading a book about D-day that he'd been trying to read for months and was determined to finish now, when he heard the distant ring tone of his cell
phone. He didn't get up.

A minute later, Lucas came out from the bungalow holding the phone
and brought it over to him. "It's for you, Dad."

Nick looked up, marked a place in his book with his forefinger, reluctantly took the phone.

"Mr. Conover?"

He recognized the voice immediately, and he felt the old tension clutch
his abdomen again. "Detective Rhimes," he said.

"I'm sorry to interrupt your family vacation."

"That's quite all right."

"Mr. Conover, this call is completely off the record, okay?"

"Okay."

"I think you should have your attorney contact the district attorney's office and arrange a plea bargain."

"Excuse me?"

"If you're willing to plead guilty to criminally negligent homicide—or maybe even just attempted tampering with evidence—the DA's willing to recommend probation with no time served."

"*What?* I don't get it."

"I don't imagine you've been reading the *Fenwick Free Press.*"

"Delivery out here's kind of spotty."

"Well, Mr. Conover, we both know that the DA is a very political animal—again, this is purely between you and me, you understand?"

"Yes, of course."

"And it seems the climate around here has changed. The news about what you did for your company—well, the DA's just not optimistic that a jury will convict. Then there's the death of one of our chief suspects, Mr. Rinaldi. The district attorney's reluctant to go to trial." She paused. "Hello? Hello?"

"I'm here."

"And—well, there was another article in the paper, this morning. Raising questions about how the police handled the Andrew Stadler case."

"Such as?"

"Oh, I'm sure you know some of it. How nothing was done to stop the stalker at your house or follow up on . . . her. I think it's become obvious that if the police hadn't been so negligent, the situation wouldn't have escalated the way it did. I had to let the DA know that my testimony would inevitably make even more of this negligence public. Which no one in this department wants."

For a long time, Nick was unable to speak. Finally, he said: "I—and how do *you* feel about this?"

"That's not for me to say. You mean, do I feel justice is being served?"

"Something like that, yeah."

"I think we both recognize that the DA's decision to drop most of the charges is motivated by political expedience. But as for justice?" Audrey

Rhimes sighed. "I don't know that there's any justice to be done here, Mr. Conover. I certainly don't think it would serve justice to cause your children to suffer anymore. But that's just my personal opinion."

"Am I allowed to thank you?"

"There's nothing to thank me for, Mr. Conover. I'm just trying to do the right thing." She was silent for a moment. "But maybe there *is* no right thing to do here. Maybe it's not so much a matter of doing the right thing as trying not to do the wrong thing."

Nick set down the cell phone and for a long while watched the sunlight dance on the blue water.

He watched the seagulls caw and swoop, the waves surge and recede, the froth dissolve into the sand.

A few minutes later, Lucas and Julia emerged from the bungalow together and announced that they wanted to go for a hike, explore the nearby tropical forest and waterfalls.

"All right," Nick said, "but listen, Luke—I want you to keep a close watch on your sister."

"Dad, she's almost eleven," Lucas said. His voice seemed to be getting even deeper.

"Dad, I'm not a baby," said Julia.

"I don't want you doing anything crazy like jumping off the waterfalls," Nick said.

"Don't give me any ideas," Lucas said.

"And stay on the trail. It's supposed to be muddy and slippery in some places, so be careful."

"Dad." Lucas rolled his eyes as the two of them started down the palm-lined path. A few seconds later he turned around. "Hey, can you give me twenty bucks?"

"What for?"

"In case we stop to get something to eat on the way."

"All right." Nick pulled a couple of twenties out of his wallet and handed them to Lucas.

He watched them walking away. They were both bronzed already. Julia's curly hair was flying wildly in the breeze. Her legs were lanky, coltish; she was neither a girl nor a woman. Lucas, taller and broader all the time, wore long surfer shorts and a white T-shirt, dazzling in the sun, that was still creased from the suitcase.

As Nick stared after his kids, Lucas suddenly turned around. "Dad?"

"What?"

A gull cawed as it spotted a fish, then dove to the water.

Lucas looked at him for a moment. "You come too."

ACKNOWLEDGMENTS

No, the Stratton Corporation is *not* a thinly disguised fictional version of Steelcase or Herman Miller—as anyone who works there knows. But I'm grateful to several key people at those great companies who understood the difference between fiction and reality and were willing to let me poke around, tour their offices and factories, and ask rude, provocative, and irrelevant-seeming questions. At Steelcase, Inc., in Grand Rapids, Michigan, I was helped immeasurably by Debra Bailey, director of corporate communications, and Jeanine Hill, public relations manager. I've visited a lot of corporations by now, but I've never encountered a PR staff as open and honest and welcoming and just damned *friendly*. Deb Bailey also gave me the consummate insider's tour of Grand Rapids that made me want to move there . . . almost. I was particularly impressed by the president and CEO of Steelcase, Jim Hackett, who was generous with his time and insights into the challenges (personal and professional) of running a major corporation, modernizing it, and getting it through some really tough times. Frank Merlotti Jr., president of Steelcase North America, told me about being a hometown kid who makes it to the top of the biggest company in town. At Herman Miller in Zeeland, Michigan, Bruce Buursma gave me a fascinating introduction to that company's very cool headquarters. Rob Kirkbride of the *Grand Rapids Press* gave me an interesting journalistic perspective on those companies. Unfortunately, in neither place did I meet anyone who remotely resembled Scott McNally.

Most of the CEOs and CFOs I talked to during the research for *Company Man* prefer to remain anonymous. They know who they are, and I thank them for setting aside precious time for this fictional enterprise. My friend Bill Teuber, chief financial officer of the EMC Corporation, contributed in innumerable ways, including explaining what the hell a CFO does. My Yale classmate Scott Schoen, senior managing director of Thomas H. Lee Partners in Boston, kindly took time away from some very high-powered deal-making to help me flesh out the fictional Fairfield Partners and its machinations. No Todd Muldaurs there either, by the way.

Once again, my old buddy Giles McNamee, managing director of McNamee Lawrence & Co., was a key unindicted coconspirator in devising creatively evil financial plots; I appreciate his complicity and generosity. Mike Bingle of Silver Lake Partners was an immense help in solving all sorts of tricky plot problems. (Thanks to Roger McNamee of Elevation Partners for introducing us.) Nell Minow, founder of the Corporate Library, clarified how corporate boards of directors work (or don't).

Many thanks to my corporate security experts, none of whom bore any resemblance to Eddie Rinaldi, including George Campbell, former chief security officer at Fidelity Investments; and the brilliant Jon Chorey, chief engineer, Fidelity Security Services, Inc. Bob McCarthy of Dedicated Micros illuminated the intricacies of digital video surveillance systems, as did Jason Lefort of Skyway Security, and particularly Tom Brigham of Brigham Scully. Thanks, too, to Rick Boucher of Seaside Alarms in South Yarmouth, Massachusetts. Skip Brandon, formerly deputy assistant director of the FBI and founding partner of the international security consulting firm Smith Brandon—a valued source, and friend, since *The Zero Hour*—provided some intriguing background on money laundering and shell corporations. And again, the attorney Jay Shapiro, of Katten Muchin Zavis Rosenman, was my main man on criminal law. If I got in trouble like Nick, I'd hire Jay in a second.

Even an ordinary homicide investigation can be complicated, but in trying to make Audrey Rhimes's job as hard as possible, I surely drove my two homicide experts half-crazy. My deepest thanks to Dean Garrison of the Grand Rapids Police Department's Forensic Services Unit—writer, firearms specialist, and mordantly funny observer of the foibles of police work—and

Detective Kenneth Kooistra, legendary homicide investigator recently retired from the GRPD Major Case Unit, whose war stories are spellbinding and whose generosity was boundless. Trooper Ryan Larrison, firearms examiner with the Michigan State Police, patiently took me through the intricacies of the Integrated Bullet Identification System. I thank, also, Gene Gietzen of Forensic Consulting in Springfield, Missouri; George Schiro of Acadiana Criminalistics Laboratory in New Iberia, Louisiana; Sergeant Kathy Murphy of the Cambridge Police Department; and Detective Lisa Holmes of the Boston Police Department. Stanton Kessler, M.D., was again my chief source on autopsy procedures and pathology. Mike Hanzlick was quite instructive on the perils of natural gas.

It's been a while since I've been a sixteen-year-old—I seem to have repressed all memories—so when it came to Lucas, I was fortunate to draw upon the trenchant observations of Eric Beam and Stefan Pappius-Lefebvre, who are both charismatic and articulate (though, alas, nowhere *near* as angry and alienated as I wanted them to be, for my purposes). Nick's family life, and particularly his relationship with Luke, owes much to Michael Gurian, therapist and bestselling author of *The Wonder of Boys*.

On the esoterica of fly-fishing, my friend Allen Smith was a great source; on hockey, I'm indebted to Steve Counihan, tennis pro and hockey star. Thanks again to my gifted researcher on this and several other of my books, Kevin Biehl, and to my wonderful former assistant, Rachel Pomerantz. And to a few good friends for chipping in, too: Joe Teig and Rick Weissbourd. My brother Dr. Jonathan Finder, contributed medical advice; my younger sister, Lisa Finder, a research librarian at Hunter College, assisted with research; and my older sister, Susan Finder, an attorney in Hong Kong, fact-checked the China stuff. I'm grateful, as always, to my terrific agent, Molly Friedrich, and her assistant, Paul Cirone, of the Aaron Priest Agency for their constant support as well as some very useful editorial contributions.

Now, as to my publisher, St. Martin's Press—man, am I lucky to have joined such an excellent and enthusiastic publishing team, and I thank them all, particularly CEO John Sargent, publisher Sally Richardson, Matthew Shear, John Cunningham, George Witte, Matt Baldacci, Christina Harcar, Nancy Trypuc, Jim DiMiero, Alison Lazarus, Jeff Capshew, Brian Heller, Ken Holland, Andy LeCount, Tom Siino, Rob Renzler, John Murphy,

Gregg Sullivan, Peter Nasaw, Steve Eichinger, and at Audio Renaissance, Mary Beth Roche, Joe McNeely, and Laura Wilson.

And to my amazing editor, Keith Kahla—well, you're the best.

My daughter, Emma, was my chief source on the lives of ten-year-old girls, from baseball to The Sims. In the frenzied last months of my work on *Company Man*, she had to suffer my long absences; but she cheerfully brought lemonade down the hill to my writing studio in Truro and always kept my spirits up. She and my wife, Michele Souda, were my great sources of support during the writing of this book.

And once again I thank, above all, my brother Henry Finder, editorial director at *The New Yorker*: perpetual-motion idea generator, tireless brainstormer, peerless editor of first and last resort. I could not have done it without you.